C000174815

STREET

Cornwall

www.philips-maps.co.uk

First published in 2003 by

Philip's, a division of
Octopus Publishing Group Ltd
www.octopusbooks.co.uk
2-4 Heron Quays, London E14 4JP
An Hachette Livre UK Company

Second edition 2006
Second impression with revisions 2008
CORBB

ISBN-10   0-540-08848-X (spiral)
ISBN-13   978-0-540-08848-5 (spiral)

© Philip's 2008

os Ordnance Survey®

This product includes mapping data licensed
from Ordnance Survey® with the permission of
the Controller of Her Majesty's Stationery Office.
© Crown copyright 2008. All rights reserved.
Licence number 100011710.

Printed by Toppan, China

Contents

II **Key to map pages**

IV **Route planning**

VIII **Administrative and Postcode boundaries**

1 **Key to map symbols**

2 **Street maps** at 1¾ inches to 1 mile

104 **Street maps** at 3½ inches to 1 mile

148 **Street map of Plymouth city centre**
at 7 inches to 1 mile

150 **Index** of towns and villages

154 **Index** of streets, hospitals, industrial estates, railway
stations, schools, shopping centres, universities
and places of interest

Digital Data

The exceptionally high-quality mapping found in this atlas is available as digital data in TIFFformat, which is easily convertible to other bitmapped (raster) image formats.

The index is also available in digital form as a standard database table. It contains all the details found in the printed index together with the National Grid reference for the map square in which each entry is named.

For further information and to discuss your requirements, please contact james.mann@philips-maps.co.uk

Key to map pages

149	Map pages at 7 inches to 1 mile
128	Map pages at 3½ inches to 1 mile
100	Map pages at 1¾ inches to 1 mile

Scale

0   5   10   15   20   25 km

0   5   10   15 miles

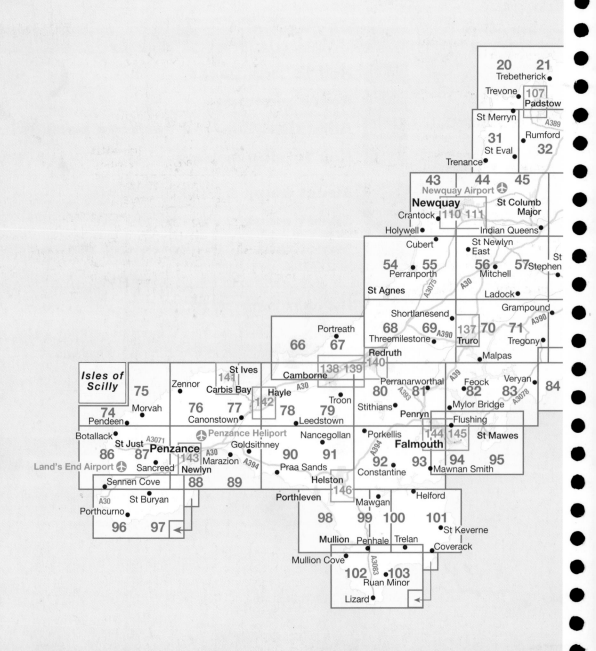

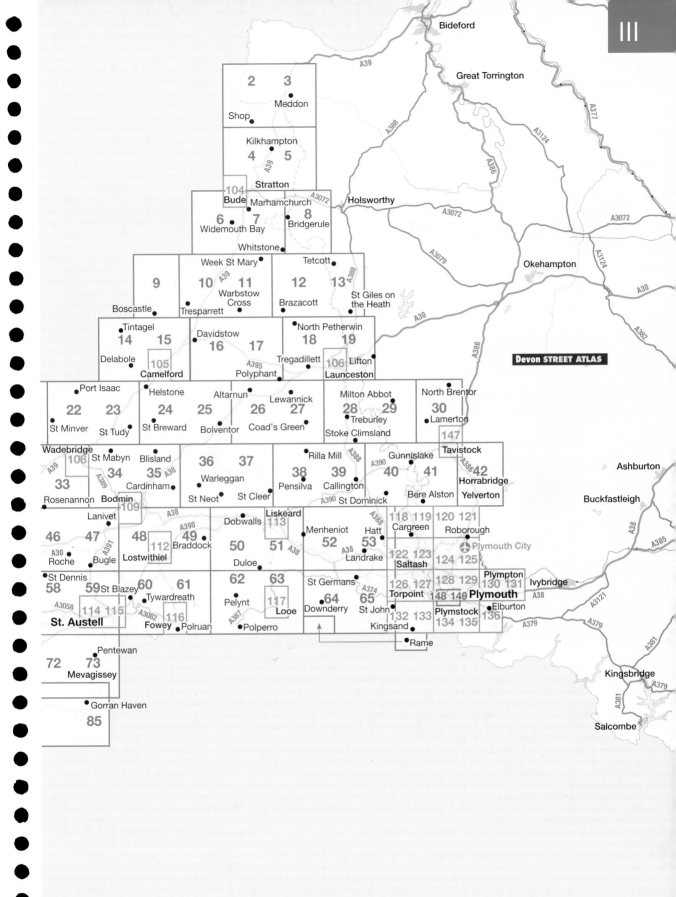

Route planning

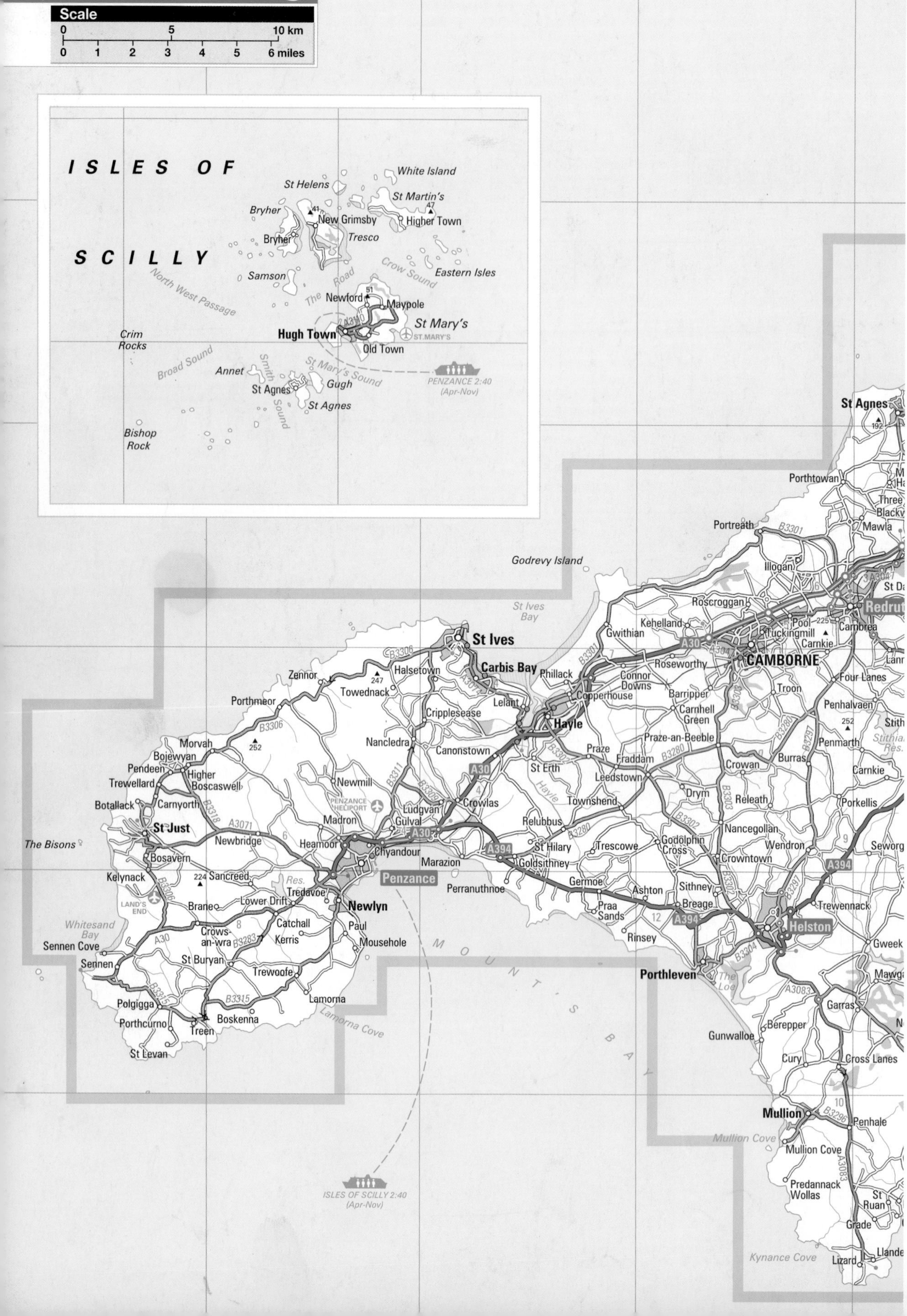

Scale

0			5			10 km
0	1	2	3	4	5	6 miles

ISLES OF

SCILLY

White Island

St Helens

St Martin's

Bryher

New Grimsby · Higher Town

Bryher · Tresco

Samson

Crow Sound

Eastern Isles

North West Passage

The Road

Newford · Maypole

Hugh Town · St Mary's

ST.MARY'S

Old Town

Crim
Rocks

Broad Sound

St Mary's Sound

Annet · Gugh

St Agnes · PENZANCE 2:40
(Apr-Nov)

St Agnes

Smith Sound

Bishop
Rock

St Agnes

Porthtowan

Mawla

Three
Blacky

Portreath · B3301

Godrevy Island

Illogan

Roscroggan

Pool · 225 · Cambrea

Redrut

St Da

St Ives
Bay

Gwithian

Kehelland · A30

Roseworthy

Tuckingmill · Carnkie

CAMBORNE

Lann

St Ives

Halsetown

Carbis Bay

Phillack

Connor
Downs

Barripper · Four Lanes

Troon

Penhalvaen

Stith

Zennor · 247

Towednack

Lelant

Copperhouse

Hayle

Praze-an-Beeble

Carnhell
Green

Stithia
Res.

Porthmeor

Cripplesease

Canonstown

Praze

Drym · B3303

Burras

Carnkie

252

Penmarth

Morvah

Bojewyan

252 · B3306

Nancledra

St Erth

Fraddam · B3280

Crowan

Releath

Porkellis

Seworg

Pendeen

Trewellard

Higher
Boscaswell

Newmill

Leedstown

Townshend

Nancegollan

9

Botallack

Carnyorth

PENZANCE
HELIPORT

Ludgvan

Crowlas

Relubbus · B3280

Godolphin
Cross

Wendron

A394

The Bisons

St Just

Newbridge · A3071

Madron

Gulval

A30

St Hilary

Trescowe

Crowntown

Heamoor

Chyandour

Marazion

Goldsithney

Sithney

Trewennack

Bosavern · 224

Sancreed

Res.

Penzance

Perranuthnoe

Germoe

Ashton

Breage · A394

Helston

Kelynack

Brane

Tredavoe

Lower Drift

Newlyn

Praa
Sands

12

Gweek

Sennen Cove

Crows-
an-wra · B3283

Catchall

Kerris

Paul

Mousehole

Rinsey

MOUNT'S

Mawga

Sennen

St Buryan

Trewoofe

Porthleven

The
Loe · A3083

Garras

Polgigga

Boskenna

Lamorna

Lamorna Cove

BAY

Berepper

Porthcurno

Treen · B3315

St Levan

Gunwalloe

Cury · Cross Lanes

ISLES OF SCILLY 2:40
(Apr-Nov)

Mullion

B3296 · Penhale

Mullion Cove

Mullion Cove

A3083

Predannack
Wollas

St
Ruan

Grade

Kynance Cove

Lizard · Llande

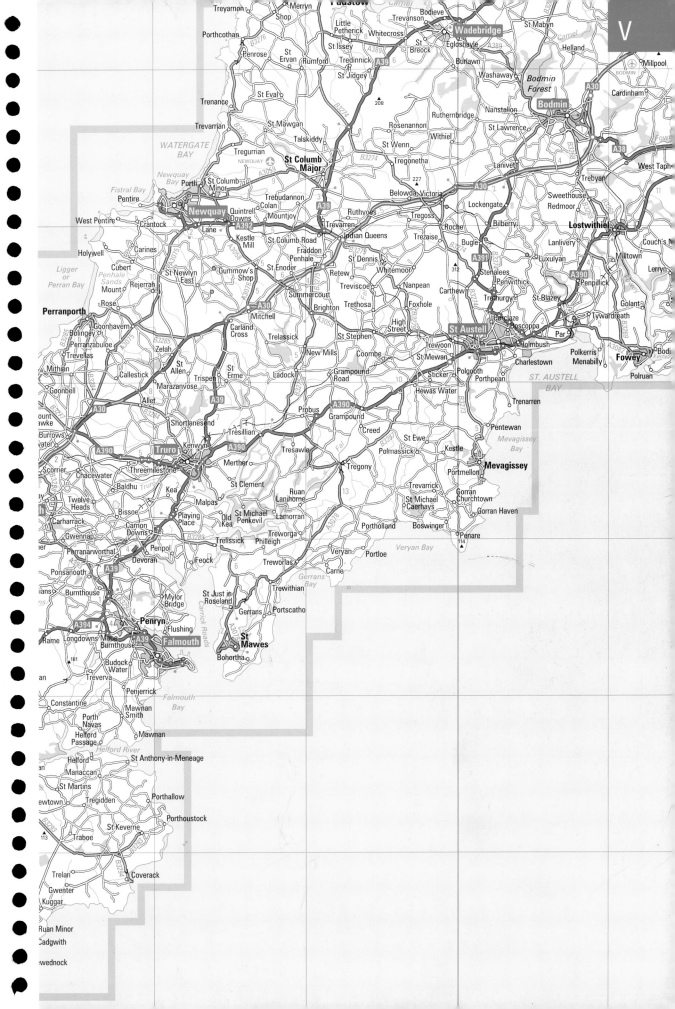

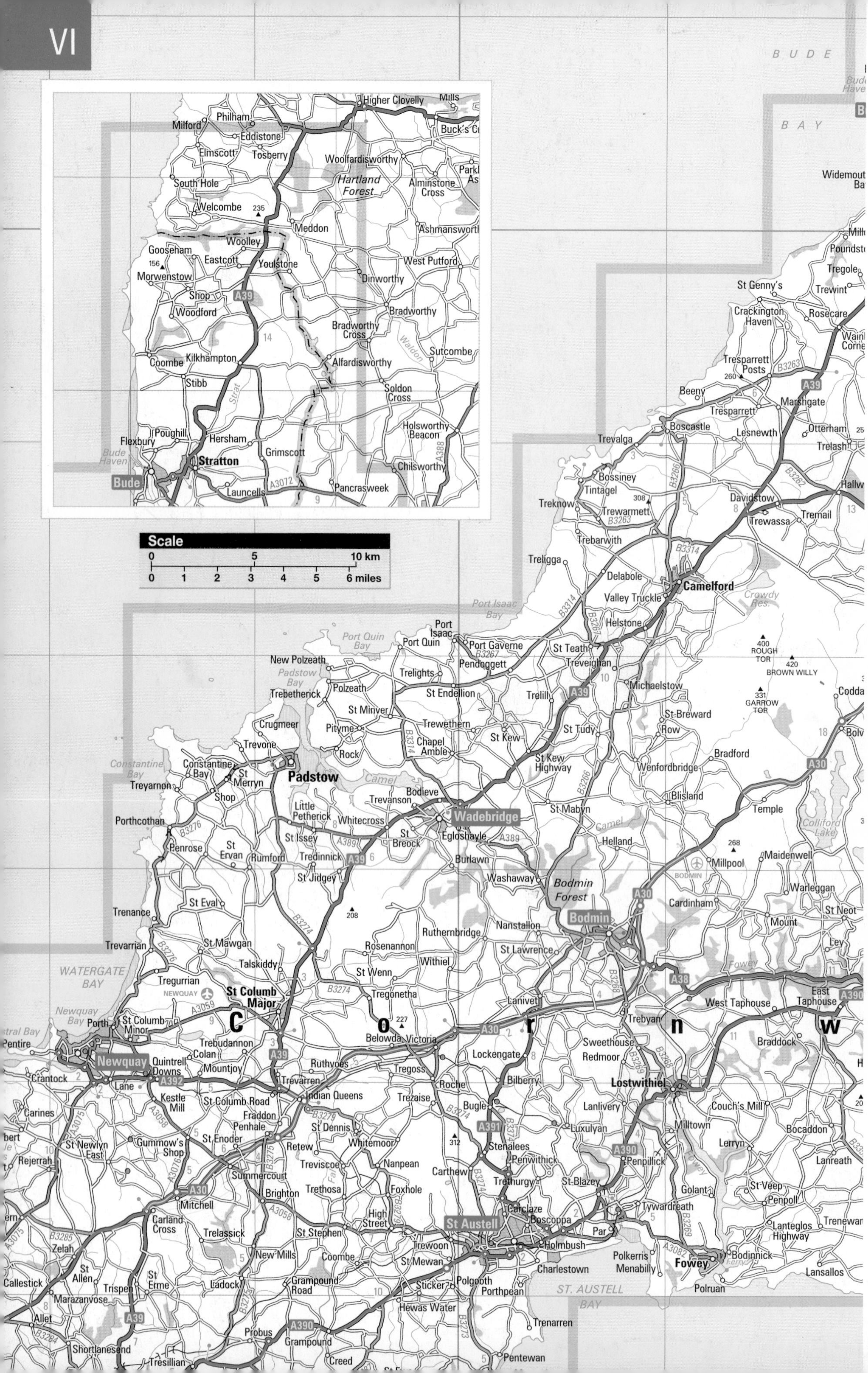

BUDE
BAY
Widemouth Bay
Higher Clovelly
Mills
Buck's Cross
Philham
Milford
Eddistone
Elmscott
Tosberry
Woolfardisworthy
Parkham Ash
Hartland Forest
Alminstone Cross
South Hole
Welcombe
235
Meddon
Ashmansworthy
Woolley
Gooseham
Eastcott
Youlstone
West Putford
156
Morwenstow
Dinworthy
Shop
A39
Woodford
Bradworthy
Bradworthy Cross
Waldon
14
Coombe
Kilkhampton
Sutcombe
Alfardisworthy
Stibb
Soldon Cross
Strat
Poughill
Holsworthy Beacon
Flexbury
Hersham
Bude Haven
Grimscott
A388
Stratton
Chilsworthy
Bude
Launcells
A3072
Pancrasweek
9
Scale
0
5
10 km
0
1
2
3
4
5
6 miles
Millook
Poundstock
Tregole
St Genny's
Trewint
Crackington Haven
Rosecare
Wainhouse Corner
Tresparrett Posts
260
B3263
A39
Beeny
Marshgate
Tresparrett
Boscastle
Otterham
Trevalga
Lesnewth
Trelash
Bossiney
B3266
B3262
Tintagel
Hallworthy
Treknow
308
Davidstow
Trewarmett
B3263
Tremail
Trewassa
13
Trebarwith
B3314
Treligga
Delabole
Camelford
Crowdy Res.
Port Isaac Bay
Valley Truckle
B3314
B3267
Helstone
Port Quin Bay
Port Isaac
Port Quin
Port Gaverne
St Teath
400 ROUGH TOR
420 BROWN WILLY
New Polzeath
B3267
Pendoggett
Treveighan
Padstow Bay
Trelights
10
Michaelstow
331 GARROW TOR
Codda
Trebetherick
Polzeath
St Endellion
Trelill
A39
St Minver
St Breward
Crugmeer
Pityme
Trewethern
St Tudy
Row
18
Bolventor
B3314
St Kew
Trevone
Chapel Amble
Rock
Bradford
Constantine Bay
Constantine Bay
St Merryn
Padstow
St Kew Highway
Wenfordbridge
A30
Treyarnon
Shop
Camel
Trevanson
Bodieve
B3266
Blisland
Little Petherick
Wadebridge
St Mabyn
Temple
Porthcothan
Whitecross
B3276
St Issey
St Breock
Egloshayle
A389
Camel
Colliford Lake
A389
Helland
Penrose
St Ervan
Rumford
Tredinnick
A39
6
Burlawn
268
Maidenwell
St Jidgey
Millpool
BODMIN
Washaway
Bodmin Forest
St Eval
A30
Warleggan
208
Cardinham
Trenance
B3274
St Neot
Bodmin
Mount
Nanstallon
Ruthernbridge
Trevarrian
St Mawgan
B3276
Rosenannon
St Lawrence
Ley
WATERGATE BAY
Talskiddy
Withiel
Fowey
St Wenn
B3268
A38
Tregurrian
NEWQUAY
St Columb Major
B3274
Tregonetha
East Taphouse
A3059
Lanivet
West Taphouse
A390
Newquay Bay
C
227
o
r
Trebyan
n
w
Porth
St Columb Minor
A30
2
11
Watergate Bay
Pentire
Trebudannon
Belowda
Victoria
Sweetshouse
Braddock
Colan
Lockengate
Redmoor
B3269
B3268
Newquay
Quintrell Downs
A39
Ruthvoes
Tregoss
8
Crantock
A392
Mountjoy
Trevarren
Roche
Bilberry
Lostwithiel
Lane
Kestle Mill
St Columb Road
Indian Queens
Trezaise
Bugle
Lanlivery
Couch's Mill
Fraddon
B3279
Carines
A3058
Penhale
St Dennis
A391
Luxulyan
Milltown
Bocaddon
St Newlyn East
St Enoder
Whitemoor
312
Stenalees
Lerryn
Gummow's Shop
Retew
B3275
A3076
Nanpean
Penwithick
A390
Penpillick
Lanreath
Rejerrah
Treviscoe
Carthew
B3274
Summercourt
Trethurgy
St Blazey
St Veep
Trethosa
Foxhole
Golant
Brighton
A30
Penpoll
Mitchell
Carclaze
Tywardreath
B3269
High Street
A3058
Carland Cross
B3279
St Austell
Boscoppa
Lanteglos Highway
Trenewan
Trelassick
St Stephen
B3285
Par
Zelah
Holmbush
New Mills
Coombe
Trewoon
St Mewan
Polkerris
Bodinnick
A3075
St Allen
Menabilly
Fowey
St Erme
Charlestown
Lansallos
Trispen
Ladock
Grampound Road
Sticker
Polgooth
Polruan
Callestick
Marazanvose
ST. AUSTELL BAY
Porthpean
10
Hewas Water
Allet
A39
B3273
A390
Trenarren
B3284
Probus
Grampound
Shortlanesend
Tresillian
Creed
Pentewan

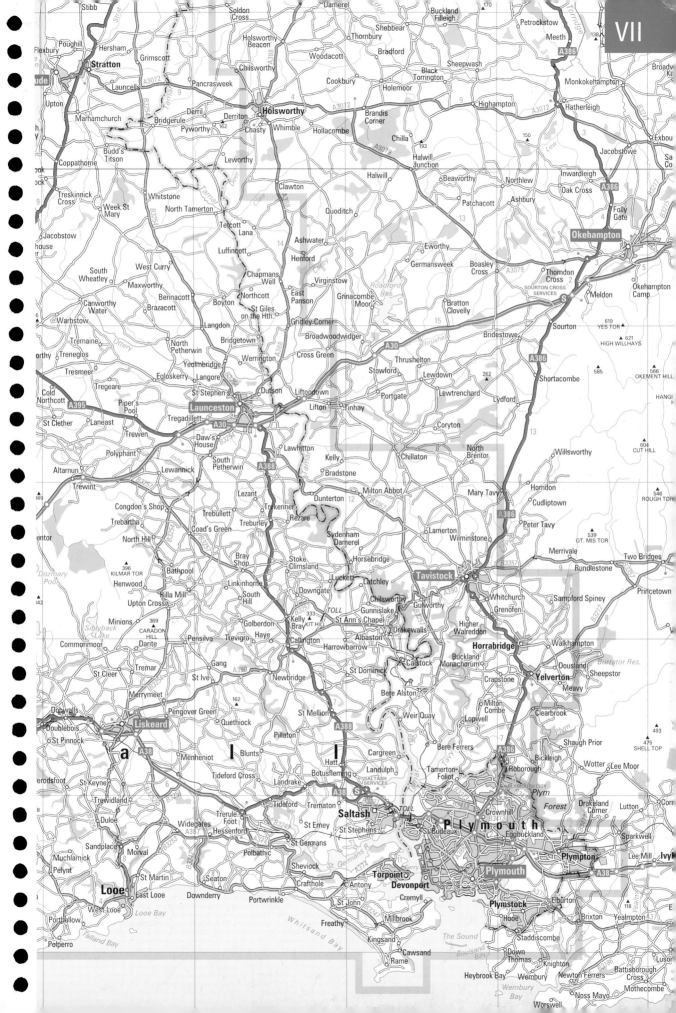

Major administrative and Postcode boundaries

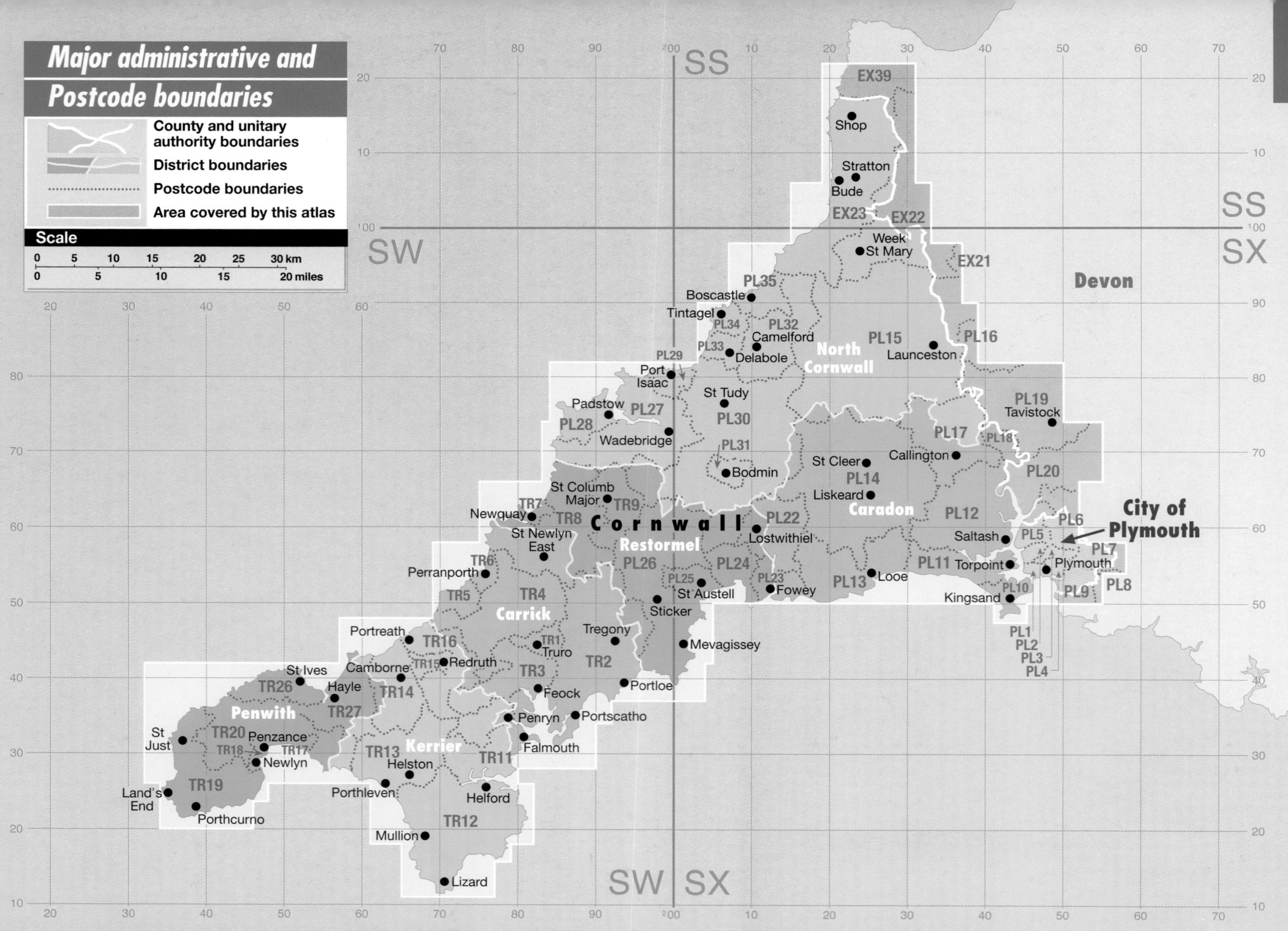

Scale

0	5	10	15	20	25	30 km	
0	5	10	15	20 miles			

County and unitary authority boundaries
District boundaries
Postcode boundaries
Area covered by this atlas

Devon

City of Plymouth

Cornwall

North Cornwall

Carrick

Caradon

Restormel

Penwith

Kerrier

SS
SX
SW
SX
SW

EX39
EX22
EX23
EX21

Shop
Stratton
Bude
Week St Mary
Launceston
Tavistock
Plymouth
Saltash
Torpoint
Kingsand
Callington
St Cleer
Liskeard
Looe
Fowey
Mevagissey
St Austell
Lostwithiel
Sticker
Bodmin
St Tudy
Delabole
Camelford
Tintagel
Boscastle
Port Isaac
Wadebridge
Padstow
St Columb Major
Newquay
St Newlyn East
Tregony
Portloe
Portscatho
Penryn
Feock
Falmouth
Truro
Redruth
Camborne
Helford
Lizard
Mullion
Porthleven
Helston
Hayle
St Ives
Penzance
Newlyn
Porthcurno
St Just
Land's End
Perranporth
Portreath

PL19 PL18 PL20 PL16 PL17 PL15 PL14 PL12 PL13 PL22 PL23 PL24 PL25 PL26 PL27 PL28 PL29 PL30 PL31 PL32 PL33 PL34 PL35 PL6 PL5 PL7 PL1 PL2 PL3 PL4 PL8 PL9 PL10 PL11
TR1 TR2 TR3 TR4 TR5 TR6 TR7 TR8 TR9 TR11 TR12 TR13 TR14 TR15 TR16 TR17 TR18 TR19 TR20 TR26 TR27

Motorway with junction number			♦ Ambulance station
Primary route – dual/single carriageway			♦ Coastguard station
A road – dual/single carriageway			♦ Fire station
B road – dual/single carriageway			♦ Police station
Minor road – dual/single carriageway			✚ Accident and Emergency entrance to hospital
Other minor road – dual/single carriageway			🅷 Hospital
Road under construction			✝ Place of worship
Tunnel, covered road			🄸 Information Centre (open all year)
Rural track, private road or narrow road in urban area			🛒 Shopping Centre
Gate or obstruction to traffic (restrictions may not apply at all times or to all vehicles)			P P&R Parking, Park and Ride
Path, bridleway, byway open to all traffic, road used as a public path			PO Post Office
Pedestrianised area			⽊ 🚐 Camping site, caravan site
DY7 **Postcode boundaries**			▷ ✕ Golf course, picnic site
County and unitary authority boundaries			Prim Sch Important buildings, schools, colleges, universities and hospitals
Railway, tunnel, railway under construction			Built up area
Tramway, tramway under construction			Woods
Miniature railway			River Medway Water name
≷ Walsall **Railway station**			River, weir, stream
⊕ **Private railway station**			Canal, lock, tunnel
● South Shields **Metro station**			Water
⊕ ⊕ **Tram stop, tram stop under construction**			Tidal water
◼ **Bus, coach station**			Church Non-Roman antiquity
			ROMAN FORT Roman antiquity

Acad	**Academy**	Inst	**Institute**	Recn Gd	**Recreation Ground**
Allot Gdns	**Allotments**	Ct	**Law Court**		
Cemy	**Cemetery**	L Ctr	**Leisure Centre**	Resr	**Reservoir**
C Ctr	**Civic Centre**	LC	**Level Crossing**	Ret Pk	**Retail Park**
CH	**Club House**	Liby	**Library**	Sch	**School**
Coll	**College**	Mkt	**Market**	Sh Ctr	**Shopping Centre**
Crem	**Crematorium**	Meml	**Memorial**	TH	**Town Hall/House**
Ent	**Enterprise**	Mon	**Monument**	Trad Est	**Trading Estate**
Ex H	**Exhibition Hall**	Mus	**Museum**	Univ	**University**
Ind Est	**Industrial Estate**	Obsy	**Observatory**	W Twr	**Water Tower**
IRB Sta	**Inshore Rescue Boat Station**	Pal	**Royal Palace**	Wks	**Works**
		PH	**Public House**	YH	**Youth Hostel**

◀ 87 **Adjoining page indicators and overlap bands**
The colour of the arrow and the band indicates the scale of the adjoining or overlapping page (see scales below)

237

Enlarged mapping only

Railway or bus station building

Place of interest

Parkland

◼ The small numbers around the edges of the maps identify the 1 kilometre National Grid lines
◼ The dark grey border on the inside edge of some pages indicates that the mapping does not continue onto the adjacent page

The scale of the maps on the pages numbered in blue is 5.52 cm to 1 km • 3½ inches to 1 mile • 1: 18103

0   ¼   ½   ¾   1 mile
0   250 m   500 m   750 m   1 kilometre

The scale of the maps on pages numbered in green is 2.76 cm to 1 km • 1¾ inches to 1 mile • 1: 36206

0   ¼   ½   ¾   1 mile
0   250m   500m   750m   1 kilometre

The scale of the maps on pages numbered in red is 11.04 cm to 1 km • 7 inches to 1 mile • 1: 9051

0   220 yards   440 yards   660 yards   ½ mile
0   125m   250m   375m   ½ kilometre

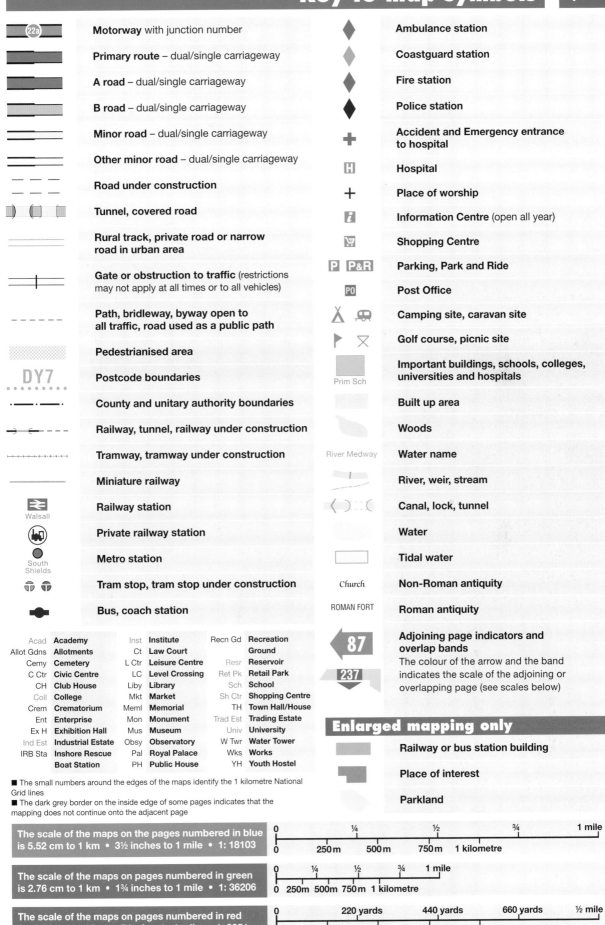

Scale: 1¾ inches to 1 mile

0   ¼   ½ mile
0 250m 500m 750m 1 km

A   B   C   D   E   F

Mansley Cliff
YH   Elmscott
Edistone

Docton

SANDHOLE CROSS

Sandhole Cliff

Mast
Hardisworthy
HARDISWORTHY CROSS
FIREBEACON CROSS
Firebeacon

Nabor Point
South Hole
Goldenpark

EX39
Wembsworthy

Embury Beacon
Putshole Farm

Embury Beach
Cranham

Knaps Longpeak
Henaford

Knap Head
Linton
LINTON LA
LANE PARK LA
KING'S CROSS

The Hermitage
Welcombe
WELL LA
Tredown
UPCOTT CROSS

Welcombe Mouth
P
OLD SMITHY COTTS
Upcott

Mead
Darraccott
MEAD CNR
Berry Park
PO
DARRAC'T HILL

Marsland Mouth
South West Coast Path
Gooseham Mill
Marsland Water

Gull Rock
Marsland Cliff

Cornakey Cliff
Marsland Manor
Hackmarsh

Yeol Mouth
Cornakey Farm
Cory
Gooseham

Henna Cliff
Westcott Farm
Bryaton
Brownspit
Lopthorne

EX23

Hawker's Hut
Well
West Beckon CL
St Mark's CE Prim Sch

Vicarage Cliff
P
Morwenstow
RULE CROSS

Lucky Hole
Crosstown
PH
JAMES'S CROSS
FURZE GDNS
PO
P
MORWENNA RD
Milton

Higher Sharpnose Point
The Tidna
Shop
SARGENTS MDW

CROSSWATER
Ruxmoor

Tonacombe
STANBURY CROSS
WOODFORD CROSS
WOODVILLE RD
Darzle Farm
Middlefields Farm

19   A   20   B   21   C   22   D   23   E   24   F

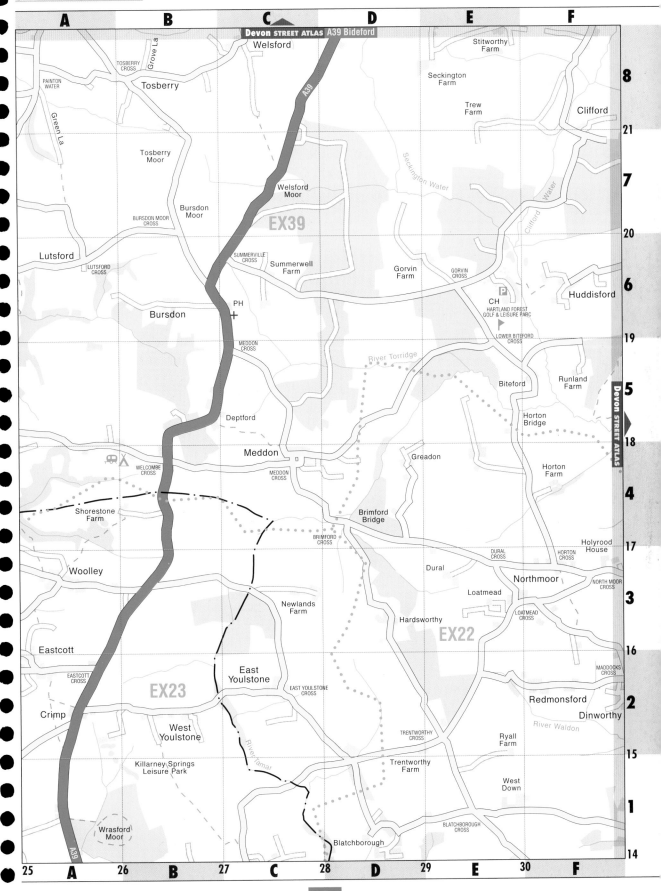

Scale: 1¾ inches to 1 mile

0   ¼   ½ mile

0   250m 500m 750m 1 km

Devon STREET ATLAS A39 Bideford

A   B   C   D   E   F

8
21
7
20
6
19
5
18
4
17
3
16
2
15
1
14

25   26   27   28   29   30

Welsford

Stitworthy
Farm

Seckington
Farm

Trew
Farm

Clifford

PAINTON
WATER

Tosberry

TOSBERRY
CROSS

Grove La

Tosberry
Moor

Green La

Bursdon
Moor

BURSDON MOOR
CROSS

Welsford
Moor

EX39

Seckington Water

Clifford Water

Lutsford

LUTSFORD
CROSS

SUMMERVILLE
CROSS

Summerwell
Farm

Gorvin
Farm

Gorvin
Cross

Huddisford

Bursdon

PH

CH

HARTLAND FOREST
GOLF & LEISURE PARC

P

LOWER BITEFORD
CROSS

MEDDON
CROSS

River Torridge

Biteford

Runland
Farm

Deptford

Meddon

MEDDON
CROSS

Greadon

Horton
Bridge

Horton
Farm

WELCOMBE
CROSS

Brimford
Bridge

BRIMFORD
CROSS

Dural

DURAL
CROSS

HORTON
CROSS

Holyrood
House

Shorestone
Farm

Northmoor

NORTH MOOR
CROSS

Woolley

Newlands
Farm

Hardsworthy

Loatmead

LOATMEAD
CROSS

EX22

Eastcott

EASTCOTT
CROSS

EX23

East
Youlstone

EAST YOULSTONE
CROSS

MADDOCKS
CROSS

Redmonsford

Dinworthy

Crimp

West
Youlstone

River Tamar

Trentworthy
Cross

Ryall
Farm

River Waldon

Killarney Springs
Leisure Park

Trentworthy
Farm

West
Down

Wrasford
Moor

Blatchborough

BLATCHBOROUGH
CROSS

A39

Devon STREET ATLAS

5

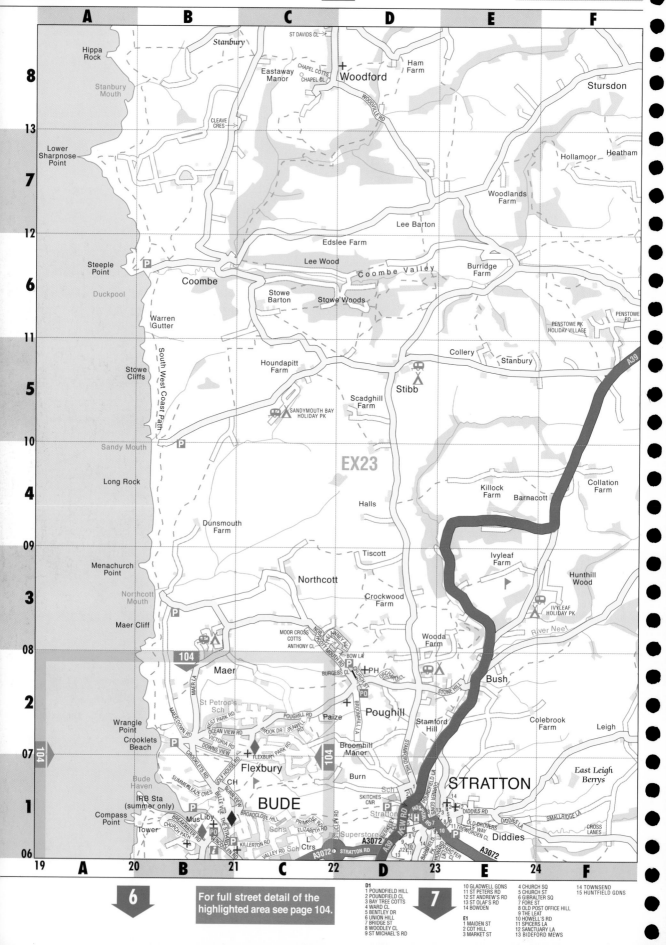

Scale: 1¾ inches to 1 mile

0   ¼   ½ mile
0 250m 500m 750m 1 km

Hippa Rock

Stanbury

St Davids Cl

Eastaway Manor

Chapel Cotts
Chapel Cl

Woodford

Ham Farm

Stursdon

Stanbury Mouth

Cleave Cres

Woodville Rd

Lower Sharpnose Point

Hollamoor

Heatham

Woodlands Farm

Lee Barton

Edslee Farm

Lee Wood

Coombe Valley

Burridge Farm

Steeple Point

Coombe

Duckpool

Stowe Barton

Stowe Woods

Penstowe Pk Holiday Village

Penstowe Rd

Warren Gutter

South West Coast Path

Stowe Cliffs

Houndapitt Farm

Collery

Stanbury

Scadghill Farm

Stibb

Sandymouth Bay Holiday Pk

Long Rock

EX23

Sandy Mouth

Killock Farm

Barnacott

Collation Farm

Menachurch Point

Halls

Tiscott

Ivyleaf Farm

Hunthill Wood

Northcott Mouth

Dunsmouth Farm

Northcott

Crockwood Farm

Ivyleaf Holiday Pk

River Neet

Maer Cliff

Moor Cross Cotts

Anthony Cl

Bow La

Wooda Farm

Bush

104

Maer

Burgess Cl

Church St

PH

Orchard Cl

Stone Hill

Maer La

St Petroc's Sch

West Park Rd

Poughill Rd

Paize

Broomhill La

Poughill

PO

Stamford Hill

Colebrook Farm

Leigh

Wrangle Point

Maer Down Rd

Ocean View Rd

Brook Dr

Stanwell Rd

Victoria Rd

Downs View

Broomhill Manor

Crooklets Beach

Crooklets Rd

Golf House Rd

Flexbury Park Rd

Flexbury

104

Burn

East Leigh Berrys

Bude Haven

Summerleaze Cres

Belle Vue

Burn View

CH

BUDE

Sch

Stratton

Skitches Cnr

STRATTON

Townsend

Smallridge La

Cross Lanes

IRB Sta (summer only)

Compass Point

Tower

Mus

Lib

Church Park Rd

Benson Dr

Killerton Rd

Broadclose Hill

Primrose

Elizabeth Rd

Schs

Valley Rd Sch

Stratton Rd

A3072

A3072

Superstore

New Rd

Hospital

Howell's Rd

Treworder Way

Old Drovers Way

Diddies Rd

Diddies

Diddies La

A39

D1
1 POUNDFIELD HILL
2 POUNDFIELD CL
3 BAY TREE COTTS
4 WARD CL
5 BENTLEY DR
6 UNION HILL
7 BRIDGE ST
8 WOODLEY CL
9 ST MICHAEL'S RD

10 GLADWELL GDNS
11 ST PETERS RD
12 ST ANDREW'S RD
13 ST OLAF'S RD
14 BOWDEN

E1
1 MAIDEN ST
2 COT HILL
3 MARKET ST

4 CHURCH SQ
5 CHURCH ST
6 GIBRALTER SQ
7 FORE ST
8 OLD POST OFFICE HILL
9 THE LEAT
10 HOWELL'S RD
11 SPICERS LA
12 SANCTUARY LA
13 BIDEFORD MEWS

14 TOWNSEND
15 HUNTFIELD GDNS

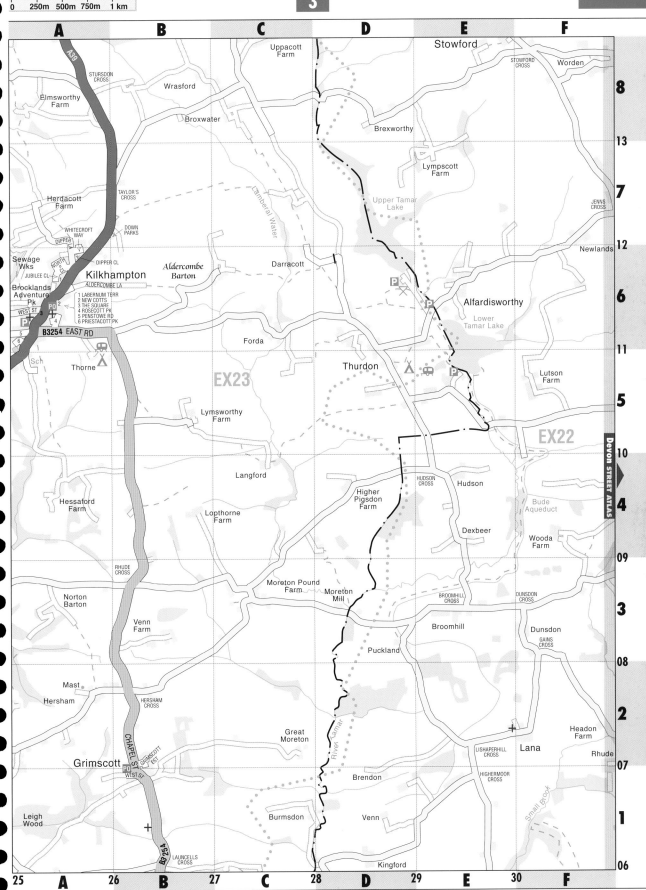

3

A   B   C   D   E   F

8

A39

STURSDON CROSS

Elmsworthy Farm

Wrasford

Uppacott Farm

Stowford

STOWFORD CROSS

Worden

13

Broxwater

Brexworthy

JENNS CROSS

7

Lympscott Farm

Upper Tamar Lake

Herdacott Farm

TAYLOR'S CROSS

WHITECROFT WAY

DOWN PARKS

Lamberal Water

12

DIPPER CL

Darracott

Aldercombe Barton

NORTH CL

Sewage Wks

JUBILEE CL

Kilkhampton

ALDERCOMBE LA

1 LABERNUM TERR
2 NEW COTTS
3 THE SQUARE
4 ROSECOTT PK
5 PENSTOWE RD
6 PRIESTACOTT PK

Newlands

Alfardisworthy

6

Brocklands Adventure Pk

WEST ST PO 3 2

Lower Tamar Lake

Lutson Farm

B3254 EAST RD

Forda

Thurdon

11

Sch

Thorne

EX23

5

Lymsworthy Farm

EX22

Devon STREET ATLAS

Langford

Higher Pigsdon Farm

HUDSON CROSS

Hudson

Bude Aqueduct

10

Hessaford Farm

Lopthorne Farm

Dexbeer

Wooda Farm

4

RHUDE CROSS

Moreton Pound Farm

Moreton Mill

BROOMHILL CROSS

DUNSDON CROSS

09

Norton Barton

Venn Farm

Broomhill

Dunsdon

GAINS CROSS

3

Puckland

08

Mast

Hersham

HERSHAM CROSS

Great Moreton

River Tamar

LISHAPERHILL CROSS

Lana

Headon Farm

2

CHAPEL ST

GRIMSCOTT EST

Brendon

Venn

HIGHERMOOR CROSS

Rhude

07

Grimscott

PO

WEST ST

Burmsdon

Small Brook

Leigh Wood

B3254

LAUNCELLS CROSS

Kingford

1

06

25   A   26   B   27   C   28   D   29   E   30   F

7   **8**

For full street detail of the highlighted area see page 104.

4

104
104

Scale: 1¾ inches to 1 mile
0   ¼   ½ mile
0   250m 500m 750m 1 km

Ebbingford Manor
Efford Beacon
Lynstone
Upton
Hotel
Phillips Farm
Phillip's Point
Higher Longbeak
Lower Longbeak
Salthouse Cottage
Bay View Inn (PH)
BRAMBLE CL
1 ATLANTIC CL
2 CRESCENT CL
MADEIRA DR
ASHTON WLK
BRANDON WLK
THE CRESCENT
Widemouth Sand
Widemouth Bay
Black Rock
Wanson Mouth
WIDEMOUTH BAY HOLIDAY VILLAGE
Widemouth Farms
COMBE LA
LEVERLAKE RD
Foxhole Point
South West Coast Path
Penhalt Cliff
PH
Wanson
WIDEMOUTH BAY CVN PK
Wanson Water
EX23
Millook Haven
PENHALT FARM HOLIDAY PK
Millook
Trevisick
BANGORS EST
Bangors
Cancleave Strand
Poundstock
VICARAGE LA
Dizzard Point
Millook Common
Cemy
Trekennard Farm
Trebarfoote
A39
Chipman Strand
Long Cliff
Bynorth Cliff
Trevoulter Farm
Treskinnick Cross
Mast
FORGE GDNS
Dizzard
The Den
Tregole
Cleave Strand

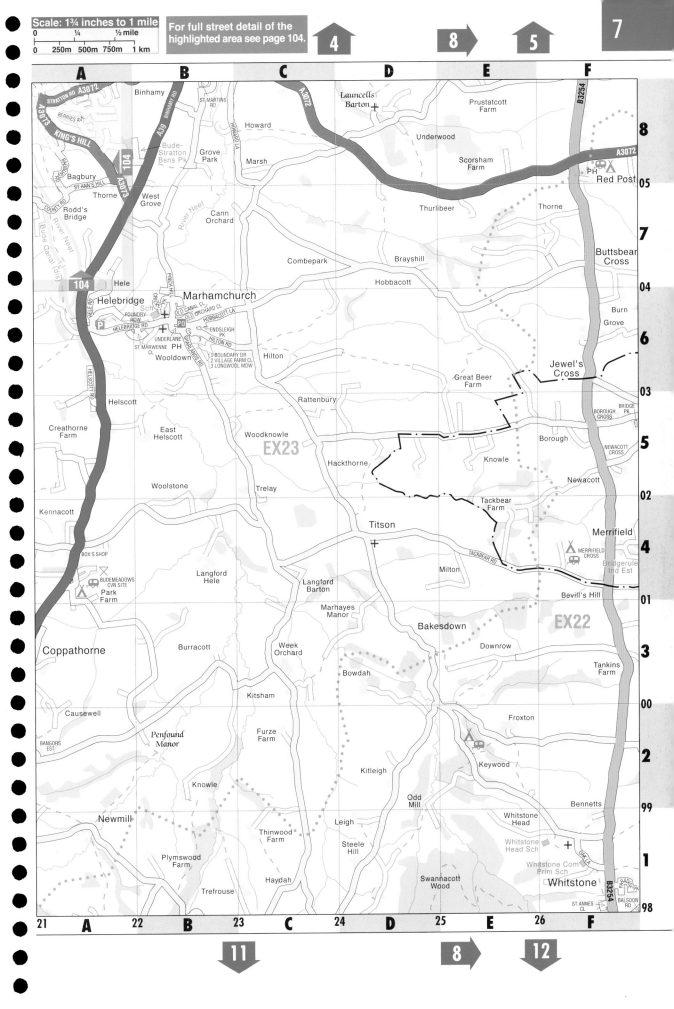

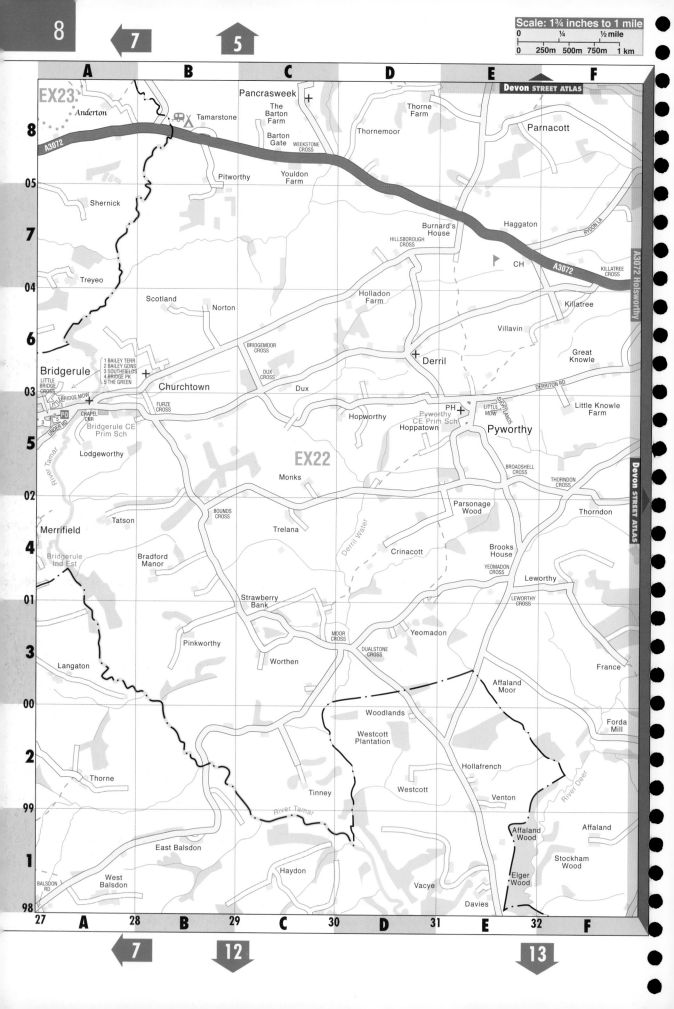

Scale: 1¾ inches to 1 mile

0   ¼   ½ mile
0   250m 500m 750m 1 km

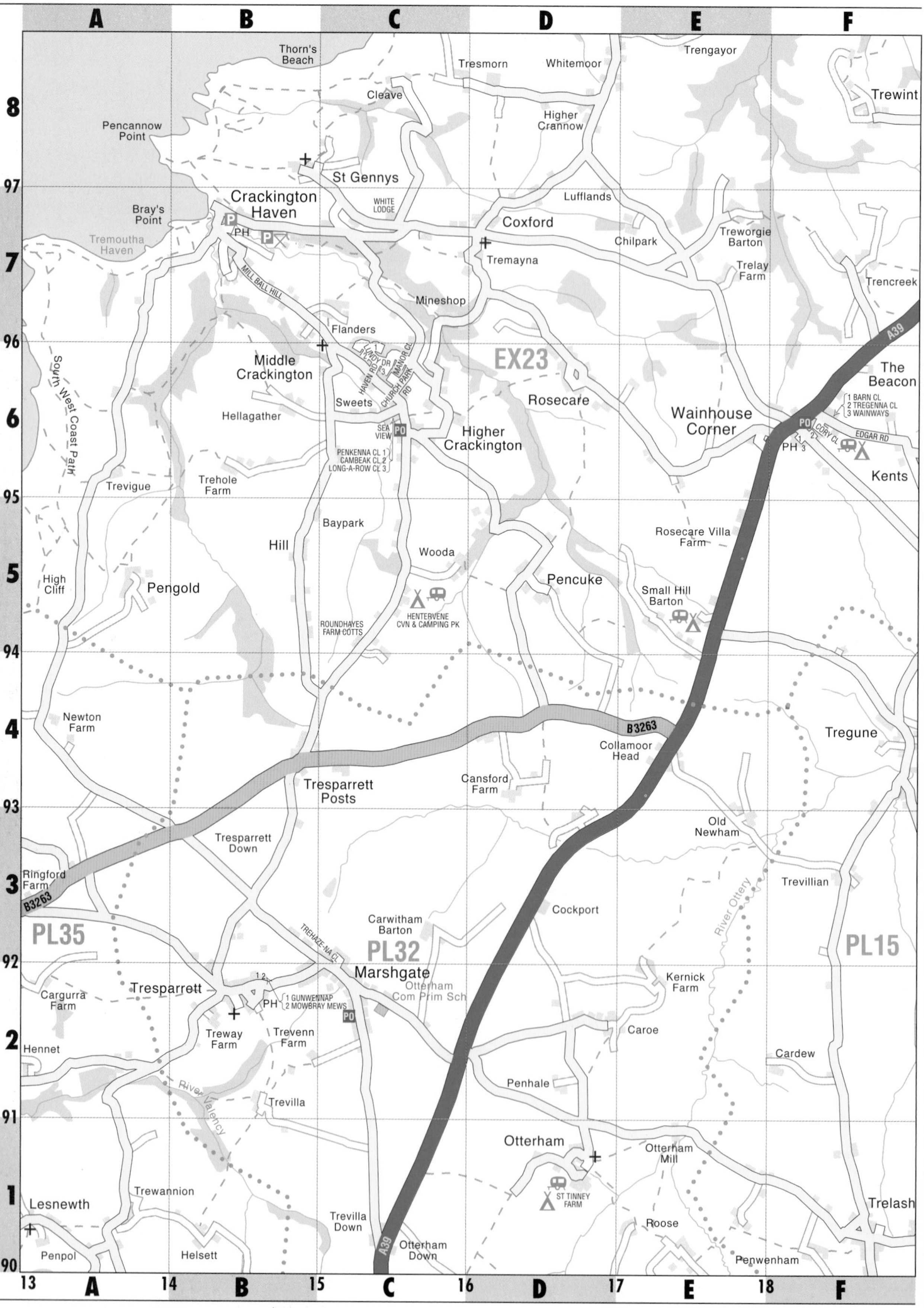

A   B   C   D   E   F

8

Thorn's Beach

Tresmorn
Whitemoor
Trengayor

Trewint

Cleave

Higher Crannow

Pencannow Point

97

St Gennys
Lufflands

Bray's Point

Crackington Haven
PH
Coxford
Chilpark
Treworgie Barton

Tremoutha Haven

Trelay Farm

Trencreek

7

MILL BALL HILL
Tremayna

Mineshop

A39

96

Flanders

EX23

The Beacon

1 BARN CL
2 TREGENNA CL
3 WAINWAYS

Middle Crackington

Rosecare

Wainhouse Corner

6

Hellagather
Sweets

Higher Crackington

PO
CORY CL
EDGAR RD
PH
Kents

SEA VIEW
PO

95

PENKENNA CL 1
CAMBEAK CL 2
LONG-A-ROW CL 3

Trevigue

Trehole Farm

Baypark

Rosecare Villa Farm

5

High Cliff

Pengold

Hill

Wooda

Pencuke

Small Hill Barton

ROUNDHAYES FARM COTTS

HENTERVENE CVN & CAMPING PK

94

Newton Farm

B3263

4

Collamoor Head

Tregune

Cansford Farm

93

Ringford Farm

Tresparrett Posts

Old Newham

Trevillian

3

B3263

Tresparrett Down

Cockport

River Ottery

PL35

PL15

Carwitham Barton

92

PL32
Marshgate
Otterham Com Prim Sch

Kernick Farm

Cargurra Farm

Tresparrett
TREHAZE-NA CL
PH
1 GUNWENNAP
2 MOWBRAY MEWS
PO

Caroe

Cardew

2

Hennet

Treway Farm
Trevenn Farm

Penhale

River Valency

Trevilla

1

Lesnewth

Trewannion

Otterham

Otterham Mill

Trelash

St TINNEY FARM

Trevilla Down

Roose

Penwenham

90

Penpol
Helsett
Otterham Down
A39

13   A   14   B   15   C   16   D   17   E   18   F

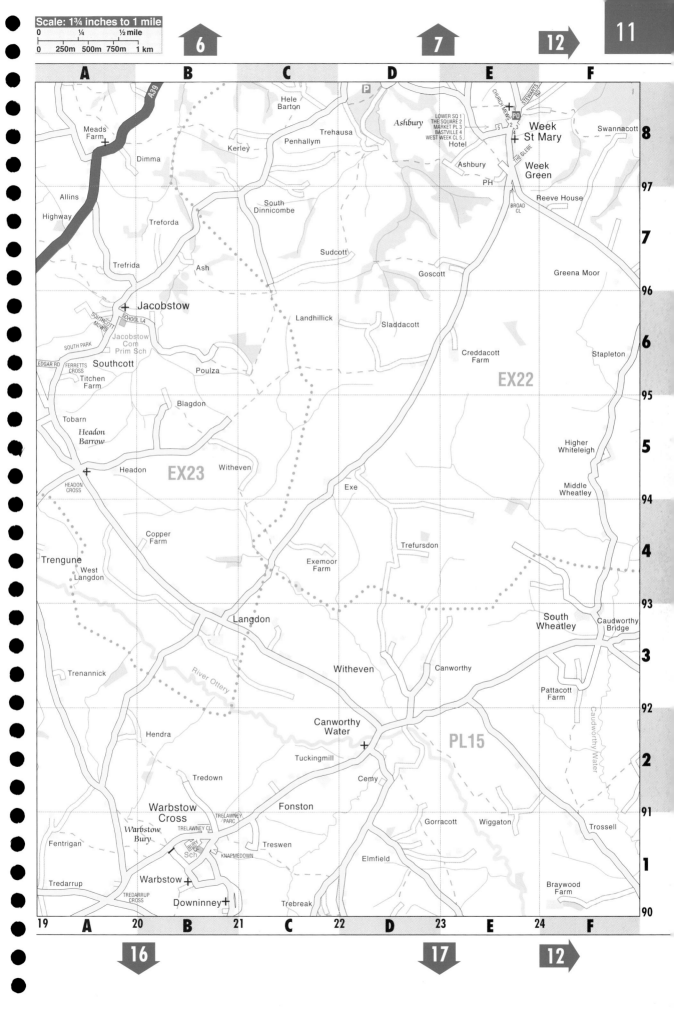

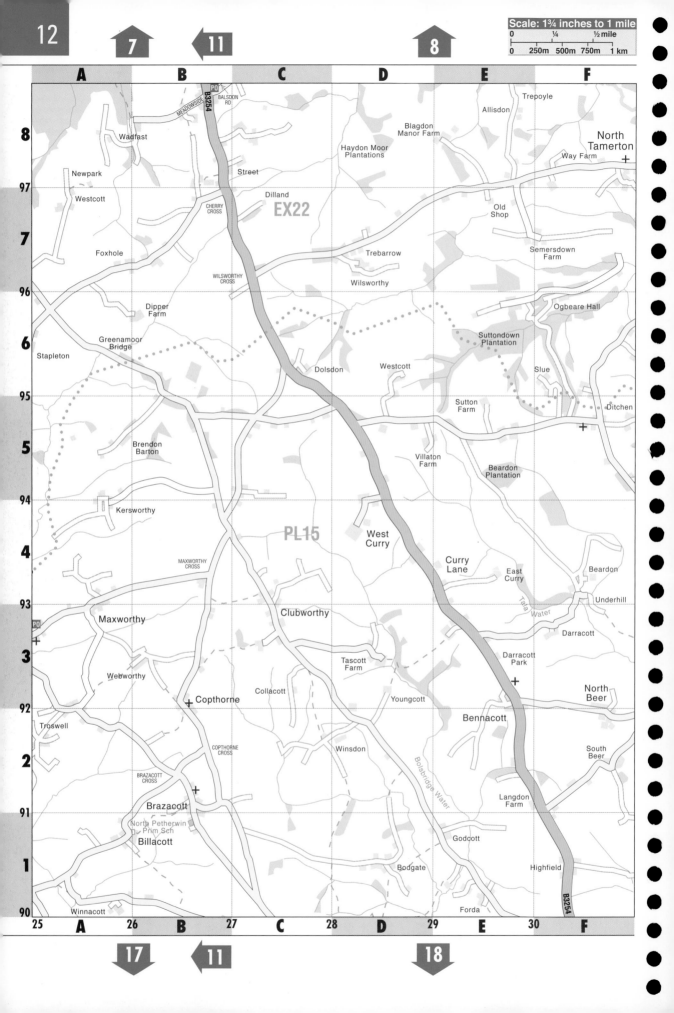

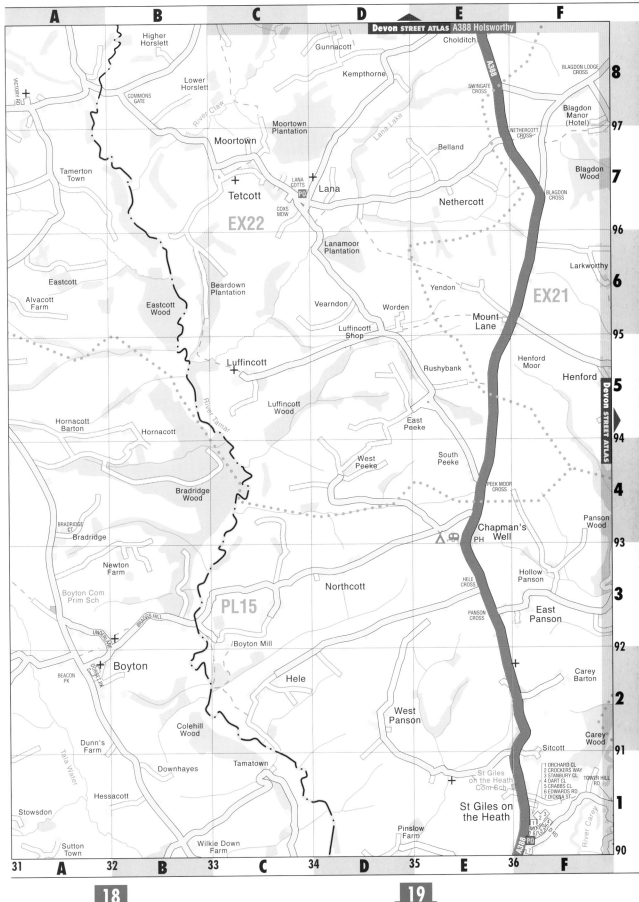

Scale: 1¾ inches to 1 mile

0   ¼   ½ mile
0 250m 500m 750m 1 km

Devon STREET ATLAS **A388 Holsworthy**

Devon STREET ATLAS

Higher Horslett

Lower Horslett

COMMONS GATE

Gunnacott

Kempthorne

Choldich

SWINGATE CROSS

BLAGDON LODGE CROSS

River Claw

Moortown Plantation

Lana Lake

Belland

NETHERCOTT CROSS

Blagdon Manor (Hotel)

Tamerton Town

Moortown

EX22

Tetcott

LANA COTTS

PO

Lana

Nethercott

Blagdon Wood

COXS MDW

BLAGDON CROSS

Lanamoor Plantation

Larkworthy

Eastcott

Beardown Plantation

Vearndon

Worden

Yendon

Mount Lane

EX21

Alvacott Farm

Eastcott Wood

Luffincott Shop

Henford Moor

Henford

Hornacott Barton

Hornacott

Luffincott

Rushybank

River Tamar

Luffincott Wood

East Peeke

South Peeke

Bradridge Wood

West Peeke

PEEK MOOR CROSS

Panson Wood

BRADRIDGE CT

Bradridge

Chapman's Well

PH

Hollow Panson

Newton Farm

Boyton Com Prim Sch

Northcott

HELE CROSS

East Panson

PL15

BRAGGS HILL

PANSON CROSS

UNDERLANE

Boyton Mill

Carey Barton

DORSET PK

Boyton

BEACON PK

Hele

West Panson

Carey Wood

Dunn's Farm

Colehill Wood

Sitcott

TOWER HILL RD

Downhayes

Tamatown

St Giles on the Heath Com Sch

1 ORCHARD CL
2 CROCKERS WAY
3 STANBURY CL
4 DART CL
5 CRABBS CL
6 EDWARDS RD
7 DICKNA ST

Hessacott

River Carey

Stowsdon

Pinslow Farm

St Giles on the Heath

A388

PO

Sutton Town

Wilkie Down Farm

Tala Water

Scale: 1¾ inches to 1 mile
0 ¼ ½ mile
0 250m 500m 750m 1 km

9

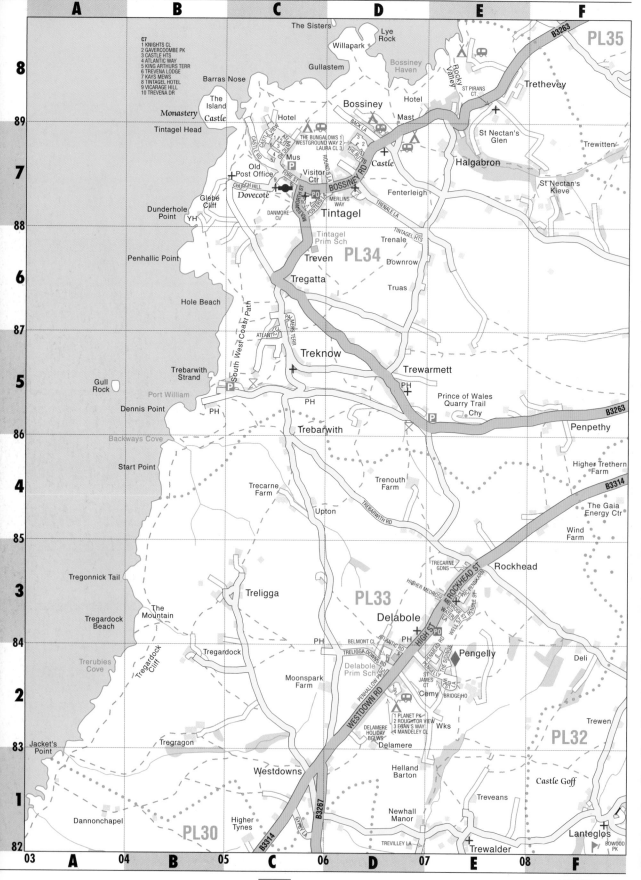

C7
1 KNIGHTS CL
2 GAVERCOOMBE PK
3 CASTLE HTS
4 ATLANTIC WAY
5 KING ARTHURS TERR
6 TREVENA LODGE
7 KAYS MEWS
8 TINTAGEL HOTEL
9 VICARAGE HILL
10 TREVENA DR

PL35

The Sisters
Willapark
Lye Rock
Gullastem
Bossiney Haven
Rocky Valley
ST PIRANS CT.
Trethevey
Barras Nose
Bossiney
Hotel
Mast
St Nectan's Glen
Trewitten
Monastery
The Island
Castle
Hotel
BACK LA
Halgabron
St Nectan's Kieve
Tintagel Head
THE BUNGALOWS 1
WESTGROUND WAY 2
LAURA CL 3
THE BUTTS
Castle
Old Post Office
Mus
Visitor Ctr
Fenterleigh
BOSSINEY RD
Dunderhole Point
Glebe Cliff
Dovecote
CHURCH HILL
PO
MERLINS WAY
TRENALE LA
YH
DANMORE CL
Tintagel
Tintagel Prim Sch
Tintagel HTS
Trenale
Penhallic Point
Treven
Downrow
Tregatta
Truas
Hole Beach
South West Coast Path
PALMERS TERR
ATLANTIC CL
Treknow
Trewarmett
Trebarwith Strand
Gull Rock
Port William
PH
Prince of Wales Quarry Trail
Chy
Dennis Point
PH
Trebarwith
PH
B3263
Penpethy
Backways Cove
Higher Trethern Farm
Start Point
B3314
Trecarne Farm
Trenouth Farm
The Gaia Energy Ctr
Upton
TREBARWITH RD
Wind Farm
TRECARNE GDNS
Tregonnick Tail
Treligga
HIGHER MEDROSE
ROCKHEAD ST
Rockhead
The Mountain
PL33
Delabole
HIGH ST
Pengelly
Deli
Tregardock Beach
PH
BELMONT CL
PH
Trerubies Cove
Tregardock Cliff
Tregardock
ATLANTIC RD
TRELIGGA DOWNS RD
Delabole Prim Sch
JAMES CT
THE SIDINGS
BRIDGE HO
Trewen
Moonspark Farm
PENHALLOW RD
WESTDOWN RD
Cemy
Wks
PL32
Tregragon
1 PLANET PK
2 ROUGHTOR VIEW
3 EGAN'S WAY
4 MANDELEY CL
DELAMERE HOLIDAY BGLWS
Delamere
Castle Goff
Westdowns
Helland Barton
Treveans
Jacket's Point
B3267
B3314
GYPSY LA
Newhall Manor
Lanteglos
Dannonchapel
PL30
Higher Tynes
TREVILLEY LA
Trewalder
BOWOOD PK

03 A 04 B 05 C 06 D 07 E 08 F

23

24

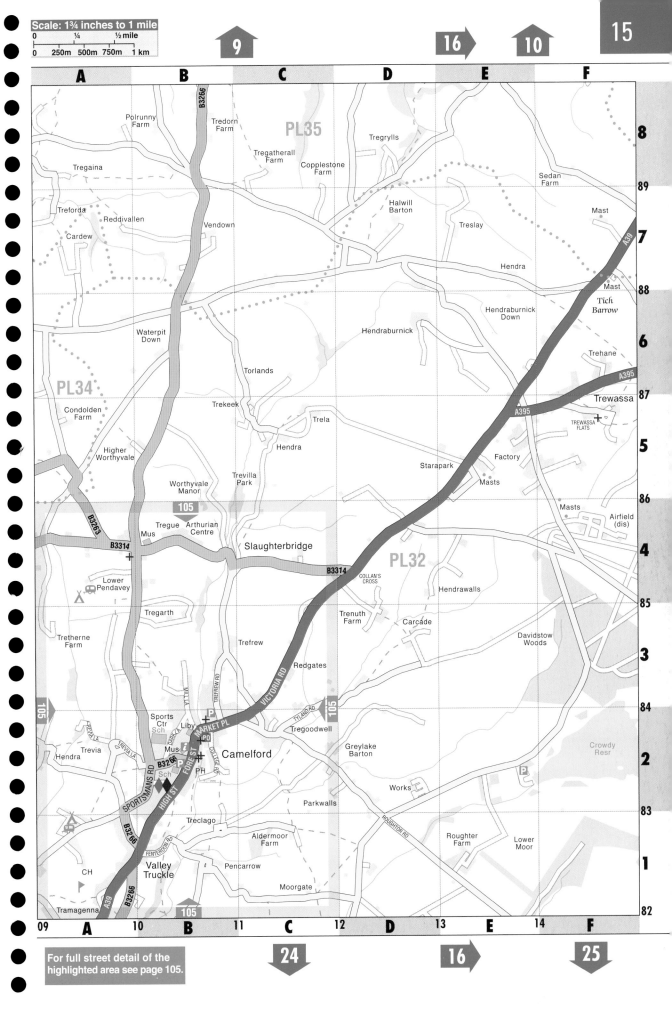

Scale: 1¾ inches to 1 mile

0   ¼   ½ mile
0 250m 500m 750m 1 km

9   16   10

A   B   C   D   E   F

Polrunny
Farm

Tredorn
Farm

PL35

Tregrylls

Sedan
Farm

Tregaina

Tregatherall
Farm

Copplestone
Farm

8

Treforda

Reddivallen

Vendown

Halwill
Barton

Treslay

89

Mast

Cardew

Hendra

Mast

A39

7

Tich
Barrow

88

Waterpit
Down

Hendraburnick
Down

Trehane

6

PL34

Torlands

Hendraburnick

A395

Trewassa

87

Condolden
Farm

Trekeek

Trela

A395

TREWASSA
FLATS

Higher
Worthyvale

Hendra

Factory

5

Worthyvale
Manor

Trevilla
Park

Starapark

Masts

86

105

B3263

Tregue
Mus

Arthurian
Centre

Masts

Masts

Airfield
(dis)

B3314

Slaughterbridge

PL32

4

Lower
Pendavey

B3314

COLLAN'S
CROSS

Hendrawalls

85

Tregarth

Trefrew

Trenuth
Farm

Carcade

Davidstow
Woods

3

Tretherne
Farm

Redgates

TREFREW RD

MILLLA

VICTORIA RD

TYLAND RD

105

Tregoodwell

84

Hendra

Trevia

TREVIA LA

FREVIA LA

Sports
Ctr
Sch

Liby

MARKET PL

P
P
PO

Camelford

Greylake
Barton

Crowdy
Resr

2

B3266

Mus
SPORTSMANS RD

FORE ST

COLLEGE RD

HIGH ST

Sch
P
PH

Works

P

83

B3266

Treclago

FENTEROON RD

Parkwalls

ROUGHTOR RD

Roughter
Farm

Lower
Moor

CH

Aldermoor
Farm

Moorgate

1

A39

B3266

Valley
Truckle

Pencarrow

Tramagenna

105

82

09   A   10   B   11   C   12   D   13   E   14   F

24   16   25

For full street detail of the
highlighted area see page 105.

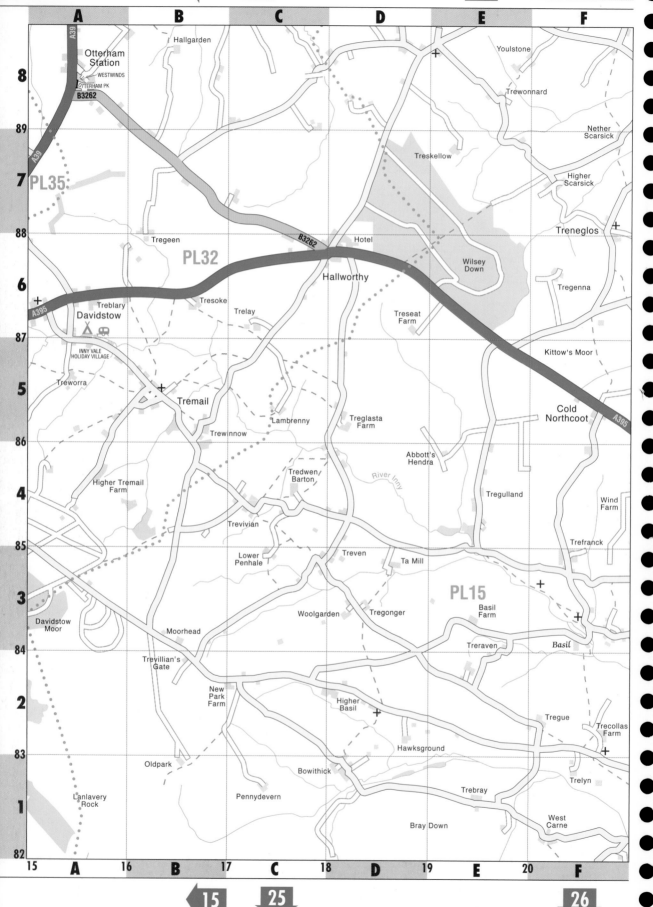

A B C D E F

8

89

7   PL35

88

6

87

5

86

4

85

3

84

2

83

1

82

15 A 16 B 17 C 18 D 19 E 20 F

A39
Otterham
Station
WESTWINDS
OTTERHAM PK
B3262
Hallgarden
Youlstone
Trewonnard
Nether
Scarsick
Higher
Scarsick
Treskellow
Treneglos
Tregeen
PL32
B3262
Hotel
Tregenna
Wilsey
Down
Hallworthy
A395
Treblary
Davidstow
Tresoke
Trelay
Treseat
Farm
Kittow's Moor
INNY VALE
HOLIDAY VILLAGE
Treworra
Tremail
Lambrenny
Treglasta
Farm
Cold
Northcoot
A395
Trewinnow
Abbott's
Hendra
Higher Tremail
Farm
Tredwen
Barton
River Inny
Tregulland
Wind
Farm
Trevivian
Trefranck
Lower
Penhale
Treven
Ta Mill
PL15
Davidstow
Moor
Moorhead
Woolgarden
Tregonger
Basil
Farm
Treraven
Basil
Tregue
Trevillian's
Gate
Trecollas
Farm
New
Park
Farm
Higher
Basil
Hawksground
Oldpark
Bowithick
Trebray
Trelyn
Lanlavery
Rock
Pennydevern
Bray Down
West
Carne

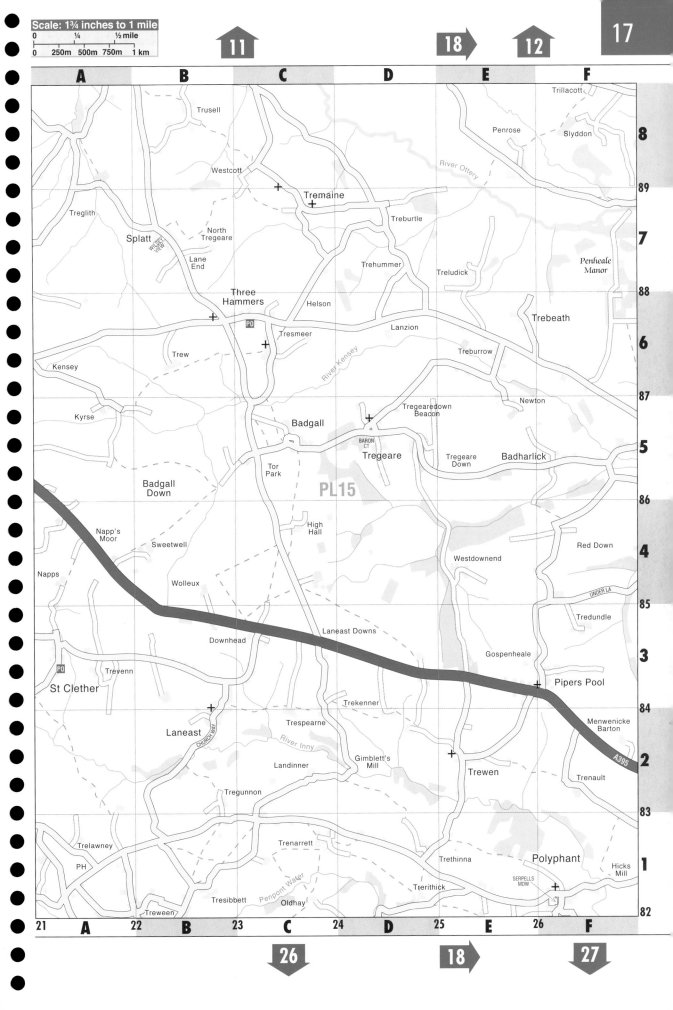

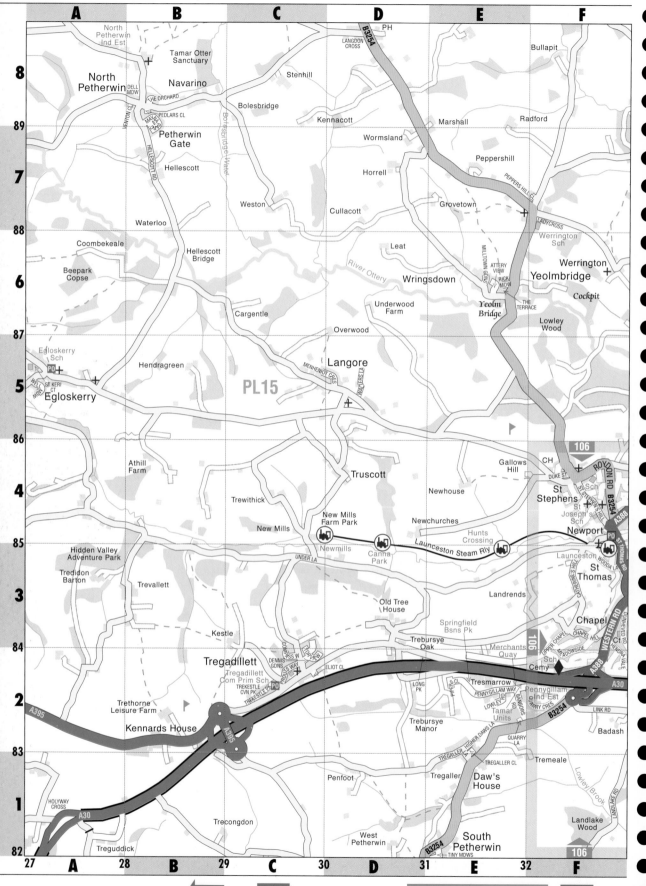

17 12

Scale: 1¾ inches to 1 mile

0   ¼   ½ mile
0 250m 500m 750m 1 km

A   B   C   D   E   F

8

North Petherwin Ind Est

Tamar Otter Sanctuary

North Petherwin

DELL MDW

Navarino

Stenhill

THE ORCHARD

PEDLARS CL

Bolesbridge

Kennacott

B3254

LANGDON CROSS

PH

Bullapit

Marshall

Radford

89

Petherwin Gate

VENTON CL

MALT

Hellescott

HELLESCOTT RD

Wormsland

Peppershill

PEPPERS HILL CL

7

Hellescott

Weston

Horrell

Cullacott

Grovetown

Werrington Sch

LADYCROSS

Werrington

88

Waterloo

Coombekeale

Hellescott Bridge

Leat

River Ottery

Wringsdown

MILLTOWN GDNS

ATTERY VIEW

RICKI MDW

Yeolmbridge

THE TERRACE

Cockpit

6

Beepark Copse

Cargentle

Underwood Farm

Yeolm Bridge

Lowley Wood

87

Egloskerry Sch

PO

Hendragreen

Overwood

Langore

MENHENIOT CRES

WATERS LA

CH

Gallows Hill

106

ROYDON RD

DUKE ST

5

WELL MDW

ST KERI CT

Egloskerry

PL15

St Stephens

ST STEPHENS HILL

St Joseph's Sch

B3254

A388

86

Athill Farm

Truscott

Newhouse

Newchurches

Hunts Crossing

Newport

PO

ST THOMAS RD

WOODA RD

4

Trewithick

New Mills Farm Park

Launceston Steam Rly

St Thomas

Trevallett

New Mills

Newmills

UNDER LA

Canna Park

Landrends

Chapel

CHAPEL HL

85

Hidden Valley Adventure Park

Tredidon Barton

Old Tree House

Springfield Bsns Pk

Merchants Quay

106

UPPER CHAPEL

MEADOWSIDE

WESTERN RD

A388

DUNHEVED RD

KENSEY VALE

3

Kestle

Treburseye Oak

Cemy

A30

84

Tregadillett

COMPASS W

TORK PKWY

DENNIS GDNS

PROUSE WAY

ELIOT CL

LONG PK

Tresmarrow

PENNYGILLAM WAY

LOWLEY

Tamar Units

BANGORS LA

Pennygillam Ind Est

QUARRY CRES

B3254

LINK RD

Badash

2

A395

Tregadillett Com Prim Sch

TREKESTLE CVN PK

TREKESTLE RD

Trethorne Leisure Farm

Treburseye Manor

Tregaller

TREGALLER

HIGHER DAWS LA

QUARRY LA

TREGALLER CL

Tremeale

LOWLEY BROOK

83

Kennards House

A395

Penfoot

Daw's House

LANDLAKE RD

1

HOLYWAY CROSS

A30

Trecongdon

West Petherwin

B3254

South Petherwin

TINY MDWS

Landlake Wood

106

82

Treguddick

17 27

For full street detail of the highlighted area see page 106.

28

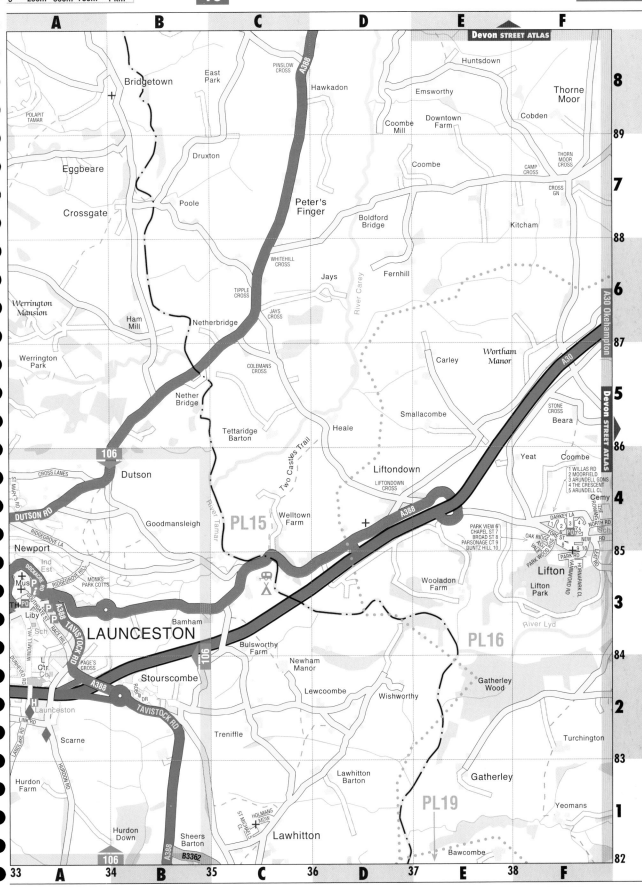

Devon STREET ATLAS

A B C D E F

8
Bridgetown
East Park
Hawkadon
Huntsdown
Emsworthy
Thorne Moor
Cobden

POLAPIT TAMAR

89
Coombe Mill
Downtown Farm
Coombe
CAMP CROSS
THORN MOOR CROSS
Eggbeare
Druxton

7
Crossgate
Poole
Peter's Finger
Boldford Bridge
Kitcham
CROSS GN

88
WHITEHILL CROSS
Fernhill

6
Werrington Mansion
Jays
River Carey
A30 Okehampton

TIPPLE CROSS
JAYS CROSS
Carley
Wortham Manor

87
Ham Mill
Netherbridge
Werrington Park
COLEMANS CROSS
Smallacombe
A30
Beara
STONE CROSS

5
Nether Bridge
Heale
Yeat
Coombe

86
Tettaridge Barton
Two Castles Trail
Liftondown
1 WILLAS RD
2 MOORFIELD
3 ARUNDELL GDNS
4 THE CRESCENT
5 ARUNDELL CL

106
Dutson
LIFTONDOWN CROSS
DARKEY LA
NORTH RD
Cemy

CROSS LANES
ST MARY'S RD
Goodmansleigh
Welltown Farm
PL15
Park View 6
CHAPEL ST 7
BROAD ST 8
PARSONAGE CT 9
DUNTZ HILL 10
OAK RIDGE HS
FORE ST
PARK RD

4
DUTSON RD
RIDGEGROVE LA

85
Newport
Ind Est
Mus
Liby
TH PO
Wooladon Farm
Lifton
Lifton Park

3
DOCKACRE RD
SOUTHGATE ST
RIDGEGROVE HILL
MONKS PARK COTTS
River Lyd
PL16

LAUNCESTON
Bamham
Bulsworthy Farm

84
Sch
PAGE'S CROSS
A388
Stourscombe
Newham Manor
Lewcoombe
Wishworthy
Gatherley Wood

2
Ctr Coll
WINDMILL HILL
RACE HILL
TAVISTOCK RD
ROBIN DR
Launceston
Treniffle
Lawhitton Barton
Gatherley
Turchington

83
LINK RD
H
Scarne
DUNHEVED RD
LANDLAKE RD
HURDON RD

1
Hurdon Farm
ST MICHAELS CL
HOLMANS MDW
Lawhitton
PL19
Yeomans

82
Hurdon Down
Sheers Barton
B3362
Bawcombe

106
A388

33 A 34 B 35 C 36 D 37 E 38 F

For full street detail of the highlighted area see page 106.

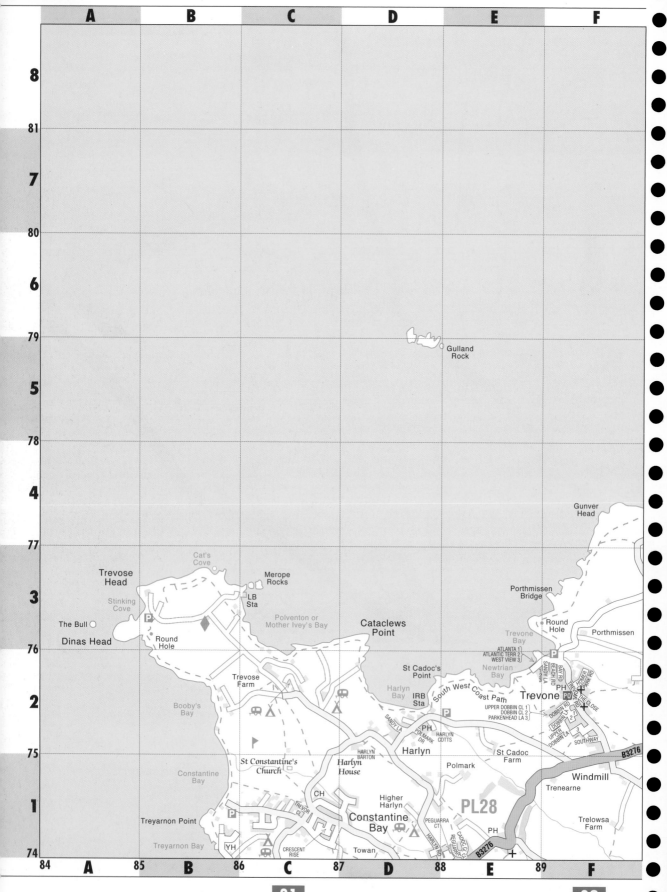

Scale: 1¾ inches to 1 mile

0 ¼ ½ mile
0 250m 500m 750m 1 km

A **B** **C** **D** **E** **F**

8
81
7
80
6
79
Gulland Rock
5
78
4
Gunver Head
77
Cat's Cove
Trevose Head
Merope Rocks
Porthmissen Bridge
3
Stinking Cove
LB Sta
Polventon or Mother Ivey's Bay
Cataclews Point
Round Hole
Porthmissen
The Bull
Round Hole
Trevone Bay
Dinas Head
76
St Cadoc's Point
ATLANTA 1
ATLANTIC TERR 2
WEST VIEW 3
Newtrian Bay
BAY RD
BEACH RD
SANDY LA
Trevose Farm
Harlyn Bay
IRB Sta
South West Coast Path
Trevone
THE CLOSE
PARK RD
2
Booby's Bay
UPPER DOBBIN CL 1
DOBBIN CL 2
PARKENHEAD LA 3
DOBBIN RD
UPPER DOBBIN LA
3
SANDY LA
PH
POLMARK DR
HARLYN COTTS
SOUTHWAY
HARLYN BARTON
Harlyn
St Cadoc Farm
75
PH
Constantine Bay
St Constantine's Church
Harlyn House
Polmark
Windmill
Trenearne
CH
TREVOR CL
Higher Harlyn
PL28
1
Treyarnon Point
P
PEGUARRA CT
CADOC CL
PEGUARRA RD
PH
Trelowsa Farm
Constantine Bay
B3276
Trelowsa Farm
YH
CRESCENT RISE
Towan
HARLYN RD
B3276
74
84 **A** 85 **B** 86 **C** 87 **D** 88 **E** 89 **F**

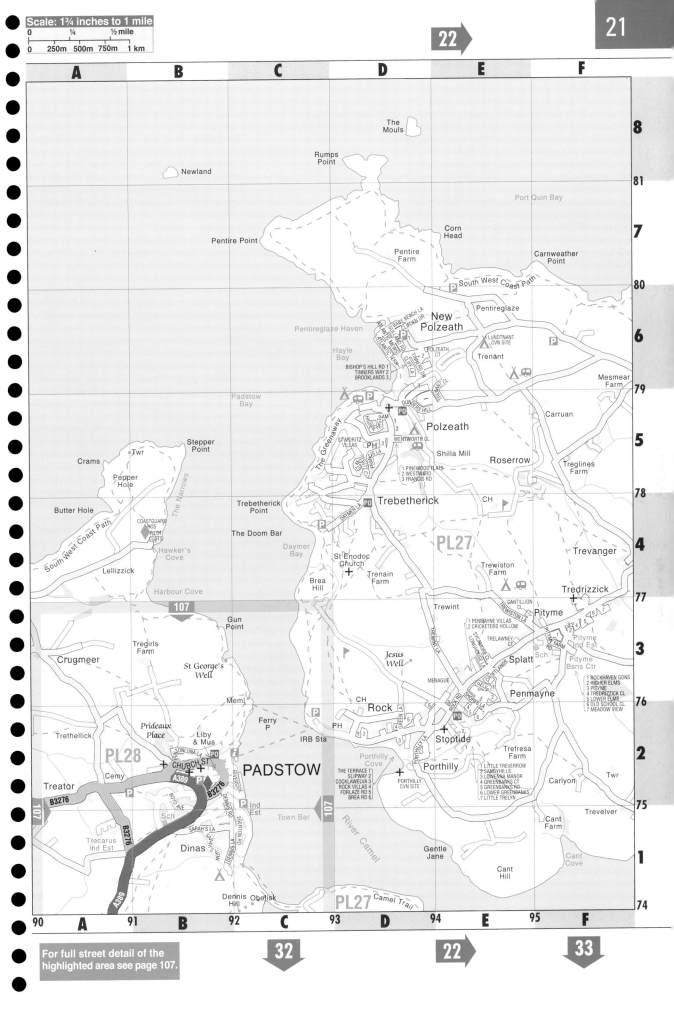

Scale: 1¾ inches to 1 mile

0   ¼   ½ mile

0   250m   500m   750m   1 km

A   B   C   D   E   F

The Mouls

Newland

Rumps Point

Port Quin Bay

Pentire Point

Corn Head

Pentire Farm

Carnweather Point

South West Coast Path

Pentireglaze

New Polzeath

Pentireglaze Haven

Hayle Bay

GT BABY BEACH LA
CLIFDON DR
GILL LANDS
ATLANTIC GDNS
ATLANTIC TERR
CLIFF LA
TINNERS DR

POLZEATH CT

Mesmear Farm

LUNDTNANT CVN SITE

Trenant

TRENANT CL

Padstow Bay

BISHOP'S HILL RD 1
TINNERS WAY 2
BROOKLANDS 3

DUNDERS HILL
PO

Polzeath

Carruan

HIGHER

ST MORITZ VILLAS
PH
JAS LA
TERR
FARM

WENTWORTH CL

Shilla Mill

Roserrow

Treglines Farm

Stepper Point

Crams

Twr

Pepper Hole

The Greenaway

1 PINEWOOD FLATS
2 WESTWARD
3 FRANCIS RD

Trebetherick

CH

Butter Hole

The Narrows

Trebetherick Point

DAYMER LA
PO

PL27

Trevanger

COASTGUARD HOS
PILOT COTTS

South West Coast Path

Hawker's Cove

The Doom Bar

Daymer Bay

St Enodoc Church

Trewiston Farm

Tredrizzick

Lellizzick

Brea Hill

Trenain Farm

Harbour Cove

107

Trewint

CANTILLON CL
TREWISTON LA

Pityme

Gun Point

Crugmeer

Tregirls Farm

St George's Well

Jesus Well

TREWINT LA

1 PENMAYNE VILLAS
2 CRICKETERS HOLLOW

TRELAWNEY CT

SYCAMORE CL
LONGMEADOW

PITYME FARM

Pityme Ind Est

1 ROCKHAVEN GDNS
2 HIGHER ELMS
3 PITYME
4 TREDRIZZICK CL
5 LOWER ELMS
6 OLD SCHOOL CL
7 MEADOW VIEW

Meml

CH

MENAGUE

CROFTLANDS

Splatt

Sch

Pityme Bsns Ctr

Trethellick

Prideaux Place

Liby & Mus

Ferry P

ROCK RD

Penmayne

Treator

PL28

ONLUNA LA
PO

CHURCH ST
A389
P

RIVERSIDE

PADSTOW

IRB Sta

CH

Rock

GREEN LA

PH

Stoptide

PO

Trefresa Farm

Cemy

BOYD AVE

DENNIS RD

Ind Est

PH

Porthilly Cove

Porthilly

1 LITTLE TREVERROW
2 SANDYHILLS
3 LONEDNA MANOR
4 GREENBANKS CT
5 GREENBANKS RD
6 LOWER GREENBANKS
7 LITTLE TRELYN

Carlyon

B3276

Sch

SARAH'S LA
SARAH'S VW

EGERTON RD

DENNIS LA

Town Bar

107

PORTHILLY
CVN SITE

THE TERRACE 1
SLIPWAY 2
COCKLAWELVA 3
ROCK VILLAS 4
FORLAZE RD 5
BREA RD 6

PORTHILLY

Twr

Trevelver

107

B3276

Trecarus Ind Est

Dinas

River Camel

Gentle Jane

Cant Farm

Cant Cove

A389

Dennis Hill

Dennis Obelisk

Camel Trail

PL27

Cant Hill

90   A   91   B   92   C   93   D   94   E   95   F

8
81
7
80
6
79
5
78
4
77
3
76
2
75
1
74

For full street detail of the highlighted area see page 107.

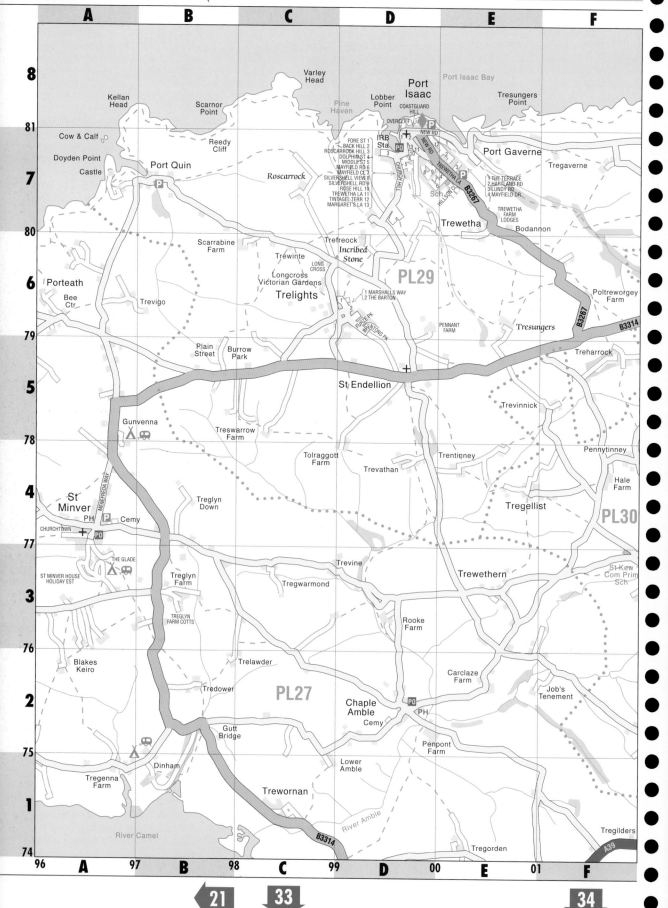

← 21

Scale: 1¾ inches to 1 mile

0 | ¼ | ½ mile

0 | 250m | 500m | 750m | 1 km

A B C D E F

8

81

Varley
Head

Port Isaac
Port Isaac Bay

Kellan
Head

Scarnor
Point

Pine
Haven

Lobber
Point

Tresungers
Point

Cow & Calf

Reedy
Cliff

COASTGUARD
HILL

OVERCLIFF

NEW RD

P

Doyden Point
Castle

Port Quin

P

Roscarrock

IRB
Sta

PO

NEW RD

TREWETHA LA

Port Gaverne

Tregaverne

7

Porteath

FORE ST 1
BACK HILL 2
ROSCARROCK HILL 3
DOLPHIN ST 4
MIDDLE ST 5
MAYFIELD RD 6
MAYFIELD CL 7
SILVERSHELL VIEW 8
SILVERSHELL RD 9
ROSE HILL 10
TREWETHA LA 11
TINTAGEL TERR 12
MARGARET'S LA 13

CHURCH HILL

P

HILLSON CL

B3267

Sch

1 THE TERRACE
2 HARTLAND RD
3 LUNDY RD
4 MAYFIELD DR

TREWETHA
FARM
LODGES

Trewetha

Bodannon

80

Scarrabine
Farm

Trefreock

Trewinte

Incribed
Stone

LONG
CROSS

PL29

6

Bee
Ctr

Trevigo

Longcross
Victorian Gardens

Trelights

1 MARSHALLS WAY
2 THE BARTON

PENNANT
FARM

Tresungers

Poltreworgey
Farm

B3267

B3314

PURZE PK

BRENTONS PK

79

Plain
Street

Burrow
Park

St Endellion

Treharrock

5

Gunvenna

△ ⊞

Treswarrow
Farm

Trevinnick

78

Tolraggott
Farm

Trevathan

Trentinney

Pennytinney

Hale
Farm

4

St
Minver

PH

MENEFREDA WAY

P

Cemy

Treglyn
Down

Tregilders

Trevine

Tregellist

PL30

CHURCHTOWN

+

PO

77

St Minver House
Holiday Est

THE GLADE

△ ⊞

Treglyn
Farm

Tregwarmond

Trewethern

St Kew
Com Prim
Sch

3

TREGLYN
FARM COTTS

Rooke
Farm

76

Blakes
Keiro

Trelawder

Carclaze
Farm

Job's
Tenement

2

Tredower

PL27

Chaple
Amble

PO

PH

Cemy

Gutt
Bridge

Penpont
Farm

75

△ ⊞

Dinham

Lower
Amble

△

Tregenna
Farm

Treworman

1

River Camel

B3314

River Amble

Tregilders

74

Tregorden

A39

96 A 97 B 98 C 99 D 00 E 01 F

← 21   33 ↓   34 ↓

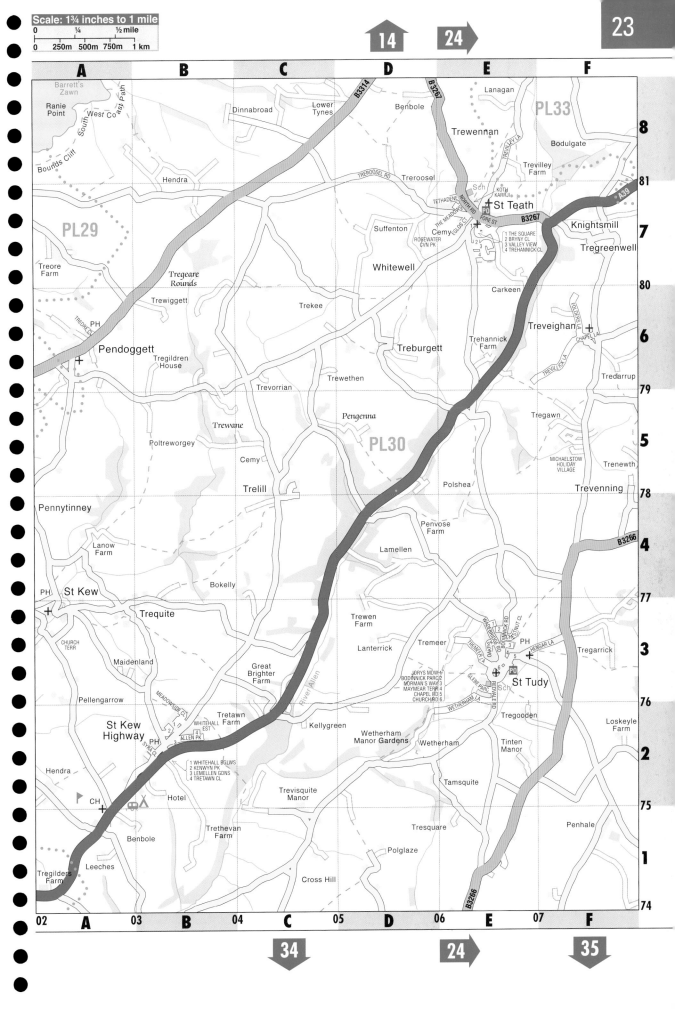

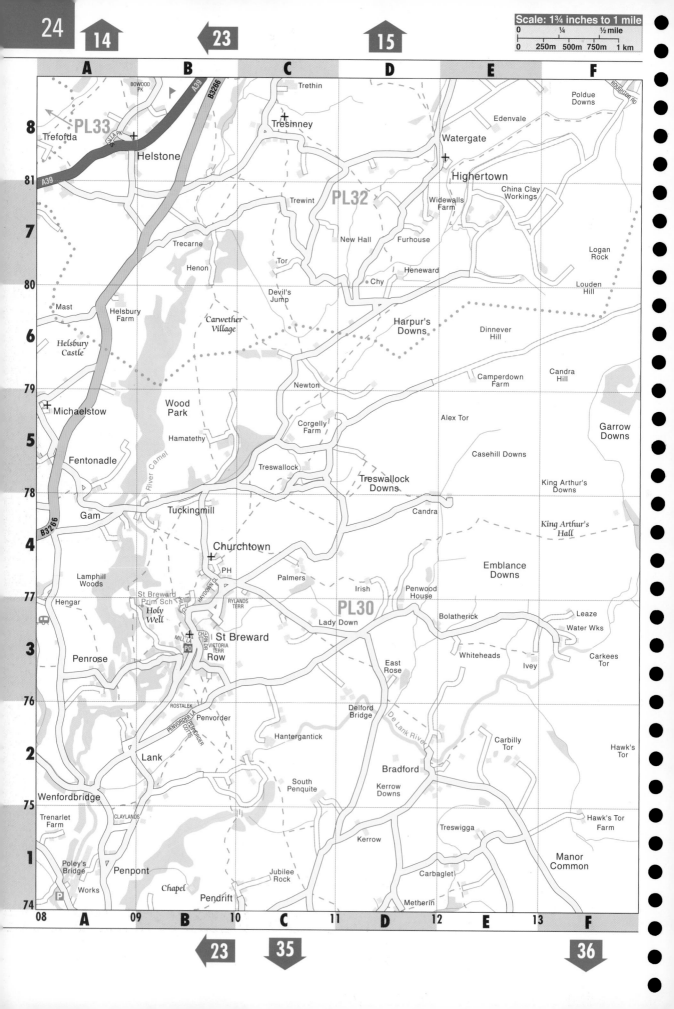

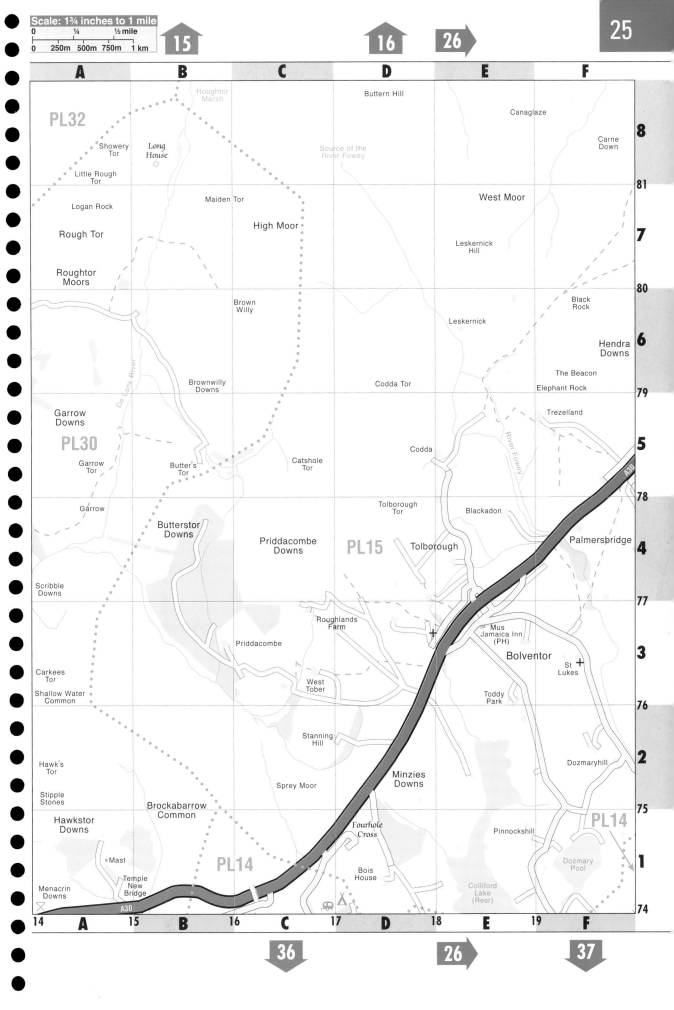

A   B   C   D   E   F

PL32

Roughtor Marsh

Buttern Hill

Canaglaze

Carne Down   8

Showery Tor   Long House

Source of the River Fowey

Little Rough Tor   81

Logan Rock   Maiden Tor   West Moor

Rough Tor   High Moor   Leskernick Hill   7

Roughtor Moors   80

Brown Willy   Leskernick   Black Rock   6

Hendra Downs

Brownwilly Downs   Codda Tor   The Beacon   79

Elephant Rock

Garrow Downs   Trezelland

PL30   Codda   5

Garrow Tor   Butter's Tor   Catshole Tor   78

Garrow   Butterstor Downs   Tolborough Tor   Blackadon   Palmersbridge   4

Priddacombe Downs   PL15   Tolborough   77

Scribble Downs   Roughlands Farm   Mus Jamaica Inn (PH)   3

Priddacombe   Bolventor   St Lukes

Carkees Tor   West Tober   Toddy Park   76

Shallow Water Common

Hawk's Tor   Stanning Hill   Dozmaryhill   2

Stipple Stones   Sprey Moor   Minzies Downs   75

Brockabarrow Common

Hawkstor Downs   Pinnockshill   PL14

PL14   Fourhole Cross   Dozmary Pool   1

Mast   Bois House

Menacrin Downs   Temple New Bridge   Colliford Lake (Resr)   74

A30

14   A   15   B   16   C   17   D   18   E   19   F

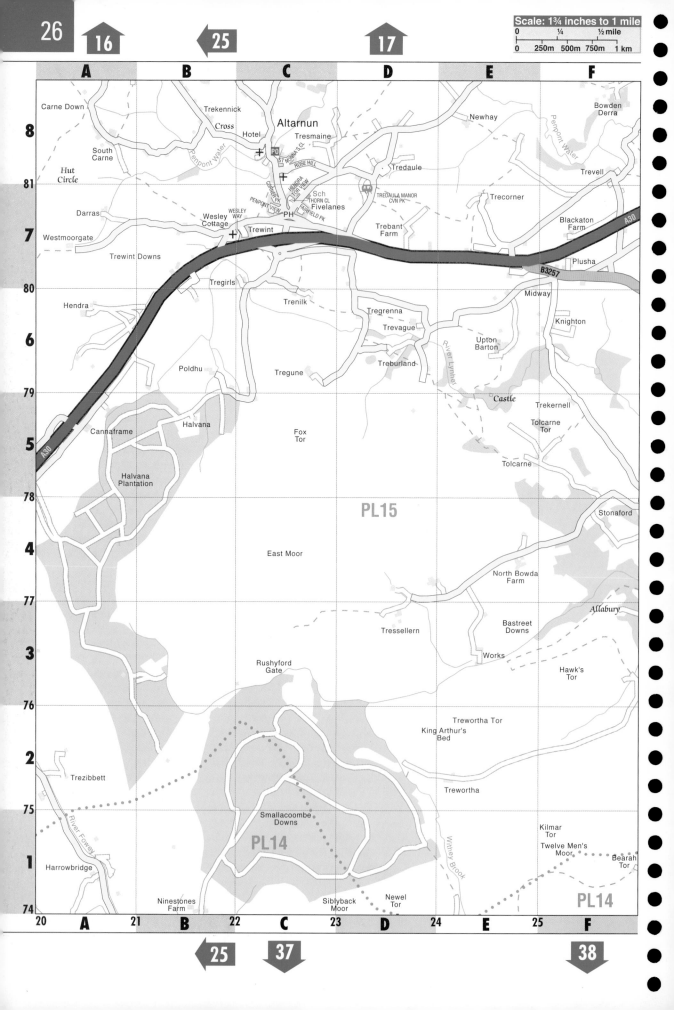

Scale: 1¾ inches to 1 mile
0   ¼   ½ mile
0 250m 500m 750m 1 km

A **B** **C** **D** **E** **F**

8
Carne Down
Trekennick
Cross
Hotel
Altarnun
Tresmaine
Newhay
Bowden Derra
South Carne
Hut Circle
PO
ST NONNA SQ.
ROSE HILL
Tredaule
Trevell

81
Darras
CORNER PK
HENDRA TOR VIEW
Sch
TREDAULA MANOR CVN PK
Trecorner
A30

7
Westmoorgate
Wesley Cottage
WESLEY WAY
PENPONT VIEW
Trewint
THORN CL
Fivelanes
FAIRFIELD PK
PH
Trebant Farm
Blackaton Farm
Trewint Downs
Plusha
B3257

80
Tregirls
Trenilk
Midway
Hendra
Trevague
Tregrenna
Knighton

6
Poldhu
Tregune
Treburland
River Lynher
Upton Barton

79
Halvana
Castle
Trekernell
Tolcarne Tor

5
Cannaframe
Fox Tor
Tolcarne
A30

78
Halvana Plantation
PL15
Stonaford

4
East Moor
North Bowda Farm

77
Tressellern
Bastreet Downs
Allabury

3
Rushyford Gate
Works
Hawk's Tor

76
Treworthia Tor
King Arthur's Bed

2
Trezibbett
Trewortha

75
River Fowey
Smallacoombe Downs
PL14
Kilmar Tor
Twelve Men's Moor
Withey Brook
Bearah Tor

1
Harrowbridge
PL14

74
Ninestones Farm
Siblyback Moor
Newel Tor

Penpont Water

A **B** **C** **D** **E** **F**
20 21 22 23 24 25

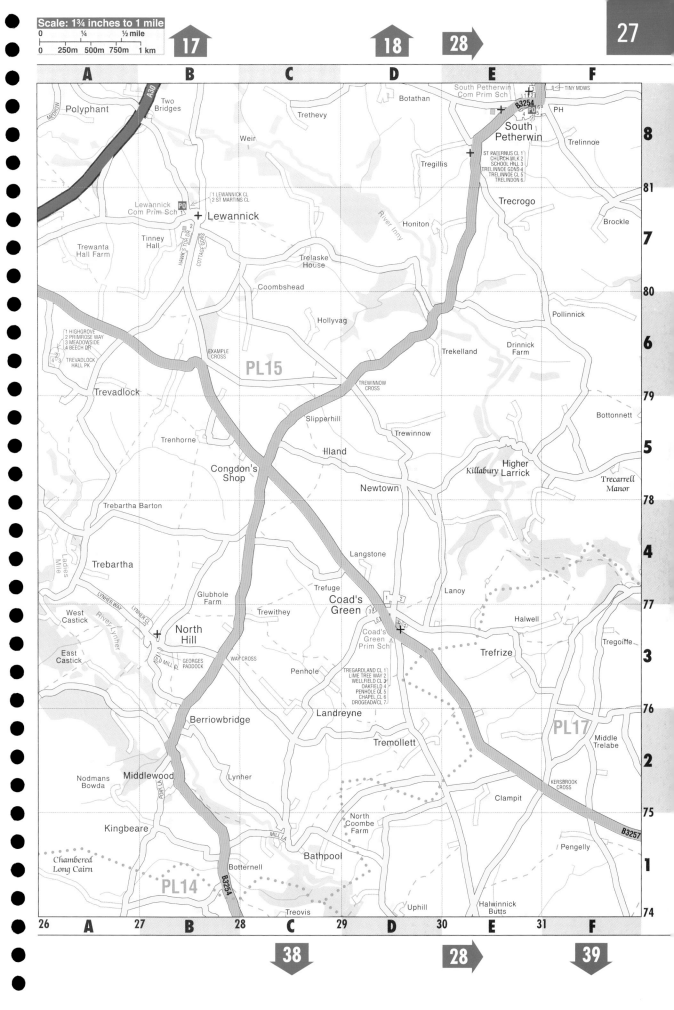

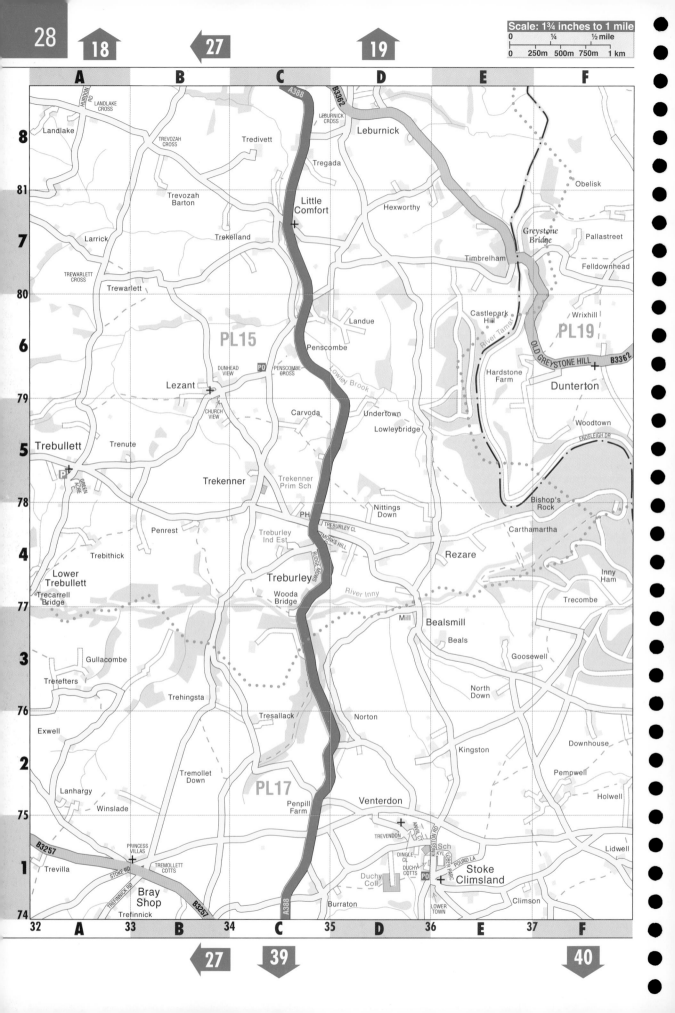

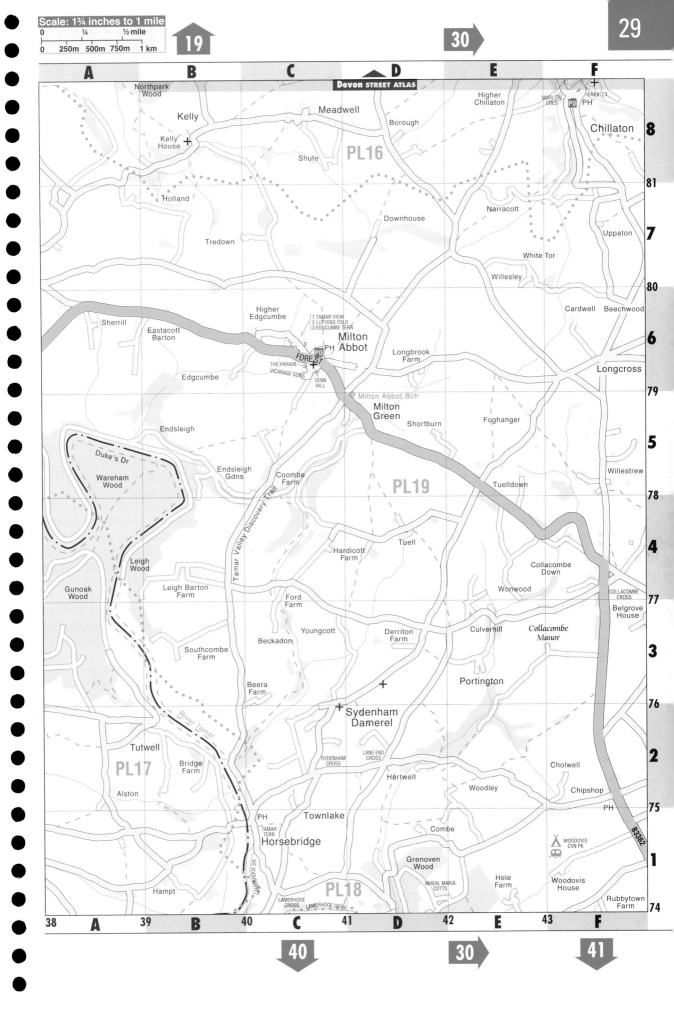

A | **B** | **C** | **D** | **E** | **F**

Northpark Wood

Kelly

Meadwell

Borough

Higher Chillaton

MARLOW CRES

PARK CT

PO

PH

Chillaton

8

Kelly House

Shute

PL16

Narracott

81

Holland

Downhouse

Uppaton

7

Tredown

White Tor

Willesley

80

Sherrill

Higher Edgcumbe

1 TAMAR VIEW
2 LUTYENS FOLD
3 EDGCUMBE TERR

Cardwell

Beechwood

Eastacott Barton

PH

Milton Abbot

Longbrook Farm

Longcross

6

Edgcumbe

FOREST

PO

THE PARADE

VICARAGE GDNS

VENN HILL

Milton Abbot Sch

Milton Green

Shortburn

Foghanger

79

Endsleigh

Coombe Farm

Tuelldown

Willestrew

5

Endsleigh Gdns

PL19

78

Duke's Dr

Wareham Wood

Hardicott Farm

Tuell

Collacombe Down

4

Leigh Wood

Leigh Barton Farm

Ford Farm

Wonwood

COLLACOMBE CROSS

77

Gunoak Wood

Youngcott

Derriton Farm

Culverhill

Collacombe Manor

Belgrove House

Southcombe Farm

Beckadon

Portington

3

Beera Farm

Sydenham Damerel

76

River Tamar

Tutwell

PL17

Bridge Farm

SYDENHAM CROSS

LANE END CROSS

Hartwell

Woodley

Cholwell

Chipshop

2

Alston

PH

TAMAR TERR

Townlake

Combe

PH

75

B3362

Horsebridge

WOODOVIS CVN PK

LAMERHOOE DR

Hampt

LAMERHOOE CROSS

LAMERHOOE DR

PL18

Grenoven Wood

WHEAL MARIA COTTS

Hele Farm

Woodovis House

Rubbytown Farm

1

74

29

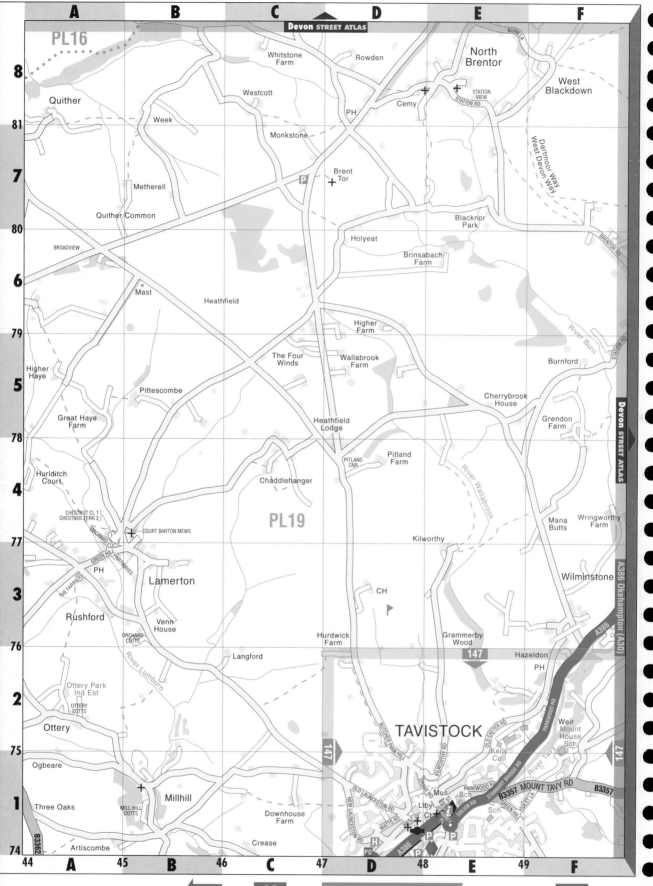

A   B   C   D   E   F

Devon STREET ATLAS

PL16

8

Quither

Whitstone Farm   Rowden   North Brentor   West Blackdown

81   Westcott   STATION VIEW   STATION RD

Week   Monkstone   PH   Cemy

7   Metherell   Brent Tor   P   Dartmoor Way / West Devon Way

Quither Common   Holyeat   Blacknor Park

80   BROADVIEW   Brinsabach Farm   River Burn

BRENTOR RD

6   Mast   Heathfield   Higher Farm   Burnford

79   Higher Haye   Pittescombe   The Four Winds   Wallabrook Farm   Cherrybrook House   Grendon Farm

5   Great Haye Farm   Heathfield Lodge   River Wallabrook   Mana Butts   Wringworthy Farm

78   Hurlditch Court   Chaddlehanger   PITLAND CNR.   Pitland Farm

Devon STREET ATLAS

4   CHESTNUT CL 1 / CHESTNUT TERR 2   PL19   Kilworthy   Wilminstone

77   ORCHARD CT / PARTWAYES   Court Barton Mews   CH   A386 Okehampton (A30)

GREEN HILL   PH   Lamerton   Grammerby Wood   Hazeldon   PH

3   THE FARRIERS   Venn House   Hurdwick Farm   147

Rushford   ORCHARD COTTS   Langford   Kelly Coll   Weir Mount House Sch

76   River Lumburn   TAVISTOCK   OLD EXETER RD   PARKWOOD RD

2   Ottery Park Ind Est   BUTCHER PARK HILL   KILWORTHY RD   STANNARY BRIDGE RD   River Tavy   147

OTTERY COTTS   147   PARKWOOD RD

75   Ottery   Mus   Sch   MOUNT TAVY RD   B3357

Ogbeare   OLD LAUNCESTON RD   TRANE RD   DOLVIN RD   GREEN HILL

1   Three Oaks   Millhill   Liby / Ct   Sch   B3357

MILL HILL COTTS   NEW LAUNCESTON RD   WATTS RD   WEST ST / DUKE ST   P   P

74   B3362   Artiscombe   Downhouse Farm   Crease   PO   H   A386

44   A   45   B   46   C   47   D   48   E   49   F

For full street detail of the highlighted area see page 147.

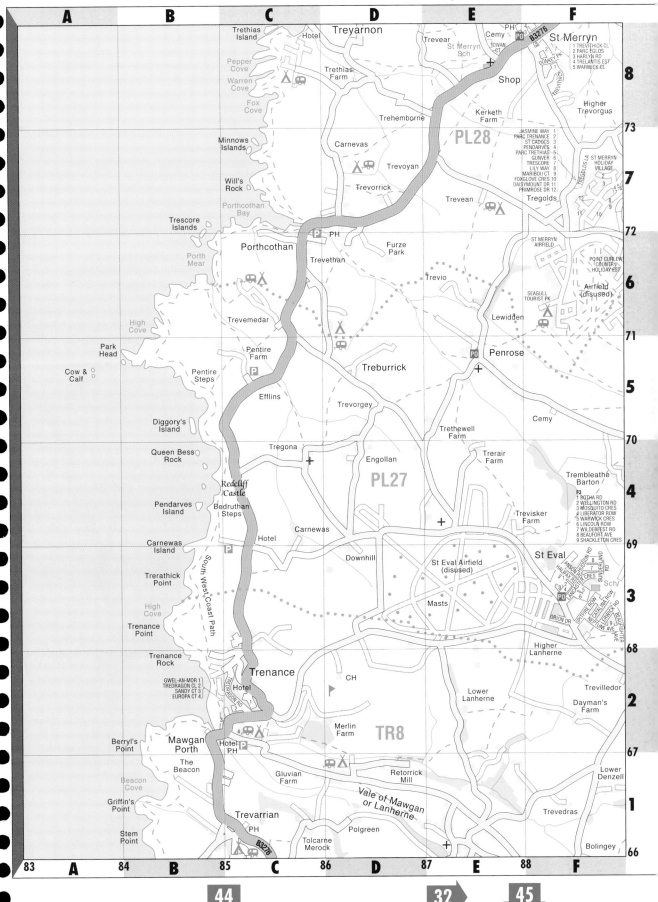

A   B   C   D   E   F

Trethias
Island

Treyarnon

Trevear

St Merryn
Sch   PH
Cemy   PO   B3276   St Merryn

Hotel

Pepper
Cove

Warren
Cove

Trethias
Farm

Trehemborne

Shop

Kerketh
Farm

TOWAN
CT

DONKEY PK

TREVITHICK

1 TREVITHICK CL
2 PARC EGLOS
3 HARLYN RD
4 TRELANTIS EST
5 WARWICK CL

Higher
Trevorgus

8

Fox
Cove

Minnows
Islands

Carnevas

Trevoyan

PL28

Trevorrick

Trevean

JASMINE WAY   1
PARC TRENANCE   2
ST CADOCS   3
PENDARVES   4
PARC TRETHIAS   5
GUNVER   6
TRESCORE   7
LILY WAY   8
MARIBOU CT   9
FOXGLOVE CRES 10
DAISYMOUNT DR 11
PRIMROSE DR 12

ST MERRYN
HOLIDAY
VILLAGE

73

7

Will's
Rock

Trescore
Islands

Porthcothan
Bay

Porth
Mear

Porthcothan

P   PH

Trevethan

Furze
Park

Trevio

Tregolds

12   3
11   10   9

St Merryn
Airfield

POINT CURLEW
COUNTRY
HOLIDAY EST

72

6

High
Cove

Trevemedar

Pentire
Farm

Park
Head

Cow &
Calf

Pentire
Steps

P

Efflins

Treburrick

Trevorgey

Penrose

Cemy

Airfield
(disused)

SEAGULL
TOURIST PK

Lewidden

PO

71

5

Diggory's
Island

Tregona

Engollan

Trethewell
Farm

Trerair
Farm

Trembleathe
Barton

70

Queen Bess
Rock

Redcliff
Castle

PL27

F3
1 BOTHA RD
2 WELLINGTON RD
3 MOSQUITO CRES
4 LIBERATOR ROW
5 WARWICK CRES
6 LINCOLN ROW
7 WILDEBEEST RD
8 BEAUFORT AVE
9 SHACKLETON CRES

4

Pendarves
Island

Bedruthan
Steps

Carnewas

Hotel

Trevisker
Farm

Carnewas
Island

P

Downhill

St Eval Airfield
(disused)

St Eval

69

Terathick
Point

South West Coast Path

High
Cove

Masts

ANSON RD
HUDSON RD
HALIFAX
CRES
LANCASTER

SUNDERLAND
RD

Sch

3

Trenance
Point

Trenance
Rock

TREDRAGON RD

Trenance

CH

Higher
Lanherne

PO   SPITFIRE ROW   ORION DR
CATALINA ROW
WARWICK   3
2   4   1
BEAUFIGHTER

LANCASTER
LANCASTER ROW
NEPTUNE AVE

68

2

GWEL-AN-MOR 1
TREDRAGON CL 2
SANDY CT 3
EUROPA CT 4

Hotel
PH

Merlin
Farm

Lower
Lanherne

Trevilledor

Dayman's
Farm

Berryl's
Point

Mawgan
Porth

The
Beacon

P

Gluvian
Farm

Retorrick
Mill

Lower
Denzell

67

1

Beacon
Cove

Griffin's
Point

Trevarrian

PH

Tolcarne
Merock

TR8

Polgreen

Vale of Mawgan
or Lanherne

Trevedras

Stem
Point

B3276

Bolingey

66

83   A   84   B   85   C   86   D   87   E   88   F

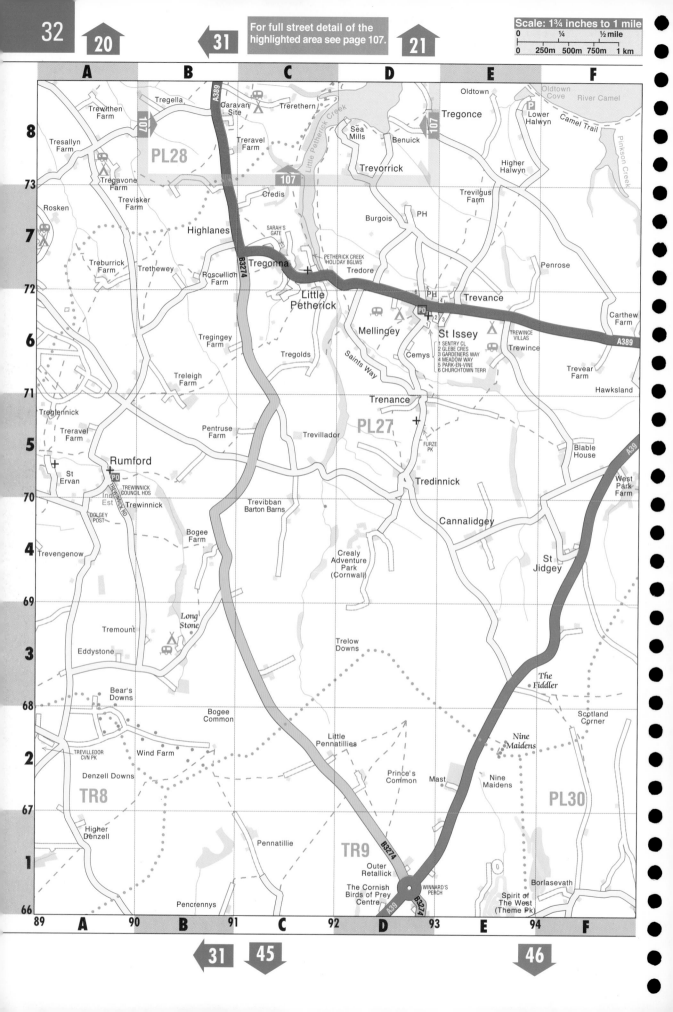

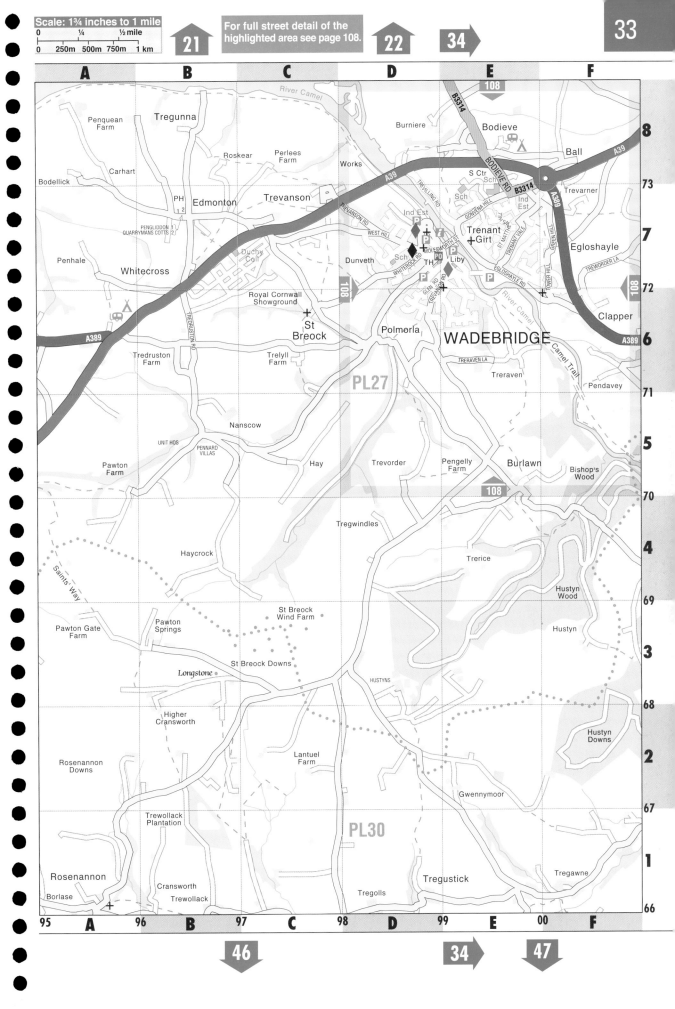

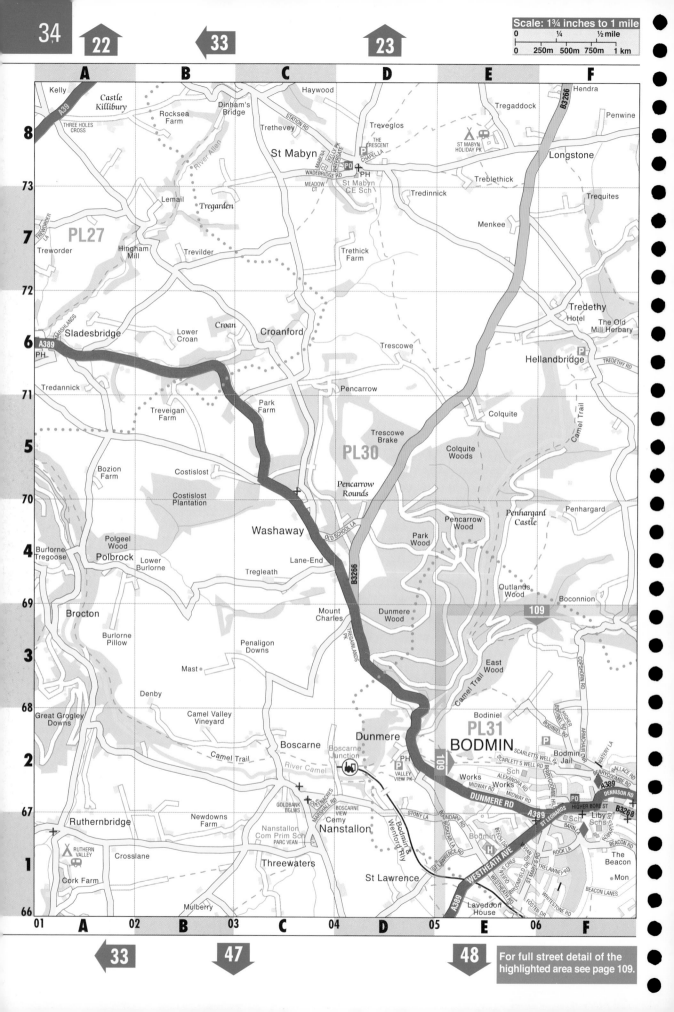

Scale: 1¾ inches to 1 mile
0 ¼ ½ mile
0 250m 500m 750m 1 km

A B C D E F

Kelly
Castle
Killibury
THREE HOLES CROSS
A39

8

Rocksea
Farm
Dinham's
Bridge
Haywood
Trethevey
STATION RD
Treveglos
Tregaddock
Penwine
Hendra
B3266
Longstone

River Allen
Lemail
St Mabyn
ST MABYN HOLIDAY PK
Treblethick
Trequites

73

Tregarden
WADEBRIDGE RD
MEADOW CT
PH
St Mabyn CE Sch
Tredinnick
Menkee
Tredethy
Hotel

PL27
Trevilder
Hingham Mill
Trethick Farm
The Old Mill Herbary

7

Treworder
Treworder
Croan
Croanford
Trescowe
Hellandbridge
TREDETHY RD
P

72

Lower Croan
Pencarrow
Colquite
Camel Trail

Sladesbridge
A389
PH
Tredannick
Treveigan Farm
Park Farm
Trescowe Brake
Colquite Woods

6

71

Bozion Farm
Costislost
Pencarrow Rounds
PL30
Pencarrow Wood
Penhargard Castle
Penhargard

Costislost Plantation
Washaway
OLD SCHOOL LA
Park Wood

5

70

Burlorne Tregoose
Polgeel Wood
Polbrock
Lower Burlorne
Lane-End
Tregleath
B3266
Dunmere Wood
Outlands Wood
Boconnion

4

69

Brocton
Burlorne Pillow
Penaligon Downs
Mount Charles
TREGARLANDS PK
Dunmere Wood
East Wood
Camel Trail
109

3

68

Great Grogley Downs
Mast
Denby
Camel Valley Vineyard
Boscarne
Camel Trail
Boscarne Junction
Dunmere
PH
VALLEY VIEW PK
P
109
Bodiniel
PL31
BODMIN
Scarletts Well
Bodmin Jail
WATERY LA
ARMCHAIR CNR
BODINIEL HIGHER
BODINIEL RD

2

Ruthernbridge
RUTHERN VALLEY
Newdowns Farm
GOLDBANK BGLWS
MARSHALL RD
Cemy
Nanstallon
Nanstallon Com Prim Sch
PARC VEAN
STONY LA
BOSCARNE VIEW
Bodmin & Wenford Rly
BOUNDARY RD
Works
Works
MIDWAY RD
ALEXANDRA RD
SCARLETTS WELL RD
Sch
BERRYCOOMBE HILL
A389
DENNISON RD
B3268
PO
HIGHER BORE ST
ST LEONARDS
Liby Schs
BEACON RD

67

Cork Farm
Crosslane
Threewaters
St Lawrence
ST LAWRENCE RD
BOSCAR LANE RD
A389
H
WESTHEATH AVE
Bodmin
Laveddon House
BROADFIELD DR
ST CREG
ROCK LA
ST MABES RD
TRELAWNE RD
WHITESTONE RD
FOSTER DR
BEACON LANES
The Beacon
Mon

1

Mulberry

66

01 A 02 B 03 C 04 D 05 E 06 F

For full street detail of the highlighted area see page 109.

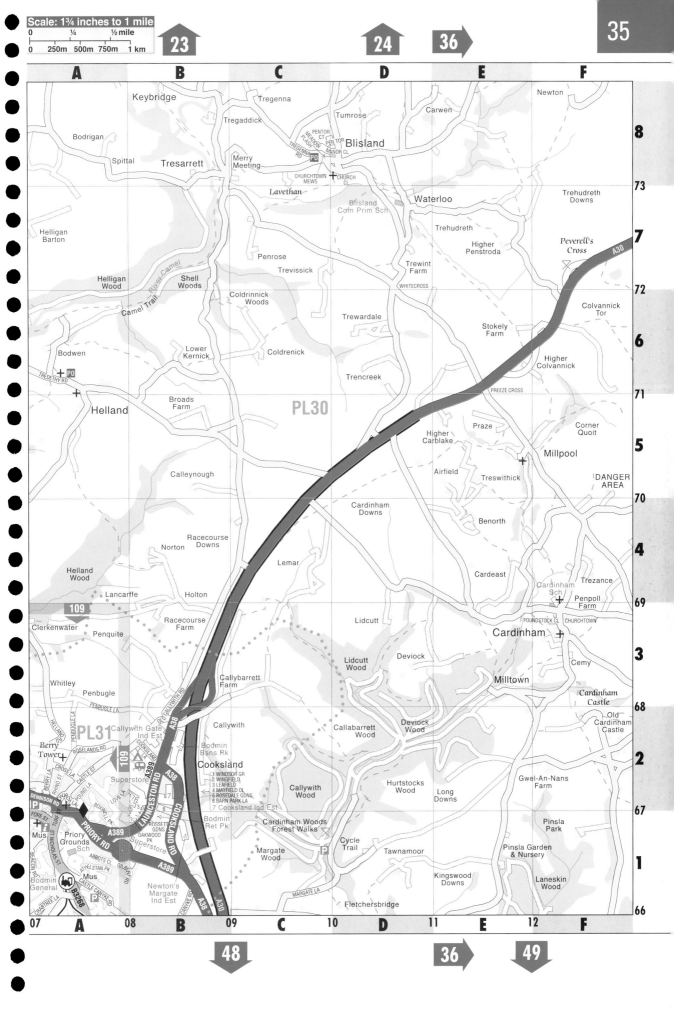

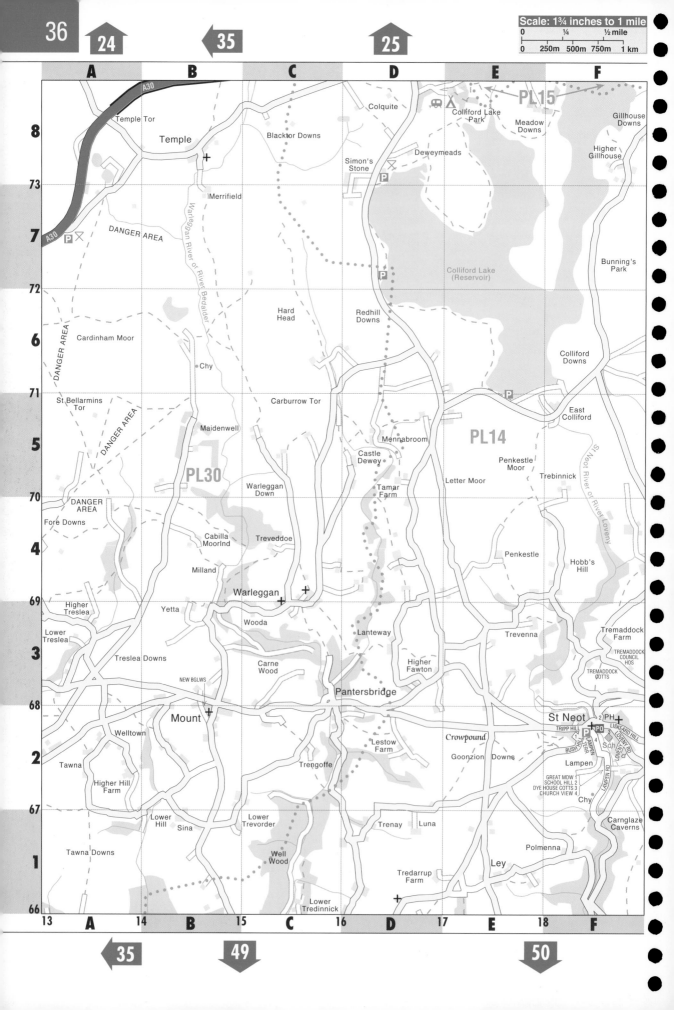

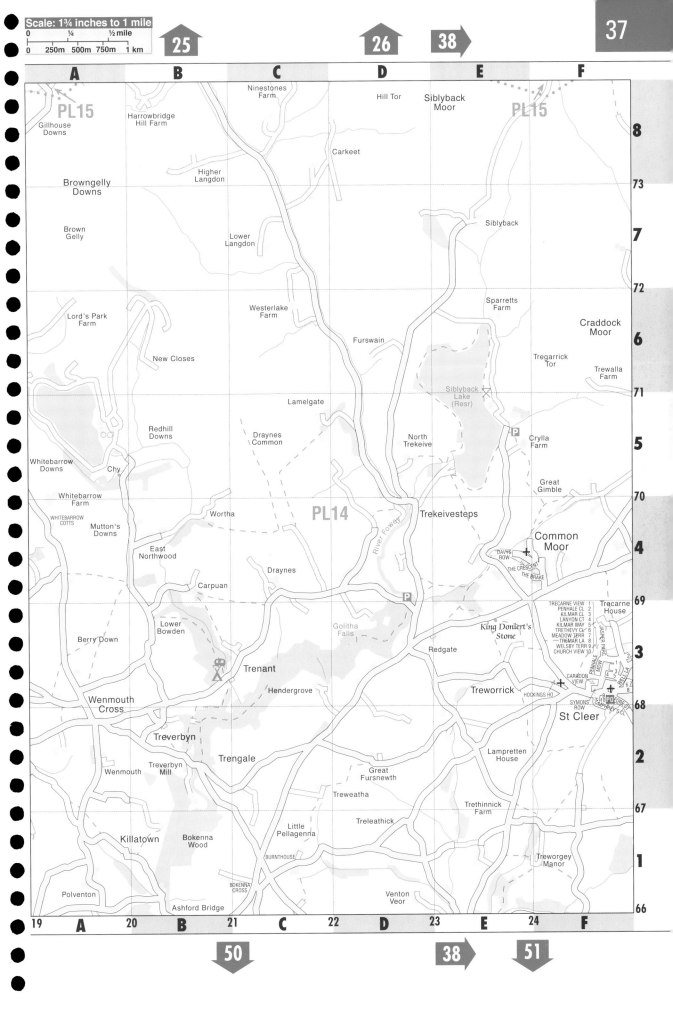

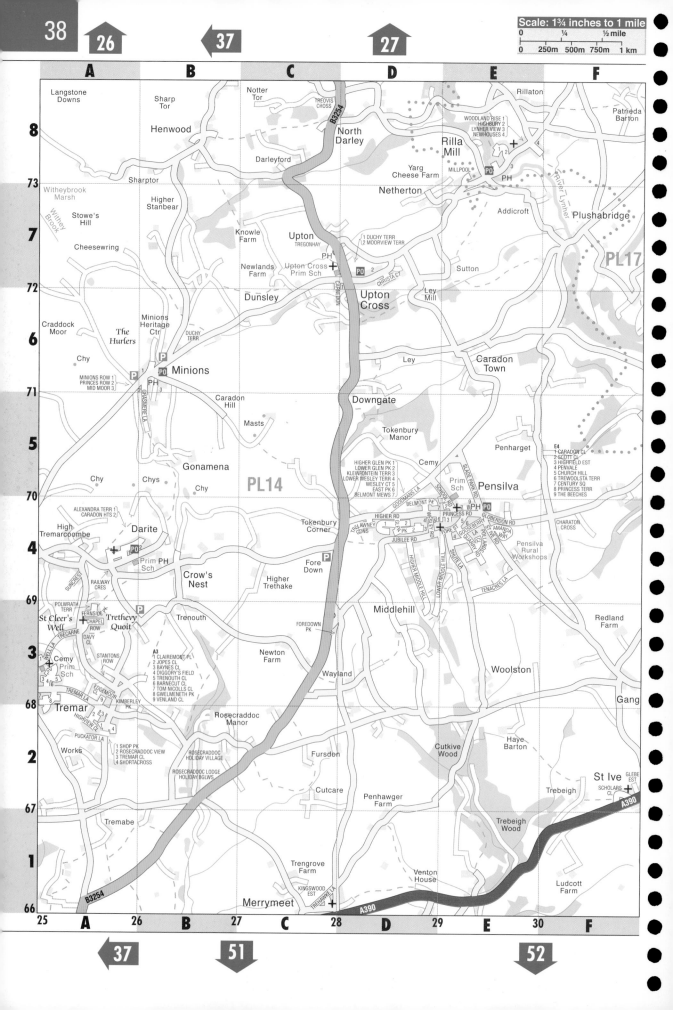

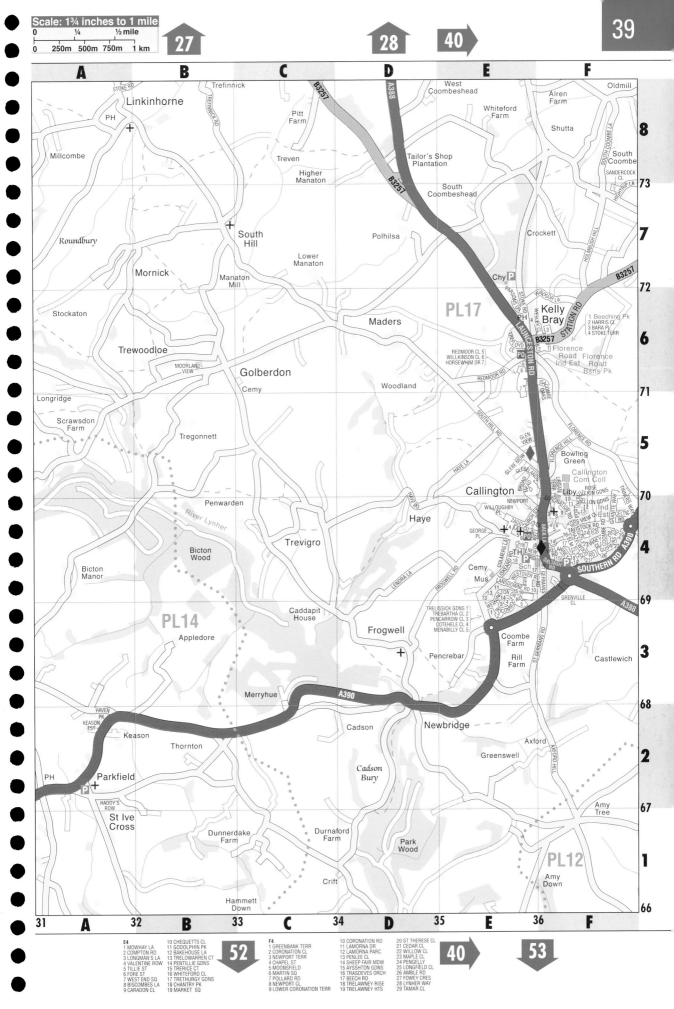

A   B   C   D   E   F

8
73
7
72
6
71
5
70
4
69
68
2
67
1
66

Linkinhorne
PH
Millcombe
Roundbury
Mornick
Stockaton
Trewoodloe
Longridge
Scrawsdon Farm
Bicton Manor
Bicton Wood
St Ive Cross
Parkfield
PH
Keason
HAVEN PK
KEASON EST
HADDY'S ROW
Thornton
Dunnerdake Farm
Appledore
Penwarden
Golberdon
Cemy
MOORLAND VIEW
South Hill
Manaton Mill
Trefinnick
Pitt Farm
Higher Manaton
Treven
Lower Manaton
Maders
Polhilsa
Tailor's Shop Plantation
South Coombeshead
West Coombeshead
Whiteford Farm
Alren Farm
Oldmill
Shutta
South Coombe
SANDERCOCK CL
SOUTH COOMBE LA
HIGHTRIP LA
HOLMBUSH HILL
Crockett
Crockett
Kelly Bray
Chy
PH
WINDSOR LA
PARSONS LA
WESLEY LA
FRED LLOYD
STOKE HILL
PO
1 Beeching Pk
2 Harris Cl
3 Bara Pl
4 Stoke Terr
Florence Road Ind Est
Florence Road Bsns Pk
STATION RD
B3257
REDMOOR CL 5
WILLKINSON CL 6
HORSEWHIM DR 7
REDMOOR RD
SOUTH HILL RD
Woodland
PL17
ISCOMBE OAKS
HAYE LA
HAYE LA
GLEN VIEW
GLEBE MDW
GLEBELANDS
BROAD LA
Bowling Green
Callington Com Coll
Liby
URBAN VALE TERR
ROSE
CELTIC
TINNERS WAY
GRANITE WAY
FLORENCE HILL
Callington
Haye
Trevigro
Tregonnett
River Lynher
PL14
Caddapit House
Frogwell
NEWPORT WILLOUGHBY
GEORGE PL
COLMERS LA
ZAGGY CHURCH LA
BACK RD
FORE LA
CORONATION RD
NEWPORT
TAVISTOCK RD
PO
TH
Sch
Cemy Mus
LENDRA LA
FROGWELL RD
ISKEARD RD
LANSDOWNE
STOVER RD
WELLINGTON
CECIL AVE
CLARENCE RD
ST GERMANS RD
SALTASH RD
GRENVILLE CL
TRELISSICK GDNS 1
TREBARTHA CL 2
PENCARROW CL 3
COTEHELE CL 4
MENABILLY CL 5
Pencrebar
Coombe Farm
Rill Farm
Castlewich
Newbridge
Axford
Greenswell
AXFORD HILL
A388
A390
A390
SOUTHERN RD
Merryhue
Cadson
Cadson Bury
Durnaford Farm
Crift
Park Wood
Amy Tree
Amy Down
PL12
Hammett Down

A390
B3257
B3257
A388
A388
STOKE RD
TREFINNICK RD
LAUNCESTON RD

31   32   33   34   35   36
A   B   C   D   E   F

E4
1 MOWHAY LA
2 COMPTON RD
3 LONGMAN'S LA
4 VALENTINE ROW
5 TILLIE ST
6 FORE ST
7 WEST END SQ
8 BISCOMBES LA
9 CARADON CL
10 CHEQUETTS CL
11 GODOLPHIN PK
12 BAKEHOUSE LA
13 TRELOWARREN CT
14 PENTILLIE GDNS
15 TRERICE CT
16 WHITEFORD CL
17 TRETHURGY GDNS
18 CHANTRY PK
19 MARKET SQ

F4
1 GREENBANK TERR
2 CORONATION CL
3 NEWPORT TERR
4 CHAPEL ST
5 MOONSFIELD
6 MARTIN SQ
7 POLLARD RD
8 NEWPORT CL
9 LOWER CORONATION TERR
10 CORONATION RD
11 LAMORNA DR
12 LAMORNA PARC
13 PENLEE CL
14 SHEEP FAIR MDW
15 AYSSHTON GDNS
16 TRASDEVES ORCH
17 BEECH RD
18 TRELAWNEY RISE
19 TRELAWNEY HTS
20 ST THERESE CL
21 CEDAR CL
22 WILLOW CL
23 MAPLE CL
24 PENGELLY
25 LONGFIELD CL
26 AMBLE RD
27 FOWEY CRES
28 LYNHER WAY
29 TAMAR CL

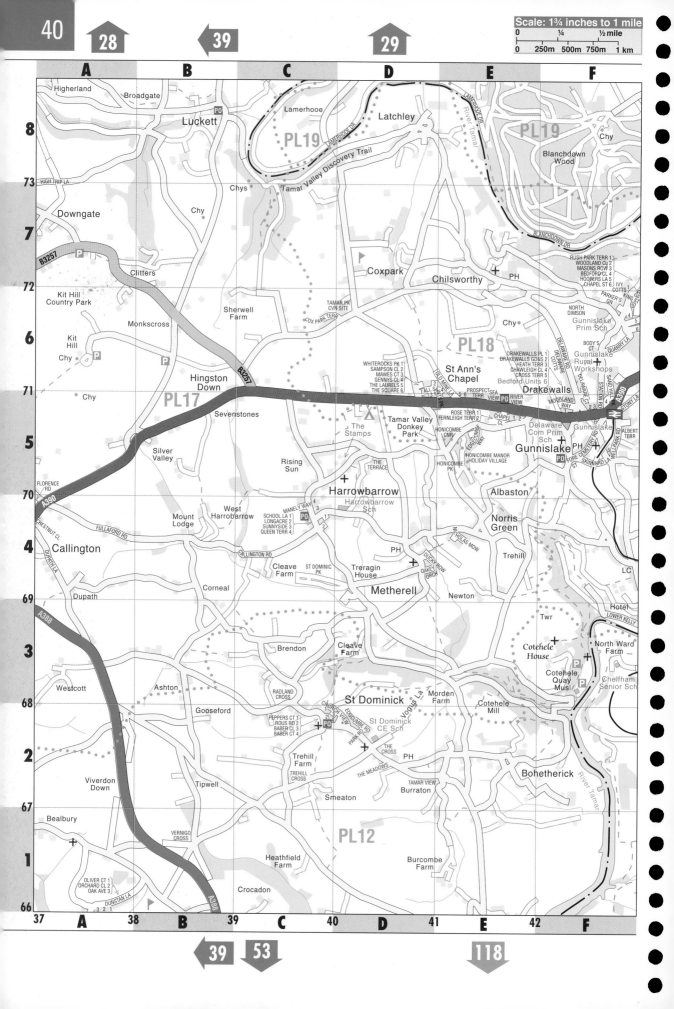

Scale: 1¾ inches to 1 mile

0   ¼   ½ mile

0   250m 500m 750m 1 km

For full street detail of the highlighted area see page 147.

29   30   42

41

119   42   120

B1
1 POUNDS PARK RD
2 JOHNSON CL
3 DRAKE'S PK
4 CHAPEL ST
5 WEST VIEW RD
6 BEDFORD PL
7 BEDFORD VILLAS
8 PARK LA
9 WHITEHALL DR

10 BEDFORD PK
11 PILGRIM CT
12 ST ANDREWS CL
13 LANGMAN CT
14 EDGCUMBE TERR
15 MARYTHORNE RD
16 THE SQUARE
17 THE CLOSE
18 TAMAR CL
19 MAYFLOWER CL

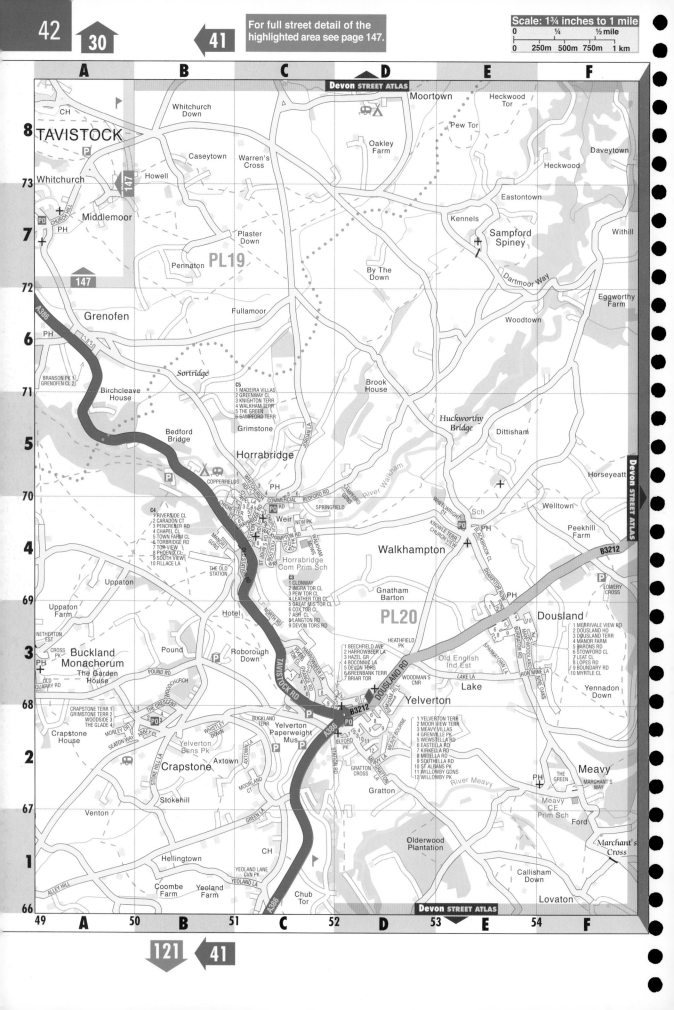

42

30

41

For full street detail of the highlighted area see page 147.

Scale: 1¾ inches to 1 mile

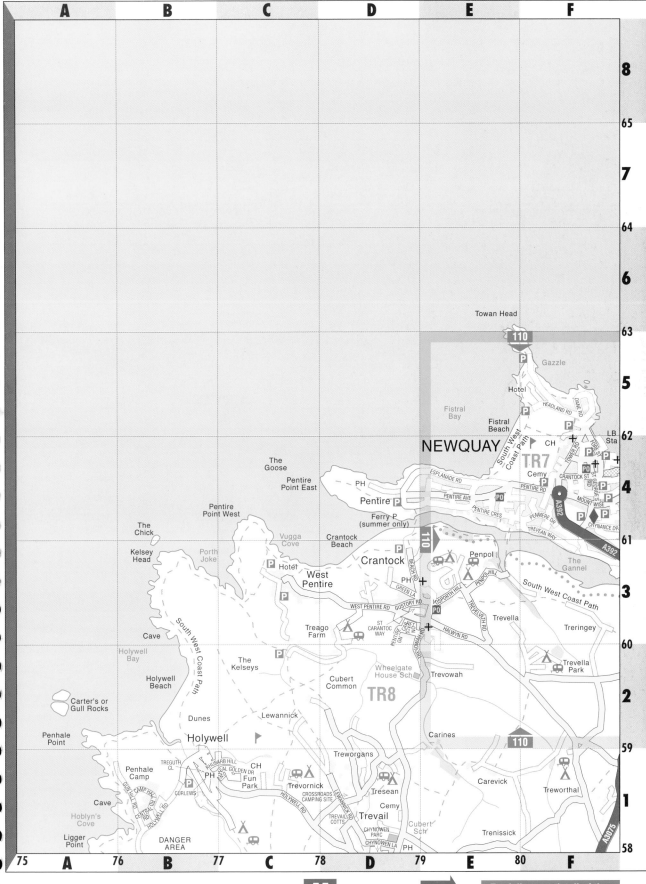

Scale: 1¾ inches to 1 mile
0   ¼   ½ mile
0   250m 500m 750m 1 km

| | A | B | C | D | E | F |

8
65
7
64
6
63
5
62
4
61
60
3
2
59
1
58

Towan Head
110
Gazzle
Hotel
Fistral
Bay
HEADLAND RD
DANE RD
Fistral
Beach
TOWER RD
FORE ST
LB Sta
NEWQUAY
CH
Cemy
TR7
CRANTOCK ST
RD
ST GEORGE'S RD
The Goose
Pentire Point East
PH
ESPLANADE RD
PENTIRE RD
PENMERE DR
MOUNT WISE
Pentire
PENTIRE AVE
PO
PENTIRE CRES
PENMERE DR
A392
Pentire Point West
Ferry P (summer only)
110
TREVEAN WAY
CHYNANCE DR
A392
The Chick
Vugga Cove
Crantock Beach
BEACH RD
The Gannel
Kelsey Head
Porth Joke
Hotel
West Pentire
Crantock
PH
GREEN LA
GUSTORY RD
VOSPORTH HILL
PENPOL HILL
Penpol
South West Coast Path
Cave
WEST PENTIRE RD
PENTIRE GN
PENTIRE CL
LANE
VOSPORTH HILL
TREPELVETH RD
Trevella
Treringey
South West Coast Path
Holywell Bay
The Kelseys
Treago Farm
ST CARANTOC WAY
HALWYN RD
PO
Wheelgate House Sch
Trevowah
Trevella Park
TR8
Holywell Beach
Cubert Common
Carines
110
Carter's or Gull Rocks
Dunes
Lewannick
Penhale Point
Holywell
Treworgans
Carevick
Treworthal
Penhale Camp
TREGUTH CL
RHUBARB HILL
SEAL GOLDEN DR
CH
PH
Fun Park
Trevornick
HOLYWELL RD
CROSSROADS CAMPING SITE
LEVANNICK RD
Tresean
Cemy
Trenissick
A3075
Cave
GUN HILL RD
CAMP RD
CENTRAL RD
HOLYWELL RD
CURLEWS
Trevail
TREVAIL COTTS
CHYNOWEN PARC
Cubert Sch
Hoblyn's Cove
Ligger Point
DANGER AREA
CHYNOWEN LA
PH

44 ▶

For full street detail of the highlighted area see page 110.

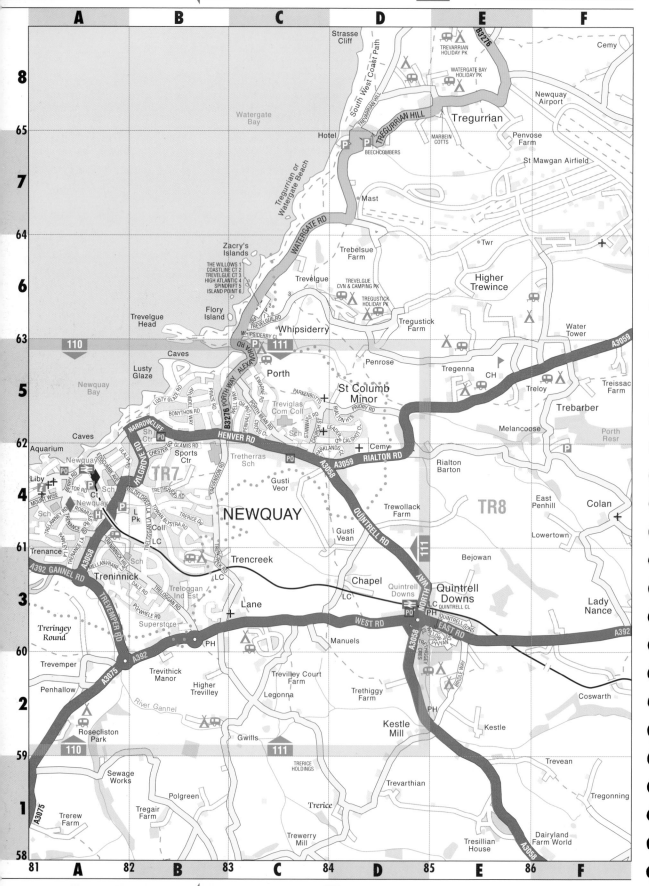

A   B   C   D   E   F

8

65

7

64

6

63

5

62

4

61

3

60

59

1

58

Cemy

Strasse Cliff

South West Coast Path

Trevarrian Hill

TREGURRIAN HILL

TREVARRIAN HOLIDAY PK

WATERGATE BAY HOLIDAY PK

Tregurrian

Newquay Airport

Penvose Farm

St Mawgan Airfield

B3216

Hotel

Beechcombers

MARBEIN COTTS

Watergate Bay

WATERGATE RD

Mast

Twr

Trebelsue Farm

Higher Trewince

Water Tower

A3059

Zacry's Islands

THE WILLOWS 1
COASTLINE CT 2
TREVELGUE CT 3
HIGH ATLANTIC 4
SPINDRIFT 5
ISLAND POINT 6

Trevelgue

TREVELGUE CVN & CAMPING PK

TREGUSTICK HOLIDAY PK

Tregustick Farm

Flory Island

Trevelgue Head

TREVELGUE RD

WHIPSIDDERY CL

Whipsidderry

Penrose

Tregenna

CH

Treloy

Trebarber

Treissac Farm

110

Caves

Lusty Glaze

Newquay Bay

PORTH WAY

ALEXANDRA RD

111

Porth

St Columb Minor

Melancoose

Porth Resr

Caves

Aquarium

Liby

Newquay

PO

Sch

BETTY RD

ULALIA RD

EDGCUMBE AVE

CHESTER

GLAMIS RD

Sch Ctr

NARROWCLIFF

Sports Ctr

LUSTY GLAZE RD

ARUNDEL WAY

BONYTHON RD

PRAZE RD

PO

PELL WAY

LEWARNE RD

PORTH BEAN RD

PORTH CROSS CL

Treviglas Com Coll

PARKENBUTTS

STANNAS RD

RIALTON HTS

PRIORY RD

LEADON RD

CALSHOT CL

Rialton Barton

HENVER RD

62

TR7

PO

Tretherras Sch

Gusti Veor

PARKLANDS

Cemy

RIALTON RD

East Penhill

Colan

Mount Wise

Sch

MILGROVE RD

WILDFLOWER CL

TREVENSON RD

TRETHERRAS RD

TR8

4

TRELAWNEY LA

TRENANCE RD

ROBARTES RD

H

Newquay

P

L Pk

Coll

TRERICE DR

TOWAN BLYSTRA RD

NEWQUAY

QUINTRELL RD

Trewollack Farm

Lowertown

61

Trenance

TRENINNICK HILL

TRENARREN CL

TRENANCE LA

RAWLEY LA

A3058

MELLANVRANE LA

DALE RD

Sch

LC

TRELOGGAN RD

Treninnick

Gusti Vean

Bejowan

Lady Nance

A392

GANNEL RD

TRELOGGAN IND EST

Trencreek

Chapel

LC

Quintrell Downs

NORTH WAY

AVON

Quintrell Downs

QUINTRELL GDNS

60

Treringey Round

TREVEMPER RD

PIZWHELE RD

Superstore

Lane

LC

PH

Manuels

WEST RD

PO

PH

EAST RD

A3058

TRELOY CRES

BRIDLE WAY

PH

Coswarth

A3075

Trevemper

Trevithick Manor

Higher Trevilley

Trevilley Court Farm

Legonna

Trethiggy Farm

Kestle

Penhallow

River Gannel

Kestle Mill

A392

Rosecliston Park

110

Gwills

111

Trevean

Trevarthian

Tregonning

Sewage Works

TRERICE HOLDINGS

Trerice

A3058

59

Trewerry Mill

Tresillian House

Dairyland Farm World

Trerew Farm

Tregair Farm

Polgreen

A3075

81   A   82   B   83   C   84   D   85   E   86   F

43

56

For full street detail of the highlighted area see pages 110 and 111.

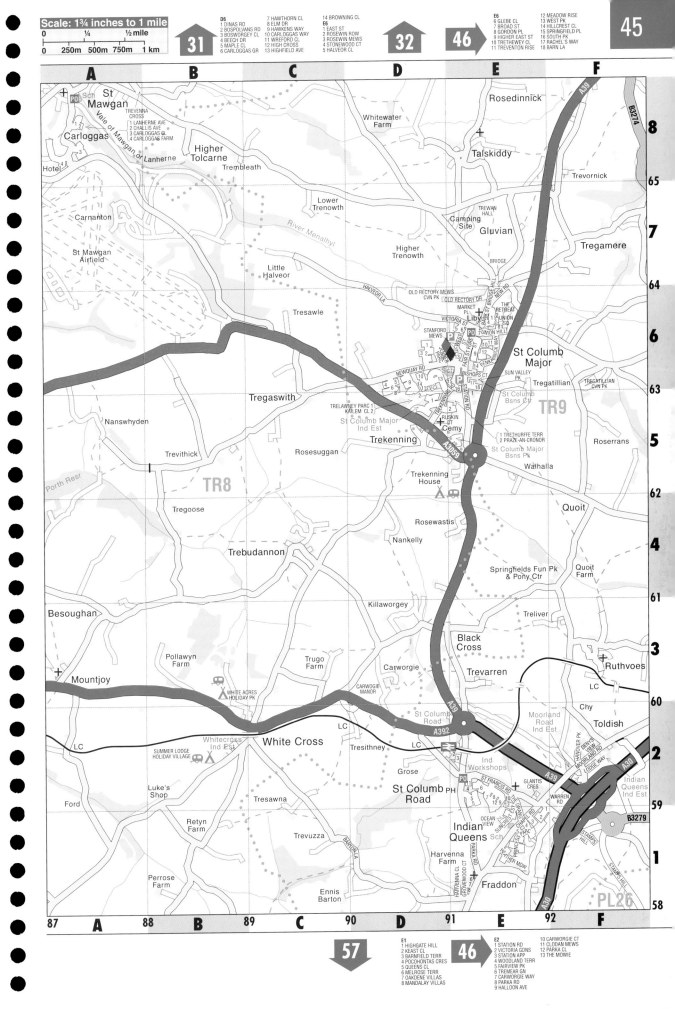

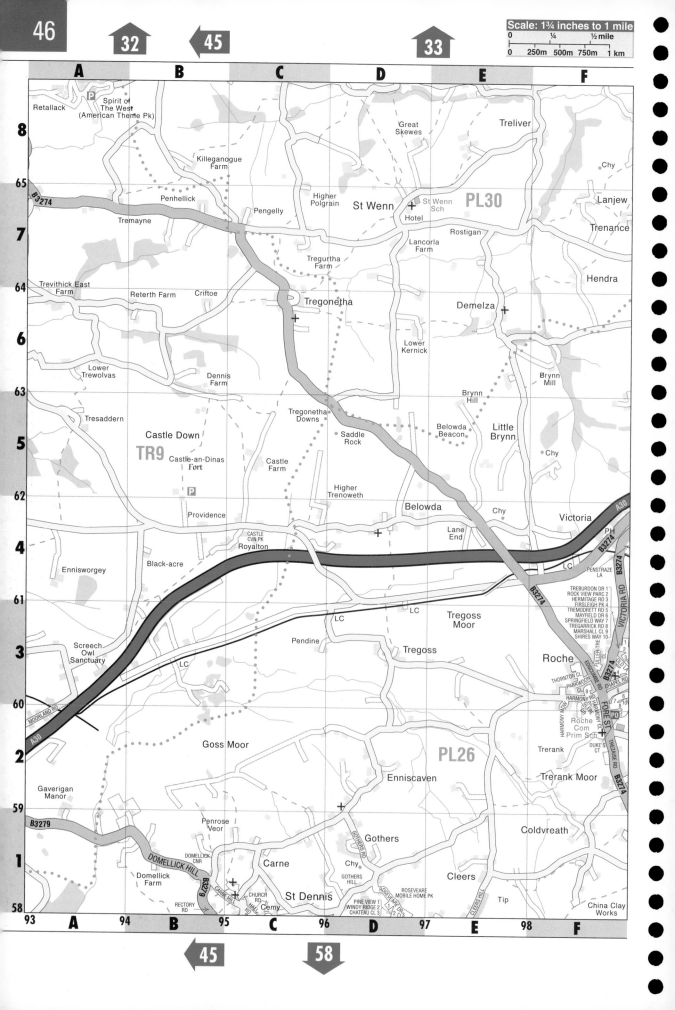

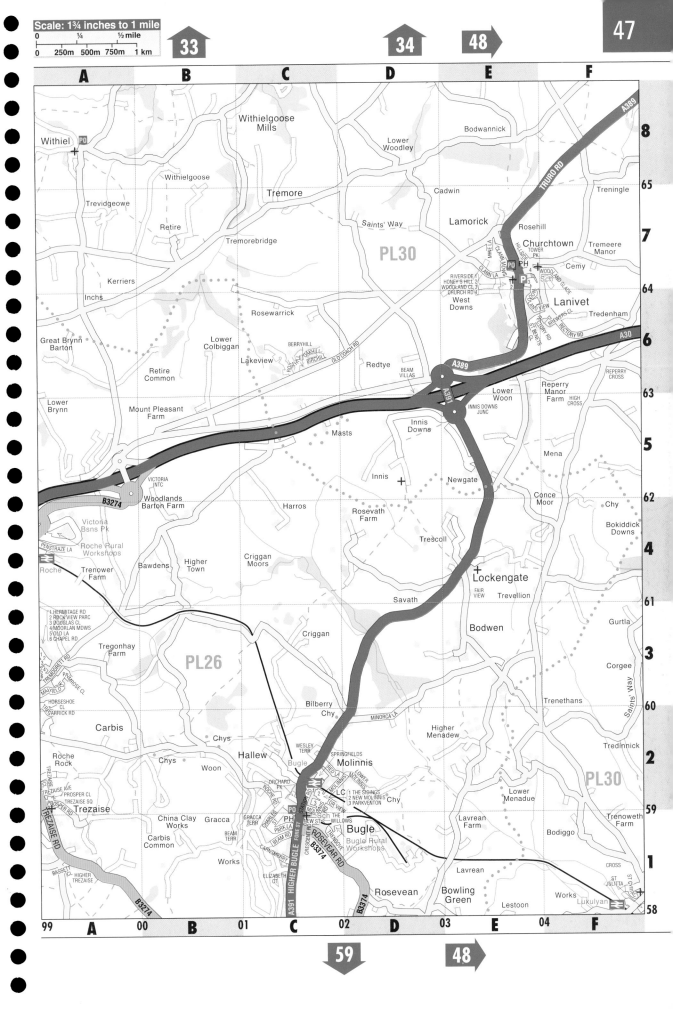

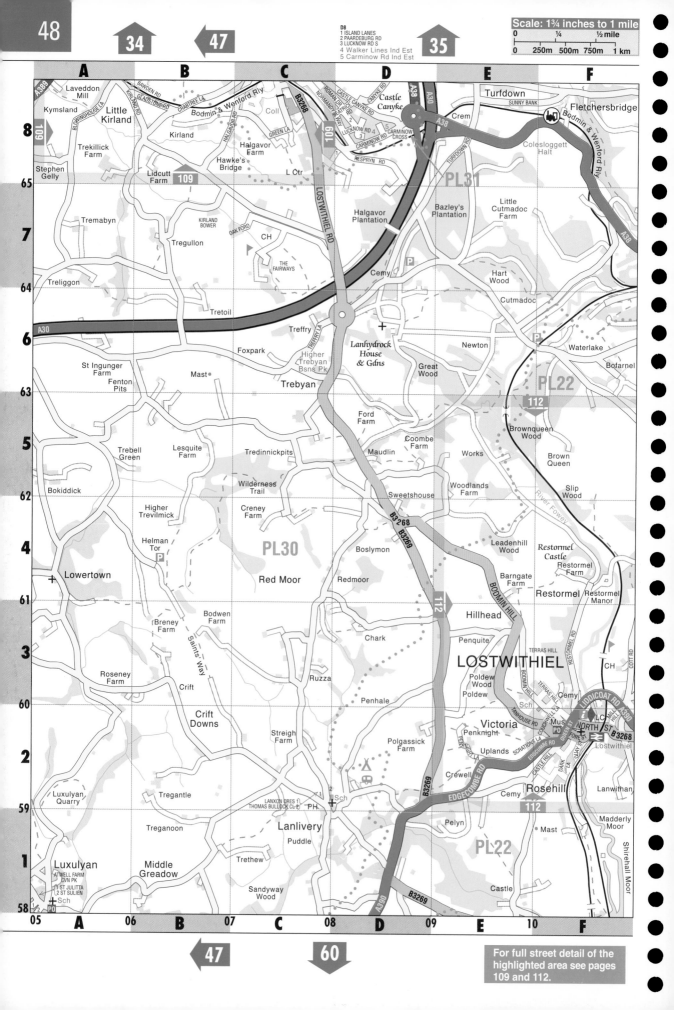

34 47 35

D8
1 ISLAND LANES
2 PAARDEBURG RD
3 LUCKNOW RD S
4 Walker Lines Ind Est
5 Carminow Rd Ind Est

Scale: 1¾ inches to 1 mile

0   ¼   ½ mile
0   250m   500m   750m   1 km

47 60

For full street detail of the highlighted area see pages 109 and 112.

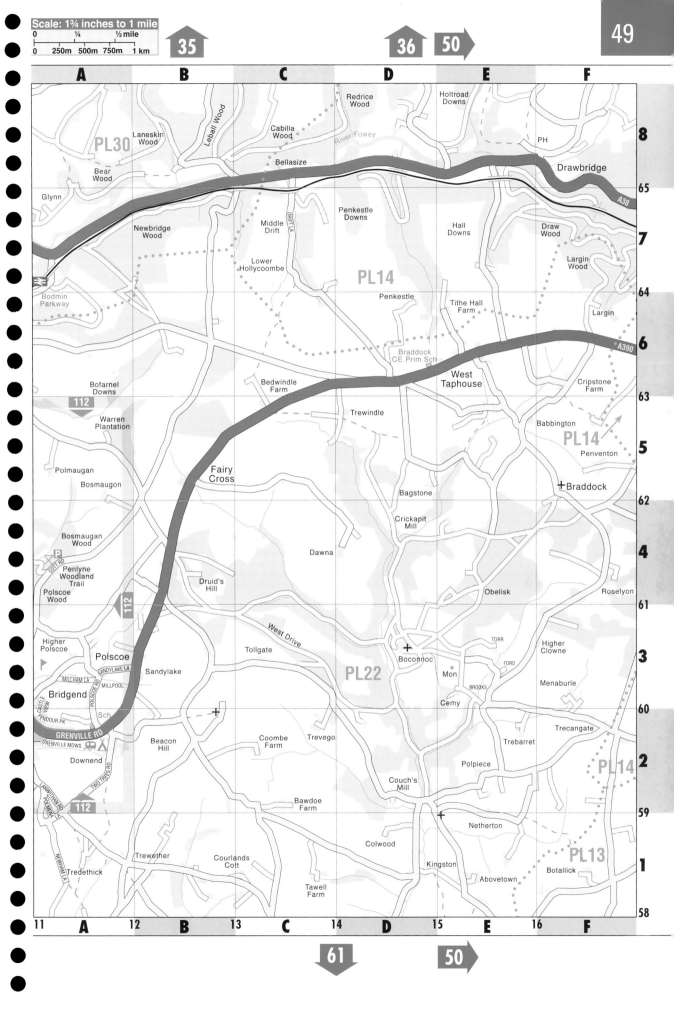

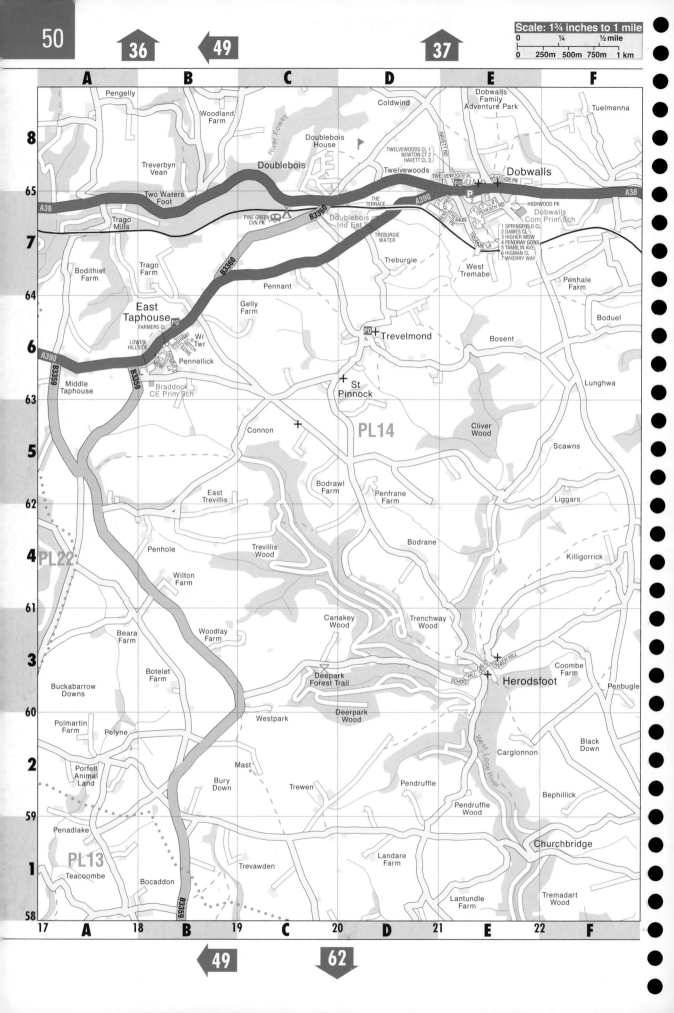

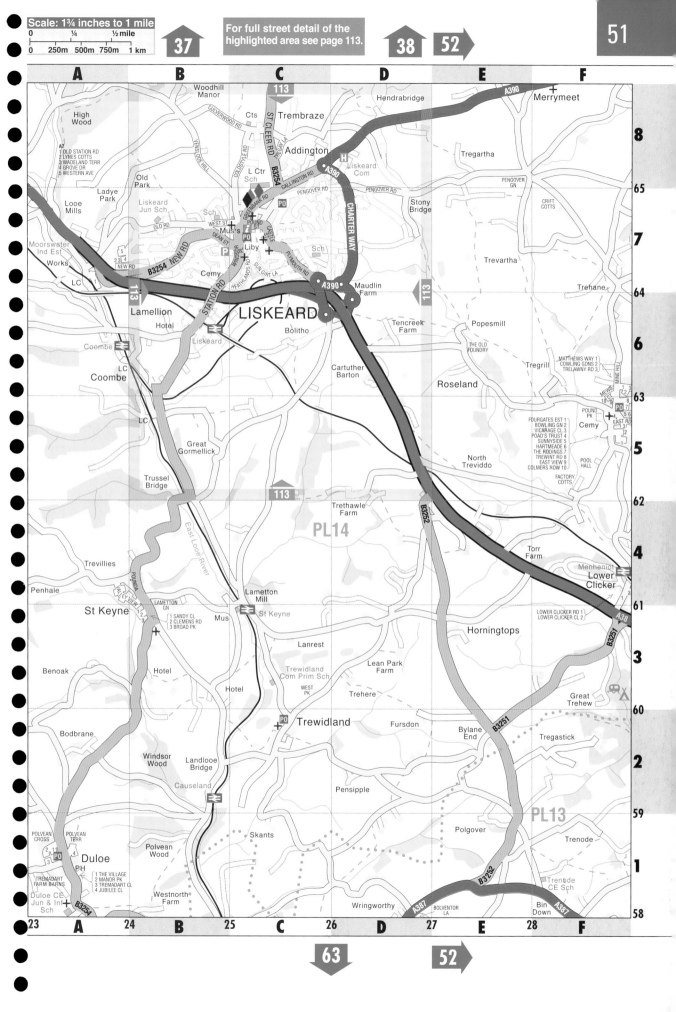

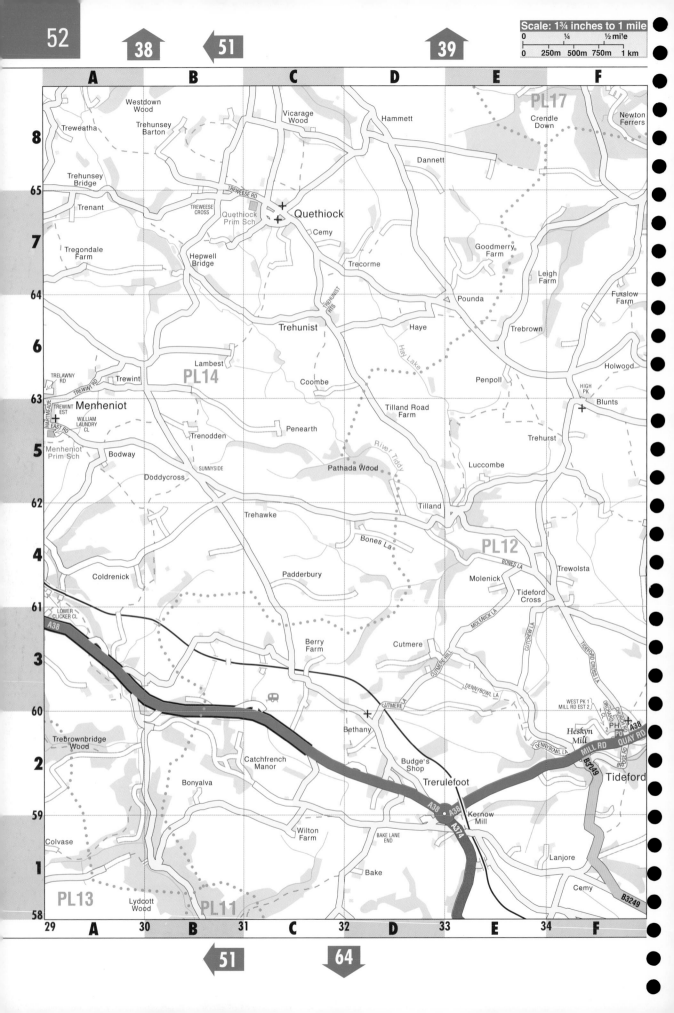

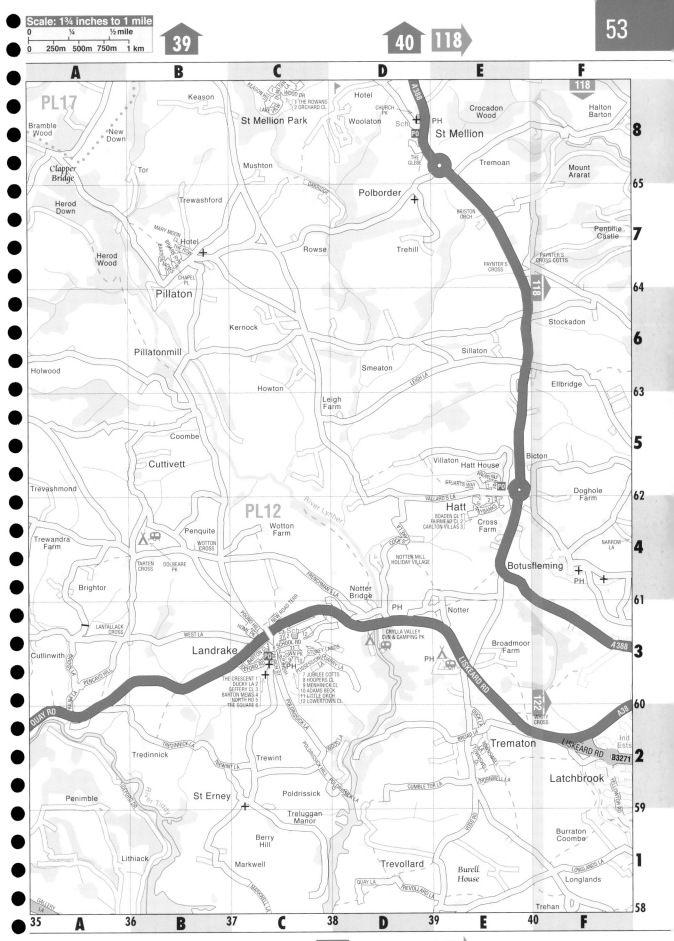

A   **B**   **C**   **D**   **E**   **F**

8
57
7
56
6
55
5
54
4
53
3
52
2
51
1
50

69   **A**   70   **B**   71   **C**   72   **D**   73   **E**   74   **F**

Shag Rock

Shafts (dis)

Cligga Head

Cligga Workshops 1
ST GEORGE'S TERR 2

B3285

Shafts (dis)

Hotel

TR6

Hanover Cove

Anchor

South West Coast Path

Airfield

Green Island

Trevellas Porth

Cross Coombe

Chy

Trevellas

Trevaunance Cove

Blue Hills

Trevellas Coombe

Blowinghouse

Newdowns Head

Heritage Trail

Shafts (dis)

PH

Wheal Kitty Workshops

PERRAN VIEW HOLIDAY PK

TR5

Crams

New Downs

Chy

Wheal Kitty

Mithian Sch

St Agnes Head

Trevaunance CL

Goonlaze Terr

Barkla Shop

Carn Gowla

Higher Bal

Chy

Peterville

PO   PH

Tubby's Head

St Agnes Sch

TOWN HILL

B3285

WATER LA

Mithian

St Agnes Beacon

Chy

Liby

Mus

Chy

St Agnes

Goonown

BEACON FARM

Cemy

B3277

C1
1 BRECON CL
2 BEACONSFIELD PL
3 WHITE'S CL
4 ANGWIN AVE
5 CHURCHTOWN
6 CHEGWYN GDNS
7 KEMP'S CL
8 BOLSTER CL
9 PENWINNICK CL

D1
1 PENGARTH
2 CASTLE MDWS
3 CASTLE MEADOWS CT
4 PENWINNICK PARC
5 MIDDLEGATES
6 GRENVILLE DR
7 LAMBOURNE AVE
8 ATLANTIC MEWS
9 HIGHFIELD CT

10 THE OLD SCHOOL
11 STIPPY STAPPY

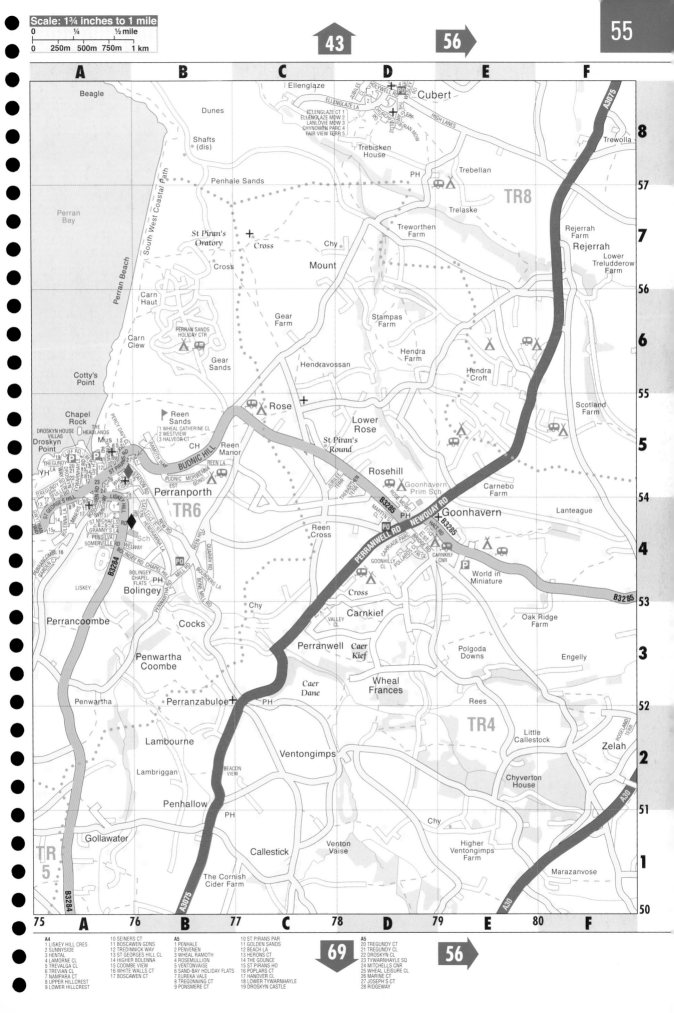

A4
1 LISKEY HILL CRES
2 SUNNYSIDE
3 HENTAL
4 LAMORNE CL
5 TREVALGA CL
6 TREVIAN CL
7 NAMPARA CT
8 UPPER HILLCREST
9 LOWER HILLCREST
10 SEINERS CT
11 BOSCAWEN GDNS
12 TREDINNICK WAY
13 ST GEORGES HILL CL
14 HIGHER BOLENNA
15 COOMBE VIEW
16 WHITE WALLS CT
17 BOSCAWEN CT

A5
1 PENHALE
2 PENVENEN
3 WHEAL RAMOTH
4 ROSEMULLION
5 VENTONVAISE
6 SAND-BAY HOLIDAY FLATS
7 EUREKA VALE
8 TREGONNING CT
9 PONSMERE CT

10 ST PIRANS PAR
11 GOLDEN SANDS
12 BEACH LA
13 HERONS CT
14 THE GOUNCE
15 ST PIRANS HO
16 POPLARS CT
17 HANOVER CL
18 LOWER TYWARNHAYLE
19 DROSKYN CASTLE

A5
20 TREGUNDY CT
21 TREGUNDY CL
22 DROSKYN CL
23 TYWARNHAYLE SQ
24 MITCHELLS CNR
25 WHEAL LEISURE CL
26 MARINE CT
27 JOSEPH S CT
28 RIDGEWAY

55
44

Scale: 1¾ inches to 1 mile
0 ¼ ½ mile
0 250m 500m 750m 1 km

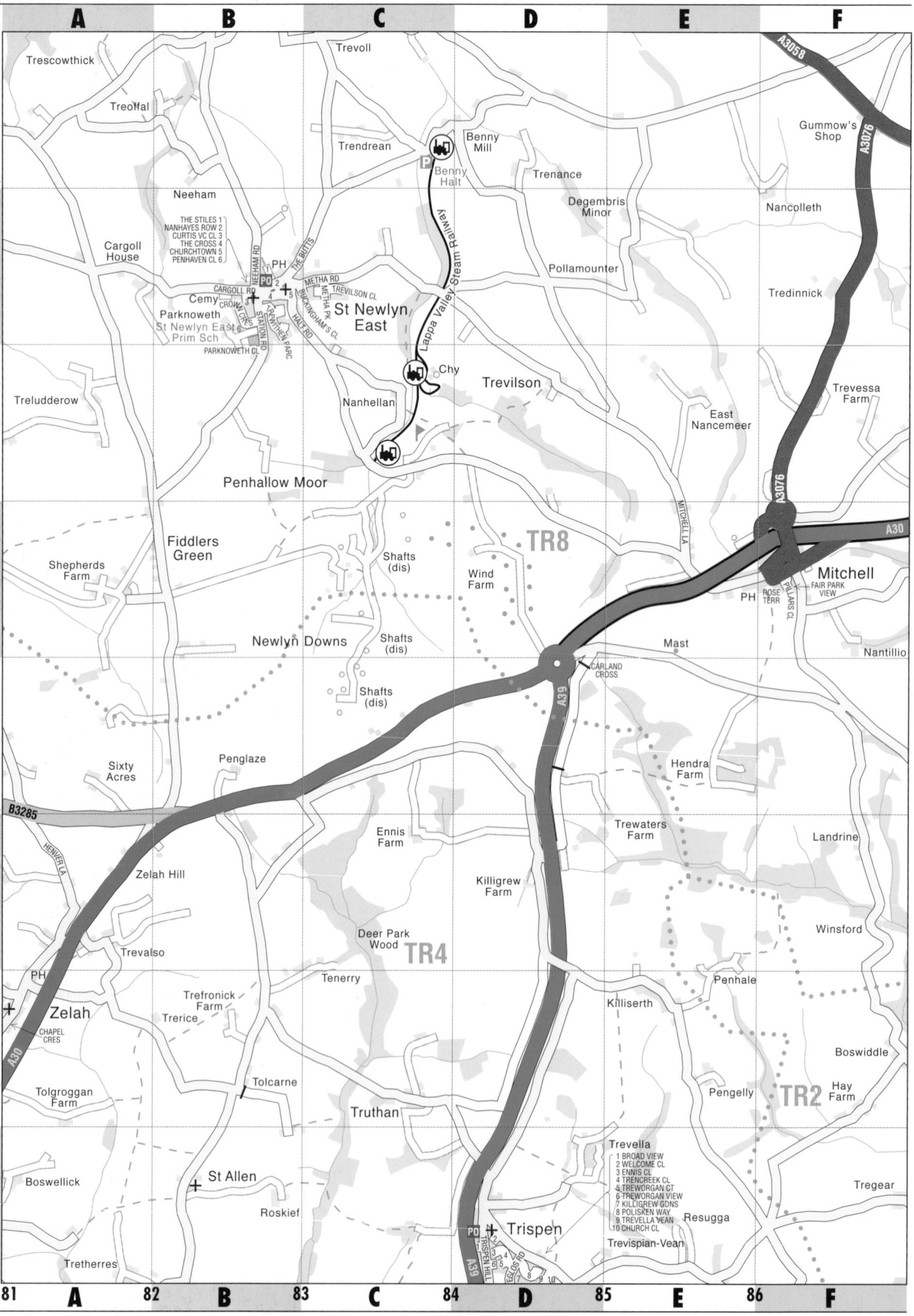
A
B
C
D
E
F
Trescowthick
Trevoll
A3058
Treoffal
Trendrean
Benny Mill
Benny Halt
Trenance
Gummow's Shop
A3076
Neeham
Degembris Minor
Nancolleth
THE STILES 1
NANHAYES ROW 2
CURTIS VC CL 3
THE CROSS 4
CHURCHTOWN 5
PENHAVEN CL 6
Cargoll House
NEEHAM RD
THE BUTTS
PH
PO
Lappa Valley Steam Railway
Pollamounter
Tredinnick
METHA RD
CARGOLL RD
TREVILSON CL
METHA PK
BUCKINGHAM'S CL
Cemy
CROWN CRES
St Newlyn East
Parknoweth
St Newlyn East Prim Sch
STATION RD
TREWITHEN PARC
HALT RD
PARKNOWETH CL
Chy
Treludderow
Trevilson
Trevessa Farm
Nanhellan
East Nancemeer
Penhallow Moor
MITCHELL LA
A3076
TR8
A30
Fiddlers Green
Shafts (dis)
Shepherds Farm
Wind Farm
Mitchell
FAIR PARK VIEW
PH
ROSE TERR
PILLARS CL
Newlyn Downs
Shafts (dis)
Mast
Nantillio
CARLAND CROSS
Shafts (dis)
A39
Sixty Acres
Penglaze
Hendra Farm
B3285
Trewaters Farm
Ennis Farm
Landrine
HENVER LA
Zelah Hill
Killigrew Farm
Deer Park Wood
TR4
Winsford
Trevalso
PH
Tenerry
Penhale
Zelah
Trefronick Farm
Trerice
Killiserth
CHAPEL CRES
A30
Boswiddle
Tolgroggan Farm
Tolcarne
Pengelly
TR2
Hay Farm
Truthan
Trevella
1 BROAD VIEW
2 WELCOME CL
3 ENNIS CL
4 TRENCREEK CL
5 TREWORGAN CT
6 TREWORGAN VIEW
7 KILLIGREW GDNS
8 POLISKEN WAY
9 TREVELLA VEAN
10 CHURCH CL
Boswellick
St Allen
Tregear
Roskief
Resugga
PO
Trispen
Trevispian-Vean
TRISPEN HILL
EGLOS RD
A39
Tretherres
8
57
7
56
6
55
5
54
4
53
3
52
2
51
1
50
81
82
83
84
85
86

55
70

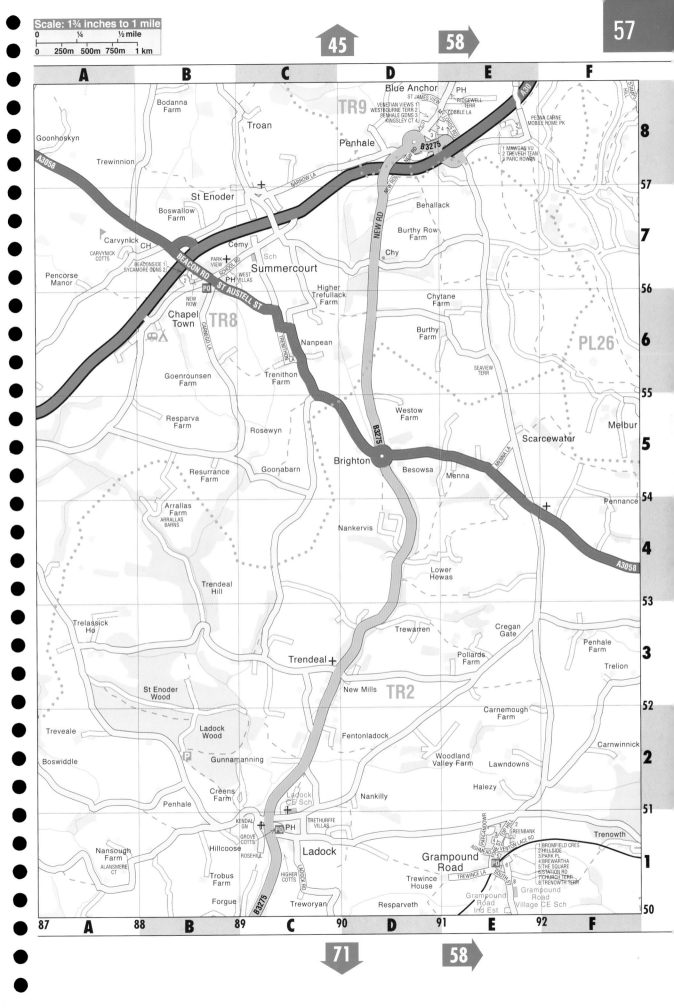

57
46

Scale: 1¾ inches to 1 mile
0 ¼ ½ mile
0 250m 500m 750m 1 km

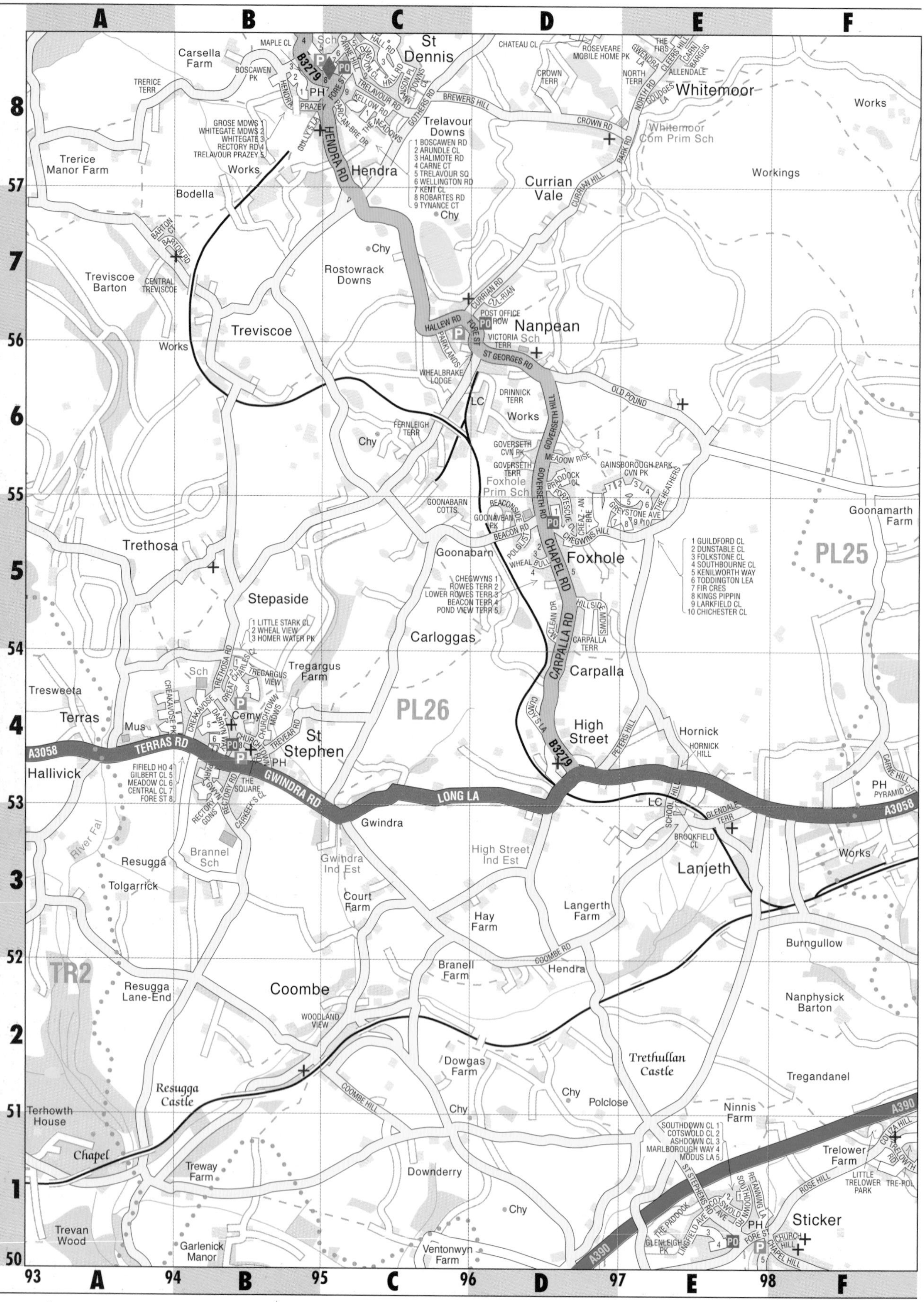

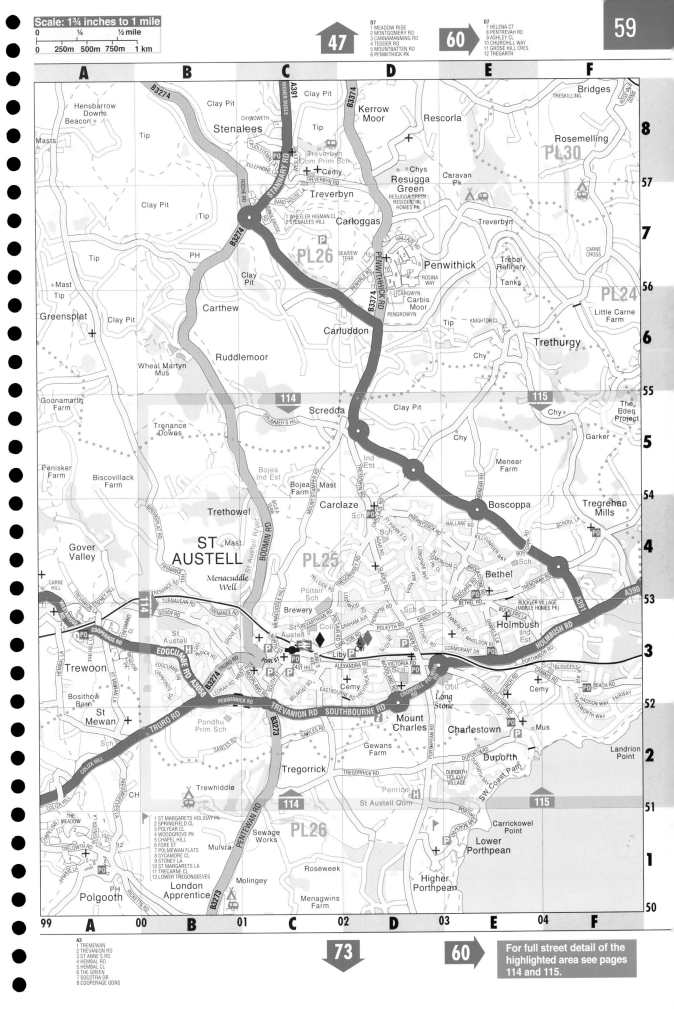

D7
1 MEADOW RISE
2 MONTGOMERY RD
3 CANNAMANNING RD
4 TEDDER RD
5 MOUNTBATTEN RD
6 PENWITHICK PK

D7
7 HELENA CT
8 PENTREVAH RD
9 ASHLEY CL
10 CHURCHILL WAY
11 GROSE HILL CRES
12 TREGARTH

47   60

Bridges
TRESKILLING

Hensbarrow
Downs
Beacon

Masts

CHYNOWETH
Clay Pit
Stenalees
Clay Pit

Kerrow
Moor

Rescorla

Rosemelling
PL30

Tip

Cemy
TREVERBYN RD
Treverbyn

Chys

Caravan
Pk

Resugga
Green

Carloggas

RESUGGA GREEN
RESIDENTIAL
HOMES PK

Treverbyn

1 WHEELER HIGMAN CL
2 STENALEES HILL

PL26

Clay Pit

Tip

PH

SEA VIEW
TERR

HALLAZE RD

Penwithick

Trebal
Refinery

Tanks

PL24

Carthew

ROSINA
WAY

CARGWYN

PENGROWYN

Carbis
Moor

Little Carne
Farm

Clay
Pit

Carluddon

KNIGHTOR CL

Tip

Chy

Trethurgy

Greensplat

Mast
Tip

Clay Pit

Ruddlemoor

Wheal Martyn
Mus

Chy

114

Scredda

Clay Pit

115

The
Eden
Project

Goonamarth
Farm

Trenance
Downs

DRUMMER'S HILL

Chy

Garker

Peniseker
Farm

Biscovillack
Farm

Bojea
Ind Est

Ind
Est

Menear
Farm

Bojea
Farm

Mast

Trethowel

MOUNT STAMPER RD

Carclaze

Boscoppa

Tregrehan
Mills

Gover
Valley

CARNE
HILL

ST
AUSTELL

Mast

Menacuddle
Well

PL25

SCHOOL LA

Bethel

Sch

Brewery

Poltair
Sch

Buckler Village
(MOBILE HOMES PK)

A391

A390

Trewoon

EDGCUMBE RD A3058

St
Austell

St
Austell
Coll

Holmbush
Ind
Est

HOLMBUSH RD

Bosithow
Barn

St
Mewan

PENWINNICK RD

TRURO RD

TREVANION RD SOUTHBOURNE RD

Cromwell Rd

Long
Stone

Cemy

BEACH RD
FAIRWAY

Pondhu
Prim Sch

B3273

Mount
Charles

Charlestown

Mus

Landrion
Point

COLIZA HILL

Trewhiddle

114

Tregorrick

TREGORRICK RD

Gewans
Farm

Duporth

DUPORTH
HOLIDAY
VILLAGE

1 ST MARGARETS HOLIDAY PK
2 SPRINGFIELD CL
3 POLYEAR CL
4 WOODGROVE PK
5 CHAPEL HILL
6 FORE ST
7 POLMEWAN FLATS
8 SYCAMORE CL
9 STONEY LA
10 ST MARGARETS LA
11 TRECARNE CL
12 LOWER TREGONGEEVES

PL26

Sewage
Works

Penrice

St Austell Com

115

Carrickowel
Point

Mulvra

Roseweek

Lower
Porthpean

London
Apprentice

B3273

Molingey

Menagwins
Farm

Higher
Porthpean

Polgooth

99   00   01   02   03   04

73   60   For full street detail of the
highlighted area see pages
114 and 115.

A3
1 TREMEWAN
2 TREVANION RD
3 ST ANNE'S RD
4 HEMBAL RD
5 HEMBAL CL
6 THE GREEN
7 SOCOTRA DR
8 COOPERAGE GDNS

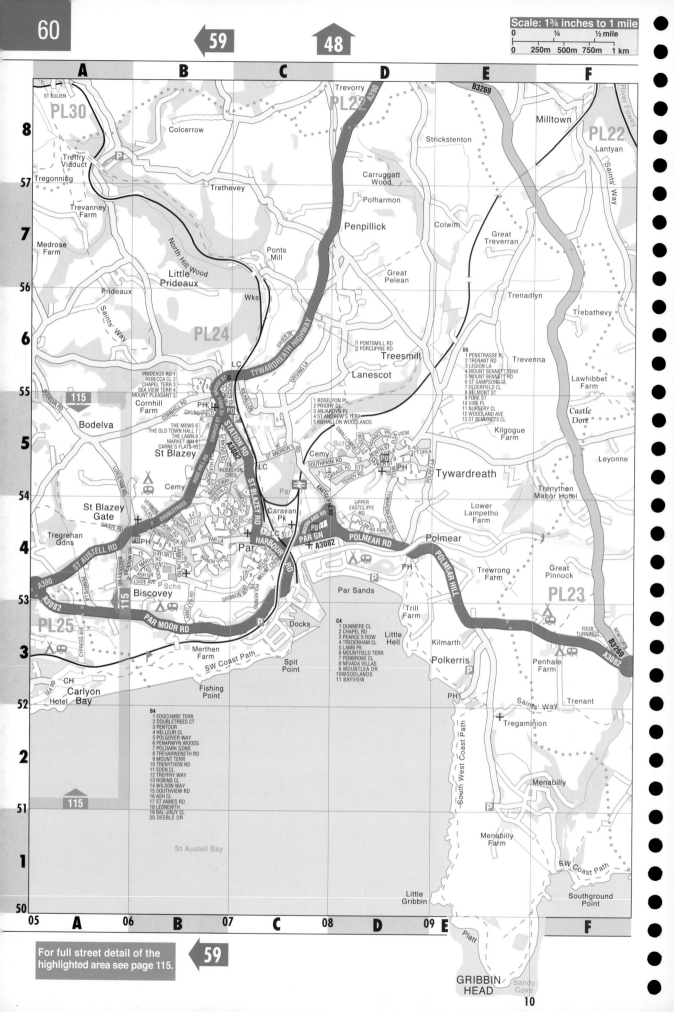

59

48

Scale: 1¾ inches to 1 mile
0   ¼   ½ mile
0   250m 500m 750m 1 km

For full street detail of the highlighted area see page 115.

59

PL30
St Sulien
Treffry Viaduct
Tregonning
Trevanney Farm
Medrose Farm
Prideaux
Saints' Way
Bodelva
115
BODELVA RD
LUXULYAN RD
Cornhill Farm
St Blazey
Colcerrow
Trethevey
North Hill Wood
Little Prideaux
PL24
Ponts Mill
Wks
GROVER LA
TYWARDREATH HIGHWAY
DRIVING LA

PRIDEAUX RD 1
REBECCA CL 2
CHAPEL TERR 3
SEA VIEW TERR 4
MOUNT PLEASANT 5

THE MEWS 6
THE OLD TOWN HALL 7
THE LAWN 8
MARKET INN 9
CARNE'S FLATS 10

CORNHILL RD
CHURCHFIELD RD
PH
CHURCH ST
ABERDEEN PL
KILHALLON
STATION RD
A3082
RISE HILL RD
POLGREAN PL
MIDDLEWAY
TREVIA CL
CHADDON
OLD ROSELYON CRES
OLD ROSELYON RD
ST ANDREW'S RD
LC
St Andrew's
Cemy
St Blazey Gate
Tregrehan Gdns
VERNON VILLAS
GROVE RD
DOUBLETREES
TRENOVISSICK RD
PONSMILL RD
Sch
Cemy
ST AUSTELL RD
A390
A3082
PH
PO
PENRYS LA
ST MARYS RD
ASH GR
BISCOVEY RD
HILLSIDE AVE
Biscovey
MANOR VIEW
PAR LA
LAMELYN RD
MOUNT CRES
HARBOUR RD
Par
Caravan Pk
Par
POLKERRIS
GRIBBIN RD
LANELYN RD
Schs
115
PAR MOOR RD
CYPRESS AVE
SEA RD
CH
Carlyon Bay Hotel
Merthen Farm
Docks
Spit Point
Fishing Point
PL25
Colcerrow

Trevorry
PL22
A390
B3269
Milltown
PL22
Strickstenton
Lantyan
Carruggatt Wood
Polharmon
Penpillick
Colwith
Great Treverran
Trenadlyn
Trebathevy
Great Pelean
Treesmill
1 PONTSMILL RD
2 PORCUPINE RD
Lanescot
1 ROSELYON PL
2 PRIORY CL
3 ANJARDYN PL
4 ST ANDREW'S TERR
5 KILHALLON WOODLANDS
D5
1 PENSTRASSE PL
2 TRENANT RD
3 LEGION LA
4 MOUNT BENNETT RD
5 MOUNT BENNETT TERR
6 ST SAMPSONS CL
7 ELDERFIELD CL
8 BELMONT ST
9 FORE ST
10 VINE PL
11 NURSERY CL
12 WOODLAND AVE
13 ST BENEDICTS CL
Trevenna
Lawhibbet Farm
Castle Dore
Leyonne
Kilgogue Farm
SWALLOWFIELD
SCHOOLFIELD
WOODLA
VANCE PK
GLEN VIEW
NORTH ST
POLDREA
CHURCH ST
WELL
VICARAGE RD
SOUTHPARK RD
TEHIDY RD
POLPEY LA
Tywardreath
EASTCLIFFE RD
UPPER EASTCLIFFE RD
TYWARDREATH HILL
POLMEAR PARC
Lower Lampetho Farm
Trenython Manor Hotel
PAR GN
A3082
POLMEAR RD
Polmear
PH
POLMEAR HILL
Trewrong Farm
Great Pinnock
PL23
Par Sands
Trill Farm
Little Hell
C4
1 DUNMERE CL
2 CHAPEL RD
3 PEARCE'S ROW
4 TREDENHAM CL
5 LAMB PK
6 MOUNTFIELD TERR
7 PEMBROKE CL
8 NEVADA VILLAS
9 MOUNTLEA DR
10 WOODLANDS
11 BAYVIEW
Kilmarth
Polkerris
Kilmarth
Penhale Farm
Trenant
FOUR TURNINGS
B3269
A3082
NEWTOWN
PH
Saints' Way
Tregaminion
Menabilly
St Austell Bay
B4
1 EDGCUMBE TERR
2 DOUBLETREES CT
3 PENTOUR
4 HELLEUR CL
5 POLGOVER WAY
6 PENARWYN WOODS
7 POLDARK GDNS
8 TREVARWENETH RD
9 MOUNT TERR
10 TRENYTHON RD
11 EDEN CL
12 TREFFRY WAY
13 ROBINS CL
14 WILSON WAY
15 SOUTHVIEW RD
16 ASH CL
17 ST ANNES RD
18 LESNEWTH
19 BAL-JINJY CL
20 DEEBLE DR
South West Coast Path
Menabilly Farm
Little Gribbin
SW Coast Path
Southground Point
Platt
GRIBBIN HEAD
Sandy Cove

10

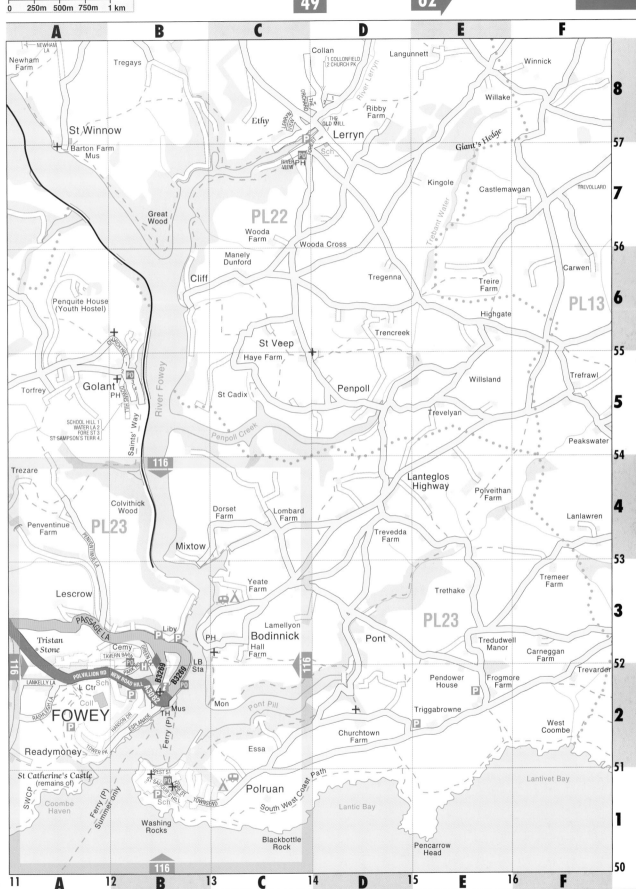

Scale: 1¾ inches to 1 mile

For full street detail of the highlighted area see page116.

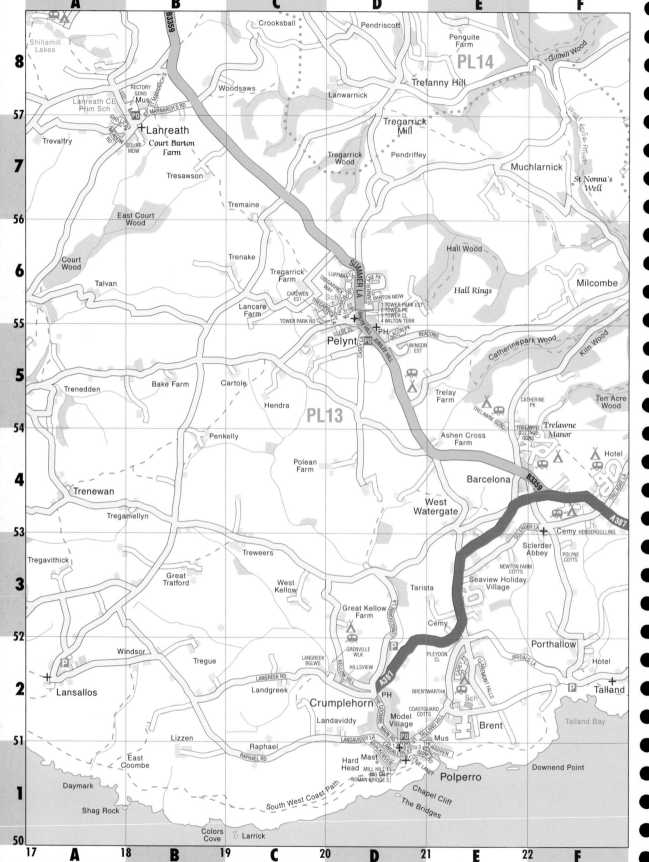

Scale: 1¾ inches to 1 mile

0   ¼   ½ mile

0   250m   500m   750m   1 km

Shillamill Lakes

Lanreath CE Prim Sch

RECTORY GDNS

Mus

PO

St MARNARCH'S RD

GRAIL'S MEADOW RD

Lanreath

COURT MDW

Court Barton Farm

Trevalfry

Trevalfry

Tresawson

B3359

Crooksball

Woodsaws

Pendriscott

Penquite Farm

PL14

Trefanny Hill

Lanwarnick

Tregarrick Mill

Pendriffey

Tregarrick Wood

Muchlarnick

St Nonna's Well

Gillhill Wood

West Looe River

Tremaine

East Court Wood

Trenake

Court Wood

Talvan

Tregarrick Farm

Lancare Farm

CARDWEN EST

TREGARRICK LA

Hall Wood

Hall Rings

Milcombe

SUMMER LA

Luffman Way

Sch

RICHMOND RD

TREGARRICK CL

BROWNE PK

1 TOWER PARK EST
2 TOWER PK
3 TOWER CL
4 WILTON TERR

SHUTE HILL

JUBILEE HILL

BEACON PK

TOWER PARK RD

GLEBE CL

Pelynt

PH

PO

CASTLE CL

BEACONS

WINSOR EST

Trelay Farm

Catherinepark Wood

Kiln Wood

Ten Acre Wood

Trenedden

Bake Farm

Cartole

Hendra

PL13

Penkelly

Polean Farm

Ashen Cross Farm

TRELAWNE GDNS

TRELAWNE COTTAGE GDNS

CATHERINE PK

Trelawne Manor

Hotel

Trenewan

Tregamellyn

Barcelona

West Watergate

B3359

SCLERDER LA

Cemy

HENDERGULLING

A387

TRELASKE LA

Tregavithick

Great Tratford

Treweers

West Kellow

Tarista

Sclerder Abbey

POLYNE COTTS

NEWTON FARM COTTS

Seaview Holiday Village

Great Kellow Farm

Cemy

Porthallow

Windsor

Tregue

LANGREEK BGLWS

LONGCOOMBE LA

GRENVILLE WLK

HILLSVIEW

KELLOW HILL

P

PLEYDON CL

CAREY PK

CLAREMONT FALLS

BRIDA'S LA

Hotel

Lansallos

P

LANGREEK RD

Landgreek

THE COOMBE

A387

PH

Crumplehorn

Brentwartha

Sch

P

Talland

Lizzen

Raphael

RAPHAEL RD

Landaviddy

Model Village

LANDAVIDDY LA

FORE ST

BRACKEN CL

LANSALLOS ST

PO

Mus

THE WARREN

QUAY RD

Brent

Talland Bay

East Coombe

Daymark

Hard Head

Mast

MILL HILL

BIG GN 2

LITTLE LANEY

TALLAND HILL

1 FORE ST
2 ...
3 ...

Polperro

Downend Point

Shag Rock

South West Coast Path

Chapel Cliff

The Bridges

Colors Cove

Larrick

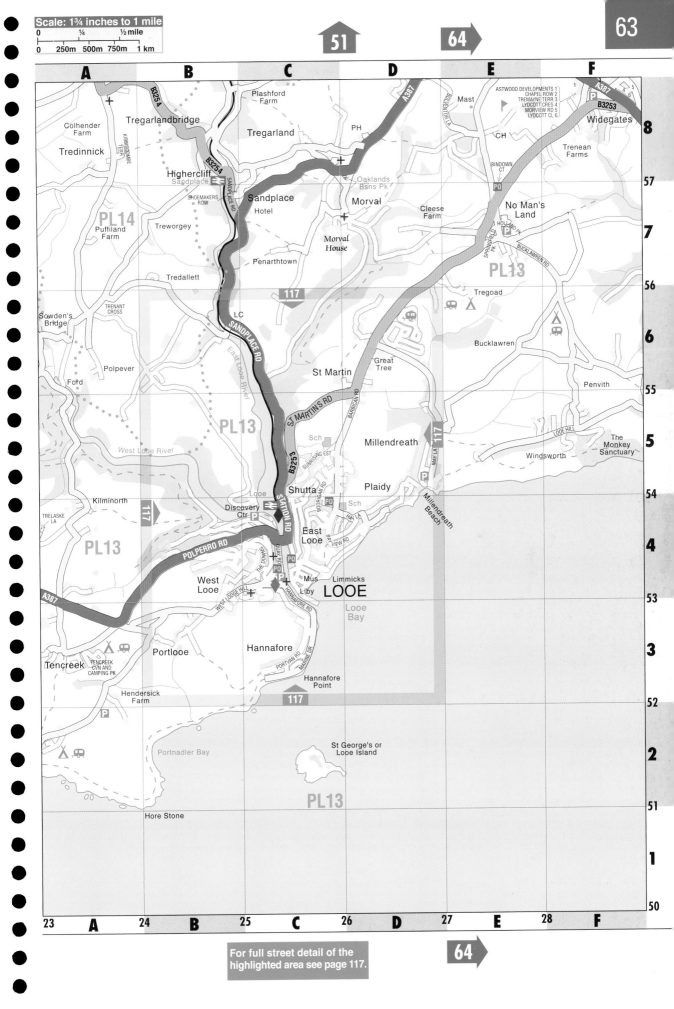

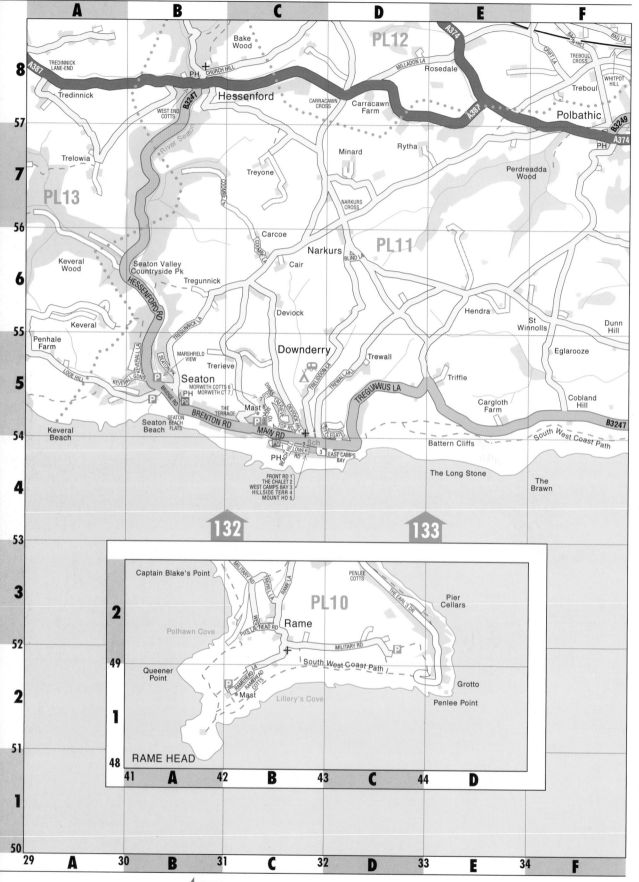

63 52

Scale: 1¾ inches to 1 mile

0   ¼   ½ mile
0 250m 500m 750m 1 km

A   B   C   D   E   F

PL12

A374

8

Tredinnick
Lane-End
A387

Tredinnick

Bake
Wood

PH
CHURCH HILL
B3247
West End
Cotts

Hessenford

Milladon La

Rosedale

Carracawn
Cross
Carracawn
Farm

A387

Polbathic

Bag La

Cruft La

Treboul
Cross

Whitpot
Hill

Treboul

B3249
A374
PH

57

River Seaton

Minard

Rytha

Perdreadda
Wood

7

Trelowia

Treyone

Narkurs
Cross

PL11

56

PL13

Keveral
Wood

Seaton Valley
Countryside Pk

Carcoe

Narkurs

Cair

Blind La

6

Hessenford Rd

Tregunnick

Deviock

Hendra

St
Winnolls

Dunn
Hill

55

Keveral

Penhale
Farm

Looe Hill

Keverall La

Keverall Gdns

Tregunnick La

Marshfield
View

Trerieve

Downderry

Seaton

Coombe La

Treveck

Top Rd

Treludick La

Trewall

Trewall La

Tregunwus La

Triffle

Cargloth
Farm

Cobland
Hill

B3247

Eglarooze

5

Seaton Rd
P
P

PH
PO

Seaton

Morweth Cotts 6
Morweth Ct 7

Mast

Main Rd

Brenton Rd

P

Dinas La

Bridge Rd

The Terrace

South West Coast Path

Battern Cliffs

4

Keveral
Beach

Seaton
Beach

Seaton Beach
Flats

PO
PH

Beach Hill

Lower
Rd

2
3

Castle Gate

Sch

East Camps
Bay

The Long Stone

The
Brawn

54

Front Rd 1
The Chalet 2
West Camps Bay 3
Hillside Terr 4
Mount Ho 5

53

132   133

Captain Blake's Point

Military Rd

Trehill La

Rame La

Penlee
Cotts

The Earl's Dr

Pier
Cellars

3

PL10

2

Polhawn Cove

Pits La

West Head Rd

Rame

Military Rd

P

52

49

Queener
Point

Ramehead La

P

Mast

Ramehead
Cotts

South West Coast Path

Grotto

Penlee Point

2

1

Lillery's Cove

51

48 RAME HEAD

41   A   42   B   43   C   44   D

1

50

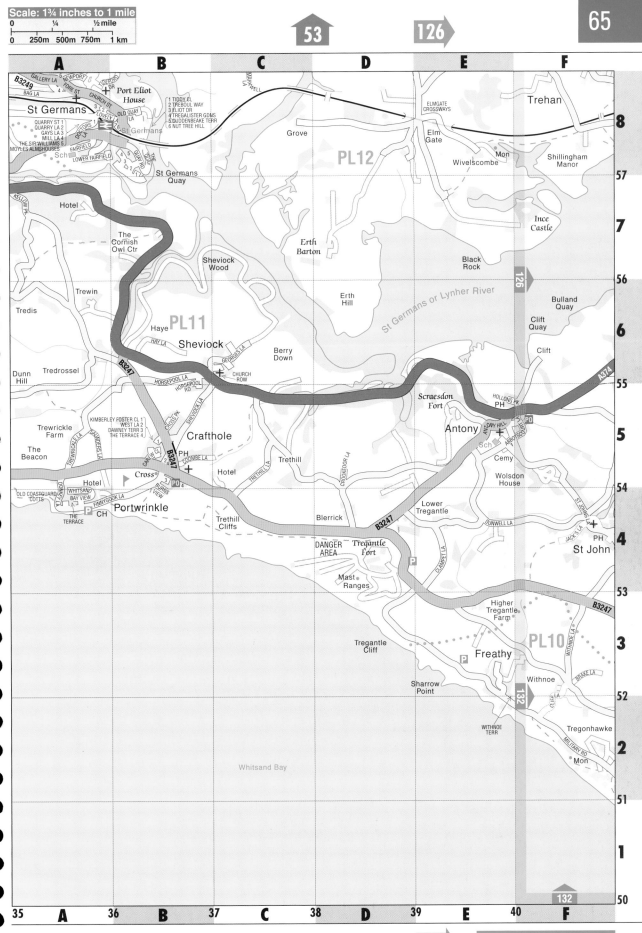

Scale: 1¾ inches to 1 mile

0   ¼   ½ mile

0   250m 500m 750m 1 km

53 | 126

A B C D E F

B3249
GALLERY LA
NEWPORT
BAG LA
FORE ST
CHURCH ST
St Germans
QUARRY ST 1
QUARRY LA 2
GAYS LA 3
MILL LA 4
THE SIR WILLIAMS 5
MOYLES ALMSHOUSES
Sch
FAIRFIELD
LOWER FAIRFIELD
Port Eliot House
Old Quay LA
LOVELY LA
DOCTORS LA
QUAY RD
THE QUAY
St Germans
St Germans Quay

1 TIDDY CL
2 TREBOUL WAY
3 ELIOT DR
4 TREGALISTER GDNS
5 CUDDENBEAKE TERR
6 NUT TREE HILL

MARWELL LA
Grove

ELMGATE CROSSWAYS
Elm Gate
Wivelscombe
Mon
Trehan

Shillingham Manor

PL12

8

57

Hotel
KELLOW PK

The Cornish Owl Ctr

Sheviock Wood

Erth Barton

Ince Castle

Black Rock

7

St Germans or Lynher River

126

56

Trewin
Tredis

PL11
Haye
HAY LA
Sheviock

Erth Hill

Bulland Quay

Clift Quay

Clift

6

Dunn Hill
Tredrossel
B3247
HORSEPOOL LA
HORSEPOOL RD
GEORGES LA
CHURCH ROW

Berry Down

Scraesdon Fort

HOLLONG PK
PH
Antony
ANTONY HILL
ABBOTSCH
Sch
A374
PO

55

Trewrickle Farm
TREWRICKLE LA
SAUNDERS LA
The Beacon
KIMBERLEY FOSTER CL 1
WEST LA 2
DAWNEY TERR 3
THE TERRACE 4
CROSS PK
SHEVIOCK LA
Crafthole
CAREW CL
COOMBE LA
PH
B3247

Trethill
TRETHILL LA
Hotel

Cemy
Wolsdon House

St JOHNS LA
PH
St John
JACK'S LA

5

54

Old Coastguard Cotts
DUNN PK
WHITSAND BAY VIEW
FINNYGOOK LA
Hotel
Cross
BURNS VIEW
PO
Portwrinkle
THE TERRACE
CH
P

Trethill Cliffs

Blerrick

B3247
Lower Tregantle
SUNWELL LA

CLAMPET LA

4

DANGER AREA
Tregantle Fort

Mast Ranges

P

53

Higher Tregantle Farm

B3247

PL10

Tregantle Cliff

Freathy
WITHNOE LA
Withnoe

BRAKE LA

3

Sharrow Point

132

Tregonhawke

MILITARY RD

52

WITHNOE TERR
CLIFF LA

Mon

2

Whitsand Bay

51

1

50

35 A 36 B 37 C 38 D 39 E 40 F

132

For full street detail of the highlighted area see pages 126 and 132.

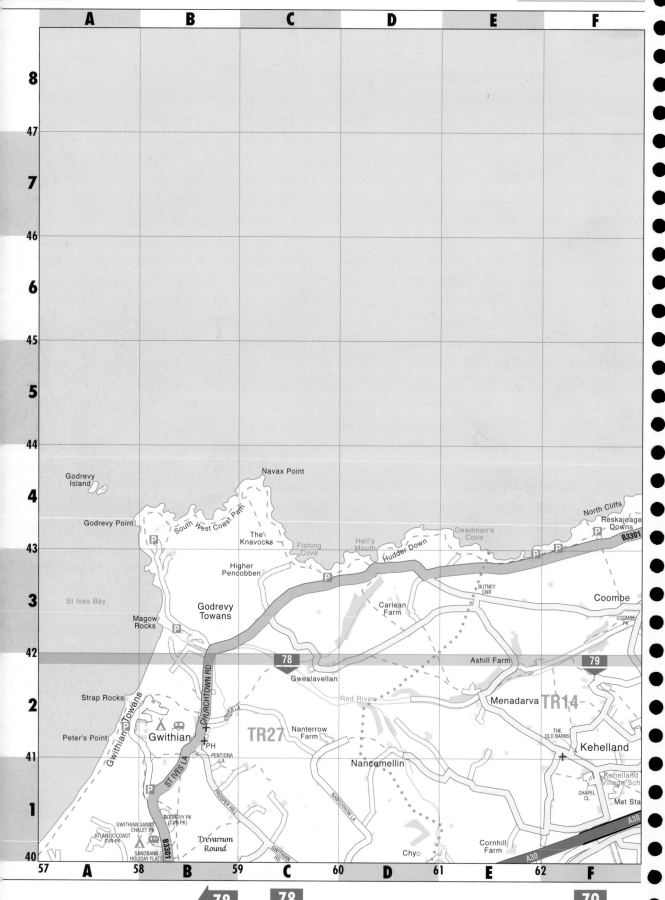

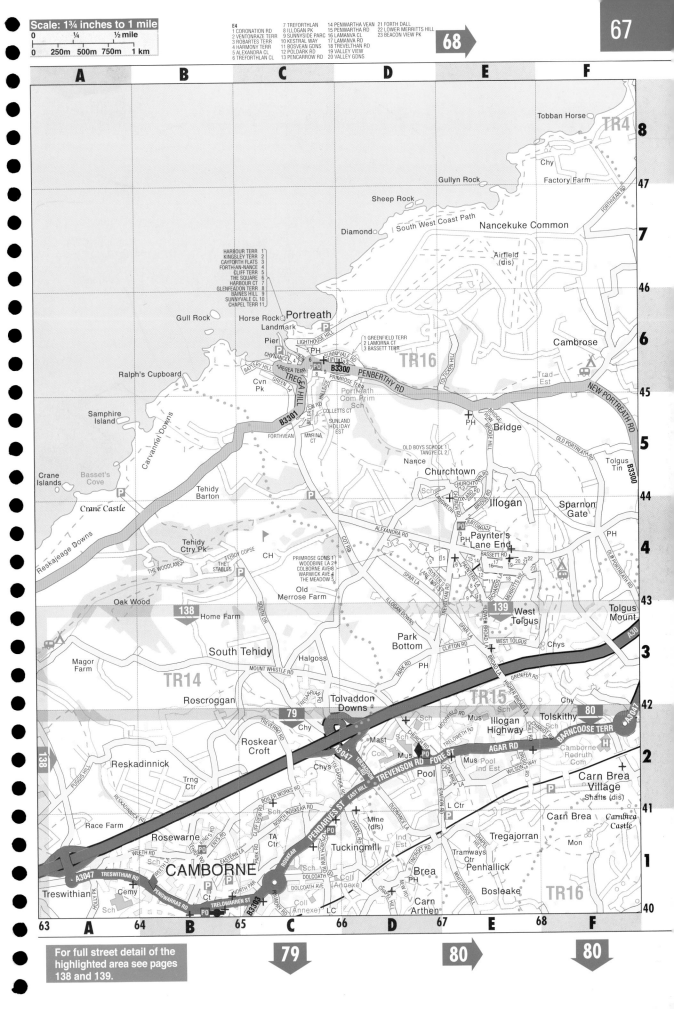

E4
1 CORONATION RD
2 VENTONRAZE TERR
3 ROBARTES TERR
4 HARMONY TERR
5 ALEXANDRA CL
6 TREFORTHLAN CL
7 TREFORTHLAN
8 ILLOGAN PK
9 SUNNYSIDE PARC
10 KESTRAL WAY
11 BOSVEAN GDNS
12 POLDARK RD
13 PENCARROW RD
14 PENWARTHA VEAN
15 PENWARTHA RD
16 LAMANVA CL
17 LAMANVA CT
18 TREVELTHAN RD
19 VALLEY VIEW
20 VALLEY GDNS
21 FORTH DALL
22 LOWER MERRITTS HILL
23 BEACON VIEW PK

A   B   C   D   E   F

Tobban Horse   TR4   8

Gullyn Rock   Chy   Factory Farm   47

Sheep Rock   Nancekuke Common

Diamond   South West Coast Path   7

Airfield (dis)   Cambrose   6

1 GREENFIELD TERR
2 LAMORNA CT
3 BASSETT TERR

HARBOUR TERR   1
KINGSLEY TERR   2
CAYFORTH FLATS   3
FORTH-AN-NANCE   4
CLIFF TERR   5
THE SQUARE   6
HARBOUR CT   7
GLENFEADON TERR   8
BAINES HILL   9
SUNNYVALE CL   10
CHAPEL TERR   11

Gull Rock   Horse Rock   Portreath   46

Landmark

Pier   PH   New Portreath Rd   45

Ralph's Cupboard   Cvn Pk   B3300   PENBERTHY RD   TR16   Trad Est

Samphire Island   B3301   Portreath Com Prim Sch   PH   Bridge   Cambrose

Crane Islands   Tehidy Barton   OLD BOYS SCHOOL 1   TANGYE CL 2   Nance   Tolgus Tin   B3300   5

Crane Castle   Churchtown   Illogan   Sparnon Gate   44

ALEXANDRA RD   Paynter's Lane End   PH

Tehidy Ctry Pk   PRIMROSE GDNS 1   BASSETT RD   4

Oak Wood   The Stables   WOODBINE LA 2   COLBORNE AVE 3   WARWICK AVE 4   THE MEADOW 5   Old Merrose Farm

138   Home Farm   139   West Tolgus   Tolgus Mount   43

Magor Farm   South Tehidy   Halgoss   Park Bottom   WEST TOLGUS   Chys

TR14   Mount Whistle Rd   PH   3

Roscroggan   Tolvaddon Downs   TR15   Illogan Highway   Tolskithy   80   42

79   Chy   Mus   Sch   BARNCOOSE TERR

Roskear Croft   Mast   AGAR RD   Camborne Redruth Com   2

Reskadinnick   Chys   TREVENSON RD   FORE ST   Pool

138   Trng Ctr   Mus   Ind Est   Carn Brea Village   Shafts (dis)   41

Race Farm   Mine (dis)   Carn Brea   Cambra Castle

Rosewarne   Tregajorran   Penhallick

Treswithian   TRESWITHIAN RD   CAMBORNE   Tuckingmill   Tramways Ctr

Cemy   Sch   PENGWARRAS RD   TRELOWARREN ST   B3303   DOLCOATH RD   DOLCOATH AVE   Coll (Annexe)   Brea   Carn Arthen   Bosleake   TR16   40

63   A   64   B   65   C   66   D   67   E   68   F

79   80   80

For full street detail of the highlighted area see pages 138 and 139.

Scale: 1¾ inches to 1 mile
0   ¼   ½ mile
0   250m   500m   750m   1 km

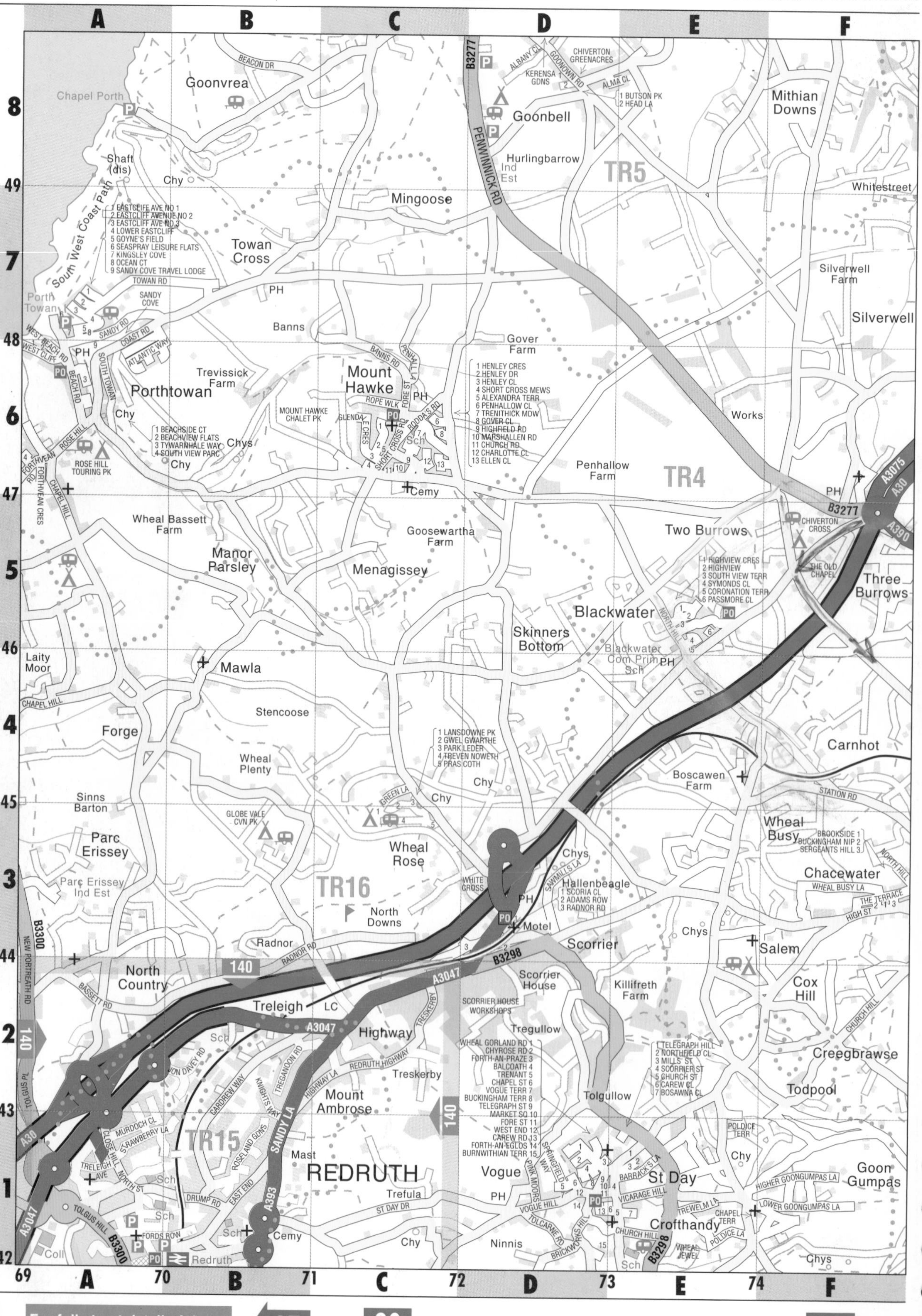

A   B   C   D   E   F

Chapel Porth
Goonvrea
BEACON DR
Goonbell
ALBANY CL
KERENSA GDNS
CHIVERTON GREENACRES
ALMA CL
1 BUTSON PK
2 HEAD LA
Mithian Downs
Shaft (dis)
Chy
Mingoose
Hurlingbarrow Ind Est
TR5
Whitestreet
South West Coast Path
1 EASTCLIFE AVE NO 1
2 EASTCLIFF AVENUE NO 2
3 EASTCLIFF AVE NO 3
4 LOWER EASTCLIFF
5 GOYNE'S FIELD
6 SEASPRAY LEISURE FLATS
7 KINGSLEY COVE
8 OCEAN CT
9 SANDY COVE TRAVEL LODGE
Towan Cross
Silverwell Farm
PH
TOWAN RD
Porth Towan
SANDY RD
Banns
Gover Farm
Silverwell
SANDY COVE
COAST RD
Trevissick Farm
Mount Hawke
1 HENLEY CRES
2 HENLEY DR
3 HENLEY CL
4 SHORT CROSS MEWS
5 ALEXANDRA TERR
6 PENHALLOW CL
7 TRENTHICK MDW
8 GOVER CL
9 HIGHFIELD RD
10 MARSHALLEN RD
11 CHURCH RD
12 CHARLOTTE CL
13 ELLEN CL
Porthtowan
Chy
MOUNT HAWKE CHALET PK
Chys
ROPE WLK
FORE ST
Penhallow Farm
Works
TR4
ROSE HILL TOURING PK
Chy
Cemy
Goosewartha Farm
Penhallow
Two Burrows
CHIVERTON CROSS
THE OLD CHAPEL
B3277
Wheal Bassett Farm
Manor Parsley
Menagissey
Blackwater
1 HIGHVIEW CRES
2 HIGHVIEW
3 SOUTH VIEW TERR
4 SYMONDS CL
5 CORONATION TERR
6 PASSMORE CL
Three Burrows
Laity Moor
Mawla
Skinners Bottom
Blackwater Com Prim Sch
PH
CHAPEL HILL
Stencoose
1 LANSDOWNE PK
2 GWEL GWARTHE
3 PARK LEDER
4 TREVEN NOWETH
5 PRAS COTH
Carnhot
Forge
Wheal Plenty
Chy
Boscawen Farm
STATION RD
Sinns Barton
GLOBE VALE CVN PK
GREEN LA
Chy
Wheal Busy
BROOKSIDE 1
BUCKINGHAM NIP 2
SERGEANTS HILL 3
Parc Erissey
Wheal Rose
Chys
Hallenbeagle
1 SCORIA CL
2 ADAMS ROW
3 RADNOR RD
Chacewater
WHEAL BUSY LA
Parc Erissey Ind Est
TR16
WHITE CROSS
PH
SAWMILLS LA
THE TERRACE
HIGH ST
North Downs
Motel
Scorrier
Salem
COX HILL
NEW PORTREATH RD
B3300
Radnor
RADNOR RD
B3298
Scorrier House
Killifreth Farm
BASSETT RD
North Country
Treleigh
LC
A3047
SCORRIER HOUSE WORKSHOPS
Tregullow
CHURCH HILL
Creegbrawse
140
Highway
REDRUTH HIGHWAY
Treskerby
Treskerby
1 TELEGRAPH HILL
2 NORTHFIELD CL
3 MILLS ST
4 SCORRIER ST
5 CHURCH ST
6 CAREW CL
7 BOSAWNA CL
Todpool
TR15
Mount Ambrose
WHEAL GORLAND RD 1
CHYROSE RD 2
FORTH-AN-PRAZE 3
BALCOATH 4
TRENANT 5
CHAPEL ST 6
VOGUE TERR 7
BUCKINGHAM TERR 8
TELEGRAPH ST 9
MARKET SQ 10
FORE ST 11
WEST END 12
CREW RD 13
FORTH-AN-EGLOS 14
BURNWITHIAN TERR 15
Tolgullow
POLDICE TERR
SANDY LA
REDRUTH
Mast
EAST END
A393
Trefula
ST DAY DR
Vogue
St Day
VICARAGE HILL
Chy
Goon Gumpas
TREGULUS HILL
B3300
Coll
Sch
FORDS ROW
Redruth
Trefula
Ninnis
Crofthandy
CHURCH RD
Wheal Jewel
Chys
TR15
TRELEIGH AVE
A30
A3047

For full street detail of the highlighted area see page 140.

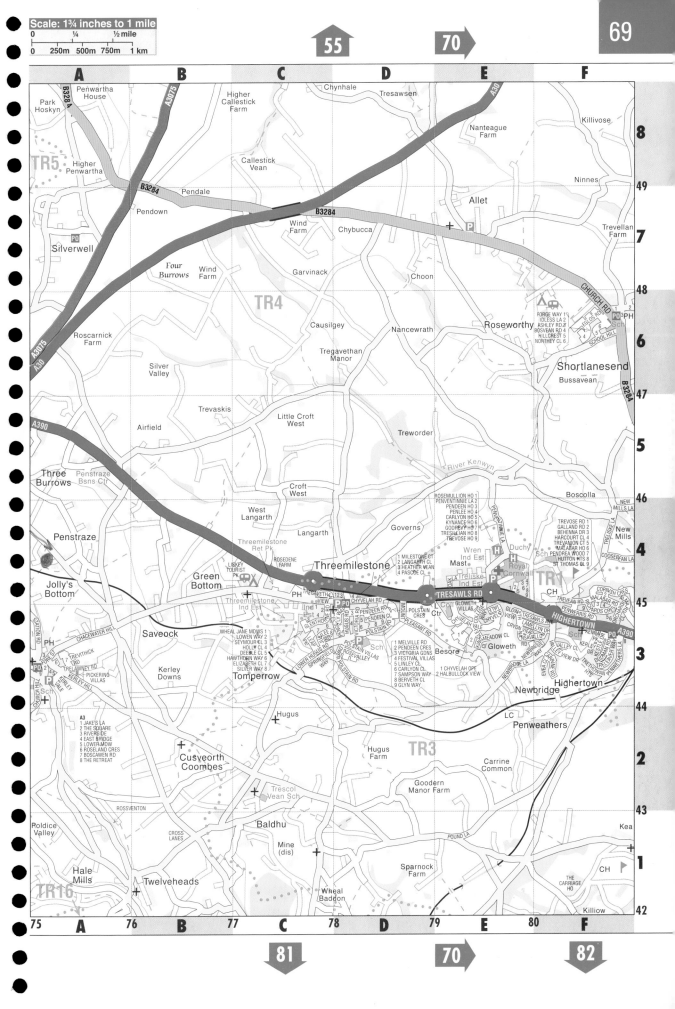

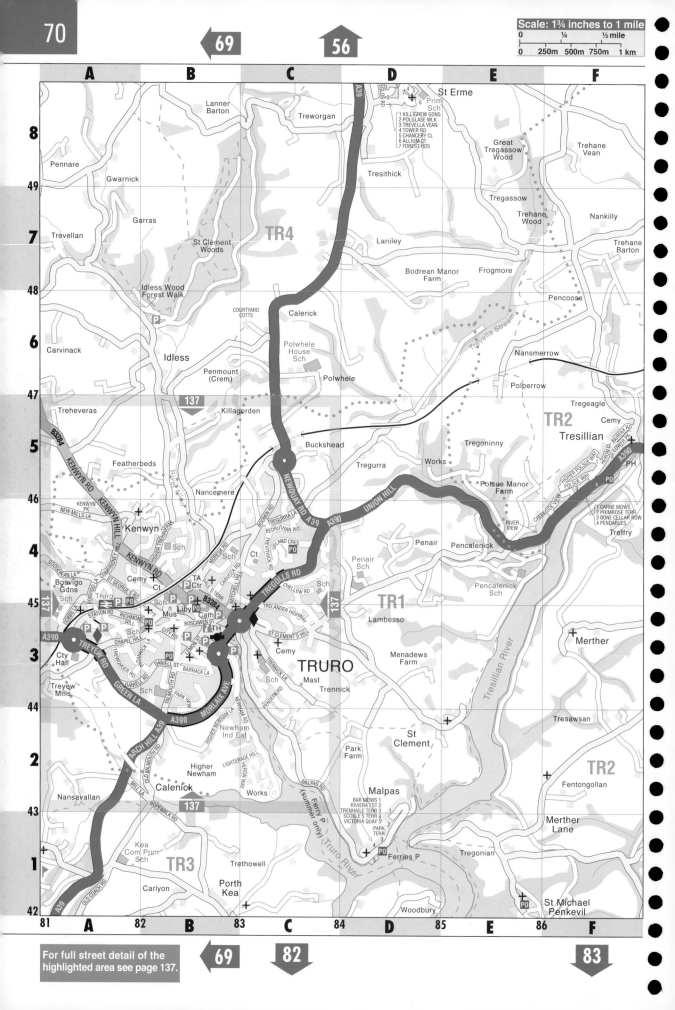

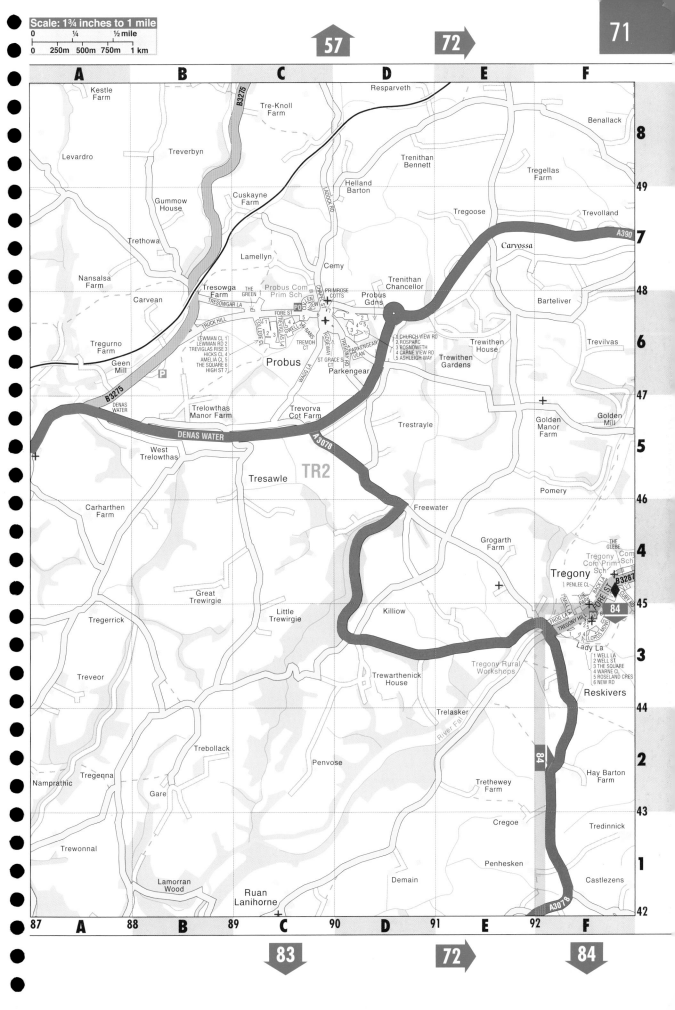

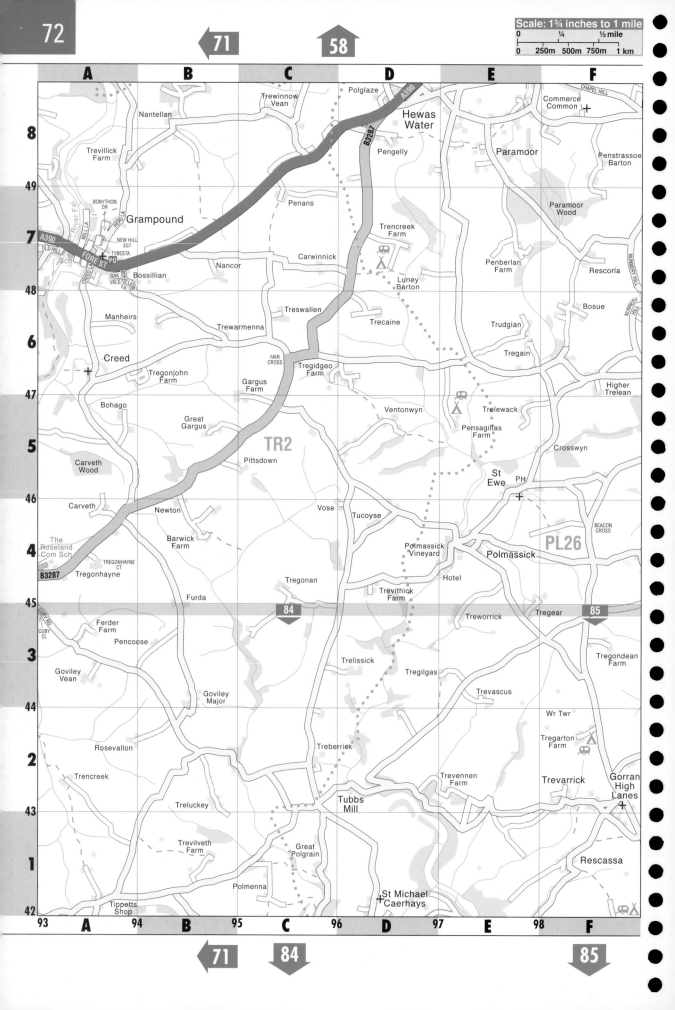

Scale: 1¾ inches to 1 mile
0   ¼   ½ mile
0 250m 500m 750m 1 km

A   B   C   D   E   F

8   Trewinnow Vean   Polglaze
Nantellan   Hewas Water   Commerce Common   CHAPEL HILL
Trevillick Farm   Pengelly   Paramoor   Penstrassoe Barton
49   BONYTHON DR   Penans   Paramoor Wood
7   Grampound   Trencreek Farm   Penberlan Farm   Rescorla
A390   NEW HILL EST   Carwinnick   Luney Barton   NUNNERY HILL
Sch   FORE ST   PO   TYBESTA
48   OAK VALE   Bossillian   Nancor   Treswallen   Trecaine   Trudgian   Bosue
Manheirs   Trewarmenna   Trecaine   NUNNERY LN
6   Creed   FAIR CROSS   Tregidgeo Farm   Tregain   Higher Trelean
Tregonjohn Farm   Gargus Farm   Ventonwyn   Trelewack
47   Bohago   Great Gargus   Pensagillas Farm   Crosswyn
5   Carveth Wood   TR2   Pittsdown   St Ewe   PH   PL26
46   Carveth   Newton   Vose   Tucoyse   Polmassick Vineyard   BEACON CROSS
The Roseland Com Sch   Barwick Farm   Polmassick   Tregear   85
4   B3287   TREGONHAYNE CT   Tregonhayne   Furda   Tregonan   Trevithick Farm   Hotel
45   84   Treworrick   Tregondean Farm
CUBY RD   Ferder Farm   Trelissick   Tregilgas
3   CUBY CL   Pencoose   Trevascus   Wr Twr
Goviley Vean   Goviley Major   Tregarton Farm   Trevarrick
2   Rosevallon   Trevennen Farm   Gorran High Lanes
Trencreek   Treberrick
Treluckey   Tubbs Mill   Rescassa
1   Trevilveth Farm   Great Polgrain
Polmenna   St Michael Caerhays
42   Tippetts Shop

93   A   94   B   95   C   96   D   97   E   98   F

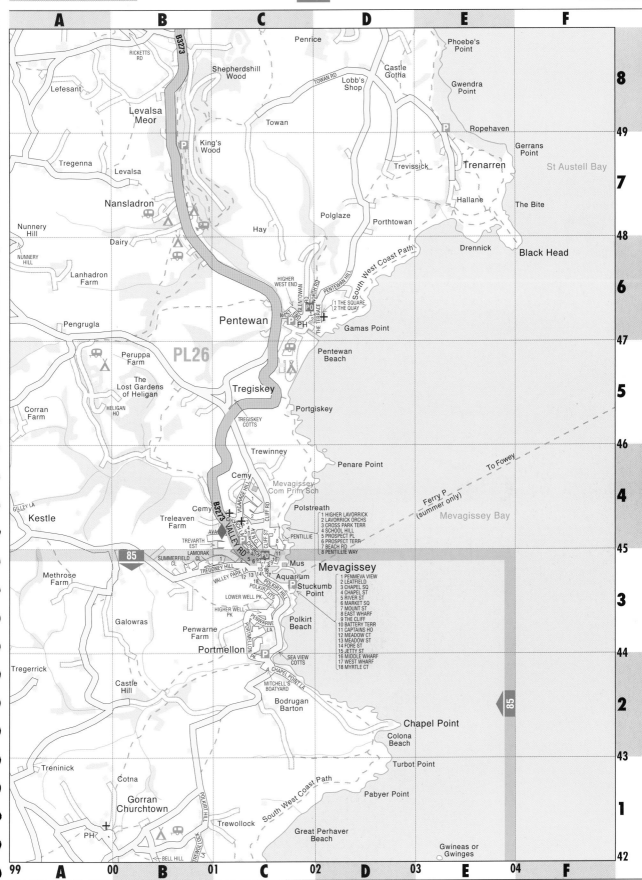

Scale: 1¾ inches to 1 mile

0   ¼   ½ mile
0 250m 500m 750m 1 km

8
49
7
48
6
47
5
46
4
45
3
44
2
43
1
42

A   B   C   D   E   F

Phoebe's Point
Gwendra Point
Ropehaven
Gerrans Point
St Austell Bay
Penrice
Castle Gotha
Lobb's Shop
TOWAN RD
Trenarren
Hallane
The Bite
Shepherdshill Wood
RICKETTS RD
B3273
Lefesant
Levalsa Meor
King's Wood
Towan
Trevissick
Porthtowan
Drennick
Black Head
Tregenna
Levalsa
Hay
Polglaze
South West Coast Path
Nansladron
Nunnery Hill
NUNNERY HILL
Dairy
HIGHER WEST END
PENTEWAN HILL
Gamas Point
1 THE SQUARE
2 THE QUAY
Lanhadron Farm
GLENTOWAN
NORTH RD
PO
WEST END
Pentewan
PH
THE TERRACE
Pentewan Beach
Pengrugla
PL26
Peruppa Farm
The Lost Gardens of Heligan
HELIGAN HO
Tregiskey
Portgiskey
Corran Farm
Tregiskey Cotts
Penare Point
To Fowey
Trewinney
Cemy
VICARAGE HILL
Mevagissey Com Prim Sch
Ferry P (summer only)
Mevagissey Bay
GILLEY LA
Kestle
Cemy
B3273
CLIFF RD
Polstreath
1 HIGHER LAVORRICK
2 LAVORRICK ORCHS
3 CROSS PARK TERR
4 SCHOOL HILL
5 PROSPECT PL
6 PROSPECT TERR
7 BEACH RD
8 PENTILLIE WAY
Treleaven Farm
VALLEY RD
PENTILLIE
CLIFF ST
TREVARTH EST
LAMORAK CL
PO
Mus
Mevagissey
1 PENMEVA VIEW
2 LEATFIELD
3 CHAPEL SQ
4 CHAPEL ST
5 RIVER ST
6 MARKET SQ
7 MOUNT ST
8 EAST WHARF
9 THE CLIFF
10 BATTERY TERR
11 CAPTAINS HO
12 MEADOW CT
13 MEADOW ST
14 FORE ST
15 JETTY ST
16 MIDDLE WHARF
17 WEST WHARF
18 MYRTLE CT
Methrose Farm
85
SUMMERFIELD CL
TREGONEY HILL
Aquarium
VALLEY PARK LA
POLKIRT HILL
Stuckumb Point
Galowras
LOWER WELL PK
HIGHER WELL PK
Polkirt Beach
PENWARNE LA
PORTMELLON
Penwarne Farm
Portmellon
PK
SEA VIEW COTTS
Castle Hill
A CHAPEL POINT LA
MITCHELL'S BOATYARD
Bodrugan Barton
85
Chapel Point
Colona Beach
Tregerrick
Turbot Point
Treninick
Cotna
Pabyer Point
Gorran Churchtown
POLKIRT HILL
PH
South West Coast Path
Trewollock
Great Perhaver Beach
Gwineas or Gwinges
BELL HILL
TREVOLLOW RD

99   00   01   02   03   04

85

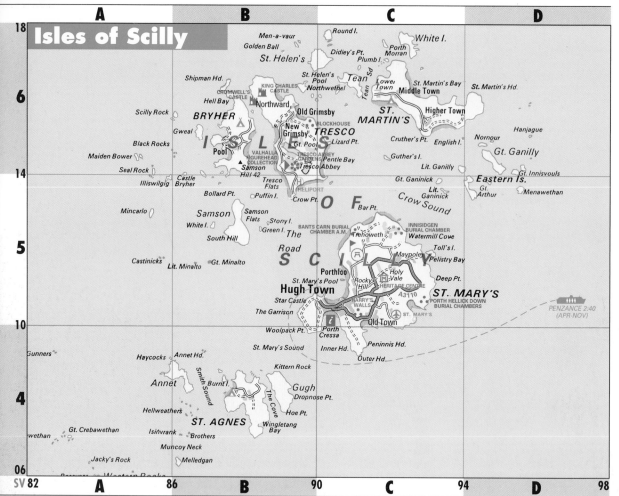

Isles of Scilly

A B C D

18

Men-a-vaur
Golden Ball
Round I.
White I.
St. Helen's
Didley's Pt.
Porth
Plumb I. Morran
Shipman Hd.
St. Helen's
Pool
Northwethel
Tean
Lower
Town
St. Martin's Bay
Middle Town
St. Martin's Hd.

6

CROMWELL'S
CASTLE
Scilly Rock
Hell Bay
KING CHARLES
CASTLE
Northward
Higher Town
BRYHER
Old Grimsby
ST.
Gweal
New
Grimsby
TRESCO
MARTIN'S
Black Rocks
ISLES
Cruther's Pt.
English I.
Pool
Gt. Pool
Lizard Pt.
Nornour
Hanjague
Maiden Bower
VALHALLA
FIGUREHEAD
COLLECTION
TRESCO ABBEY
GARDENS
Pentle Bay
Gt. Ganilly
Seal Rock
Samson
Hill 42
Tresco Abbey
Eastern Is.

14

Illiswilgig
Castle
Bryher
Tresco
Flats
HELIPORT
Crow Pt.
Gt. Ganinick
Lit.
Ganinick
Gt.
Arthur
Gt. Innisvouls
Menawethan
Bollard Pt.
Puffin I.
OF
Crow Sound
Mincarlo
Samson
Flats
Bar Pt.
Samson
Stony I.
White I.
Green I.
The
SCILLY
Trehoweth
INNISIDGEN
BURIAL CHAMBER
Watermill Cove
South Hill
BANTS CARN BURIAL
CHAMBER A.M.
Road
Toll's I.

5

Castinicks
Lit. Minalto
Gt. Minalto
Maypole
Pelistry Bay
Porthloo
Deep Pt.
Holy
Vale
St. Mary's Pool
Rocky
Hill
Hugh Town
HERITAGE CENTRE
ST. MARY'S
A3110
PORTH HELLICK DOWN
BURIAL CHAMBERS
Star Castle
HARRY'S
WALLS
PENZANCE 2:40
(APR-NOV)
The Garrison
Old Town
ST. MARY'S

10

Woolpack Pt.
Porth
Cressa
Peninnis Hd.
St. Mary's Sound
Inner Hd.
Haycocks
Annet Hd.
Outer Hd.
Kittern Rock
Gunners
Annet
Burnt I.
Gugh
Dropnose Pt.
Smith Sound
The Cove
Hoe Pt.
Hellweathers
ST. AGNES
Wingletang
Bay

4

wethan
Gt. Crebawethan
Isinvrank
Brothers
Muncoy Neck
Melledgan

06

Jacky's Rock
Western Rocks

SV 82   A   86   B   90   C   94   D   98

A B C D E F

37

3

The Wra or
Three Stone Oar

36

Lighthouse
Pendeen Watch

2

The Enys

CARN ROS 1
BOSCASWELL RD 2
LOWER BOSCASWELL PARC 3
BOSCASWELL EST 4
MOORLAND CL 5
The Avarack
Pendeen
Old Cliff
Carn Ros
Lower
Boscaswell
Trewellard Zawn

35

Levant Zawn
South West Coast Path
Chys

1

Levant
Beam Engine
Geevor
Tin Mine
Carn Du
TR19
CRESCENT
PL.
Chy
Geevor Tin
Mine Mus
Carn Vellan
Chy
B3306

34

32   A   33   B   34   C   35   D   36   E   37   F

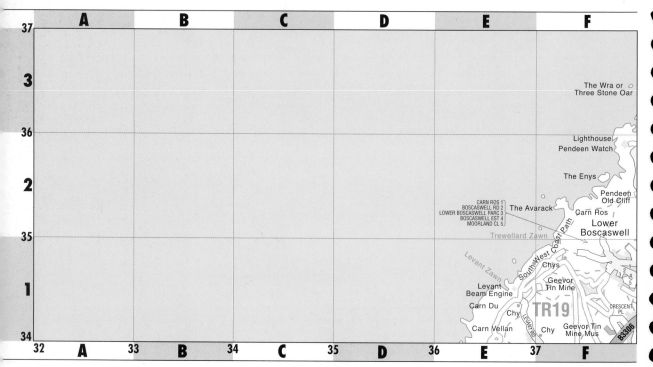

75

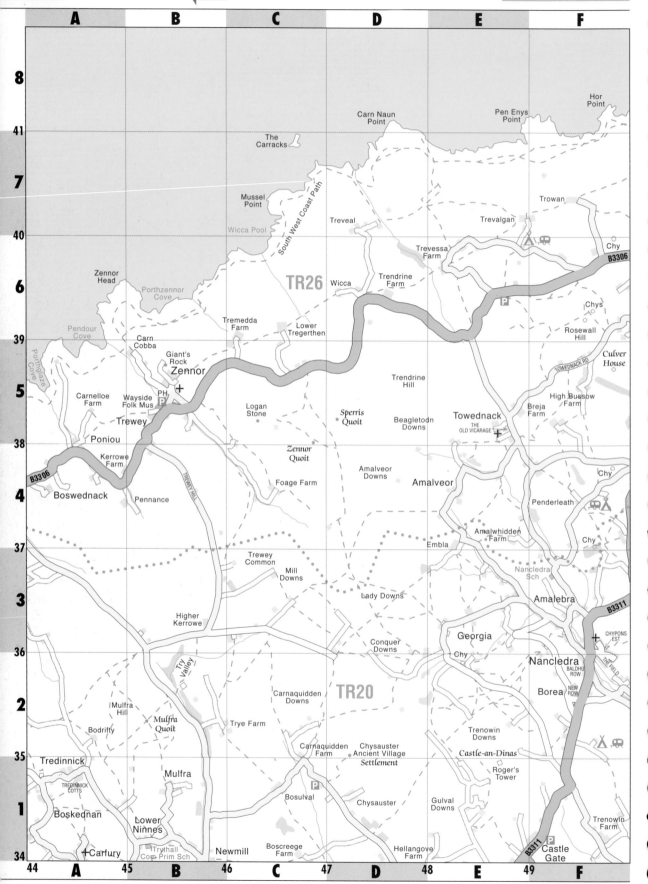

A   B   C   D   E   F

8
41
7
40
6
39
5
38
4
37
3
36
2
35
1
34

44   A   45   B   46   C   47   D   48   E   49   F

Hor Point
Pen Enys Point
Carn Naun Point
The Carracks
Mussel Point
Trowan
Wicca Pool
South West Coast Path
Treveal
Trevalgan
Chy
B3306
TR26
Trevessa Farm
Wicca
Trendrine Farm
Chys
Zennor Head
Porthzennor Cove
Tremedda Farm
Lower Tregerthen
Rosewall Hill
Pendour Cove
Carn Cobba
Giant's Rock
Trendrine Hill
Culver House
Porthglaze Cove
Zennor
TOWEDNACK RD
Carnelloe Farm
Wayside Folk Mus
PH
P
Logan Stone
Sperris Quoit
Beagletodn Downs
Towednack
THE OLD VICARAGE
High Bussow Farm
Breja Farm
Trewey
Zennor Quoit
Poniou
Chy
Kerrowe Farm
Foage Farm
Amalveor Downs
Amalveor
Penderleath
B3306
Boswednack
Pennance
Amalwhidden Farm
Chy
Embla
Trewey Common
Mill Downs
Nancledra Sch
Lady Downs
Amalebra
B3311
Higher Kerrowe
Conquer Downs
Georgia
CHYPONS EST
Try Valley
Chy
Nancledra
BALDHU ROW
Borea
NEW ROW
THE FIELD
Carnaquidden Downs
TR20
Mulfra Hill
Mulfra Quoit
Trye Farm
Trenowin Downs
Castle-an-Dinas
Bodrifty
Carnaquidden Farm
Chysauster Ancient Village
Settlement
Roger's Tower
Tredinnick
P
Mulfra
Bosulval
Chysauster
Gulval Downs
Trenowin Farm
TREDINNICK COTTS
Boskednan
Lower Ninnes
Newmill
Boscreege Farm
Hellangove Farm
P
B3311
Castle Gate
Carfury
Trythall Com Prim Sch

75
88

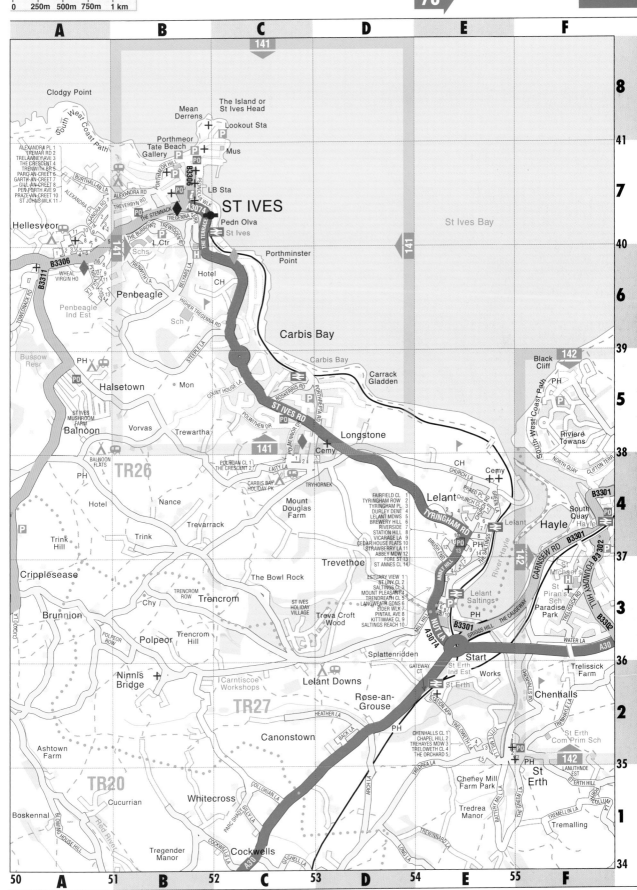

78

Scale: 1¾ inches to 1 mile

| 0 | ¼ | ½ mile |
| 0 | 250m | 500m | 750m | 1 km |

A B C D E F

8
41
7
40
6
39
5
38
4
37
3
36
2
35
1
34

Clodgy Point

South West Coast Path

ALEXANDRA PL 1
TREMAR RD 2
TRELAWNEY AVE 3
THE CRESCENT 4
TRENWITH BR 5
PARC-AN-CREET 6
GARTH-AN-CREET 7
GILL-AN-CREET 8
PEN-PORTH AVE 9
PRAZE-AN-CREET 10
ST JOHNS WLK 11

Hellesveor

Mean Derrens

The Island or St Ives Head

Lookout Sta

Porthmeor Tate Beach Gallery

Mus

ST IVES

Pedn Olva

St Ives

Porthminster Point

St Ives Bay

WHEAL VIRGIN HO

Penbeagle

Hotel
CH

Penbeagle Ind Est

Carbis Bay

Carbis Bay

Carrack Gladden

Black Cliff

142

Bussow Resr

Halsetown

Mon

ST IVES RD

Longstone

Riviere Towans

South West Coast Path

North Quay

South Quay

Balnoon

Vorvas

Trewartha

Cemy

141

Lelant

Hayle

B3301

Hayle

TR26

Balnoon Flats

PH

Carbis Bay Holiday Pk

Tryhornek

Mount Douglas Farm

FAIRFIELD CL 1
TYRINGHAM ROW 2
TYRINGHAM PL 3
DURLEY DENE 4
LELANT MDWS 5
BREWERY HILL 6
RIVERSIDE 7
STATION HILL 8
VICARAGE LA 9
CEDAR HOUSE FLATS 10
STRAWBERRY LA 11
ABBEY MDW 12
FORE ST 13
ST ANNES CL 14

CH
Cemy

Lelant

TYRINGHAM RD

Michael's Sch
St Piran's Sch

Paradise Park

Trink Hill

Trink

Trevarrack

Trevethoe

Lelant Saltings

Crippleseace

The Bowl Rock

ESTUARY VIEW 1
ST LIVY CL 2
SALTINGS CL 3
MOUNT PLEASANT 4
TRENDREATH 5
LANGWEATH GDNS 6
EIDER WLK 7
PINTAIL AVE 8
KITTIWAKE CL 9
SALTINGS REACH 10

Brunnion

Chy

Trencrom

Trencrom Row

Trencrom Hill

St Ives Holiday Village

Treva Croft Wood

Splattenridden

Start

Works

Trelissick Farm

Polpeor

Ninnis Bridge

Carntiscoe Workshops

Lelant Downs

Gateway Ct

St Erth Ind Est

St Erth

Chenhalls

Ashtown Farm

TR27

Rose-an-Grouse

PH

CHENHALLS CL 1
CHAPEL HILL 2
TREHAYES MDW 3
TRELOWETH CL 4
THE ORCHARD 5

St Erth Com Prim Sch

Boskennal

TR20

Cucurrian

Whitecross

Canonstown

Cheney Mill Farm Park

Tredrea Manor

St Erth

142

Lanuthnoe Est

Tregender Manor

Cockwells

Tremalling

50 A 51 B 52 C 53 D 54 E 55 F

A6
1 CHY-AN-DOUR CL
2 HELLESVEAN
3 HELLESVEAN CL
4 PARC-AN-STAMPS
5 CROWS-AN-EGLOS
6 PARC-AN-FORTH
7 PENBEAGLE TERR
8 PENBEAGLE CRES
9 CORVA RD
10 PRIORS CL
11 CORVA CL
12 PORTHIA RD
13 CARNSTABBA RD
14 ALAN HARVEY CL
15 JUBILEE CT
16 TINNERS WAY
17 PENBEAGLE CL

For full street detail of the highlighted area see pages 141 and 142.

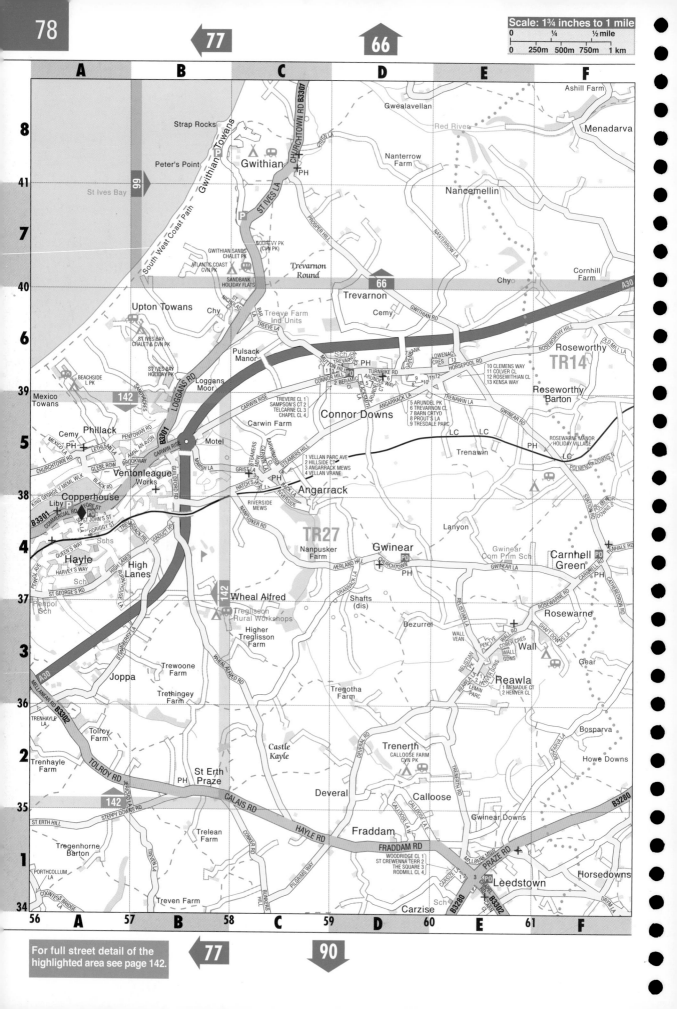

A B C D E F

8

41

7

40

6

39

5

38

4

37

3

36

2

35

1

34

56 A 57 B 58 C 59 D 60 E 61 F

Ashill Farm
Gwealavellan
Red River
Menadarva
Strap Rocks
Gwithian Towans
Nanterrow Farm
Gwithian
PH
Nancemellin
Peter's Point
P
St Ives Bay
66
St Ives Bay
ST IVES LA
Prosper Hill
Naxterrow La
Cornhill Farm
A30
South West Coast Path
P
Godrevy Pk (CVN PK)
Gwithian Sands Chalet Pk
Atlantic Coast CVN.Pk
Sandbank Holiday Flats
Trevarnon Round
66
Trevarnon
Chyo
Upton Towans
St Nicholas
Chy
Treeve Farm Ind Units
Cemy
Gwithian Rd
St Ives Bay Chalet & CVN Pk
Treeve La
Pulsack Manor
Sch
PH
Turnpike Rd
Horsepool Rd
Roseworthy
TR14
St Ives Bay Holiday Pk
Loggans Rd
Loggans Moor
Mutton Hill
Connor Hill
PO
Arundel Way
Greenbank
Lowenac Cres
13
10 Clemens Way
11 Colver Cl
12 Rosewithian Cl
13 Kensa Way
Roseworthy Barton
Beachside L Pk
Mexico Towans
142
Sandacres
Carwin Rise
Trevere Cl 1
Sampson's Ct 2
Telcarne Cl 3
Chapel Cl 4
Angarrack La
5 Arundel Pk
6 Trevarnon Cl
7 Barn Crtyd
8 Prout S La
9 Tresdale Parc
Trenawin La
Gwinear Rd
Rosewanne Manor Holiday Village
Cemy
Phillack
Pentowan Rd
Carwin Farm
Connor Downs
LC
LC
PH
LC
Mexico La
PH
Lethlean La
Amal La Avon
Brookway
Carwin Rise
B3301
Motel
Steamers Mews
Carnwinnick
Steamers Hill
1 Vellan Parc Ave
2 Hillside Cl
3 Angarrack Mews
4 Vellan Vrane
Trenawin
Polmewor Downs
Churchtown Rd
Glebe Row
Black Rd
Guildford Rd
Marsh La
Gris La
Hatch Ch La
Back La
PH
Riverside
Angarrack
Lanyon
Station Rd
Ventonleague
Works
King George V Meml Wlk
Copperhouse
Foxe St
PO
St John's St
Boriggy St
Trans'ck Hill
Viaduct Hill
Nampusker Rd
Riverside Mews
TR27
Nanpusker Farm
Gwinear
PO
Churchtown
PH
Gwinear Com Prim Sch
Gwinear La
Carnhell Green
PO
PH
Conhale Rd
Catherstown Rd
B3301
Commercial Rd
Liby
P
Queen's Way
Sohs
High Lanes
Burhouse La
Herland Hl
Drannack La
142
Wheal Alfred
Shafts (dis)
Bezurrel
Relistian La
Rosewarne
Percy Ave
Hayle
Harvey's Way
St George's Rd
Sch
High Lanes
Wheal Alfred Rd
Treglisson Rural Workshops
Higher Treglisson Farm
Wall Vean
Pen Tye
Cober Cres
Wall Gdns
Wall Rd
Wall
Rosewarne La
Shaft Downs La
Gear
Hempol Sch
A30
Mellanear Rd
Trewoone Farm
Trethingey Farm
Reawla La
Lemin Parc
Reawla
1 Menadue Ct
2 Henver Cl
Havel Downs
Joppa
B3302
Trenhaylp La
Tolroy Farm
Castle Kayle
Tregotha Farm
Trenerth
Bosparva
Howe Downs
Trenhayle Farm
Tolroy Rd
Jericho Rd
St Erth Praze
PH
Deveral
Calloose Farm CVN Pk
Trenerth Rd
Calloose
Barsva La
St Erth Hill
142
Calais Rd
Steppy Downs Rd
Hayle Rd
Fraddam
Calloose La E
Calloose La W
Gwinear Downs
B3280
Tregenhorne Barton
Trelean Farm
Connor Rd
Pilgrims Way
Fraddam Rd
Woodridge Cl 1
St Crewenna Terr 2
The Square 3
Rodmill Cl 4
Millbank Mdw
Prazo Rd
Leedstown
Horsedowns
Porthcollum La
Countess Bridge La
Treven Farm
Bunkers Hill
Carsize La
Sch
B3280
B3302
Drylla
Carzise

77 90

For full street detail of the highlighted area see page 142.

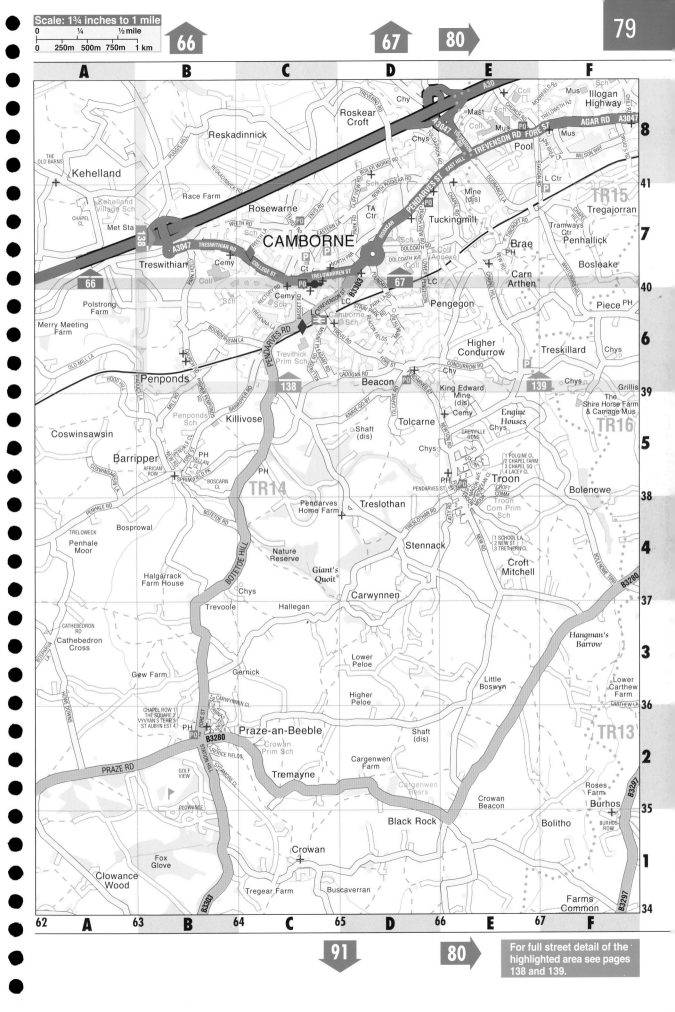

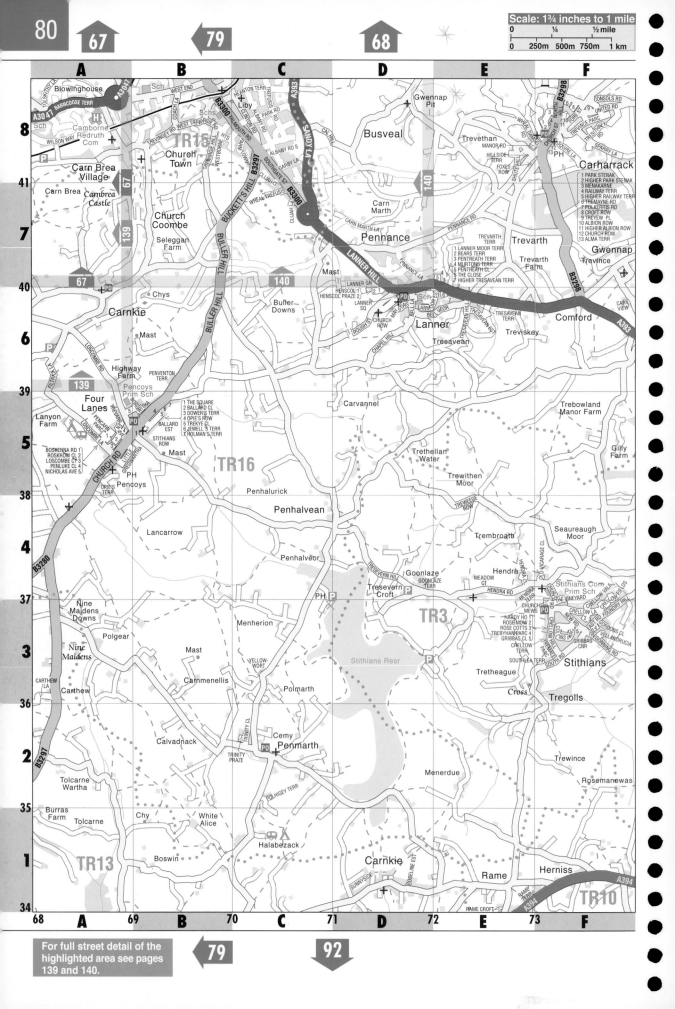

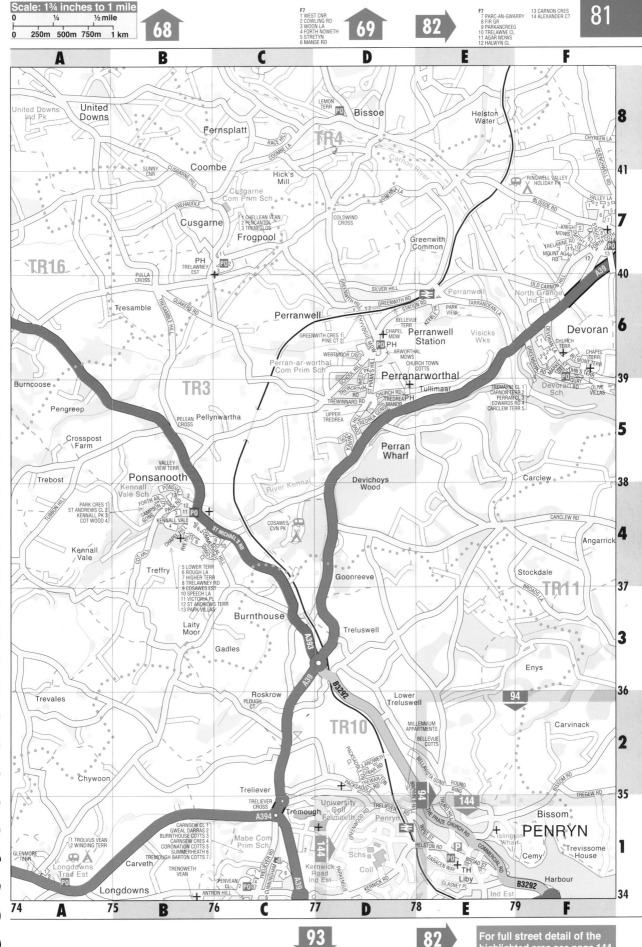

Scale: 1¾ inches to 1 mile

0 ¼ ½ mile
0 250m 500m 750m 1 km

68

F7
1 WEST CNR
2 COWLING RD
3 WOON LA
4 FORTH NOWETH
5 STRETYN
6 MANSE RD

69

82

F7
7 PARC-AN-GWARRY
8 FIR GR
9 PARKANCREEG
10 TRELAWNE CL
11 AGAR MDWS
12 HALWYN CL

13 CARNON CRES
14 ALEXANDER CT

81

A B C D E F

8

UNITED DOWNS
Ind Pk

United Downs

Fernsplatt

Bissoe
LEMON TERR
PO

Helston Water

CHYREEN LA

QUENCHWELL RD

41

Coombe

RACE HILL

COOMBE LA

CUSGARNE HILL

TR4

Carnon River

RINGWELL VALLEY HOLIDAY PK

VALLEY LA

7

SUNNY CNR

Hick's Mill

TREHADDLE

Cusgarne Com Prim Sch

BISSOE RD

GWENNA LA

KNIGHT'S MDWS

STAGG RD

FORTH COTH

PO

TR16

Cusgarne

Frogpool

1 CHELLEAN VEAN
2 PENCANTOL
3 TRENEGLOS

COLDWIND CROSS

Greenwith Common

TRELAWNE RD
MOUNT AGAR RD

A39

40

PULLA CROSS

PH
TRELAWNEY EST
PO

QUAKERS RD

TRESAMBLE HILL

SILVER HILL

Perranwell

GREENWITH HILL

STATION RD

TARRANDEAN LA

PARK VIEW

OLD CARNON HILL

North Grange Ind Est

Devoran

6

Tresamble

TR3

Perranwell

Perranwell Station

GREENWITH CRES 1
PINE CT 2

CHAPEL MDW
PO PH

BELLEVUE TERR

ARWORTHAL MDWS

Visicks Wks

CHURCH TERR
BELMONT TERR

GREENBANK RD

MARKET

DEVORAN LA

CHURCH TERR

39

Burncoose

Perran-ar-worthal Com Prim Sch

WESTMOOR CRES

SCHOOL HILL

WEST HILL

ST PIRANS HILL

CHURCH TOWN COTTS

Perranarworthal

CHURCH RD

TREDREA
PH MANOR

Tullimaar

TREMAYNE CL 1
CARNON TERR 2
PERRAN CL 3
EDWARDS RD 4
CARCLEW TERR 5

JOHN'S TERR

PO QUAY

Devoran Sch

OLIVE VILLAS

Pengreep

PELEAN CROSS

Pellynwartha

TRENWORTHAL RD

TREWINNARD RD

UPPER TREDREA

DOVE LA

SOUVREA

Carclew

5

Crosspost Farm

VALLEY VIEW TERR

Ponsanooth

Perran Wharf

38

Trebost

TURBON HILL

Kennall Vale Sch

FORTH AN

PONSILLE

PARK RD

PO

PARK CRES 1
ST ANDREWS CL 2
KENNALL PK 3
COT WOOD 4

SAMPSON GDNS

CHAPEL HILL

RYE TERR

ST MICHAEL'S RD

COMMERCIAL HILL

DINGLE

River Kennal

COSAWES CVN PK

Devichoys Wood

CARCLEW RD

Angarrick

4

Kennall Vale

COT HILL

Treffry

4 LOWER TERR
6 ROUGH LA
7 HIGHER TERR
8 TRELAWNEY RD
9 COSAWES EST
10 SPEECH LA
11 VICTORIA PL
12 ST ANDREWS TERR
13 PARK VILLAS

Goonreeve

Stockdale

BROADS LA

TR11

37

Laity Moor

Burnthouse

A393

Treluswell

3

Gadles

A39

Enys

B3292

Trevales

Roskrow

PLOUGH CT

Lower Treluswell

94

Carvinack

36

TR10

MILLENNIUM APARTMENTS

BELLEVUE COTTS

2

Chywoon

PACKSADDLE CL

LANOWETH

SQUNAR RD

TREWARTH RD

PACKSADDLE

BROWNS HILL

BELLAVISTA GDNS

Round Ring

144

BISSOM RD

TREGEW RD

35

Treliever

TRELIEVER CROSS

Tremough

A394

University Coll Falmouth

GREENWOOD RD

TRELIEVER RD

94

THE PRAZE

TRURO HILL

CHURCH RD

Bissom

PENRYN

Trevissome House

1

1 TROLVUS VEAN
2 WINDING TERR

GLENMORE TERR

Longdowns Trad Est

PO

Carveth

TRELIEVER RD

CUNNINGHAM RD

CARNSEW CL 1
GWEAL DARRAS 2
BURNTHOUSE COTTS 3
CARNSEW CRES 4
CORONATION COTTS 5
SUMMERHEATH 6
TREMOUGH BARTON COTTS 7

Mabe Com Prim Sch

TRENOWETH VEAN

PENVEAN LA
PO

144

Kernwick Road Ind Est

PARKENGUE

KERNICK RD

Schs
Coll

HELSTON RD

WEST ST

P

SARACEN WAY

BROAD ST

COMMERCIAL RD

Islington Wharf

Cemy

TH
Liby

Harbour

B3292

GLASNEY PL

Ind Est

Trevissome House

Longdowns

ANTRON HILL

A39

34

74 A 75 B 76 C 77 D 78 E 79 F

93

82

For full street detail of the highlighted area see page 144.

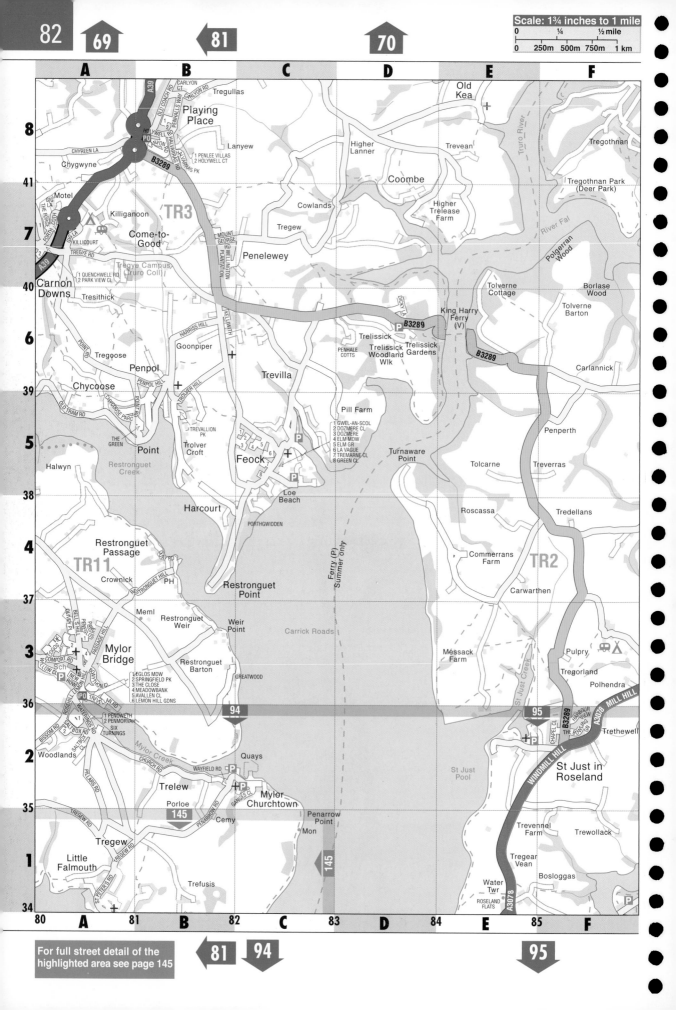

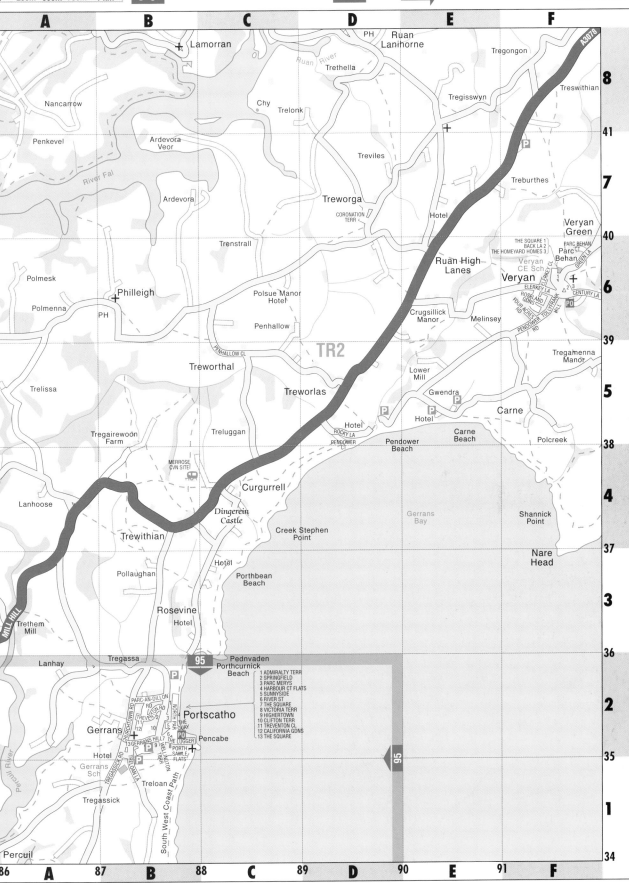

Scale: 1¾ inches to 1 mile

0   ¼   ½ mile
0   250m 500m 750m 1 km

70   71   84

A B C D E F

Lamorran
Nancarrow
Penkevel
Ardevora Veor
Ardevora
Trenstrall
Polmesk
Philleigh
Polmenna
PH
Trelissa
Treworthal
Tregairewoon Farm
Treluggan
Trelissa
Lanhoose
Trewithian
Pollaughan
Rosevine
Hotel
Lanhay
Tregassa
Gerrans
Hotel
Gerrans Sch
Tregassick
Percuil
Trethem Mill
MILL HILL
River Fal
Chy
Trelonk
Trethella
Trelonk
Ruan River
Ruan Lanihorne
PH
Tregongon
Treswithian
Tregisswyn
Treviles
Treworga
CORONATION TERR
Hotel
Ruan High Lanes
Treburthes
Veryan Green
Parc Behan
THE SQUARE 1
BACK LA 2
THE HOMEYARD HOMES 3
Veryan CE Sch
Veryan
ELERKEY CL
ROSELAND GDNS
FOUR ACRES
CENTURY LA
GREEN LA
PO
Polsue Manor Hotel
Penhallow
PENHALLOW CL
Crugsillick Manor
Melinsey
Tregamenna Manor
TR2
Treworlas
Lower Mill
Gwendra
Carne
Polcreek
Hotel
ROCKY LA
PENDOWER CT
Hotel
Pendower Beach
Carne Beach
PENDOWER RD
TOLVERNE
TOLLYTRUK
MILL LA
Curgurrell
Dingerein Castle
Creek Stephen Point
Gerrans Bay
Shannick Point
MERROSE CVN SITE
Nare Head
Hotel
Porthbean Beach
Tregassa
Pednvaden
Porthcurnick Beach
95
1 ADMIRALTY TERR
2 SPRINGFIELD
3 PARC MERYS
4 HARBOUR CT FLATS
5 SUNNYSIDE
6 RIVER ST
7 THE SQUARE
8 VICTORIA TERR
9 HIGHERTOWN
10 CLIFTON TERR
11 TREVENTON CL
12 CALIFORNIA GDNS
13 THE SQUARE
PARC-AN-DILLON RD
CHURCHTOWN RD
TREVARTH RD
NORTH PAR
THE QUAY
Portscatho
Pencabe
THE LUGGER
PO
PORTH SAWL E FLATS
WELLINGTON TERR
GERRANS HILL
TREGASSICK RD
TRELOAN LA
South West Coast Path
Percuil River
95
95
A3078

8 41 7 40 6 39 5 38 4 37 3 36 2 35 1 34

86 87 88 89 90 91

A B C D E F

95

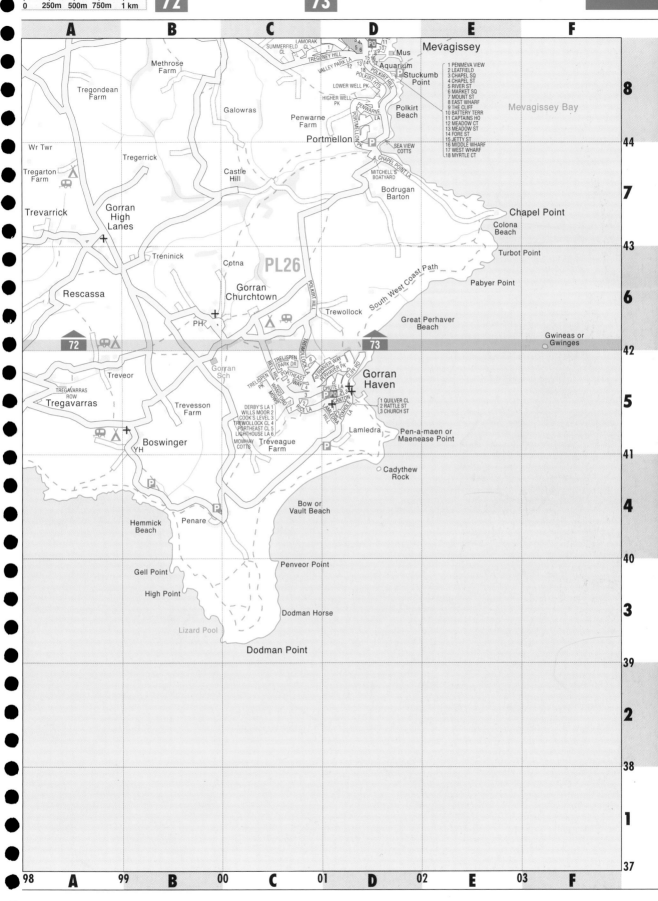

Scale: 1¾ inches to 1 mile

| 0 | ¼ | ½ mile |

| 0 | 250m | 500m | 750m | 1 km |

72   73

A   B   C   D   E   F

Mevagissey

1 PENMEVA VIEW
2 LEATHFIELD
3 CHAPEL SQ
4 CHAPEL ST
5 RIVER ST
6 MARKET SQ
7 MOUNT ST
8 EAST WHARF
9 THE CLIFF
10 BATTERY TERR
11 CAPTAINS HO
12 MEADOW CT
13 MEADOW ST
14 FORE ST
15 JETTY ST
16 MIDDLE WHARF
17 WEST WHARF
18 MYRTLE CT

Mevagissey Bay

Tregondean Farm

Methrose Farm

Galowras

Penwarne Farm

Aquarium
Stuckumb Point
Polkirt Beach

SUMMERFIELD CL
LAMORAK CL
TREGONEY HILL
VALLEY PARK LA
LOWER WELL PK
HIGHER WELL PK
PENWARNE LA
POLKIRT HILL
PORTMELLON PK
Mus

Wr Twr

Tregarton Farm

Tregerrick

Trevarrick

Gorran High Lanes

Castle Hill

Portmellon

SEA VIEW COTTS

CHAPEL POINT LA

MITCHELL'S BOATYARD

Bodrugan Barton

Chapel Point
Colona Beach

Turbot Point

Treninick

Cotna

PL26

Pabyer Point

Rescassa

Gorran Churchtown

PH

Trewollock

South West Coast Path

Great Perhaver Beach

Gwineas or Gwinges

72   73

Treveor

Gorran Sch

TRELISPEN PARK DR
TRELISPEN PK
BELL HILL
PORTHEAST WAY
MONGLEATH
PERHAVER WAY
PERHAVER PK
CLIFF LA
TREWOLLOCK LA

Gorran Haven

Tregavarras ROW

Tregavarras

Trevesson Farm

DERBY'S LA 1
WILLS MOOR 2
COOK'S LEVEL 3
TREWOLLOCK CL 4
PORTHEAST CL 5
LIGHTHOUSE LA 6

MOWHAY COTTS

Tréveague Farm

CHUTE LA
CANTON
PICE LA
FOXHOLE HILL
RANDLE

1 QUILVER CL
2 RATTLE ST
3 CHURCH ST

Lamledra

Pen-a-maen or Maenease Point

Boswinger

YH

Cadythew Rock

Hemmick Beach

Penare

Bow or Vault Beach

Gell Point

Penveor Point

High Point

Dodman Horse

Lizard Pool

Dodman Point

8
44
7
43
6
42
5
41
4
40
3
39
2
38
1
37

Scale: 1¾ inches to 1 mile
0   ¼   ½ mile
0   250m   500m   750m   1 km

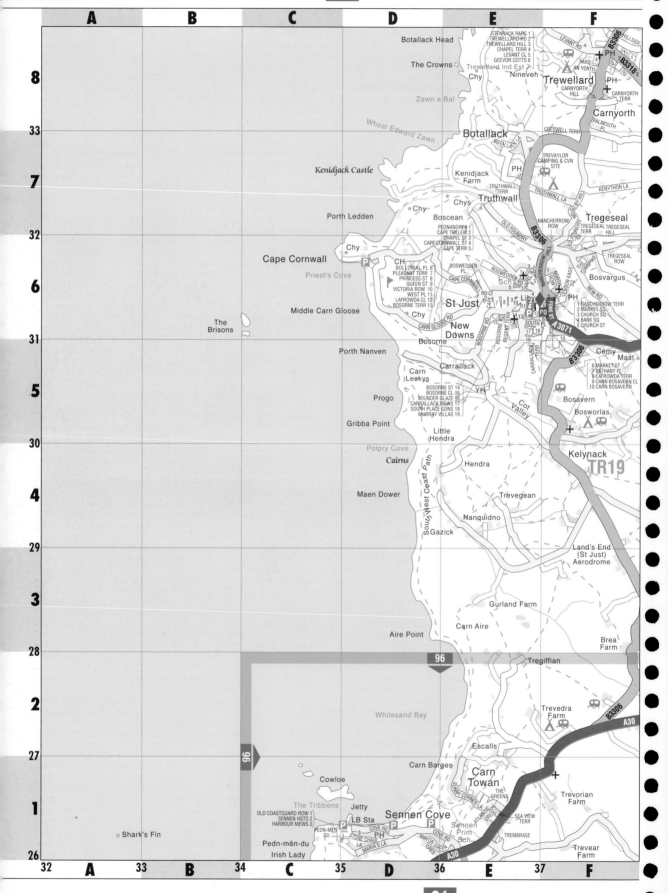

A B C D E F

8

33

7

32

6

31

5

30

4

3

28

2

27

1

26

32 A 33 B 34 C 35 D 36 E 37 F

Botallack Head

The Crowns

Zawn a Bal

Wheal Edward Zawn

Kenidjack Castle

Porth Ledden

Cape Cornwall

Priest's Cove

The Brisons

Middle Carn Gloose

Porth Nanven

Carn Leskys

Progo

Gribba Point

Polpry Cove

Cairns

Maen Dower

Aire Point

Whitesand Bay

Shark's Fin

Pedn-mên-du
Irish Lady

Cowloe

The Tribbens

OLD COASTGUARD ROW 1
SENNEN HGTS 2
HARBOUR MEWS 3
PEDN-MÊN-DU

Jetty
LB Sta
Sennen Cove

STENNACK PARC 1
TREWELLARD RD 2
TREWELLARD HILL 3
CHAPEL TERR 4
LEVANT CL 5
GEEVOR COTTS 6
LEVANT RD
HILLSIDE
B3306
B3318

PARC
AN YORTH
PH
Trewellard Ind Est
Nineveh
Chy
Trewellard
CARNYORTH
HILL
Carnyorth
CARNYORTH
TERR

Carnyorth
FALMOUTH
PL
CRESWELL TERR
Botallack
BOTALLACK
PH
Kenidjack
Farm
TRUTHWALL
TERR
TREVAYLOR
CAMPING & CVN
SITE
TRUTHWALL LA
KENYTHON LA

Truthwall
OLD FOUNDRY
NANCHERROW
ROW
Tregeseal
TREGESEAL TREGESEAL
TERR   HILL

Chy
Chys
Boscean
B3306

PEDNANDREA 1
CAPE TRELEW 2
CHAPEL ST 3
CAPE CORNWALL ST 4
CAPE TERR 5
BOSWEDDEN
PL.
TREGESEAL
ROW

Chy
BOLLOWAL PL 6
PLEASANT TERR 7
PRINCESS ST 8
QUEEN ST 9
VICTORIA ROW 10
WEST PL 11
LAFROWDA CL 12
BOSORNE TERR 13
CH
Bosvargus

CAPE CORNWALL
St Just
Sch
Lib
PO
PH

Bosorne
New
Downs
CARN GLOOSE RD
CARN CL
BOSORNE RD
REGENT TERR

1 NANCHERROW TERR
2 MARKET SQ
3 CHURCH SQ
4 BANK SQ
5 CHURCH ST

Carrallack
A3071
B3306
Cemy
Mast

BOSORNE ST 14
BOSORNE CL 15
VOUNDER GLAZE 16
CARRALLACK MEWS 17
SOUTH PLACE GDNS 18
MURRAY VILLAS 19
YH
Cot
Valley

6 MARKET ST
7 BETHANY PL
8 LAFROWDA TERR
9 CARN BOSAVERN CL
10 CARN BOSAVERN

Little
Hendra
Bosavern
Bosworlas

Hendra
Kelynack
TR19

Trevegean
Nanquidno
Land's End
(St Just)
Aerodrome

South West Coast Path
Gazick
Gurland Farm
Carn Aire
Brea
Farm

Tregiffian
96
Trevedra
Farm
B3306
A30

Escalls
Carn Barges
Carn
Towan
Trevorian
Farm

96
THE
GREENS
STONE CHAIR LA
MARIA'S LA
COVE HILL
COVE RD
PH
ATLANTIC CREST
ST JOHN'S CORNER LA
Sennen
Prim
Sch.
SEA VIEW
TERR
TREMBRASE

MAYON GREEN
A30
Trevear
Farm

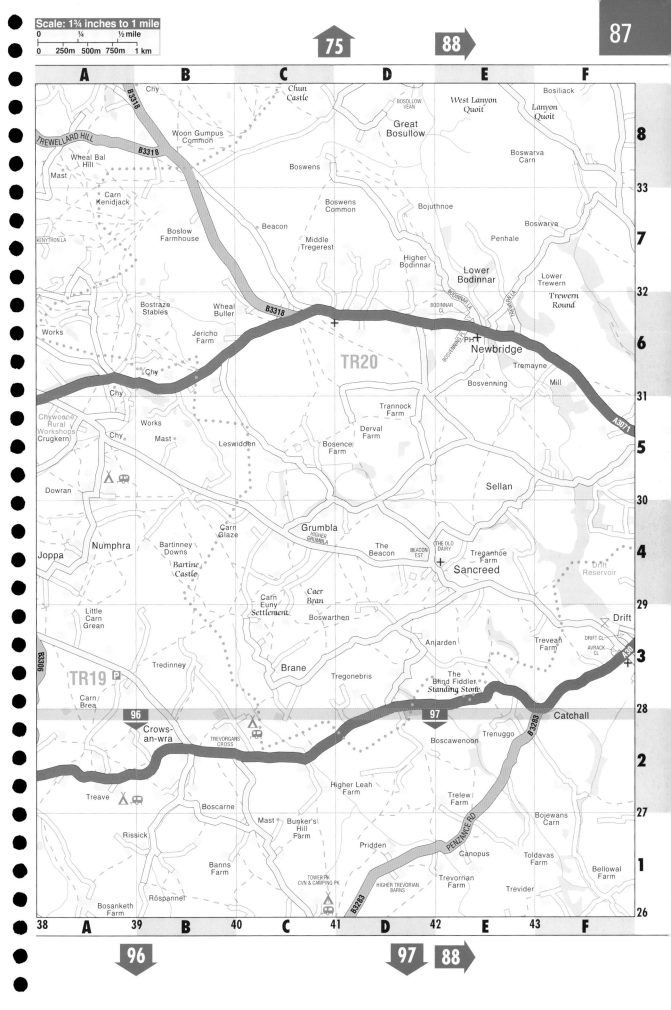

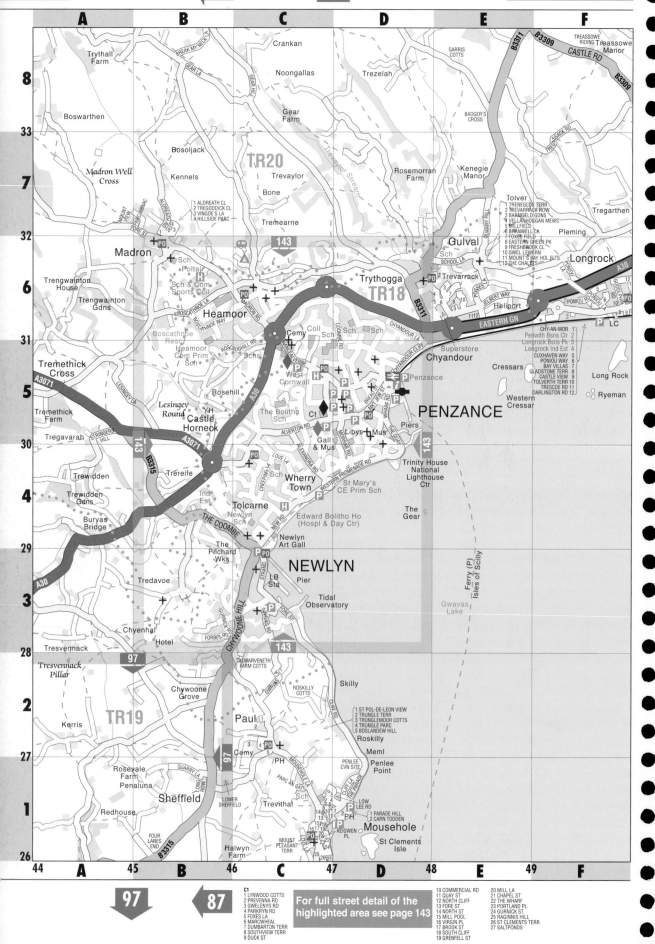

A · B · C · D · E · F

8

Trythall Farm

Crankan

Noongallas

Trezelah

Garris Cotts

B3311 · B3309

CASTLE RD

TREASSOWE RIDING · Treassowe Manor

B3309

33

Boswarthen

Bosoljack

TR20

Gear Farm

Rosemorran Farm

BADGER'S CROSS

7

Madron Well Cross

Kennels

Trevaylor

Bone

Tremearne

Trevaylor Stream

Kenegie Manor

Tolver
1 TRENEGLOS TERR
2 TREVARRACK ROW
3 BARNFIELD GDNS
4 VELLANHOGGAN MEWS
5 MILLFIELD
6 BRANWELL LA
7 FOXES FIELD
8 EASTERN GREEN PK
9 FRESHBROOK CL
10 GWEL LEWERN
11 MOUNT S BAY HOL FLTS
12 THE CHALETS

Tregarthen

Pleming

32

Trengwainton House

1 ALDREATH CL
2 TREGODDICK CL
3 VINGOE'S LA
4 HILLSIDE PARC

PO

Madron

Sch

Poltair

Gulval

Longrock

A30

Trengwainton Gdns

Sch & Com Sports Coll

Heamoor

MADRON RD

Trythogga

TR18

B3311

CHYANDOUR LA

SCHOOL LA

PO

Trevarrack

QUARRY HILL

ALBERT WAY

Heliport

CHY-AN-MOR 1
PONIOU WAY
GODOLPHIN
LC

6

Trengwainton House

BOSCATHNOE LA

BOSCATHNOE WAY

Cemy

Coll

Sch

Sch

EASTERN GN

1112

Penwith Bsns Ctr 2
Longrock Bsns Pk 3
Longrock Ind Est 4
CUXHAVEN WAY 5
PONIOU WAY 6
BAY VILLAS 7
GLADSTONE TERR 8
CASTLE VIEW 9
TOLVERTH TERR 10
TRESCOE RD 11
DARLINGTON RD 12

31

Tremethick Cross

A3071

Heamoor Com Prim Sch

Boscathnoe Resr

ROSCADGHILL RD

Schs

COOMBE RD

CHYANDOUR CLIFF

Superstore

Chyandour

Cressars

Long Rock

Western Cressar

Ryeman

5

Tremethick Farm

LESINGEY LA

Rosehill

H

West Cornwall

P

P

BREAK ST

WHARF RD

PENZANCE

30

Tregavarah

STRINGERS HILL

143

B3315

A3071

Trereife

Castle Horneck

YH

Lesingey Round

The Bolitho Sch

Ct

ALVERTON RD

Libys

Mus

THE QUAY

Piers

143

4

Trewidden

Trewidden Gdns

Buryas Bridge

Ind Est

Newlyn Sch

ALEXANDRA RD

LOVE LA

CREEPING LA

Gall & Mus

PO

Wherry Town

WESTERN PROMENADE RD

St Mary's CE Prim Sch

Edward Bolitho Ho (Hospl & Day Ctr)

The Gear

Trinity House National Lighthouse Ctr

29

A30

Tredavoe

THE COOMBE

Tolcarne

NEW RD

H

The Pilchard Wks

PO

Newlyn Art Gall

Ferry (P) Isles of Scilly

3

Chyenhal

GURNICK RD

FORBES RD

CHYWOONE HILL

STRAND

LB Sta

FORE ST

GWAVAS RD

NEWLYN

Pier

Tidal Observatory

Gwavas Lake

28

Tresvennack

97

143

Trewarveneth Farm Cotts

2

Tresvennack Pillar

Chywoone Grove

GWAVAS

Paul

ROSKILLY COTTS

CLIFF RD

Skilly

1 ST POL-DE-LEON VIEW
2 TRUNGLE TERR
3 TRUNGLEMOOR COTTS
4 TRUNGLE PARC
5 BOSLANDEW HILL

Roskilly

Karris

TR19

Cemy

PO

PH

MOUSEHOLE LA

Meml

PENLEE CVN SITE

Penlee Point

1

Rosevale Farm · Penaluna

QUARRY LA

LONG ROW

PARC AN GATE

Sheffield

LOWER SHEFFIELD

Trevithal

CLIFF LA

THE PARADE

LOW LEE RD

PH

KEIGWIN PL

1 PARADE HILL
2 CARN TODDEN

Mousehole

St Clements Isle

Redhouse

FOUR LANES END

B3315

Halwyn Farm

MOUNT PLEASANT TERR

PO

26

44 · A · 45 · B · 46 · C · 47 · D · 48 · E · 49 · F

C1
1 LYNWOOD COTTS
2 PREVENNA RD
3 GWELENYS RD
4 PARKRYN RD
5 FOXES LA
6 MARCWHEAL
7 DUMBARTON TERR
8 SOUTHVIEW TERR
9 DUCK ST

For full street detail of the highlighted area see page 143

10 COMMERCIAL RD
11 QUAY ST
12 NORTH CLIFF
13 FORE ST
14 NORTH ST
15 MILL POOL
16 VIRGIN PL
17 BROOK ST
18 SOUTH CLIFF
19 GRENFELL ST

20 MILL LA
21 CHAPEL ST
22 THE WHARF
23 PORTLAND PL
24 GURNICK ST
25 RAGINNIS HILL
26 ST CLEMENTS TERR
27 SALTPONDS

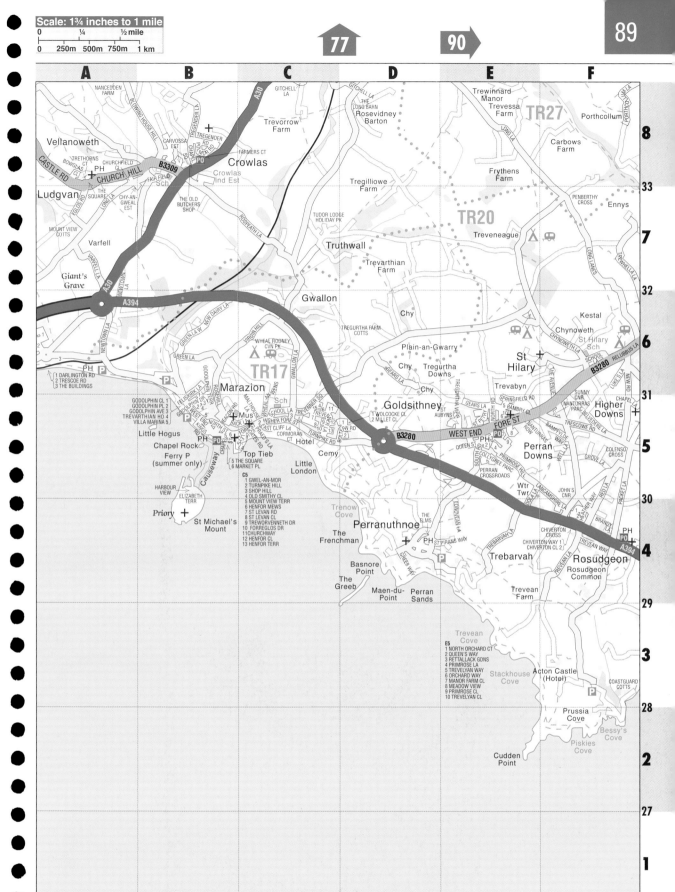

Scale: 1¾ inches to 1 mile

0   ¼   ½ mile
0   250m   500m   750m   1 km

A   B   C   D   E   F

NANCEDDEN FARM

Vellanoweth

TREWINNARD MANOR
TREVESSA FARM

TR27

Porthcollum

CASTLE RD
TRETHORNS CT
PH   BOWGLAS
CHURCHFIELD CL
THE SQUARE
Ludgvan
EGLOS RD
LONG LA

CARVOSSA EST
TREGENDER RD
CHAPEL RD
POLMENNOR RD
CHAPEL HILL
B3309
CHURCH HILL
FAIR FIELD

FARMERS CT

Crowlas
Crowlas Ind Est
Crowlas Sch

Carbows Farm

8

THE OLD BUTCHERS SHOP

Frythens Farm

33

MOUNT VIEW COTTS

CHY-AN-GWEAL EST

TUDOR LODGE HOLIDAY PK

Tregilliowe Farm

TR20

PENBERTHY CROSS

Ennys

Varfell

VARFELL

ROSEATH LA

Truthwall

Trevarthian Farm

Treveneague

7

32

Giant's Grave

A30

A394

NEWTOWN LA
NEW DAIRY LA

Gwallon

Chy

TREGURTHA FARM COTTS

Kestal

Chynoweth
CHYNOWETH LA
St Hilary Sch

PH
P
1 DARLINGTON RD
2 TRESCOE RD
3 THE BUILDINGS

GREEN LA W
GREEN LA
VIRGIN HILL
WHEAL RODNEY CVN PK
TR17

GODOLPHIN TERR
GODOLPHIN DR
WEST END

Plain-an-Gwarry

Chy
Tregurtha Downs

St Hilary

B3280
RELUBBUS LA

6

31

GODOLPHIN CL 1
GODOLPHIN PL 2
GODOLPHIN AVE 3
TREVARTHIAN HO 4
VILLA MARINA 5

FELISKIRK LA
ROSELVA
Marazion
Mus
MALTHOUSE LA

SCHOOL LA
TREVENNER SQ

GEARS LA

Goldsithney

GEARS LA

Trevabyn

THE AVENUE
SCHOOL LA
LUKE'S LA
NEW RD
SUNNY CNR
NANTURRAS PARC
BELVEDERE LA

Higher Downs

31

Little Hogus
Chapel Rock
Ferry P
(summer only)

BACK RD
FORE ST
ST CLIFF
P
CHAPEL
HIGHER FORE RD
ST CLIFF
CORMORAN CT
Hotel

1 WOLCOCKE CL
2 MILLET CL

B3280
WEST END
FORE ST

PH
PO

NANTURRAS ROW
BAMPY CL
TRESCOWE RD
COLENSO CROSS

Perran Downs

5

30

HARBOUR VIEW
ELIZABETH TERR
Priory

Top Tieb
5 THE SQUARE
6 MARKET PL
C5
1 GWEL-AN-MOR
2 TURNPIKE HILL
3 SHOP HILL
4 OLD SMITHY CL
5 MOUNT VIEW TERR
6 HENFOR MEWS
7 ST LEVAN RD
8 ST LEVAN CL
9 TREWORVENNETH DR
10 FORREGLOS DR
11 CHURCHWAY
12 HENFOR CL
13 HENFOR TERR

Little London

Cemy

Trenow Cove

Trebarvah

ROSUDGEON COMMON

Causeway

St Michael's Mount

The Frenchman

Perranuthnoe

PH
ST PIRANS WAY

Wtr Twr

LANCASTRIE LA
JOHN S CNR

HEATHER WAY
RED LA
PACKET LA

PH
PO
A394

Rosudgeon

4

30

Basnore Point
The Greeb

GREEB WAY

THE ELMS
EDDYSTONE LA

TREBARVAH LA

CHIVERTON CROSS
CHIVERTON WAY 1
CHIVERTON CL 2

BRANDY LA
TREVEAN WAY

Rosudgeon Common

Maen-du-Point
Perran Sands

Trevean Farm

29

Trevean Cove

E5
1 NORTH ORCHARD CT
2 QUEEN'S WAY
3 RETTALLACK GDNS
4 PRIMROSE LA
5 TREVELYAN WAY
6 ORCHARD WAY
7 MANOR FARM CL
8 MEADOW VIEW
9 PRIMROSE CL
10 TREVELYAN CL

Stackhouse Cove

Acton Castle (Hotel)

COASTGUARD COTTS

3

P

Prussia Cove

28

Bessy's Cove

Cudden Point

Piskies Cove

2

27

1

26

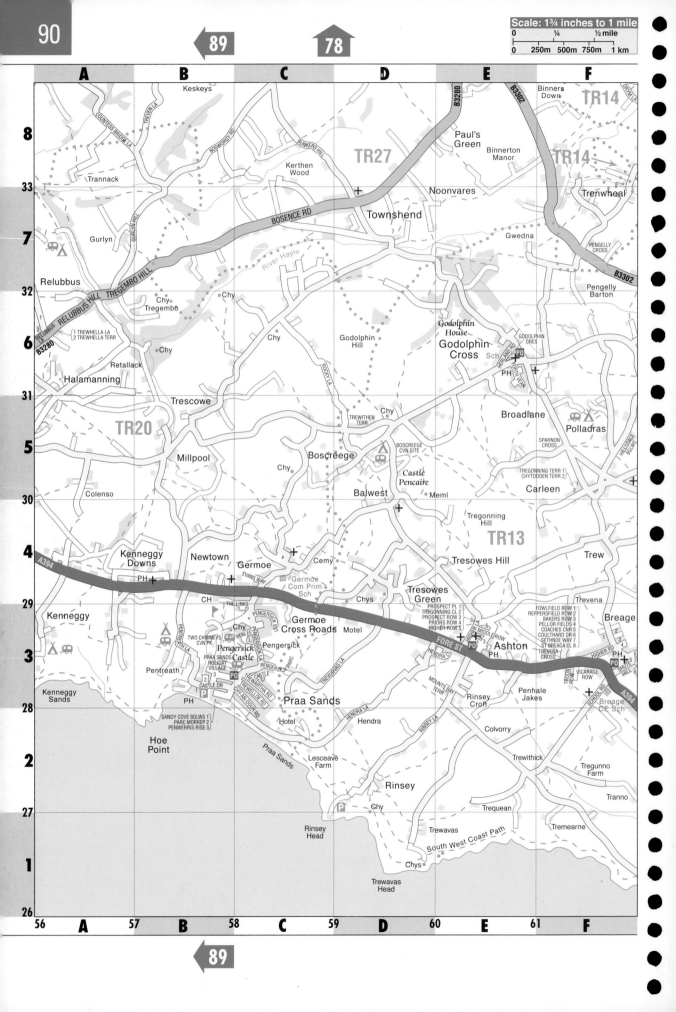

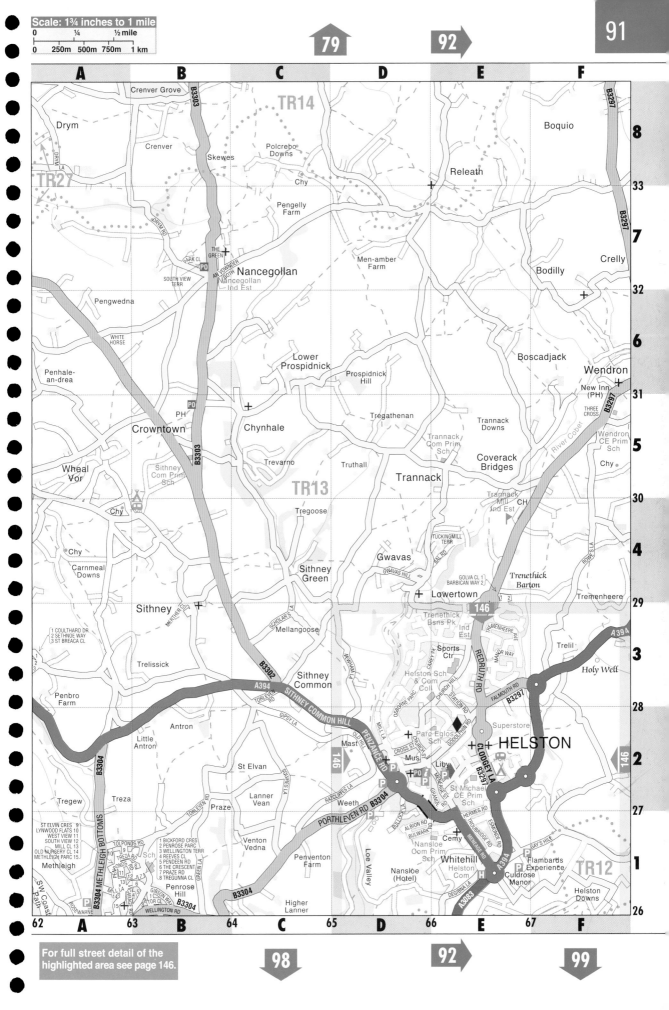

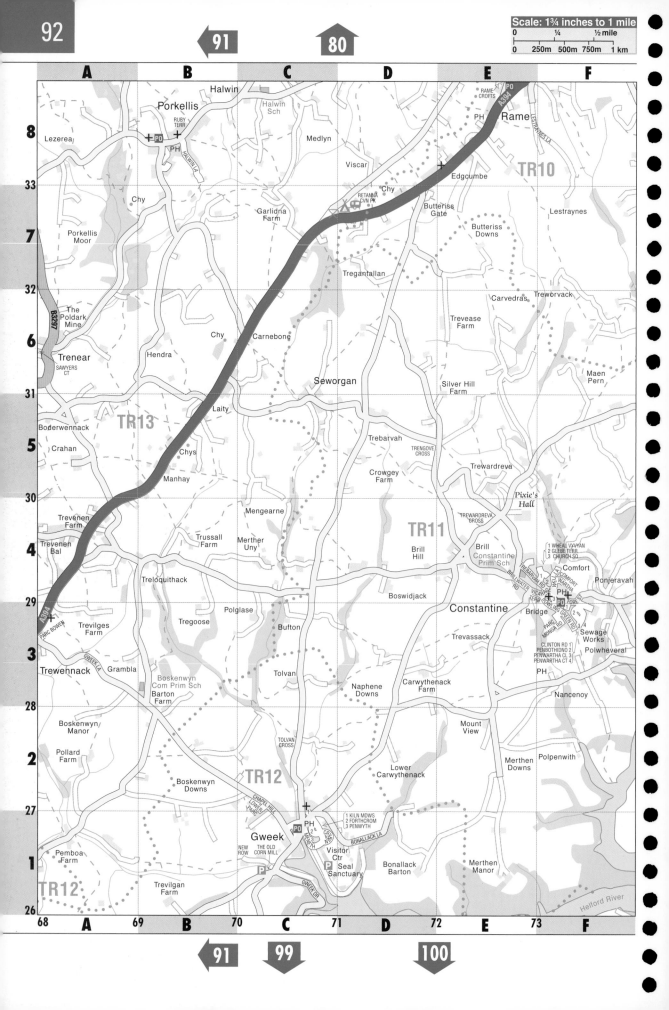

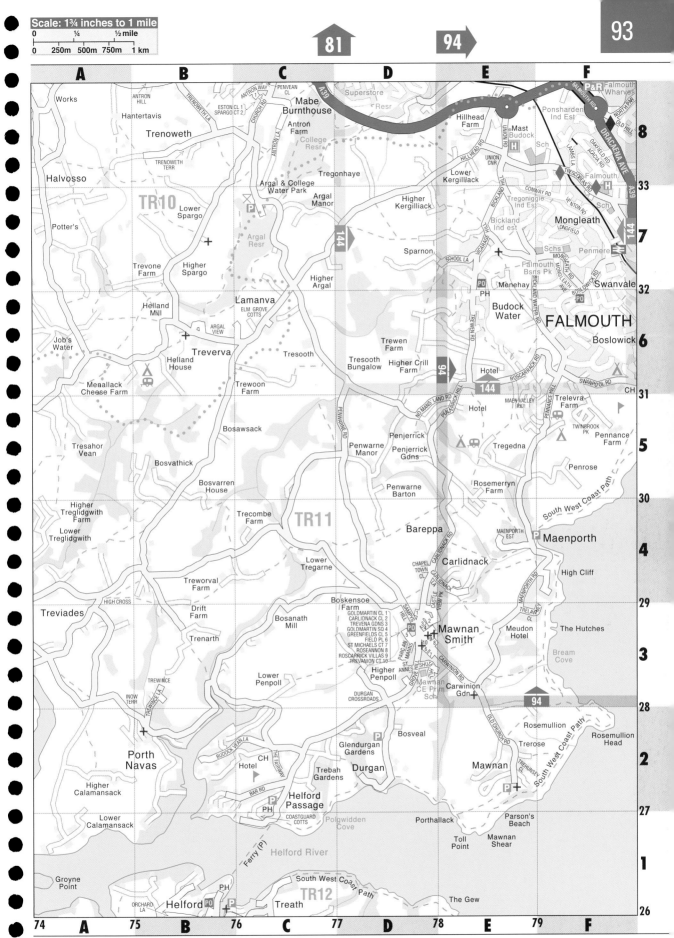

81

94

A39

Works

ANTRON HILL

Hantertavis

Trenoweth

TRENOWETHLA

CHURCH LA

ANTRON LA

ESTON CL 1
SPARGO CT 2

ANTRON WAY

PENVEAN CL

Mabe Burnthouse

Antron Farm

Superstore

College Resr

Resr

Hillhead Farm

UNION RD

Mast Budock

H

Ponsharden Ind Est

FALMOUTH RD

P&R

Falmouth Wharves

NORTH PAR

OLD HILL

DRACAENA AVE

A39

Halvosso

TRENOWETH TERR

Tregonhaye

Lower Kergilliack

UNION CNR

Sch

8

33

Potter's

TR10

Lower Spargo

Argal & College Water Park

Argal Manor

Higher Kergilliack

HILL HEAD RD

VICARAGE RD

BICKLAND

Tregoniggie Ind Est

CONWAY RD

VENTON RD

TRESCOBEAS RD

H

Falmouth

ACAGA RD

OAKFIELD RD

Sch

A39

144

Mongleath

LONGFIELD

Penmere

144

7

Trevone Farm

Higher Spargo

Argal Resr

P

Higher Argal

Sparnon

SCHOOL LA

Bickland Ind est

MONGLEATH RD

MONGLEATH AVE

BOSLOWICK RD

BICKLAND WATER RD

Schs

PO

Swanvale

32

Helland Mill

Lamanva

ELM GROVE COTTS

Higher Argal

PD

PH

Menehay

Budock Water

FALMOUTH

Boslowick

6

Job's Water

ARGAL VIEW

Treverva

Tresooth

Trewen Farm

Helland House

Tresooth Bungalow

Higher Crill Farm

TREWEN RD

94

Hotel

Hotel

ROSCARRACK RD

SWANPOOL RD

CH

31

Menallack Cheese Farm

Trewoon Farm

PENWARNE RD

NO MANS LAND RD

PENJERRICK HILL

144

MAEN VALLEY PK

Trelevra Farm

TWINBROOK PK

Pennance Farm

Tresahor Vean

Bosawsack

Penwarne Manor

Penjerrick

Penjerrick Gdns

PENNANCE HILL

Tregedna

Penrose

5

Bosvathick

Bosvarren House

Penwarne Barton

Rosemerryn Farm

30

Higher Treglidgwith

Trecombe Farm

TR11

Bareppa

South West Coast Path

MAENPORTH EST

P

Maenporth

4

Lower Treglidgwith

Carlidnack

CARLIDNACK RD

High Cliff

Treviades

Treworval Farm

Lower Tregarne

CHAPEL TOWN CL

CASTLE VIEW PK

CARLIDNACK LA

MAENPORTH RD

TRELAWNE CL

29

HIGH CROSS

Drift Farm

Bosanath Mill

Boskensoe Farm

GOLDMARTIN CL 1
CARLIDNACK CL 2
TREVENA GDNS 3
GOLDMARTIN SQ 4
GREENFIELDS CL 5
FIELD PL 6
ST MICHAELS CT 7
ROSEANNON 8
ROSCARRICK VILLAS 9
TREVANION CT 10

PARC AN MANIS

SEAMPS HILL

PO

Mawnan Smith

Meudon Hotel

The Hutches

Bream Cove

3

Trenarth

TREWINCE

TREWINCE LA

Trewince

INOW TERR

Lower Penpoll

Higher Penpoll

DURGAN CROSSROADS

ST ANNES HILL

GROVE HILL

CARWINION RD

Mawnan CE Prim Sch

Carwinion Gdn

94

28

Porth Navas

BUDOCK VEAN LA

THE FAIRWAY

CH

Hotel

BAR RD

P

Glendurgan Gardens

Trebah Gardens

Bosveal

Durgan

OLD CHURCH RD

Rosemullion

Trerose

TREHUNSEY CL

Mawnan

P

South West Coast Path

Rosemullion Head

2

Higher Calamansack

P

PH

COASTGUARD COTTS

Helford Passage

Polgwidden Cove

Porthallack

Toll Point

Parson's Beach

Mawnan Shear

27

Lower Calamansack

Ferry (P)

Helford River

South West Coast Path

The Gew

1

Groyne Point

ORCHARD LA

Helford

PO

P

PH

Treath

TR12

26

100

101

For full street detail of the highlighted area see page 144.

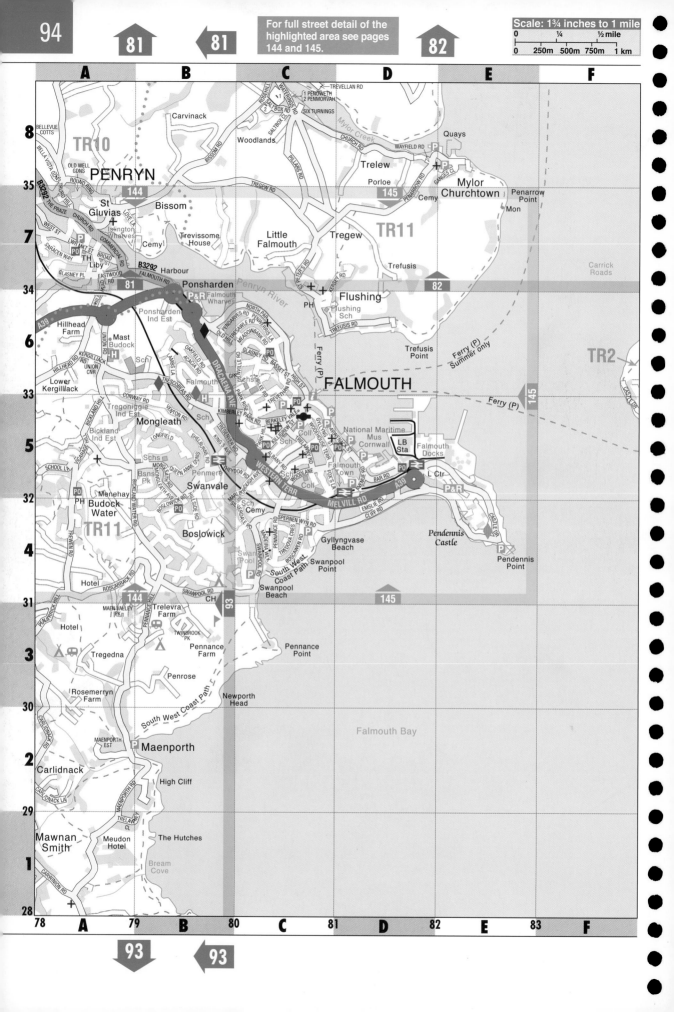

For full street detail of the highlighted area see pages 144 and 145.

Scale: 1¾ inches to 1 mile

0   ¼   ½ mile
0   250m   500m   750m   1 km

Scale: 1¾ inches to 1 mile
0 ¼ ½ mile
0 250m 500m 750m 1 km

82

83

A6
1 MANOR CT
2 ST AUSTELL ROW
3 THE SQUARE
4 KINGS RD
5 COMMERCIAL RD
6 GIBRALTAR TERR
7 CHURCH HILL
8 PEN-EGLOS
9 THE ROPE WLK
10 CHAPEL TERR
11 SEA VIEW CRES
12 SEA VIEW RD
13 NEWTON PK
14 HANCOCK LA
15 PLACE VIEW RD
16 KENNERLEY TERR
17 BROOKLYN TERR
18 BROOKLYN FLATS
19 BEECH HALL FLATS
20 BOHELLA RD

1 PORTH VIEW
2 PERCUIL VIEW
3 PEN BREA CL

1 ADMIRALTY TERR
2 SPRINGFIELD
3 PARC MERYS
4 HARBOUR CT FLATS
5 SUNNYSIDE
6 RIVER ST
7 THE SQUARE
8 VICTORIA TERR
9 HIGHERTOWN
10 CLIFTON TERR
11 TREVENTON CL
12 CALIFORNIA GDNS
13 THE SQUARE

Messack Point
St Just Pool
WINDMILL HILL
Trethewell
Lanhay
Tregassa
Tregassick
Pednvadan
Porthcurnick Beach
Porthcurnick
St Just in Roseland
PARC-AN-DILLON
Gerrans
Portscatho
Pencabe
PORTH SAWLE FLATS
THE LUGGER
THE QUAY
Hotel
Gerrans Sch
Trevennel Farm
Trewollack
Tregear Vean
Bosloggas
Water Twr
ROSELAND FLATS
TR2
Treloan
Trewince
TREWINCE MANOR
Rosteague
Greeb Point
Percuil
Percuil River
St Mawes
Quay
Froe
South West Coast Path
UPPER CASTLE RD
POLVARTH RD
TREDENHAM RD
RIVIERA
MARINE PAR
LOWER CASTLE RD
CASTLE DR
A3078
St Mawes Castle
Castle Point
St Mawes Harbour
Ferry P (summer only)
Carricknath Point
Bohortha
St Anthony
Place House
Place Barton
MILITARY RD
Porth Farm
Towan Beach
Killigerran Head
Porthbeor Beach
Porthmellin Head
St Anthony Head
Zone Point

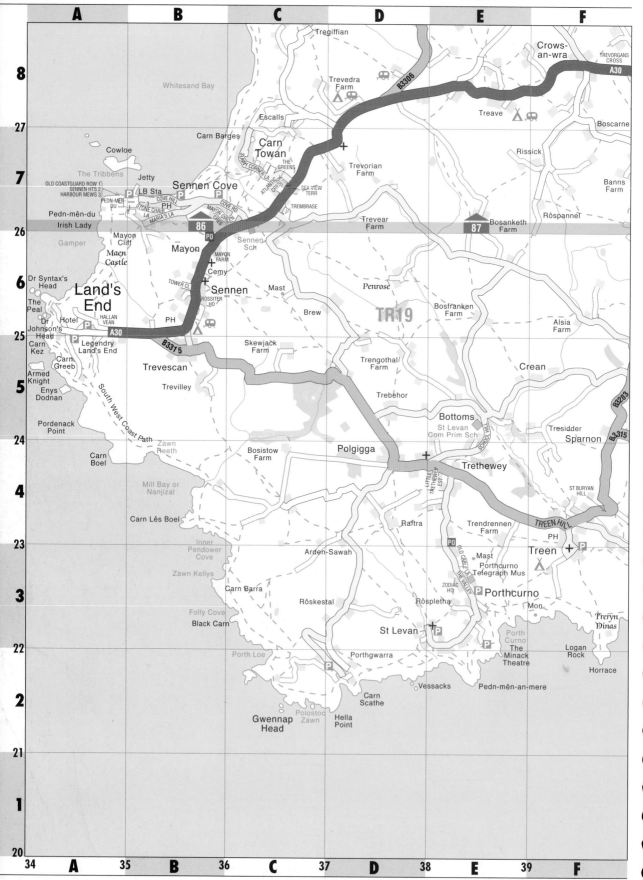

86

87

Scale: 1¾ inches to 1 mile

0   ¼   ½ mile
0   250m 500m 750m 1 km

A   B   C   D   E   F

Crows-an-wra

TREVORGANS CROSS

A30

Tregiffian

Trevedra Farm

Boscarne

Whitesand Bay

Escalls

Treave

Carn Barges

Carn Towan

THE GREENS

Rissick

Cowloe

The Tribbens

Jetty

Sennen Cove

SANDY CORNER LA

ATLANTIC CREST

SEA VIEW TERR

Trevorian Farm

Banns Farm

OLD COASTGUARD ROW 1
SENNEN HTS 2
HARBOUR MEWS 3

LB Sta

COVE HILL

TREMBRASE

Pedn-mên-du

PEDN-MEN-DU

STONE CHAIR

PH

COVE RD

MAYON GREEN CRB

Trevear Farm

Bosanketh Farm

Rôspannel

Irish Lady

LA MARIA'S LA

86

87

Gamper

Mayon Cliff

Mayon

PO

Sennen Sch

Dr Syntax's Head

Maen Castle

MAYON FARM

Penrose

The Peal

Land's End

TOWER CL

Cemy

Sennen

Mast

Bosfranken Farm

TR19

Alsia Farm

Dr Johnson's Head

Hotel

HALLAN VEAN

ROSSITER HO

Brew

Carn Kez

A30

PH

Crean

Carn Greeb

Legendry Land's End

B3315

Skewjack Farm

Trengothal Farm

Trebehor

Tresidder

Sparnon

B3283

Armed Knight

Trevescan

Trevilley

B3315

Enys Dodnan

Bottoms

St Levan Com Prim Sch

SCHOOL HILL

Pordenack Point

Zawn Peeth

Bosistow Farm

Polgigga

Trethewey

ST BURYAN HILL

Carn Boel

LITTLE TRETHEWEY EST

TREEN HILL

Mill Bay or Nanjizal

Raftra

Trendrennen Farm

PH

Treen

Carn Lês Boel

Inner Pendower Cove

Arden-Sawah

PO

OLD CABLE LA

Mast

THE VALLEY

Porthcurno Telegraph Mus

Zawn Kellys

Carn Barra

ZODIAC HO

Rôspletha

Porthcurno

Mon

Treryn Dinas

Folly Cove

Rôskestal

St Levan

Black Carn

Porth Curno

The Minack Theatre

Logan Rock

Porth Loe

Porthgwarra

Horrace

Pedn-mên-an-mere

Vessacks

Carn Scathe

Gwennap Head

Polostoc Zawn

Hella Point

34 A 35 B 36 C 37 D 38 E 39 F

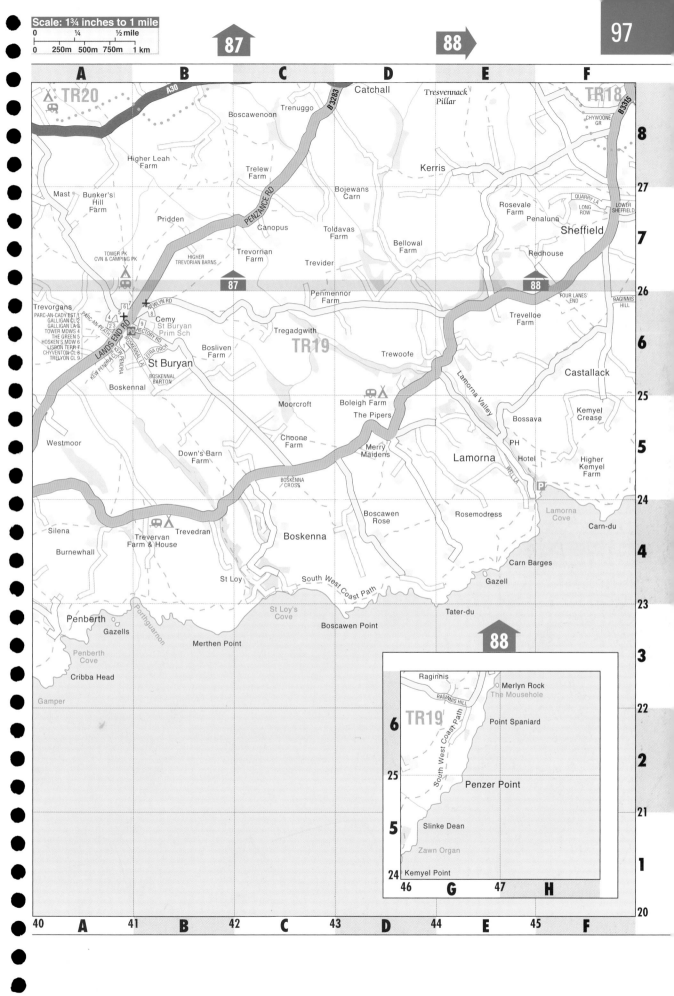

98

90

For full street detail of the highlighted area see page 146.

91

Scale: 1¾ inches to 1 mile

0   ¼   ½ mile

0   250m 500m 750m 1 km

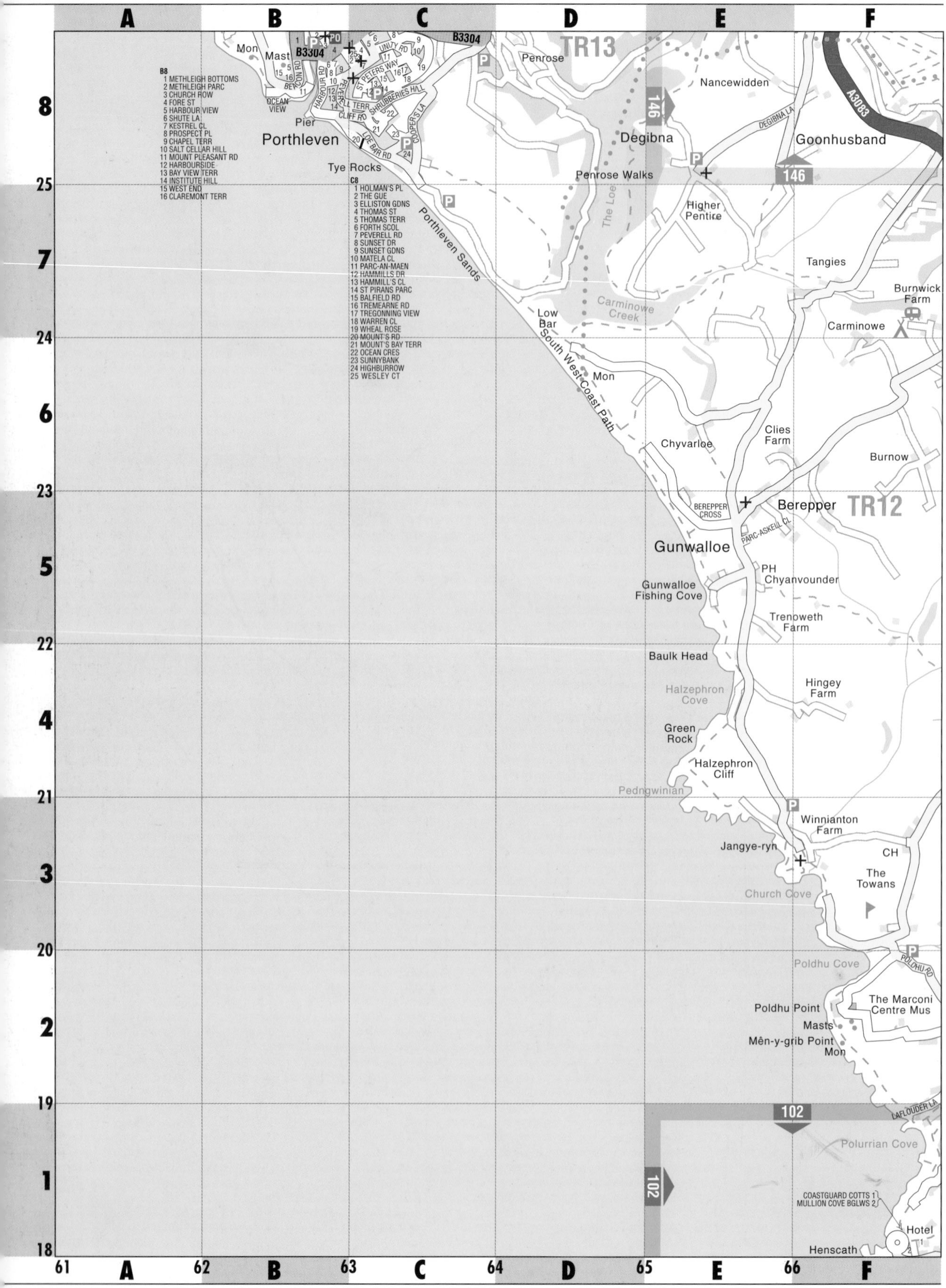

A **B** **C** **D** **E** **F**

B8
1 METHLEIGH BOTTOMS
2 METHLEIGH PARC
3 CHURCH ROW
4 FORE ST
5 HARBOUR VIEW
6 SHUTE LA
7 KESTREL CL
8 PROSPECT PL
9 CHAPEL TERR
10 SALT CELLAR HILL
11 MOUNT PLEASANT RD
12 HARBOURSIDE
13 BAY VIEW TERR
14 INSTITUTE HILL
15 WEST END
16 CLAREMONT TERR

C8
1 HOLMAN'S PL
2 THE GUE
3 ELLISTON GDNS
4 THOMAS ST
5 THOMAS TERR
6 FORTH SCOL
7 PEVERELL RD
8 SUNSET DR
9 SUNSET GDNS
10 MATELA CL
11 PARC-AN-MAEN
12 HAMMILL'S DR
13 HAMMILL'S CL
14 ST PIRANS PARC
15 BALFIELD RD
16 TREMEARNE RD
17 TREGONNING VIEW
18 WARREN CL
19 WHEAL ROSE
20 MOUNT'S RD
21 MOUNT'S BAY TERR
22 OCEAN CRES
23 SUNNYBANK
24 HIGHBURROW
25 WESLEY CT

Mon Mast
B3304
OCEAN VIEW
Pier
Porthleven
Tye Rocks

B3304

TR13

Penrose

Nancewidden

Degibna

Penrose Walks

Goonhusband

Higher Pentire

Tangies

Burnwick Farm

Carminowe

Porthleven Sands

Low Bar

Mon

Carminowe Creek

The Loe

South West Coast Path

Chyvarloe

Clies Farm

Burnow

Berepper Cross

Berepper

TR12

Gunwalloe

Gunwalloe Fishing Cove

PH Chyanvounder

Trenoweth Farm

Baulk Head

Hingey Farm

Halzephron Cove

Green Rock

Halzephron Cliff

Pedngwinian

Winnianton Farm

Jangye-ryn

CH

The Towans

Church Cove

Poldhu Cove

Poldhu Point

The Marconi Centre Mus

Masts

Mên-y-grib Point Mon

102

LAFLOUDER LA

Polurrian Cove

102

COASTGUARD COTTS 1
MULLION COVE BGLWS 2

Hotel

Henscath

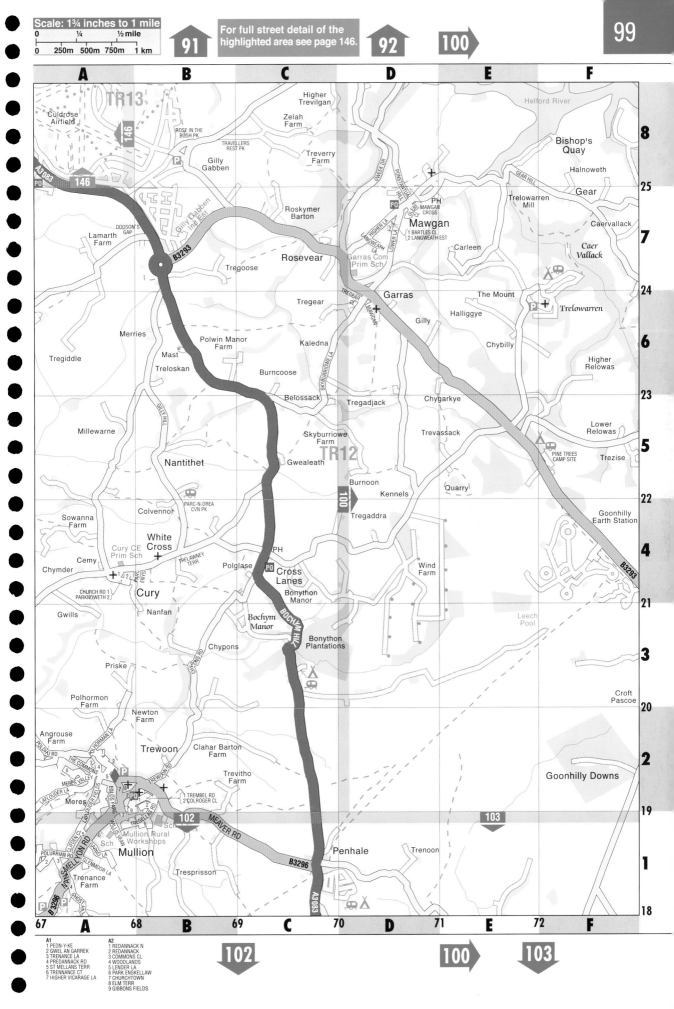

Scale: 1¾ inches to 1 mile
0   ¼   ½ mile
0   250m 500m 750m 1 km

For full street detail of the
highlighted area see page 146.

91
92
100
99

A   B   C   D   E   F

TR13

Culdrose Airfield

146

A3083
PO
146
B3293

Higher Trevilgan
Zelah Farm
ROSE IN THE BUSH PK
TRAVELLERS REST PK
Treverry Farm
Gilly Gabben
Roskymer Barton
Gilly Gabben Ind Est
DODSON'S GAP
Lamarth Farm
Rosevear

Helford River
Bishop's Quay
Halnoweth
Gear
PH
Mawgan Cross
PO
CREEK DR
PONSANTUEL
GEAR HILL
Trelowarren Mill
Caervallack
Caer Vallack
Mawgan
1 BARTLES CL
2 LANGWEATH EST
GLEBE
HIGHER LA
LANGWEATH LA
LOWER LA
Garras Com Prim Sch
Carleen
The Mount
Trelowarren
PO
Garras
LANGENAR
TREGEAR CL
Gilly
Halliggye
Chybilly

Tregoose
Tregear
Kaledna
Polwin Manor Farm
Mast
Treloskan
Burncoose
Belossack
Merries
Tregiddle
SKYBURRIOWE LA
Tregadjack
Chygarkye
Trevassack
Higher Relowas
Lower Relowas
Trezise
PINE TREES CAMP SITE
Goonhilly Earth Station

Millewarne
Nantithet
PARC-N-DREA CVN PK
Skyburriowe Farm
Gwealeath
TR12
Burnoon
Kennels
Tregadra
100
Quarry
Tregaddra

Sowanna Farm
Colvennor
White Cross
Cury CE Prim Sch
Cemy
Chymder
PARC ENYS
TRELAWNEY TERR
Polglase
PH
Cross Lanes
PO
Bonython Manor
Wind Farm
Leech Pool
Goonhilly Downs

CHURCH RD 1
PARKNOWETH 2
Cury
Gwills
Nanfan
Bochym Manor
BOCHYM HILL
Bonython Plantations
Croft Pascoe

Priske
Chypons
CHYPONS RD

Polhormon Farm
Newton Farm
Angrouse Farm
POLDHU RD
RD HORMAN LA
Trewoon
Clahar Barton Farm
Trevitho Farm

THE COMMONS
MERES VALLEY
Meres
LAFLOUDER LA
LAFLOUDER FIELDS
CLIFDEN CL
P
PO
Z
Mullion Rural Workshops
102
MEAVER RD
1 TREMBEL RD
2 COLROGER CL
Penhale
Trenoon
103

POLURRIAN RD
NANSMELLYON RD
GLENMOOR LA
GARIO LA
WILLIS LA
TREBELLAN RD
EGLOS PARC
Sch
Mullion
Trenance Farm
GHOST LA
B3296
A3083
Trespisson
B3296
Meaver Rd
Penhale

67   A   68   B   69   C   70   D   71   E   72   F

8
25
7
24
6
23
5
22
4
21
3
20
2
19
1
18

A1
1 PEDN-Y-KE
2 GWEL AN GARREK
3 TRENANCE LA
4 PREDANNACK RD
5 ST MELLANS TERR
6 TRENNANCE CT
7 HIGHER VICARAGE LA

A2
1 REDANNACK N
2 REDANNACK
3 COMMONS CL
4 WOODLANDS
5 LENDER LA
6 PARK ENSKELLAW
7 CHURCHTOWN
8 ELM TERR
9 GIBBONS FIELDS

99 92
93

Scale: 1¾ inches to 1 mile

0   ¼   ½ mile
0   250m   500m   750m   1 km

A   B   C   D   E   F

Helford River

Bishop's
Quay

Tremayne   Trevedor
Kestle

Halnoweth   Mudgeon
Gear Hill   Farm   Frenchman's
Pill

25   Gear   Withan
Trelowarren
Mill   Tregithew

Owek Dr   Ponsanooth Hill   Caervallack   Landrivick   Tregonwell
PH   Carleen   Caer
Mawgan Cross   Vallack   Choon
7   Higher La   PO   Mawgan
Langweath La   1 BARTLES CL   Fords Hill
Lower La   2 LANGWEATH EST

B3293   Garras Com
Prim Sch   The Mount   Sch   1 PORK ST
24   Tregear Ct   Garras   P   PO   2 THE GREEN
Skyburriowe La   Gilly   Halliggye   Trelowarren   Green Hill   3 BOSKERNOW
Langwan   2   Tregevis
Chybilly   Moor Parc   Farm   Trevaddra
6   Green Hill   Higher
Higher   St Martin   Trenower
Relowas   PH
Trethewey   Newtown-
in-St Martin   Tregidden Hill
23   Tregadjack   Chygarkye   Tregidden
Trevassack   Lower   Tretharrup
Relowas   Trewoon
5   Trezise   TR12   Trewince   Trelease
Pine Trees   Trelaminney   Mill
Burnoon   Camp Site   Trenithon
Quarry   Tregeague
Kennels   99
22   Tregaddra   Goonhilly   Polkerth   Traboe   Zoar
Earth Station
4   Rosuick   Grugwith
Wind   Roscrowgey   Roskilly
Farm   B3293
Kernewas
21   Leech   Traboe
Pool   P   Cross
3   Trelanvean
Croft   The Lizard
Pascoe   Nature Reserve
20   Croft Pascoe
Pool
2   Goonhilly Downs

19
Trenoon   Trelan
1   The Lizard
Nature Reserve
18
70   A   71   B   72   C   73   D   74   E   75   F

102
103
102   99   103

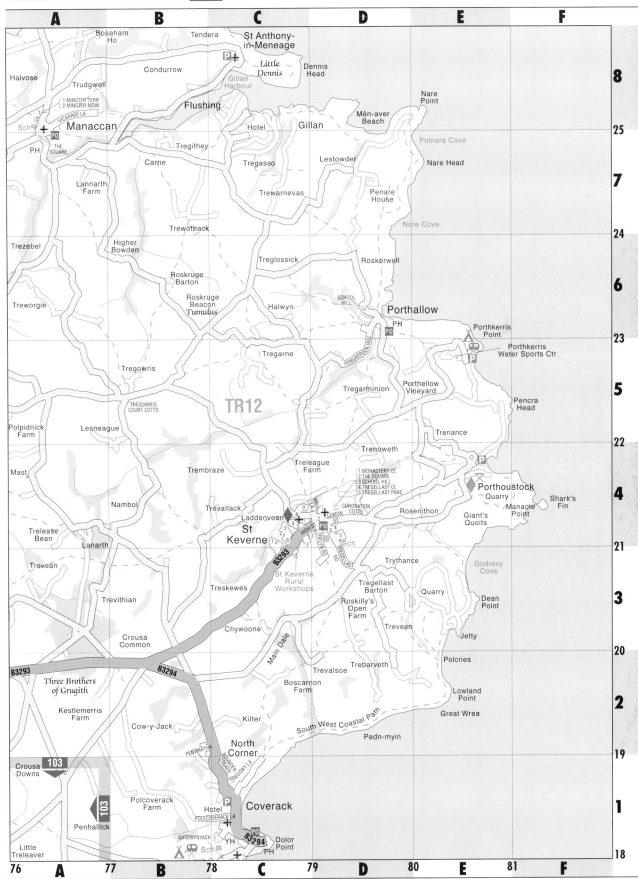

C4
1 TRESKEWES EST
2 TREVALLACK VIEW
3 TREVALLACK PARC
4 LANHEVERNE PARC
5 DOCTORS HILL
6 POLVENTON PARC
7 PENMENNER EST
8 COMMERCIAL RD
9 TREGONNING PARC

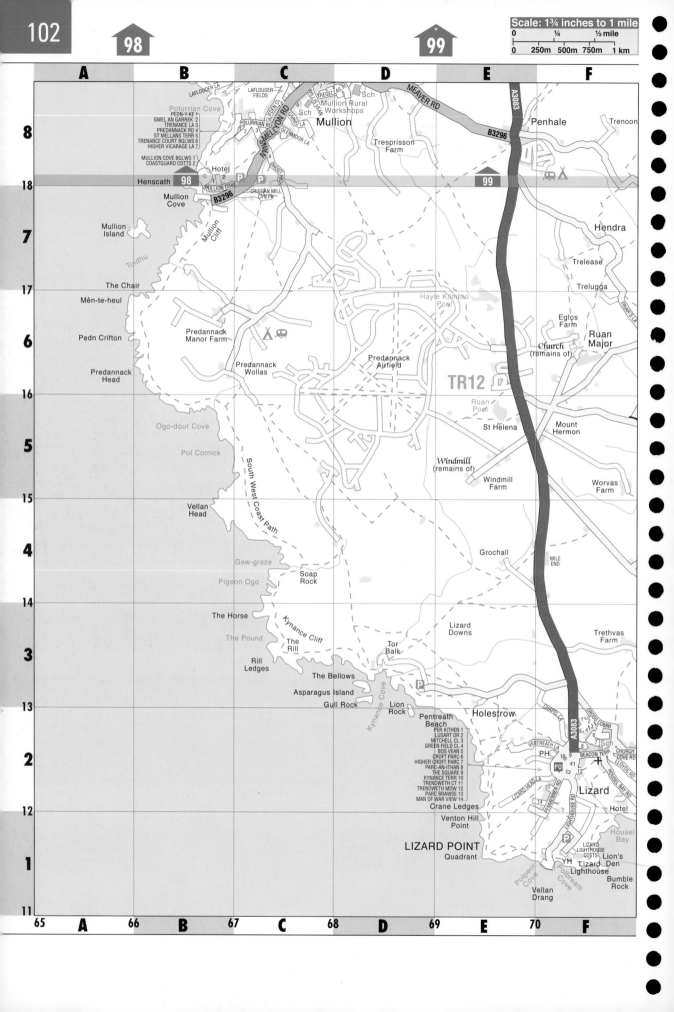

Scale: 1¾ inches to 1 mile

Mullion

Polurrian Cove
PEDN-Y-KE 1
GWEL AN GARREK 2
TRENANCE LA 3
PREDANNACK RD 4
ST MELLANS TERR 5
TRENANCE COURT BGLWS 6
HIGHER VICARAGE LA 7

MULLION COVE BGLWS 1
COASTGUARD COTTS 2

LAFLOUDER LA
LAFLOUDER FIELDS
TREGELLAS RD
WILLIS LEAN
MEAVER RD

Sch
Sch
Mullion Rural Workshops

Penhale
Trenoon

B3296

POLURRIAN RD
CLEBEN CL
ANSMELLYON RD
GLENMADOR LA
GHOST HILL

Tresprisson Farm

Hotel

Henscath   98
Mullion Cove
B3296

CRIGGAN MILL CVN PK

99

Hendra

Mullion Island

Mullion Cliff

Trelease

Trelugga

Toldhu

The Chair

Eglos Farm

Mên-te-heul

Hayle Kimbro Pool

Ruan Major

Pedn Crifton

Predannack Manor Farm

Church (remains of)

Predannack Wollas

Predannack Airfield

FRIARS LA

Predannack Head

TR12

Ruan Pool

Mount Hermon

Ogo-dour Cove

St Helena

South West Coast Path

Pol Cornick

Windmill (remains of)

Windmill Farm

Worvas Farm

Vellan Head

Gew-graze

Grochall

MILE END

Pigeon Ogo

Soap Rock

The Horse

Kynance Cliff

Lizard Downs

Trethvas Farm

The Pound

The Rill

Tor Balk

Rill Ledges

The Bellows

Asparagus Island

Gull Rock

Kynance Cove

Lion Rock

Holestrow

CHAPEL LA

CROSS COMM

A3083

Pentreath Beach
PER KITHEN 1
LUSART DR 2
MITCHELL CL 3
GREEN FIELD CL 4
BOS VEAN 5
CROFT PARC 6
HIGHER CROFT PARC 7
PARC-AN-ITHAN 8
THE SQUARE 9
KYNANCE TERR 10
TRENOWETH CT 11
TRENOWETH MDW 12
PARC BRAWSE 13
MAN OF WAR VIEW 14

Sch

PENTREATH LA
PH
PO

BEACON TERR
CHURCH COVE RD

Lizard
Hotel

Crane Ledges

Venton Hill Point

LIZARD POINT
Quadrant

LIZARD HEAD LA
PENMENNER RD
LIGHTHOUSE RD

Housel Bay

P
LIZARD LIGHTHOUSE COTTS
YH
Lizard Lighthouse

Lion's Den

Bumble Rock

Polpeor Cove

Polbream Cove

Vellan Drang

ROSSEL RD
LLOYDS RD

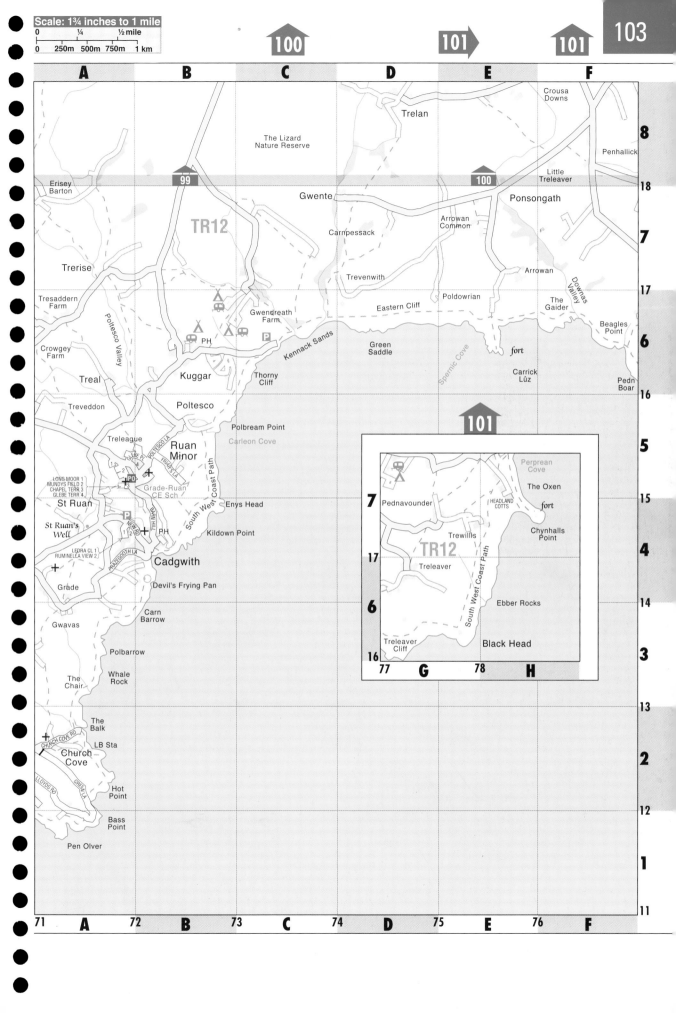

A B C D E F

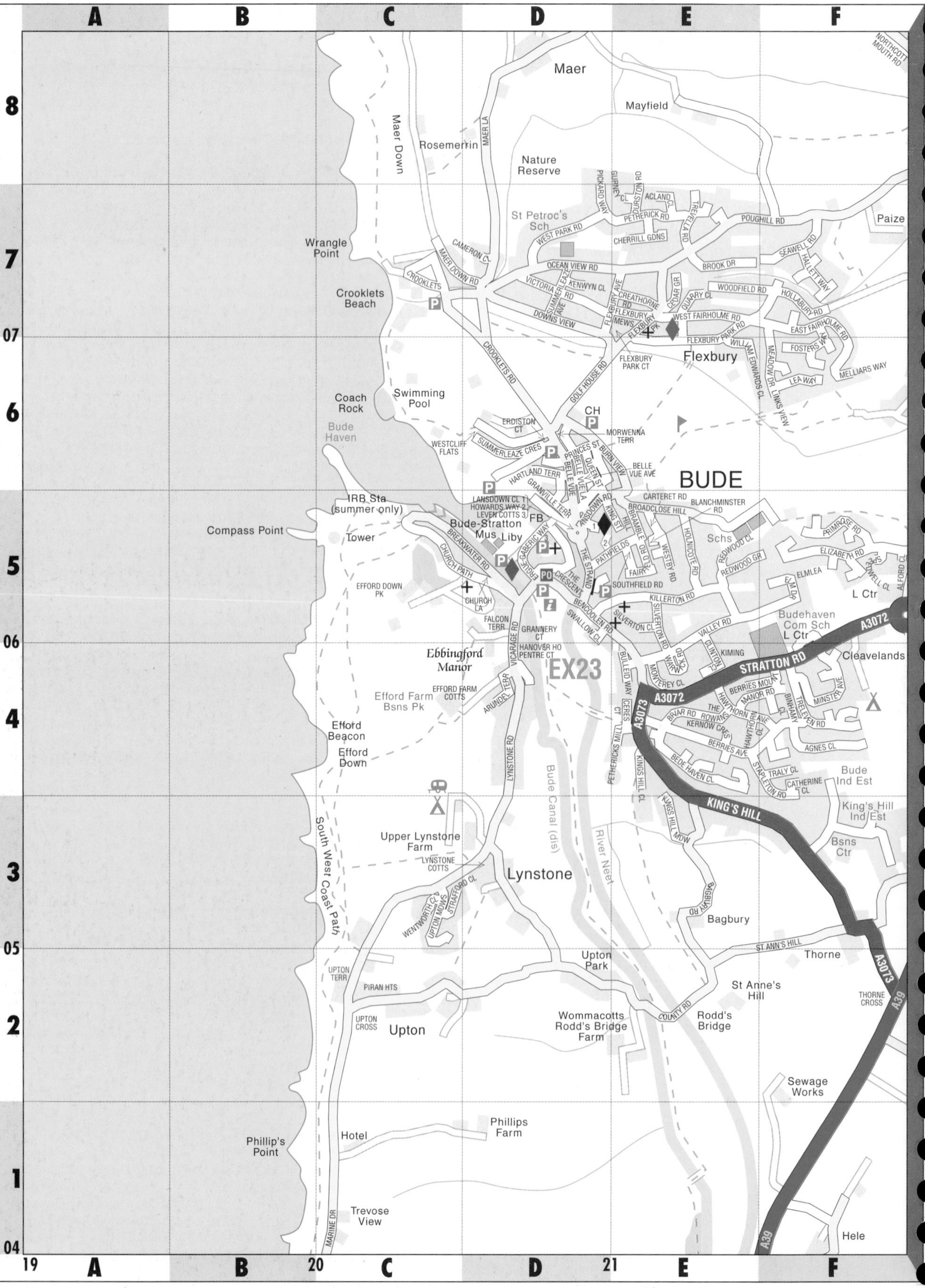

4 4

8

Maer

Mayfield

Rosemerrin

Maer Down

Nature
Reserve

7

Wrangle
Point

St Petroc's
Sch

Paize

Crooklets
Beach

CAMERON CL

OCEAN VIEW RD

WEST PARK RD

GURNEY
CL

OLD
POUGHILL RD

ACLAND

PETHERICK RD

TRELLA RD

CHERRILL GDNS

POUGHILL RD

SEAWELL RD

HALLETT WAY

07

Coach
Rock

Swimming
Pool

CROOKLETS RD

VICTORIA
RD

KENWYN CL

CREATHORNE
RD

WOODFIELD RD

HOLLABURY RD

EAST FAIRHOLME RD

WEST FAIRHOLME RD

FLEXBURY
MEWS

FLEXBURY PARK RD

FLEXBURY PARK CT

Flexbury

FOSTERS WAY

MEADOW

MELLIARS WAY

LEA WAY

6

Bude
Haven

WESTCLIFF
FLATS

ERDISTON
CT

SUMMERLEAZE CRES

CH

MORWENNA
TERR

BELLE
VUE AVE

BUDE

Compass Point

IRB Sta
(summer only)

Tower

HARTLAND TERR

PRINCES ST

GRANVILLE TERR

BURN VIEW

BELLE VUE

CARTERET RD

BLANCHMINSTER
RD

BROADCLOSE HILL

Schs

PRIMROSE

ELIZABETH RD

LOWELL CL

5

EFFORD DOWN
PK

LANSDOWN CL 1
HOWARDS WAY 2
LEVEN COTTS 3

Bude-Stratton
Mus Liby

CHURCH PATH

BREAKWATER RD

GLEBE

CROSS RD

PO

THE CRESCENT

FB

THE STRAND

PATHFIELDS

WESTBY RD

HOLNICOTE RD

REDWOOD CL

REDWOOD GR

ELMLEA

L Ctr

06

CHURCH
LA

FALCON
TERR

GRANNERY
CT

HANOVER HO
PENTRE CT

BENZOOLEN RD

SWALLOW CL

SOUTHFIELD RD

KILLERTON RD

SILVERTON CL

VALLEY RD

KIMING

Budehaven
Com Sch
L Ctr

Cleavelands

Ebbingford
Manor

EX23

BULLEDD WAY

MONTEREY CL

STRATTON RD

BERRIES MOU

MANOR RD

BIRHAM

MINSTER

A3072

4

Efford Farm
Bsns Pk

EFFORD FARM
COTTS

ARUNDEL TERR

CERES

A3072

BRIAR RD

HAWTHORN AVE

ROWAN CL

KERNOW CRES

BERRIES AVE

AGNES CL

Bude
Ind Est

Efford
Beacon

Efford
Down

VICARAGE RD

LYNSTONE RD

PETHERICKS WAY

KINGS HILL CL

BEDE HAVEN CL

TRALY CL

SHIPTON RD

CATHERINE
CL

King's Hill
Ind/Est

Bude Canal (dis)

River Neet

KINGS HILL

King's Hill

Bsns
Ctr

3

South West Coast Path

Upper Lynstone
Farm

LYNSTONE
COTTS

Lynstone

Bagbury

05

WENTWORTH CL

UPTON MDWS

STRATFORD CL

Upton
Park

ST ANN'S HILL

Thorne

UPTON
TERR

PIRAN HTS

Upton

Wommacotts
Rodd's Bridge
Farm

COUNTY RD

St Anne's
Hill

Rodd's
Bridge

THORNE
CROSS

A39

2

UPTON
CROSS

Sewage
Works

Phillip's
Point

Hotel

Phillips
Farm

1

MARINE DR

Trevose
View

Hele

04
19 A B 20 C D 21 E F

6 6 7 7

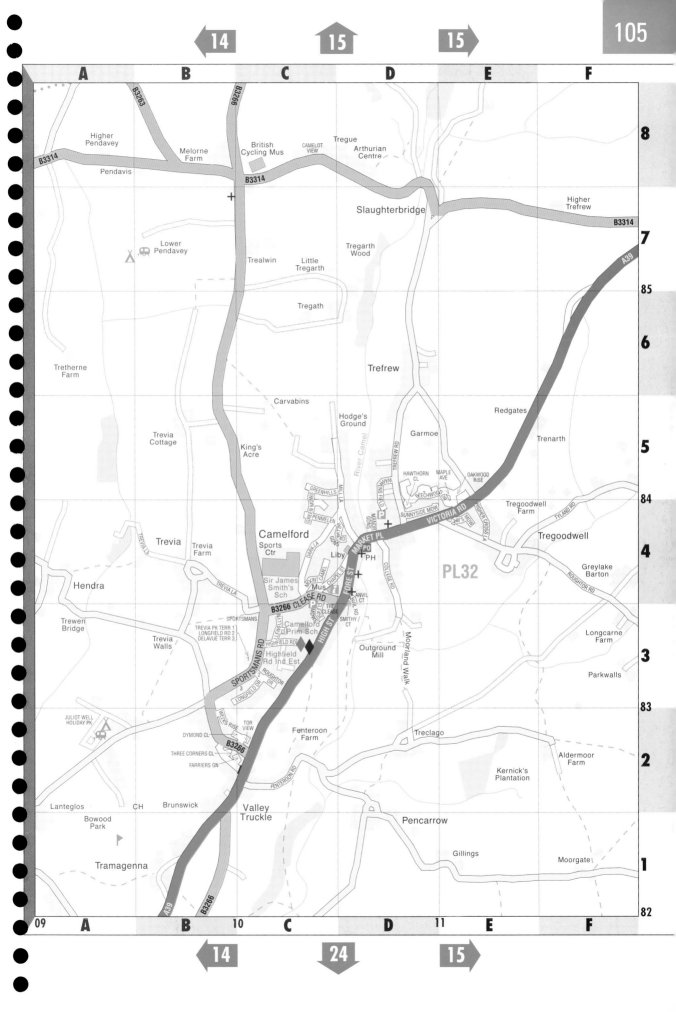

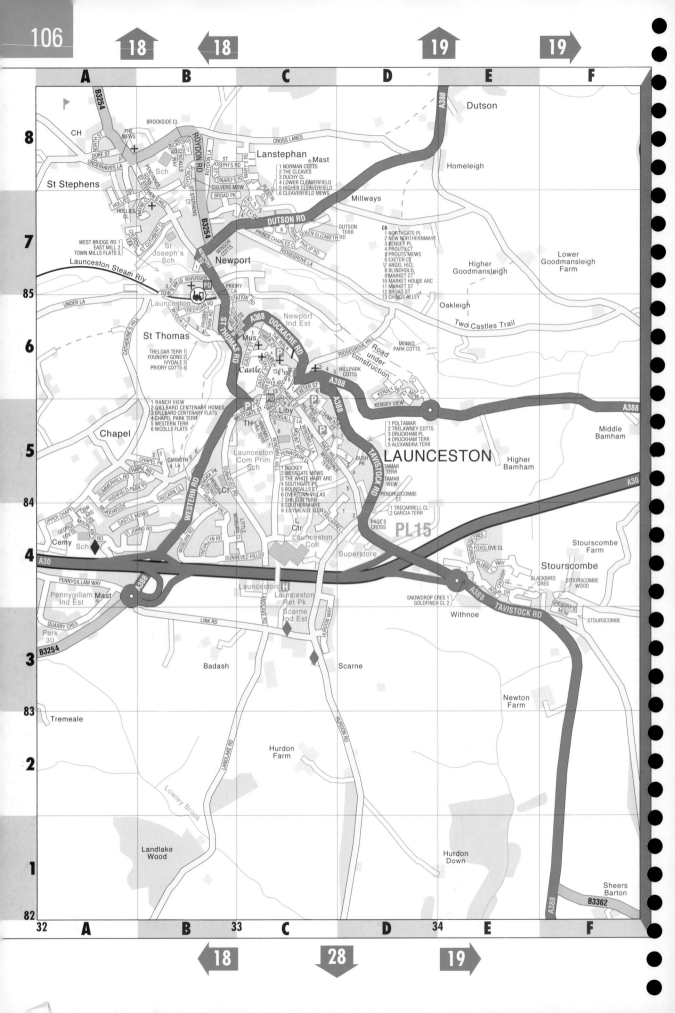

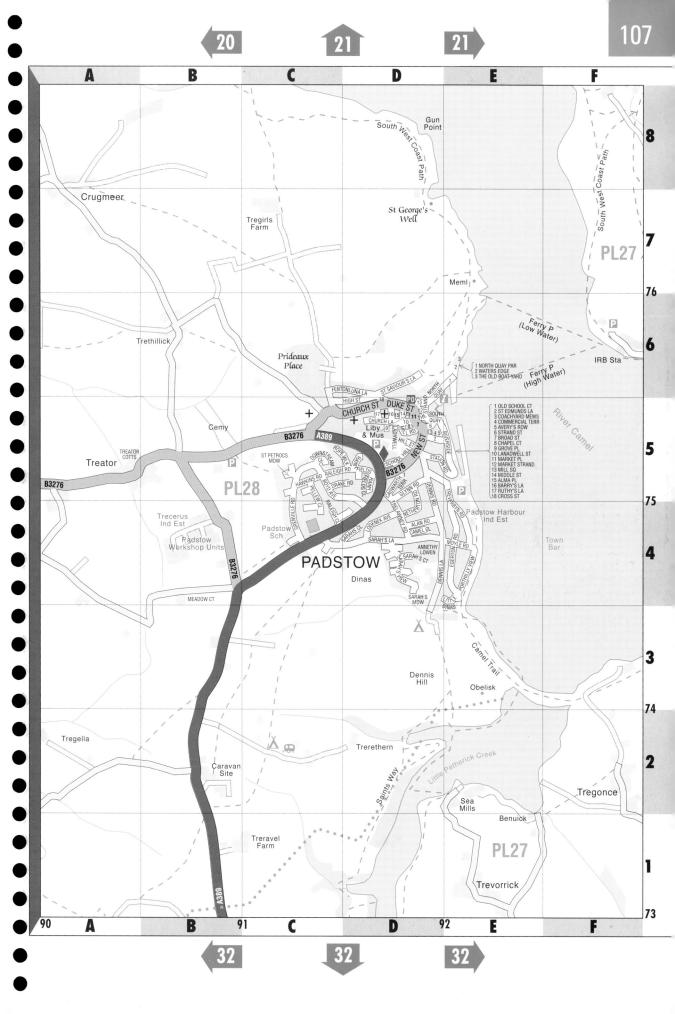

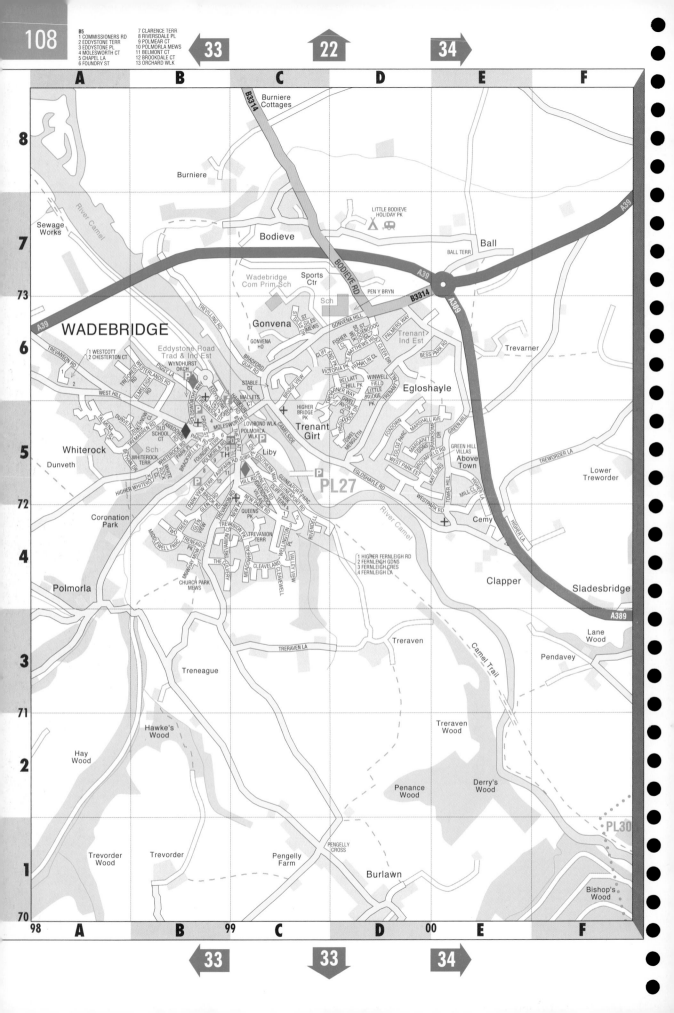

108

B5
1 COMMISSIONERS RD
2 EDDYSTONE TERR
3 EDDYSTONE PL
4 MOLESWORTH CT
5 CHAPEL LA
6 FOUNDRY ST
7 CLARENCE TERR
8 RIVERSDALE PL
9 POLMEAR CT
10 POLMORLA MEWS
11 BELMONT CT
12 BROOKDALE CT
13 ORCHARD WLK

33   22   34

A   B   C   D   E   F

8

Burniere Cottages
B3314

Burniere

Bodieve

Little Bodieve Holiday Pk

Ball
BALL TERR

A39

7

Sewage Works

River Camel

Wadebridge Com Prim Sch

Sports Ctr

BODIEVE RD

A39

B3314

73

A39

WADEBRIDGE

Gonvena

Pen y Bryn

Sch

Trevarner

A389

6

1 WESTCOTT
2 CHESTERTON CT

Eddystone Road Trad & Ind Est

WYNDHURST ORCH

Gonvena Hill

St Giles Mews

Gonvena Ho

Trenant Ind Est

Egloshayle

Trevarner

TREVANSON RD

TREVILLING RD

BRADFORD QUAY RD

STABLE CT

MALLETS CT

BRIDGE VIEW

HIGHER BRIDGE PK

WINWELL FIELD

Trenant Girt

Lovibond Wlk

Camelside

POLMORLA WLK

Above Town

Green Hill Villas

TREWORDER LA

Lower Treworder

5

Whiterock

Sch

WHITEROCK TERR

Old School CT

HIGHER WHITE...

Dunveth

TH

Liby

P

PL27

River Camel

EGLOSHAYLE RD

WEST PARK EST

Cemy

4

Coronation Park

CHURCH PARK MEWS

Treneague

Cleaveland

Clearwell

1 HIGHER FERNLEIGH RD
2 FERNLEIGH GDNS
3 FERNLEIGH CRES
4 FERNLEIGH LA

Clapper

Sladesbridge

A389

Polmorla

Lane Wood

3

Treneague

TRERAVEN LA

Treraven

Camel Trail

Pendavey

71

Hawke's Wood

Treraven Wood

2

Hay Wood

Penance Wood

Derry's Wood

PL30

1

Trevorder Wood

Trevorder

Pengelly Farm

PENGELLY CROSS

Burlawn

Bishop's Wood

70

98   A   B   99   C   D   00   E   F

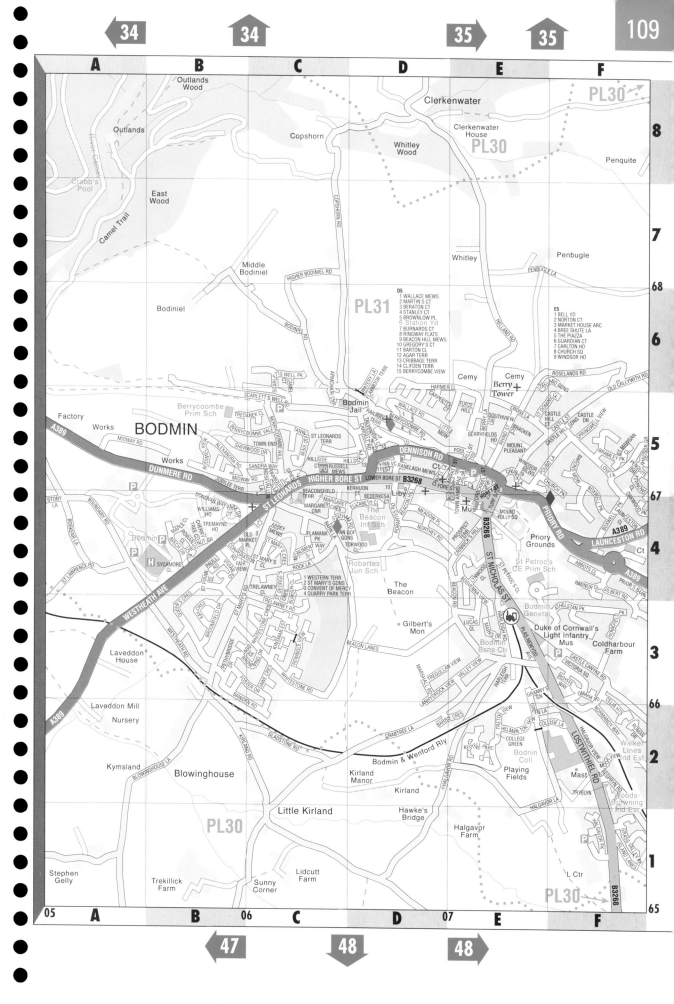

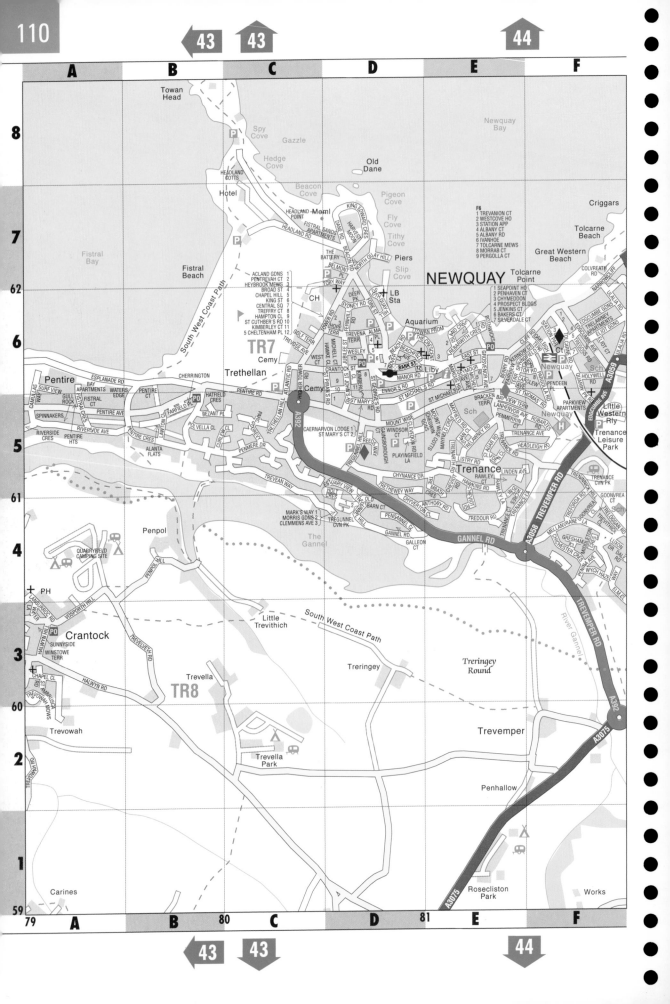

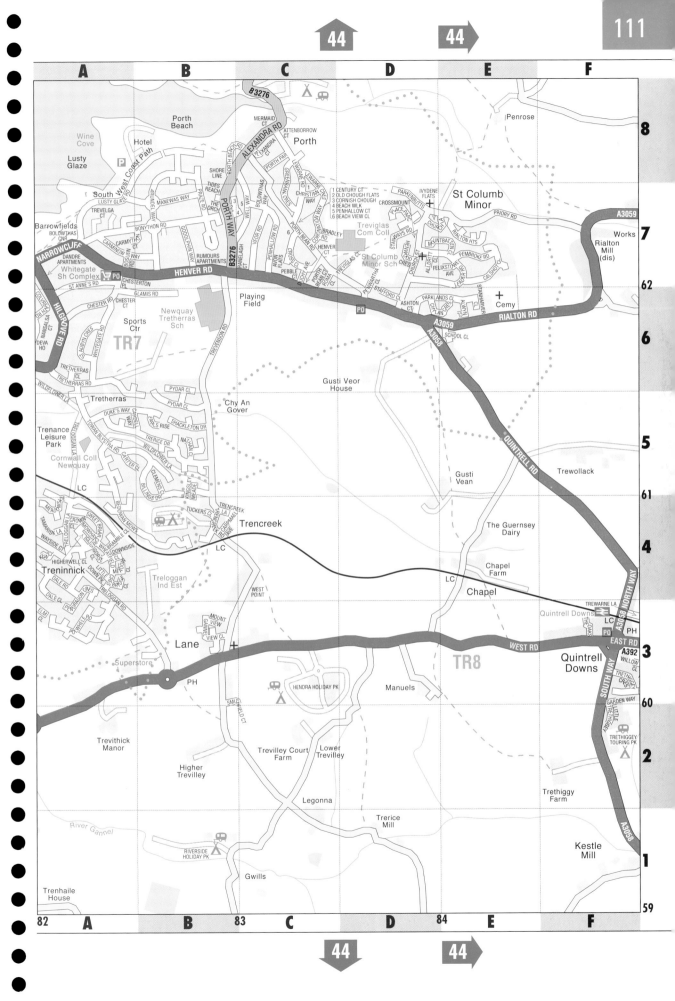

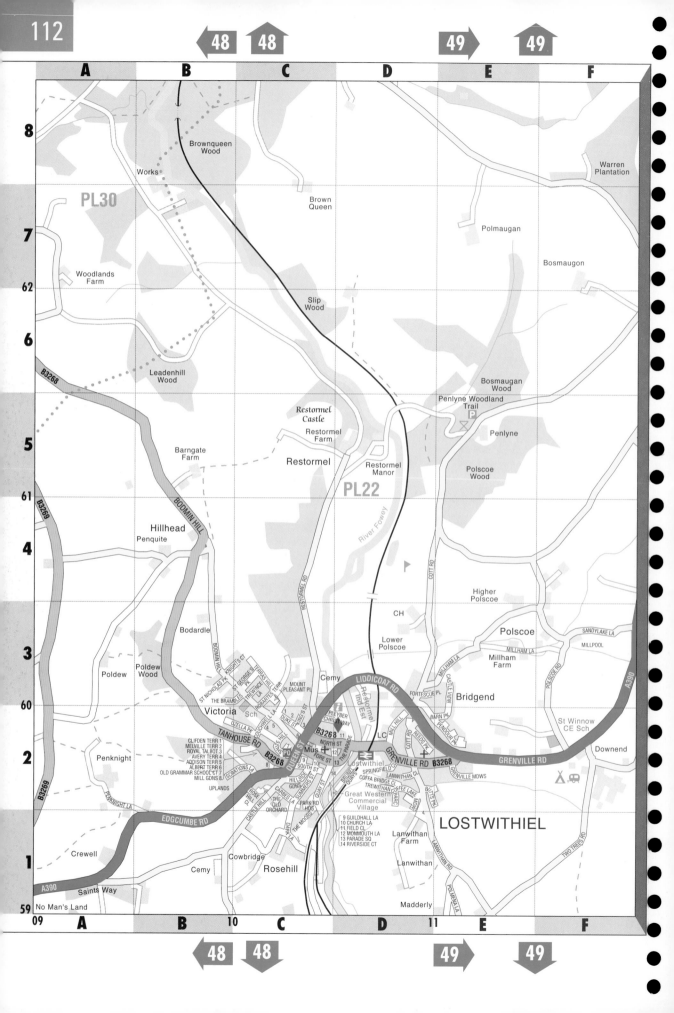

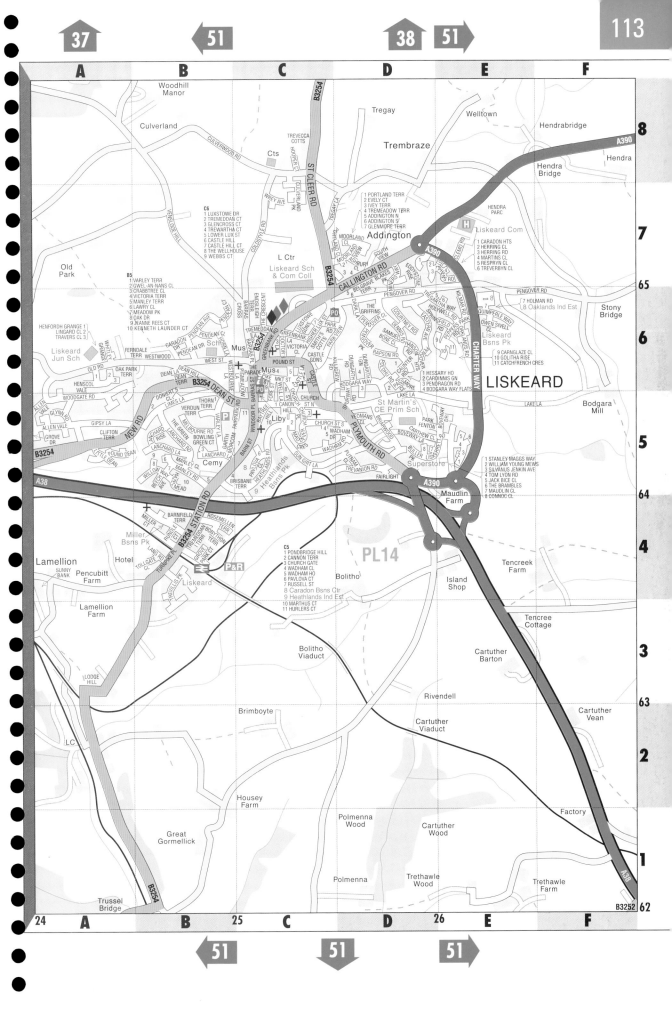

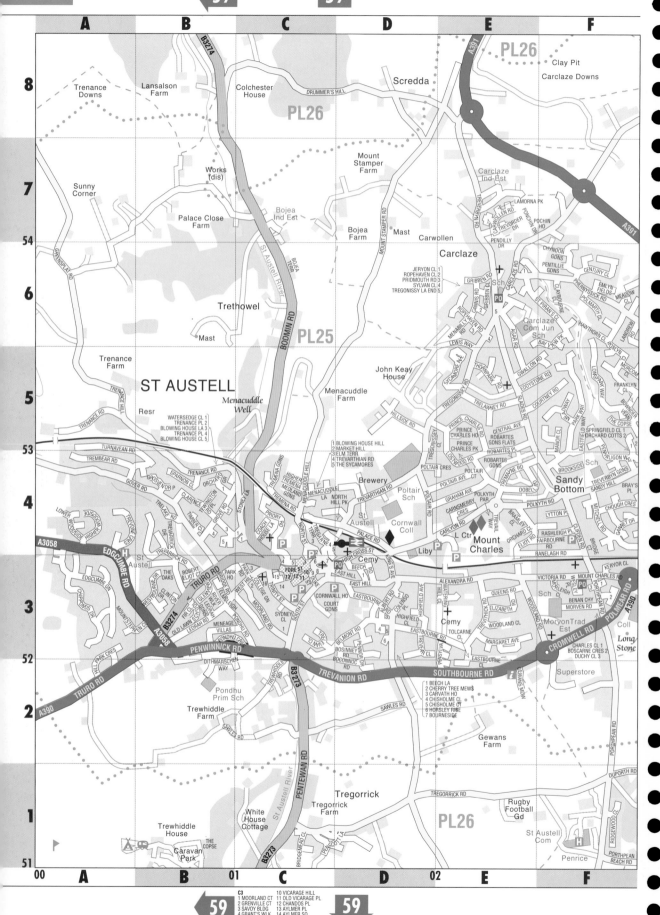

C3
1 MOORLAND CT
2 GRENVILLE CT
3 SAVOY BLDG
4 GRANT'S WLK
5 BIDDICK'S CT
6 MARKET ST
7 CROSS LA
8 CHURCH ST
9 VICTORIA PL
10 VICARAGE HILL
11 OLD VICARAGE PL
12 CHANDOS PL
13 AYLMER PL
14 AYLMER SQ
15 BURTON HO
16 WEST HILL CT

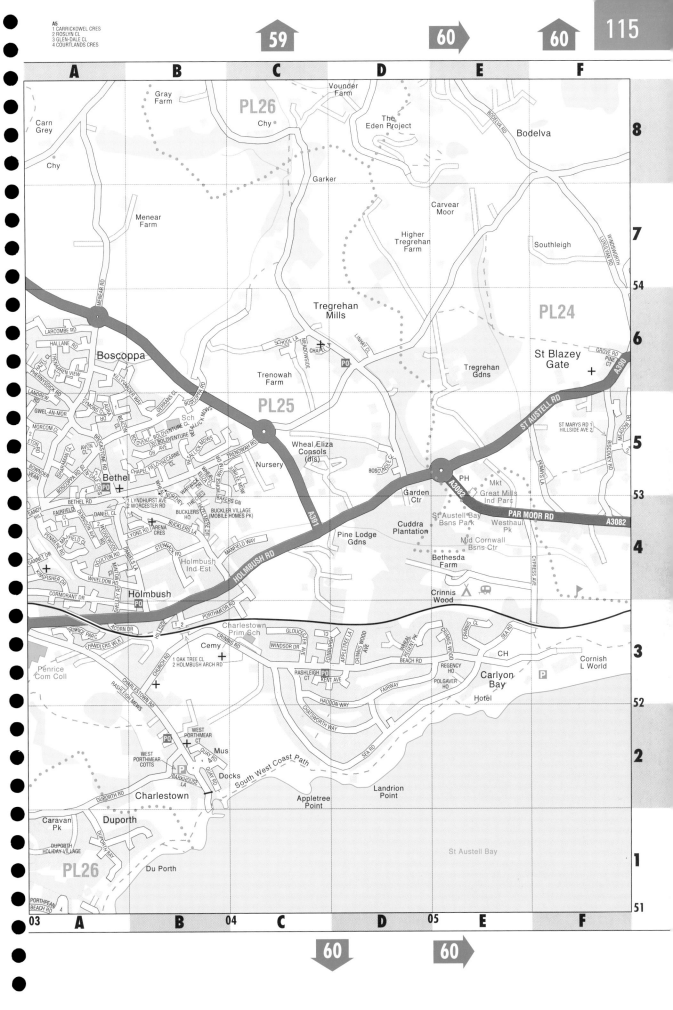

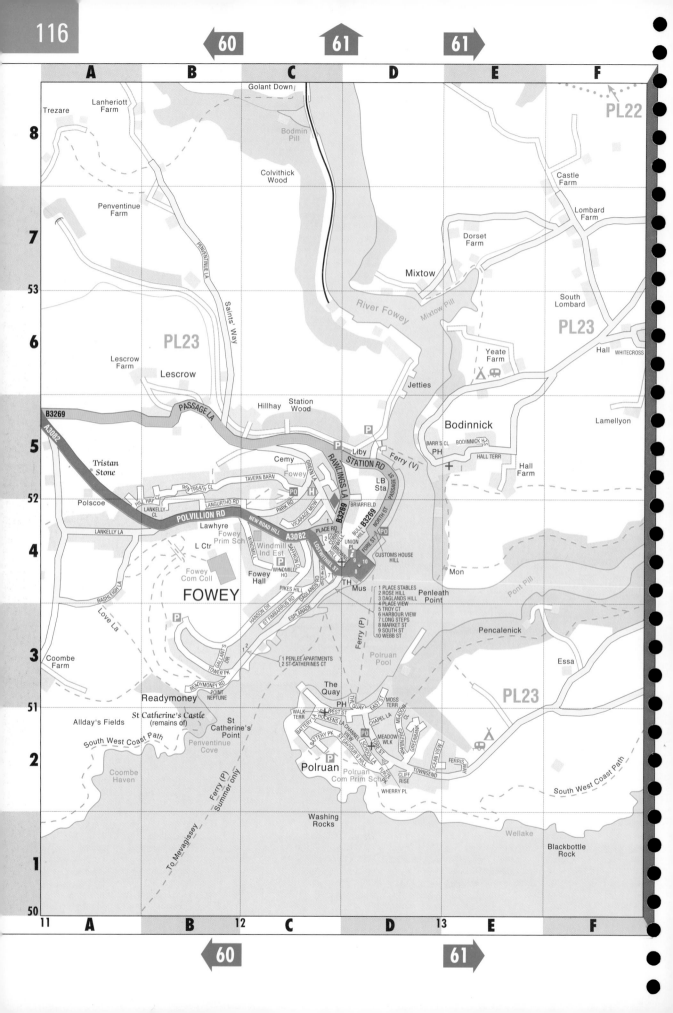

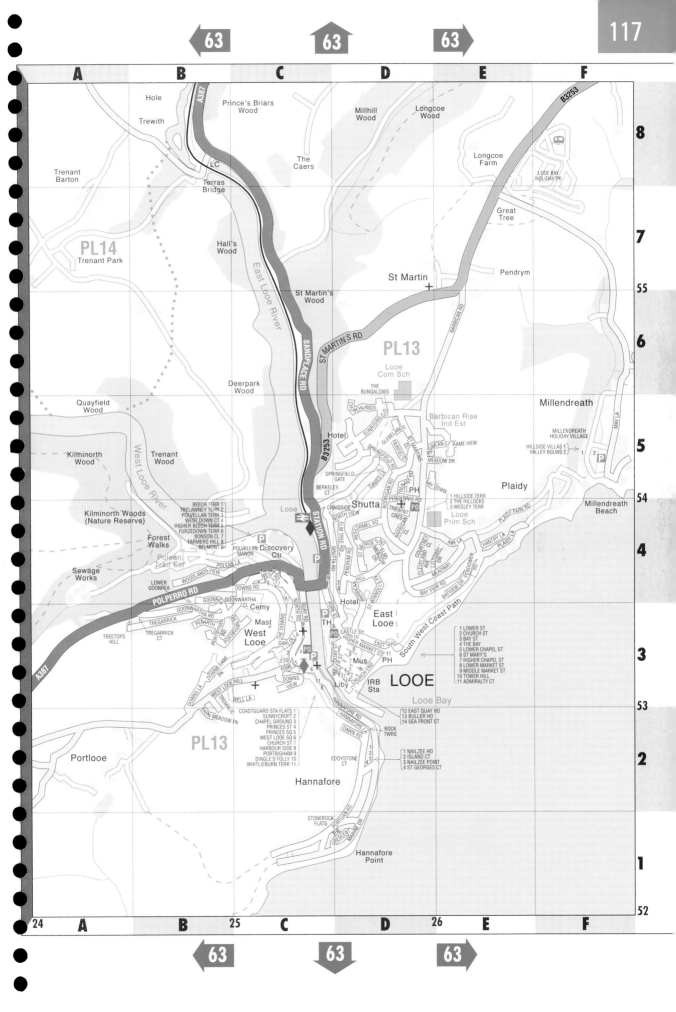

63
63
63

A B C D E F

8

Hole

Prince's Briars Wood

Millhill Wood

Longcoe Wood

Trewith

LC

The Caers

Longcoe Farm

Loose Bay Holiday Pk

Trenant Barton

Terras Bridge

Great Tree

7

PL14
Trenant Park

Hall's Wood

St Martin's Wood

St Martin

Pendrym

55

6

Quayfield Wood

Deerpark Wood

PL13

Looe Com Sch

Millendreath

Kilminorth Wood

Trenant Wood

THE BUNGALOWS

Barbican Rise Ind Est

MILLENDREATH HOLIDAY VILLAGE

HILLSIDE VILLAS 1
VALLEY BGLWS 2

5

Hotel

Springfield Gate

RAME VIEW

MEADOW DR

Plaidy

54

Kilminorth Woods (Nature Reserve)

BERKELEY CT

Shutta

BAY DOWN

Looe Prim Sch

Millendreath Beach

Forest Walks

BEECH TERR 1
TRELAWNEY TERR 2
POLVELLAN TERR 3
WEST DOWN CT 4
HIGHER BEECH TERR 5
FURZEDOWN TERR 6
BONSON CT 7
FARMERS HILL 8
BELMONT 9

Looe

Polean Trad Est

Polvellan Manor

Discovery Ctr

CRAIGSIDE

NORTH VIEW

4

Sewage Works

WOODLANDS VIEW

LOWER GOONREA

POLEAN LA

DOWNS RD

Hotel

East Looe

South West Coast Path

POLPERRO RD

GOONREA

GOONWARTHA

Cemy

TH

PO

1 LOWER ST
2 CHURCH ST
3 BAY ST
4 THE BAY
5 LOWER CHAPEL ST
6 ST MARY'S
7 HIGHER CHAPEL ST
8 LOWER MARKET ST
9 MIDDLE MARKET ST
10 TOWER HILL
11 ADMIRALTY CT

3

A387

Mast

TREGARRICK

West Looe

CASTLE ST

HIGHER MARKET ST

PH

LOOE

Looe Bay

TREETOPS HILL

TREGARRICK CT

Mus

Liby

IRB Sta

12 EAST QUAY HO
13 BULLER HO
14 SEA FRONT CT

53

West Looe Hill

WELL LA

DOWNS VIEW

HANNAFORE RD

ROCK TWRS

COASTGUARD STA FLATS 1
SUNNYCROFT 2
CHAPEL GROUND 3
PRINCES ST 4
PRINCES SQ 5
WEST LOOE SQ 6
CHURCH ST 7
HARBOUR SIDE 8
PORTBIGHAM 9
DINGLE'S FOLLY 10
WHITLIEBURN TERR 11

DAWN RD

1 NAILZEE HO
2 ISLAND CT
3 NAILZEE POINT
4 ST GEORGES CT

2

Portlooe

PL13

EDDYSTONE CT

Hannafore

STONEROCK FLATS

1

Hannafore Point

52

24 A B 25 C D 26 E F

63
63
63

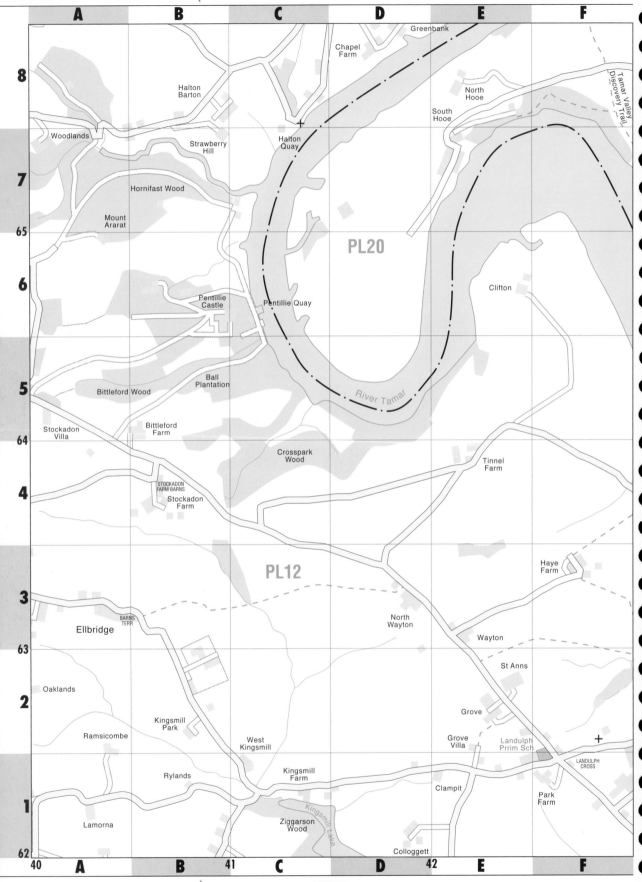

A   B   C   D   E   F

8

Greenbank

Chapel
Farm

Halton
Barton

North
Hooe

Tamar Valley Discovery Trail

Woodlands

Strawberry
Hill

Halton
Quay

South
Hooe

7

Hornifast Wood

Mount
Ararat

65   PL20

6

Pentillie
Castle   Pentillie Quay   Clifton

5   Bittleford Wood   Ball
Plantation

Stockadon
Villa   Bittleford
Farm   River Tamar

64
                              Crosspark
                              Wood   Tinnel
                                                      Farm

4   STOCKADON
           FARM BARNS
           Stockadon
           Farm

                    PL12   Haye
                                                                  Farm

3   BARNS
                     TERR   North
                                                       Wayton
    Ellbridge   Wayton

63   St Anns

2   Oaklands   Grove

    Ramsicombe   Kingsmill
                  Park   Grove
                                                     Villa   Landulph
           West   Prrim Sch
           Kingsmill   LANDULPH
                                                                   CROSS

    Rylands   Kingsmill   Clampit
                   Farm   Park
1   Farm

    Lamorna   Ziggarson   Colloggett
                   Wood   Kingsmill Lake

62
    40   A   B   41   C   D   42   E   F

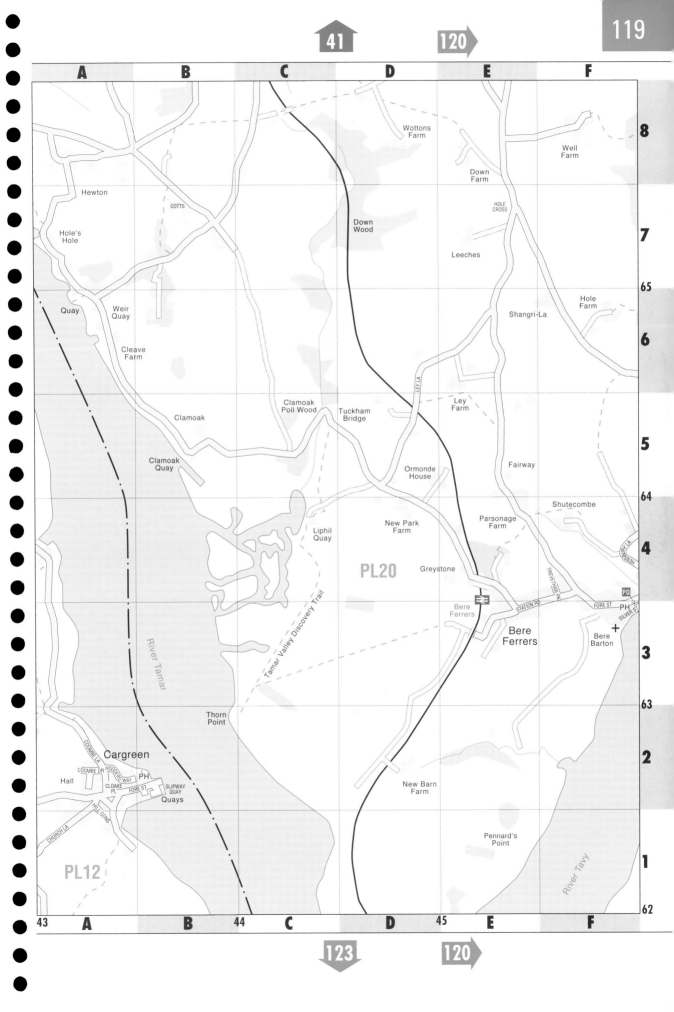

A B C D E F

8

Wottons
Farm

Well
Farm

Hewton

COTTS

Down
Farm

HOLE
CROSS

Hole's
Hole

Down
Wood

7

Leeches

65

Quay

Weir
Quay

Hole
Farm

Shangri-La

6

Cleave
Farm

LEY LA

Clamoak

Clamoak
Poll Wood

Tuckham
Bridge

Ley
Farm

Clamoak
Quay

Fairway

5

Ormonde
House

Shutecombe

64

Liphil
Quay

New Park
Farm

Parsonage
Farm

HENSBURY LA

4

PL20

Greystone

TREVETHAN PK

PO

FORE ST

PH

Tamar Valley Discovery Trail

Bere
Ferrers

STATION RD

SILVER ST

Bere
Ferrers

Bere
Barton

River Tamar

Bere
Ferrers

3

Thorn
Point

63

COOMBE LA

Cargreen

2

COOMBE DR

HOODES WAY

PH

Hall

CLOAKE
PL

FORE ST

SLIPWAY

QUAY

New Barn
Farm

Quays

HILL GDNS

CHURCH LA

Pennard's
Point

1

PL12

River Tavy

62

43 A B 44 C D 45 E F

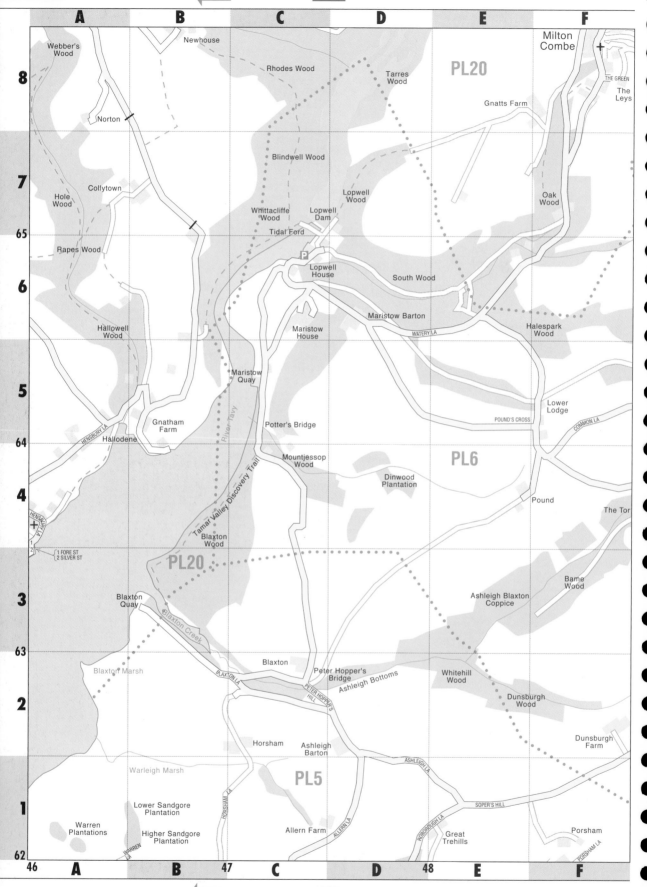

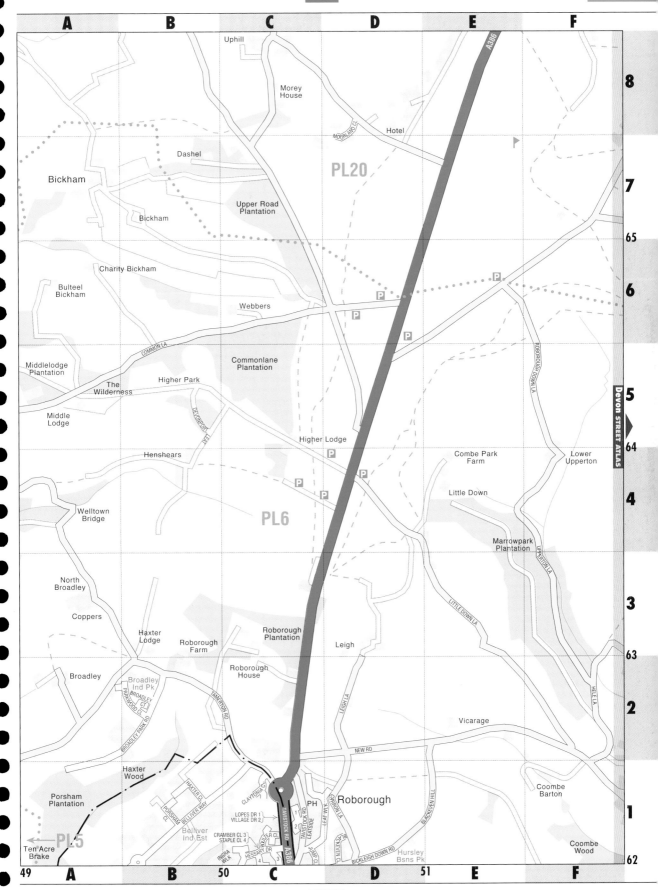

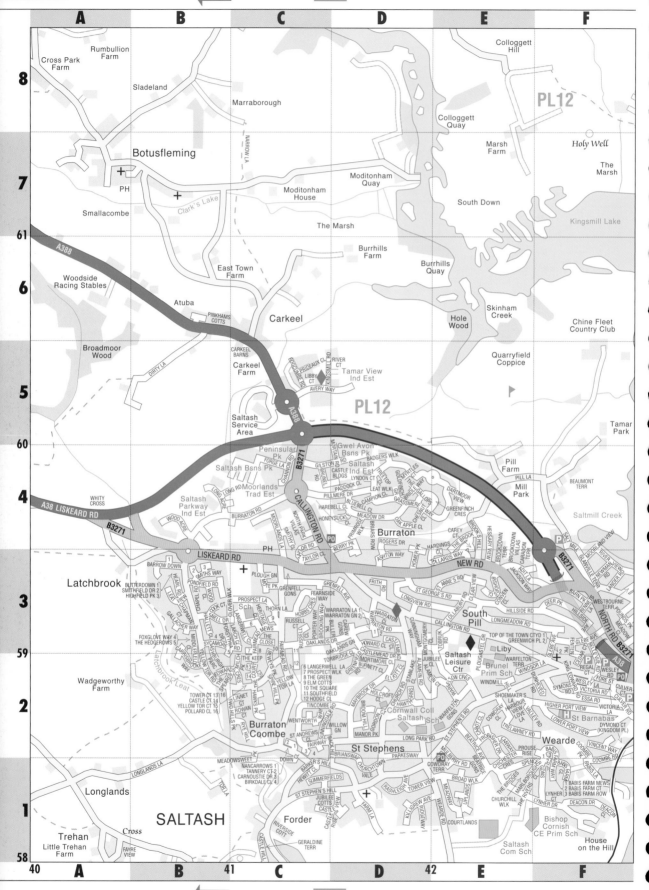

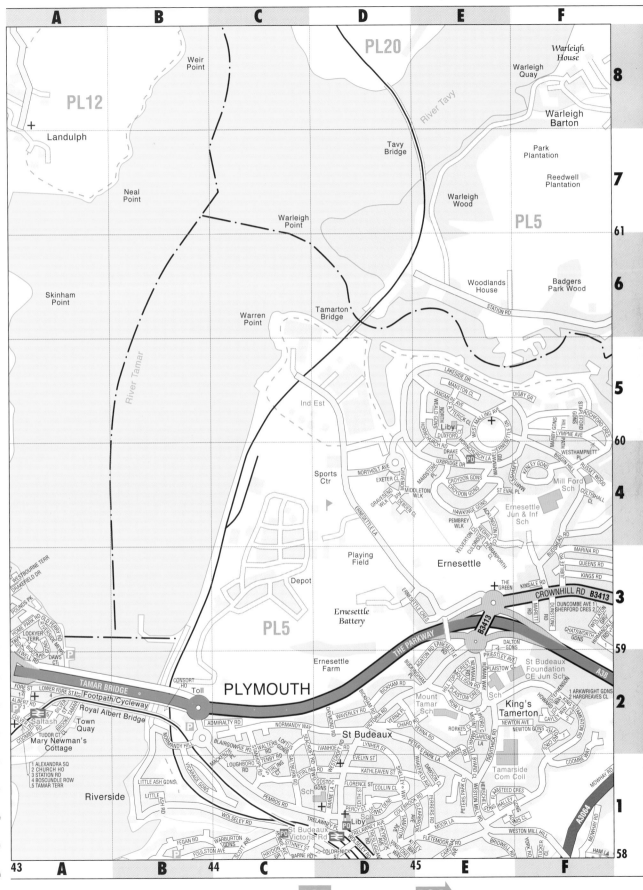

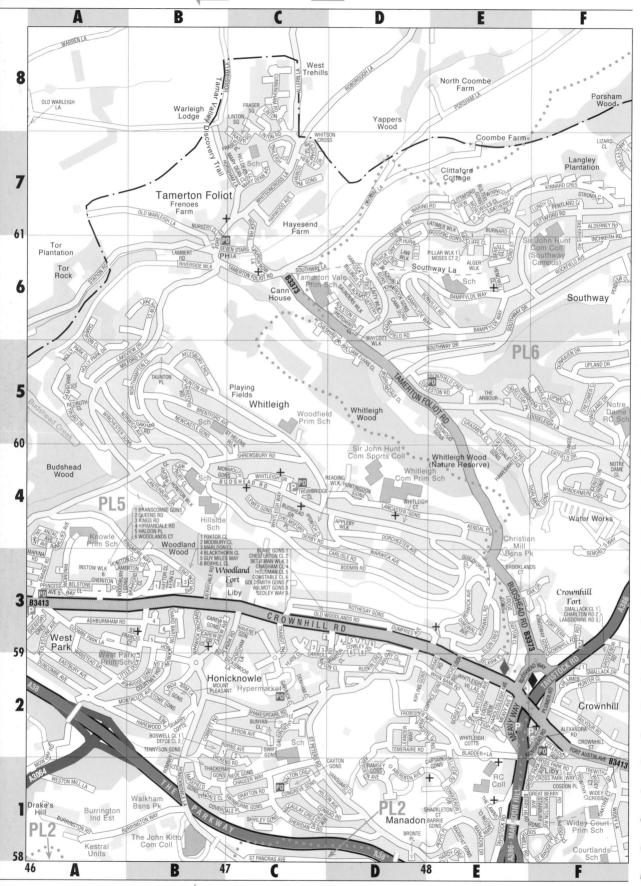

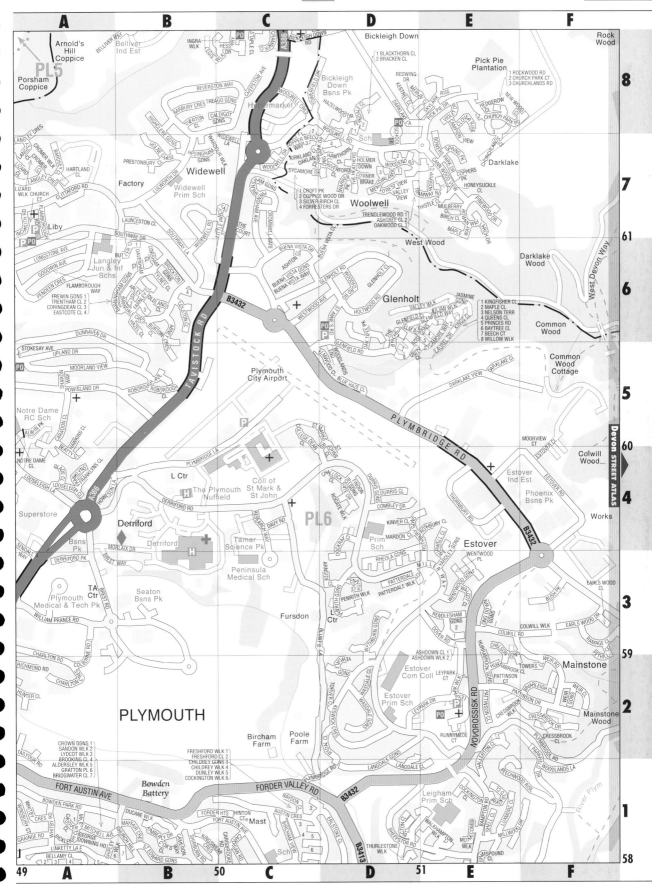

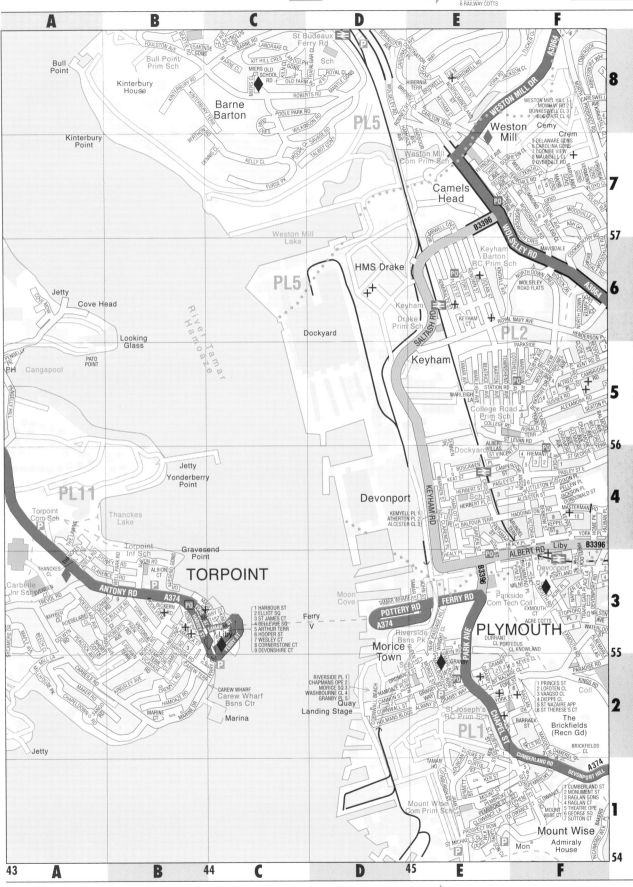

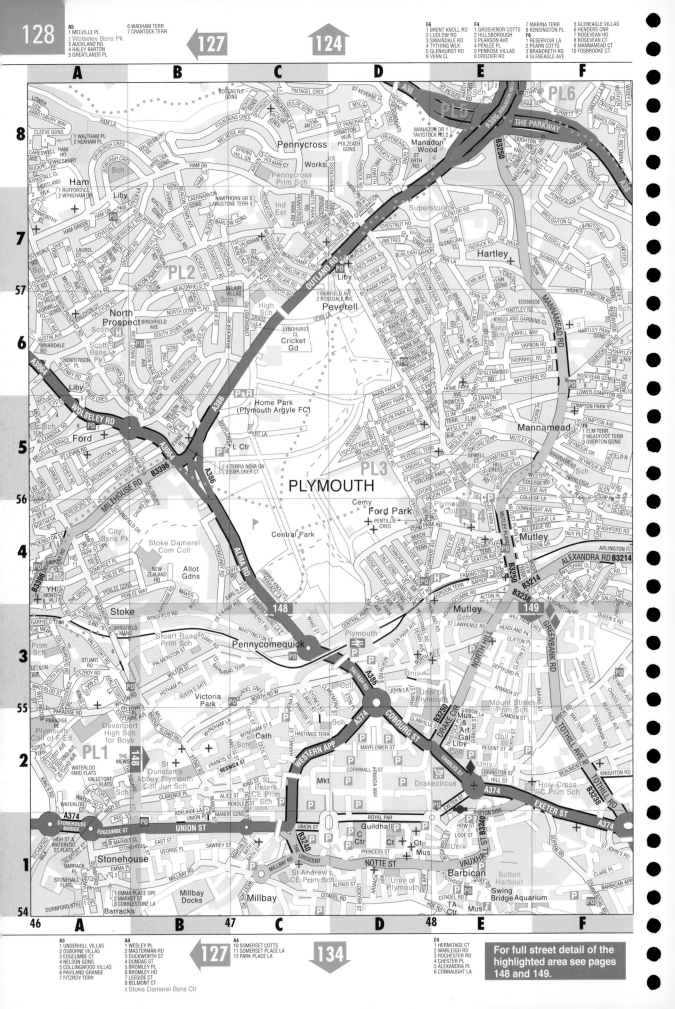

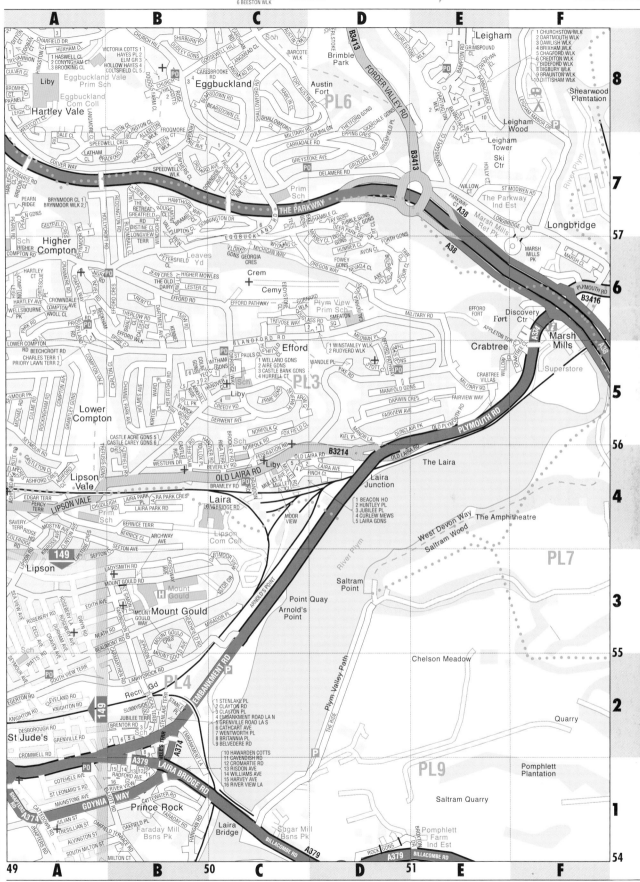

For full street detail of the highlighted area see page 149.

129

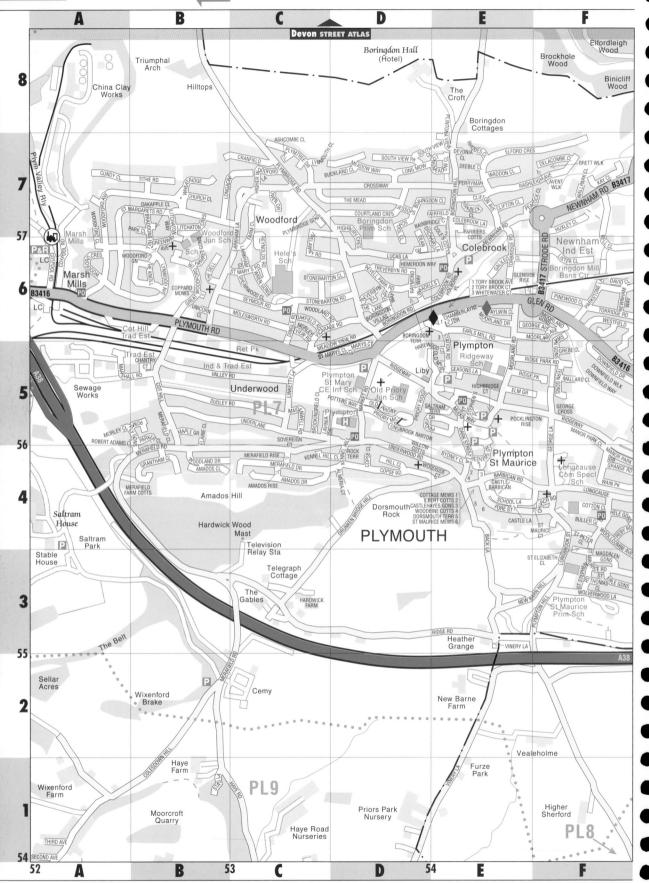

Devon STREET ATLAS

129

136

Devon STREET ATLAS

B5
1 CALEDONIA CL
2 ELDER CL
3 MAGNOLIA CL
4 TURBILL GDNS
5 PAYNTER WLK

C5
1 EIGHT ACRE CL
2 LAWN CL
3 ORCHARD CL
4 GREAT PARK CL
5 LONG TERRACE CL
6 CYPRESS CL

7 CAMPION CL
8 RODDICK WAY
9 BRANSON CT

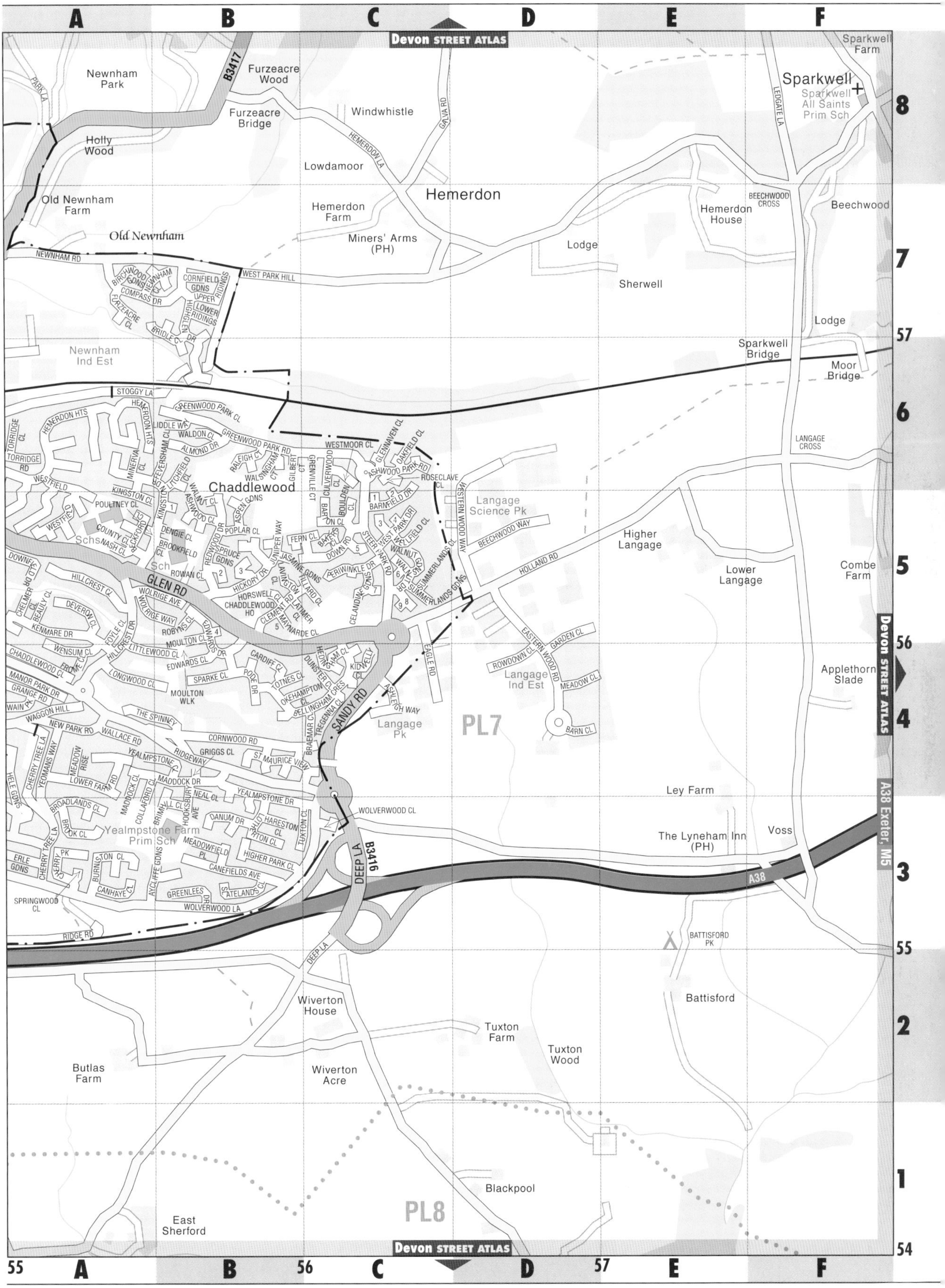

Sparkwell Farm

Sparkwell

Sparkwell All Saints Prim Sch

Newnham Park

Furzeacre Wood

Windwhistle

BEECHWOOD CROSS

Beechwood

Holly Wood

Furzeacre Bridge

Lowdamoor

Hemerdon

Hemerdon House

Old Newnham Farm

Hemerdon Farm

Lodge

Old Newnham

Miners' Arms (PH)

Sherwell

Lodge

NEWNHAM RD

WEST PARK HILL

Sparkwell Bridge

57

Moor Bridge

Newnham Ind Est

STOGGY LA

LANGAGE CROSS

6

GREENWOOD PARK CL

WESTMOOR CL

Chaddlewood

ROSECLAVE

Langage Science Pk

Higher Langage

Combe Farm

5

GLEN RD

Lower Langage

HOLLAND RD

56

Langage Ind Est

Applethorn Slade

SANDY RD

Langage Pk

PL7

BARN CL

4

DEEP LA
B3416

WOLVERWOOD CL

Ley Farm

The Lyneham Inn (PH)

Voss

A38

3

WOLVERWOOD LA

RIDGE RD

BATTISFORD PK

55

Wiverton House

Battisford

Butlas Farm

Wiverton Acre

Tuxton Farm

Tuxton Wood

2

Blackpool

East Sherford

PL8

1

Devon STREET ATLAS

54

Devon STREET ATLAS

A38 Exeter, M5

55 A   B   56   C   D   57   E   F

65
126

A B C D E F

8

Ford
Vanderbands
St John's Lake
SUNWELL LA
ST JOHN'S LA
GOOSEFORD LA
CHURCH LA
Sango Island
PH
Vanderbands Farm
JACK'S LA
MOWHAY
7
St John's Down
Penhale
Mendennick
Penhale Lake
53
B3247
Mendennick Hill
PL11
6
Works
Insworke
EDGCUMBE CRES
Millbrook Bsns Pk
MANOR GDNS
CAMPERKNOWLE
HERON CL
CALVEZ CL
INSWORKE CRES
Sewage Wks
WITHNOE LA
OLD CHAPEL WAY
SANGO CT
BARTON
WELHAM MEW
SOUTHDOWN RD
TREFUSIS TERR
New Barn
POTTERY EST
PRIESTHOOD TERR
ST JOHN'S RD
1
2
1 HEANTON TERR
2 CLINTON TERR
MILL RD
5
BRAKE LA
Millbrook Resr
Millbrook CE Prim Sch
Blindwell
PH
MILL VIEW GDNS
MILL VIEW TERR
MOLESWORTH TERR
LOWER ANDERTON RD
LAKE MDNS
NEW ST
NEWPORT ST
GREENLAND
HIGHER ANDERTON RD
LEE POINT CRES
SPEEDWELL
BROOKS CL
52
Withnoe Barton
RICHARDS TERR 1
THE PARADE 2
KNILL CROSS COTTS 3
ST ANDREW ST
MOUNT PLEASANT
PO
P
KING ST
KNILL CROSS
AMHERST
Millbrook
Anderton
Withnoe
CLIFF LA
Higher Hounster Farm
HOUNSTER HILL
HOUNSTER DR
WEST ST
Cemy
MAKER LA
4
Tregonhawke Farm
RADFORD LA
Dadbrook
Sollack
Tregonhawke
BONKET LA
Treninnow Grove
B3247
WHITSAND BAY HOLIDAY PK
Mon
MILITARY RD
Treninnow
Fourlanesend Com Prim Sch
Treninnow Plantation
51
TRENINNOW & WIGGLE CHALETS
The Hats
2
Whitsand Bay
South West Coast Path
PL10
Wiggle
HTT LA
Wringford Down
Wringford Farm
TRENCHER LA
1
Wiggle Cliff
P
Hotel
Forder
FORDER HILL
FORDER LA
RAME LA
Knatterbury
50
40 A 41 B C 42 D E F

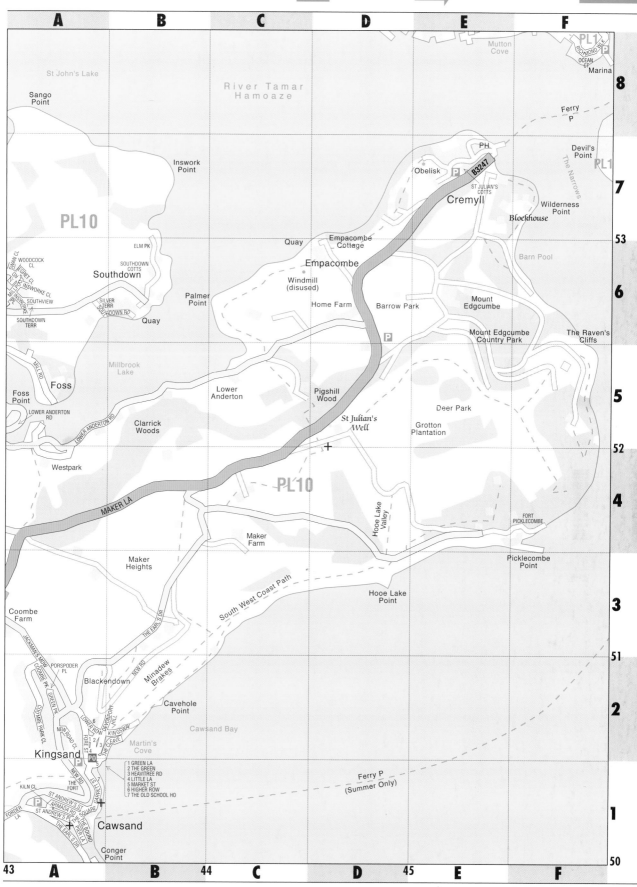

Mutton Cove
PL1
OCEAN CT
Marina

St John's Lake

River Tamar Hamoaze

Sango Point

Ferry P

Devil's Point
PL1

Inswork Point

The Narrows

8

PH

Obelisk
P
B3247
ST JULIAN'S COTTS
Cremyll

Wilderness Point
Blockhouse

7

PL10

ELM PK
SOUTHDOWN COTTS

Quay
Empacombe Cottage

Barn Pool

53

WOODCOCK CL
SWAN CL
EGRET CL
OW CL
INSWORKE CL

Southdown

Empacombe

Mount Edgcumbe

6

MT INSMORE
SOUTHVIEW
SILVER TERR
SOUTHDOWN TERR
SOUTHDOWN RD
Quay

Palmer Point

Windmill (disused)

Home Farm

Barrow Park

Mount Edgcumbe Country Park

The Raven's Cliffs

Millbrook Lake

Lower Anderton

Pigshill Wood

Deer Park

5

Foss
Foss Point

MILL RD
LOWER ANDERTON RD
LOWER ANDERTON RD

Clarrick Woods

St Julian's Well

Grotton Plantation

52

Westpark

+

PL10

4

MAKER LA

Maker Farm

Hoe Lake Valley

FORT PICKLECOMBE

Maker Heights

South West Coast Path

Hoe Lake Point

Picklecombe Point

3

Coombe Farm

THE EARL'S TER

51

JACKMAN'S MDW
PORSPODER PL
Blackendown
Minadew Brakes
NEW RD

Cavehole Point

2

COOMBE PK
GREEN PK
COOMBE PARK CL
NEW ROAD CL
LONGFIELD HILL
6
7
THE KINGSWAY
Cawsand Bay

Martin's Cove

NEW RD
FORE ST
THE CLEAVE
1
2/3
4
5
Kingsand
P
PO

1 GREEN LA
2 THE GREEN
3 HEAVITREE RD
4 LITTLE LA
5 MARKET ST
6 HIGHER ROW
7 THE OLD SCHOOL HO

Ferry P (Summer Only)

KILN CL
THE FORT

FORDER LA
ST ANDREW'S ST
ARMADA RD
ST ANDREW'S PL
THE SQUARE
THE ROUND
PIER LA
CARROL CARE
THE EARL'S TER
NEW RD

+
Cawsand

Conger Point

133
128

For full street detail of the highlighted area see pages 148 and 149.

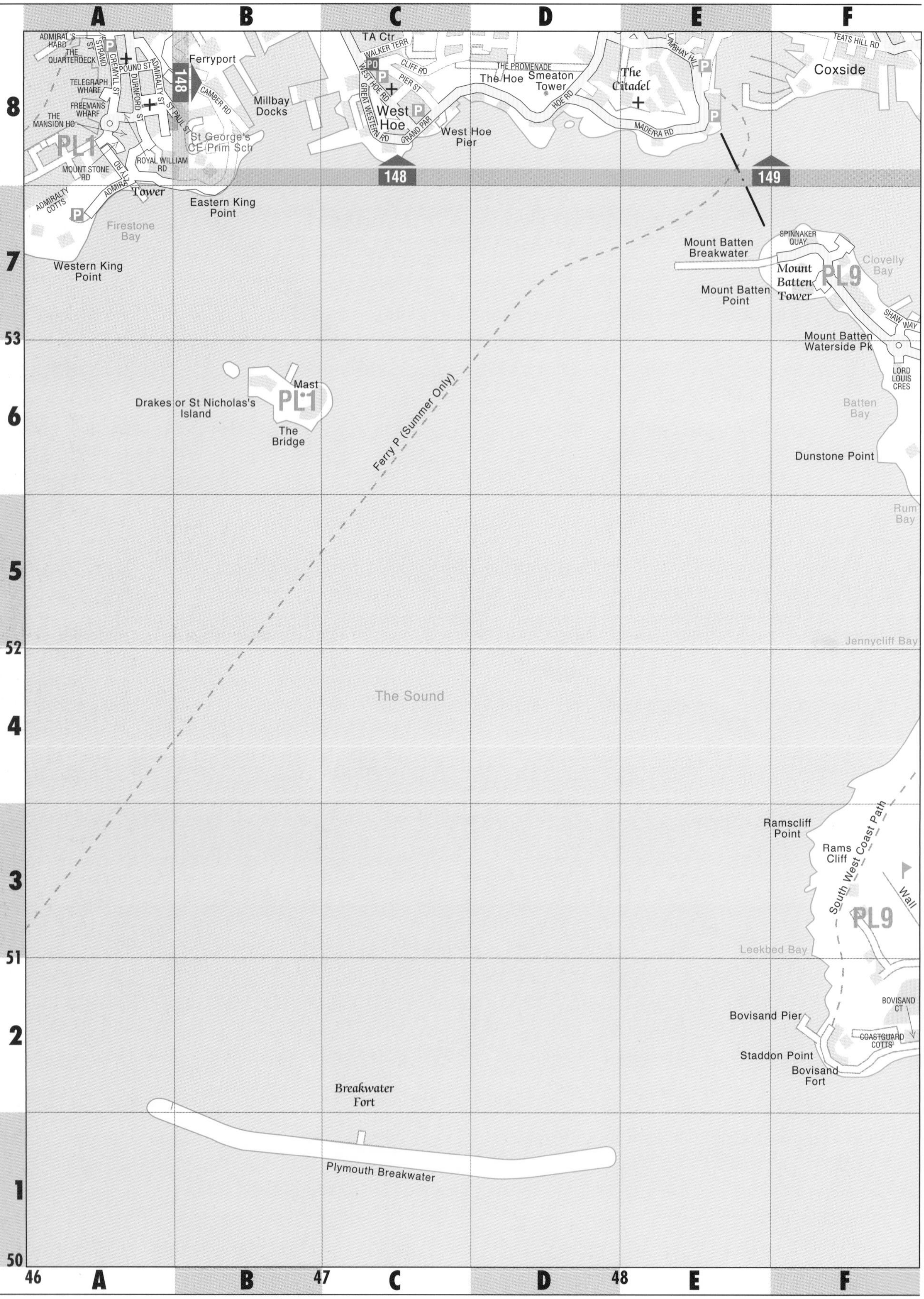

A B C D E F

8

ADMIRAL'S HARD
THE QUARTERDECK
TELEGRAPH WHARF
THE MANSION HO
FREEMANS WHARF
PL1
MOUNT STONE RD
ADMIRALTY COTTS
Tower

TA Ctr
WALKER TERR
CLIFF RD
PIER ST
West Hoe
West Hoe Pier
THE PROMENADE
The Hoe
Smeaton Tower
HOE RD
The Citadel
MADEIRA RD
LAMBHAY HL
Coxside
TEATS HILL RD

Ferryport
CAMBER RD
Millbay Docks
St George's CE Prim Sch
ROYAL WILLIAM RD

148
149

7

Eastern King Point
Western King Point
Firestone Bay

Mount Batten Breakwater
SPINNAKER QUAY
Mount Batten Point
Mount Batten Tower
PL9
Clovelly Bay
SHAW WAY
Mount Batten Waterside Pk
LORD LOUIS CRES

53

6

Drakes or St Nicholas's Island
Mast PL1
The Bridge
Ferry P (Summer Only)

Batten Bay
Dunstone Point
Rum Bay

5

52

The Sound

Jennycliff Bay

4

3

Ramscliff Point
Rams Cliff
South West Coast Path
Wall
PL9

51

Leekbed Bay

2

Breakwater Fort
Bovisand Pier
Staddon Point
Bovisand Fort
BOVISAND CT
COASTGUARD COTTS

1

Plymouth Breakwater

50

46 A B 47 C D 48 E F

133

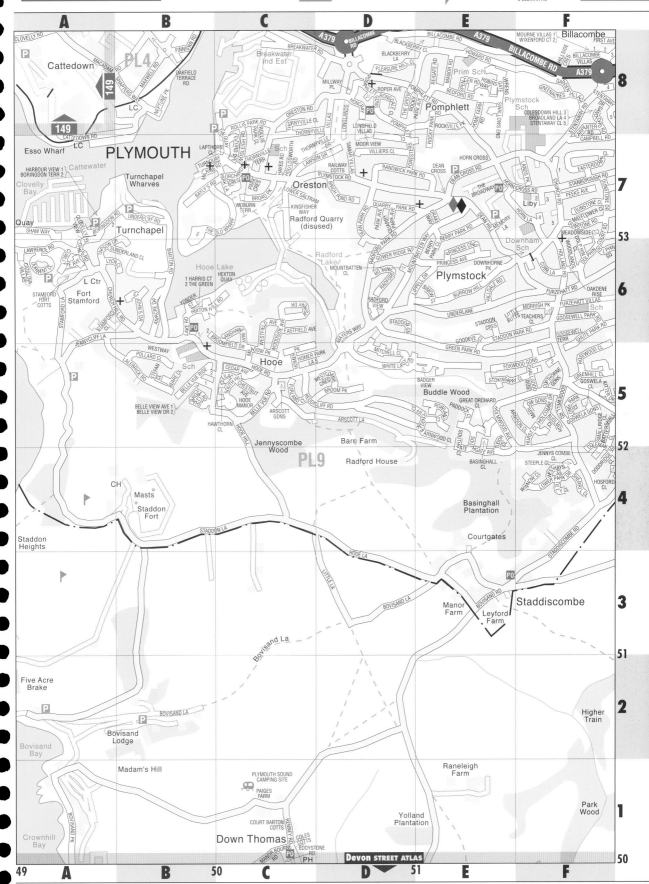

For full street detail of the highlighted area see page 149.

129
136
135

F5
1 CHALLGOOD CL
2 ORCHARDTON TERR

F7
1 THE DUKES RYDE
2 MAPLE CT
3 MAGNOLIA CT
4 HORN LANE FLATS
5 SELKIRK HO

A B C D E F

Clovelly Rd
Cattedown
PL4
149
LC
MACADAM RD
MAXWELL RD
SHAPTERS WAY
NEPTUNE PK
FINNIGAN RD
OAKFIELD TERRACE RD

Breakwater Ind Est
BREAKWATER RD

A379
BILLACOMBE RD
BLACKBERRY CL
BLACKBERRY LA
PLEASURE HILL CL
BILLACOMBE RD
A379
MOURNE VILLAS 1
WIXENFORD CT 2
Billacombe
FIRST AVE
HILLSIDE CRES
BILLACOMBE VILLAS
A379

PLYMOUTH
149
LC
CATTEDOWN RD
Esso Wharf

LAPTHORN CL
HEXTON QUAY
ROLLIS PARK RD
ROLLIS PARK CL
ROLLS QUAY
OSBOROUGH
THORNYVILLE VILLAS
THORNYVILLE CL
THORNVILLE
Sch
ORESTON RD
OSTON RD

MILLWAY PL
HOWARD RD
ROPER AVE
THE GROVE
POMPHLETT RD
BEDFORD RD
REIGATE RD
ROBINS WAY
WRENS GATE
Prim Sch
SWALLOWS END
Pomphlett
ROCKVILLE PK
ROCKY PARK RD
Plymstock Sch
GOLESDOWN HILL 3
BROADLAND LA 4
STENTAWAY CL 5
GREENACRES
GAXTON VILLAS
STENTAWAY RD
CAMPERDEN
CAMPBELL RD

Harbour View 1
Boringdon Terr 2
Cattewater
Clovelly Bay
Quay
CLOVELLY RD
BORINGDON RD
SHAW WAY
UNDERCLIFF RD
Turnchapel
TAPSOM DR
SUNDERLAND CL

Turnchapel Wharves

THE QUAY
BAYLY'S RD
BROAD PK
LOWER SALTRAM
WOBURN TERR
THE OLD WHARF
Oreston
Kingfisher Way
Radford Quarry (disused)
Radford Lake
MOUNTBATTEN CL
RAILWAY COTTS
TAMAR VILLAS
VILLIERS CL
MOOR VIEW
LONGFIELD VILLAS
FORESTERS
RANDWICK PARK RD
DEAN CROSS
DEAN CROSS RD
HORN CROSS
Liby
THE BROADWAY PO
HORN CROSS RD
LAIRA PK
CHURCH RD
STANBOROUGH RD
PEEKS AVE
TUNSTONE
MAYFLOWER DR
DUNSTONE CL
DUNSTONE RD
EASTERDEN
MEADOWSIDE
COURT

Lawrence Rd
Fort Stamford
STAMFORD FORT COTTS
CAROLINA VILLAS
RYE AVE
TRENT CL
STAMFORD LA
JENNYCLIFF LA
CHURCH HILL
ST JOHN'S DR
AMADEU DR
YONDER ST
HEXTON HILL RD
LAKE RD
PO
BROADFIELD RD
PLYMSTOCK RD
Hooe Lake
1 Harris Ct
2 The Green
Hexton Quay
QUARRY AVE
PARK AVE
RADFORD PARK RD
RADFORD VIEW
Radford House
GOWER RIDGE RD
RADFORD
PARK RD
DEAN PARK RD
PARK AVE
QUARRY PK
DEAN HILL
MEMORY LA
Downham Sch
DOWNHORNE PK
PRINCESS AVE
PRINCESS CRES
UPPER DELL
SIMON CL
BERRY PARK RD
BERRY PARK CL
MOUNT BATTEN WAY
NAYERS WAY
Plymstock
53
6
COBB LA
HOLLAND
DOWN PK
DRIVE DOWN
HILL
HILL
PVN
COURT
52

FINNIGAN
PL4

Fort Stamford
L Ctr
Westway
POLLARD CL
STEFAN
TALEBRICK RD
Sch
BELLE VUE RISE
South Hill
Hooe
BROOMFIELD DR
WESTFIELD AVE
EASTFIELD AVE
MEADOW PK
HOMER PARK LA
CEDAR AVE
CHESTNUT AVE
HAWTHORN CL
ARSCOTT GDNS
Hooe Manor
BELLE VALE RD
HOOE HILL
WESTCOMBE CRES
BROOM PK
REDDICLIFF RD
FURLAND CL
Jennyscombe Wood
Barn Farm
ARSCOTT LA
STADDON GN
STADDON CRES
GOODEVE CL
STADDON PARK RD
GREEN PARK RD
MITCHELL CL
WHITE LADY RD
FOXWOOD GDNS
STOKINGWAY CL
CHAPEL RD
Badger Wood
Buddle Wood
Great Orchard CL
PADDOCK
ROWL
CARNWOOD CL
BASINGHALL CL
JENNYS COMBE CL
STEEPLE CL
FURZEHATT VILLAS
FURZEHATT RD
LITTLE BUTTS
TEACHERS CL
MORRISH PK
GOOSEWELL PARK
GOOSEWELL TERR
SHUTE PARK RD
ROSEWOOD CL
GREENHILL RD
GOSWELA CL
GOSWELA GDNS
Sch
Oakdene Rise
KNITTERS
PARK
BATTERSBY
SMALL RIDGE
COLEMAN DR
HOSFORD CL
DODBROOKE
LOWER PARK DR
WINNOW CL
HAYS CL
DERRY CL
TIL CL
52

Belle View Ave 1
Belle View Dr 2
PL9
Radford House

CH
Masts
Staddon Fort
Staddon Heights
STADDON LA
Courtgates
Basinghall Plantation
HOOE LA
LITTLE LA
STADDISCOMBE RD
BOVISAND RD
PO
Manor Farm
Leyford Farm
Staddiscombe
BOVISAND LA
4
3
51

Five Acre Brake
P
BOVISAND LA
P
Bovisand Lodge
Madam's Hill
Bovisand Bay
BOVISAND PK
Higher Train
2

Crownhill Bay
Plymouth Sound Camping Site
Paiges Farm
Court Barton Cotts
REINNY RD
Down Thomas
MANOR BOURNE
COLES COTTS
EDDYSTONE RD
PH
PO
Yolland Plantation
Raneleigh Farm
Park Wood
1

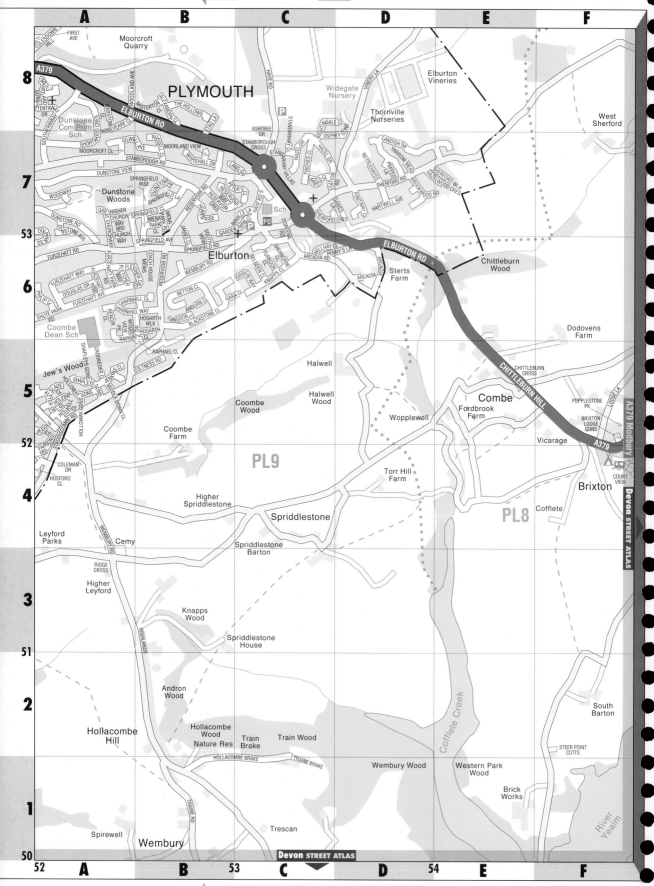

PLYMOUTH

ELBURTON RD

Elburton Vineries

West Sherford

Widegate Nursery

Thornville Nurseries

Dunstone Com Prim Sch

Dunstone Woods

Elburton

Chittleburn Wood

Sterts Farm

Coombe Dean Sch

Jew's Wood

Dodovens Farm

CHITTLEBURN HILL

Halwell

Halwell Wood

Combe

Coombe Wood

Wopplewell

Fordbrook Farm

Popplestone Pk

Coombe Farm

PL9

Brixton Lodge Gdns

Vicarage

Torr Hill Farm

Brixton

Cofflete

Higher Spriddlestone

Spriddlestone

PL8

Leyford Parks

Cemy

Spriddlestone Barton

Ridge Cross

Higher Leyford

Knapps Wood

Spriddlestone House

South Barton

Coflete Creek

Andron Wood

Steer Point Cotts

Hollacombe Hill

Hollacombe Wood Nature Res

Train Brake

Train Wood

HOLLACOMBE BRAKE

TRAINE BRAKE

Wembury Wood

Western Park Wood

Brick Works

River Yealm

Spirewell

Wembury

Trescan

A379 Modbury Devon STREET ATLAS

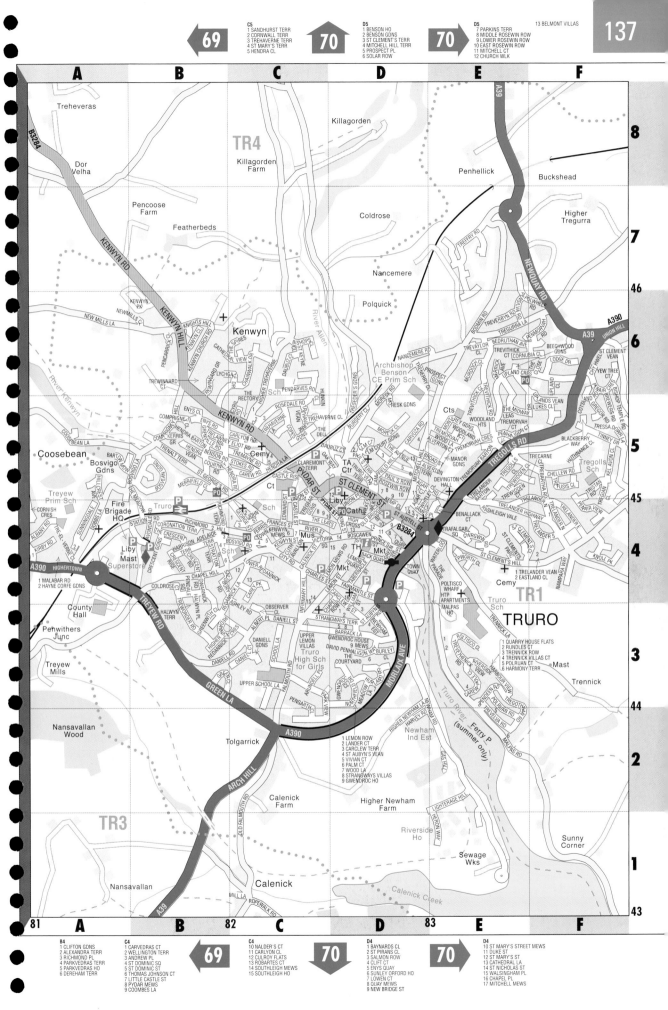

C5
1 SANDHURST TERR
2 CORNWALL TERR
3 TREHAVERNE TERR
4 ST MARY'S TERR
5 HENDRA CL

D5
1 BENSON HO
2 BENSON GDNS
3 ST CLEMENT'S TERR
4 MITCHELL HILL TERR
5 PROSPECT PL
6 SOLAR ROW

D5
7 PARKINS TERR
8 MIDDLE ROSEWIN ROW
9 LOWER ROSEWIN ROW
10 EAST ROSEWIN ROW
11 MITCHELL CT
12 CHURCH WLK

13 BELMONT VILLAS

B4
1 CLIFTON GDNS
2 ALEXANDRA TERR
3 RICHMOND PL
4 PARKVEDRAS TERR
5 PARKVEDRAS HO
6 DEREHAM TERR

C4
1 CARVEDRAS CT
2 WELLINGTON TERR
3 ANDREW PL
4 ST DOMINIC SQ
5 ST DOMINIC ST
6 THOMAS JOHNSON CT
7 LITTLE CASTLE ST
8 PYDAR MEWS
9 COOMBES LA

C4
10 NALDER'S CT
11 CARLYON CL
12 CULROY FLATS
13 ROBARTES CT
14 SOUTHLEIGH MEWS
15 SOUTHLEIGH HO

D4
1 BAYNARDS CL
2 ST PIRANS CL
3 SALMON ROW
4 CLIFT CT
5 ENYS QUAY
6 SUNLEY ORFORD HO
7 LOWEN CT
8 QUAY MEWS
9 NEW BRIDGE ST

D4
10 ST MARY'S STREET MEWS
11 DUKE ST
12 ST MARY'S ST
13 CATHEDRAL LA
14 ST NICHOLAS ST
15 WALSINGHAM PL
16 CHAPEL LA
17 MITCHELL MEWS

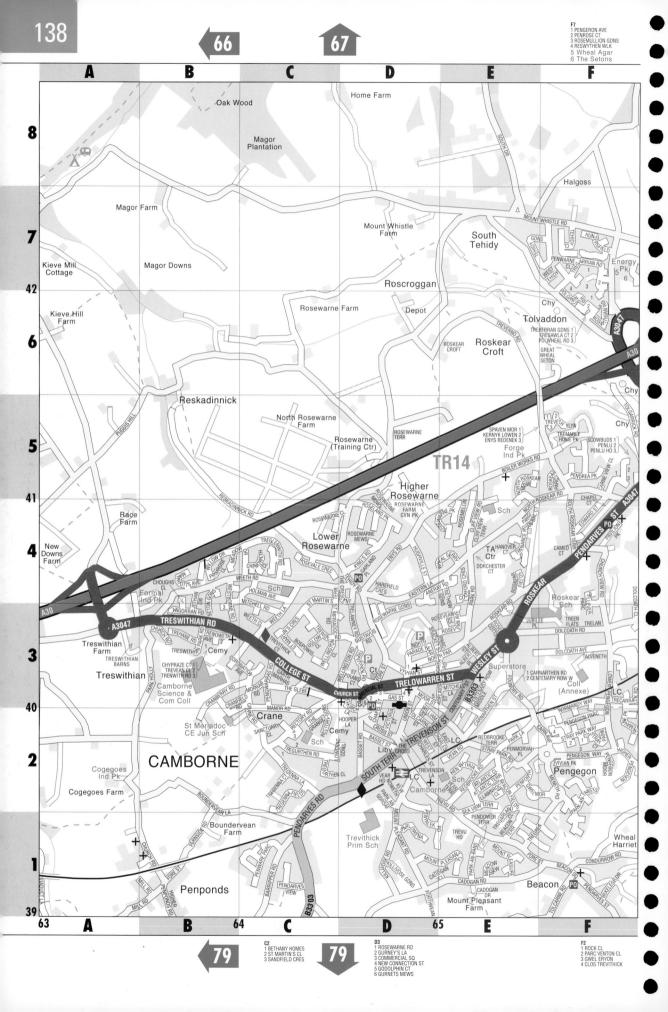

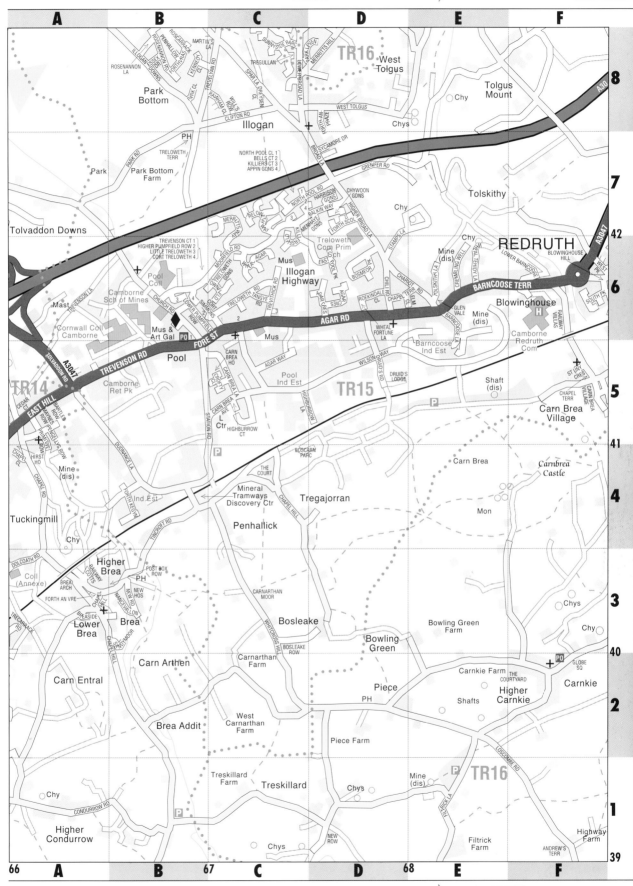

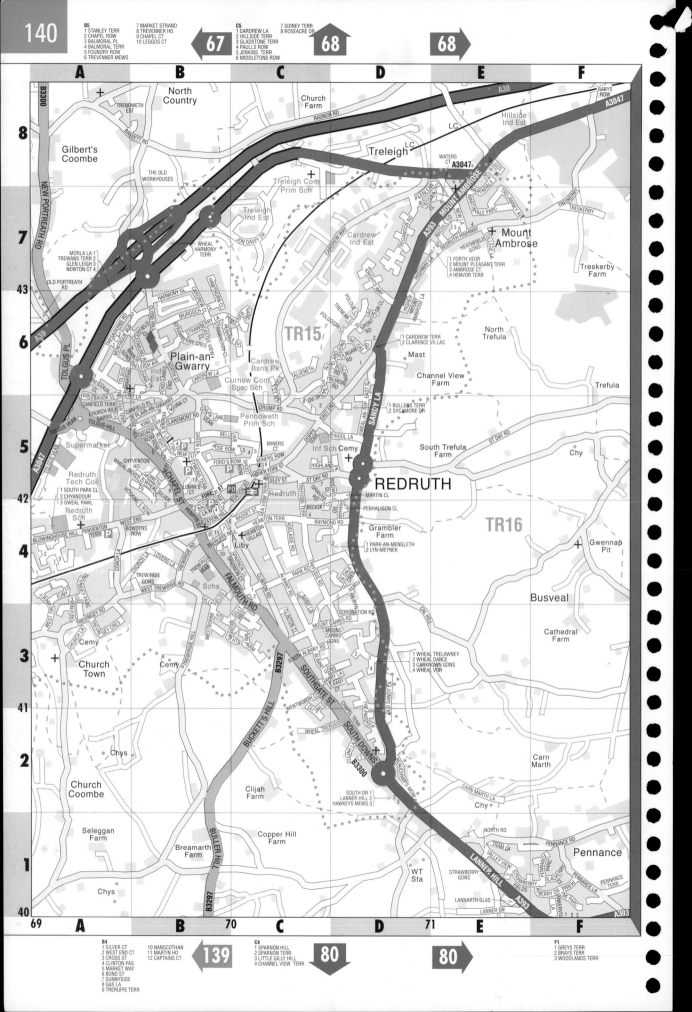

B6
1 ST NICHOLAS CT	22 BUNKERS HILL
2 SAIL LOFT FLATS	23 ROSE LA
3 THE ROPE WLK	24 LOVE LA
4 ISLAND RD	25 THE DIGEY
5 PENAMEYNE CT	26 VIRGIN ST
6 PORTHMEORE RD	27 MEADOW FLATS
7 BACK RD E	28 GODREVY TERR
8 ISLAND SQ	29 BARNOON TERR
9 FISH ST	30 ACADEMY TERR
10 BETHESDA PL	31 MARKET STRAND
11 VICTORIA RD	32 LIFEBOAT HILL
12 VICTORIA PL	33 MARKET SQ
13 BARNALOFT	34 BOWLING GN
14 PIAZZA	35 BOWLING GN TERR
15 NORTH PL	36 CARRACK DHU EST
16 ST PETERS ST	37 CARRACK DHU
17 BACK LA	38 BELLAIR TERR
18 CHURCH PL	39 MOUNT PLEASANT
19 CHY-AN-CHY	40 RICHMOND PL
20 BAILEYS LA	41 TREWYN FLATS
21 PORTHMEOR SQ	42 BACK ST
	43 ATLANTIC TERR
	44 CLODGY VIEW

45 WEST PL
46 THE GALLERIES
47 THE MEADOW
48 CRUSOE FLATS
49 DIGEY FLATS
50 PORTHMEOR STUDIOS
51 PORTHMEOR CT
52 MOUNT ZION
53 WILLS LA

CARTHEW CT 1
CARTHEW TERR 2
AYR TERR 3
WHEAL AYR TERR 4
OCEAN VIEW TERR 5
PARC BEAN TERR 6
BELMONT TERR 7
CHANNEL VIEW 8
VENTNOR TERR 9
BELMONT PL 10
ALEXANDRA ROW 11

A5
1 AYR CT	10 BOSTENNACK PL
2 TREGARTHEN	11 BOSTENNACK TERR
3 SOUTHFIELDS PL	12 PEARCE'S LA
4 WINDSOR TERR	13 MIDDLE STENNACK COTTS
5 BULLANS TERR	14 STENNACK GDNS
6 TRERICE RD	15 SANDOWS LA
7 CARNELLS RD	16 ROSEWALL COTTS
8 NANJIVEY PL	17 ROSEWALL TERR
9 NANJIVEY TERR	18 FERN GLEN
	19 LITTLE-IN-SIGHT

B5
1 ST ANDREW'S ST	10 ALMA TERR
2 REDFERN ST	11 TRENWITH TERR
3 STREET-AN-POL	12 NORTH TERR
4 TREGENNA PL	13 UMFULLA PL
5 GABRIEL ST	14 TRENWITH PL
6 BEDFORD PL	15 DOVE ST
7 WESLEY PL	16 TREGENNA HILL
8 WINDSOR HILL	17 STREET-AN-GARROW
9 DRILLFIELD LA	18 SKIDDEN HILL

B5
19 FERN LEE TERR	28 ROSEMORRAN
20 SEA VIEW TERR	29 TALLAND CT
21 ALBERT PL	30 STONES CT
22 PADNOVER TERR	
23 PORTHMINSTER TERR	
24 PETES PL	
25 CARRACK WIDDEN	
26 ALBERT TERR	
27 HARLEQUINS	

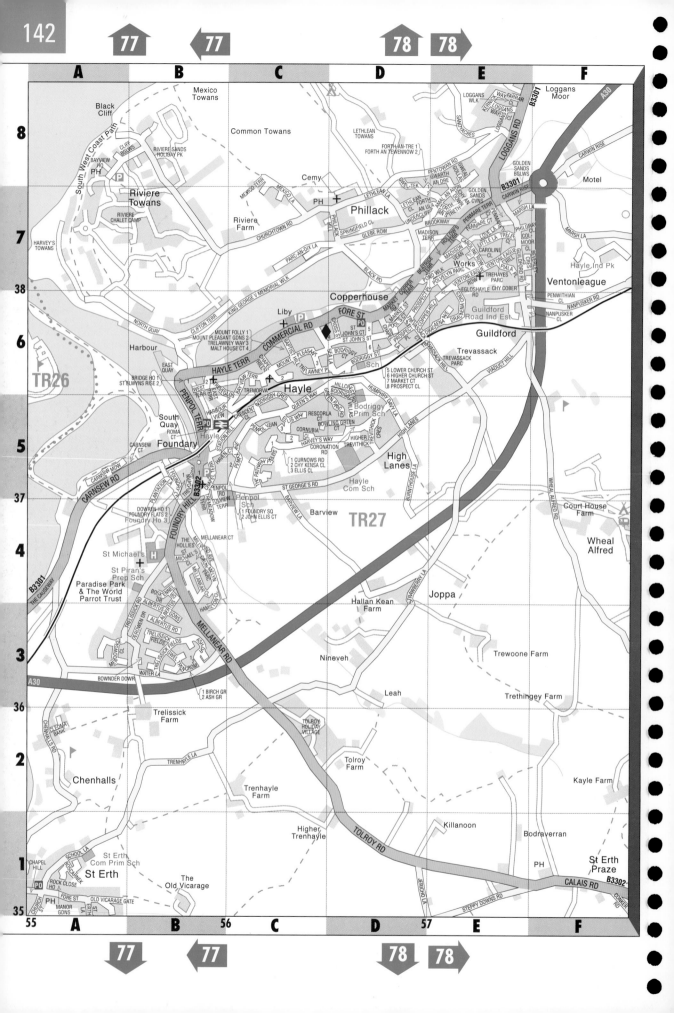

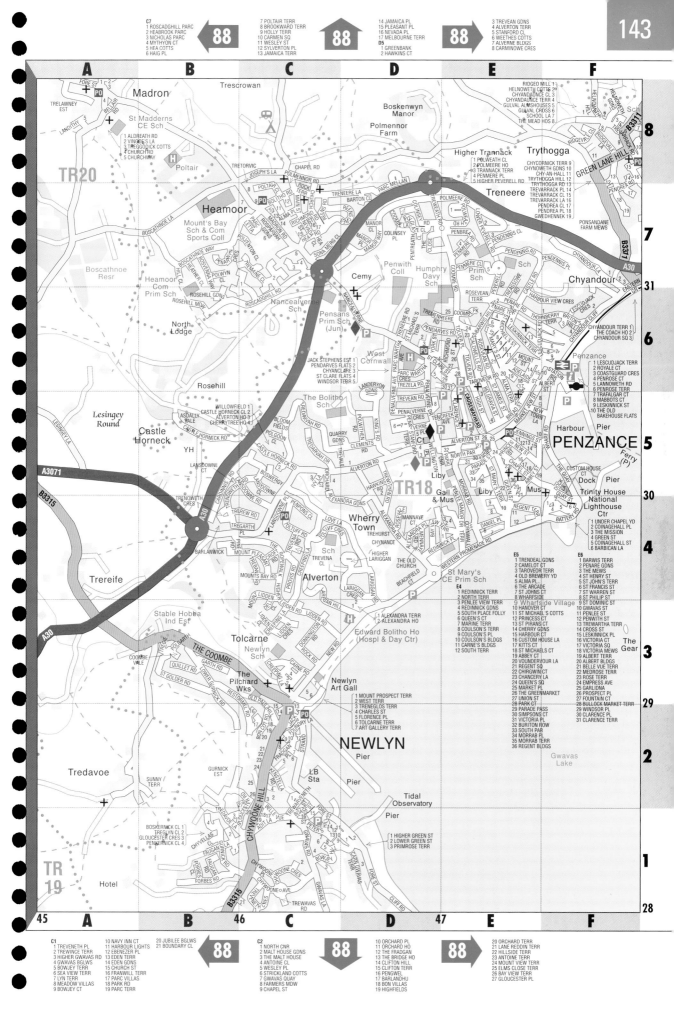

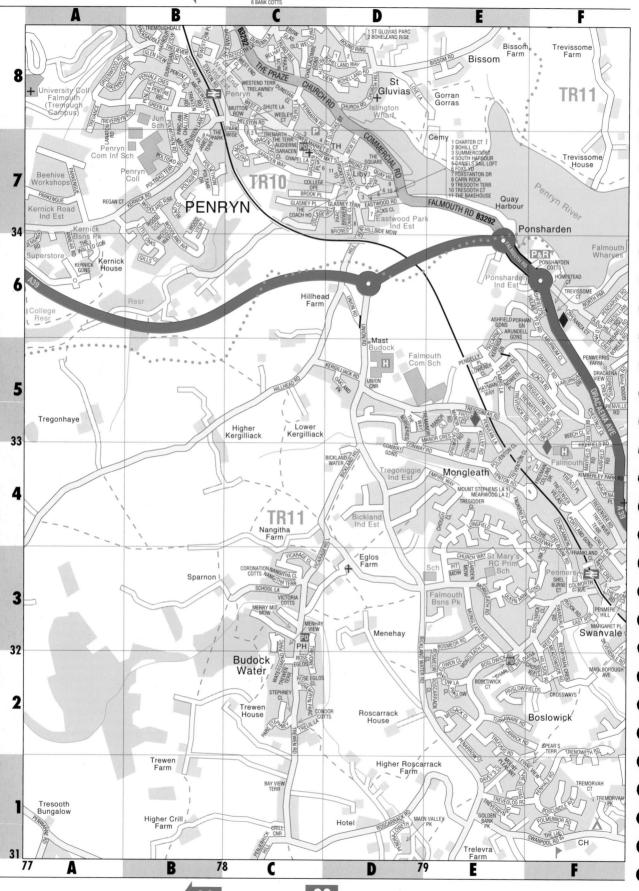

C7
1 HARRIS CT
2 SLADES LA
3 BENNETTS COTTS
4 RUSSELL WAY
5 SARACEN HO
6 BANK COTTS

8

University Coll
Falmouth
(Tremough
Campus)

Penryn

St
Gluvias

Bissom

TR11

Gorran
Gorras

Bissom
Farm

Trevissome
Farm

Trevissome
House

Beehive
Workshops

Penryn
Com Inf Sch

Penryn
Coll

TR10

PENRYN

Islington
Wharf

Cemy

1 CHARTER CT
2 BOHILL CT
3 SUMMERCOURT
4 SOUTH HARBOUR
5 DANIELS SAIL LOFT
6 FOXS YD
7 FOXSTANTON DR
8 CARN ROCK
9 TRESOOTH TERR
10 TRESOOTH CT
11 THE BAKEHOUSE

7

Kernick Road
Ind Est

Superstore

Kernick
Bsns Pk

Kernick
House

Regan Ct

The Square

Eastwood Park
Ind Est

FALMOUTH RD   B3292

Quay Harbour

Penryn River

Quay Hill

Ponsharden

Falmouth
Wharves

34

A39

College
Resr

Resr

Hillhead
Farm

P&R
Ponsharden
Cotts

Ponsharden
Ind Est

Homestead
Trevissome
CT

North Par

6

Tregonhaye

Higher
Kergilliack

Lower
Kergilliack

Mast
Budock

Union
Cnr

Falmouth
Com Sch

Ashfield
Gdns

Porhan
Gn

Arundell
Gdns

Penwerris
Farm

Dracaena
View

5

Nangitha
Farm

Bickland
Water

Tregoniggie
Ind Est

Empire Way

Trescobeas Rd

Manor Cres

Mongleath

Beech Cl

Highfield Rd

Falmouth

H

33

TR11

Sparnon

Coronation
Cotts

Victoria
Cotts

Merry Mit
Mdw

School La

Vicarage Cl

Eglos
Farm

Bickland
Ind Est

Mount Stephens La 1
Mearwood La 2
Tresidder
Cl

Longfield

The
Causeway

Frankland
Cl

A39

4

Menehay
View

PH

Rose
Eglos

Budock
Water

Menehay

Church Way St Mary's
RC Prim
Sch

Sch

Pit
Mdw

Falmouth
Bsns Pk

Penmere

Swanvale

Penmere
Hill

3

Trewen
House

Stephney
Cl

Condor
Cotts

Roscarrack
House

Boslowick

Margaret Pl

Crossways

Marlborough
Ave

32

2

Bay View
Terr

Trewen
Farm

Higher Roscarrack
Farm

Spear's
Terr

Tremorvah
Ct

Tremorvah
Pk

1

Tresooth
Bungalow

Higher Crill
Farm

Crill
Cnr

Hotel

Maen Valley
Pk

Golden
Bank
Pk

CH

Trelevra
Farm

31

77   A   78   B   C   78   D   E   79   F

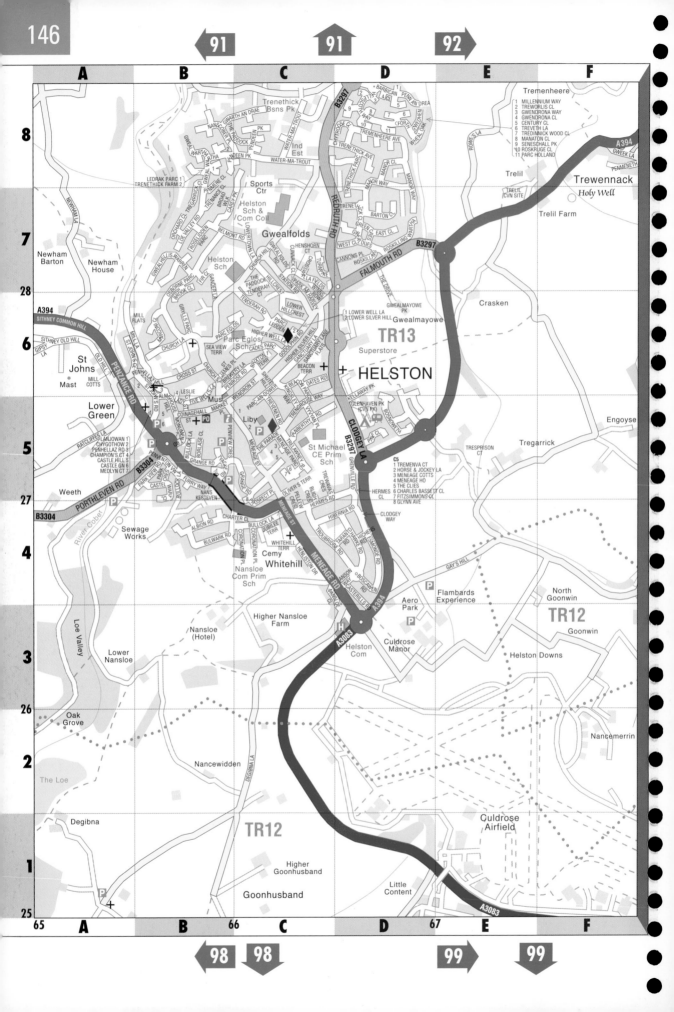

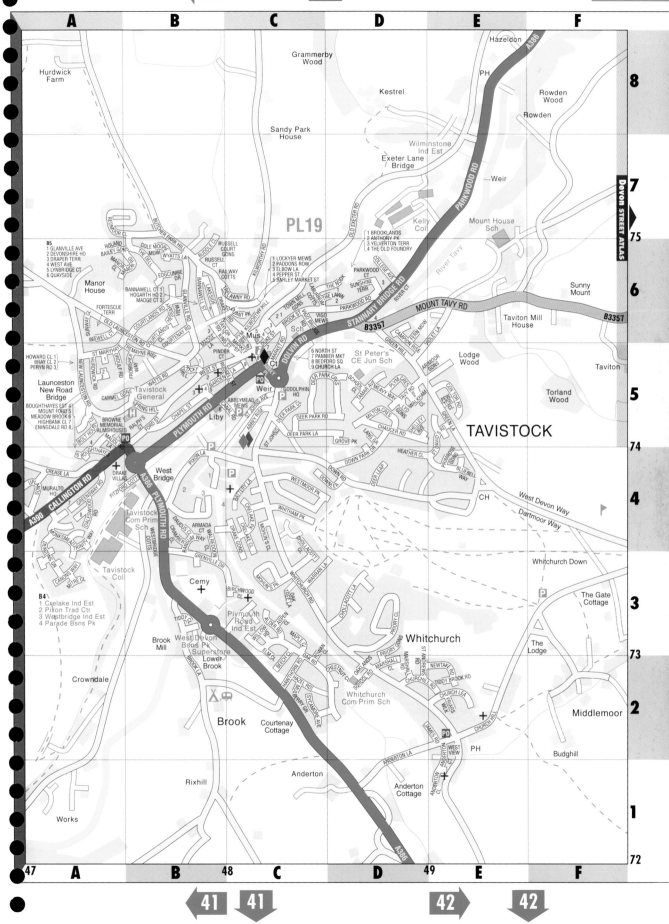

DEVON STREET ATLAS

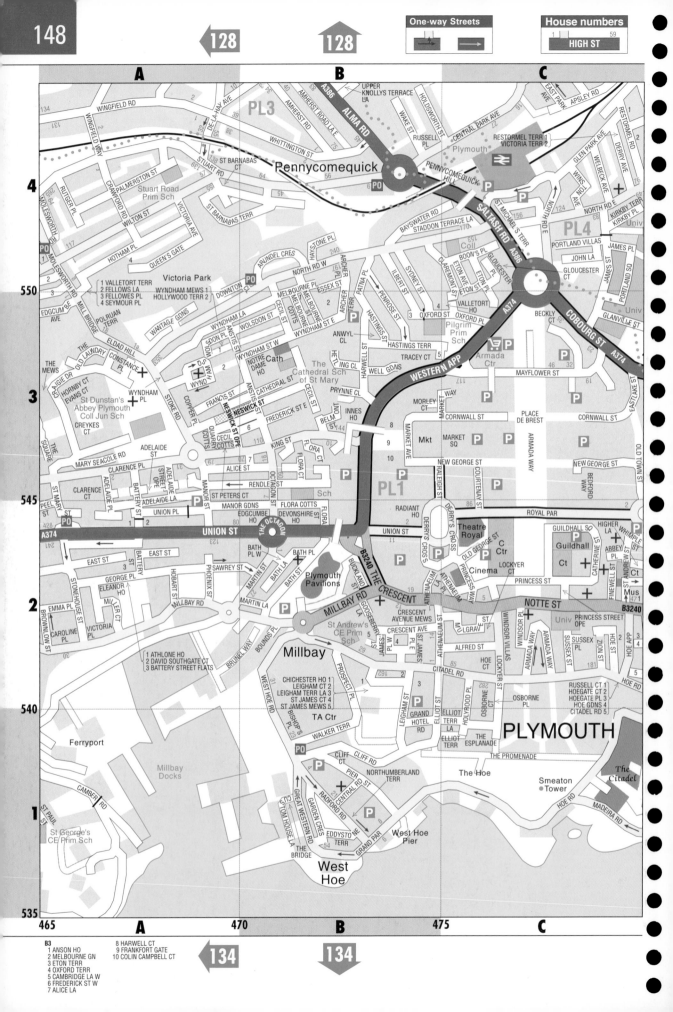

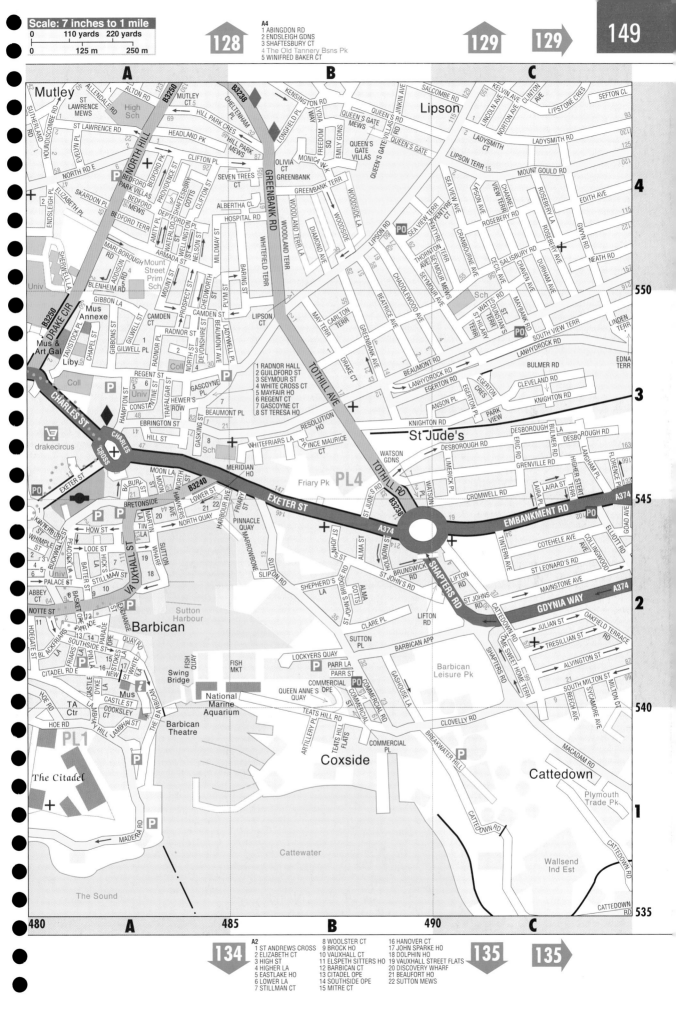

Index

Place name May be abbreviated on the map

Location number Present when a number indicates the place's position in a crowded area of mapping

Locality, town or village Shown when more than one place has the same name

Postcode district District for the indexed place

Page and grid square Page number and grid reference for the standard mapping

Church Rd **6** Beckenham BR2..........**53** C6

Public and commercial buildings are highlighted in magenta **Places of interest** are highlighted in blue with a star*

Abbreviations used in the index

Acad	**Academy**	Comm	**Common**	Gd	**Ground**	L	**Leisure**	Prom	**Promenade**
App	**Approach**	Cott	**Cottage**	Gdn	**Garden**	La	**Lane**	Rd	**Road**
Arc	**Arcade**	Cres	**Crescent**	Gn	**Green**	Liby	**Library**	Recn	**Recreation**
Ave	**Avenue**	Cswy	**Causeway**	Gr	**Grove**	Mdw	**Meadow**	Ret	**Retail**
Bglw	**Bungalow**	Ct	**Court**	H	**Hall**	Meml	**Memorial**	Sh	**Shopping**
Bldg	**Building**	Ctr	**Centre**	Ho	**House**	Mkt	**Market**	Sq	**Square**
Bsns, Bus	**Business**	Ctry	**Country**	Hospl	**Hospital**	Mus	**Museum**	St	**Street**
Bvd	**Boulevard**	Cty	**County**	HQ	**Headquarters**	Orch	**Orchard**	Sta	**Station**
Cath	**Cathedral**	Dr	**Drive**	Hts	**Heights**	Pal	**Palace**	Terr	**Terrace**
Cir	**Circus**	Dro	**Drove**	Ind	**Industrial**	Par	**Parade**	TH	**Town Hall**
Cl	**Close**	Ed	**Education**	Inst	**Institute**	Pas	**Passage**	Univ	**University**
Cnr	**Corner**	Emb	**Embankment**	Int	**International**	Pk	**Park**	Wk, Wlk	**Walk**
Coll	**College**	Est	**Estate**	Intc	**Interchange**	Pl	**Place**	Wr	**Water**
Com	**Community**	Ex	**Exhibition**	Junc	**Junction**	Prec	**Precinct**	Yd	**Yard**

Index of localities, towns and villages

A

Addington 113 D7
Albaston 40 E5
Alfardisworthy 5 E6
Altarnun 26 C8
Alverton 143 C4
Amalebra 76 F3
Amalveor 76 E4
Anderton 132 F4
Angarrack 78 C5
Antony 65 E5
Ashton 90 E3

B

Badgall 17 C5
Badharlick 17 E5
Bakesdown 7 D3
Baldhu 69 C1
Ball 108 E7
Balnoon 77 A5
Balwest 90 D5
Bangors 6 F2
Barbican 149 A2
Barcelona 62 E4
Bareppa 93 D4
Barkla Shop 54 E1
Barne Barton 127 C8
Barripper 79 B5
Bathpool 27 C1
Beacon 138 F1
Bealsmill 28 E3
Beeny 9 E3
Belowda 46 D4
Bennacott 12 E2
Bere Alston 41 B1
Bere Ferrers 119 E3
Berepper 98 F5
Berriowbridge 27 B2
Besoughan 45 A3
Bethel 115 A5
Bickham 121 A7
Billacombe 135 F8
Billacott 12 B1
Biscovey 60 B4
Bishop's Quay 99 F8
Bissoe 81 D8
Bissom 144 E8
Black Cross 45 E3
Black Rock 79 D1
Blackwater 68 D5
Blindwell 132 E5
Blisland 35 D8
Blowinghouse
Bodmin 109 B2
Redruth 139 F6
Blue Anchor 57 D8
Bodelva 115 F8
Bodieve 108 C7
Bodilly 91 F7
Bodinnick 116 E5
Bodmin 109 B5
Bodwen 47 E3
Bohetherick 40 F2
Bohortha 95 C5
Bolenowe 79 F5
Bolingey 55 B4
Bolitho 79 F1
Bolventor 25 E3
Boquio 91 F8
Borea 76 F2
Boscadjack 91 F6
Boscarne 34 C2
Boscastle 9 C1
Boscoppa 115 A6
Boscreege 90 C5
Boskednan 76 A1
Boskenna 97 C4
Bosleake 139 C3
Boslowick 144 F2
Bosporthennis 75 F3
Bossiney 14 D8
Boswednack 76 A4
Boswinger 85 B5
Botallack 86 E7
Bottoms 96 E5
Botusfleming 122 B7
Bowling Green
Bugle 47 E1
Redruth 139 D3
Boyton 13 B2
Braddock 49 F5
Bradford 24 D2
Brane 87 C3
Bray Shop 28 B1
Brazacott 12 B2
Brea 139 B3
Brea Addit 139 B2
Breage 90 F3
Brent 62 E2
Bridge 67 E5
Bridgend 112 E3
Bridgerule 8 A6
Bridges 59 F8
Bridgetown 19 B8
Brighton 57 D5
Brixton 136 F4
Broadlane 90 E5
Brocton 34 A3
Brook 147 B2
Brunnion 77 A3
Buckland Monachorum 42 A3
Bude 104 E6
Budock Water 144 C2
Bugle 47 D1
Burhos 79 F2
Burlawn 108 D1
Burraton 122 D4
Burraton Coombe 122 C2
Bursdon 3 B6
Busveal 140 F4
Buttsbear Cross 7 F7

C

Cadgwith 103 B4
Calenick 137 C1
Callestick 55 C1
Callington 39 E5
Calloose 78 D2
Calstock 41 A3
Camborne 138 B2
Cambrose 67 F6
Camelford 105 C4
Camels Head 127 E7
Cannalidgey 32 E4
Canonstown 77 C2
Canworthy Water 11 D2
Caradon Town 38 E6
Carbis 47 A2
Carbis Bay 141 D3
Carclaze 114 E6
Cardinham 35 E3
Carfury 76 A1
Cargreen 119 A2
Carharrack 80 F8
Carkeel 122 C6
Carleen 90 F5
Carlidnack 93 E4
Carloggas
Foxhole 58 C5
Penwithick 59 D7
St Mawgan 45 A8
Carluddon 59 D6
Carlyon Bay 115 E3
Carn Arthen 139 B2
Carn Brea Village 139 F5
Carne
St Dennis 46 C1
Veryan 83 F5
Carn Entral 139 A2
Carnhell Green 78 F4
Carnhot 68 F4
Carnkie 139 F2
Carnkief 55 D3
Carnon Downs 82 A7
Carn Towan 96 C7
Carnyorth 86 F8
Carpalla 58 D4
Carthew 59 B6
Carwynnen 79 D4
Carzise 78 D1
Castallack 97 F6
Castle Gate 76 F1
Castle Horneck 143 B5
Catchall 97 D8
Cattedown 149 C1
Cawsand 133 B1
Chacewater 68 F3
Chaddlewood 131 B6
Chapel
Launceston 106 A5
Quintrell Downs 111 E4
Chapel Town 57 B6
Chaple Amble 22 D2
Chapman's Well 13 E4
Charlestown 115 B2
Chenhalls 142 A2
Chillaton 29 F8
Chilsworthy 40 E7
Churchbridge 50 F1
Church Combe 140 A2
Church Cove 103 A2
Churchtown
Bridgerule 8 B6
Camborne 67 E5
Lanivet 47 E7
St Breward 24 B4
Church Town 140 A3
Chyandour 143 F7
Chy-an-Gweal 141 B2
Chycoose 82 A6
Chynhale 91 C5
Clapper 108 E4
Cleers 46 E1
Clerkenwater 109 D8
Cliff 61 B6
Clifford 3 F8
Clowance Wood 79 A1
Clubworthy 12 C3
Coad's Green 27 D4
Cocks 55 B3
Cockwells 77 C1
Colan 44 F4
Cold Northcoot 16 F5
Coldvreath 46 F1
Colebrook 130 E6
Combe 136 E5
Come-to-Good 82 B7
Comford 80 F6
Common Moor 37 F4
Condon's Shop 27 B5
Connor Downs 78 D5
Constantine 92 E3
Constantine Bay 20 D1
Cooksland 35 B2
Coombe
Camborne 66 F3
Perranarworthal 81 B8
Playing Place 82 D8
St Stephen 58 B2
Coosebean 137 A5
Coppathorne 7 A3
Copperhouse 142 D6
Copthorne 12 B3
Coswinsawsin 79 A5
Coverack 101 C1
Coverack Bridges 91 E5
Coxford 10 D7
Cox Hill 68 F2
Coxpark 40 D7
Coxside 149 B1
Crabtree 129 E5
Crackington Haven 10 B7
Crafthole 65 B5
Crane 138 C2
Crantock 43 D3
Crapstone 42 B2
Crean 96 F5
Creed 72 A6
Creegbrawse 68 F2
Crelly 91 F7
Cremyll 133 E7
Crimp 3 A2
Cripplesease 77 A3
Croanford 34 C6
Crofthandy 68 E1
Croft Mitchell 79 E4
Crossgate 19 A7
Cross Lanes 99 C4
Crosstown 2 B1
Crowan 79 C1
Crowlas 89 C8
Crownhill 124 F2
Crowntown 91 B5
Crows-an-wra 96 F8
Crow's Nest 38 B4
Crugmeer 107 A7
Crumplehorn 62 D2
Cubert 55 D8
Curgurrell 83 C4

Currian Vale ... 58 D8
Curry Lane ... 12 E4
Cury ... 99 B4
Cusgarne ... 81 B7
Cusveorth Coombes ... 69 B2
Cuttivett ... 53 B5

D

Dadbrook ... 132 E4
Darite ... 38 B4
Darraccott ... 2 D4
Davidstow ... 16 A6
Daw's House ... 18 E1
Delabole ... 14 D3
Demelza ... 46 E6
Derriford ... 125 B4
Derril ... 8 D6
Deveral ... 78 D2
Devonport ... 127 D4
Devoran ... 81 F6
Dinworthy ... 3 F2
Dizzard ... 6 B1
Dobwalls ... 50 E8
Docton ... 2 F8
Doublebois ... 50 C8
Dousland ... 42 F3
Downderry ... 64 C5
Downgate
  Kelly Bray ... 40 A7
  Pensilva ... 38 D5
Downinney ... 11 B1
Down Thomas ... 135 C1
Drawbridge ... 49 F8
Drift ... 87 F3
Drym ... 91 A8
Duloe ... 51 A1
Dunmere ... 34 D2
Dunsley ... 38 C6
Dunterton ... 28 F6
Duporth ... 115 A1
Durgan ... 93 D2
Dutson ... 106 E8

E

Eastcott ... 3 A3
East Looe ... 117 D3
East Panson ... 13 F3
East Portholland ... 84 E5
East Taphouse ... 50 B6
East Youlstone ... 3 C2
Edistone ... 2 F8
Efford ... 129 C5
Eggbeare ... 19 A7
Eggbuckland ... 129 C8
Egloskerry ... 18 A5
Egoshayle ... 108 D6
Elburton ... 136 B6
Elmscott ... 2 E8
Empacombe ... 133 D6
Enniscaven ... 46 D2
Ernesettle ... 123 E3
Estover ... 125 E4

F

Fairy Cross ... 49 B5
Falmouth ... 145 C4
Farms Common ... 79 F1
Feock ... 82 C5
Fernsplatt ... 81 C8
Fiddlers Green ... 56 B5
Fletchersbridge ... 48 F8
Flexbury ... 104 E6
Flushing
  Manaccan ... 101 B8
  Penryn ... 145 C6
Fonston ... 11 C2
Ford ... 128 A5
Forder
  Cawsand ... 132 F1
  Saltash ... 122 C1
Ford Park ... 128 D4
Forge ... 68 A4
Forrabury ... 9 C2
Foss ... 133 A5
Foundry ... 142 B5
Four Lanes ... 80 A5
Fowey ... 116 B4
Foxhole ... 58 D5
Fraddam ... 78 D1
Fraddon ... 45 E1
Freathy ... 65 E3
Frogpool ... 81 C7
Frogwell ... 39 D3

G

Gam ... 24 A4
Gang ... 38 F3
Garras ... 99 D6
Gatherley ... 19 E1
Gear ... 99 F7
Georgia ... 76 E3
Germoe ... 90 C4
Germoe Cross Roads ... 90 C3
Gerrans ... 83 B2
Gilbert's Coombe ... 140 A8
Gillan ... 101 C6
Glenholt ... 125 D6

Gloweth ... 69 E3
Gluvian ... 45 E7
Godolphin Cross ... 90 E6
Godrevy Towans ... 66 B3
Golant ... 61 A5
Golberdon ... 39 C6
Goldsithney ... 89 D5
Gollawater ... 55 A1
Gonamena ... 38 B5
Gonvena ... 108 C6
Goonbell ... 68 D8
Goon Gumpas ... 68 F1
Goonhavern ... 55 C4
Goonhusband ... 146 C1
Goonown ... 54 D1
Goonvrea ... 68 B8
Gooseham ... 2 E3
Gorran Churchtown ... 73 B1
Gorran Haven ... 85 D5
Gorran High Lanes ... 72 F2
Gothers ... 46 D1
Gover Valley ... 59 A4
Grampound ... 72 B7
Grampound Road ... 57 E1
Great Bosullow ... 87 D8
Green Bottom ... 69 B4
Greensplat ... 59 A6
Grenofen ... 42 A6
Grimscott ... 5 A2
Grumbla ... 87 C4
Guildford ... 142 E6
Gulval ... 88 E6
Gulworthy ... 41 B8
Gunnislake ... 40 F5
Gunwalloe ... 98 E5
Gwallon ... 89 C6
Gwavas ... 91 D4
Gwealfolds ... 146 C7
Gweek ... 92 C1
Gwennap ... 80 F7
Gwinear ... 78 D4
Gwithian ... 66 B2
Gwithian Towans ... 66 A2

H

Halamanning ... 90 A6
Hale Mills ... 69 A1
Halgabron ... 14 E7
Hallew ... 47 C2
Hallivick ... 58 A4
Hallworthy ... 16 D6
Halsetown ... 77 A5
Halvosso ... 93 A8
Halwin ... 92 B8
Ham ... 128 A8
Hannafore ... 117 C2
Harcourt ... 82 B4
Hardisworthy ... 2 D7
Harlyn ... 20 D2
Harrowbarrow ... 40 D5
Hartley ... 128 E7
Hartley Vale ... 129 A8
Hatt ... 53 E4
Haye ... 39 D4
Hayle ... 142 C6
Heamoor ... 143 B7
Hele ... 13 C2
Helebridge ... 7 A6
Helford ... 93 B1
Helford Passage ... 93 C2
Helland ... 35 A5
Hellandbridge ... 34 F6
Hellesveor ... 77 A7
Helston ... 146 D6
Helstone ... 24 B8
Hemerdon ... 131 D7
Henaford ... 2 F5
Hendra
  Bodmin ... 46 F7
  Camelford ... 105 A4
  Mullion ... 102 F7
  St Dennis ... 58 C8
Henford ... 13 F5
Henwood ... 38 B8
Herniss ... 80 F1
Herodsfoot ... 50 E3
Hessenford ... 64 C8
Hewas Water ... 72 D8
Higher Bal ... 54 B2
Higher Boscaswell ... 75 A1
Higher Brea ... 139 B3
Higher Carnkie ... 139 F2
Highercliff ... 63 B8
Higher Compton ... 129 A6
Higher Condurrow ... 139 A1
Higher Crackington ... 10 C6
Higher Downs ... 89 F5
Higher Larrick ... 27 E5
Higher Porthpean ... 59 D1
Higher Rosewarne ... 138 D5
Higher Tolcarne ... 45 B8
Highertown
  Camelford ... 24 E8
  Truro ... 69 F3
Higher Trewince ... 44 E6
Highlanes ... 32 B7
High Lanes ... 142 D5
High Street ... 58 D4
Hill ... 10 B5
Hingston Down ... 40 B6
Holestrow ... 102 E2
Hollacombe Hill ... 136 A2
Holmbush ... 115 B4
Holywell ... 43 B2

Honicknowle ... 124 B2
Hooe ... 135 C5
Horningtops ... 51 E3
Horrabridge ... 42 C5
Horsebridge ... 29 C1
Horsedowns ... 78 F1
Huddisford ... 3 F6

I

Idless ... 70 B6
Illogan ... 67 E4
Illogan Highway ... 139 C6
Indian Queens ... 45 E1
Insworke ... 132 F6

J

Jacobstow ... 11 B6
Jewel's Cross ... 7 F6
Jolly's Bottom ... 69 A4
Joppa
  Hayle ... 142 E4
  St Just ... 87 A4

K

Kehelland ... 66 F2
Kelly ... 29 B8
Kelly Bray ... 39 F6
Kelynack ... 86 F4
Kennards House ... 18 B2
Kenneggy ... 90 A3
Kenneggy Downs ... 90 B4
Kents ... 10 E7
Kenwyn ... 137 C6
Kerris ... 97 E8
Kerrow Moor ... 59 D8
Kestle ... 73 A4
Kestle Mill ... 111 F1
Keybridge ... 35 B8
Keyham ... 127 E5
Kilkhampton ... 5 A6
Killatown ... 37 B1
Killivose ... 79 C5
Kingbeare ... 27 A1
Kingsand ... 133 A2
King's Tamerton ... 123 F2
Knightsmill ... 23 F7
Kuggar ... 103 B6

L

Ladock ... 57 C1
Lady Nance ... 44 F3
Laira ... 129 C4
Lake ... 42 E3
Lamanva ... 93 C6
Lambourne ... 55 B2
Lamellion ... 113 A4
Lamerton ... 30 B3
Lamorick ... 47 E7
Lamorna ... 97 E5
Lamorran ... 83 C8
Lana ... 13 D7
Landrake ... 53 B3
Landreyne ... 27 C2
Landulph ... 123 A7
Lane ... 111 B3
Laneast ... 17 B2
Lanescot ... 60 D6
Langdon ... 11 C3
Langore ... 18 D5
Lanivet ... 47 F6
Lanjeth ... 58 E3
Lanjew ... 46 F7
Lank ... 24 B2
Lanlivery ... 48 C1
Lanner ... 80 D6
Lanreath ... 62 B7
Lansallos ... 62 A2
Lanstephan ... 106 C8
Lanteglos ... 14 F1
Lanteglos Highway ... 61 E4
Latchley ... 40 D8
Launceston ... 106 D5
Lawhitton ... 19 C1
Leburnick ... 28 D8
Leedstown ... 78 E1
Leigham ... 129 E8
Lelant ... 77 E4
Lelant Downs ... 77 D2
Lerryn ... 61 D8
Lescrow ... 116 B6
Lesnewth ... 10 A1
Levalsa Meor ... 73 B8
Lewannick ... 27 B7
Ley ... 36 E1
Lezant ... 28 B6
Lifton ... 19 F3
Liftondown ... 19 D4
Linkinhorne ... 39 B8
Lipson ... 149 C4
Lipson Vale ... 129 A4
Liskeard ... 113 E6
Little Bosullow ... 75 D1
Little Brynn ... 46 E5
Little Comfort ... 28 C7
Little Falmouth ... 145 B7
Little Kirland ... 109 C1
Little Petherick ... 32 C6
Little Prideaux ... 60 B7

Lizard ... 102 F2
Lockengate ... 47 E4
London Apprentice ... 59 B1
Longbridge ... 129 F7
Longcross ... 29 F6
Longdowns ... 81 A1
Longlands ... 122 A1
Longrock ... 88 F6
Longstone
  Carbis Bay ... 141 E1
  St Mabyn ... 34 F8
Looe ... 117 D3
Lostwithiel ... 112 E1
Lovaton ... 42 F1
Lower Bodinnar ... 87 E7
Lower Boscaswell ... 74 F2
Lower Brea ... 139 A3
Lower Clicker ... 51 F4
Lower Compton ... 129 A5
Lower Green ... 146 A5
Lower Ninnes ... 76 B1
Lower Porthpean ... 59 E1
Lower Prospidnick ... 91 C6
Lower Rose ... 55 D5
Lower Rosewarne ... 138 C4
Lowertown
  Helston ... 91 E4
  Lostwithiel ... 48 A4
Lower Trebullett ... 28 A4
Luckett ... 40 B8
Ludgvan ... 89 A7
Luffincott ... 13 C5
Lutsford ... 3 A6
Luxulyan ... 48 A1
Lynstone ... 104 D3

M

Mabe Burnthouse ... 93 C8
Maders ... 39 D6
Madron ... 143 B8
Maenporth ... 93 F4
Maer ... 104 D8
Mainstone ... 125 F2
Malpas ... 70 D2
Manaccan ... 101 A8
Manadon ... 124 D1
Mannamead ... 128 F5
Manor Parsley ... 68 B5
Marazion ... 89 B6
Marhamchurch ... 7 B6
Marshgate ... 10 C2
Marsh Mills ... 130 A6
Mawgan ... 99 D7
Mawgan Porth ... 31 B2
Mawla ... 68 B4
Mawnan ... 93 E2
Mawnan Smith ... 93 E3
Maxworthy ... 12 A3
Mayon ... 96 B6
Mead ... 2 D4
Meadwell ... 29 C8
Meavy ... 42 F2
Meddon ... 3 C4
Melbur ... 57 F5
Mellingey ... 32 D6
Melorn ... 83 D6
Menadarva ... 66 E2
Menagissey ... 68 C5
Mendennick ... 132 C2
Menheniot ... 52 A5
Merrifield ... 7 F4
Merrymeet ... 38 C1
Merther ... 70 F3
Merther Lane ... 70 F1
Metherell ... 40 D4
Mevagissey ... 73 D3
Michaelstow ... 24 A5
Middle Crackington ... 10 B6
Middle Greadow ... 48 B1
Middlehill ... 38 D3
Middlemoor ... 147 F2
Middlewood ... 27 B2
Milcombe ... 62 F6
Millbay ... 148 B2
Millbrook ... 132 E5
Millendreath ... 117 F5
Millhill ... 30 B1
Millook ... 6 D2
Millpool
  Cardinham ... 35 F5
  Praa Sands ... 90 B5
Milltown
  Cardinham ... 35 E3
  Lostwithiel ... 60 F8
Milton Abbot ... 29 D6
Milton Combe ... 120 F8
Milton Green ... 29 D5
Mingoose ... 68 C7
Minions ... 38 B6
Mitchell ... 56 F5
Mithian ... 54 F1
Mithian
  Downs ... 68 F8
Mixtow ... 116 D7
Molinnis ... 47 C2
Mongleath ... 144 E4
Moortown
  Tavistock ... 42 D8
  Tetcott ... 13 C7
Morice Town ... 127 D3
Mornick ... 39 B7
Morvah ... 75 C2
Morval ... 63 D7
Morwellham ... 41 B4
Morwenstow ... 2 B2

Mount
  Cardinham ... 36 B2
  Cubert ... 55 C7
Mount Ambrose ... 140 E7
Mount Charles ... 114 E4
Mount Gould ... 129 B3
Mount Hawke ... 68 C6
Mountjoy ... 45 A3
Mount Lane ... 13 E6
Mount Wise ... 127 F1
Mousehole ... 88 D1
Muchlarnick ... 62 E7
Mulfra ... 76 B1
Mullion ... 99 A1
Mutley ... 128 F4
Myler Churchtown ... 82 C2
Mylor Bridge ... 82 A3

N

Nancegollan ... 91 C7
Nancemellin ... 66 D1
Nancledra ... 76 F2
Nanpean ... 58 D7
Nansladron ... 73 B7
Nanstallon ... 34 C1
Nantithet ... 99 B5
Narkurs ... 64 D6
Navarino ... 18 B8
Nethercott ... 13 E7
Netherton ... 38 D7
Newbridge
  Callington ... 39 D2
  Penzance ... 87 E6
  Truro ... 69 F3
New Downs
  St Agnes ... 54 B2
  St Just ... 86 E6
Newlyn ... 143 D2
Newmill
  Penzance ... 76 B1
  Poundstock ... 7 A1
New Polzeath ... 21 E6
Newport ... 106 B7
Newquay ... 110 E7
Newtown
  Coad's Green ... 27 D5
  Praa Sands ... 90 B4
Newtown-in-St Martin ... 100 E6
Ninnis Bridge ... 77 B2
No Man's Land ... 63 E7
Noonvares ... 90 E7
Norris Green ... 40 E4
North Beer ... 12 F3
North Brenton ... 30 E8
North Corner ... 101 C2
Northcott
  Bude ... 4 C3
  St Giles on the Heath ... 13 D3
North Country ... 140 B8
North Darley ... 38 D8
North Hill ... 27 B3
Northmoor ... 3 F3
North Petherwin ... 18 A8
North Prospect ... 128 A6
North Tamerton ... 12 F8
Numphra ... 87 A4

O

Old Kea ... 82 E8
Oreston ... 135 C7
Otterham ... 10 D1
Otterham Station ... 16 A8
Ottery ... 30 A2

P

Padstow ... 107 C4
Palmersbridge ... 25 F4
Pancrasweek ... 8 C8
Pantersbridge ... 36 D3
Par ... 60 C4
Paramoor ... 72 E8
Parc Erissey ... 68 A3
Park Bottom ... 139 B8
Parkfield ... 39 A2
Parnacott ... 8 E8
Paul ... 88 C2
Paul's Green ... 90 E8
Paynter's Lane End ... 67 E4
Pelynt ... 62 D5
Penbeagle ... 141 A4
Penberth ... 97 A3
Pencarrow ... 105 D1
Pencuke ... 10 D5
Pendeen ... 75 A1
Pendoggett ... 23 A6
Pendrift ... 24 B1
Penelewey ... 82 C7
Pengegon ... 138 F2
Pengelly ... 14 E2
Pengold ... 10 A5
Penhale
  Indian Queens ... 57 D8
  Millbrook ... 132 D2
  Mullion ... 99 D1
Penhallick ... 139 C4
Penhallow ... 55 B2
Penhalvean ... 80 C4
Penmarth ... 80 C2
Penmayne ... 21 E3
Pennance ... 140 F1

Pennycomequick 148 B4
Pennycross 128 C8
Pennytinney 23 A4
Penpethy 14 F5
Penpillick 60 D7
Penpol 82 B6
Penpoll 61 D5
Penponds 138 B1
Penpont 24 A1
Penrose
  St Breward 24 A3
  St Eval 31 E5
Penryn 144 B7
Pensilva 38 E5
Penstraze 69 A4
Pentewan 73 C6
Pentire 43 D4
Penwartha Coombe 55 B3
Penweathers 69 F2
Penwithick 59 E7
Penzance 143 F5
Percuil 83 A1
Perranarworthal 81 D6
Perrancoombe 55 A3
Perran Downs 89 E5
Perranporth 55 B5
Perranuthnoe 89 D4
Perranwell
  Goonhavern 55 C3
  Perranarworthal 81 C6
Perranzabuloe 55 B3
Peter's Finger 19 C7
Peterville 54 D1
Petherwin Gate 18 B7
Peverell 128 D6
Phillack 142 D7
Philleigh 83 B6
Piece 139 D2
Pillaton 53 B6
Pillatonmill 53 B6
Pipers Pool 17 F3
Pityme 21 F3
Plaidy 117 E5
Plain-an-Gwarry 140 B6
Playing Place 82 B8
Plushabridge 38 F7
Plymouth 148 C1
Plympton 130 E5
Plympton St Maurice 130 E4
Plymstock 135 E6
Point 82 B5
Polbathic 64 F8
Polborder 53 D7
Polbrock 34 A4
Polgigga 96 D4
Polgooth 59 A1
Polkerris 60 E3
Polladras 90 F5
Polmassick 72 E4
Polmear 60 E4
Polmorla 108 A4
Polpeor 77 B3
Polperro 62 E1
Polruan 116 C2
Polscoe 112 E3
Poltesco 103 B5
Polyphant 17 F1
Polzeath 21 E5
Pomphlett 135 E8
Poniou 76 A5
Ponsanooth 81 B5
Ponsharden 144 E7
Ponsongath 103 E7
Pont 61 D3
Pool 139 B5
Porkellis 92 B8
Porteath 22 A6
Port Gaverne 22 E7
Porth 111 C8
Porthallow
  Looe 62 F2
  St Keverne 101 D6
Porthcothan 31 C6
Porthcurno 96 E3
Porthilly 21 D2
Porth Kea 70 B1
Porthleven 98 B8
Porthmeor 75 F4
Porth Navas 93 B2
Porthoustock 101 E4
Porthtowan 68 A6
Portington 29 E3
Port Isaac 22 D8
Portloe 84 B3
Portlooe 117 A2
Portmellon 73 C3
Port Quin 22 B7
Portreath 67 C6
Portscatho 83 B2
Portwrinkle 65 B4
Poughill 4 D2
Poundstock 6 E2
Praa Sands 90 C3
Praze-an-Beeble 79 C2
Prince Rock 129 B1
Probus 71 C6
Pyworthy 8 E5

Q

Quethiock 52 C7
Quintrell Downs 44 E3
Quither 30 A8
Quoit 45 F4

R

Rame
  Cawsand 64 B2
  Stithians 92 E8
Readymoney 116 B3
Reawla 78 E3
Redmonsford 3 F2
Red Post 7 F8
Redruth 140 D5
Rejerrah 55 F7
Releath 91 E8
Relubbus 90 A7
Rescassa 72 F1
Rescorla 59 D8
Reskadinnick 138 B5
Reskivers 71 F3
Restormel 112 C5
Restronguet Passage 82 A4
Resugga Green 59 D7
Rezare 28 E4
Rilla Mill 38 E8
Rinsey 90 D2
Riverside 123 A1
Riviere Towans 142 B7
Roborough 121 D1
Roche 46 F3
Rock 21 D2
Rockhead 14 E3
Roscroggan 138 D7
Rose 55 C5
Rose-an-Grouse 77 D2
Rosecare 10 D6
Rosedinnick 45 E8
Rosehill
  Goonhavern 55 D5
  Lostwithiel 112 C1
Roseland 51 E6
Rosemelling 59 F8
Rosemergy 75 D3
Rosenannon 33 A1
Roserrow 21 E5
Rosevean 47 D1
Rosevear 99 C7
Rosevine 83 B3
Rosewarne 78 F3
Roseworthy
  Camborne 78 F6
  Shortlanesend 69 E6
Roseworthy Barton 78 F6
Roskear Croft 138 E6
Rosudgeon 89 F4
Row 24 B3
Ruan High Lanes 83 E6
Ruan Lanihorne 83 E8
Ruan Major 102 F6
Ruan Minor 103 B5
Ruddlemoor 59 B6
Rumford 32 A5
Rushford 30 A3
Ruthernbridge 34 A1
Ruthvoes 45 F3

S

St Agnes 54 D1
St Agnes Beacon 54 B1
St Allen 56 B1
St Ann's Chapel 40 E6
St Anthony 95 B5
St Anthony-in-Meneage 101 C8
St Austell 114 B5
St Blazey 60 B5
St Blazey Gate 115 F6
St Breock 33 C6
St Breward 24 B3
St Budeaux 123 D2
St Buryan 97 B6
St Cleer 37 F2
St Clement 70 D2
St Clether 17 A3
St Columb Major 45 E6
St Columb Minor 111 E7
St Columb Road 45 D2
St Day 68 E1
St Dennis 58 C8
St Dominick 40 D3
St Endellion 22 D5
St Enoder 57 B7
St Erme 70 E8
St Erney 53 B2
St Erth 142 A1
St Erth Praze 142 F1
St Eval 31 F3
St Ewe 72 E5
St Gennys 10 C8
St Germans 65 A8
St Giles on the Heath 13 E1
St Gluvias 144 D8
St Hilary 89 E6
St Issey 32 E6
St Ive 38 F2
St Ive Cross 39 A1
St Ives 141 C6
St Jidgey 32 F4
St John 132 C8
St Johns 146 A6
St Jude's 149 B3
St Just 86 E6
St Just In Roseland 82 F2
St Keverne 101 C4
St Kew 23 A4
St Kew Highway 23 A2
St Keyne 51 A3
St Lawrence 34 D1
St Levan 96 D3
St Mabyn 34 C8
St Martin
  Looe 117 D7
  Mawgan 100 D6
St Mawes 95 B6
St Mawgan 45 A8
St Mellion 53 E8
St Mellion Pk 53 C8
St Merryn 31 F8
St Mewan 59 A2
St Michael Caerhays 72 D1
St Michael Penkevil 70 F1
St Minver 22 A4
St Neot 36 F2
St Newlyn East 56 C7
St Pinnock 50 D6
St Ruan 103 A4
St Stephen 58 B4
St Stephens
  Launceston 106 A8
  Saltash 122 D2
St Teath 23 E7
St Thomas 106 B6
St Tudy 23 E3
St Veep 61 C6
St Wenn 46 D7
St Winnow 61 A8
Salem 68 F3
Saltash 122 B1
Sampford Spiney 42 E7
Sancreed 87 E4
Sandplace 63 C7
Sandy Bottom 114 F4
Saveock 69 B3
Scarcewater 57 E5
Scorrier 68 D3
Scredda 114 D8
Seaton 64 B5
Sellan 87 E5
Sennen 96 B6
Sennen Cove 96 B7
Seworgan 92 C6
Sheffield 97 F7
Sheviock 65 B6
Shop
  Morwenstow 2 D1
  St Merryn 31 E8
Shortlanesend 69 F6
Shutta 117 D4
Silverwell 68 F7
Sithney 91 B3
Sithney Common 91 C3
Sithney Green 91 C4
Skinners Bottom 68 D5
Sladesbridge 34 A6
Slaughterbridge 105 D7
Southcott 11 A6
Southdown 133 B6
South Hill 39 C7
South Hole 2 D7
South Petherwin 27 E8
South Pill 122 E3
South Tehidy 138 E7
Southway 124 F6
South Wheatley 11 F3
Sparkwell 131 F8
Sparnon 96 F5
Sparnon Gate 67 F4
Splatt
  Rock 21 E3
  Warbstow Cross 17 B7
Spriddlestone 136 C4
Staddiscombe 135 F3
Start 77 E3
Stenalees 59 B8
Stennack 79 D4
Stepaside 58 B5
Stibb 4 D5
Sticker 58 F1
Stithians 80 F3
Stoke 128 A3
Stoke Climsland 28 E1
Stonehouse 128 A1
Stoptide 21 E2
Stourscombe 106 F4
Stowford 5 E8
Stratton 4 E1
Summercourt 57 C7
Swanvale 144 F3
Sydenham Damerel 29 D2

T

Talland 62 F2
Talskiddy 45 E8
Tamerton Foliot 124 B7
Tavistock 147 E5
Temple 36 B8
Tencreek 63 A3
Terras 58 A4
Tetcott 13 C7
The Beacon 10 F6
Thorne Moor 19 F8
Three Burrows 68 F5
Three Hammers 17 C6
Threemilestone 69 D4
Threewaters 34 C1
Thurdon 5 D5
Tideford 52 F2
Tintagel 14 D7
Titson 7 D4
Todpool 68 F2
Tolborough 25 E4
Tolcarne
  Camborne 79 D5
  Newlyn 143 C3
Toldish 45 F2
Tolgus Mount 139 E8
Tolskithy 139 E7
Tolvaddon 138 F6
Tolvaddon Downs 139 A7
Torpoint 127 C3
Tosberry 3 B8
Towan Cross 68 B7
Towednack 76 E5
Townlake 29 C1
Townshend 90 D7
Traboe 100 E4
Tramagenna 105 A1
Trannack 91 D5
Treal 103 A6
Treath 93 C1
Treator 107 A5
Trebarber 44 F5
Trebartha 27 A4
Trebarvah 89 E4
Trebarwith 14 C5
Trebeath 17 F6
Trebetherick 21 D4
Trebudannon 45 C4
Trebullett 28 A5
Treburgett 23 D6
Treburley 28 C4
Treburrick 31 D5
Trebyan 48 C6
Trecrogo 27 E7
Tredavoe 143 A2
Tredethy 34 F6
Tredinnick
  Looe 63 A8
  Penzance 76 A1
  St Issey 32 D5
Tredown 2 E5
Tredrizzick 21 F4
Treen
  Porthcurno 96 F3
  Zennor 75 F4
Treesmill 60 D6
Trefanny Hill 62 D8
Trefofda 24 A8
Trefrew 105 D6
Trefrize 27 E3
Tregadillett 18 C2
Tregajorran 139 D4
Tregamere 45 F7
Tregarland 63 C8
Tregarlandbridge 63 B8
Tregarrick Mill 62 D7
Tregaswith 45 C5
Tregatta 14 C6
Tregavarras 85 A5
Tregeare 17 D5
Tregellist 22 E4
Tregeseal 86 F7
Tregew 145 B8
Tregiskey 73 C5
Tregole 6 E1
Tregolls 80 F3
Tregonce 107 F2
Tregonetha 46 C6
Tregonhawke 132 B4
Tregonna 32 C7
Tregony 71 F4
Tregoodwell 105 F4
Tregorrick 114 D1
Tregoss 46 D3
Tregreenwell 23 F7
Tregrehan Mills 115 D6
Tregune 10 F4
Tregunna 33 B8
Tregurrian 44 E8
Tregustick 33 D1
Trehan 122 A1
Trehunist 52 C6
Trekeivesteps 37 E4
Trekenner 28 B5
Trekenning 45 D5
Treknow 14 C5
Trelan 100 E1
Trelash 10 F1
Treleigh 140 D8
Trelew 82 B2
Treligga 14 C3
Trelights 22 C6
Trelill 23 C5
Treliver 46 E8
Trelyon 141 B3
Tremail 16 B5
Tremar 38 A2
Trematon 53 E2
Tremayne 79 C2
Trembraze 113 D8
Tremethick Cross 88 A5
Tremollett 27 D2
Tremore 47 C7
Trenance
  Newquay 110 E5
  Roche 46 F7
  St Issey 32 D5
  Tregurrian 31 C2
Trenant 37 C3
Trenant Girt 108 C5
Trenarren 73 E7
Trencreek 111 C4
Trencrom 77 B3
Trendeal 57 C3
Trenear 92 A6
Treneere 143 E7
Treneglos 16 F7
Trenerth 78 D2
Trenewan 62 A4
Trengale 37 C2
Trengune 11 A4
Treninnick 111 A4
Trenoweth 93 B8
Trenwheal 90 F7
Trequite 23 B3
Trerise 103 A7
Trerulefoot 52 D2
Tresarrett 35 B8
Tresawle 71 C5
Trescowe 90 B5
Tresillian 70 F5
Tresinney 24 C8
Treskillard 139 C1
Treskinnick Cross 6 F1
Treslothan 79 D4
Tresowes Green 90 D4
Tresowes Hill 90 E4
Tresparrett 10 B2
Tresparrett Posts 10 C4
Treswithian 138 A3
Trethellan 110 C6
Trethevey 14 F8
Trethewey 96 E4
Trethosa 58 A5
Trethowel 114 C6
Trethurgy 59 F6
Trevadlock 27 A6
Trevail 43 D1
Trevalga 9 B1
Trevance 32 E6
Trevanger 21 F4
Trevanson 33 C7
Trevarnon 78 D6
Trevarren 45 E3
Trevarrian 31 C1
Trevarrick 72 F2
Trevarth 80 E7
Treveighan 23 F6
Trevellas 54 F2
Trevelmond 50 D6
Trevemper 110 E2
Treven 14 C6
Trevenning 23 F5
Treverbyn
  Penwithick 59 C7
  St Cleer 37 B2
Treverva 93 B6
Trevescan 96 B5
Trevethoe 77 D3
Trevia 105 B4
Treviades 93 A3
Trevigro 39 C4
Trevilla 82 C6
Trevilson 56 D6
Treviscoe 58 B7
Trevollard 53 D1
Trevone 20 E2
Trevorrick 107 E1
Trevowhan 75 C2
Trew 90 F4
Trewalder 14 E1
Trewarmett 14 D5
Trewassa 15 F5
Trewellard 86 F8
Trewen 17 E2
Trewennack 146 F8
Trewennan 23 E8
Trewetha 22 E7
Trewethern 22 E3
Trewey 76 B5
Trewidland 51 C2
Trewint 10 F8
Trewithian 83 B4
Trewold 9 E1
Trewoodloe 39 B6
Trewoon
  Mullion 99 B2
  St Austell 59 A3
Treworga 83 D7
Treworlas 83 D5
Trewornan 22 C1
Treworrick 37 E3
Treworthal 83 C5
Trezaise 47 A2
Trispen 56 D1
Troan 57 C8
Troon 79 E5
Truro 137 E3
Truscott 18 D4
Truthan 56 C2
Truthwall
  Marazion 89 D7
  St Just 86 E7
Trythogga 143 F8
Tubbs Mill 72 D2
Tuckermarsh 41 B2
Tuckingmill
  Camborne 139 A4
  St Breward 24 B4
Turfdown 48 E8
Turnchapel 135 B7
Tutwell 29 A2
Twelveheads 69 B1
Two Burrows 68 E5
Tywardreath 60 E5

U

Underwood 130 C5
United Downs 81 A8
Upcott 2 F4

Upton
Bude 104 C2
Upton Cross. 38 C7
Upton Cross 38 D6
Upton Towans 78 B6

V

Valley Truckle 105 C2
Vellanoweth 89 A8
Venterdon 28 D2
Ventongimps 55 C2
Ventonleague. 142 F7
Veryan 83 F6
Veryan Green 83 F7
Victoria
Lostwithiel. 112 B2
Roche. 46 F4
Vogue 68 D1

W

Wadebridge 108 A6
Wainhouse Corner 10 E6
Walkhampton. 42 D4
Wall. 78 E3
Wanson 6 F3
Warbstow 11 B1
Warbstow Cross 11 B2
Warleggan. 36 C4
Warleigh Barton 123 F8
Washaway 34 C4
Watergate 24 E8
Waterloo 35 D7
Wearde. 122 F2
Week Green 11 E8
Week St Mary 11 E8
Welcombe. 2 D5
Welsford 3 C8
Wembury. 136 B1

Wendron 91 F6
Wenfordbridge 24 A2
Wenmouth Cross. 37 A3
Werrington 18 F6
West Blackdown 30 F8
West Curry 12 D4
Westdowns 14 C1
West Hoe 148 B1
West Looe 117 C3
Weston Mill. 127 E8
West Panson. 13 D2
West Park 124 A3
West Pentire. 43 C3
West Portholland 84 D5
West Taphouse 49 E6
West Tolgus 139 D8
West Watergate. 62 E4
West Youlstone 3 B2
Wheal Alfred 142 F4
Wheal Busy 68 F3
Wheal Frances 55 D3

Wheal Rose. 68 C3
Wheal Vor 91 A5
Wherry Town 143 D4
Whipsiderry 44 C6
Whitchurch. 147 D3
Whitecross
Crowlas 77 C1
Wadebridge. 33 B7
White Cross
Mullion. 99 B4
St Columb Road. 45 C2
Whitehill 146 C4
Whitemoor 58 E8
Whiterock 108 A5
Whitewell 23 D7
Whitleigh 124 C5
Whitstone 7 F1
Widegates 63 F8
Widemouth Bay 6 F5
Widewell 125 B7
Wilminstone 30 F3

Windmill 20 F1
Witheven 11 D3
Withiel 47 A8
Withielgoose Mills 47 C8
Withnoe 132 A4
Woodford
Plymouth 130 C7
Shop. 4 D8
Woolley 3 A3
Woolston 38 E3
Woolwell 125 D7
Wringsdown 18 E6

Y

Yelverton. 42 D3
Yeolmbridge. 18 F6

Index of streets, hospitals, industrial estates, railway stations, schools, shopping centres, universities and places of interest

154 Abb–Bal

A

Abbey Cl PL20 42 B2
Abbey Ct
10 Penzance TR18 143 E5
Plymouth PL1 149 A2
Abbey Hill TR26 77 E3
Abbey Mdw TR26 77 E4
Abbeymead Mews PL19 147 C5
Abbey Mews PL31 109 C4
Abbey Pl
Plymouth PL1 148 C2
Tavistock PL19 147 C5
Abbey Rise PL19 147 C5
Abbey St TR18 143 E5
Abbotsbury Way PL2 127 F8
Abbots Cl PL31 109 F4
Abbotscourt La PL11 126 A2
Abbotsfield Cl PL19 41 D8
Abbotsfield Cres PL19 41 D8
Abbotts Rd PL3 128 E6
Aberdeen Ave PL5 124 D1
Aberdeen Cl PL24 60 B6
Aberfal Ho 1 TR11 145 C3
Abingdon Rd 1 PL4 149 A4
Abney Cres PL6 125 B6
Abscott La PL9 135 C5
Acacia Rd TR11 144 F5
Academy Terr 30 TR26 141 B6
Acklington Pl PL5 123 E4
Acland Cl EX23 104 E7
Acland Gdns TR7 110 D6
Acorn Dr PL25 115 A3
Acre Cotts PL1 127 F3
Acre Pl PL1 127 F3
Adams Cl
Plymouth PL5 123 F1
Torpoint PL11 126 F3
Adams Cres PL11 126 E3
Adams Row TR16 68 D3
Addington N PL14 113 D6
Addington S PL14 113 D6
Addison Rd PL4 149 A4
Addison Terr PL22 112 C2
Adelaide La PL1 148 A2
Adelaide Pl PL1 148 A3
Adelaide Rd TR15 140 C4
Adelaide St
Camborne TR14 138 E3
Penzance TR18 143 E6
2 Plymouth, Ford PL2 127 F5
Plymouth PL1 148 A3
Adelaide Street Ope PL1 148 A3
Adelaide Terr TR1 137 B4
Adela Rd PL11 127 A3
Adit La
Newlyn TR18 143 C1
Saltash PL12 122 E3
Adits The PL18 41 A3
Admiral's Hard PL1 134 A8
Admirals Quay 4 TR11 145 B5
Admiralty Cotts PL1 134 A7
Admiralty Ct PL13 117 D3
Admiralty Rd
Plymouth, Millbay PL1 134 A8
Plymouth, St Budeaux PL5 123 C2
Admiralty St
Plymouth, Keyham PL2 127 E6
Plymouth, Millbay PL1 134 A8
Admiralty Terr TR2 83 B2
African Row TR14 79 B5
Agar Cres TR15 139 D6
Agar Ct
2 Camborne TR15 139 C6
Truro TR1 137 D5
Agar Mdws 11 TR3 81 F7
Agar Rd
Camborne TR15 139 D6
Newquay TR7 110 E5
St Austell PL25 114 E6
Truro TR1 137 E5
Agar Terr 12 PL31 109 D5
Agar Way TR15 139 C5
Agaton Rd PL5 123 E3
Agnes Cl EX23 104 F4
Ainslie Terr PL2 127 E7
Aire Gdns PL3 129 B5
Alamein Ct PL12 122 E2
Alamein Rd PL12 122 D2
Alan Harvey Cl 14 TR26 77 A6
Alan Rd PL28 107 D4
Alansmere Ct TR2 57 A1
Alanta Flats TR7 110 B5
Albany Cl TR5 68 D8
Albany Ct
4 Newquay TR7 110 F6
Redruth TR15 140 D3
Albany Gdns TR15 140 C3
Albany La TR15 140 C4
Albany Pl TR11 145 A3
Albany Rd
Falmouth TR11 145 A3
5 Newquay TR7 110 F6
Redruth TR15 140 C4
Truro TR1 137 A4
Albany St PL1 127 E2
Albany Terr TR26 141 B4
Albemarle Villas PL1 127 F3
Albert Bldgs 20 TR18 143 E6
Albert Cotts TR11 145 B4
Albertha Cl PL4 149 B4
Albert Pl
Camborne TR14 138 E3
21 St Ives TR26 141 B5
Truro TR1 137 C3
Albert Rd
Plymouth PL2 127 F3
Saltash PL12 123 A2
St Austell PL25 114 D3
St Ives TR26 141 B5
Albert St
Camborne TR14 138 E3
Penzance TR18 143 F6
Albert Terr
Gunnislake PL18 40 F5
Lostwithiel PL22 112 C2
19 Penzance TR18 143 E6
26 St Ives TR26 141 B5
Albertus Dr TR27 142 B3
Albertus Gdns TR27 142 B3
Albertus Rd TR27 142 B3
Albert Villas PL2 127 E4
Albion Ct PL11 127 B3
Albion Dr PL2 128 B7
Albion Rd
Helston TR13 146 B4
Torpoint PL11 127 B3
Albion Row TR16 80 F8
Alcester Cl PL2 127 E4
Alcester St PL2 127 F4
Alden Wlk PL6 129 B7
Aldercombe La EX23 5 A6
Alderney Rd PL6 124 F7
Alder Rd PL19 147 C3
Aldersley Wlk PL6 125 A1
Aldreath Cl TR20 88 B7
Aldreath Rd TR20 88 B7
Alexander Ct
14 Carnon Downs TR3 81 F7
Gorran Haven PL26 85 D5
Alexandra Cl
5 Illogan TR16 67 E4
Plymouth PL9 136 B8
St Ives TR26 77 A7
Alexandra Ct TR7 111 C8
Alexandra Dr PL20 41 C1
Alexandra Gdns TR18 143 D4
Alexandra Ho TR18 143 D3
Alexandra Pl
Penzance TR18 143 D4
5 Plymouth PL4 128 E4
St Ives TR26 77 A7
Alexandra Rd
Bodmin PL31 109 B5
Illogan TR16 67 D4
Newquay TR7 111 C8
Penzance TR18 143 D4
Plymouth, Crownhill PL6 124 F2
Plymouth, Ford PL2 127 F5
Plymouth, Mutley PL4 128 F4
St Austell PL25 114 E3
St Ives TR26 77 A7
Alexandra Sq PL12 123 A2
Alexandra Terr
Mount Hawke TR4 68 C6
Penzance TR18 143 D3
Plymouth PL2 127 F5
St Ives TR26 141 A5
Tremar PL14 38 A4
2 Truro TR1 137 B4
Alford Cl EX23 104 F5
Alfred Pl PL2 127 F5
Alfred Rd PL2 127 F5
Alfred St PL1 148 C2
Alger Wlk PL6 124 E6
Alice La 7 PL1 148 B3
Alice St PL1 148 A3
Alldritt Cl TR7 111 D7
Allenby Rd PL2 128 A6
Allendale PL26 58 E8
Allendale Rd PL4 149 A4
Allen Pk PL30 23 B2
Allen Vale PL14 113 A5
Allern La PL5 120 D1
Allerton Wlk PL6 129 B7
Alley Hill PL20 42 A1
Alleyn Gdns PL3 128 E8
Allium Ct TR4 70 D8
All Saints Pk PL18 40 E5
Alma Cl TR5 68 D8
Alma Cotts PL4 149 B2
Alma Pl
Heamoor TR18 143 C7
Newquay TR7 110 D6
Padstow PL28 107 D5
5 Penzance TR18 143 E5
Redruth TR15 140 B5
Alma Rd
Plymouth PL3 128 C4
Truro TR1 69 F3
Alma St PL4 149 B2
Alma Terr
Carharrack TR16 80 F8
Gunnislake PL18 41 A6
Penzance TR18 143 E5
10 St Ives TR26 141 B5
Almeria Ct PL7 130 D4
Almond Dr PL7 131 B6
Almshouse Hill TR13 146 B5
Altarnun Com Prim Sch
PL15 26 C7
Alton Pl PL4 128 E4
Alton Rd PL4 149 A4
Alverne Bldgs 7 TR18 143 D5
Alverton Com Prim Sch
TR18 143 C4
Alverton Ct TR1 137 E5
Alverton Ho TR18 143 C5
Alverton Rd TR18 143 D5
Alverton St TR18 143 E5
Alverton Terr
4 Penzance TR18 143 D5
Truro TR1 137 D5
Alvington St PL4 149 C2
Alwin Pk PL6 125 A5
Alwyn Cl TR7 111 E6
Amacre Dr PL9 135 B6
Amados Cl PL7 130 B4
Amados Dr PL7 130 C4
Amados Rise PL7 130 C4
Amal An Avon TR27 142 E7
Amanda Way PL14 38 E4
Amble Rd 26 PL17 39 F4
Ambrose Ct TR15 140 E7
Amelia Cl TR2 71 C6
Amherst Rd PL3 148 B4
Amherst Road La E PL3 148 B4
Amity Pl PL4 149 A4
Anderton Cl PL19 147 E1
Anderton Ct PL19 147 E2
Anderton La PL19 147 D2
Anderton Rise PL10 132 F4
Andrewartha Rd TR10 144 B8
Andrew Pl 3 TR1 137 C4
Andrew's Terr TR16 139 F1
Andrews Way PL12 53 E5
Andurn Cl PL9 136 B6
Aneray Rd TR14 138 D4
Angarrack La TR27 78 D5
Angarrack Mews TR27 78 C5
Angavran Mdw TR8 55 D8
Angel Hill 7 PL15 106 C6
An Gof Gdns PL31 109 C4
Angwin Ave 4 TR5 54 C1
Anjardyn Pl PL24 60 C5
Ankervis La TR16 140 F1
Annear Rd TR10 144 A6
Ann's Pl PL3 128 A4
Anson Ho 1 PL1 148 B3
Anson Pl
Plymouth, Devonport
PL2 127 F4
Plymouth, St Jude's PL4 149 C3
Anson Rd PL27 31 F3
Anson Way TR13 146 D4
Anstis St
Plymouth PL1 148 A3
Plymouth PL1 148 B3
Anthony Cl EX23 4 C3
Anthony Lowen PL28 107 D4
Anthony Pk PL19 147 D6
Anthony Rd TR7 110 E4
Antoine Cl 4 TR18 143 C2
Antoine Terr 23 TR18 143 C2
Antony CE Sch PL11 65 E5
Antony Gdns PL2 128 C8
Antony Hill PL11 65 E5
Antony House★ PL11 126 D5
Antony Rd PL11 127 B3
Antony Woodland Gdn★
PL11 126 D6
Antron Hill TR10 81 B1
Antron La TR10 93 C8
Antron Way TR10 93 C8
Anvil Ct
Camelford PL32 105 D3
Venterdon PL17 28 D1
Anvil Rd PL32 105 D4
An Vownder Goth TR13 91 B7
Anwyl Cl PL1 148 B3
Anzac Ave PL5 124 A4
Appin Gdns TR15 139 C7
Appleby Wlk PL5 124 D4
Appleton Tor Cl PL3 129 F5
Appletree La PL25 115 D3
Apsley Rd PL4 128 D4
Arbour The PL6 124 E5
Arcade The 6 TR18 143 E5
Arcadia PL9 136 D6
Arcadia Rd PL9 136 C6
Archbishop Benson CE Prim
Sch TR1 137 D6
Archer Pl PL1 148 B4
Archer Terr PL1 148 B3
Arch Hill TR1 137 C2
Arch La TR27 77 D1
Archway Ave PL4 129 B3
Arden Gr PL2 128 C8
Arena Cres PL25 115 B4
Argal & College Water
Park★ TR10, TR11 93 C7
Argal View TR10 93 B6
Arimoor Gdns PL19 147 E5
Ark Royal Cl PL5 127 D8
Arkwright Gdns PL5 123 F2
Arley Cl PL6 125 B6
Arlington Rd PL4 128 F4
Armada Ct PL19 147 B4
Armada Ctr PL1 148 C3
Armada Rd PL10 133 A1
Armada St PL4 149 A4
Armada Way
Plymouth PL1 148 C2
Plymouth PL1 148 C3
Armchair Cnr PL31 109 C5
Arnheim Terr TR11 145 B7
Arnison Cl PL9 135 F5
Arnold's Point PL4 129 C3
Arnside Cl PL6 125 D3
Arrallas Barns TR2 57 B4
Arscott Gdns PL9 135 C5
Arscott La PL9 135 D5
Art Gallery Terr TR18 143 C3
Arthurian Centre The★
PL32 105 D8
Arthur Terr PL11 127 B2
Artillery Pl PL4 149 B1
Arun Cl PL3 129 C5
Arundel Cres PL1 148 B4
Arundel Terr TR27 78 D6
Arundell Cl PL16 19 F4
Arundell Gdns
Falmouth TR11 144 E6
Lifton PL16 19 F4
Arundell Pl TR1 137 C3
Arundell Pk TR27 78 D6
Arundel Terr
Bude EX23 104 D4
Plymouth PL2 127 F4
Arundel Way
Connor Downs TR27 78 D6
Newquay TR7 111 B7
Arundle Cl PL26 58 C8
Arwenack Ave TR11 145 C3
Arwenack Ho 4 TR11 145 C3
Arwenack St TR11 145 C4
Arworthal Mdws TR3 81 D6
Arwyn Cotts 6 TR11 145 C3
Arwyn Pl 7 TR11 145 C3
Asdally Vale TR18 143 B5
Ashburgh Parc PL12 122 B3
Ashburnham Rd PL5 124 A3
Ashbury Cl PL14 113 D7
Ash Cl
16 Par PL24 60 B4
7 Yelverton PL20 42 C3
Ashcombe Cl PL7 130 C7
Ashdown Cl
Plymouth PL6 125 E3
Sticker PL26 58 E1
Ashdown Wlk PL6 125 E3
Ash Dr TR27 142 B3
Ashery Dr PL9 135 C6
Ashfield Gdns TR11 144 E6
Ashfield Rd TR11 144 F6
Ashfield Villas TR11 144 F6
Ashford Cl PL3 129 A4
Ashford Cres PL3 129 A4
Ashford Hill PL4 129 A4
Ashford Rd PL4 128 F4
Ash Gr
Hayle TR27 142 B3
Par PL24 60 B4
Plymouth PL2 127 F7
Ashleigh Cl PL5 124 C7
Ashleigh La PL5 120 D1
Ashleigh Way
Plymouth PL7 131 C4
Probus TR2 71 D6
Ashley Cl 9 PL26 59 D7
Ashley Rd
Shortlanesend TR4 69 F6
Truro TR1 137 C4
Ashmead TR2 57 E1
Ashridge Gdns PL5 124 B2
Ashton Cl PL6 125 C6
Ashton Ct TR7 111 D6
Ashton Way PL12 122 D3
Ashton Wlk EX23 6 F5
Ashtree Cl PL6 125 D7
Ashtree Gr PL9 136 C8
Ash Vale PL16 19 F4
Ashwood Cl PL7 131 B5
Ashwood Park Rd PL7 131 C6
Aspen Cl PL19 147 C3
Aspen Gdns PL7 131 B5
Astor Dr PL4 129 C3
Astwood Developments
PL13 63 F8
Athelstan Pk PL31 109 F3
Athenaeum La PL1 148 B2
Athenaeum Pl PL1 148 C2
Athenaeum St PL1 148 B2
Atherton Pl PL2 127 E4
Athlone Ho PL1 148 A2
Atlanta PL28 20 E2
Atlantic Cl
Camborne TR14 138 E2
Treknow PL34 14 C5
Widemouth Bay EX23 6 F5
Atlantic Coast Cvn Pk
TR27 66 B1
Atlantic Cres TR19 96 C7
Atlantic Mews
New Polzeath PL27 21 D6
8 St Agnes TR5 54 D1
Atlantic Rd
Delabole PL33 14 D2
Newquay TR7 110 C6
Tintagel PL34 14 C7
Atlantic Terr
Camborne TR14 138 E2
New Polzeath PL27 21 D6
Atlantic Terr *continued*
43 St Ives TR26 141 B6
Trevone PL28 20 E2
Atlantic Way
Porthtowan TR4 68 A6
4 Tintagel PL34 14 C7
Attenborrow Ct TR7 111 C8
Attery View PL15 18 E6
Atwell Farm Cvn Pk PL30 48 A1
Auckland Rd 3 PL2 128 A5
Audierne TR10 144 C7
Austin Ave PL2 128 A6
Austin Cres PL6 125 C1
Austin Farm Prim Sch
PL6 129 C7
Automobilia Motor Mus★
PL26 58 A4
Ava PL26 73 C4
Avallen Cl TR11 82 A3
Avent Wlk PL7 130 F7
Avenue Rd TR11 145 C3
Avenue The
St Hilary TR20 89 F6
Truro TR1 137 D5
Avery's Row PL28 107 D5
Avery Terr PL22 112 C2
Avery Way PL12 122 C5
Avon Cl
Plymouth PL3 129 D6
St Austell PL25 115 A5
Avondale Rd TR1 137 B4
Avon Flats TR7 111 C7
Avrack Cl TR19 87 F3
Axe Cl PL3 129 D6
Axford Hill PL17 39 F2
Axtown La PL20 42 C2
Aycliffe Gdns PL7 131 A3
Aylesbury Cres PL5 124 B5
Aylmer Pl 13 PL25 114 C3
Aylmer Sq 14 PL25 114 C3
Aylwin Cl PL7 130 E6
Ayr Ct 1 TR26 141 A5
Ayreville Rd PL2 128 B7
Ayr La TR26 141 B6
Ayr Terr TR26 141 A6
Aysshton Gdns 15 PL17 39 F4

B

Babbacombe Cl PL6 129 E8
Baber Cl PL12 40 C2
Baber Ct PL12 40 D2
Babis Farm Cl PL12 122 F1
Babis Farm Ct PL12 122 F1
Babis Farm Mews PL12 122 F2
Babis Farm Row PL12 122 F1
Babis Farm Way PL12 122 F2
Babis La PL12 122 F1
Baby Beach La PL27 21 D6
Back Hill
Port Isaac PL29 22 D7
Saltash PL12 122 D2
Back La
Angarrack TR27 78 C5
Callington PL17 39 F4
Marazion TR17 89 B5
Plymouth PL7 130 E4
St Erth TR27 77 D2
17 St Ives TR26 141 B6
Tintagel PL34 14 D7
Tregony TR2 71 F4
Veryan TR2 83 F6
Back La W TR15 140 B4
Back Quay TR1 137 D4
Back Rd PL18 41 A3
Back Rd E 7 TR26 141 B6
Back Rd W TR26 141 B6
Back St 42 TR26 141 B6
Badger's Cross TR20 88 E8
Badgers Wlk PL12 122 D4
Badger View PL9 135 E5
Bagbury Rd EX23 104 E3
Bag La
Polbathic PL12 64 F8
St Germans PL12 65 A8
Bahavella Dr TR26 141 B4
Bailey Gdns EX22 8 A5
Baileys La 20 TR26 141 B6
Bailey Terr EX22 8 A5
Bainbridge Ave PL3 128 F7
Bainbridge Ct PL7 130 E7
Baines Hill TR16 67 C6
Bakehouse La 12 PL17 39 E4
Bakehouse The TR10 144 D7
Bake Lane End PL12 52 D1
Bakers Cl PL7 131 C5
Bakers Ct TR7 110 E6
Bakers Gn PL25 115 B4
Bakers Pl PL1 127 F1
Bakers Row TR13 90 F3
Balcoath TR16 68 D1
Baldhu Row TR20 76 F2
Balfield Rd 15 TR13 98 C8
Balfour Terr PL2 127 E4
Bal-Jinjy Cl 19 PL24 60 B4
Balkin Way TR15 139 D7
Ballard Cl TR16 80 B5
Ballard Est TR16 80 B5
Ball Terr PL27 108 E7
Balmoral Ave PL2 127 F5
Balmoral Pl 3 TR15 140 B5

Balmoral Terr 4 TR15 . . 140 B5
Balnoon Flats TR26 . . 77 A4
Bal Rd TR13 . . 91 E4
Bambry Cl TR20 . . 89 E5
Bampflyde Way PL6 . . 124 D6
Bampfylde Way
  Goldsithney TR20 . . 89 F5
  Plymouth PL6 . . 124 E6
Bampton Rd PL6 . . 125 E1
Band House La PL26 . . 59 C7
Bangors Est EX23 . . 6 F2
Bangors Rd PL15 . . 18 E2
Bank Cotts 6 TR10 . . 144 C7
Bank Pl TR11 . . 145 C3
Bank Sq TR19 . . 86 F6
Bank St
  Newquay TR7 . . 110 D6
  St Columb Major TR9 . . 45 E6
Bannawell Ct PL19 . . 147 B6
Bannawell St PL19 . . 147 B6
Banns Rd TR4 . . 68 C6
Baptist Hill TR27 . . 142 C6
Baptist St PL17 . . 41 A3
Bara Pl PL17 . . 39 F6
Barbara Hepworth Mus & Sculpture Gdn★ TR26 . . 141 B6
Barbican App PL4 . . 149 B2
Barbican Cl
  Helston TR13 . . 146 D8
  Looe PL13 . . 117 D4
Barbican Ct
  Looe PL13 . . 117 D5
  12 Plymouth PL4 . . 149 A2
Barbican Hill PL13 . . 117 D4
Barbican La TR18 . . 143 F4
Barbican Leisure Pk PL4 149 C2
Barbican Rd
  Looe PL13 . . 117 E6
  Plymouth PL7 . . 130 E4
Barbican Rise Ind Est PL13 . . 117 E5
Barbican The PL1 . . 149 A2
Barbican Theatre PL1 . . 149 A1
Barbican Way TR13 . . 91 E4
Barbury Cres PL6 . . 125 B8
Barcote Wlk PL6 . . 129 C8
Bardsey Cl PL6 . . 125 A7
Baring St PL4 . . 149 B4
Barker's Hill PL12 . . 122 C1
Barkhouse La PL25 . . 115 B2
Bar La
  Connor Downs TR27 . . 78 C6
  Falmouth TR11 . . 145 C3
Barlandhu 17 TR18 . . 143 C2
Barlanwick TR18 . . 143 B4
Barley Market St PL19 . . 147 C6
Barlowena TR14 . . 138 D1
Barlow Gdns PL2 . . 128 B7
Bar Mdws TR1 . . 70 D2
Barnaloft 13 TR26 . . 141 B6
Barn Cl
  Plymouth PL7 . . 131 D4
  Wainhouse Corner EX23 . . 10 F6
Barncoose Ind Est TR15 . 139 E5
Barncoose La TR15 . . 139 E6
Barncoose Terr TR15 . . 139 E6
Barn Crtyd TR27 . . 78 D6
Barndale Cres PL6 . . 125 B6
Barne Barton Prim Sch PL5 . . 127 D8
Barne Cl PL5 . . 127 C8
Barnecut Cl 6 PL14 . . 38 A3
Barne La PL5 . . 123 D1
Barne Rd PL5 . . 127 C8
Barnfield Dr PL7 . . 131 C5
Barnfield Gdns TR18 . . 88 E6
Barnfield Pk EX23 . . 4 E1
Barnfield Terr
  3 Indian Queens TR9 . . 45 E1
  Liskeard PL14 . . 113 B4
Barn Hill
  Cadgwith TR12 . . 103 B4
  Polbathic PL12 . . 64 F8
  Tideford PL12 . . 52 F1
Barningham Gdns PL6 . . 125 B6
Barn La
  Bodmin PL31 . . 109 C4
  18 St Columb Major TR9 . . 45 E6
Barn Meadow Pk PL13 . . 117 B2
Barnoon Hill TR26 . . 141 B6
Barnoon Terr 29 TR26 . . 141 B6
Barn Park La PL31 . . 35 B2
Barnpark Rd PL35 . . 9 C1
Barn Park Rd PL3 . . 128 D6
Barn Pk
  Lostwithiel PL22 . . 112 E2
  Saltash PL12 . . 122 F3
Barn St PL14 . . 113 C5
Barnstaple Cl PL6 . . 129 E7
Barns Terr PL12 . . 118 A3
Barnwood Cl PL9 . . 135 E5
Baron Ct PL15 . . 17 D5
Barons Mdw PL31 . . 109 F5
Barons Rd PL20 . . 42 E3
Barossa Rd PL11 . . 127 B3
Barrack La TR1 . . 137 D3
Barrack Pl PL1 . . 128 A1
Barrack's La TR16 . . 68 E1
Barrack St PL1 . . 127 E2
Barras Cross PL14 . . 113 C6
Barras Pl PL14 . . 113 C6
Barras St PL14 . . 113 C6
Bar Rd
  Falmouth TR11 . . 145 C3
  Mawnan Smith TR11 . . 93 C2
Barrepta Cl TR26 . . 141 D1
Barrie Cres PL31 . . 109 E2
Barripper Rd
  Camborne TR14 . . 138 C1
  Penponds TR14 . . 79 C5
Barrow Down PL12 . . 122 B3
Barr's Cl PL23 . . 116 D5
Barry's La PL28 . . 107 D5
Bar Terr 8 TR11 . . 145 C3
Bartholomew Rd PL2 . . 128 B5
Bartles Cl TR12 . . 99 D7
Bartles Ind Est TR15 . . 140 B6
Bartles Row TR14 . . 139 A5
Barton Ave PL2 . . 127 E5
Barton Cl
  11 Bodmin PL31 . . 109 D5
  Heamoor TR18 . . 143 D7
  Helston TR13 . . 146 D7
  Landrake PL12 . . 53 C3
  Plymouth PL7 . . 131 C5
Barton Ct PL26 . . 58 A7
Barton La TR9 . . 45 D1
Barton Mdw
  Pelynt PL13 . . 62 D6
  Truro TR1 . . 137 A5
Barton Mdws PL12 . . 53 B7
Barton Mews
  Landrake PL12 . . 53 C3
  Millbrook PL10 . . 132 F6
Barton Rd
  Plymouth PL9 . . 135 B6
  St Dennis PL26 . . 58 A7
Barton The PL29 . . 22 D6
Barview La TR27 . . 142 C4
Barwis Hill TR18 . . 143 E6
Barwis Terr 1 TR18 . . 143 E6
Basinghall Cl PL9 . . 135 E5
Basket Ope PL4 . . 149 A2
Basset Rd TR14 . . 138 D2
Basset St
  Camborne TR14 . . 138 D2
  Falmouth TR11 . . 145 A5
  Redruth TR15 . . 140 C4
Bassett Cl PL26 . . 47 A1
Bassett Pl 11 TR11 . . 145 A5
Bassett Rd
  Illogan TR16 . . 67 E4
  Redruth TR15 . . 140 B8
Bassett Terr TR16 . . 67 D6
Bastville EX22 . . 11 E8
Bath La PL1 . . 148 B2
Bath Pl PL1 . . 148 B2
Bath Pl W PL1 . . 148 B2
Bath St PL1 . . 148 B2
Battershall Cl PL9 . . 135 F5
Batter St PL4 . . 149 A2
Battery Hill TR16 . . 67 C6
Battery La
  Polruan PL23 . . 116 C2
  Tavistock PL19 . . 147 C4
Battery Mill La TR27 . . 77 E1
Battery Pk PL23 . . 116 C2
Battery Rd TR18 . . 143 F4
Battery St PL1 . . 148 A2
Battery Street Flats PL1 . 148 A2
Battery Terr PL26 . . 73 C3
Battery The TR7 . . 110 D7
Battisford Pk PL7 . . 131 E3
Bawden Rd PL31 . . 109 B3
Bay Apartments TR7 . . 110 A6
Bay Ct TR11 . . 145 C2
Baydon Cl PL6 . . 125 C1
Bay Down PL13 . . 117 D5
Bayly's Rd PL9 . . 135 B7
Baynards Cl 1 TR1 . . 137 D4
Baynes Cl 3 PL14 . . 38 A3
Bay Rd PL28 . . 20 F2
Bay St PL13 . . 117 D3
Bayswater Rd PL1 . . 148 B4
Bay The PL13 . . 117 D3
Baytree Cl PL6 . . 125 D6
Bay Tree Cotts 3 EX23 . . 4 D1
Baytree Gdns PL2 . . 128 A7
Baytree Hill PL14 . . 113 C5
Bayview 11 PL24 . . 60 C4
Bay View Cres TR11 . . 145 D3
Bayview Dr PL13 . . 117 E4
Bayview Ho TR27 . . 142 A8
Bay View Pk PL25 . . 114 F6
Bay View Rd PL13 . . 117 D4
Bay View Terr
  Budock Water TR11 . . 144 C1
  Hayle TR27 . . 142 C6
  26 Newlyn TR18 . . 143 C2
  Newquay TR7 . . 110 E5
  Penzance TR18 . . 143 D4
  13 Porthleven TR13 . . 98 B8
Bay Villas TR20 . . 88 F6
Beach Ct TR26 . . 141 C6
Beachfield Ave TR7 . . 110 D6
Beachfield Ct TR18 . . 143 D4
Beach Hill PL11 . . 64 C4
Beach La 12 TR6 . . 55 A5
Beach Rd
  Carbis Bay TR26 . . 141 D2
  Crantock TR8 . . 43 D3
  Mevagissey PL26 . . 73 C4
  Newquay TR7 . . 110 D6
  Perranporth TR6 . . 55 A5
  Porthtowan TR4 . . 68 A6
  St Austell PL25 . . 115 D3
  St Ives TR26 . . 141 A6
  Trevone PL28 . . 20 F2
Beachside Ct TR4 . . 68 A6
Beachside L Pk TR27 . . 78 A6
Beach View Cl TR7 . . 111 C7
Beachview Flats TR4 . . 68 A6
Beach Wlk TR7 . . 111 C7
Beacon Cl
  Falmouth TR11 . . 145 A5
Beacon Cl *continued*
  St Austell PL25 . . 115 A5
Beacon Com Jun Sch TR11 . . 145 A5
Beacon Cross PL26 . . 72 F4
Beacon Down Ave PL2 . . 128 B7
Beacon Dr TR5 . . 54 B1
Beacon Est TR20 . . 87 D4
Beacon Farm TR5 . . 54 C1
Beaconfield Rd PL2 . . 128 B7
Beacon Fields TR14 . . 138 E2
Beacon Hill PL31 . . 109 D4
Beacon Hill Mews 9 PL31 . . 109 D5
Beacon Ho PL3 . . 129 D4
Beacon Inf Sch TR11 . . 145 A5
Beacon Inf Sch The PL31 . . 109 D4
Beacon Lanes PL31 . . 109 D3
Beacon Parc TR13 . . 146 C6
Beacon Park Rd PL2 . . 128 B7
Beacon Pk
  Boyton PL15 . . 13 A2
  Pelynt PL13 . . 62 D5
Beacon Rd
  Bodmin PL31 . . 109 E3
  Falmouth TR11 . . 145 A5
  Foxhole PL26 . . 58 D5
  Marazion TR17 . . 89 B5
  Newquay TR7 . . 110 D7
  Porthleven TR13 . . 98 B8
  St Agnes TR5 . . 54 C1
  Summercourt TR8 . . 57 B7
Beacons PL13 . . 62 E5
Beaconsfield Pl 2 TR5 . . 54 C1
Beaconsfield Terr PL31 . 109 C5
Beaconside
  Foxhole PL26 . . 58 D5
  Summercourt TR8 . . 57 B7
Beacon Sq TR14 . . 138 F1
Beacon St TR11 . . 145 B5
Beacon Terr
  Camborne TR14 . . 138 E1
  5 Falmouth TR11 . . 145 A5
  Foxhole PL26 . . 58 D5
  Helston TR13 . . 146 C6
  Lizard TR12 . . 102 F2
Beacon The TR11 . . 145 A5
Beacon View TR4 . . 55 B2
Beacon View Pk 23 TR16 . 67 E4
Bealswood Cl PL18 . . 41 A6
Bealswood Rd PL18 . . 41 A6
Beam Rd PL26 . . 47 C1
Beam Terr PL26 . . 47 B1
Beam Villas PL30 . . 47 D5
Beare Cl PL9 . . 135 B5
Bearsdown Cl PL6 . . 129 C8
Bearsdown Rd PL6 . . 129 C8
Bears Terr TR16 . . 80 E7
Beatrice Ave
  Plymouth, Keyham PL2 . . 127 E5
  Plymouth, St Jude's PL4 . . 149 B3
  Saltash PL12 . . 122 E2
Beatrice Gdns PL12 . . 122 E1
Beatrice Rd PL31 . . 48 D8
Beatrice Terr TR27 . . 142 D7
Beattie Rd PL5 . . 127 B8
Beatty Cl PL6 . . 125 A4
Beauchamp Cres PL2 . . 128 C7
Beauchamp Rd PL2 . . 128 C7
Beauchamps Mdw TR15 . 140 D2
Beaudyn Wlk 5 PL6 . . 129 C7
Beaufighter Ave PL27 . . 31 F3
Beaufort Ave 8 PL27 . . 31 F3
Beaufort Ho 21 PL4 . . 149 A2
Beauly Cl PL7 . . 131 A5
Beaumaris Gdns PL3 . . 128 F8
Beaumaris Rd PL3 . . 128 F7
Beaumont Ave PL4 . . 149 A3
Beaumont Pl PL4 . . 149 A3
Beaumont Rd PL4 . . 149 B3
Beaumont St PL2 . . 128 A5
Beaumont Terr PL12 . . 122 F4
Beck Adams PL12 . . 53 C3
Beckett Cl TR15 . . 140 C4
Beckford Cl PL7 . . 131 A5
Beckham Pl PL3 . . 129 A6
Beckly Ct PL1 . . 148 C3
Bede Gdns PL5 . . 124 C1
Bede Haven Cl EX23 . . 104 E4
Bederkesa Ct PL31 . . 109 D4
Bedford Cl PL18 . . 40 F6
Bedford Mews PL4 . . 149 A4
Bedford Park Villas PL4 . 149 A4
Bedford Pk
  10 Bere Alston PL20 . . 41 B1
  Plymouth PL4 . . 149 A4
Bedford Pl
  6 Bere Alston PL20 . . 41 B1
  6 St Ives TR26 . . 141 B5
Bedford Rd
  Horrabridge PL20 . . 42 C4
  Plymouth PL9 . . 135 E8
  St Ives TR26 . . 141 B5
Bedford Sq PL19 . . 147 C5
Bedford St
  Bere Alston PL20 . . 41 B1
  Plymouth PL2 . . 127 F5
Bedford Terr PL4 . . 149 A4
Bedford Units PL18 . . 40 F5
Bedford Villas 7 PL20 . . 41 B1
Bedford Way PL1 . . 148 C3
Bedowan Mdws TR7 . . 111 A4
Bedruthan Ave TR1 . . 137 E6
Bedruthan Steps★ PL27 . . 31 B4
Beech Ave
  Liskeard PL14 . . 113 B5
  Plymouth PL4 . . 149 C2
Beech Cl
  Falmouth TR11 . . 144 F5
  Tavistock PL19 . . 147 C2
  Torpoint PL11 . . 127 A3
Beechcombers TR8 . . 44 D7
Beechcroft Rd
  Plymouth, Lower Compton PL3 . . 129 A6
  Plymouth, North Prospect PL2 . . 128 B7
Beech Ct PL6 . . 125 D5
Beech Dr
  Bodmin PL31 . . 109 B4
  Lewannick PL15 . . 27 A6
  4 St Columb Major TR9 . . 45 D6
Beeches The 9 PL14 . . 38 E4
Beechfield Ave PL20 . . 42 D3
Beechfield Gr PL3 . . 128 E6
Beech Hall Flats 19 TR2 . . 95 A6
Beeching Pk PL17 . . 39 F6
Beech La PL25 . . 114 D3
Beech Rd
  17 Callington PL17 . . 39 F4
  Falmouth TR11 . . 144 F5
  St Austell PL25 . . 114 D3
Beech Terr PL13 . . 117 C4
Beechwood Ave PL4 . . 128 D4
Beechwood Cross PL7 . . 131 F7
Beechwood Dr PL32 . . 105 D5
Beechwood Gdns TR1 . . 137 E6
Beechwood Rise PL6 . . 125 E1
Beechwood Terr PL4 . . 128 D4
Beechwood Way PL7 . . 131 D5
Beehive Workshops TR10 . . 144 A7
Beeston Wlk 6 PL6 . . 129 C7
Behenna Dr TR1 . . 69 F3
Bekelege Dr TR14 . . 138 F1
Belair Rd PL2 . . 128 C7
Belair Villas PL2 . . 128 C7
Belerion Rd TR16 . . 67 C5
Belgrave La PL4 . . 128 F4
Belgrave Rd PL4 . . 128 F4
Belgrave Terr PL14 . . 113 D6
Belgravia St TR18 . . 143 E5
Belhay TR10 . . 144 C8
Bellair Rd TR20 . . 143 A8
Bellair Terr 38 TR26 . . 141 B6
Bellamy Cl PL6 . . 125 A1
Bellatt PL27 . . 108 D6
Bella Vista Gdns TR10 . . 81 E2
Bell Cl PL7 . . 130 F6
Belle Acre Cl PL3 . . 128 F6
Bellever Parc TR14 . . 138 F4
Bellevue TR15 . . 140 C5
Belle Vue
  Bude EX23 . . 104 D6
  Newlyn TR18 . . 143 C1
Belle Vue Ave
  Bude EX23 . . 104 D6
  Plymouth PL9 . . 135 B5
Bellevue Cotts TR10 . . 81 E2
Belle Vue Dr PL9 . . 135 B5
Belle Vue La EX23 . . 104 D6
Belle Vue Rd
  Plymouth PL9 . . 135 C5
  Saltash PL12 . . 122 F2
Belle Vue Rise PL9 . . 135 B5
Bellevue Sq PL11 . . 127 B2
Bellevue Terr TR3 . . 81 D6
Belle Vue Terr
  Gunnislake PL18 . . 41 A6
  21 Penzance TR18 . . 143 E6
Bell Hill PL26 . . 85 C5
Belliers La TR26 . . 141 B5
Bellingham Cres PL7 . . 131 C4
Belliver Ind Est PL6 . . 121 B1
Belliver Way PL6 . . 121 B1
Bell La
  Bodmin PL31 . . 109 E5
  Lanner TR16 . . 80 D6
Bells Ct TR15 . . 139 C7
Bell's Ct TR11 . . 145 B4
Bell's Hill TR11 . . 82 A3
Bell Veor TR16 . . 80 E6
Bell Yd 1 PL31 . . 109 E5
Belmont PL13 . . 117 C4
Belmont Cl PL33 . . 14 D2
Belmont Ct
  8 Plymouth PL3 . . 128 A4
  11 Wadebridge PL27 . . 108 B5
Belmont Mews PL14 . . 38 D4
Belmont Pk PL14 . . 38 D4
Belmont Pl
  Newquay TR7 . . 110 D7
  Plymouth PL3 . . 128 A4
  St Ives TR26 . . 141 A6
Belmont Rd
  Falmouth TR11 . . 145 A3
  Helston TR13 . . 146 B7
  St Austell PL25 . . 114 D3
Belmont St
  Plymouth PL1 . . 148 B3
  8 Tywardreath PL24 . . 60 D5
Belmont Terr
  Devoran TR3 . . 81 F6
  St Ives TR26 . . 141 A6
Belmont Villas 13 TR1 . . 137 D5
Belstone Cl PL5 . . 124 A3
Belvedere La TR20 . . 89 F5
Belvedere Rd PL4 . . 129 B2
Belyars Ct TR26 . . 141 B4
Belyars La TR26 . . 141 B4
Benallack Ct TR1 . . 137 E4
Benan Chy PL25 . . 114 F3
Benbow St PL2 . . 127 F4
Bencoolen Rd EX23 . . 104 D5
Beneathway PL14 . . 50 E7
Bennets La PL12 . . 122 F3
Bennetts Cotts 3 TR10 . . 144 C7
Bennett St PL1 . . 127 E1
Benny Halt Sta★ TR8 . . 56 C8
Benson Gdns 2 TR1 . . 137 D5
Benson Ho 1 TR1 . . 137 D5
Benson Rd TR1 . . 137 B5
Bentley Dr 5 EX23 . . 4 D1
Beramic Cl TR27 . . 78 D6
Beraton Ct 3 PL31 . . 109 D5
Bere Alston Prim Sch PL20 . . 41 B1
Bere Alston Sta PL20 . . 41 B2
Bere Ferrers Sta PL20 . . 119 E3
Berepper Cross TR12 . . 98 E5
Beresford St PL2 . . 128 A4
Berkeley Cl EX23 . . 4 D1
Berkeley Cotts TR11 . . 145 A4
Berkeley Ct
  Falmouth TR11 . . 145 B4
  Looe PL13 . . 117 C5
Berkeley Hill TR11 . . 145 A4
Berkeley Mews 4 TR11 . 145 A4
Berkeley Path 3 TR11 . . 145 A4
Berkeley Vale TR11 . . 145 A4
Berkshire Dr PL2 . . 127 F5
Bernice Cl PL4 . . 129 B4
Bernice Terr PL4 . . 129 B4
Berries Ave EX23 . . 104 E4
Berries Mount EX23 . . 104 F4
Berrow Park Rd PL3 . . 128 E6
Berrycombe View 15 PL31 . . 109 D5
Berrycoombe Hill PL31 . . 109 C5
Berrycoombe Prim Sch PL31 . . 109 B5
Berrycoombe Rd PL31 . . 109 D5
Berrycoombe Vale PL31 . 109 C5
Berryfields Ho PL31 . . 109 E5
Berry Head Gdns PL6 . . 124 E1
Berryhill PL30 . . 47 C6
Berry La PL31 . . 109 E5
Berryman Cres TR11 . . 144 F3
Berry Park Cl PL9 . . 135 E6
Berry Park Rd PL9 . . 135 E7
Berry Pk PL12 . . 122 D4
Berry Rd TR7 . . 110 E6
Berthon Rd PL5 . . 127 C8
Berveth Cl TR3 . . 69 D3
Berwick Ave PL5 . . 124 E3
Bess Park Rd PL27 . . 108 E6
Bethan Dr PL27 . . 108 B5
Bethany Homes 1 TR14 . 138 C2
Bethany Pl TR19 . . 86 F6
Bethel Rd PL25 . . 115 A4
Bethesda Pl 10 TR26 . . 141 B6
Betjeman Wlk PL5 . . 124 C3
Beverley Cres TR27 . . 142 E7
Beverley Rd PL3 . . 129 C4
Beverston Way PL6 . . 125 B8
Beweys Pk PL12 . . 122 C2
Beyrout Pl 6 PL1 . . 127 F3
Bezant Pl TR7 . . 110 B5
Bickern Rd PL11 . . 127 B3
Bickford Cres TR13 . . 91 B1
Bickford Rd PL15 . . 106 B8
Bickham Park Rd PL3 . . 128 D7
Bickham Rd PL5 . . 123 D2
Bickland Hill TR11 . . 144 D4
Bickland Ind Est TR11 . . 144 D4
Bickland Water Rd TR11 144 D2
Bickland Wlk TR11 . . 144 D4
Bickleigh Cl PL6 . . 125 A1
Bickleigh Down Bsns Pk PL6 . . 125 D8
Bickleigh Down CE Prim Sch PL6 . . 125 D7
Bickleigh Down Rd PL6 . 121 D1
Bicton Cl PL6 . . 125 D1
Biddick Dr PL2 . . 127 F6
Biddick's Ct 5 PL25 . . 114 C3
Bideford Mews 13 EX23 . . 4 E1
Bideford Wlk PL6 . . 129 E8
Bigbury Wlk PL6 . . 129 E8
Biggin Hill PL5 . . 123 F4
Big Gn PL13 . . 62 D1
Bilbury St PL4 . . 149 A3
Billacombe Rd PL9 . . 129 E1
Billacombe Villas PL9 . . 135 F8
Billings Cl PL6 . . 124 D6
Billings Dr TR7 . . 111 B5
Billington Cl PL6 . . 129 B7
Bindown Ct PL13 . . 63 E8
Binhamy Cl EX23 . . 104 F4
Binhamy Rd EX23 . . 7 B8
Binkham Hill PL20 . . 42 D3
Bircham View PL6 . . 125 C1
Birch Cl PL6 . . 125 E7
Birches The PL6 . . 125 D6
Birchfield Ave PL2 . . 128 B6
Birch Gr TR27 . . 142 B3
Birchill PL30 . . 47 C6
Birch Pond Rd PL9 . . 135 D7
Birchwood Cl PL19 . . 147 C3
Birchwood Gdns PL7 . . 131 A7
Birkbeck Cl PL7 . . 130 E7
Birkdale Cl PL12 . . 122 C2
Biscombe Gdns PL12 . . 123 A2
Biscombes La 8 PL17 . . 39 E4
Biscovey Jun & Inf Schs PL24 . . 60 B4
Biscovey Rd PL24 . . 115 F5
Bishop Bronescombe CE Sch PL25 . . 115 B5

Bishop Cornish CE Prim Sch PL12 122 F1
Bishop's CE Prim Sch The TR7 110 F4
Bishops Cl
Saltash PL12 122 E3
Truro TR1 137 C6
Bishops Ct TR9 45 E6
Bishop's Hill Rd PL27 21 D6
Bishop's Pl PL1 148 B1
Bishop's Rd TR26 141 B5
Bishop Temple Rd TR1 137 F6
Bissom Rd TR10, TR11 81 F2
Blackberry Cl PL9 135 E8
Blackberry La PL9 135 E8
Blackberry Way TR1 137 F5
Blackbird Cres PL15 106 E4
Blackbrook Cl PL20 42 E4
Blackerry Cl TR16 140 F1
Blackeven Cl PL6 121 D1
Blackeven Hill PL6 121 E1
Blackfriars La PL1 149 A2
Blackhall Gdns PL6 124 D6
Blackmore Cres PL6 124 D6
Black Rd TR27 142 D7
Blacksmith La TR27 78 D6
Blackstone Cl PL9 136 B6
Blackthorn Cl
Plymouth, Honicknowle PL5 124 B3
Plymouth, Woolwell PL6 125 D8
Blackwater Com Prim Sch TR4 68 E5
Bladder La PL5 124 E2
Blagdon Cross EX21 13 F7
Blagdon Lodge Cross EX21 13 F8
Blairgowrie Rd PL5 123 C2
Blake Gdns PL5 124 C3
Blakes Pk PL14 113 D7
Blanchard Pl 2 PL7 130 E7
Blanchdown Dr PL18 40 F7
Blanchminster Rd EX23 104 E5
Blandford Rd PL3 129 C6
Blatchborough Cross EX22 3 E1
Blaxton La PL5 120 C2
Blenheim Rd PL4 149 A4
Bligh Cres TR13 146 C5
Blight's Row TR15 140 B5
Blindhole 8 PL15 106 C6
Blind La PL11 64 D6
Blindwell Hill PL10 132 E5
Blisland Com Prim Sch PL30 35 D7
Blissoe Rd TR3 81 F7
Bloomball Cl PL3 129 B6
Bloom Fields TR18 143 C5
Blowing House Cl PL25 114 B4
Blowinghouse Hill TR15 140 A4
Blowing House Hill
Crowlas TR20 89 B8
Hayle TR20 77 A1
St Austell PL25 114 C4
Blowinghouse La PL30 109 B2
Blowing House La PL25 114 B4
Bluebell Cl PL12 122 D4
Bluebell Way
Launceston PL15 106 E4
Tavistock PL19 147 E4
Blue Haze Cl PL6 125 D5
Blue Reef Aquarium★ TR7 110 D6
Blunt's La PL6 125 C3
Boaden Cl PL12 53 E5
Boase St TR18 143 C1
Bobs Rd PL24 60 B4
Bochym Hill TR12 99 C3
Boconnic La PL20 42 D3
Boconnoc Ave PL17 39 F3
Boconnoc Rd PL25 114 D2
Bodelva Rd PL24 115 E8
Bodgara Way PL14 113 D6
Bodgara Way Flats PL14 113 D6
Bodieve Rd PL27 108 D7
Bodinar Rd TR10 81 D2
Bodiniel Rd PL31 109 C6
Bodiniel View PL31 109 B5
Bodinnar Cl TR20 87 E6
Bodinnar La TR20 87 E6
Bodinnick Hts PL23 116 E5
Bodinnick Parc PL30 23 E3
Bodinnick Rd PL30 23 E3
Bodmin Bsns Ctr PL31 109 E3
Bodmin Bsns Pk PL31 35 B2
Bodmin Coll PL31 109 F2
Bodmin General Sta★ PL31 109 E3
Bodmin Hill PL22 112 B4
Bodmin Hospl PL31 109 B4
Bodmin Jail★ PL31 109 D5
Bodmin Parkway Sta PL30 49 A7
Bodmin Rd
Plymouth PL5 124 D3
St Austell PL25 114 C6
Truro TR1 137 E6
Bodmin Ret Pk PL31 35 B1
Bodmin Town Mus★ PL31 109 E4
Bodmin & Wenford Rly★ PL30, PL31 109 D2
Bodrigan Rd PL13 117 D5
Bodriggy Cres TR27 142 C5
Bodriggy Ct TR27 142 D6
Bodriggy Prim Sch
Hayle TR27 142 D5
Hayle TR27 142 D6
Bodriggy St TR27 142 D6
Bodriggy Villas TR27 142 D6
Body's Ct PL18 40 F6
Bohelland Rd TR10 144 D8
Bohelland Rise TR10 144 D8
Bohelland Way TR10 144 D8
Bohella Rd 20 TR2 95 A6
Bohill TR10 144 D7
Bohill Ct TR10 144 D7
Boiler Works Rd TR14 138 E5
Bojea Ind Est PL25 114 C7
Bojea Terr PL25 114 C6
Bojewyan Stennack TR19 75 B1
Bokenna Cross PL14 37 C1
Boldventure Ave PL25 115 B5
Boldventure Cl PL25 115 B5
Boldventure Rd PL25 115 B5
Bolenna La TR6 55 A4
Bolenowe Terr TR14 79 F4
Bolingey Chapel Flats TR6 55 B4
Bolingey Rd TR6 55 A4
Bolitho Rd TR18 143 C7
Bolitho Sch The TR18 143 C5
Bollowal Pl TR19 86 E6
Bolowthas Cnr TR7 111 A7
Bolowthas Way TR7 111 C7
Bolster Cl 8 TR5 54 C1
Boltern Rd TR17 89 C5
Bolt House Cl PL19 147 A5
Bolventor La PL13 63 E8
Bonallack La TR12 92 D1
Bon Cot Rd TR18 143 C2
Bond St
Plymouth PL6 124 E6
6 Redruth TR15 140 B4
Bone Cellar Row TR2 70 F5
Bone Mill Rd TR6 55 B4
Bones La PL12 52 E4
Bonson Cl PL13 117 C4
Bon Villas 18 TR18 143 C2
Bonville Rd PL6 124 E6
Bonython Cl TR11 82 A3
Bonython Dr TR2 72 A7
Bonython Rd TR7 111 B7
Bonython Terr PL14 113 B4
Boon's Pl PL1 148 C4
Borgwitha TR16 80 B5
Boringdon Ave PL5 127 D8
Boringdon Cl PL7 130 D7
Boringdon Hill PL7 130 E7
Boringdon Mill Bsns Ctr PL7 130 F6
Boringdon Prim Sch PL7 130 D7
Boringdon Rd
Plymouth, Plympton PL7 130 D6
Plymouth, Turnchapel PL9 135 A7
Boringdon Terr
Plymouth, Plympton PL7 130 D6
Plymouth, Turnchapel PL9 135 A7
Boringdon Villas PL7 130 D6
Borlase Cl TR13 146 B5
Borough Cross EX22 7 F5
Borough Ct PL11 126 E4
Borough Pk PL11 126 E4
Borrowdale Cl PL6 124 D5
Bosawna Cl TR16 68 E1
Boscarn Cl TR14 79 B5
Boscarne Cres PL25 114 F3
Boscarne Junction Sta★ PL30 34 D2
Boscarnek TR27 142 A1
Boscarne View PL30 34 D2
Boscarn Parc TR15 139 C4
Boscarn Rd TR15 140 D6
Boscastle Com Prim Sch PL35 9 C1
Boscastle Gdns PL2 128 C8
Boscastle Visitor Ctr★ PL35 9 D2
Boscaswell Downs TR19 75 A1
Boscaswell Est TR19 74 F1
Boscaswell Rd TR19 75 A1
Boscaswell Terr TR19 75 A1
Boscathnoe La TR18 143 B7
Boscathnoe Way TR18 143 B7
Boscawen Ct 17 TR6 55 A4
Boscawen Gdns 11 TR6 55 A4
Boscawen Pk PL26 58 B8
Boscawen Pl PL2 127 E4
Boscawen Rd
7 Chacewater TR4 69 A3
Falmouth TR11 145 B2
Helston TR13 146 D4
Perranporth TR6 55 A4
St Dennis PL26 58 C8
Boscawen St TR1 137 D4
Boscean Cl TR14 79 E4
Boscoppa Cl TR15 140 D7
Boscoppa Rd
St Austell, Bethel PL25 115 A5
St Austell, Boscoppa PL25 115 B5
Boscowan TR11 145 C2
Boscreege Cvn Site TR13 90 D5
Boscundle Ave TR11 144 F1
Boscundle Cl PL25 115 D5
Boscundle Row PL12 123 A2
Bosence Rd TR27 90 C7
Bosillion La TR2 72 A7
Bosinney Rd PL25 114 D3
Bosinver La PL26 59 A1
Boskear La PL31 109 A4
Boskenna Cross TR19 97 C5
Boskennal Barton TR19 97 B6
Boskennal La TR19 97 B6
Boskenna Rd TR16 80 A5
Boskennel Dr TR27 142 B4
Boskenwyn Com Prim Sch TR13 92 B3
Boskenza Ct TR26 141 C2
Boskernick Cl TR18 143 B1
Boskernow TR12 100 D6
Boskerris Cres TR26 141 D2
Boskerris Mews TR26 141 D1
Boskerris Rd TR26 141 D2
Boslandew Hill TR19 88 C2
Bosleake Row TR15 139 C3
Bosloggas Mews 9 TR11 145 C3
Boslowick Cl TR11 144 F3
Boslowick Ct TR11 144 E2
Boslowick Rd TR11 144 E2
Bosmeor Cl TR11 144 E2
Bosmeor Pk TR15 139 D6
Bosmeor Rd TR11 144 E3
Bosnoweth
Helston TR13 146 D5
Probus TR2 71 D6
Bosollow Vean TR20 87 D8
Bosorne Cl TR19 86 E6
Bosorne Rd TR19 86 E6
Bosorne St TR19 86 E6
Bosorne Terr TR19 86 E6
Bosparva La
Leedstown TR27 78 F2
Praze-an-Beeble TR14 79 A3
Bospolvans Rd 2 TR9 45 D6
Bospowis TR14 138 C3
Bossiney Rd PL34 14 D7
Bostennack Pl 10 TR26 141 A5
Bostennack Terr 11 TR26 141 A5
Bosuen Rd TR7 111 A7
Bos Vean TR12 102 F2
Bosvean Gdns
11 Illogan TR16 67 E4
Truro TR1 137 B5
Bosvean Rd TR4 69 F6
Bosvenna View PL31 109 E4
Bosvenna Way TR18 143 B7
Bosvenning Pl TR20 87 E6
Bosvigo Gdns★ TR1 137 A5
Bosvigo La TR1 137 B5
Bosvigo Rd TR1 137 C4
Bosvigo Sch TR1 137 C4
Boswedden Pl TR19 86 E6
Boswedden Rd TR19 86 E6
Boswell Cl PL5 124 B2
Boswergy TR18 143 C5
Boswithian Rd TR14 138 F6
Bosworgey Cl 3 TR9 45 D6
Bosworgy Rd TR20, TR27 90 B8
Botallack La TR19 86 E7
Botetoe Hill TR14 79 C4
Botetoe Rd TR14 79 B4
Botha Rd 1 PL27 31 F3
Bothwicks Rd TR7 110 E6
Boughthayes Est PL19 147 A5
Boulden Cl PL7 131 C5
Boulter Cl PL6 121 C1
Boundary Cl 21 TR18 143 C1
Boundary Dr EX23 7 B6
Boundary Rd
Bodmin PL31 109 A4
Dousland PL20 42 E3
Bounders La TR6 55 B4
Bounder Treath TR12 101 C1
Boundervean La TR14 138 B2
Bounds Cross EX22 8 B4
Bounds Pl PL1 148 B2
Bound The PL10 133 A1
Bounsalls Ct PL15 106 C5
Bounsall's La PL15 106 C5
Bourne Cl PL3 129 D6
Bourneside PL25 114 D3
Boveway Dr PL14 113 E5
Boveway La PL14 113 D5
Boville La PL9 136 C7
Bovisand Ct PL9 134 F2
Bovisand La
Down Thomas PL9 135 B2
Staddiscombe PL9 135 D3
Bovisand Pk PL9 135 A1
Bovisand Rd PL9 135 E3
Bowden 14 EX23 4 D1
Bowden Park Rd PL6 125 A1
Bowdens Row TR15 140 A4
Bowers Park Dr PL6 125 E7
Bowers Rd PL2 128 B5
Bowglas Cl TR20 89 A8
Bowhays Wlk 2 PL6 129 C7
Bowjey Ct 9 TR18 143 C1
Bowjey Hill TR18 143 C1
Bowjey Terr 5 TR18 143 C1
Bow La EX23 4 D2
Bowles Rd TR11 145 A6
Bowling Gn
Menheniot PL14 51 F5
34 St Ives TR26 141 B6
Bowling Gn Terr 35 TR26 141 B6
Bowling Gn The TR2 82 F2
Bowling Green Ct
Hayle TR27 142 D5
Liskeard PL14 113 B5
Bowling Green Rd TR11 92 F3
Bownder Dowr TR27 142 B3
Bownder Vean PL25 115 A5
Bowood Pk
Delabole PL33 14 F1
Helstone PL32 24 B8
Boxhill Cl PL5 124 B3
Boxhill Gdns PL2 128 C8
Box's Shop EX23 7 A4
Boxwell Pk PL31 109 F4
Boyd Ave PL28 107 C5
Boyton Com Prim Sch PL15 13 A3
Bracken Cl
Bodmin PL31 109 E5
Plymouth PL6 125 D8
Brackenside PL13 62 D1
Bracken Terr TR7 110 E5
Brackwell Pl PL27 108 B5
Braddock CE Prim Sch
East Taphouse PL14 50 B6
Lostwithiel PL22 49 D6
Braddock Cl PL26 58 D6
Braddons Hill PL7 130 B7
Bradfield Cl PL6 125 E1
Bradford Cl PL6 129 B7
Bradford Quay Rd PL27 108 C6
Bradley Rd
Newquay TR7 111 C7
Plymouth PL4 128 F4
Bradridge Ct PL15 13 A4
Braemar Cl PL7 131 C4
Braeside Pk PL14 50 E8
Braggs Hill PL15 13 B3
Brake La PL10 132 B5
Brake Rd PL5 124 E2
Brake The PL14 37 F4
Bramblebank TR11 145 B7
Bramble Cl
Newquay TR7 111 A4
Plymouth PL3 129 B7
Widemouth Bay EX23 6 F5
Bramble Hill EX23 104 E5
Brambles The
Liskeard PL14 113 E5
Lostwithiel PL22 112 C3
Bramble Wlk 1 PL6 129 C7
Bramfield Pl PL6 129 D7
Bramley Cl PL25 114 E4
Bramley Pk PL31 109 F5
Bramley Rd PL3 129 C4
Brancker Rd PL2 128 C6
Brandon Rd PL3 129 C4
Brandon Wlk EX23 6 F5
Brandreth Rd 3 PL3 128 F6
Brandy La TR20 89 F4
Branksome Dr PL27 108 E5
Brannel Sch PL26 58 B3
Branscombe Gdns PL5 124 A3
Branson Ct 9 PL7 131 C5
Branson Pk PL19 42 A6
Branwell La TR18 88 E6
Braunton Wlk PL6 129 E8
Bray Cl PL19 147 A5
Brayford Cl PL5 124 B3
Bray's Pl PL25 114 F4
Brays Terr 2 TR16 140 F1
Brazacott Cross PL15 12 B2
Brea Arch TR14 139 A3
Bread St TR18 143 E5
Breage CE Sch TR13 90 F3
Break My Neck La TR20 88 B8
Breakwater Hill PL4 149 C1
Breakwater Ind Est PL9 135 C8
Breakwater Rd
Bude EX23 104 D5
Plymouth PL9 135 C8
Brean Down Cl PL3 128 E6
Brean Down Rd PL3 128 E7
Brea Rd PL27 21 D2
Breaside TR14 139 A3
Brecon Cl
Plymouth PL3 129 A7
1 St Agnes TR5 54 C1
Bree Shute La 4 PL31 109 E5
Brentford Ave PL5 124 B5
Brent Knoll Rd 1 PL3 128 E6
Brenton Rd PL11 64 B5
Brentons Pk PL29 22 D6
Brentor Rd
Mary Tavy PL19 30 F6
Plymouth PL4 129 B2
Brent Tor★ PL19 30 D7
Brentwartha PL13 62 E2
Brest Rd PL6 125 A3
Brest Way PL6 125 A3
Bretonside PL4 149 A2
Brett Wlk PL7 130 F7
Brewartha TR2 57 E1
Brewers Cl PL30 47 F6
Brewers Hill PL26 58 C8
Brewers Rd TR1 137 F5
Brewery Hill TR26 77 E4
Brewery La TR13 146 B6
Briansway PL12 122 D2
Briardale Rd PL2 127 F6
Briarfield PL23 116 D4
Briarleigh Cl PL6 125 F2
Briar Rd
Bude EX23 104 E4
Plymouth PL3 128 F7
Briars Row PL12 122 D4
Briars Ryn PL12 53 B7
Briar Tor PL20 42 D3
Briarwood PL14 113 D5
Brickfields Cl PL1 127 F1
Brickworks Hill TR16 68 D1
Bridals La PL13 62 E2
Bridge TR9 45 E7
Bridge Cl TR7 111 A4
Bridge Ct PL25 114 F4
Bridge Hill
Illogan TR16 67 E5
St Column Major TR9 45 E6
Bridge Ho
Delabole PL33 14 E2
Hayle TR27 142 B6
Bridge Ho The 13 TR18 143 C2
Bridge La PL12 53 A3
Bridgemead Cl PL26 114 C1
Bridgemoor Cross EX22 8 C6
Bridge Pk EX22 8 A5
Bridge Rd
Goonhavern TR4 55 D4
Illogan TR16 67 E4
Seaton PL11 64 B5
St Austell PL25 114 B3
Tideford PL12 52 F2
Bridge Row TR16 67 E5
Bridgerule CE Prim Sch EX22 8 A5
Bridgerule Ind Est EX22 7 F4
Bridge St
Par PL24 60 B6
7 Stratton EX23 4 D1
Bridges The PL12 122 E1
Bridge The PL1 148 B1
Bridge View PL27 108 C6
Bridge Wlk 2 PL35 9 C2
Bridgwater Cl PL6 125 B1
Bridle Cl PL7 131 B7
Bridle Way
Quintrell Downs TR8 44 E3
Saltash PL12 122 D4
Bridwell Cl PL5 127 E8
Bridwell La N PL5 127 E8
Bridwell Rd PL5 127 E8
Brillwater Rd TR11 92 E4
Brimford Cross EX22 3 D4
Brimhill Cl PL7 131 B3
Brisbane Terr PL14 113 C5
Brismar Wlk 3 PL6 129 C7
Briston Orch PL12 53 E7
Britannia Pl PL4 129 B2
British Cycling Mus★ PL32 105 C8
British Rd TR5 54 D1
Briton's Hill TR18 143 F6
Brixham Wlk PL6 129 E8
Brixton Lodge Gdns PL8 136 F5
Brixton Terr TR13 146 C6
Broad Cl EX22 11 E7
Broadclose Hill EX23 104 E5
Broad La
Illogan TR15 139 D7
Trematon PL12 53 E2
Broadland Gdns PL9 136 A8
Broadland La PL9 135 F8
Broadlands Cl PL7 131 A3
Broadley Ct PL6 121 B2
Broadley Ind Pk PL6 121 B2
Broadley Park Rd PL6 121 B2
Broad Mead PL17 39 E5
Broad Park Rd
Bere Alston PL20 41 B2
Plymouth PL3 128 D6
Broad Pk
Launceston PL15 106 B7
Plymouth PL9 135 C7
St Keyne PL14 51 B3
Broadshell Cross EX22 8 E5
Broads La TR11 81 F3
Broad St
12 Launceston PL15 106 C6
Lifton PL16 19 F4
Newquay TR7 110 D6
Padstow PL28 107 D5
Penryn TR10 144 D7
7 St Columb Major TR9 45 E6
Truro TR1 137 E5
Broads Yd PL11 64 C5
Broadview PL19 30 A6
Broad View TR4 56 D1
Broadway The PL9 135 E7
Broad Wlk
Helston TR13 146 B7
Saltash PL12 122 E1
Brock Ho 9 PL4 149 A2
Brocklands Adventure Pk★ EX23 5 A6
Brockley Rd PL3 129 C4
Brocks La PL10 132 F5
Brockstone Rd PL25 115 A5
Brockton Gdns PL6 125 B6
Bromfield Cres TR2 57 E1
Bromhead Ct PL6 129 A8
Bromley Ho 6 PL2 128 A4
Bromley Pl 5 PL2 128 A4
Bronescombe Cl TR10 144 D7
Bronte Pl PL5 124 D1
Brook Cl
Helston TR13 146 B7
Plymouth PL7 131 A3
Brook Ct 6 TR11 145 A4
Brookdale Ct 12 PL27 108 B5
Brookdown Terr PL12 122 E3
Brookdown Villas PL12 122 E3
Brook Dr EX23 104 E7
Brooke Cl PL12 123 A2
Brookfield Cl
Lanjeth PL26 58 E3
Plymouth PL7 131 B5
Brooking Cl PL6 129 A8
Brookingfield Cl PL7 130 C5
Brooking Way PL12 122 C3
Brook La PL19 147 B2
Brooklands
New Polzeath PL27 21 D6
Tavistock PL19 147 D6
Brooklands Ct PL6 124 E3
Brooklyn Flats 18 TR2 95 A6
Brooklyn Terr 17 TR2 95 A6

Bro–Cas 157

Brook Pl
Falmouth TR11 145 A4
Penryn TR10 144 C7
Brook Rd
Falmouth TR11 144 F3
Wadebridge PL27 108 B5
Brooks PL22 49 E3
Brookside
Chacewater TR4 68 F3
St Austell PL25 114 F4
Brookside Cl PL15 106 B8
Brook St
Falmouth TR11 145 A4
17 Mousehole TR19 88 C1
Tavistock PL19 147 C6
Brook The PL12 122 E4
Brookward Terr 8 TR18 143 C7
Brookway TR27 142 E7
Brookwood Rd PL9 136 D7
Broomfield Dr
Bodmin PL31 109 B3
Plymouth PL9 135 C5
Broomfield Rd PL27 108 D5
Broom Hill PL12 122 D2
Broomhill Cross EX22 5 E3
Broomhill La EX23 4 D2
Broom Pk PL9 135 D5
Broughton Cl PL3 128 F7
Browne Memorial Almshouses PL19 147 A5
Browning Cl 14 TR9 45 D6
Browning Dr PL31 109 C3
Browning Rd PL2 128 A5
Brownlow Pl 5 PL31 109 D5
Brownlow St PL1 148 A2
Browns Hill PL23 116 C4
Brown's Hill TR10 144 C8
Broxton Dr PL9 129 E1
Brunel Ave PL2 127 F5
Brunel Prim Sch PL12 122 E2
Brunel Quays PL22 112 D2
Brunel Rd PL12 122 C4
Brunel Terr 3 PL2 127 F5
Brunel Way PL1 148 A2
Brunswick Pl 10 PL2 127 F4
Brunswick Rd PL4 149 B2
Brush End TR26 77 E4
Brynmoor Cl PL3 129 A7
Brynmoor Pk PL3 129 A6
Brynmoor Wlk PL3 129 A6
Bryny Cl PL30 23 E7
Buckett's Hill TR15 140 C2
Buckeys La TR2 95 B6
Buckfast Cl PL2 128 A8
Buckingham Nip TR4 68 F3
Buckingham Pl PL5 123 E2
Buckingham's Cl TR8 56 B7
Buckingham Terr TR16 68 D1
Buckland Abbey★ PL20 41 F1
Buckland Cl PL7 130 D7
Buckland St PL1 148 B2
Buckland Terr PL20 42 C2
Bucklawren Rd PL13 63 E7
Bucklers Ho PL25 115 B4
Bucklers La PL25 115 B4
Buckler Village (Mobile Homes Pk) PL25 115 B4
Buckwell St PL1, PL4 149 A2
Buctor Pk PL19 41 D8
Buddle Cl
Plymouth PL9 136 A5
Tavistock PL19 147 B6
Budehaven Com Sch EX23 104 F5
Bude Ind Est EX23 104 F4
Bude Inf Sch EX23 104 E5
Bude Jun Sch EX23 104 E5
Budemeadows Cvn Site EX23 7 A4
Bude-Stratton Bsns Pk EX23 7 B8
Bude-Stratton Mus★ EX23 104 D5
Budge Mdws PL15 28 C4
Budleigh Cl PL9 135 F5
Budnic Est TR6 55 B5
Budnic Hill TR6 55 B5
Budock Hospl TR11 144 D5
Budock Pl TR11 145 B4
Budock Terr TR11 145 B3
Budock Vean La TR11 93 B2
Budshead Gn PL5 124 C4
Budshead Rd PL5 124 C4
Budshead Way PL5 124 E2
Buena Vista Cl PL6 125 D6
Buena Vista Dr PL6 125 C6
Buena Vista Gdns PL6 125 C6
Buena Vista Way PL6 125 C6
Bugle Rural Workshops PL26 47 C1
Bugle Sch PL26 47 C1
Bugle Sta PL26 47 C2
Buildings The TR20 89 A6
Bullan's La TR26 141 A5
Bullans Terr 5 TR26 141 A5
Bulleid Cl PL2 127 F7
Bulleid Way EX23 104 E4
Buller Cl
Plymouth PL7 130 F4
Torpoint PL11 127 A3
Buller Hill TR16 80 B6
Buller Ho PL13 117 D3
Buller Pk
Liskeard PL14 113 D5
Saltash PL12 122 D3
Buller Rd PL11 127 B3
Buller St PL13 117 C3
Bullers Terr TR15 140 D5
Bull Hill PL23 116 D4
Bullock La
Helston, Lower Green TR13 146 B5
Helston, Whitehill TR13 146 C4
Bullock Market Terr 28 TR18 143 E6
Bull Point Prim Sch PL5 127 B8
Bulmer Rd PL4 149 C3
Bulteel Gdns PL6 124 E7
Bulwark Rd TR13 146 B4
Bungalows The
Looe PL13 117 D6
Tintagel PL34 14 D7
Bunkers Hill
22 St Ives TR26 141 B6
Townshend TR27 90 C8
Bunyan Cl PL5 124 C2
Burden Cl PL31 109 C4
Burgess Cl EX23 4 D2
Burhos Row TR13 79 F1
Buriton Row 32 TR18 143 E5
Burleigh La PL3 128 D7
Burleigh Manor PL3 128 D7
Burleigh Park Rd PL3 128 D6
Burley Cl TR1 137 D3
Burley Ct TR11 145 B4
Burnard Cl PL6 124 E7
Burnards Ct 7 PL31 109 D5
Burnett Cl PL12 122 D2
Burnett Rd PL6 128 F8
Burnham Park Rd PL3 128 D6
Burniston Cl PL7 131 A3
Burnistone Cl PL7 131 A3
Burn La PL19 30 E8
Burns Ave PL5 124 C2
Burns View PL11 65 B5
Burnthouse PL14 37 C1
Burnthouse Cotts TR10 81 C1
Burnthouse La TR27 142 D5
Burn View EX23 104 D6
Burnwithian Terr TR16 68 D1
Burraton Com Prim Sch PL12 122 C3
Burraton Rd PL12 122 C4
Burrator Rd PL20 42 E3
Burrington Ind Est PL5 124 A1
Burrington Rd PL5 124 A1
Burrington Way PL5 124 B1
Burrow Hill PL9 135 E6
Burrows The TR26 141 A5
Bursdon Moor Cross EX39 3 B7
Burthallan La TR26 77 A7
Burton Cl PL6 125 B6
Burton Ho 15 PL25 114 C3
Burwell Cl PL6 125 E4
Bury Cl PL15 11 B1
Bush Hill PL14 36 F2
Bush Pk
Launceston PL15 106 D5
Plymouth PL6 125 F3
Butcher Park Hill PL19 147 B7
Bute Rd PL4 129 A4
Butler Cl PL6 125 B6
Butney Cnr TR14 66 E3
Butson Pk TR5 68 D8
Butterdown PL12 122 B3
Buttlegate PL11 64 D5
Butt Park Rd PL5 124 B3
Butts La PL35 9 D1
Butts Pk PL22 112 D2
Butts The
St Newlyn East TR8 56 B7
Tintagel PL34 14 D7
Byard Cl PL5 123 E1
Byland Rd PL3 129 A6
Byron Ave PL5 124 C2

C

Cabot Cl PL12 122 E2
Cades Parc TR13 146 C6
Cadoc Cl PL28 20 E1
Cadogan Cl TR14 138 E1
Cadogan Dr TR14 138 E1
Cadogan Rd TR14 138 E1
Cadover Cl PL6 125 A1
Caernarvon Gdns PL2 128 B7
Caernarvon Lodge TR7 110 D5
Calais Rd TR27 78 C2
Calartha Rd TR19 75 A1
Calartha Terr TR19 75 A1
Calder Cl PL3 129 B6
Caldicot Gdns PL6 125 C8
Caldwells Rd TR18 143 E6
Caledonia Cl 1 PL7 131 B5
Calenick St TR1 137 C4
Cal Hill TR16 140 D3
California Gdns
Plymouth PL3 129 D6
Portscatho TR2 83 B2
Callington Com Coll PL17 39 F5
Callington Mus★ PL17 39 E4
Callington Prim Sch PL17 39 E4
Callington Rd
Harrowbarrow PL17 40 C4
Liskeard PL14 113 D7
Saltash PL12 122 E3
Tavistock PL19 147 A4
Calloose Farm Cvn Pk TR27 78 D2
Calloose La E TR27 78 D1
Calloose La W TR27 78 D1
Callywith Gate Ind Est PL31 35 B2
Calshot Cl TR7 111 E7
Calstock Com Prim Sch PL18 41 A3
Calstock Rd PL18 41 A6
Calstock Sta PL17 41 A3
Calvez Cl PL10 132 F6
Camaret Dr TR26 141 B4
Cambeak PL35 9 C1
Cambeak Cl EX23 10 C6
Camber Rd PL1 148 A1
Camborne Cl PL5 124 A5
Camborne Geological Mus & Art Gal★ TR15 139 B6
Camborne Redruth Com Hospl TR15 139 F6
Camborne Ret Pk TR15 139 B5
Camborne Sch of Mines TR15 139 B6
Camborne Science & Com Coll TR14 138 B3
Camborne Sta TR14 138 D2
Cambridge La W 5 PL1 148 B3
Cambridge Pl TR11 145 A3
Cambridge Rd PL2 127 F5
Camden Ct PL4 149 A3
Camden St PL4 149 A3
Camel Cl PL28 107 D4
Camel Ct PL30 109 C6
Camelford Com Prim Sch PL32 105 C3
Camelot Ct 2 TR18 143 E5
Camelot View PL32 105 C8
Camelside PL27 108 C5
Camel Valley Vineyard★ PL30 34 B2
Cameo Ct TR14 138 F4
Cameron Cl EX23 104 D7
Cameron Way PL6 125 B1
Camilla Terr PL2 128 D7
Campbell Rd PL9 135 F7
Campbeltown Way TR11 145 C3
Camp Cross PL15 19 F7
Camperdown St PL2 127 F4
Camperknowle Cl PL10 132 F6
Campfield Hill TR1 137 D5
Camp Hall Rd TR8 43 B1
Campion Cl
7 Plymouth PL7 131 C5
Saltash PL12 122 D4
Campion Rise PL19 147 D6
Campion View PL6 125 E8
Camullas Way TR7 110 A5
Canal Rd PL19 147 B5
Candish Dr PL9 136 D7
Canefields Ave PL7 131 B3
Canfield Pl TR15 140 A5
Canfield Terr TR15 140 A5
Canhaye Cl PL7 131 A3
Cannamanning Rd 3 PL26 59 D7
Canna Park Sta★ PL15 18 D3
Cann Gdns PL6 124 D6
Cannis Rd PL25 114 E6
Cannon Hill PL14 113 C5
Cannons Pl TR13 146 D7
Cannon St PL1 127 D2
Cannon Terr 2 PL14 113 C5
Cann Wood View PL6 125 E7
Canons Way PL19 147 A3
Canterbury Dr PL5 124 B4
Cantillion Cl PL27 21 E3
Canton PL26 85 D5
Canyke Rd PL31 48 D8
Cape Cl TR19 86 E6
Cape Cornwall Rd TR19 86 E6
Cape Cornwall Sch TR19 86 E6
Cape Cornwall St TR19 86 E6
Cape Terr TR19 86 E6
Cape Trelew TR19 86 E6
Captains Gdns PL5 124 E1
Captains Ho PL26 73 C3
Captain's Wlk TR11 145 A2
Caradon Bsns Ctr 8 PL14 113 C5
Caradon Cl
9 Callington PL17 39 E4
1 Pensilva PL14 38 E4
Plymouth PL6 125 A5
Caradon Ct 2 PL20 42 C4
Caradon Dr PL14 113 B6
Caradon Hts
Liskeard PL14 113 D7
Tremar PL14 38 B4
Caradon Terr PL12 122 E3
Caradon View PL14 37 F3
Carbeile Jnr Sch PL11 127 A3
Carbeile Rd PL11 127 A2
Carbes La PL22 112 C2
Carbis Bay Holiday Pk TR26 77 C4
Carbis Bay Sta TR26 141 D2
Carbis Beach Apartments TR26 141 D2
Carbis Ct TR15 140 A5
Carboth La PL15 106 B5
Carclaze Com Inf Sch PL25 114 E6
Carclaze Com Jun Sch PL25 114 E6
Carclaze Ind Est PL25 114 E7
Carclaze Rd PL25 114 E6
Carclew Ave TR7 110 E6
Carclew Rd TR11 81 F4
Carclew St TR1 137 D3
Carclew Terr
Devoran TR3 81 F6
Truro TR1 137 D3
Cardell Rd PL31 109 D5
Cardell Way TR7 111 A5
Cardiff Cl PL7 131 B4
Cardigan Rd PL6 125 C1
Cardinal Ave PL5 127 D8
Cardinham Sch PL30 35 F3
Cardinham Woods Forest Walks★ PL30 35 C1
Cardinnis Gn PL14 113 D6
Cardinnis Rd TR18 143 B5
Cardrew Bsns Pk TR15 140 C6
Cardrew Cl TR15 140 B6
Cardrew Ind Est TR15 140 D7
Cardrew La 1 TR15 140 C5
Cardrew Terr TR15 140 D6
Cardrew Way TR15 140 D7
Cardwen Est PL13 62 C6
Careswell Ave PL2 127 F8
Carew Ave PL5 124 B3
Carew Cl
Crafthole PL11 65 B5
St Day TR16 68 E1
Carew Gdns
Plymouth PL5 124 B3
Saltash PL12 122 D3
Carew Gr PL5 124 B3
Carew-Pole Cl TR1 137 E3
Carew Rd
St Day TR16 68 D1
Truro TR1 137 C5
Carew Terr PL11 127 B2
Carew Wharf PL11 127 C2
Carew Wharf Bsns Ctr PL11 127 C2
Carey Ct PL12 122 E3
Carey Pk
Helston TR13 146 B7
Polperro PL13 62 E2
Truro TR1 137 C4
Cargoll Rd TR8 56 B7
Cargwyn PL26 59 D6
Carisbrooke Rd PL6 125 C1
Carkeek's Cl PL26 58 B3
Carkeel Barns PL12 122 C5
Carland Cross TR8 56 D4
Carlidnack Cl TR11 93 D3
Carlidnack La TR11 93 D4
Carlidnack Rd TR11 93 E4
Carlisle Rd PL5 124 D3
Carloggas Cl TR8 45 A8
Carloggas Farm TR8 45 A8
Carloggas Gr 6 TR9 45 D6
Carloggas Way 10 TR9 45 D6
Carlton Cl PL3 129 B5
Carlton Ho 7 PL31 109 E5
Carlton Terr
Plymouth, Lipson PL4 149 B3
Plymouth, Weston Mill PL5 127 E8
Carlton Vills PL12 53 E4
Carlyon Cl
Threemilestone TR3 69 D3
Torpoint PL11 126 F4
11 Truro TR1 137 C4
Carlyon Ct TR3 82 B8
Carlyon Ho TR1 69 E4
Carlyon Rd
Playing Place TR3 82 B8
St Austell PL25 114 E4
Truro TR1 137 C5
Carmarthen Rd PL4 129 B2
Carmel Gdns PL19 147 A5
Carmen Sq 10 TR18 143 C7
Carminow Cross PL30 48 D8
Carminowe Cres 8 TR18 143 D5
Carminow Rd PL31 48 D8
Carminow Road Ind Est 5 PL31 48 D8
Carminow Way TR7 111 A7
Carmython Ct TR7 111 B7
Carnarthan Moor TR15 139 C3
Carnarthen Rd TR14 138 E3
Carnarthen St TR14 138 E2
Carn Ave TR14 138 F2
Carn Bargus PL26 58 E8
Carn Bosavern TR19 86 F6
Carn Bosavern Cl TR19 86 F6
Carn Brea Ave TR15 139 C5
Carn Brea Ho TR15 139 C5
Carn Brea La TR15 139 C5
Carn Brea Village TR15 139 F5
Carn Cl TR27 78 E1
Carncrows Rd TR26 141 C6
Carncrows St TR26 141 C6
Carne Cross PL24 59 F7
Carne Ct PL26 58 C8
Carnedon PL14 38 C7
Carnego La TR8 57 B6
Carne Hill
St Dennis PL26 46 C1
Trewoon PL25 58 F4
Carnellis Rd 7 TR26 141 A5
Carne Mdws TR2 70 F5
Carne Rd TR18 143 C3
Carne's Bldgs 11 TR18 143 E4
Carnes Ct TR11 145 C2
Carne's Flats PL24 60 B5
Carneton Cl TR8 43 D3
Carn Euny Settlement★ TR20 87 C3
Carne View Cl TR14 138 F5
Carne View Rd TR2 71 D6
Carnglaze Caverns★ PL14 36 F1
Carnglaze Cl PL14 113 E6
Carn Gloose Rd TR19 86 D6
Carn Gwavas Terr TR18 143 D1
Carnhell Rd TR14, TR27 78 F4
Carninney La TR26 141 C1
Carnkief Cnr TR4 55 D4
Carn Marth La TR16 140 E2
Carnock Rd PL2 128 D8
Carnon Cres 13 TR3 81 F7
Carnon Terr TR3 81 F6
Carnoustie Dr PL12 122 C2
Carn Rock TR10 144 D7
Carn Ros TR19 74 F1
Carnsew Cl TR10 81 C1
Carnsew Cres TR10 81 C1
Carnsew Ct TR27 142 B5
Carnsew Mdw TR27 142 A5
Carnsew Rd TR27 142 A5
Carnsmerry PL26 47 C1
Carnsmerry Cres PL25 114 E4
Carnstabba Rd 13 TR26 77 A6
Carntiscoe Workshops TR27 77 C2
Carn Todden TR19 88 D1
Carn View TR16 80 F6
Carn View Terr TR19 75 A1
Carnyorth Hill TR19 86 F8
Carnyorth Terr TR19 86 F8
Carolina Gdns PL2 127 F7
Caroline Cl TR27 142 E7
Caroline Pl PL1 148 A2
Caroline Row TR27 142 E7
Carpalla Rd PL26 58 D5
Carpalla Terr PL26 58 D5
Carpenter Ct PL31 109 D5
Carpenter Rd PL9 135 F8
Carpmael Ave TR8 111 B4
Carracawn Cross PL12 64 D8
Carrack Dhu 37 TR26 141 B6
Carrack Dhu Est 36 TR26 141 B6
Carrack Gladden TR26 141 D2
Carrack Widden 25 TR26 141 B5
Carradale Rd PL6 129 C7
Carrallack Mews TR19 86 E6
Carrallack Terr TR19 86 E5
Carriage Ho The TR3 69 F1
Carriage Parc TR4 55 D4
Carrickowel Cres 1 PL25 115 A5
Carrick Rd TR11 144 E2
Carrick Way TR2 95 A6
Carrine Rd TR1 69 F3
Carrisbrooke Way PL12 122 B2
Carrnown Gdns TR15 140 D3
Carroll Rd PL5 124 C2
Carron La PL6 121 D1
Carsize La TR27 78 E1
Carter Cl TR7 111 A5
Carteret Rd EX23 104 E5
Carthew Cl
Liskeard PL14 113 D5
St Ives TR26 141 A6
Carthew Ct TR26 141 A6
Carthew La
Four Lanes TR13 80 A3
Praze-an-Beeble TR13 79 F2
Carthew Terr TR26 141 A6
Carthew Way TR26 141 A6
Carvath Ho PL25 114 D3
Carvedras Ct 5 TR1 137 C4
Carvossa Est TR20 89 B8
Carvoza Rd TR1 137 D5
Carvynick Cotts TR8 57 A7
Carwinard Cl TR27 78 C5
Carwinion Gdn★ TR11 93 E3
Carwinion Rd TR11 93 E3
Carwin La TR27 78 C5
Carwin Rise
Angarrack TR27 78 C5
Hayle TR27 142 E7
Carwollen Rd PL25 114 E7
Carworgie Ct 10 TR9 45 E2
Carworgie Manor TR8 45 D3
Carworgie Way 7 TR9 45 E2
Carwynnen Cl TR14 79 B3
Casey La PL13 62 D5
Castel Wary Cl TR13 146 B5
Casterills Rd TR13 146 D4
Castle Acre Gdns PL3 129 B5
Castle Bank Gdns PL3 129 B5
Castle Barbican PL7 130 E4
Castle Bldgs PL12 122 D4
Castle Canyke Rd PL31 109 F3
Castle Carey Gdns PL3 129 B5
Castle Cl TR11 145 E3
Castle Ct
Praa Sands TR20 90 C3
Saltash PL12 122 C2
Castle Dr
Bodmin PL31 109 F5
Falmouth TR11 145 F2
Praa Sands TR20 90 B3
St Mawes TR2 94 F5
Castle Dyke PL15 106 C6
Castle Dyke La PL1 149 A2
Castle Gdns PL14 113 C6
Castle Gn TR13 146 B5
Castlehayes Gdns PL7 130 E4
Castle Hill
Helston TR13 146 B5
6 Liskeard PL14 113 C6
Lostwithiel PL22 112 C2
Saltash PL12 122 C1
Castle Hill Ct
Bodmin PL31 109 E5
7 Liskeard PL14 113 C6
Castle Hill Gdns PL31 109 F5
Castle Horneck Cl TR18 143 C5
Castle Horneck Rd TR18 143 C5
Castle Hts 3 PL34 14 C7
Castle La
Liskeard PL14 113 C6

Castle La *continued*
Plymouth PL7 130 E4
Castle Mdws
Launceston PL15 106 A4
2 St Agnes TR5 54 D1
Castlemead Cl PL12 122 D3
Castlemead Dr PL12 122 D3
Castle Meadows Ct 3 TR5 54 D1
Castle Rd
Longrock TR20 88 F8
Ludgvan TR20 89 A8
Penzance TR18 143 E7
Tintagel PL34 14 C7
Castle Rise
Plymouth PL3 129 B4
Saltash PL12 122 D1
Truro TR1 137 C5
Castle St
Bodmin PL31 109 F5
Launceston PL15 106 C6
Liskeard PL14 113 C6
Looe PL13 117 D3
Plymouth PL1 149 A2
Truro TR1 137 C4
Castleton Cl PL3 129 A4
Castle View
Longrock TR20 88 F6
Lostwithiel PL22 112 E3
Saltash PL12 122 D1
Tintagel PL34 14 C7
Castle View Cl TR15 140 B6
Castle View Pk TR11 93 D3
Caswarth Terr PL28 107 D5
Catalina Row PL27 31 F3
Catalina Villas PL9 135 A6
Catchfrench Cres PL14 113 E6
Cathcart Ave PL4 129 B2
Cathebedron Rd
Carnhell Green TR14 78 F4
Praze-an-Beeble TR14 79 A3
Cathedral Church of the Blessed Virgin Mary★ TR1 137 D4
Cathedral La 13 TR1 137 D4
Cathedral School of St Mary The PL1 148 B3
Cathedral St PL1 148 B3
Cathedral View TR1 137 C6
Catherine Cl EX23 104 F4
Catherine Pk PL13 62 E5
Catherine's Hill PL15 106 A6
Catherine St PL1 148 C2
Cath of St Mary & St Boniface PL1 148 B3
Cattedown Rd PL4 149 C1
Catterick Cl PL5 123 E5
Cattewater Rd PL4 129 B1
Caudledown La PL26 59 C8
Caunter Rd PL14 113 D6
Causeland Sta PL14 51 B2
Causewayhead TR18 143 E5
Causeway The
Falmouth TR11 144 F4
Hayle TR27 142 A4
Causley Cl PL15 106 C7
Cavendish Rd PL4 129 B1
Caxton Gdns PL5 124 C1
Cayforth Flats TR16 67 C6
Cayley Way PL5 123 F2
Cecil Ave PL4 149 C4
Cecil Cotts PL1 148 A3
Cecil St PL1 148 B3
Cedar Ave PL9 135 C5
Cedar Cl
21 Callington PL17 39 F4
Torpoint PL11 126 F2
Cedarcroft Rd PL2 128 B7
Cedar Ct
Camborne TR14 139 A5
Saltash PL12 122 F2
Cedar Dr PL11 126 F2
Cedar Gr EX23 104 E7
Cedar House Flats TR26 77 E4
Celandine Gdns PL7 131 C5
Celia Hts PL31 109 F2
Celtic Rd PL17 39 F4
Cemetery Rd PL18 40 F5
Centenary Row Middle TR14 138 E3
Centenary Row W TR14 138 E2
Centenary St TR14 138 E3
Central Ave PL25 114 E5
Central Cl PL26 58 B4
Central Park Ave PL4 148 C4
Central Rd
Holywell TR8 43 B1
Plymouth PL1 148 B1
Central Sq TR7 110 D6
Central Treviscoe PL26 58 A7
Century Cl
Helston TR13 146 D8
St Austell PL25 114 F6
Century Ct TR7 111 C7
Century La TR2 83 F6
Century Sq 7 PL14 38 E4
Ceres Ct EX23 104 E4
Chacewater Com Prim Sch TR4 69 A3
Chacewater Hill TR4 69 A3
Chaddlewood Ave PL4 149 B3
Chaddlewood Cl PL7 131 A4
Chaddlewood Ho PL7 131 B5
Chaddlewood Inf Sch PL7 131 A5
Chaddlewood Jun Sch PL7 131 A5
Chagford Wlk PL6 129 E8
Chainwalk Dr TR1 137 C6
Chalets The TR18 88 E6
Chalet The PL11 64 C4
Challacombe Gdns TR10 144 C8
Challenger Quay 12 TR11 145 C3
Challgood Cl 1 PL9 135 F5
Challgood Rise PL9 135 F5
Challis Ave TR8 45 A8
Challock Cl PL6 125 D4
Chamberlayne Dr PL7 130 E6
Champion's Ct TR13 146 B6
Chancery Cl TR4 70 D8
Chancery La 23 TR18 143 E5
Chandlers Wlk PL25 115 A3
Chandos Pl 12 PL25 114 C3
Channel Park Ave PL3 129 B5
Channel View
Polruan PL23 116 D2
St Ives TR26 141 A6
Channel View Terr
Plymouth PL4 149 C4
4 Redruth TR15 140 C4
Channon Rd PL12 122 C4
Chantry Ct PL7 130 B5
Chantry La PL13 117 E4
Chantry Pk 18 PL17 39 E4
Chapel Cl
Camborne, Kehelland TR14 66 F1
Camborne, Tuckingmill TR14 139 A4
Coad's Green PL15 27 D3
Connor Downs TR27 78 D6
Crantock TR8 110 A3
Gunnislake PL18 40 E5
4 Horrabridge PL20 42 C4
St Just In R TR2 82 F2
Chapel Cnr EX22 8 A5
Chapel Cotts EX23 4 C8
Chapel Cres TR4 56 A2
Chapel Ct
Camborne TR14 138 F4
Padstow PL28 107 D5
9 Redruth TR15 140 B5
Chapeldown Rd PL11 127 A2
Chapel Farm TR14 79 E5
Chapel Field PL25 115 B5
Chapel Gn PL26 59 A1
Chapel Ground PL13 117 C3
Chapel Hill
Camborne, Brea TR14 139 A3
Camborne, Tregajorran TR15 139 C4
Gweek TR12 92 C2
Hayle TR27 142 C6
Lanner TR16 80 D6
Launceston PL15 106 B5
Newquay TR7 110 D6
Perranporth TR6 55 B4
Polgooth PL26 59 A1
Ponsanooth TR3 81 B4
Porthtowan TR4 68 A5
Redruth TR16 68 A4
St Erth TR27 142 A1
Sticker PL26 58 F1
Truro TR1 137 B4
Chapel La
Bodmin PL31 109 D5
Goldsithney TR20 89 F5
Hayle TR27 142 D6
Horrabridge PL20 42 C4
Lizard TR12 102 F2
Penryn TR10 144 C7
Polruan PL23 116 D2
St Austell PL25 115 C6
St Mabyn PL30 34 D8
St Teath PL30 23 F6
5 Wadebridge PL27 108 B5
Chapel Mdw
Buckland Monachorum PL20 41 F3
Perranarworthal TR3 81 D6
Chapel Park Terr PL15 106 B5
Chapel Pk PL15 106 B5
Chapel Pl
Pillaton PL12 53 B7
16 Truro TR1 137 D4
Chapel Point La PL26 73 C2
Chapel Rd
Camborne TR14 139 A4
Foxhole PL26 58 D5
Heamoor TR18 143 C8
Indian Queens TR9 45 E1
Leedstown TR27 78 E1
2 Par PL24 60 C4
Roche PL26 46 F3
Saltash PL12 122 B3
St Just TR19 86 E6
St Tudy PL30 23 E3
Chapel Row
Praze-an-Beeble TR14 79 B2
2 Redruth TR15 140 B5
Tremar PL14 38 A3
Truro TR1 137 D4
Widegates PL13 63 F8
Chapel Sq
Crowlas TR20 89 B8
Mevagissey PL26 73 C3
Troon TR14 79 E5
Chapel St
4 Bere Alston PL20 41 B1
4 Callington PL17 39 F4
Camborne TR14 138 D2
Camelford PL32 105 C4
Chapel St *continued*
Grimscott EX23 5 B2
Gunnislake PL18 40 F6
Lifton PL16 19 F4
Marazion TR17 89 B5
Mevagissey PL26 73 C3
21 Mousehole TR19 88 C1
9 Newlyn TR18 143 C2
Penzance TR18 143 E5
Plymouth, Mount Wise PL1 127 E2
Plymouth PL4 149 A3
Probus TR2 71 C6
Redruth TR15 140 B5
St Day TR16 68 D1
St Ives TR26 141 B5
St Just TR19 86 E6
Tavistock PL19 147 B5
Chapel Terr
Camborne TR15 139 D6
Devoran TR3 81 F6
Falmouth TR11 145 B4
Hayle TR27 142 B5
Par PL24 60 B6
9 Porthleven TR13 98 B8
Portreath TR16 67 C6
Redruth, Carn Brea Village TR15 139 F5
Redruth TR15 140 D2
Ruan Minor TR12 103 A5
St Day TR16 68 E1
10 St Mawes TR2 95 A6
Trewellard TR19 86 F8
Chapel Town Cl TR11 93 D4
Chapel Way PL3 129 A6
Chapman Ct PL12 122 B3
Chapmans Ope PL1 127 D2
Charaton Cross PL14 38 F4
Chard Barton PL5 124 B3
Chard Rd PL5 123 D2
Chard Terr 6 TR11 145 A3
Charfield Dr PL6 129 A8
Chariot Rd TR15 139 E6
Charles Ave TR11 144 E2
Charles Bassett Cl 6 TR13 146 C5
Charles Cl PL25 114 F3
Charles Cross PL4 149 A3
Charles St
Bugle PL26 47 C1
Newlyn TR18 143 C3
Plymouth PL1 149 A3
Truro TR1 137 C4
Charles Terr PL3 129 A6
Charlestown Prim Sch PL25 115 C3
Charlestown Rd PL25 115 B3
Charlestown Shipwreck, Rescue & Heritage Ctr★ PL25 115 B2
Charlotte Cl TR4 68 C6
Charlotte St PL2 127 E4
Charlton Cres PL6 125 A2
Charlton Rd PL6 125 A3
Charnhill Cl PL9 136 A6
Charnhill Way PL9 136 A6
Charter Cl TR13 146 C4
Charter Ct TR10 144 D7
Charter Way PL14 113 E6
Chateau Cl PL26 46 D1
Chatsworth Gdns PL5 123 F3
Chatsworth Way PL25 115 C2
Chaucer Prim Sch PL5 124 C2
Chaucer Rd PL19 147 D5
Chaucer Way PL5 124 C1
Chawleigh Cl PL18 40 F5
Chedworth St PL4 149 A3
Chegwin Gdns TR7 110 E5
Chegwins Hill PL26 58 D5
Chegwyn Gdns 6 TR5 54 C1
Chegwyns PL26 58 D5
Chelfham Senior Sch PL20 40 F3
Chellean Vean TR4 81 C7
Chellew Rd TR1 137 F5
Chelmer Cl PL7 131 A5
Chelmsford Pl PL5 124 C4
Chelson Gdns PL6 125 E3
Cheltenham Pl
Newquay TR7 110 D6
Plymouth PL4 149 B4
Cheney Mill Farm Park★ TR27 77 E1
Chenhalls Cl TR27 77 E2
Chenhalls Rd TR27 142 A2
Chenoweth Cl TR14 138 C4
Chepstow Ave PL6 125 C8
Chequetts Cl 10 PL17 39 E4
Cheriton Cl PL5 124 A3
Cherrill Gdns EX23 104 E7
Cherrington TR7 110 B5
Cherry Cross EX22 12 B7
Cherry Gdns 14 TR18 143 E5
Cherry Pk PL7 131 A3
Cherry Tree Cl PL31 109 B4
Cherrytree Ho TR18 143 C5
Cherry Tree La PL7 131 A4
Cherry Tree Mews PL25 114 D3
Cheshire Dr PL6 124 D6
Chesnut Cl PL12 122 D4
Chester Ct TR7 111 A6
Chesterfield Rd PL3 129 B4
Chester Pl 4 PL4 128 E4
Chester Rd TR7 111 A6
Chesterton Cl PL5 124 C3
Chesterton Ct PL27 108 A6
Chesterton Pl TR7 111 A7
Chestnut Ave PL9 135 C5
Chestnut Cl
Callington PL17 40 A4
Falmouth TR11 144 F5
Lamerton PL19 30 A4
St Tudy PL30 23 E3
Tavistock PL19 147 D2
Torpoint PL11 126 F3
Chestnut Gr PL31 109 B4
Chestnut Rd PL3 128 D7
Chestnut Terr PL19 30 A4
Cheviot Rd TR7 110 E4
Chichester Cl PL26 58 E5
Chichester Cres
Newquay TR7 110 F4
Saltash PL12 122 E1
Chichester Ct PL20 42 C4
Chichester Ho PL1 148 B2
Childrey Gdns PL6 125 C1
Childrey Wlk PL6 125 C1
Chili Rd TR15 139 D6
Chilton Cl PL6 129 B7
Chings Alley 13 PL15 106 C6
Chipponds Dr PL25 114 A3
Chirgwin Ct 22 TR18 143 E5
Chirgwin Rd TR1 137 E4
Chisholme Cl PL25 114 D3
Chisholme Ct PL25 114 D3
Chittleburn Cross PL8 136 E5
Chittleburn Hill PL8 136 E5
Chivenor Ave PL5 123 D4
Chiverton Cl TR20 89 F4
Chiverton Cross
Blackwater TR4 68 F5
Rosudgeon TR20 89 F4
Chiverton Greenacres TR5 68 D8
Chiverton Way TR20 89 F4
Chollacott Cl PL19 147 C4
Chollacott La PL19 147 D3
Chough Cl
Falmouth TR11 144 E4
Launceston PL15 106 E4
Chough Cres PL25 114 F4
Choughs Cl TR14 138 B3
Christa Ct PL14 38 D7
Christian Mill Bsns Pk PL6 124 E4
Christian Way TR7 111 C7
Chubb Dr PL3 128 B4
Chudleigh Rd PL4 129 A4
Chun Castle★ TR20 87 C8
Church Cl
Blisland PL30 35 D8
Lelant TR26 77 E4
Plymouth PL7 130 B7
Trispen TR4 56 D1
Church Cove Rd TR12 103 A2
Church Ct PL6 125 A7
Church End PL13 117 D3
Churchfield Cl TR20 89 A8
Churchfield Pl PL24 60 B5
Churchfields Rd TR8 55 D8
Church Gate 3 PL14 113 C5
Church Hill
Calstock PL18 41 A3
Chacewater TR4 68 F2
Golant PL23 61 B6
Helston TR13 146 C7
Herodsfoot PL14 50 E3
Hessenford PL11, PL12 64 B8
Ludgvan TR20 89 A8
Milton Combe PL20 41 F1
Penryn TR10 144 D8
5 Pensilva PL14 38 E4
Plymouth PL6 125 B1
Port Isaac PL29 22 D7
St Day TR16 68 E1
Sticker PL26 58 F1
7 St Mawes TR2 95 A6
Tavistock PL19 147 E2
Tintagel PL34 14 C7
Church Hill Rd PL9 135 A6
Church Ho PL12 123 A2
Churchill Rd PL19 147 D2
Churchill Way
10 Penwithick PL26 59 D7
Plymouth PL3 128 E6
Churchill Wlk PL12 122 E1
Church La
Bodmin PL31 109 E5
Bude EX23 104 D5
Calstock PL18 41 A3
Camborne TR14 138 D3
Cargreen PL12 119 A1
Flushing TR11 145 B7
Helston TR13 146 B6
Lelant TR26 77 E4
Lostwithiel PL22 112 C2
Mevagissey PL26 73 C4
Padstow PL28 107 D5
Redruth TR15 140 A3
St Columb Minor TR7 111 E7
St John PL11 132 B8
Tavistock PL19 147 C5
Churchlands PL13 117 D5
Churchlands Cl PL6 125 E7
Churchlands Rd PL6 125 E8
Church Lea
Launceston PL15 106 A7
Tavistock PL19 147 E2
Church Mews
Stithians TR3 80 F3
Week St Mary EX22 11 E8
Church Park Ct PL6 125 E8
Church Park Mews PL27 108 B4
Church Park Rd
Crackington Haven EX23 10 C6
Plymouth PL6 125 E8
Church Path EX23 104 C5
Church Pk
Bodmin PL31 109 F5
Horrabridge PL20 42 C4
Lerryn PL22 61 D8
St Mellion PL12 53 D8
Church Pl
Liskeard PL14 113 C5
18 St Ives TR26 141 B6
Church Rd
Camborne TR15 139 B6
Cury TR12 99 A4
Four Lanes TR16 80 A5
Heamoor TR18 143 C7
Illogan TR16 67 E4
Lanivet PL30 47 E7
Lelant TR26 77 E4
Mabe Burnthouse TR10 93 C8
Madron TR20 143 A8
Mount Hawke TR4 68 C6
Mylor Bridge TR11 82 B2
Pendeen TR19 75 A1
Penponds TR14 138 B1
Penryn TR10 144 C8
Perranarworthal TR3 81 D5
Plymouth, Plympton PL7 130 F4
Plymouth, Plymstock PL9 135 F7
Saltash PL12 122 D2
Shortlanesend TR4 69 F6
St Austell PL25 115 B3
St Dennis PL26 46 C1
Stithians TR3 80 F4
St Tudy PL30 23 E3
Tideford PL12 52 F2
Church Row
Carharrack TR16 80 F8
Lanner TR16 80 D6
3 Porthleven TR13 98 B8
Sheviock PL11 65 C6
Church Row La PL5 124 C6
Church St N PL14 113 C5
Church St S PL14 113 C5
Church Sq
8 Bodmin PL31 109 E5
Constantine TR11 92 F4
St Just TR19 86 F6
4 Stratton EX23 4 E1
Church St
Callington PL17 39 E4
Calstock PL18 41 A3
Camborne TR14 138 D3
Carharrack TR16 80 F8
Falmouth TR11 145 B4
Gorran Haven PL26 85 D5
Helston TR13 146 B6
Landrake PL12 53 C3
Launceston PL15 106 C6
Liskeard PL14 113 C5
Looe, East Looe PL13 117 D3
Looe, West Looe PL13 117 C3
Mevagissey PL26 73 C3
15 Newlyn TR18 143 C1
Padstow PL28 107 D5
Par PL24 60 B5
Plymouth PL3 128 A4
Poughill EX23 4 D2
8 St Austell PL25 114 C3
St Columb Minor TR7 111 D7
St Day TR16 68 E1
St Erth TR27 142 A1
St Germans PL12 65 A8
St Just TR19 86 F6
5 Stratton EX23 4 E1
Tywardreath PL24 60 D5
Churchstow Wlk PL6 129 E8
Church Terr
Devoran TR3 81 F6
Grampound Road TR2 57 E1
St Kew PL30 23 A3
Churchtown
Cardinham PL30 35 F3
Gwinear TR27 78 D4
7 Mullion TR12 99 A2
5 St Agnes TR5 54 C1
St Minver PL27 22 A4
St Newlyn East TR8 56 B7
Church Town Cotts TR3 81 D5
Churchtown Mdws PL26 58 B4
Churchtown Mews PL30 35 C8
Churchtown Rd
Gwithian TR27 66 B2
Illogan TR16 67 E5
Phillack TR27 142 C7
Portscatho TR2 83 B2
St Stephen PL26 58 B4
Churchtown Terr PL27 32 D6
Churchtown Vale PL12 122 D1
Church View
St Cleer PL14 37 F3
St Dominick PL12 40 D2
St Neot PL14 36 F2
Treburley PL15 28 B5
Walkhampton PL20 42 E4
Church View Rd
Camborne TR14 138 F4
Probus TR2 71 D6
Churchway
Madron TR20 143 A8
11 Marazion TR17 89 C5
Church Way
Falmouth TR11 144 E3
Plymouth PL5 127 E8
St Clether PL15 17 B2
Church Wlk
Redruth TR15 140 A5
South Petherwin PL15 27 E8
12 Truro TR1 137 D5
Chute La PL26 85 D5

Chy-An-Chy 19 TR26 141 B6
Chyanclare TR18 143 D6
Chyandaunce Cl TR18 143 F8
Chyandaunce Terr TR18 143 F8
Chyandor Cl PL24 60 C4
Chyandour TR15 140 A4
Chy-An-Dour Cl 1 TR26 77 A6
Chyandour Cliff TR18 143 F6
Chyandour La TR18 143 F7
Chy-An-Dour Rd TR20 90 C3
Chyandour Sq TR18 143 F7
Chyandour Terr TR18 143 F7
Chy An Dowr TR27 142 E7
Chy-an-Gweal Est TR20 89 A7
Chy-an-hall TR18 143 F8
Chy-an-Mor TR20 88 F6
Chy Cober TR27 142 E7
Chycoose Parc TR3 82 A5
Chycornick Terr TR18 143 F8
Chygothow TR13 146 B6
Chy Hwel TR1 137 F6
Chy Kensa Cl TR27 142 C5
Chylan Cres TR7 111 E6
Chymeddon TR7 110 E6
Chy Nampara 1 TR11 145 A4
Chynance
Penzance TR18 143 D4
Portreath TR16 67 C6
Chynance Dr TR7 110 D5
Chynoon Gdns PL25 114 F6
Chynowen La TR8 43 D1
Chynowen Parc TR8 43 D1
Chynoweth PL26 59 C8
Chynoweth Gdns TR18 143 F8
Chynoweth La TR20 89 F6
Chypons Est TR 20 76 F3
Chypons Rd TR12 99 B3
Chypraze Ct TR14 138 B3
Chyreen La
Carnon Downs TR3 81 F8
Playing Place TR3 82 A8
Chyrn Dr PL30 24 B3
Chyrose Rd TR16 68 D1
Chysauster Ancient Village Settlement★ TR 20 76 D2
Chytodden Terr TR13 90 F5
Chytroose Cl TR13 146 D8
Chyvelah Ope TR1 69 E3
Chyvelah Rd TR3 69 D4
Chyvelah Vale TR1 69 E3
Chyvellas Cl TR18 143 B1
Chyventon Cl TR19 97 B6
Chyventon Ho TR15 140 B5
Chyverton Cl TR7 110 D4
Chyvogue Mdw TR3 81 D6
Chywoone Ave TR18 143 C1
Chywoone Cres TR18 143 C1
Chywoone Gr TR19 97 F8
Chywoone Hill TR18 143 C1
Chywoone Pl TR18 143 C1
Chywoone Rural Workshops TR19 87 A5
Chywoon Gdns TR15 139 D7
Citadel Ope 13 PL1 149 A2
Citadel Rd PL1 148 C2
Citadel Rd E PL1 149 A2
Citadel The★ PL1 149 A1
City Bsns Pk PL3 128 A4
City Mus & Art Gal★ PL4 149 A3
City Mus & Art Gal Annexe★ PL4 149 A3
City Rd TR1 137 C4
Clairemont Pl 1 PL14 38 A3
Clampet La PL11 65 E4
Clann La PL30 47 E7
Clann Mdws PL30 47 E7
Claremont Cotts 1 TR11 145 A5
Claremont Falls PL13 62 E2
Claremont Rd TR15 140 B5
Claremont St PL1 148 C4
Claremont Terr
3 Falmouth TR11 145 A5
16 Porthleven TR13 98 B8
Truro TR1 137 C5
Clarence Ct PL1 148 A3
Clarence Pl
30 Penzance TR18 143 E6
Plymouth, Morice Town PL2 127 E4
Plymouth, Stonehouse PL1 148 A3
Clarence Rd
St Austell PL25 114 B4
Torpoint PL11 127 B3
Clarence St TR18 143 E5
Clarence Terr
31 Penzance TR18 143 E6
7 Wadebridge PL27 108 B5
Clarence Villas TR15 140 D6
Clarendon Ho 1 PL1 127 F3
Clare Pl PL4 149 B2
Clare Terr TR11 145 B4
Claybourne Cl PL25 114 F6
Claylands PL30 24 A1
Claytonia Cl PL6 121 C1
Clayton Pl PL4 129 B2
Clayton Rd PL4 129 B2
Clearbrook Ave PL5 123 E1
Clear View PL12 122 E3
Clease Mdws PL32 105 C3
Clease Rd PL32 105 C4
Clease The PL32 105 C3
Cleave Cres EX23 4 B8
Cleaveland PL27 108 C4
Cleaverfield Mews PL15 106 C7
Cleaves The PL15 106 C7
Cleave The PL10 133 B2
Cleavewell PL27 108 C4
Cledma Bank TR27 142 A2
Cleers Hill
St Dennis PL26 46 E1
Whitemoor PL26 58 E8
Cleeve Gdns PL2 128 A8
Clegg Ave PL11 126 E3
Clemens Cl TR7 111 B5
Clemens Rd PL14 51 B3
Clemens Way TR27 78 D6
Clement Rd PL7 131 B5
Clements Rd TR18 143 D5
Clemmens Ave TR7 110 D4
Clemo Rd PL14 113 E7
Clevedon Park Ave PL2 128 B6
Clevedon Rd TR7 110 D5
Cleveland Ave PL13 117 D4
Cleveland Rd PL4 149 C3
Clies The 5 TR13 146 C5
Clifden Cl
Mullion TR12 99 A1
Newquay TR7 110 E5
Clifden Dr PL27 21 D6
Clifden Rd PL25 114 F4
Clifden Terr
14 Bodmin PL31 109 D5
Lostwithiel PL22 112 C2
Cliff Bglws TR27 142 A8
Cliff Ct
Falmouth TR11 145 B3
Plymouth PL1 148 B1
Cliff End Pk PL27 108 D6
Cliff La
Millbrook PL10 132 A4
Mousehole TR19 88 D1
New Polzeath PL27 21 D6
Clifford Cl PL5 123 E2
Cliff Park Terr PL27 108 C5
Cliff Rd
Falmouth TR11 145 C2
Gorran Haven PL26 85 D5
Mevagissey PL26 73 C4
Mousehole TR19 88 D2
Newlyn TR18 143 D1
Newquay TR7 110 F6
Perranporth TR6 55 A5
Plymouth PL1 148 B1
Porthleven TR13 98 B8
Cliff Rise PL23 116 D2
Cliff St PL26 73 C4
Cliff Terr TR16 67 C6
Cliff The PL26 73 C3
Cliff View Rd TR14 138 E4
Cliff View Terr TR14 138 E4
Clift Ct 4 TR1 137 D4
Clifton Ave PL7 130 E7
Clifton Cl PL7 130 E7
Clifton Cres 16 TR11 145 A4
Clifton Gdns 1 TR1 137 B4
Clifton Hill 14 TR18 143 C2
Clifton Pl
14 Falmouth TR11 145 A4
Plymouth PL4 149 A4
Clifton Rd TR15 139 C8
Clifton St PL4 149 A4
Clifton Terr
15 Falmouth TR11 145 A4
Hayle TR27 142 B6
Liskeard PL14 113 A5
15 Newlyn TR18 143 C2
Portscatho TR2 83 B2
Cligga Workshops TR6 54 F4
Clijah Cl TR15 140 C2
Clijah La TR15 140 D2
Clinton Ave PL4 129 A4
Clinton Cl
Bude EX23 104 E4
Redruth TR15 140 C3
Clinton Dr PL25 114 B3
Clinton Pas 4 TR15 140 B4
Clinton Rd
Constantine TR11 92 F3
Redruth TR15 140 C4
Clinton Terr PL10 132 F6
Clittaford Rd PL6 124 F7
Clittaford View PL6 124 E7
Cloake Pl PL12 119 A2
Clodan Mews 11 TR9 45 E2
Clodgey La TR13 146 D5
Clodgey Way TR13 146 D4
Clodgy View 44 TR26 141 B6
Clonway 1 PL20 42 C3
Close Hill TR15 140 B6
Close The
17 Bere Alston PL20 41 B1
Lanner TR16 80 E6
Mylor Bridge TR11 82 A3
Penzance TR18 143 D7
Saltash PL12 122 C3
Trevone PL28 20 F2
Truro TR1 137 F6
Clos Trevithick 4 TR14 138 F2
Clovelly Rd PL4 149 C1
Clovelly View PL9 135 A7
Clover Lane Cl 6 PL35 9 C1
Clover Rise PL6 125 E8
Clover Wlk PL12 122 C3
Clowance TR14 79 B2
Clowance Cl PL1 127 F1
Clowance La PL1 127 E1
Clowance St PL1 127 F1
Clyde St PL2 127 F5
Coaches Cnr TR13 90 F3
Coach Ho The
Penryn TR10 144 D7
Penzance TR18 143 F7
Coach House La PL25 114 C4
Coach House Mews PL9 136 B6
Coach La TR15 140 A4
Coachyard Mews PL28 107 D5
Coad's Green Prim Sch PL15 27 D3
Coastguard Cotts
Down Thomas PL9 134 F2
Mawnan Smith TR11 93 C1
Mullion TR12 98 F1
Polperro PL13 62 E2
Rosudgeon TR20 89 F3
Coastguard Cres TR18 143 F6
Coastguard Hill PL29 22 D8
Coastguard Hos PL28 21 B4
Coastguard Sta Flats PL13 117 C3
Coastguard Terr TR2 84 B3
Coastline Ct TR8 44 C6
Coast Rd TR4 68 A7
Cobbett Rd PL5 124 B2
Cobb La PL9 135 F6
Cobble La TR9 57 E8
Cobblestone La PL1 128 A1
Cobbs Well PL23 116 C4
Cober Cres TR27 78 E3
Cobourg St PL1 148 C3
Cockington Cl PL6 125 E1
Cockington Wlk PL6 125 C1
Cocklawelva PL27 21 D2
Cock's Lake La PL12 53 D4
Cockwells La TR26 77 C1
Codiford Cres TR14 138 E4
Coffa Bridge Cl PL22 112 D2
Coffee Lake Mdw PL22 112 D2
Cogegoes Ind Pk TR14 138 A2
Cogos Pk TR11 82 A3
Coinagehall Pl TR18 143 F4
Coinagehall St
Helston TR13 146 B5
Penzance TR18 143 F4
Colborne Ave TR16 67 D4
Colborne Rd PL6 125 A2
Coldrenick St PL5 123 D1
Coldrose Ct TR1 137 B4
Coldstyle Rd PL14 113 C7
Coldwind Cross TR3 81 D7
Colebrook Cl TR15 140 A5
Colebrook La PL7 130 E7
Colebrook Rd
Plymouth, Plympton PL7 130 E6
Plymouth, St Budeaux PL5 123 D1
Coleman Dr PL9 135 F4
Colemans Cross PL15 19 C5
Cole Moore Mdw PL19 147 B6
Colenso Cross TR20 89 F5
Colenso Pl PL25 114 D3
Coleridge Ave PL6 124 F2
Coleridge Rd PL4 129 A4
Coles Cotts PL9 135 C1
Cole's Cotts PL7 130 E6
Colesdown Hill PL9 130 B1
Colesloggett Halt PL30 48 F8
Colin Campbell Ct 10 PL1 148 B3
Colinsey Pl TR18 143 D7
Colinsey Rd TR18 143 D7
Coliza Hill PL26 59 A2
Collacombe Cross PL19 29 F4
Collaford Cl PL7 131 A4
Collan's Cross PL32 15 D4
College Ave
Plymouth PL3 128 E5
Tavistock PL19 147 D6
College Ct TR2 71 C6
College Dean Cl PL6 125 C5
College Gn
Bodmin PL31 109 E2
St Austell PL25 114 C3
College Hill TR10 144 C7
College La
Bodmin PL31 109 F2
Plymouth PL4 128 F4
Redruth TR15 140 E7
College Ope TR10 144 D7
College Park Pl PL3 128 E5
College Rd
Camelford PL32 105 D4
Plymouth PL2 127 E5
College Road Prim Sch PL2 127 E5
College St TR14 138 C3
College View PL3 128 E4
College Way TR1 69 E3
Colletts Ct TR16 67 C5
Colliford Lake Pk★ PL14 36 E8
Collin Cl PL5 123 D1
Collingwood Ave PL4 149 C2
Collingwood Rd PL1 128 A3
Collingwood Villas 5 PL1 128 A3
Collins Parc TR3 80 F3
Coll of St Mark & St John PL6 125 C4
Collon Field PL22 61 D8
Collorian La TR26 77 C1
Collygree Parc TR20 89 E5
Colmers La PL17 39 E4
Colmers Row PL14 51 F5
Col-Moor Cl TR27 142 E7
Colne Gdns PL3 129 B5
Colroger Cl TR12 99 B2
Colston Cl PL6 125 B6
Coltishall Cl PL5 123 F4
Coltness Rd PL9 136 B5
Coltsfield Cl PL6 129 B8
Colver Cl TR27 78 D6
Colvreath Rd TR7 110 F6
Colwill Rd PL6 125 E3
Colwill Wlk PL6 125 F3
Colworth Ave TR11 144 F3
Colwyn Rd PL11 127 A3
Combe La EX23 6 F4
Combley Dr PL6 125 D4
Comfort Rd TR11 82 A3
Comfort Wartha TR11 92 F4
Commercial Hill TR3 81 B4
Commercial Ope PL4 149 B2
Commercial Pl PL4 149 B1
Commercial Rd
Calstock PL18 41 A3
Hayle TR27 142 C6
Horrabridge PL20 42 C4
10 Mousehole TR19 88 C1
Penryn TR10 144 D7
Plymouth PL4 149 B2
8 St Keverne TR12 101 C4
5 St Mawes TR2 95 A6
Commercial Sq 3 TR14 138 D3
Commercial St
Camborne TR14 138 D3
Gunnislake PL18 41 A6
Plymouth PL4 149 B2
Commercial Terr PL28 107 D5
Commissioners Rd 1 PL27 108 B5
Common La PL6 121 B5
Commons Cl 3 TR12 99 A2
Commons Gate EX22 13 B8
Commons The TR12 99 A2
Compass Dr PL7 131 A7
Compass Point TR26 141 D2
Compass W PL15 18 C2
Comprigney Cl TR1 137 B5
Comprigney Hill TR1 137 B5
Compton Ave PL3 129 A5
Compton CE Prim Sch PL3 129 A6
Compton Knoll Cl PL3 129 A6
Compton Leigh PL3 129 A6
Compton Park Rd PL3 128 F5
Compton Rd 2 PL17 39 E4
Compton Vale PL3 129 A5
Condor Cotts TR11 144 C2
Condurrow Rd TR14 139 A1
Congreve Gdns PL5 124 C1
Coniston Gdns PL6 124 F4
Conker Rd TR27 78 C1
Connaught Ave PL4 128 F4
Connaught La 6 PL4 128 E4
Connoc Cl PL14 113 D5
Connor Downs Prim Sch TR27 78 D6
Connor Hill TR27 78 D6
Conqueror Dr PL5 124 E1
Conrad Rd PL5 124 D1
Consols Rd TR16 80 F8
Consort Cl PL3 128 E7
Consort Ho PL5 123 B2
Constable Cl PL5 124 D3
Constance Pl PL1 148 A3
Constantine Prim Sch TR11 92 E4
Constantine St PL4 149 A3
Convent Cl PL12 122 E3
Convent of Mercy PL31 109 C4
Conway Cl TR11 144 E4
Conway Gdns
Falmouth TR11 144 D4
Plymouth PL2 128 B7
Conway Rd TR11 144 D4
Conyngham Ct PL6 129 A8
Cooban Ct PL6 129 A8
Cook Ct PL12 122 B3
Cooksland Ind Est PL31 35 B2
Cooksland La PL31 35 B2
Cooksland Rd PL31 35 B1
Cook's Level PL26 85 C5
Cooksley Ct PL1 149 A1
Cookworthy Rd PL2 127 F6
Coombe Dean Sch PL9 136 A6
Coombe Dr PL12 119 A2
Coombe Hill PL26 58 C2
Coombe La
Cargreen PL12 119 A2
Crafthole PL11 65 B5
Penzance TR18 143 D7
Plymouth PL5 124 D7
Seaton PL11 64 B7
Truro TR4 81 C8
Coombe Park Cl PL10 133 A2
Coombe Park La PL5 124 A3
Coombe Pk
Camborne TR14 66 F3
Kingsand PL10 133 A2
Penzance TR18 143 E6
Saltash PL12 122 F2
Coombe Rd
Callington PL17 39 F4
Lanjeth PL26 58 D3
Penzance TR18 143 E7
Saltash PL12 123 A2
Coombes La 9 TR1 137 C4
Coombe Sta PL14 51 A6
Coombe The
Crumplehorn PL13 62 D2
Newlyn TR18 143 B3
Coombe Vale TR18 143 B3
Coombe View
15 Perranporth TR6 55 A4
Plymouth PL2 127 F7
Coombe Way PL5 123 F1
Cooperage Gdns 8 PL25 59 A3
Cooperage Rd PL25 59 A3
Cooper's La TR13 98 C8
Coosebean La TR4 137 A5
Copes Gdns TR1 137 C5
Copleston Rd PL6 124 E5
Coppard Mdws PL7 130 B6
Copper Beech Way PL6 125 C7
Copperfields PL20 42 B5
Copper Hill TR27 142 D6
Copper Pl PL1 148 A3
Coppers Pk PL6 125 E7
Copper Terr TR27 142 D7
Coppice Gdns PL5 124 E2
Coppice Wood Dr PL6 125 C7
Copse Cl PL7 130 D4
Copse Rd PL7 130 D4
Copse The
St Austell, Sandy Bottom PL25 114 F5
St Austell, Tregorrick PL26 114 B1
Copshorn Rd PL31 109 C7
Copthorne Cross PL15 12 B2
Copthorne Gdns PL9 135 F5
Corea Terr PL1 128 A2
Corfe Ave PL3 128 F8
Coringdean Cl PL6 125 B6
Cormoran Ct TR17 89 C5
Cormorant Dr PL25 115 A4
Corner Brake PL6 125 D7
Corner Gdns EX23 4 D1
Corner Pk PL15 26 C7
Cornerstone Ct PL11 127 B3
Cornfield Gdns PL7 131 B7
Cornhill Rd PL24 60 B5
Cornish Beam Engine Mus★ TR15 139 C6
Cornish Birds of Prey Ctr The★ TR9 32 D1
Cornish Chough TR7 111 B7
Cornish Cider Farm The★ TR4 55 B1
Cornish Cres TR1 69 F4
Cornish Engines Mus★ TR15 139 C6
Cornish Owl Ctr The★ PL11 65 B7
Cornubia Cl
Hayle TR27 142 C5
Truro TR1 137 F6
Cornwall Beach PL1 127 D2
Cornwall Coll PL25 114 D4
Cornwall Coll Camborne TR15 139 B6
Cornwall Coll Newquay TR7 111 A5
Cornwall Coll of F & H Ed (Annexe)
Camborne TR14 138 F3
Camborne TR14 139 A3
Cornwall Coll Saltash PL12 122 D2
Cornwall Ho PL25 114 C3
Cornwallis TR26 141 E2
Cornwall St
Bere Alston PL20 41 B1
Plymouth, Morice Town PL1 127 D2
Plymouth PL1 148 C3
Cornwall Terr
Penzance TR18 143 E4
2 Truro TR1 137 C5
Cornwood Rd PL7 131 B4
Cornworthy Cl PL2 128 A7
Coronation Ave TR14 138 C3
Coronation Cl 2 PL17 39 F4
Coronation Cotts
Budock Water TR11 144 C3
Mabe Burnthouse TR10 81 C1
St Keverne TR12 101 D4
Coronation Pl
Helston TR13 146 C4
Plymouth PL5 127 E8
Coronation Rd
10 Callington PL17 39 F4
Hayle TR27 142 D5
1 Illogan TR16 67 E4
Redruth TR15 140 D4
Coronation Terr
Blackwater TR4 68 E5
Truro TR1 137 B4
Veryan TR2 83 D7
Coronation Way TR7 111 C7
Corondale Rd PL2 128 B7
Corporation Rd
Bodmin PL31 109 B4
Plymouth PL2 128 D7
Corsham Cl PL6 125 B6
Cort Simmons TR15 139 C6
Cort Treloweth TR15 139 B6
Corva Cl 11 TR26 77 A6
Corva Rd 9 TR26 77 A6
Cory Cl EX23 10 F6
Cosawes Cvn Pk TR3 81 C4
Cosawes Est TR3 81 B4
Cosdon Pl PL6 124 F1
Coswinsawsin La TR14 79 A5
Cotehele Ave
Plymouth, Keyham PL2 127 F5
Plymouth, Prince Rock PL4 149 C2
Cotehele Cl PL17 39 E3
Cotehele Ho★ PL12 40 F3
Cotehele Quay Mus★ PL12 40 F3
Cotehele View PL18 41 A3
Cot Hill
Plymouth PL7 130 B5
Ponsanooth TR3 81 B4
2 Stratton EX23 4 E1
Cot Hill Trad Est PL7 130 B6
Cot Rd TR15, TR16 67 D4

Cotsland Rd TR1 .... 137 F5
Cotswold Ave PL26 .... 58 E1
Cotswold Cl PL26 .... 58 E1
Cottage Gdns PL15 .... 27 B7
Cottage Mews PL7 ...... 130 E4
Cotton Cl PL7 .... 130 F4
Cott Rd
Lostwithiel PL22 .... 112 D2
Lostwithiel, Polscoe PL22 . 112 D4
Cotts PL20 .... 119 B7
Cot Wood TR3 .... 81 B4
Couchwell La PL22 ...... 112 C2
Coulson's Bldgs 10 TR18 143 E4
Coulson's Pl 9 TR18 .... 143 E4
Coulson's Terr 8 TR18 .. 143 E4
Coulthard Dr TR13 .... 91 A3
Countess Bridge La TR27 . 90 A8
Count House La TR26 ... 141 C2
County Cl PL7 .... 131 A5
County Rd EX23 .... 104 E2
Court Barton Cotts PL9 .. 135 C1
Court Barton Mews PL19 . 106 B4
Courtenay Rd PL19 ...... 147 B6
Courtenay St PL1 .... 148 C3
Courtfield Rd PL3 .... 128 F5
Court Gdns PL25 .... 114 C3
Courtland Cres PL7 ..... 130 D7
Courtlands PL12 .... 122 E1
Courtlands Cl PL19 ...... 147 B6
Courtlands Cres 4 PL25 . 115 A5
Courtlands Rd PL19 ..... 147 B6
Courtlands Sch PL6 ..... 124 F1
Court Mdw PL13 .... 62 B7
Courtney Cl PL13 .... 117 D4
Courtney Ho PL5 .... 124 B2
Courtney Rd
Liskeard PL14 .... 113 D6
St Austell PL25 .... 114 F5
Truro TR1 .... 137 B5
Court The
Camborne TR15 .... 139 C4
Plymouth PL6 .... 125 C7
Saltash PL12 .... 122 C2
Court View PL8 .... 136 F4
Courtyard Cotts TR4 ..... 70 C6
Courtyard The
Redruth TR16 .... 139 F2
Truro TR1 .... 137 D3
Cove Hill
Perranarworthal TR3 ...... 81 D5
Sennen Cove TR19 .... 96 B7
Cove Mdw PL11 .... 127 A6
Coventry Rd TR11 .... 145 B6
Coverack Com Prim Sch
TR12 .... 101 C1
Cove Rd TR19 .... 96 C7
Coverdale Pl PL5 .... 124 C1
Cowdray Cl PL12 .... 122 E2
Cowdray Terr PL12 ...... 122 E1
Cow Lard Cl PL15 .... 106 A4
Cowley Rd PL5 .... 124 D3
Cowling Gdns PL14 ...... 51 F6
Cowling Rd 2 TR3 .... 81 F7
Cox Park Terr PL18 ...... 40 C6
Cox's Cl PL6 .... 125 B1
Coxs Mdw EX22 .... 13 C7
Cox Tor Cl 6 PL20 .... 42 C3
Cox Tor Rd PL19 .... 147 E5
Coypool Rd PL7 .... 130 A6
Crabbs Cl PL15 .... 13 F1
Crabbtree Cl 3 PL14 .... 113 B5
Crabtree Cl PL3 .... 129 F5
Crabtree La PL30, PL31 .. 109 D2
Crabtree Villas PL3 ..... 129 E5
Crackston Cl PL6 .... 129 B7
Craigie Dr PL1 .... 148 A3
Craigmore Ave PL2 ..... 127 F5
Craigside PL13 .... 117 D4
Cramber Cl
Roborough PL6 .... 125 C8
Tavistock PL19 .... 147 B4
Cranberry Rd TR14 ...... 138 B3
Cranbourne Ave PL4 .... 149 C4
Crane Rd TR14 .... 138 C2
Cranfield PL7 .... 130 C7
Cranfield Rd TR14 ...... 138 B3
Cranmere Rd PL3 .... 129 A6
Crantock St TR7 .... 110 D6
Crantock Terr 7 PL2 .... 128 A5
Crapstone Terr PL20 ..... 42 B2
Crashaw Cl PL5 .... 124 D3
Craven Ave PL4 .... 149 C4
Crawford Rd PL1 .... 148 A4
Creakavose PL26 .... 58 B4
Creakavose Pk PL26 ...... 58 A4
Crealy Adventure Park
(Cornwall)★ PL27 .... 32 D4
Crease La PL19 .... 147 A4
Creathorne Rd EX23 ..... 104 E7
Creaz - An - Bre PL26 .... 58 D5
Crediton Wlk PL6 .... 129 E8
Creed La TR2 .... 72 A7
Creedy Rd PL3 .... 129 C5
Creekside View TR2 ...... 70 F4
Creeping La
Newlyn TR18 .... 143 C3
Penzance TR18 .... 143 C4
Crelake Cl PL19 .... 147 C4
Crelake Ind Est 1 PL19 . 147 B4
Crelake Pk PL19 .... 147 C4
Crellow Fields TR3 .... 80 F3
Crellow Hill TR3 .... 80 F3
Crellow La TR3 .... 80 F3
Crellow Terr TR3 .... 80 F3
Crellow Vale TR3 .... 80 F3
Crembling Well TR15 .... 139 E6
Cremyll Rd PL11 .... 127 B2
Cremyll St PL1 .... 134 A8
Crescent Ave PL1 .... 148 B2
Crescent Avenue Mews
PL1 .... 148 B2
Crescent Cl
Hayle TR27 .... 142 C5
Widemouth Bay EX23 .... 6 F5
Crescent Gdns TR1 ...... 137 B4
Crescent Pl TR19 .... 74 F1
Crescent Rd
Bugle PL26 .... 47 C1
Truro TR1 .... 137 B4
Crescent Rise
Constantine Bay PL28 ..... 20 C1
Truro TR1 .... 137 B4
Crescent The
Bude EX23 .... 104 D5
Camborne TR14 .... 138 D4
Carbis Bay TR26 .... 77 C4
Common Moor PL14 ...... 37 F4
Crapstone PL20 .... 42 B3
Gunnislake PL18 .... 41 A6
Landrake PL12 .... 53 C3
Lifton PL16 .... 19 F4
Liskeard PL14 .... 113 C6
Looe PL13 .... 117 D1
Newquay TR7 .... 110 E6
Plymouth PL1 .... 148 B2
Porthleven TR13 .... 91 B1
St Ives TR26 .... 77 A7
St Mabyn PL30 .... 34 D8
Truro TR1 .... 137 B4
Widemouth Bay EX23 .... 6 F5
Cressbrook Cl PL6 ...... 125 F2
Cressbrook Dr PL6 ...... 125 F2
Cressbrook Wlk PL6 .... 125 E2
Cres The PL25 .... 115 B5
Cresthill Rd PL2 .... 128 B7
Creswell Terr TR19 .... 86 F7
Creykes Ct PL1 .... 148 A3
Cribbage Terr 13 PL31 ... 109 D5
Cricketers Hollow PL27 .. 21 E3
Cricket Pk EX23 .... 7 B6
Crift Cotts PL14 .... 51 F7
Crift La PL12 .... 64 F8
Criggan Mill Cvn Pk
TR12 .... 102 C7
Crill Cnr TR11 .... 144 C1
Crinnick's Hill PL31 .... 109 E4
Crinnis Cl PL25 .... 115 E3
Crinnis Rd PL25 .... 115 B3
Crinnis Wood PL25 ...... 115 E3
Crinnis Wood Ave PL25 . 115 D3
Crocker's Row PL18 ..... 41 A6
Crockers Way PL15 ...... 13 F1
Crockwell St PL31 ...... 109 E5
Croft Comm TR14 .... 79 E5
Croftlands PL27 .... 21 E3
Croft Parc TR12 .... 102 F2
Croft Pk PL6 .... 125 C7
Croft Rd TR18 .... 143 C4
Croft Row TR16 .... 80 F8
Crofty Cl TR15 .... 139 C5
Cromartie Rd PL4 .... 129 B1
Cromer Cl PL6 .... 125 A7
Cromer Wlk PL6 .... 125 A7
Cromwell Gate PL6 ..... 125 C7
Cromwell Rd
Plymouth PL4 .... 149 C3
St Austell PL25 .... 114 F3
Crookeder Cl PL9 .... 136 A5
Crookedor La PL11 .... 65 D5
Crooklets EX23 .... 104 C7
Crooklets Rd EX23 ...... 104 D6
Cross PL30 .... 47 F1
Cross Cl TR7 .... 111 C7
Cross Comm TR12 .... 102 F2
Cross Gn PL15 .... 19 F7
Cross Hill PL2 .... 127 E4
Cross La
Bodmin PL31 .... 109 E5
7 St Austell PL25 .... 114 C3
Cross Lanes
Chacewater TR4 .... 69 B1
Cross Lanes TR12 .... 99 C4
Launceston PL15 .... 106 C8
Stratton EX23 .... 4 F1
Crossmount TR7 .... 111 D7
Cross Park Ave PL6 ..... 124 F1
Cross Park Rd PL6 ...... 124 F1
Cross Park Terr PL26 ..... 73 C4
Cross Park Way PL6 ..... 124 F1
Cross Pk
Buckland Monachorum
PL20 .... 42 A3
Crafthole PL11 .... 65 B5
Crossroads Camping Site
TR8 .... 43 D1
Cross St
Camborne TR14 .... 138 D2
Hayle TR27 .... 142 D6
Helston TR13 .... 146 B6
Padstow PL28 .... 107 D5
14 Penzance TR18 ...... 143 E6
3 Redruth TR15 .... 140 B4
Wadebridge PL27 .... 108 B5
Cross Terr PL18 .... 40 F5
Cross The
Camborne TR14 .... 138 D2
St Dominick PL12 .... 40 D2
St Newlyn East TR8 ...... 56 B7
Crosswalla Fields TR13 .. 146 C7
Crosswater EX23 .... 2 C1
Crossway PL7 .... 130 D7
Crossway Ave PL4 ...... 129 B3
Crossways TR11 .... 144 F2
Crowan Prim Sch TR14 ... 79 C2
Crowlas Ind Est TR20 ..... 89 B8
Crown Cl TR7 .... 111 A4
Crown Cres TR8 .... 56 B7
Crowndale Ave PL3 ..... 129 A6
Crown Gdns PL6 .... 125 A1
Crownhill Ct PL6 .... 124 F2
Crownhill Fort★ PL6 .... 124 F3
Crownhill Fort Rd PL6 ... 124 F3
Crownhill Rd PL5 .... 124 C3
Crown Rd PL26 .... 58 D8
Crown Terr PL26 .... 58 D8
Crow Pk PL3 .... 128 F5
Crows-An-Eglos 5 TR26 . 77 A6
Croydon Gdns PL5 ...... 123 E4
Crozier Rd 6 PL4 .... 128 F4
Crun-Melyn Parc TR27 .. 142 B4
Crusoe Flats 43 TR26 .... 141 B6
Cryben TR12 .... 92 C1
Crylla Valley Cvn & Camping
Pk PL12 .... 53 D3
Cryon View TR1 .... 69 E3
Cubert Sch TR8 .... 43 D1
Cuby Cl TR2 .... 72 A3
Cuby Rd TR2 .... 71 F4
Cuckoo La TR20 .... 77 A3
Cuddenbeake Terr PL12 .. 65 B8
Cuffe Rd PL3 .... 128 C4
Culbin Gn PL6 .... 129 D7
Culdrose Airfield TR12 .. 146 E1
Culdrose Cl PL5 .... 123 E4
Cullen View TR2 .... 71 C6
Culme Rd PL3 .... 129 A5
Cul-Rian PL26 .... 58 D7
Culroy Flats 12 TR1 .... 137 C4
Culver Cl PL6 .... 129 A8
Culver Ct PL12 .... 122 F2
Culverland Pk PL14 ..... 113 C7
Culver Rd PL12 .... 122 F2
Culvers Mdw PL15 ...... 106 B8
Culver Way PL6 .... 129 A7
Culverwood Cl PL7 ..... 131 C6
Culverwood Rd PL14 .... 113 B8
Culvery The PL27 .... 108 B4
Cumberland Rd PL1 ..... 127 F1
Cumberland St PL1 ..... 127 E2
Cumble Tor La PL12 ..... 53 D2
Cundy Cl PL7 .... 130 A7
Cundy's La PL26 .... 58 D4
Cunliffe Ave PL9 .... 135 A6
Cunnack Cl TR13 .... 146 C7
Cunningham Pk TR10 .... 81 C1
Cunningham Rd PL5 .... 124 C8
Cunningham Way PL12 .. 122 D3
Curlew Cl TR7 .... 110 B5
Curlew Mews PL3 .... 129 C4
Curlew Pk Ind Est TR4 ... 69 C3
Curlews TR8 .... 43 B1
Curnow Com Spec Sch
TR15 .... 140 B6
Curnows Rd TR27 .... 142 C5
Currian Hill PL26 .... 58 D8
Currian Rd PL26 .... 58 D7
Curtis St PL1 .... 127 E1
Curtis VC Cl TR8 .... 56 B7
Cury CE Prim Sch TR12 ... 99 A4
Cusgarne Com Prim Sch
TR4 .... 81 C7
Cusgarne Hill TR4, TR16 .. 81 B8
Custom House Ct TR18 .. 143 F5
Custom House La
16 Penzance TR18 ...... 143 E5
Plymouth PL1 .... 148 B1
Customs House Hill
PL23 .... 116 D4
Cutcrew La PL12 .... 52 E3
Cuth Avallon TR1 .... 137 C4
Cutmere Hill PL12 .... 52 D3
Cutmere La PL12 .... 52 D3
Cuxhaven Way TR20 ...... 88 F6
Cuxton Mdws PL20 .... 41 F3
Cypress Ave PL25 .... 115 F4
Cypress Cl 6 PL7 .... 131 C5
Cyril Rd TR1 .... 137 C5

D

Dabryn Way PL26 .... 58 B4
Daglands Hill PL23 ..... 116 C4
Daglands Rd PL23 ...... 116 C4
Dairyland Farm World★
TR8 .... 44 F1
Daisymount Dr PL28 ..... 31 F7
Dale Ave PL6 .... 129 C7
Dale Cl TR7 .... 111 A4
Dale Gdns PL4 .... 128 D4
Dale Rd
Newquay TR7 .... 111 A4
Plymouth PL4 .... 128 D4
Daleswood Rd PL19 ..... 147 A4
Dalton Gdns PL5 .... 123 E3
Damerel Cl PL1 .... 127 F2
Dandre Apartments TR7 . 111 A7
Dane Rd TR7 .... 110 D7
Daniel Cl PL25 .... 115 A4
Daniell Ct TR1 .... 137 C3
Daniell Gdns TR1 .... 137 C3
Daniell Rd TR1 .... 137 B3
Daniell St TR1 .... 137 C3
Daniel Pl TR18 .... 143 E4
Daniels La PL25 .... 115 B4
Daniels Sail Loft TR10 .. 144 D7
Danmore Cl PL34 .... 14 C7
Danum Dr PL7 .... 131 B3
Daphne Du Maurier's
Smugglers at Jamaica Inn
Mus★ PL15 .... 25 E3
Darite Prim Sch PL14 .... 38 A4
Darkey La PL16 .... 19 F4
Dark La
Camelford PL32 .... 105 C4
Liskeard PL14 .... 113 D6
Lostwithiel PL22 .... 112 C1
Darklake Cl PL6 .... 125 E5
Darklake La PL6 .... 125 D8
Darklake View PL6 ...... 125 E5
Dark Street La PL7 ..... 130 E4
Darlington Rd TR20 ...... 88 F6
Darloe La PL13 .... 117 C3
Darracott Hill EX39 .... 2 E4
Dart Cl
Plymouth PL3 .... 129 D7
St Giles on t H PL15 ..... 13 F1
Dartington Wlk PL6 ..... 129 E8
Dartmeet Ave PL3 ...... 129 B6
Dartmoor View
Plymouth PL4 .... 129 C3
Saltash PL12 .... 122 E4
Dartmouth Wlk PL6 ..... 129 E8
Darwin Cres PL3 .... 129 D5
Dashwood Ho TR11 ..... 145 A6
Daubuz Cl TR1 .... 137 C6
Daubuz Ct TR1 .... 137 D5
Daucus Cl PL19 .... 147 B4
Davenham Cl PL6 .... 125 B6
Davey's Cl TR11 .... 144 E1
David Cl PL7 .... 130 F6
David Penhaligon Way
TR1 .... 137 D3
David Southgate Ct PL1 . 148 A2
Davy Cl
Torpoint PL11 .... 126 F3
Tremar PL14 .... 38 A3
Davy Rd PL6 .... 125 C4
Davys Row PL14 .... 37 E4
Dawe Cres PL31 .... 109 C3
Dawes Cl PL14 .... 50 E7
Dawes La
Looe PL13 .... 117 D5
Millbrook PL10 .... 132 E5
Plymouth PL9 .... 136 D7
Dawlish Wlk PL6 .... 129 E8
Dawney Terr PL11 .... 65 B5
Dawn Rd PL13 .... 117 D2
Daws Ct PL12 .... 123 A2
Daw's Mdw PL32 .... 105 E4
Dawson Cl PL5 .... 123 E1
Daymer La PL27 .... 21 D4
Daymond Rd PL5 .... 123 D2
Dayton Cl PL6 .... 124 E3
Deacon Dr PL12 .... 122 F1
Deacons Gn PL19 ...... 147 A3
Dean Cross PL9 .... 135 E7
Dean Cross Rd PL9 ..... 135 E7
Dean Hill
Liskeard PL14 .... 113 B6
Plymouth PL9 .... 135 E7
Dean La PL14 .... 113 B6
Dean Park Rd PL9 ...... 135 D7
Dean Rd PL7 .... 130 D6
Dean St PL14 .... 113 B5
Dean Terr PL14 .... 113 B6
Debden Cl PL5 .... 123 D4
Deeble Cl
Plymouth PL7 .... 130 E7
Threemilestone TR3 ...... 69 C3
Deeble Dr 20 PL24 .... 60 B4
Deep La PL7 .... 131 C3
Deer Leap PL19 .... 147 D4
Deer Park Cl PL19 ..... 147 C5
Deer Park Cres PL19 .... 147 C5
Deer Park Dr PL3 ...... 129 D7
Deerpark Forest Trail★
PL14 .... 50 C3
Deer Park La PL19 ..... 147 C5
Deer Park Rd PL19 ..... 147 C5
Deer Pk
Newquay TR7 .... 110 D6
Saltash PL12 .... 122 F3
Defoe Cl PL5 .... 124 C1
Degibna La TR12, TR13 .. 146 C2
Delabole Com Prim Sch
PL33 .... 14 D2
Delacombe Cl PL7 ...... 130 F7
De-La-Hay Ave PL3 ..... 148 A4
Delamere Holiday Bglws
PL33 .... 14 D2
Delamere Rd PL6 .... 129 D7
Delavue Terr PL32 ...... 105 C3
Delaware Com Prim Sch
PL18 .... 40 F5
Delaware Cotts PL18 .... 40 F6
Delaware Ct PL18 .... 40 F5
Delaware Gdns PL2 .... 127 F7
Delaware Rd PL18 .... 40 F6
Dell Cl TR18 .... 143 C3
Dell Mdw PL15 .... 18 B8
Dell The
Plymouth PL7 .... 130 B6
Tavistock PL19 .... 147 B6
Truro TR1 .... 137 C5
Denas Water TR2 .... 71 A5
Dengie Cl PL7 .... 131 B5
Denham Cl PL5 .... 124 C2
Dennis Cl PL5 .... 127 C7
Dennis Gdns PL15 .... 18 C2
Dennis La PL28 .... 107 D4
Dennison Ave PL25 ..... 115 A4
Dennison Rd PL31 ...... 109 D5
Dennis Rd
Liskeard PL14 .... 113 D6
Padstow PL28 .... 107 D5
Dennybowl La
Tideford PL12 .... 52 E3
Tideford PL12 .... 52 F2
Denyer Ct TR11 .... 145 A6
Denys View TR9 .... 45 F2
De Pass Gdns TR11 ..... 145 C3
De Pass Rd TR11 .... 145 C2
Deptford Pl PL4 .... 149 A4
Derby Rd PL5 .... 124 C4
Derby's La PL26 .... 85 C5
Dereham Terr 6 TR1 .... 137 B4
Derowen Dr TR27 .... 142 B3
Derriford Bsns Pk PL6 .. 125 A4
Derriford Hospl PL6 ..... 125 B4
Derriford Pk PL6 .... 125 A3
Derriford Rd PL6 .... 125 B4
Derriton Rd EX22 .... 8 F6
Derry Ave PL4 .... 148 C4
Derry's Cross PL1 ...... 148 B2
Derwent Ave PL3 .... 129 C5
Desborough La PL4 ..... 149 C3
Desborough Rd PL4 .... 149 C3
Deva Ho TR7 .... 111 A6
Deveral Rd TR27 .... 78 D2
Deveron Cl PL7 .... 131 A5
Devington Ct TR11 ..... 145 C2
Devington Hall TR1 ..... 137 E5
Deviock Hill PL11 .... 64 C5
Devonia Cl PL7 .... 130 E7
Devonport High Sch for Boys
PL1 .... 128 A2
Devonport High Sch for Girls
PL2 .... 128 C6
Devonport Hill
Kingsand PL10 .... 133 A2
Plymouth PL1 .... 127 F1
Devonport Leat PL6 .... 121 B5
Devonport Rd PL3 ...... 127 F3
Devonport Sta PL1 ..... 127 F3
Devonshire Ct PL11 .... 127 B3
Devonshire Ho
Plymouth PL1 .... 148 B2
2 Tavistock PL19 .... 147 B5
Devonshire St PL4 ..... 149 A3
Devon Terr PL3 .... 128 E5
Devon Tors PL20 .... 42 D3
Devon Tors Rd 9 PL20 ... 42 C3
Devoran La TR3 .... 81 F6
Devoran Sch TR3 .... 81 F6
Diamond Ave PL4 ...... 149 B4
Diana Cl TR11 .... 144 E2
Dickens Rd PL5 .... 124 B1
Dickiemoor La PL5 ..... 124 C2
Dickna St PL15 .... 13 F1
Dicky La TR3 .... 82 D6
Diddies La EX23 .... 4 E1
Diddies Rd EX23 .... 4 E1
Dieppe Cl PL1 .... 127 F2
Digby Gr PL5 .... 123 F5
Digey Flats 49 TR26 .... 141 B6
Digey The 25 TR26 ..... 141 B6
Diggory's Field 4 PL14 .. 38 A3
Dinas Ct PL11 .... 64 C5
Dinas Rd 1 TR9 .... 45 D6
Dingle Cl PL17 .... 28 D1
Dingle Rd
Plymouth, North Prospect
PL2 .... 128 A6
Plymouth, Plympton PL7 .. 130 C6
Dingles Cl TR3 .... 81 B4
Dingle's Folly PL13 ..... 117 C3
Dingwall Ave PL5 ...... 124 E3
Dipper Cl EX23 .... 5 A6
Dipper La EX23 .... 5 A7
Dirty La PL12 .... 122 B5
Discovery Wharf 20 PL4 . 149 A2
Distine Cl PL3 .... 129 B7
Dithmarschen Way PL25 . 114 B2
Dittisham Wlk PL6 ..... 129 E8
Ditton Ct PL6 .... 129 A8
Dixon Pl PL2 .... 127 F4
Dobbin Cl PL28 .... 20 F2
Dobbin La PL28 .... 20 F2
Dobbin Rd PL28 .... 20 F2
Dobbs La TR1 .... 137 A4
Dobell Rd PL25 .... 114 E4
Dobwalls Com Prim Sch
PL14 .... 50 E7
Dobwalls Family Adventure
Park★ PL14 .... 50 E8
Dockacre Rd PL15 ...... 106 C6
Dockey PL15 .... 106 C5
Dock La TR18 .... 143 F5
Dockray Cl PL6 .... 125 D4
Dockyard PL2 .... 127 E4
Doctors Hill
8 Boscastle PL35 .... 9 C1
5 St Keverne TR12 ...... 101 C4
Doctors La PL12 .... 65 A8
Doctor's La PL14 .... 113 C6
Doddridge Cl PL9 ...... 135 F4
Dodson's Gap TR12 ...... 99 B7
Doidges Farm Cl PL6 ... 129 B8
Dola La TR20 .... 89 E5
Dolbeare Pk (Cvn Pk)
PL12 .... 53 B4
Dolcoath Ave TR14 ..... 138 F3
Dolcoath Cl TR14 ...... 138 F3
Dolcoath Rd TR14 ...... 138 F3
Dolgey Post PL27 .... 32 A4
Dolphin Cl PL9 .... 135 F6
Dolphin Court Rd PL9 ... 135 F6
Dolphin Ho 18 PL4 ..... 149 A2
Dolphin Sq PL9 .... 135 F6
Dolphin St PL29 .... 22 D7
Dolvin Rd PL19 .... 147 C5
Domellick Cnr PL26 ..... 46 B1
Domellick Hill PL26 ..... 46 B1
Doniert's Cl PL14 ...... 113 B5
Donkey La
Millbrook PL10 .... 132 C4

Don–Est 161

Donkey La *continued*
Portwrinkle PL11 . . . . 65 A4
Donkey Pk PL28 . . . . 31 F8
Donnington Dr PL3 . . . . . 129 C7
Donnington Rd TR18 . . . . 143 C3
Donovan Way PL31 . . . . . 109 B4
Dopps Terr TR15 . . . . 140 C5
Dorchester Ave PL5 . . . . . 124 D4
Dorchester Ct TR14 . . . . . 138 E4
Doreena Rd PL9 . . . . 136 C7
Dormy Ave PL3 . . . . 128 F5
Dorset Pk PL15 . . . . 13 A2
Dorsmouth Terr PL7 . . . . 130 E4
Doublebois Ind Est PL14 . 50 D7
Doubletrees PL24 . . . . 60 B4
Doubletrees Ct 2 PL24 . . . 60 B4
Doubletrees Sch PL24 . . . 60 B4
Douglas Cl PL26 . . . . 47 A3
Douglas Dr PL9 . . . . 136 A6
Douglass Rd PL3 . . . . . . 129 C6
Doulton Rd PL25 . . . . 115 A4
Dousland Ho PL20 . . . . . . 42 E3
Dousland Rd PL20 . . . . . . 42 D3
Dousland Terr PL20 . . . . . 42 E3
Dovedale Rd PL2 . . . . 128 A7
Dove Gdns PL3 . . . . 129 D7
Dover Rd PL6 . . . . 125 E3
Dove St 15 TR26 . . . . 141 B5
Dower's Terr TR16 . . . . . . 80 B5
Down Cl PL12 . . . . 122 C2
Downfield Dr PL7 . . . . . . 130 F5
Downfield Way PL7 . . . . . 130 F5
Downfield Wlk PL7 . . . . . 130 F5
Downgate Gdns PL2 . . . . 128 D8
Downham Gdns PL5 . . . . 124 C7
Downham Sch PL9 . . . . . 135 F7
Downhorne Pk PL9 . . . . . 135 F6
Downlea PL19 . . . . 147 D4
Down Park Dr PL19 . . . . . 147 D4
Down Parks EX23 . . . . 5 B7
Down Rd
Plymouth PL7 . . . . 131 C5
Tavistock PL19 . . . . 147 D4
Downs Cl PL26 . . . . 58 C8
Downs Hill PL23 . . . . 61 B5
Downside Ave PL6 . . . . . 129 C7
Downside Cl TR7 . . . . . . 111 A4
Downs La PL13 . . . . 117 B3
Downs Lane Pk PL13 . . . . 117 B3
Downs Rd PL13 . . . . 117 C4
Downs The PL13 . . . . 117 C3
Downstream Cl PL28 . . . . 107 C5
Downs View
Bude EX23 . . . . 104 D7
Looe PL13 . . . . 117 C3
Down The PL20 . . . . 41 C1
Downton Cl PL1 . . . . 148 A4
Dowren Ho TR27 . . . . 142 B5
Dozmere TR3 . . . . 82 C5
Dozmere Cl TR3 . . . . 82 C5
Dracaena Ave
Falmouth TR11 . . . . 144 F5
Hayle TR27 . . . . 142 E6
Dracaena Cres TR27 . . . . 142 E6
Dracaena Pl TR11 . . . . . . 144 F4
Dracaena View TR11 . . . . 144 F5
Drake Cir PL1, PL4 . . . . . 149 A3
drakecircus Sh Ctr PL1 . . 149 A3
Drake Ct
Plymouth, Ernesettle
PL5 . . . . 123 E4
Plymouth, St Jude's PL4 . . 149 B3
Drakefield Dr PL12 . . . . . 123 A3
Drake Gdns PL19 . . . . 147 C4
Drake Prim Sch PL2 . . . . 127 E6
Drake Rd
Padstow PL28 . . . . 107 C5
Tavistock PL19 . . . . 147 C6
Drakes Cl PL6 . . . . 124 F4
Drake's Pk 3 PL20 . . . . . . 41 B1
Drake Villas PL19 . . . . 147 A4
Drakewalls Gdns PL18 . . . . 40 F5
Drakewalls Pl PL18 . . . . . . 40 F5
Drake Way PL9 . . . . 135 E7
Drang The TR9 . . . . 45 E1
Drannack La TR27 . . . . . . 78 D4
Draper Terr 3 PL19 . . . . . 147 B5
Drax Gdns PL6 . . . . 128 E8
Draycott Terr TR26 . . . . . 141 C4
Drayton Rd PL5 . . . . 124 C1
Dreysen Cl TR15 . . . . 139 C8
Drift Cl TR20 . . . . 87 F3
Drift La PL14 . . . . 49 C7
Drillfield La 9 TR26 . . . . 141 B5
Drinnick Terr PL26 . . . . . . 58 D6
Drive The
Helston TR13 . . . . 146 D7
Plymouth PL3 . . . . 128 E7
Driving La PL24 . . . . 60 C6
Drogeada Cl PL15 . . . . 27 D3
Droskyn Castle 19 TR6 . . . 55 A5
Droskyn Cl 22 TR6 . . . . . . 55 A5
Droskyn House Villas TR6 55 A5
Droskyn Way TR6 . . . . 55 A5
Druckham Pl PL15 . . . . . . 106 D5
Druckham Terr PL15 . . . . 106 D5
Druid's Lodge TR15 . . . . . 139 D5
Druid's Rd TR15 . . . . 139 D5
Drummer's Hill PL26 . . . . 114 C8
Drummond Cl PL2 . . . . . . 127 F7
Drummond Pl PL1 . . . . . . 127 F3
Drump Rd TR15 . . . . 140 C5
Drunken Bridge Hill PL7 130 D4
Dryburgh Cres PL2 . . . . . 128 A8
Dryden Ave PL5 . . . . 124 C1
Drym La
Leedstown TR14 . . . . 78 F1
Nancegollan TR14 . . . . 91 A8
Drym Rd TR13 . . . . 91 B7
Dualstone Cross EX22 . . . . . 8 D3
Ducane Wlk PL6 . . . . 125 B1
Duchy Ave TR7 . . . . 111 C7
Duchy Cl
Launceston PL15 . . . . 106 C7
St Austell PL25 . . . . 114 F3
Duchy Coll
St Breock PL27 . . . . 33 C7
Stoke Climsland PL17 . . . . 28 D1
Duchy Cotts PL17 . . . . 28 D1
Duchy Hospl TR1 . . . . 69 E4
Duchy Terr
Minions PL14 . . . . 38 B6
Upton Cross PL14 . . . . 38 D7
Duck La PL12 . . . . 53 E2
Duck St 9 TR19 . . . . 88 C1
Duckworth St 3 PL2 . . . . 128 A4
Ducky La PL12 . . . . 53 C3
Ducky Row PL17 . . . . 40 D4
Dudley Gdns PL6 . . . . 129 B8
Dudley Rd PL7 . . . . 130 B5
Dudman Rd TR1 . . . . 69 F3
Dudnance La TR15 . . . . . . 139 B4
Duke of Cornwall's Light
Infantry Mus★ PL31 . . . . 109 F3
Duke's Ct PL26 . . . . 46 F3
Dukes Dr PL19 . . . . 41 B4
Dukes Ryde The 1 PL9 . . 135 F7
Duke St
Launceston PL15 . . . . 106 A8
Lostwithiel PL22 . . . . 112 C2
Padstow PL28 . . . . 107 D5
Plymouth PL1 . . . . 127 E2
St Austell PL25 . . . . 114 C3
Tavistock PL19 . . . . 147 C6
11 Truro TR1 . . . . 137 D4
Duke's Way TR7 . . . . 111 A5
Duloe CE Jun & Inf Sch
PL14 . . . . 51 A1
Duloe Gdns PL2 . . . . 128 C8
Dumbarton Terr 7 TR19 . 88 C1
Dumfries Ave PL5 . . . . . . 124 D3
Duncannon Dr TR11 . . . . 144 F4
Duncan St PL1 . . . . 127 E1
Dunclair Pk PL3 . . . . 129 D5
Duncombe Ave PL5 . . . . . 124 A2
Dundas St 4 PL2 . . . . 128 A4
Dunders Hill PL27 . . . . 21 D5
Dundonald St PL2 . . . . . . 127 F4
Dungarth Gn PL14 . . . . . . 113 D6
Dungarth Rd PL14 . . . . . . 113 D6
Dunhead View PL15 . . . . . 28 B6
Dunheved Fields PL15 . . . 106 C4
Dunheved Rd
Launceston PL15 . . . . 106 C5
Saltash PL12 . . . . 122 F2
Dunkeswell Cl PL2 . . . . . 127 F8
Dunley Wlk PL6 . . . . 125 C1
Dunmere Cl 1 PL24 . . . . . 60 C4
Dunmere Rd PL31 . . . . . . 109 B5
Dunnet Rd PL6 . . . . 124 D7
Dunn St 10 PL35 . . . . 9 C1
Dunraven Dr PL6 . . . . 125 A6
Dunsdon Cross EX22 . . . . . 5 F3
Dunstable Cl PL26 . . . . 58 D6
Dunstan Cl TR10 . . . . 144 C8
Dunstan La PL12 . . . . 40 A1
Dunstanville Terr 12
TR11 . . . . 145 A5
Dunster Cl PL7 . . . . 131 C4
Dunston Cl PL26 . . . . 58 C8
Dunstone Ave PL9 . . . . . . 136 A7
Dunstone Cl PL9 . . . . 135 F7
Dunstone Com Prim Sch
PL9 . . . . 136 A8
Dunstone Dr PL9 . . . . 135 F7
Dunstone La PL9 . . . . 136 B7
Dunstone Rd
Plymouth, Plymstock PL9 . 135 F7
Plymouth, St Budeaux PL5 . 123 F3
Dunstone View PL9 . . . . . 136 A7
Duntz Hill PL16 . . . . 19 F4
Dunvegan Rd TR10 . . . . . 144 B8
Dunveth Rd PL27 . . . . 108 A5
Dupath La PL17 . . . . 40 A4
Duporth Bay PL26 . . . . . . 115 A1
Duporth Holiday Village
PL26 . . . . 115 A1
Duporth Rd PL25, PL26 . . . 115 A2
Dural Cross EX22 . . . . 3 E3
Durban Rd PL3 . . . . 128 D5
Durgan Crossroads TR11 . 93 D3
Durgan La TR10 . . . . 144 C8
Durham Ave PL4 . . . . 149 C4
Durley Dene TR26 . . . . 77 E4
Durnford St PL1 . . . . 128 A1
Durnford Street Ope
PL1 . . . . 128 A1
Durning Rd TR5 . . . . 54 C1
Durrant Cl PL1 . . . . 127 E3
Durris Cl PL6 . . . . 125 D4
Durris Gdns PL6 . . . . 125 D4
Durston Rd EX23 . . . . 104 E7
Durwent Cl PL9 . . . . 135 A6
Dutson Rd PL15 . . . . 106 C7
Dutson Terr PL15 . . . . 106 C7
Dux Cross EX22 . . . . 8 C6
Duxford Cl PL5 . . . . 123 E5
Dye House Cotts PL14 . . . 36 F2
Dymond Cl PL32 . . . . 105 B2
Dymond Ct (Kingdom Pl)
PL12 . . . . 122 F2
Dynas-la Rd TR26 . . . . . . 141 B4
Dynevor Cl PL3 . . . . 128 F7

E

Eagle Rd PL7 . . . . 131 C4
Earle's Retreat TR11 . . . . 145 B3
Earl's Acre PL3 . . . . 128 C4
Earl's Dr The
Cawsand PL10 . . . . 133 A1
Kingsand PL10 . . . . 133 B3
Earls Mill Rd PL7 . . . . 130 E6
Earls Rise TR7 . . . . 111 B5
Earls Wood Cl PL6 . . . . . . 125 F3
Earls Wood Dr PL6 . . . . . 125 F3
Eastbourne Cl PL25 . . . . . 114 E3
Eastbourne Rd PL25 . . . . 114 D3
East Bridge 4 TR4 . . . . 69 A3
Eastbury Ave PL5 . . . . . . 124 A2
East Camps Bay PL11 . . . . 64 D4
East Charles St TR14 . . . . 138 E2
East Cl TR13 . . . . 146 D7
East Cliff PL13 . . . . 117 D3
Eastcliff Ave TR4 . . . . 68 A7
Eastcliff Avenue No 2
TR4 . . . . 68 A7
Eastcliffe Rd PL24 . . . . 60 C5
East Cliff La TR17 . . . . 89 C5
Eastcote Cl PL6 . . . . 125 B6
Eastcott Cross EX23 . . . . . . 3 A2
Eastella Rd PL20 . . . . 42 D2
East End TR15 . . . . 140 C5
Easterdown Cl PL9 . . . . . 135 F7
Eastern Ave PL14 . . . . . . 113 D6
Eastern Gn
Gulval TR18 . . . . 88 E6
Penzance TR18 . . . . 143 F7
Eastern Green Pk TR18 . . . 88 E6
Eastern La TR14 . . . . 138 D4
Eastern Wood Rd PL7 . . . 131 D4
East Fairholme Rd EX23 . 104 F7
Eastfield Ave PL9 . . . . . . 135 C6
Eastfield Cres PL3 . . . . . . 129 A6
Eastfield Way PL25 . . . . . 114 F5
East Hill
Camborne TR14 . . . . 139 A5
St Austell PL25 . . . . 114 D3
Eastlake Ho 5 PL1 . . . . . 149 A2
Eastlake St PL4 . . . . 148 C3
Eastland Cl TR1 . . . . 137 F4
East Mill PL15 . . . . 106 B7
East Park Ave PL4 . . . . . . 148 C4
East Pk
Pensilva PL14 . . . . 38 D4
Redruth TR15 . . . . 140 D6
East Pool Pk TR15 . . . . . . 139 D6
East Quay TR27 . . . . 142 B6
East Quay Ho PL13 . . . . . 117 D3
East Rd
Kilkhampton EX23 . . . . 5 A6
Menheniot PL14 . . . . 52 A5
Quintrell Downs TR8 . . . . . 44 E3
Stithians TR3 . . . . 80 F3
East Rise TR11 . . . . 144 F3
East Rosewin Row 10
TR1 . . . . 137 D5
East St
Newquay TR7 . . . . 110 E6
Plymouth PL1 . . . . 148 A2
Polruan PL23 . . . . 116 D3
1 St Columb Major TR9 . . . 45 E6
East Terr TR27 . . . . 142 B6
East View PL14 . . . . 51 F5
East Wharf PL26 . . . . 73 C3
Eastwood Park Ind Est
TR10 . . . . 144 D7
Eastwood Rd TR10 . . . . . . 144 D7
East Youlstone Cross EX23 3 C2
Ebenezer Pl 12 TR18 . . . . 143 C1
Ebrington St PL4 . . . . 149 A3
Eddystone Cl PL3 . . . . . . 129 C6
Eddystone Ct PL13 . . . . . 117 D2
Eddystone Pl 3 PL27 . . . 108 B5
Eddystone Rd
Down Thomas PL9 . . . . . . 135 C1
St Austell PL25 . . . . 114 E5
Wadebridge PL27 . . . . . . 108 B6
Eddystone Rise PL14 . . . . 113 D7
Eddystone Road Trad & Ind
Est PL27 . . . . 108 B6
Eddystone Terr
Plymouth PL1 . . . . 148 B1
2 Wadebridge PL27 . . . . 108 B5
Eden Cl 11 PL24 . . . . 60 B4
Eden Gdns 14 TR18 . . . . . 143 C1
Eden Project The★ PL24,
PL26 . . . . 115 D8
Edenside PL3 . . . . 128 F6
Eden Terr 13 TR18 . . . . . 143 C1
Edgar Rd
Jacobstow EX23 . . . . 11 A6
Wainhouse Corner EX23 . . . 10 F6
Edgar Terr PL4 . . . . 129 A4
Edgcumbe Ave
Newquay TR7 . . . . 110 F5
Plymouth PL1 . . . . 148 A3
Edgcumbe Cl PL18 . . . . . . 41 A6
Edgcumbe Cres PL10 . . . . 132 F6
Edgcumbe Ct 3 PL3 . . . . 128 A3
Edgcumbe Dr PL19 . . . . . 147 B6
Edgcumbe Gdns TR7 . . . . 110 F6
Edgcumbe Gn PL25 . . . . . 114 A3
Edgcumbe Ho PL1 . . . . . . 148 B2
Edgcumbe Park Rd PL3 . 128 D6
Edgcumbe Rd
Lostwithiel PL22 . . . . 112 B1
Roche PL26 . . . . 46 F3
Saltash PL12 . . . . 122 C5
St Austell PL25 . . . . 114 A3
St Dominick PL12 . . . . 40 D2
Edgcumbe St PL1 . . . . 128 A1
Edgcumbe Terr
Milton Abbot PL19 . . . . 29 C6
1 Par PL24 . . . . 60 B4
Edgecombe Way PL18 . . . . 40 E5
Edgecumbe Terr 10 PL20 . 41 B1
Edgemoor Cl PL14 . . . . 38 A3
Edinburgh Cl PL25 . . . . . 115 C3
Edinburgh St PL1 . . . . . . 127 E1
Edith Ave PL4 . . . . 149 C4
Edith St PL5 . . . . 123 D1
Edmonton PL27 . . . . 33 B7
Edmund Rd TR15 . . . . 140 B6
Edna Terr PL4 . . . . 149 C3
Ednovean La TR20 . . . . . . 89 E4
Edward Bolitho Ho (Hospl &
Day Ctr) TR18 . . . . 143 D3
Edward Hain Hospl TR26 141 B5
Edwards Cl PL7 . . . . 131 B4
Edwards Cres PL12 . . . . . 122 C2
Edwards Dr PL7 . . . . 131 B5
Edwards Rd
Devoran TR3 . . . . 81 F6
St Giles on t H PL15 . . . . . 13 F1
Edward St
Camborne TR14 . . . . 138 F4
Truro TR1 . . . . 137 C4
Edymeade Ct PL15 . . . . . 106 C5
Edymeade Gdn PL15 . . . . 106 C5
Effingham Cres PL3 . . . . . 128 D7
Efford Cres PL3 . . . . 129 B6
Efford Down Pk EX23 . . . 104 C5
Efford Farm Bsns Pk
EX23 . . . . 104 C4
Efford Farm Cotts EX23 . 104 C4
Efford Fort PL3 . . . . 129 E6
Efford La PL3 . . . . 129 B5
Efford Pathway
Plymouth PL3 . . . . 129 C6
Plymouth PL3 . . . . 129 D5
Efford Rd PL3 . . . . 129 B6
Efford Wlk PL3 . . . . 129 B6
Egan's Way PL33 . . . . 14 D2
Egerton Cres PL4 . . . . . . 149 C3
Egerton Pl PL4 . . . . 149 C3
Egerton Rd
Padstow PL28 . . . . 107 E4
Plymouth PL4 . . . . 149 C3
Eggbuckland Com Coll
PL6 . . . . 129 A8
Eggbuckland Rd PL3 . . . . 129 C7
Eggbuckland Vale Prim Sch
PL6 . . . . 129 A8
Eglos Ct PL30 . . . . 23 E7
Egloshayle Rd
Hayle TR27 . . . . 142 E6
Wadebridge PL27 . . . . . . 108 D5
Egloskerry Sch PL15 . . . . . 18 A5
Eglos Mdw TR11 . . . . 82 A3
Eglos Parc
Mullion TR12 . . . . 99 A2
Wadebridge PL27 . . . . . . 108 D5
Eglos Rd
Ludgvan TR20 . . . . 89 A7
Shortlanesend TR4 . . . . . . 69 F6
St Erme TR4 . . . . 70 D8
Eglos View 2 PL35 . . . . 9 C1
Egret Cl PL10 . . . . 133 A6
Eider Wlk TR27 . . . . 77 E3
Eight Acre Cl 1 PL7 . . . . 131 C5
Elaine Cl PL7 . . . . 130 B5
Elbow La PL19 . . . . 147 C6
Elburton Prim Sch PL9 . . 136 C7
Elburton Rd PL9 . . . . 136 B8
Eldad Hill PL1 . . . . 148 A3
Elder Cl 2 PL7 . . . . 131 B5
Elderfield Cl 7 PL24 . . . . . 60 D5
Eleanor Ho PL1 . . . . 148 A2
Elerkey Cl TR2 . . . . 83 F6
Elerkey La TR2 . . . . 83 F6
Elford Cres PL7 . . . . 130 E7
Elford Dr PL9 . . . . 135 C7
Elford Pk PL20 . . . . 42 D2
Elgin Cres PL5 . . . . 124 E3
Elim Ct PL3 . . . . 128 E5
Elim Terr PL3 . . . . 128 E5
Eliot Cl PL15 . . . . 18 C2
Eliot Ct TR7 . . . . 110 F6
Eliot Dr PL12 . . . . 65 B8
Eliot Gdns TR7 . . . . 110 F6
Eliot Rd
St Austell PL25 . . . . 114 E4
Truro TR1 . . . . 137 C5
Eliot St PL5 . . . . 127 E8
Elizabethan House (Mus)
The★ PL1 . . . . 149 A2
Elizabeth Cl
Bodmin PL31 . . . . 109 D4
Threemilestone TR3 . . . . . . 69 C3
Elizabeth Ct
Bugle PL26 . . . . 47 C1
2 Plymouth PL1 . . . . 149 A2
Elizabeth Pl PL4 . . . . 149 A4
Elizabeth Rd
Bude EX23 . . . . 104 F5
St Austell PL25 . . . . 114 E3
Elizabeth Terr TR17 . . . . . 89 B5
Ellen Cl TR4 . . . . 68 C6
Ellenglaze Ct TR8 . . . . 55 D8
Ellenglaze La TR8 . . . . 55 D8
Ellenglaze Mdw TR8 . . . . . 55 D8
Elliot Sq PL11 . . . . 127 B3
Elliot St PL1 . . . . 148 B1
Elliott Cl PL12 . . . . 122 D2
Elliot Terr PL1 . . . . 148 C1
Elliot Terrace La PL1 . . . . 148 C1
Elliott Rd PL4 . . . . 129 B1
Ellis Cl TR27 . . . . 142 C5
Elliston Gdns 3 TR13 . . . . 98 C8
Ellis Way TR27 . . . . 142 C5
Elm Cl
Callington PL17 . . . . 39 F4
Camborne TR15 . . . . 139 D6
Newquay TR7 . . . . 110 F4
Tavistock PL19 . . . . 147 C3
Elm Cotts PL12 . . . . 122 C3
Elm Court Gdns TR1 . . . . 137 D5
Elm Cres PL3, PL4 . . . . . . 129 A4
Elm Croft PL2 . . . . 128 B7
Elm Ct TR1 . . . . 137 D5
Elm Dr
Bude EX23 . . . . 104 F5
8 St Columb Major TR9 . . . 45 D6
Elmgate Crossways PL12 . 65 E8
Elm Gr
Feock TR3 . . . . 82 C5
Plymouth, Eggbuckland
PL6 . . . . 129 B8
Plymouth, Plympton PL7 . . 130 E5
Elm Grove Cotts TR10 . . . . 93 C6
Elmlea EX23 . . . . 104 F5
Elm Mdw TR3 . . . . 82 C5
Elm Meadow Dr PL13 . . . 117 D4
Elm Pk PL10 . . . . 133 B6
Elm Rd
Plymouth, Glenholt PL6 . . . 125 D6
Plymouth, Mannamead PL4 128 F4
Elms Close Terr 25 TR18 . 143 C2
Elmsleigh PL25 . . . . 114 B3
Elmsleigh Rd PL27 . . . . . 108 B6
Elms The
Perranuthnoe TR20 . . . . . . 89 D4
Plymouth PL3 . . . . 128 A3
Elm Terr
8 Mullion TR12 . . . . 99 A2
1 Plymouth PL3 . . . . 128 F5
St Austell PL25 . . . . 114 C4
Elm Tree Rd PL13 . . . . . . 117 D4
Elmwood Cl PL6 . . . . 125 D5
Elowen Cl TR11 . . . . 144 E2
Elphinstone Rd PL2 . . . . 128 C7
Elspeth Sitters Ho 11
PL4 . . . . 149 A2
Elwell Rd PL12 . . . . 123 A2
Elwick Gdns PL3 . . . . 129 B5
Embankment La PL4 . . . . 129 B2
Embankment Rd PL4 . . . . 129 B2
Embankment Road La N
PL4 . . . . 129 B2
Emily Gdns PL4 . . . . 149 B4
Emlyn Fields PL25 . . . . . . 114 F6
Emma Pl PL1 . . . . 128 A1
Emma Place Ope PL1 . . . 128 A1
Empire Way TR11 . . . . . . 144 E4
Empress Ave 24 TR18 . . . 143 E6
Emslie Rd TR11 . . . . 145 C2
Endsleigh Dr PL15, PL19 . . 28 F5
Endsleigh Gdns
Milton Abbot PL19 . . . . 29 B5
2 Plymouth PL4 . . . . 149 A4
Endsleigh Park Rd PL3 . . 128 D6
Endsleigh Pk EX23 . . . . 7 B6
Endsleigh Pl PL4 . . . . 149 A4
Endsleigh Rd PL9 . . . . . . 135 C7
Endsleigh Terr PL14 . . . . 113 C6
Eningdale Rd PL19 . . . . . 147 A4
Ennerdale Gdns PL6 . . . . 124 E5
Ennis Cl TR4 . . . . 56 D1
Ennor's Rd TR7 . . . . 110 D6
Enys Cl
Carbis Bay TR26 . . . . 141 D1
Truro TR1 . . . . 137 B5
Enys Cotts TR19 . . . . 75 A2
Enys Quay 5 TR1 . . . . 137 D4
Enys Rd
Camborne TR14 . . . . 138 D4
Truro TR1 . . . . 137 B5
Enys Redenek TR14 . . . . . 138 F5
Epping Cres PL6 . . . . 129 D7
Epworth Cl TR1 . . . . 137 E4
Epworth Terr 4 PL2 . . . . 127 F5
Erdiston Ct EX23 . . . . 104 D6
Ergue-Gaberic Way
EX23 . . . . 104 D5
Eric Rd
Calstock PL18 . . . . 41 B3
Plymouth PL4 . . . . 149 C3
Erisey Terr TR11 . . . . 145 B4
Erith Ave PL2 . . . . 127 E7
Erle Gdns PL7 . . . . 130 F3
Erlstoke Cl PL6 . . . . 125 D1
Erme Gdns PL3 . . . . 129 C5
Ermington Terr PL4 . . . . 128 E4
Ernesettle Com Prim Sch
PL5 . . . . 123 F4
Ernesettle Cres PL5 . . . . 123 E3
Ernesettle Gn PL5 . . . . . . 123 E4
Ernesettle La PL5 . . . . . . 123 D4
Ernesettle Rd PL5 . . . . . . 123 E3
Erow Glas TR10 . . . . 144 C8
Esmonde Gdns PL5 . . . . . 127 B8
Esmonde Rd TR13 . . . . . . 146 D4
Esperanza Ct TR11 . . . . . 144 F6
Esplanade PL23 . . . . 116 C3
Esplanade Rd TR7 . . . . . . 110 A6
Esplanade The PL1 . . . . . 148 C1
Essa Rd PL12 . . . . 122 F2
Essex Dr TR15 . . . . 139 B8
Essex St PL1 . . . . 148 B4
Eston Cl TR10 . . . . 93 C8
Estover Cl PL6 . . . . 125 F5
Estover Com Coll PL6 . . . 125 D2
Estover Ind Est PL6 . . . . . 125 E4

Estover Prim Sch PL6 125 D2
Estover Rd PL6 125 F4
Estuary View
2 Falmouth TR11 145 B5
Lelant TR26 77 E3
Newquay TR7 110 D5
Eton Ave PL1 148 C4
Eton Pl PL1 148 C4
Eton St PL1 148 C4
Eton Terr 3 PL1 148 B3
Euny Cl TR15 140 A4
Eureka Vale 7 TR6 55 A5
Europa Ct TR8 31 C2
Evans Ct PL1 148 A3
Evans Pl PL2 128 B5
Evans Way TR20 90 C4
Evea Cl TR1 69 F3
Evely Ct PL14 113 D7
Evelyn Pl PL4 149 A4
Evelyn St PL5 123 D1
Evenden Ct PL11 127 A3
Example Cross PL15 27 B6
Exchange St PL1 149 A2
Exe Gdns PL3 129 C7
Exeter Cl PL5 123 D4
Exeter Ct 6 PL15 106 C6
Exeter St
Launceston PL15 106 C6
Plymouth, Barbican PL4 149 A3
Plymouth, St Jude's PL4 149 B2
Exmouth Ct PL1 127 F3
Exmouth Rd PL1 127 F3
Explorer Ct PL2 128 B5

F

Factory Cotts PL14 51 F5
Fairbourne Rd PL25 114 F4
Fair Cross TR2 72 C6
Fairfax Rd TR2 70 F5
Fairfax Terr 5 PL2 127 F4
Fairfield
Plymouth PL7 130 E7
St Germans PL12 65 A8
Fair Field TR20 89 B8
Fairfield Ave PL2 128 C7
Fairfield Cl
Lelant TR26 77 E4
St Austell PL25 115 A4
Fairfield Pk PL15 26 C7
Fairfield Rd
Bude EX23 104 E5
Falmouth TR11 144 F4
Fairfields PL13 117 D5
Fairlight PL14 113 D5
Fairmantle St TR1 137 D4
Fairmead Cl PL12 53 E4
Fairmead Mews PL12 122 C3
Fairmeadow TR10 144 B7
Fairmead Rd PL12 122 C2
Fairpark Rd
Liskeard PL14 113 C5
Wadebridge PL27 108 B5
Fair Park View TR8 56 F5
Fair St TR9 45 E6
Fair View
Bodmin PL31 109 B4
Lanivet PL26 47 E4
Fairview Ave PL3 129 D5
Fairview Pk 5 TR9 45 E2
Fairview Pl TR11 145 B4
Fairview Terr TR7 110 E6
Fair View Terr TR4 55 D8
Fairview Way PL3 129 E5
Fairway
Saltash PL12 122 C2
St Austell PL25 115 D3
Fairways The PL30 48 C7
Fairway The TR11 93 C2
Falcon Terr EX23 104 D5
Falmouth Bsns Pk TR11 144 E3
Falmouth Com Sch TR11 144 D5
Falmouth Docks Sta TR11 145 D3
Falmouth Hospl TR11 144 F4
Falmouth Marine Sch TR11 145 B4
Falmouth Pl TR19 86 F8
Falmouth Rd
Helston TR13 146 D7
Penryn TR10 144 E7
Redruth TR15 140 C4
Truro TR1 137 C3
Falmouth Town (The Dell) Sta TR11 145 C3
Falmouth Wharves TR11 145 A6
Fanshawe Way PL9 135 C6
Faraday Mill Bsns Pk PL4 129 B1
Faraday Rd PL4 129 B1
Farfield Pl TR7 110 B5
Faringdon Rd PL4 129 B3
Farm Cl PL7 130 C7
Farmers Cl PL14 50 B6
Farmers Ct TR20 89 B8
Farmers Hill PL13 117 C4
Farmer's La PL14 50 B6
Farmers Mdw 8 TR18 143 C2
Farm La
Plymouth PL5 124 B2
Saltash PL12 122 D1
Farm Town TR15 140 C3
Farnley Cl PL6 125 B6
Farrar Cl TR27 142 E8
Farriers Cotts PL7 130 E7
Farriers Gn PL32 105 B2
Farriers The PL19 30 A3
Faugan La TR18 143 B1
Faugan Rd TR18 143 B1
Faukener Cl TR11 144 E4
Fayre View PL12 122 B1
Fearnside Way PL12 122 C3
Federation Rd PL3 129 C4
Fegan Rd PL5 123 B1
Feliskirk La TR17 89 B6
Felixstowe Ave TR7 111 E7
Fellowes Pl PL1 128 A2
Fellows La PL1 148 A4
Fenten Pk PL12 122 F3
Fenteroon Rd PL32 105 C2
Fentonluna La PL28 107 D6
Fenwick Rd TR11 145 B2
Fern Cl PL7 131 C5
Ferndale Ave PL2 127 E7
Ferndale Cl PL6 125 D8
Ferndale Rd
Falmouth TR11 145 A2
Plymouth PL2 127 F7
Ferndale Terr PL14 113 B6
Fern Glen 18 TR26 141 A5
Fernhill Rd TR7 110 D6
Fern Lee Terr 19 TR26 141 B5
Fernleigh Cres PL27 108 C4
Fernleigh Gdns PL27 108 C4
Fernleigh La PL27 108 C4
Fernleigh Rd
Plymouth PL3 128 F5
Wadebridge PL27 108 C5
Fernleigh Terr
Gunnislake PL18 40 E5
Nanpean PL26 58 C6
Fern Mdw PL19 147 D6
Fernside Pk PL14 38 A3
Fernside Rd TR14 138 B1
Ferrers Rd PL5 123 E1
Ferretts Cross EX23 11 A6
Ferris Town TR1 137 C4
Ferris Way PL23 116 E2
Ferry La PL11 126 D5
Ferry Rd PL1 127 E3
Ferry St PL11 127 C3
Festival Villas TR3 69 D3
Feversham Cl PL7 131 B6
Field Cl PL22 112 D2
Field Pl TR11 93 D3
Field The TR20 76 F2
Fifield Ho PL26 58 B4
Fillace La 10 PL20 42 C4
Fillace Pk PL20 42 C4
Filtrick La TR16 139 E1
Finch Cl PL3 129 D4
Finches Cl PL9 136 C7
Findon Gdns PL6 125 D4
Finewell St PL1 148 C2
Finnigan Rd PL4 129 B1
Finn VC Est PL31 109 D5
Finnygook La PL11 65 A4
Fir Cl
Goonhavern TR4 55 D4
Helston TR13 146 B7
St Austell PL25 114 B3
Fir Cres PL26 58 D5
Fircroft Rd PL2 128 B7
Firebeacon Cross EX39 2 F7
Fir Gr 8 TR3 81 F7
Firsleigh Pk PL26 46 F3
First Ave
Plymouth, Billacombe PL9 135 F8
Plymouth, Stoke PL1 128 A2
Firs The PL26 58 E8
Fisgard Way PL11 126 D3
Fisher Cl PL27 108 D6
Fisher Rd PL2 128 A5
Fish Mkt PL4 149 B2
Fish Quay PL4 149 A2
Fish St 9 TR26 141 B6
Fish Strand Hill TR11 145 B4
Fish Strand Quay TR11 145 B4
Fistral Cl PL11 126 F4
Fistral Cres TR7 110 A5
Fistral Ct TR7 110 A5
Fistral Sands Apartments TR7 110 D7
Fitzford Cotts PL19 147 B4
Fitzroy Rd PL1 128 A3
Fitzroy Terr 7 PL1 128 A3
Fitzsimmons Cl 7 TR13 146 C5
Five Fields La TR11 145 A5
Five Wells La TR13 146 B5
Flamank Pk PL31 109 C4
Flambards Experience★ TR13 146 E4
Flamborough Rd PL6 125 A7
Flamborough Way PL6 125 A6
Flamsteed Cres PL5 123 E1
Flaxmoor Terr PL31 109 D5
Fleet St PL2 127 E6
Fletcher Cres PL9 136 B6
Fletcher Way PL9 136 A6
Fletemoor Rd PL5 123 E1
Flexbury Ave EX23 104 E7
Flexbury Mews EX23 104 E7
Flexbury Park Ct EX23 104 E7
Flexbury Park Rd EX23 104 E6
Flexbury Pk EX23 104 E7
Flora Cotts PL1 148 B2
Flora Ct PL1 148 B3
Flora St PL1 148 B2
Florence Hill PL17 39 F5
Florence Pl
Falmouth TR11 145 B3
Newlyn TR18 143 C3
Plymouth PL4 149 C3
Florence Rd PL17 39 F5
Florence Road Bsns Pk PL17 39 F6
Florence Road Ind Est PL17 39 F6
Florence St PL5 123 D1
Florence Terr TR11 145 B3
Florida Gdns PL3 129 C6
Floyd Cl PL2 127 F7
Flushing Sch TR11 145 B6
Folders La PL30 23 F6
Foliot Ave PL2 128 A6
Foliot Rd PL2 128 A6
Folkstone Cl PL26 58 E6
Forbes Cl TR18 143 B1
Forbes Rd TR18 143 B1
Ford PL22 49 E3
Forder Hill PL10 132 F1
Forder Hts PL6 125 B1
Forder La PL10 132 F1
Forder Valley Rd PL6 129 D8
Ford Hill PL2 128 A5
Ford Park La PL4 128 E4
Ford Park Rd PL4 128 D4
Ford Prim Sch PL2 128 A5
Fords Hill TR12 100 D7
Ford's Row TR15 140 B5
Ford St PL19 147 B5
Foredown Pk PL14 38 C3
Fore St
Ashton TR13 90 E3
Barripper TR14 79 B5
Bere Alston PL20 41 B1
Bere Ferrers PL20 119 F3
Bodmin PL31 109 D5
Boscastle PL35 9 C1
Bugle PL26 47 C1
6 Callington PL17 39 E4
Calstock PL18 41 A3
Camborne TR15 139 B6
Camelford PL32 105 D4
Cargreen PL12 119 A2
Carharrack TR16 80 F8
Chacewater TR4 69 A3
Constantine TR11 92 F4
Crumplehorn PL13 62 D1
Fowey PL23 116 D4
Golant PL23 61 B5
Goldsithney TR20 89 E5
Grampound Road TR2 57 E1
Grampound TR2 72 A7
Gunnislake PL18 40 F5
Gunnislake PL18 41 A6
Hayle TR27 142 D6
Herodsfoot PL14 50 E3
Kingsand PL10 133 A2
Lelant TR26 77 E4
Lerryn PL22 61 C7
Lifton PL16 19 F4
Liskeard PL14 113 C6
Looe PL13 117 C3
Lostwithiel PL22 112 C2
Madron TR20 88 B7
Marazion TR17 89 C5
Mevagissey PL26 73 C3
Millbrook PL10 132 E5
Milton Abbot PL19 29 C6
Mount Hawke TR4 68 C6
13 Mousehole TR19 88 C1
Nanpean PL26 58 D7
Newlyn TR18 143 C1
Newquay TR7 110 D6
Par PL24 60 B5
Penponds TR14 138 B1
Pensilva PL14 38 E4
Plymouth, Devonport PL1 127 F2
Plymouth, Plympton PL7 130 E4
Plymouth, Tamerton Foliot PL5 124 B6
Polgooth PL26 59 A1
Polruan PL23 116 D2
4 Porthleven TR13 98 B8
Port Isaac PL29 22 D7
Praze-an-Beeble TR14 79 B2
Probus TR2 71 C6
Redruth TR15 140 B5
Roche PL26 46 F2
Saltash PL12 122 F2
St Austell PL25 114 C3
St Cleer PL14 37 F3
St Columb Major TR9 45 E6
St Day TR16 68 D1
St Dennis PL26 58 C8
St Erth TR27 142 A1
St Germans PL12 65 A8
Sticker PL26 58 E1
St Ives TR26 141 B6
St Just TR19 86 F6
7 Stratton EX23 4 E1
St Stephen PL26 58 B4
St Teath PL30 23 E7
Tintagel PL34 14 C7
Torpoint PL11 127 B3
Tregony TR2 71 F3
Troon TR14 79 E5
9 Tywardreath PL24 60 D5
Forest Ave PL2 128 C7
Foresters Rd PL9 135 D7
Forest Hos TR4 70 D8
Forest View PL6 125 D7
Forge Gdns EX23 6 F1
Forge Ind Pk TR14 138 E5
Forge La PL12 122 C4
Forge The TR3 82 A7
Forge Way TR4 69 F6
Forlaze Rd PL27 21 D2
Formal Ind Pk TR14 138 B4
Forrabury Hill 5 PL35 9 C1
Forreglos Dr 10 TR17 89 C5
Forresters Dr PL6 125 D7
Forsythia Dr PL12 122 C3
Fort Austin Ave PL6 125 C1
Fortescue Cl PL26 58 D6
Fortescue Pl
Lostwithiel PL22 112 D3
Plymouth PL3 129 A6
Fortescue Terr PL19 147 A6
Forth An Cos TR3 81 B4
Forth-an-Eglas TR16 68 D1
Forth-An-Nance TR16 67 C6
Forth-An-Praze
Illogan TR15 139 D8
St Day TR16 68 D1
Forth-An-Ryn TR15 140 D4
Forth An Streth TR27 142 E7
Forth An Tewennow TR27 142 D7
Forth-An-Tre TR27 142 D7
Forth An Ula TR27 142 E7
Forth An Vre TR14 139 A3
Forth Coth TR3 82 A7
Forthcrom TR12 92 C1
Forth Gwel 21 TR16 67 E4
Forth Gdns PL3 129 D6
Forth Gwedhen TR13 146 D8
Forth Kegyn TR15 139 B4
Forthnoweth TR15 140 B5
Forth Noweth 4 TR3 81 F7
Forth Scol
Camborne TR15 139 D7
6 Porthleven TR13 98 C8
Forthvean
Camborne TR14 138 D1
Portreath TR16 67 C5
Forth Vean TR13 90 E6
Forthvean Cres TR4 68 A6
Forthvean Rd TR4, TR16 67 E7
Forth Veor TR15 140 E7
Forthvras TR15 139 B8
Fort Picklecombe PL10 133 F4
Fort Terr PL6 124 F3
Fort The PL10 133 A1
Fosbrooke Ct 10 PL3 128 F6
Foster Dr PL31 109 C3
Fosters La PL34 14 C7
Fosters Way EX23 104 F6
Foulston Ave PL5 127 B8
Foundry Flats TR27 142 B5
Foundry Gdns PL15 106 B6
Foundry Hill
Hayle TR27 142 B4
Stithians TR3 80 F3
Foundry Ho TR27 142 B5
Foundry La
Hayle TR27 142 B5
Newlyn TR18 143 C2
Foundry Rd TR14 138 E3
Foundry Row
Marhamchurch EX23 7 B6
5 Redruth TR15 140 B5
Foundry Sq TR27 142 B5
Foundry St 6 PL27 108 B5
Foundry Terr PL27 108 B5
Fountain Ct 27 TR18 143 E6
Fountains Cres PL2 128 C8
Four Acres Rd TR2 83 F6
Fourgates Est PL14 51 F5
Four Lanes' End TR19 97 F6
Fourlanesend Com Prim Sch PL10 132 F3
Four Turnings PL23 60 F3
Fowey Com Coll PL23 116 B4
Fowey Cres 27 PL17 39 F4
Fowey Gdns PL3 129 D6
Fowey Hospl PL23 116 C5
Fowey Mus★ PL23 116 D4
Fowey Prim Sch PL23 116 C4
Fowlfield Row TR13 90 F3
Foxdown PL27 108 D5
Foxes Field TR18 88 E6
Foxes La 5 TR19 88 C1
Foxes Row TR16 80 E8
Fox Field Cl PL3 129 C5
Foxglove Cl PL15 106 E4
Foxglove Cres PL28 31 F7
Foxglove Way PL12 122 B3
Foxhole La PL26 85 D5
Foxhole Prim Sch PL26 58 D5
Fox's La TR11 145 B3
Foxstanton Dr TR10 144 D7
Foxs Yd TR10 144 D7
Foxtor Cl PL5 124 B3
Foxwood Gdns
Plymouth, Plymstock PL9 135 F5
Plymouth, Southway PL6 124 E5
Foyle Cl PL7 131 A5
Fraddam Rd TR27 78 D1
Fradgan Pl TR18 143 C2
Fradgan The 12 TR18 143 C2
Frances St TR1 137 C4
Francis La PL27 21 D5
Francis Rd PL27 21 D5
Francis St PL1 148 A3
Frankfort Gate 9 PL1 148 B3
Frankland Cl TR11 144 F3
Franklin Cl PL27 108 D6
Franklyn Cl PL25 114 F5
Franklyns' PL6 125 A4
Franklyns Cl PL6 125 A4
Franwill Terr 15 TR18 143 C1
Fraser Pl PL5 124 C7
Fraser Rd PL5 124 C7
Fraser Sq PL5 124 C7
Frederick St E PL1 148 B3
Frederick St W 6 PL1 148 B3
Fredington Gr PL2 128 B6
Freedom Sq PL4 149 B4
Freeman Collins Dr TR11 144 F4
Freemans Wharf PL1 134 A8
Fremantle Gdns 4 PL2 127 F4
Fremantle Pl PL2 127 F4
Frenchman's La PL12 53 C4
Frensham Ave PL6 125 C7
Frensham Gdns PL6 125 C7
Freshbrook Cl TR18 88 E6
Freshford Cl PL6 125 C1
Freshford Wlk PL6 125 C1
Freshwater La TR2 95 B6
Frewin Gdns PL6 125 B6
Friar's La TR12 102 F6
Friars' La PL1 149 A2
Friar's La TR12 103 B5
Friars Wlk PL19 147 E2
Friary Pk PL4 149 B3
Friary St PL4 149 B3
Frith Rd PL12 122 D3
Frobisher App PL5 124 D2
Frobisher Dr PL12 122 E2
Frobisher Terr 9 TR11 145 A5
Frobisher Way
Tavistock PL19 147 B5
Torpoint PL11 126 D3
Frog La TR2 71 F3
Frogmore Ave
Plymouth PL6 129 B7
Plymouth PL6 129 C7
Frogmore Ct PL6 129 B7
Frogwell Rd PL17 39 E4
Frome Cl PL7 131 A4
Frontfield Cres PL6 124 E5
Front Rd PL11 64 C4
Frost Ct TR11 144 E5
Fuggoe Croft TR26 141 C3
Fuggoe La TR26 141 C2
Fullaford Rd PL17 40 A4
Fuller Rd TR6 55 A5
Fullerton Rd PL2 128 A5
Fuller-Tre Cl PL26 46 F3
Furland Cl PL9 135 C5
Furneaux Ave PL2 128 B5
Furneaux Rd PL2 128 B6
Furry Way TR13 146 B5
Fursdon Cl PL9 136 C6
Furse Pk PL5 127 C7
Furzeacre Cl PL7 131 A7
Furze Cross EX22 8 B5
Furzedown Terr PL13 117 C4
Furze Gdns EX23 2 D1
Furzehatt Ave PL9 136 A6
Furzehatt Park Rd PL9 136 A6
Furzehatt Rd PL9 135 F6
Furzehatt Rise PL9 136 A6
Furzehatt Villas PL9 135 F6
Furzehatt Way PL9 136 A6
Furze Hill PL31 109 E5
Furzehill Rd PL4 128 F4
Furze Pk
Polruan PL23 116 D2
St Issey PL27 32 D5
Trelights PL29 22 D6

G

Gabriel St 5 TR26 141 B5
Gaia Energy Ctr The★ PL32 14 F4
Gainsborough Ct TR7 110 D5
Gainsborough Ho PL19 147 B6
Gainsborough Park Cvn Pk PL26 58 E6
Gains Cross EX22 5 F3
Galileo Cl PL7 130 E6
Gallacher Way PL12 122 B3
Galland Rd TR1 69 F4
Gallant's Dr PL23 116 B3
Galleon Ct TR7 110 D4
Galleries The 46 TR26 141 B6
Gallery La
Landrake PL12 53 A1
St Germans PL12 65 A8
Galligan Cl TR19 97 A6
Galligan La TR19 97 A6
Gallops The PL12 122 D4
Galsworthy Cl PL5 124 C2
Galva Rd PL7 131 C8
Gander La TR13 146 B6
Ganges Cl TR11 82 C2
Ganges Rd PL2 128 A5
Ganna Park Rd PL3 128 D6
Gannel Rd TR7 110 E4
Gannel View Cl TR8 111 B3
Gannet Dr PL25 114 F4
Gara Cl PL9 136 B6
Garby La TR15 140 C3
Garcia Terr PL15 106 D4
Garden Cl PL7 131 D5
Garden Cres PL1 148 B1
Gardeners Way PL27 32 E6
Garden House The★ PL20 42 A3
Garden La PL19 147 B5
Garden Mdw TR11 144 E3
Garden Park Cl PL9 136 C7
Garden St PL2 127 E4
Garden Village PL9 135 F8
Garden Way TR8 111 F3
Gards La PL5 123 E2
Garfield Terr PL1, PL3 128 A3
Garland Pl TR14 138 D4

Garlidna 25 TR18 143 E6
Garras Com Prim Sch
TR12 99 D7
Garrett St PL10 133 A1
Garrick Cl PL5 124 C2
Garris Cotts TR20 88 E8
Garrison Cl PL1 127 E1
Garro La TR12 99 A1
Garston Cl PL9 136 A8
Garth-An-Creet TR26 77 A7
Garth Marhas TR14 138 C3
Garth Morcom PL14 113 B5
Garth Rd TR18 143 B3
Gascoyne Ct PL4 149 A3
Gascoyne Pl PL4 149 A3
Gas Hill TR1 137 E2
Gashouse La PL4 149 B2
Gasking St PL4 149 A3
Gas La 8 TR15 140 B4
Gas St TR14 138 D3
Gateway Ct TR27 77 E2
Gatewynyack TR12 101 C1
Gavercoombe Pk 2 PL34 14 C7
Gay's Hill TR12, TR13 146 E4
Gays La PL12 65 A8
Gdynia Way PL4 149 C2
Gear Hill
Madron TR20 88 C8
Mawgan TR12 99 E8
Gear La TR20 88 B8
Gears La
Goldsithney TR17, TR20 89 D6
Goldsithney TR20 89 E5
Geasons La PL7 130 E5
Geevor Cotts TR19 86 F8
Geevor Tin Mine★ TR19 74 F1
Geevor Tin Mine Mus★
TR19 74 F1
Geffery Cl PL12 53 C3
Gendalls Way PL15 106 B8
Gennys Cl PL18 40 E6
George Ave PL7 130 F6
George Cross PL7 130 F5
George Downing Ho
PL6 125 A1
George Fox Cl PL15 106 A4
George La PL7 130 F5
George Pl
Callington PL17 39 E4
Plymouth PL1 148 A2
Georges La PL11 65 C6
Georges Paddock PL15 27 B3
George Sq PL1 127 F1
George St
Plymouth PL1 127 F1
Truro TR1 137 C4
Georgia Cres PL3 129 C6
Geraldine Terr PL12 122 C1
Germoe Com Prim Sch
TR20 90 C4
Gerrans Cl PL25 115 B5
Gerrans Hill TR2 83 B2
Gerrans Sch TR2 83 B1
Gerrans Sq TR2 83 B2
Gewans Mdw PL25 114 E2
Ghost Hill TR12 99 A1
Gibbon La PL4 149 A3
Gibbons Fields 9 TR12 99 A2
Gibbons St PL4 149 A3
Gibbs La PL35 9 C1
Gibraltar Terr 6 TR2 95 A6
Gibralter Sq 6 EX23 4 E1
Gibson Way TR13 91 B1
Gifford Pl PL3 128 D4
Gifford Terrace Rd PL3 128 E5
Gig La TR3 82 A7
Gilbert Cl PL26 58 B4
Gilbert Ct PL7 131 B6
Gilbert La PL2 128 C5
Gilbert Rd PL31 109 F4
Gill-An-Creet TR26 77 A7
Gillbard Centenary Flats
PL15 106 B5
Gillbard Centenary Homes
PL15 106 B5
Gilley La PL26 73 A4
Gill Pk PL3 129 B5
Gills Cl TR10 144 B6
Gilly Fields TR15 140 B3
Gilly Gabben Ind Est TR12 99 B7
Gilly Hill
Cury TR12 99 B5
Redruth TR15 140 C3
Gilly La TR26 77 C1
Gilston Rd PL12 122 D4
Gilwell Ave PL9 136 B7
Gilwell Pl PL4 149 A3
Gilwell St PL4 149 A3
Gipsy La
Liskeard PL14 113 A5
Sithney TR13 91 C2
Gitchell La
Crowlas TR20 89 C8
St Erth TR26 77 C1
Glade Cl PL6 125 A4
Glade The
Crapstone PL20 42 B2
St Minver PL27 22 A3
Gladstone Rd PL30 109 C2
Gladstone Terr
Longrock TR20 88 F6
3 Redruth TR15 140 C5
Gladwell Gdns 10 EX23 4 D1
Glamis Rd TR7 111 B6
Glantis Cres TR9 45 E2
Glanville Ave 1 PL19 147 B5
Glanville Rd PL19 147 B6
Glanville St PL1, PL4 148 C3
Glanville Terr PL12 122 F3
Glasney Pl TR10 144 C7
Glasney Rd TR11 145 A5
Glasney Terr TR10 144 D7
Glebe Ave PL12 122 F3
Glebe Cl
Mawgan TR12 99 D7
Pelynt PL13 62 D5
6 St Columb Major TR9 45 E6
Glebe Cres PL27 32 D6
Glebe Dr PL26 46 F3
Glebe Est PL14 38 F2
Glebelands
Callington PL17 39 E5
Looe PL13 117 D5
Glebe Mdw PL17 39 E5
Glebe Parc PL30 23 E3
Glebe Pl TR12 103 B5
Glebe Row TR27 142 D7
Glebe Terr
Constantine TR11 92 F4
Ruan Minor TR12 103 B5
Glebe The
Camborne TR14 138 C3
Cubert TR8 55 D8
St Mellion PL12 53 D8
Tregony TR2 71 F4
Week St Mary EX22 11 E8
Glenavon Rd PL3 128 E5
Glenburn Cl PL3 128 E7
Glencross Ct 3 PL14 113 C6
Glen-Dale Cl 3 PL25 115 A5
Glendale Cres TR4 68 C6
Glen Dale Cres TR15 140 D4
Glen-Dale Cres PL25 115 A5
Glendale Terr PL26 58 E3
Glendower Rd PL3 128 D5
Glendurgan Gdns★ TR11 93 D2
Gleneagle Ave 4 PL3 128 F6
Gleneagle Rd PL3 128 F6
Gleneagle Villas 5 PL3 128 F6
Glenfeadon Terr TR16 67 C6
Glenfield Cl PL6 125 D6
Glenfield Rd PL6 125 D5
Glenfield Way PL6 125 E6
Glenhaven Pk (Cvn Pk)
TR13 146 D5
Glenholt Cl PL6 125 D6
Glenholt Rd PL6 125 D6
Glenhurst Rd 5 PL3 128 E6
Glen Leigh TR15 140 A6
Glenleigh Pk PL26 58 E1
Glenmoor La TR12 99 A1
Glenmore Ave PL2 127 F5
Glenmore Terr
Liskeard PL14 113 D6
Mabe Burnthouse TR10 81 A1
Glennaven Cl PL7 131 C6
Glen Park Ave PL4 148 C4
Glen Park Prim Sch PL7 131 B5
Glen Pk PL14 38 D4
Glen Rd
Plymouth, Mannamead
PL3 128 F5
Plymouth, Plympton PL7 130 F6
Wadebridge PL27 108 B5
Glenside Rise PL7 130 E6
Glenthorne Rd TR3 69 C3
Glentor Rd PL3 128 E7
Glentowan Rd PL26 73 C6
Glen Vale TR15 139 E6
Glenview PL25 114 B3
Glen View
Callington PL17 39 E5
Penryn TR10 144 B8
Tywardreath PL24 60 D5
Wadebridge PL27 108 B4
Glenwood Rd PL3 128 E6
Globerdon Rd PL14 38 E4
Globe Sq TR16 139 F2
Globe Vale Cvn Pk TR16 68 B3
Gloucester Ave PL25 115 C3
Gloucester Cres TR18 143 B1
Gloucester Ct PL1 148 C4
Gloucester Pl
27 Newlyn TR18 143 C2
Plymouth PL1 148 C4
Gloucester Rd TR18 143 C2
Gloweth View TR1 69 E3
Gloweth Villas TR1 69 E3
Gluyas The TR11 144 E1
Glynn Ave 8 TR13 146 C5
Glynn Rd
Liskeard PL14 113 A5
Padstow PL28 107 D5
Glyn Way TR3 69 D3
Goad Ave
Plymouth PL4 149 C2
Torpoint PL11 126 E3
Goad Cl PL11 126 F3
Godding Gdns PL6 124 E6
Godolphin Ave TR17 89 B5
Godolphin Cl TR17 89 B6
Godolphin Cres TR13 90 E6
Godolphin Ct 5 TR14 138 D3
Godolphin Dr TR17 89 B5
Godolphin Ho
Godolphin Cross TR13 90 E6
Tavistock PL19 147 C5
Godolphin Pk 11 PL17 39 E4
Godolphin Pl TR17 89 B5
Godolphin Prim Sch TR13 90 E6
Godolphin Rd
Falmouth TR11 144 F5
Helston TR13 146 C6
Longrock TR20 88 F6
Godolphin Terr TR17 89 B5
Godolphin Way TR7 111 B7
Godrevy Ct TR26 141 D2
Godrevy Ho TR1 69 E4
Godrevy Pk (Cvn Pk)
TR27 66 B1
Godrevy Terr 28 TR26 141 B6
Goldbank Bglws PL30 34 C2
Golden Bank Pk TR11 144 E1
Golden Sands 11 TR6 55 A5
Golden Sands Bglws
TR27 142 E7
Golden Sands Cvns TR27 142 E7
Goldfinch Cl PL15 106 E4
Goldfinch Gr PL12 122 D4
Goldmartin Cl TR11 93 D3
Goldmartin Sq TR11 93 D3
Goldsmith Gdns PL5 124 D3
Goldsworthy Way PL27 108 B5
Golf House Rd EX23 104 D6
Golf Terr TR7 110 C6
Golf View TR14 79 B2
Golitha Falls★ PL14 37 D3
Golitha Rise PL14 113 E6
Golva Cl TR13 91 E4
Gonvena Hill PL27 108 D6
Gonvena Ho PL27 108 C6
Goodeve Cl PL9 135 E6
Goodmans La PL14 38 D4
Goodwin Ave PL6 125 A6
Goodwin Cres PL2 128 A6
Goonabarn Cotts PL26 58 C5
Goonavean Pk PL26 58 D5
Goongumpas La TR16 68 E1
Goonhavern Ind Est TR4 55 D4
Goonhavern Prim Sch
TR4 55 D4
Goonhilly Cl TR4 55 D4
Goonhilly Earth Station★
TR12 99 F4
Goonlaze Terr
St Agnes TR5 54 D1
Stithians TR3 80 D4
Goonown La TR5 54 D1
Goonown Rd
Goonbell TR5 68 D8
St Agnes TR5 54 D1
Goonrea PL13 117 B4
Goonvrea TR3 81 D5
Goonvrea Cl TR7 110 F4
Goonvrea Ct TR7 110 F4
Goonvrea Rd TR5 54 C1
Goonwartha Cl PL13 117 C4
Goonwartha Rd PL13 117 B3
Gooseberry La
Pensilva PL14 38 E4
Plymouth PL1 148 B2
Gooseford La PL11 132 C8
Goosewell Hill PL6 129 C8
Goosewell Park Rd PL9 135 F6
Goosewell Prim Sch PL9 135 F6
Goosewell Rd PL9 135 F5
Goosewell Terr PL9 135 F6
Gordon Ct PL12 122 D2
Gordon Pl 8 TR9 45 E6
Gordons Cl TR3 80 F3
Gordon Terr PL4 128 E4
Gorran Sch PL26 85 B5
Gorse Cl TR7 111 A4
Gorsey Cl PL5 124 E2
Gorvin Cross EX39 3 E6
Goswela Cl PL9 135 F5
Goswela Gdns PL9 135 F5
Gotch Gdns PL14 50 B6
Gothers Hill PL26 46 D1
Gothers Rd
St Dennis, Gothers PL26 46 D1
St Dennis, Hendra PL26 58 C8
Goudges La PL26 58 E8
Gounce The 14 TR6 55 A5
Gover Cl TR4 68 C6
Gover La TR7 110 D6
Gover Rd PL25 114 B4
Goverseth Cvn Pk PL26 58 D6
Goverseth Hill PL26 58 D6
Goverseth Rd PL26 58 D6
Goverseth Terr PL26 58 D6
Gower Ridge Rd PL9 135 D6
Goyne's Field TR4 68 A7
Gracca Terr PL26 47 C1
Grade-Ruan CE Sch
TR12 103 B5
Grafton Rd PL4 128 E4
Graham Ave PL25 114 E4
Graham Rd
Redruth TR15 140 C5
Redruth TR15 140 D4
Grainge Rd PL6 125 A1
Grampound Road Ind Est
TR2 57 E1
Grampound Road Village CE
Sch TR2 57 E1
Grampound-with-Creed CE
Sch TR2 72 A7
Granby Ct PL1 127 E2
Granby Gn PL1 127 E2
Granby Pl PL1 127 E2
Granby St PL1 127 E2
Granby Way PL1 127 E2
Grand Hotel Rd PL1 148 B1
Grand Par PL1 148 B1
Grange Rd
Helston TR13 146 B5
Plymouth PL7 131 A4
Yelverton PL20 42 C3
Grange The TR14 138 C2
Granite Way PL17 39 F4
Grannery Ct EX23 104 D5
Granny's Gn PL31 109 E3
Granny's La TR6 55 A4
Grantham Cl PL7 130 B4
Grantley Gdns PL3 129 A5
Grant's Ct PL25 114 C3
Grant's Wlk 4 PL25 114 C3
Granville Terr EX23 104 D5
Grasmere Cl PL6 124 E5
Grasmere La PL14 38 B5
Grassendale Ave PL2 127 F7
Grass La PL2 128 C6
Grassmere Way PL12 122 D4
Grass Valley Pk PL31 109 F1
Gratton Cross PL20 42 D2
Gratton La PL20 42 D2
Gratton Pl PL6 125 A1
Gravesend Gdns PL11 127 B3
Gravesend Wlk PL5 123 D4
Graybridge Rd PL20 42 C4
Gray Cres PL5 127 C8
Great Berry Rd PL6 124 F1
Great Charles Cl PL26 58 B4
Great Churchway PL9 136 A7
Greatfield Rd PL3 129 B7
Greatlands Cres PL2 128 A6
Greatlands Pl 5 PL2 128 A5
Great Mdw PL14 36 F2
Great Mills Ind Parc
PL25 115 E4
Great Mis Tor Cl 5 PL20 42 C3
Great Orchard Cl PL9 135 E5
Great Park Cl 4 PL7 131 C5
Great Western Commercial
Village PL22 112 D2
Great Western Rd PL1 148 B1
Great Wheal Seton TR14 138 F6
Greatwood TR11 82 C3
Great Woodford Dr PL7 130 B6
Grebe Cl PL7 130 F5
Greeb Way TR20 89 D4
Green Acre PL15 28 A5
Greenacres
Bodmin PL30 34 C2
Plymouth PL9 135 F8
Greenbank
Connor Downs TR27 78 D6
1 Penzance TR18 143 D5
Plymouth PL4 149 B4
Polruan PL23 116 D2
Greenbank Ave PL4 149 B3
Greenbank Cl TR2 57 E1
Greenbank Cres TR7 111 C7
Greenbank La PL14 113 C6
Greenbank Rd
Devoran TR3 81 F6
Liskeard PL14 113 C6
Plymouth PL4 149 B4
Greenbanks Ct PL27 21 E2
Greenbanks Rd PL27 21 E2
Greenbank Terr
1 Callington PL17 39 F4
Plymouth PL4 149 B4
Yelverton PL20 42 D3
Green Cl
Feock TR3 82 C5
Truro TR1 137 B3
Green Cres TR13 146 D7
Greendale Rd PL2 128 A7
Green Field Cl TR12 102 F2
Greenfield Rd PL12 122 D2
Greenfields Cl TR11 93 D3
Greenfield Terr TR16 67 D6
Greenfinch Cres PL12 122 E4
Green Hill
Lamerton PL19 30 A3
St Martin TR12 100 D6
Tavistock PL19 147 D5
Wadebridge PL27 108 E5
Greenhill Cl PL9 135 F5
Greenhills PL32 105 C5
Green Hill Terr TR12 100 D6
Green Hill Villas PL27 108 E5
Green La
Bodmin PL31 109 F2
Boscastle PL35 9 C1
Crantock TR8 43 D3
Fowey PL23 116 C5
Gwithian TR27 66 B2
Kingsand PL10 133 A2
Lelant TR26 77 E4
Lizard TR12 103 A2
Marazion TR17 89 B6
Penryn TR10 144 B8
Porthleven TR13 91 B1
Portreath TR16 67 C6
Redruth, Plain-an-Gwarry
TR15 140 B5
Redruth, Wheal Rose TR16 68 C4
Rock PL27 21 D2
Tavistock PL19 147 E5
Truro TR1 137 B3
Veryan TR2 83 F6
Yelverton PL20 42 C1
Greenland PL10 132 F5
Greenlands Est PL19 147 D5
Green Lane Cl TR10 144 B8
Green Lane Hill TR18 143 F8
Green Lane Vean TR15 140 B5
Green La The TR27 77 F1
Green La W TR17 89 B6
Greenlees Dr PL7 131 B3
Greenmarket The 26
TR18 143 E5
Green Mdws PL32 105 C4
Green Parc Rd TR27 142 D5
Green Park Ave PL4 128 D4
Green Park Rd PL9 135 E5
Green Pk PL10 133 A2
Greensplat Rd PL25 114 A6
Green St
Penzance TR18 143 F4
Truro TR1 137 D4
Greens The TR19 96 C7
Greensway Rd PL19 147 A4
Green The
Bridgerule EX22 8 A5
Carnon Downs TR3 82 A5
5 Horrabridge PL20 42 C5
Kingsand PL10 133 A2
Liskeard PL14 113 B5
Meavy PL20 42 F2
Milton Combe PL20 120 F8
Nancegollan TR13 91 B7
Plymouth, Ernesettle PL5 123 E3
Plymouth, Hooe PL9 135 B6
Probus TR2 71 C6
Saltash PL12 122 C3
St Buryan TR19 97 A6
St Martin TR12 100 D6
6 Trewoon PL25 59 A3
Greenway Ave PL7 130 B6
Greenway Cl 2 PL20 42 C5
Greenwich Pl PL12 122 F3
Greenwith Cl TR1 137 B3
Greenwith Cres TR3 81 D6
Greenwith Hill TR3 81 D6
Greenwith Rd TR3 81 D6
Greenwood Cres TR10 144 A8
Greenwood Park Cl PL7 131 B6
Greenwood Park Rd PL7 131 B6
Greenwood Rd TR10 144 A8
Gregor Rd TR1 137 F5
Gregory's Ct 10 PL31 109 D5
Gregory's Mdw PL15 106 F3
Grenfell Ave PL12 122 D3
Grenfell Gdns PL12 122 C3
Grenfell St 19 TR19 88 C1
Grenifer Rd TR15 139 D7
Grenna La TR3 81 D7
Grenofen Cl PL19 42 A6
Grenville Cl PL17 39 F4
Grenville Cres TR11 144 F5
Grenville Ct
Plymouth PL7 131 C6
2 St Austell PL25 114 C3
Grenville Dr
6 St Agnes TR5 54 D1
Tavistock PL19 147 B3
Grenville Gdns TR14 79 E5
Grenville Mdws PL22 112 E2
Grenville Pk PL20 42 D2
Grenville Rd
Falmouth TR11 145 A5
Helston TR13 146 D5
Lostwithiel PL22 112 D2
Padstow PL28 107 C4
Plymouth PL4 149 C3
Truro TR1 137 B5
Grenville Road La S PL4 129 B2
Grenville Wlk PL13 62 D2
Gresham Cl
Newquay TR7 110 F4
Plymouth PL5 124 C7
Greyfriars TR11 145 C2
Greys Terr 1 TR16 140 F1
Greystoke Ave PL6 129 D7
Greystone Ave PL26 58 E5
Gribbas Cl TR3 80 F3
Gribbas Cnr TR3 80 F3
Gribben Cl PL25 114 E6
Gribben Rd PL25 114 E6
Gribbon Way PL24 60 C4
Griffins The PL14 113 D6
Griffin Way PL9 136 C6
Griggs Cl PL7 131 B4
Griggs Hill TR27 77 E3
Grimscott Est EX23 5 B2
Grimspound Cl PL6 129 E8
Grimstone Terr PL20 42 B2
Grist La TR27 78 C5
Grizedale Rd PL6 129 D7
Grose Hill Cres 11 PL26 59 D7
Grose Mdws PL26 58 B8
Grosvenor Ave TR7 110 E6
Grosvenor Cotts 1 PL4 128 F4
Grosvenor Pl PL25 114 B4
Grosvenor Rd PL6 124 F2
Grove Cotts TR2 57 C1
Grove Dr 4 PL14 51 A7
Grove Hill
Mawnan Smith TR11 93 D3
St Mawes TR2 95 A6
Grovehill Cres TR11 145 C3
Grovehill Dr TR11 145 C3
Grovehill Ho TR11 145 B3
Grove La TR20 89 F5
Grove Park Ct PL14 113 B4
Grove Pk
Par PL24 60 C6
Tavistock PL19 147 D5
Torpoint PL11 126 E3
Grove Pl
3 Falmouth TR11 145 C3
Padstow PL28 107 D5
Grove Rd
Par PL24 115 F6
St Austell PL25 114 B4
Grove The
Plymouth, Plymstock
PL9 135 D8
Plymouth, Stoke PL3 128 A4
Grovewood Ct TR9 45 E1
Grylls Parc TR13 146 B6
Grylls Pk PL13 62 A7

Guardian Ct 6 PL31 109 E5
Gue The 2 TR13 98 C8
Guildford Cl
Foxhole PL26 58 D6
Plymouth PL5 124 E3
Guildford Rd TR27 142 E7
Guildford Road Ind Est TR27 142 E6
Guildford St PL4 149 A3
Guildhall La PL22 112 C2
Guildhall Sq PL1 148 C2
Guineaport Parc PL27 108 C5
Guineaport Rd PL27 108 C5
Guipavas Rd PL17 39 F4
Gulland Rd PL27 21 D6
Gull Rock TR7 110 A5
Gully's La PL26 58 B8
Gulval Almshouses TR18 143 F8
Gulval Com Prim Sch TR18 88 E6
Gulval Cross TR18 143 F8
Gulworthy Cotts PL19 41 B7
Gulworthy Cross PL19 41 B7
Gulworthy Prim Sch PL19 41 B7
Gun Hill Rd TR8 43 B1
Gunnislake Prim Sch PL18 40 F6
Gunnislake Rural Workshops PL18 40 F6
Gunnislake Sta PL18 40 F5
Gunpool La 9 PL35 9 C1
Gunver PL28 31 F7
Gunwennap PL32 10 B2
Gurlyn Hill TR20 90 A7
Gurnard Wlk PL3 129 C6
Gurney Cl
Bude EX23 104 E7
Torpoint PL11 126 F3
Gurney's La 2 TR14 138 D3
Gurneys Mews 6 TR14 138 D3
Gurnick Est TR18 143 B2
Gurnick Rd TR18 143 B1
Gurnick St 24 TR19 88 C1
Gustavus Rd TR14 138 D3
Gustory Rd TR8 43 D3
Guy Miles Way PL5 124 B3
Gwallon La TR17 89 C6
Gwallon Rd PL25 114 E5
Gwarnick Rd TR1 137 B4
Gwarth An Drae TR13 146 C8
Gwarth An Dre TR27 142 E8
Gwavas Bglws 4 TR18 143 C1
Gwavas La TR18 88 C2
Gwavas Quay 7 TR18 143 C2
Gwavas Rd TR18 143 C1
Gwavas St 10 TR18 143 E6
Gweal-An-Top TR15 140 D5
Gweal-an-Top Inf Sch TR15 140 C5
Gweal Darras TR10 81 C1
Gwealdues TR13 146 D7
Gwealfolds Rd TR13 146 C7
Gweal Gollas TR27 142 E8
Gwealhellis Warren TR13 146 B7
Gwealmayowe Pk TR13 146 D6
Gweal Pawl TR15 140 A4
Gweal Wartha TR13 146 B8
Gwedhennek TR18 143 F7
Gweek Dr
Gweek TR12 92 C1
Mawgan TR12 99 D8
Gweek La TR13 92 A3
Gwel An Garrek 2 TR12 99 A1
Gwel-an-mor
1 Marazion TR17 89 C5
St Austell PL25 115 A5
Trenance TR8 31 C2
Gwel-an-mor Apartments TR26 141 C4
Gwelanmor Cl TR26 141 D2
Gwelanmor Rd TR26 141 D2
Gwel-An-Nans Cl 2 PL14 113 B5
Gwel-An-Scol TR3 82 C5
Gwel An Wheal TR26 141 A4
Gwel An Wheal Cres TR26 141 A4
Gwel Avon Bsns Pk PL12 122 D4
Gwelavon Cl PL27 108 D5
Gwelenys Rd 3 TR19 88 C1
Gwel Eryon 3 TR14 138 F2
Gwel Gwarthe TR16 68 C3
Gwell-An-Nans TR2 71 C6
Gwel Lewern TR18 88 E6
Gwel Marten Flats TR26 141 E2
Gwelmeneth Pk 8 PL14 38 A3
Gwel Mengleth PL27 108 D5
Gwelmor TR14 138 E2
Gwel-Mor TR19 75 A1
Gwel-Tek TR27 142 D8
Gwel Trencrom TR27 142 B3
Gwendra La PL26 58 E8
Gwendroc Cl TR1 137 D3
Gwendroc Ho TR1 137 D3
Gwendroc House Mews TR1 137 D3
Gwendrock Villas PL27 108 C5
Gwendrona Cl TR13 146 D8
Gwendrona Way TR13 146 D8
Gwennap Pit★ TR16 140 F4
Gwindra Ind Est PL26 58 C3
Gwindra Rd PL26 58 B4
Gwinear Com Prim Sch TR27 78 E4
Gwinear La TR27 78 E4
Gwinear Rd TR27 78 E5
Gwithian Cl PL11 126 F4
Gwithian Rd TR27 78 D6
Gwithian Sands Chalet Pk TR27 66 B1
Gwyn Rd PL4 149 C4
Gwythian Way TR6 55 A4
Gyllyng Hall TR11 145 B3
Gyllyng St TR11 145 B4
Gyllyngvase Hill TR11 145 B2
Gyllyngvase Rd TR11 145 C2
Gyllyngvase Terr TR11 145 C2
Gypsy La PL33 14 C1

H

Haddington Rd PL2 127 F4
Haddon Way PL25 115 D3
Haddy's Row PL14 39 A2
Haig Pl 6 TR18 143 C7
Hain Wlk TR26 141 C4
Halbullock View TR1 69 E3
Halcyon Ct PL2 128 A6
Halcyon Rd PL2 128 A6
Haldon Pl PL5 124 A3
Haley Barton 4 PL2 128 A5
Halgavor La PL31 109 E2
Halgavor Pk PL31 109 F1
Halgavor Rd PL30, PL31 109 D2
Halgavor View PL31 109 F2
Halifax Rd PL27 31 F3
Halimote Rd PL26 58 C8
Hallane Rd PL25 115 A6
Hallan Vean TR19 96 A6
Hallaze Rd PL26 59 D7
Hallerton Cl PL6 125 E2
Hallett Cl PL12 122 B3
Hallett Way EX23 104 F7
Hallew Rd PL26 58 C7
Halley Gdns PL5 123 E1
Halloon Ave 9 TR9 45 E2
Hall Rd PL26 58 C8
Hall Terr PL23 116 E5
Halt Rd
Goonhavern TR4 55 D4
St Newlyn East TR8 56 B7
Halvarras Pk TR3 82 B8
Halvarras Rd TR3 82 B8
Halveor Cl 5 TR9 45 E6
Halveor Ct TR6 55 B5
Halveor La TR9 45 D6
Halwin La TR13 92 B8
Halwin Sch TR13 92 C8
Halwyn Cl 12 TR3 81 F7
Halwyn Hill TR8 110 A3
Halwyn Pl TR1 137 B4
Halwyn Rd TR8 110 A3
Halwyn Terr TR1 137 B3
Hamble Cl PL3 129 D7
Ham Cl PL2 128 B8
Ham Dr PL2 128 B8
Ham Gn PL2 128 A7
Ham Green Ct PL2 128 A7
Ham Green La PL2 128 A7
Ham Ho PL2 128 A8
Hamilton Cl TR27 142 B4
Hamilton Gdns PL4 128 D4
Hamilton Pl TR11 145 D3
Ham La PL2 128 A8
Hammill's Cl 13 TR13 98 C8
Hammills Dr 12 TR13 98 C8
Hamoaze Ave PL5 127 D8
Hamoaze Pl PL1 127 D2
Hamoaze Rd PL11 127 B2
Hampton Cl TR7 110 D6
Hampton St PL4 149 A3
Hancock Cl PL6 124 D6
Hancock La 14 TR2 95 A6
Hangmans Wlk TR11 145 A1
Hannaford Rd PL16 19 F3
Hannafore PL13 117 C3
Hannafore La PL13 117 D2
Hannafore Rd PL13 117 D2
Hanover Cl
17 Perranporth TR6 55 A5
Plymouth PL3 129 B5
Hanover Ct
Camborne TR14 138 E4
10 Penzance TR18 143 E5
16 Plymouth PL1 149 A2
Hanover Ho EX23 4 D4
Hanover Pk TR9 45 F2
Hanover Rd PL3 129 C4
Hanson Dr PL23 116 C3
Hanson Rd PL14 113 D6
Harbour Ave
Plymouth, Camels Head PL5 127 E8
Plymouth PL4 149 A2
Harbour Ct
Falmouth TR11 145 B4
15 Penzance TR18 143 E5
Portreath TR16 67 C6
Harbour Ct Flats TR2 83 B2
Harbour Lights 11 TR18 143 C1
Harbour Mews TR19 96 B7
Harbour Rd
Par PL24 60 C4
Porthleven TR13 98 B8
Wadebridge PL27 108 C5
Harbourside 12 TR13 98 B8
Harbour Side PL13 117 C3
Harbour St PL11 127 B3
Harbour Terr
Falmouth TR11 145 B5
Portreath TR16 67 C6
Harbour View
Fowey PL23 116 C4
Hayle TR27 142 B5
Marazion TR17 89 B5
Penryn TR10 144 B8
Plymouth PL9 135 A7
5 Porthleven TR13 98 B8
Saltash PL12 122 E2
Truro TR1 137 E3
Harbour View Cres TR18 143 E6
Harcourt Cl TR1 69 F3
Hardings Cl PL12 122 E3
Hardisworthy Cross EX39 2 E7
Hardwick Farm PL7 130 C3
Hardy Cres PL5 124 E1
Hardy Ho TR3 80 F3
Harebell Cl PL12 122 D4
Harefield Cres TR14 138 D4
Hareston Cl PL7 131 B3
Harewood Cl PL7 130 E5
Harewood Cres PL5 124 B2
Harewood Rd PL18 41 A3
Hargood Terr 6 PL2 127 F4
Hargreaves Cl PL5 123 F2
Harlech Cl PL3 129 A7
Harleigh Rd PL31 109 E3
Harleigh Terr PL31 109 E3
Harlequins 27 TR26 141 B5
Harlyn Barton PL28 20 D2
Harlyn Cotts PL28 20 D2
Harlyn Rd PL28 20 D1
Harmer Cl PL31 109 D6
Harmony Cl
Redruth TR15 140 B6
Roche PL26 46 F3
Harmony Mdw PL26 46 F3
Harmony Rd PL26 46 F3
Harmony Terr
4 Illogan TR16 67 E4
Truro TR1 137 E2
Harnorlen Rd PL2 128 D7
Haroldsleigh Ave PL5 124 E2
Harriet Gdns PL7 130 B6
Harriet Pl TR11 145 A5
Harris Cl PL17 39 F6
Harris Ct
1 Penryn TR10 144 C7
Plymouth PL9 135 B6
Harrison Gdns TR15 139 D7
Harrison St 7 PL2 127 F4
Harrison Terr TR1 137 B4
Harriss Hill TR3 82 A7
Harrowbarrow Sch PL17 40 D4
Harrowbeer La PL20 42 C3
Hartland Cl PL6 125 A7
Hartland Forest Golf & Leisure Parc EX39 3 E6
Hartland Rd PL29 22 E7
Hartland Terr EX23 104 D6
Hartley Ave PL3 129 A6
Hartley Ct PL3 129 A6
Hartley Park Gdns PL3 128 F6
Hartley Rd PL3 128 E6
Hartmeade PL14 52 A5
Hartwell Ave PL9 136 D7
Harvenna Cl TR9 45 E1
Harvest Moon TR7 110 D7
Harvey Ave PL4 129 B1
Harvey Rd TR1 137 D2
Harvey St PL11 127 B3
Harvey's Towans TR27 142 A7
Harvey's Way TR27 142 C5
Harwell Ct 8 PL1 148 B3
Harwell St PL1 148 B3
Harwood Ave PL5 124 C7
Hastings St PL1 148 B3
Hastings Terr PL1 148 B3
Haswell Cl PL6 129 A8
Hatch's Hill TR27 78 C5
Hatfield Cres TR7 110 B5
Hat La PL10 132 F2
Havelock Terr PL2 127 F3
Haven Ct TR27 142 C5
Haven Pk PL14 39 A2
Haven Rd EX23 10 C6
Havett Cl PL14 50 E8
Havett Rd PL14 50 E8
Hawarden Cotts PL4 129 B1
Haweswater Cl PL6 124 E4
Hawke Cl TR7 110 D6
Hawkens Way 9 TR9 45 D6
Hawke Rd TR13 146 D4
Hawkers Ave PL4 149 A2
Hawkers La PL3 128 E5
Hawkeys Mews TR15 140 D2
Hawkinge Gdns PL5 123 E4
Hawkins Cl PL6 125 A5
Hawkins Ct 2 TR18 143 D5
Hawkins Rd
Newquay TR7 110 E5
Padstow PL28 107 C5
Penzance TR18 143 D5
Hawkins Way 12 TR11 145 A4
Hawks Pk PL12 122 C2
Hawk's Tor Dr PL15 27 B7
Hawthorn Ave
Bude EX23 104 E4
Torpoint PL11 126 F3
Hawthorn Cl
Bude EX23 104 E4
Camelford PL32 105 D4
Plymouth, Hooe PL9 135 C5
Plymouth, Woolwell PL6 125 D7
Redruth TR15 140 B6
St Austell PL25 114 F6
7 St Columb Major TR9 45 D6
Hawthorn Gr PL2 128 C7
Hawthorn Rd PL19 147 C2
Hawthorns PL12 122 D2
Hawthorn Way
Plymouth PL3 129 B7
Threemilestone TR3 69 C3
Haxter Cl PL6 121 B1
Haydon Gr PL5 123 C1
Haydown Cl PL30 24 B4
Haye La PL17 39 E5
Haye Rd
Callington PL17 39 D4
Plymouth PL7, PL9 130 C1
Haye Rd S PL9 136 C7
Hayes Pl PL6 129 B8
Hayes Rd PL9 135 C7
Hay La
Looe PL13 117 E4
Sheviock PL11 65 B6
Hayle Com Sch TR27 142 D5
Hayle Ind Pk TR27 142 F7
Hayle Rd TR27 78 C1
Hayle Sta TR27 142 B5
Hayle Terr TR27 142 C6
Hayman Way TR11 144 E5
Hayne Corfe Gdns TR1 137 A4
Haystone Pl PL1 148 B4
Haytor Cl PL5 124 B3
Hazel Cl
Plymouth PL6 125 B6
St Austell PL25 115 A6
Hazel Dr PL9 136 C7
Hazel Gr
Plymouth PL9 136 C7
Yelverton PL20 42 D3
Hazelmead PL14 113 B5
Hazelmere Dr PL25 115 B4
Hazel Rd PL19 147 C2
Hazelwood Cres PL9 136 D7
Hazelwood Dr PL6 125 D8
Hazelwood Rd PL17 39 F4
Heabrook Parc 2 TR18 143 C7
Hea Cl TR18 143 C7
Hea Cotts 5 TR18 143 C7
Head La TR5 68 D8
Headland Cl TR26 141 E2
Headland Cotts
Coverack TR12 103 H7
Newquay TR7 110 C8
Headland Ct TR26 141 E2
Headland Pk PL4 149 A4
Headland Point TR7 110 C7
Headland Rd
Carbis Bay TR26 141 E2
Newquay TR7 110 C7
Headlands The TR6 55 A5
Headleigh Rd TR7 110 F5
Headon Cross EX23 11 A5
Healy Ct 9 PL2 127 F4
Healy Pl PL2 127 F4
Heamoor Com Prim Sch TR18 143 B6
Heanton Terr
Millbrook PL10 132 E6
Redruth TR15 140 C4
Heanton Villas TR15 140 C4
Hea Rd TR18 143 C7
Hearl Rd PL12 122 B3
Heatherbell Gdns TR26 141 E1
Heather Cl
Heamoor TR18 143 B7
Tavistock PL19 147 D4
Heather La TR27 77 D2
Heather Mdw TR9 45 E1
Heathers The
Foxhole PL26 58 E5
Plymouth PL6 125 D7
Heather Vean TR3 69 D4
Heather Way TR20 89 F4
Heathfield Gdns TR15 140 E7
Heathfield Pk PL20 42 D3
Heathfield Rd PL4 129 B3
Heathlands Bsns Pk PL14 113 C5
Heathlands Ind Est 9 PL14 113 C5
Heathlands Rd PL14 113 C5
Heath Terr PL18 40 F5
Heavitree Rd PL10 133 A2
Hedgerow Cl PL6 125 E8
Hedgerows The PL12 122 B3
Hedingham Cl PL7 131 C4
Hedingham Gdns PL6 125 B7
Helca Dr TR26 141 C3
Helebridge Rd EX23 7 B6
Hele Cross PL15 13 E3
Hele Gdns PL7 131 A4
Hele La PL6 121 F2
Helena Ct 7 PL26 59 D7
Hele Rd EX23 7 A6
Hele's Sch PL7 130 C6
Hele's Terr PL4 129 B2
Heligan Ho PL26 73 A5
Helland Rd PL31 109 E6
Hellescoth Way TR13 146 D8
Hellescott Rd PL15 18 B7
Hellesvean 2 TR26 77 A6
Hellesvean Cl 3 TR26 77 A6
Hellesvoer Cvn & Camping Site TR26 141 A6
Helleur Cl 4 PL24 60 B4
Helman Tor View PL31 109 E2
Helnoweth Cotts TR18 143 F8
Helnoweth Gdns TR18 143 F8
Helnoweth Hill TR18 143 F8
Helscott Rd EX23 7 A6
Helston Com Hospl TR13 146 D3
Helston Folk Mus★ TR13 146 B5
Helston Rd TR10 144 C8
Helston Sch TR13 146 B7
Helston Sch & Com Coll TR13 146 C7
Hembal Cl 5 PL25 59 A3
Hembal La PL25 59 A3
Hembal Rd 4 PL25 59 A3
Hemerdon House★ PL7 131 E7
Hemerdon Hts PL7 131 A6
Hemerdon La PL7 131 C8
Hemerdon Way PL7 130 D6
Hendergulling PL13 62 F4
Henders Cnr 6 PL3 128 F6
Henderson Pl PL2 127 F6
Hendra Barton TR1 137 B5
Hendra Cl
Ashton TR13 90 E3
Stithians TR3 80 E4
5 Truro TR1 137 C5
Hendra Gdns PL15 106 B5
Hendra Holiday Pk TR8 111 C3
Hendra La
Ashton TR13 90 D2
Truro TR1 137 C5
Hendra Parc PL14 113 E7
Hendra Pk PL15 106 B5
Hendra Prazey PL26 58 B8
Hendra Rd
St Dennis PL26 58 C8
Stithians TR3 80 E4
Truro TR1 137 C5
Hendras Ct TR26 141 E2
Hendras Parc TR26 141 D2
Hendra Terr TR3 80 E4
Hendra Tor View PL15 26 C7
Hendra Vale PL15 106 B4
Hendra Vean
Carbis Bay TR26 141 E1
Truro TR1 137 B5
Hendrawna La TR6 55 B4
Hendwell Cl PL6 124 E6
Henfor Cl 12 TR17 89 C5
Henfordh Grange PL14 113 A6
Henfor Mews 6 TR17 89 C5
Henfor Terr 13 TR17 89 C5
Hengar La PL30 23 F3
Henley Cl TR4 68 C6
Henley Cres TR4 68 C6
Henley Dr
Mount Hawke TR4 68 C6
Plymouth PL5 124 C7
Henliston Dr TR13 146 C4
Henry Scott Tuke Ho 5 TR11 145 A4
Hensbury La PL20 119 F4
Henscol TR16 80 D6
Henscol Praze TR16 80 D6
Henscol Vale PL14 113 A6
Henshorn Ct TR13 146 C7
Hental 3 TR6 55 A4
Hentervene Cvn & Camping Pk EX23 10 C5
Henver Cl TR27 78 E3
Henver Ct TR7 111 C7
Henver Gdns TR27 78 E3
Henver La TR4 56 A3
Henver Rd TR7 111 B7
Henvor Cl TR15 140 D6
Henvor Terr TR15 140 E7
Henwood Cres TR7 111 D7
Hen Wythva TR14 138 E2
Herbert Pl PL2 127 E4
Herbert St PL2 127 E4
Hereford Rd PL5 124 B5
Heritage Cl PL12 122 C3
Herland Hill TR27 78 D4
Herland Rd TR13 90 E6
Hermes Cl TR13 146 D5
Hermes Rd TR13 146 C4
Hermitage Ct 1 PL4 128 E4
Hermitage Rd
Plymouth PL3 128 E5
Roche PL26 46 F3
Heron Cl
Millbrook PL10 132 F6
Tresillian TR2 70 F5
Herons Ct 13 TR6 55 A5
Heron Way TR1 137 E1
Herring Cl PL14 113 D7
Herring Rd PL14 113 D7
Herschel Gdns PL5 123 E1
Hersham Cross EX23 5 B2
Hertland Wlk PL2 128 A7
Hessary Dr PL6 121 C1
Hessary Ho PL14 113 D6
Hessary View
Saltash PL12 122 E4
Tavistock PL19 147 B6
Hessenford Rd PL13, PL11 64 B6
Hetling Cl PL1 148 B3
Hewer's Row PL4 149 A3
Hewitt Cl PL12 122 C1
Hexham Pl PL2 128 A8
Hexton Hill Rd PL9 135 B6
Hexton Quay PL9 135 C6
Heybrook Ave PL5 123 D1
Heybrook Mews TR7 110 D6
Hibernia Rd TR13 146 D4
Hibernia Terr PL5 127 E8
Hichens La TR11 145 A5
Hichens Rd TR13 146 D4
Hickory Dr PL7 131 B5
Hicks Cl TR2 71 C6
Hick's La PL4 149 A2
Hidden Valley Adventure Pk★ PL15 18 A3
High Atlantic TR8 44 C6
Highbank Cl PL19 147 A4

Hig–Jam 165

Highbridge Ct PL7 130 E5
Highburrow 24 TR13 98 C8
Highburrow Ct TR15 139 C5
Highburrow La TR15 139 C5
Highbury PL17 38 E8
Highbury Cres PL7 130 D7
Highclere Gdns PL6 125 B8
Highcliffe PL27 21 D5
High Cross
Lanivet PL30 47 F5
Porth Navas TR11 93 A4
12 St Columb Major TR9 45 D6
Truro TR1 137 D4
High Cross St PL25 114 D4
Higher Albion Row TR16 80 F8
Higher Anderton Rd
PL10 132 F5
Higher Beech Terr PL13 117 C4
Higher Bodiniel Rd PL31 109 C7
Higher Bojewyan TR19 75 B1
Higher Bolenna 14 TR6 55 A4
Higher Bore St PL31 109 C5
Higher Boskerris TR26 141 D1
Higher Bridge Pk PL27 108 D5
Higher Broad La TR15 139 D7
Higher Bugle
Bugle PL26 47 C1
Stenalees PL26 59 C8
Higher Burrow Cl TR26 141 A4
Higher Chapel St PL13 117 D3
Higher Church St TR27 142 D6
Higher Churchway PL9 136 A7
Higher Cleaverfield
PL15 106 C7
Higher Compton Rd PL3 128 F6
Higher Cotts TR2 57 C1
Higher Croft Parc TR12 102 F2
Higher Cross La PL32 105 E4
Higher Daws La PL15 18 E2
Higher East St 9 TR9 45 E6
Higher Efford Rd PL3 129 B5
Higher Elms PL27 21 F3
Higher Fernleigh Rd
PL27 108 C4
Higher Fore St
Marazion TR17 89 C5
Redruth TR15 140 C5
Higher Glen Pk PL14 38 D4
Higher Goongumpas La
TR16 68 F1
Higher Green St TR18 143 D1
Higher Grumbla TR20 87 C4
Higher Gwavas Rd 3
TR18 143 C1
Higher Kelly PL18 41 A3
Higher La
Ashton TR13 90 E3
Mawgan TR12 99 D7
Plymouth PL1 148 C2
Wadebridge PL27 108 E4
Wadebridge PL27 108 E5
Higher Lariggan TR18 143 D4
Higher Lavorrick PL26 73 C4
Higher Lidden Rd TR18 143 C3
Higher Lux St PL14 113 C6
Higher Market St
Looe PL13 117 D3
Penryn TR10 144 C7
Higher Mdw PL14 50 E7
Higher Medrose PL33 14 E3
Higher Middle Hill PL14 38 D4
Highermoor Cross EX22 5 E1
Higher Mount Ambrose La
TR15 140 D6
Higher Mowles PL3 129 B6
Higher Newham La TR1 137 D2
Higher Park Cl PL7 131 B3
Higher Park Stenak TR16 80 F8
Higher Pengegon TR14 138 F2
Higher Penponds Rd
TR14 79 B5
Higher Peverell Rd TR18 143 E7
Higher Polsue Way TR2 70 F5
Higher Port View PL12 122 F2
Higher Pumpfield Row
TR15 139 B6
Higher Railway Terr TR16 80 F8
Higher Rd
Breage TR13 90 F3
Pensilva PL14 38 D4
Higher Redannick TR1 137 B3
Higher Row
Ashton TR13 90 E3
Kingsand PL10 133 A2
Higher Silver Hill TR13 146 C6
Higher Stennack TR26 141 A5
Higher Stert Terr PL4 149 C3
Higher Tamar Terr PL18 41 A7
Higher Terr TR3 81 B4
Higher Tower Rd TR7 110 C6
Highertown
Portscatho TR2 83 B2
Truro TR1 69 F3
Highertown Pk PL12 53 C3
Higher Trebyan Bsns Pk
PL30 48 C6
Higher Tregenna Rd
TR26 141 B3
Higher Trehaverne TR1 137 C6
Higher Tremena PL25 114 C4
Higher Tresavean Terr
TR16 80 E6
Higher Trevithick TR27 142 D5
Higher Trevorian Barns
TR19 97 B7
Higher Trewidden Rd
TR26 141 B4
Higher Trezaise PL26 47 A1
Higher Tristram PL27 21 D5
Higher Vicarage La 7
TR12 99 A1
Higherwell Cl TR7 111 A4
Higher Well La TR13 146 C6
Higher Well Pk PL26 73 C3
Higher West End PL26 73 C6
Higher Whiterock PL27 108 B5
Higher Woodford La
PL7 130 C7
Higher Woodside PL25 114 A4
Highfield Ave
St Austell PL25 114 D3
13 St Columb Major TR9 45 D6
Highfield Cl
Plymouth PL3 129 C5
St Austell PL25 114 D3
Highfield Ct 9 TR5 54 D1
Highfield Est 3 PL14 38 E4
Highfield Park Rd PL15 106 A5
Highfield Pk PL12 122 B3
Highfield Prim Sch PL3 129 C5
Highfield Rd
Camelford PL32 105 C3
Falmouth TR11 144 F4
Mount Hawke TR4 68 C6
Highfield Rd Ind Est
PL32 105 C3
Highfields 19 TR18 143 C2
Highgate Hill 1 TR9 45 E1
Highglen Dr PL7 131 B7
Highgrove PL15 27 A6
Highland Pk
Penryn TR10 144 B8
Redruth TR15 140 C5
Highlands PL9 136 B3
High Lanes
Cubert TR8 55 E8
Hayle TR27 142 D5
High Pk PL12 52 F6
High St
Boscastle PL35 9 D1
Camelford PL32 105 C3
Chacewater TR4 68 F3
Delabole PL33 14 D3
Falmouth TR11 145 B5
Launceston PL15 106 C6
Padstow PL28 107 D5
Penzance TR18 143 E5
3 Plymouth PL1 149 A2
Plymouth, Stonehouse PL1 128 A2
Probus TR2 71 C6
St Ives TR26 141 B6
St Keverne TR12 101 C4
High Street Ind Est PL26 58 D3
High Street Prim Sch
PL1 128 A2
High Street & Waterloo
Street Flats PL1 128 A1
Hightrip La PL17 39 F7
High Trip La PL17 40 A8
Highview TR4 68 E5
Highview Cl PL14 38 A2
Highview Cres TR4 68 E5
Highway PL14 50 B6
Highway La TR15 140 D7
Highwood Pk PL14 50 E7
Higman Cl PL14 50 E7
Hilgrove Rd TR7 111 A6
Hill Church TR4 68 F2
Hill Cl
Heamoor TR18 143 B7
Plymouth PL7 130 D4
St Breward PL30 24 B3
Hillcrest
Helston TR13 146 C7
Shortlanesend TR4 69 F6
Hill Crest PL3 128 E5
Hillcrest Ave TR1 137 A5
Hillcrest Cl
Plymouth PL7 131 A5
14 St Columb Major TR9 45 E6
Hillcrest Dr PL7 131 A4
Hillcrest Rd TR27 142 D6
Hilldale Rd PL9 135 E6
Hilldean Cl PL5 124 C7
Hill Gdns PL12 119 A2
Hill Hay Cl PL23 116 A4
Hillhead TR2 95 A6
Hill Head TR10 144 D6
Hillhead Gdns PL32 105 D4
Hillhead Rd TR11 144 C5
Hill La PL3 128 F7
Hillocks The PL13 117 D4
Hillpark Cotts PL15 106 D6
Hill Park Cres
Plymouth PL4 149 A4
St Austell PL25 114 A2
Hill Park Mews PL4 149 B4
Hill Path PL5 123 F5
Hill Pk PL27 108 D6
Hill Rd PL27 108 C5
Hillsborough 2 PL4 128 F4
Hillsborough Cross EX22 8 D7
Hillsdale Bglws TR13 90 F5
Hillsdunne Rd PL3 128 E6
Hillside
Grampound Road TR2 57 E1
Lanivet PL30 47 E7
Portreath TR16 67 C6
St Austell PL25 115 B3
Trewellard TR19 86 F8
Hillside Ave
Par PL24 60 B4
Plymouth PL4 128 D4
Saltash PL12 122 F3
Hillside Cl PL20 41 F3
Hillside Cres PL9 135 F8
Hillside Ct
Angarrack TR27 78 C5
Bodmin PL31 109 C5
Hillside Gdns PL22 112 C2
Hillside Ind Est TR16 140 E8
Hillside Mdw TR10 144 D7
Hillside Mdws PL26 58 D5
Hillside Parc TR20 88 B7
Hillside Pk PL31 109 D5
Hillside Rd
Falmouth TR11 144 F2
Saltash PL12 122 E3
St Austell PL25 114 D5
Hillside Sch PL5 124 B4
Hillside Terr
Carharrack TR16 80 E8
Downderry PL11 64 C5
Looe PL13 117 D4
22 Newlyn TR18 143 C2
2 Redruth TR15 140 C5
Hillside Villas PL13 117 F5
Hillson Cl PL29 22 E7
Hill St
Padstow PL28 107 D5
Plymouth PL4 149 A3
Hillsview PL13 62 D2
Hill Top Crest PL5 123 E2
Hill View PL20 41 F3
Hilton Ave PL5 124 D1
Hilton Rd EX23 7 B6
Hingston Ct PL6 129 A8
Hinton Ct PL6 125 C1
Hirmandale Rd PL5 123 F3
Hirst Ho TR14 139 A4
Hobart St PL1 148 A2
Hobbacott La EX23 7 B6
Hobbs Cres PL12 122 C3
Hockens La PL23 116 C2
Hockings Ho PL14 37 F3
Hodders Way PL12 119 A2
Hodge Cl PL12 122 C2
Hoe App PL1 148 C2
Hoe Ct PL1 148 C2
Hoegate Ct PL1 148 C2
Hoegate Pl PL1 148 C2
Hoegate St PL1 149 A2
Hoe Gdns PL1 148 C2
Hoe Rd PL1 148 C1
Hoe St PL1 148 C2
Hoe The PL1 148 C1
Hogarth Cl PL9 136 B6
Hogarth Ho PL19 147 B6
Hogarth Wlk PL9 136 B6
Holborn Pl PL7 130 E6
Holborn St PL4 149 B2
Holcombe Dr PL9 135 F5
Holcroft Cl PL12 122 D2
Holdsworth St PL4 148 B4
Holebay Cl PL9 136 A5
Hole Cross PL20 119 E7
Hollabury Rd EX23 104 F7
Hollacombe Brake PL9 136 C1
Holland Rd
Plymouth, Chaddlewood
PL7 131 D5
Plymouth, Peverell PL3 128 E6
Plymouth, Plymstock PL9 135 F6
Widegates PL13 63 E7
Hollies Cl PL15 106 B7
Hollies Rd PL15 106 A7
Hollies The TR27 142 B4
Hollong Pk PL11 65 E5
Holloway Gdns PL9 136 A5
Hollowell Ho 1 PL35 9 C2
Hollowgutter La PL11 126 C2
Hollow Hayes PL6 129 B8
Hollow's Terr TR27 142 E7
Hollows The PL9 136 B8
Holly Cl TR3 69 C3
Hollycroft Rd PL3 129 A7
Holly Ct PL6 129 E7
Holly Park Cl PL5 124 A5
Holly Park Dr PL5 124 A5
Holly Terr 9 TR18 143 C7
Hollywell Bay Fun Pk★
TR8 43 C1
Hollywood Terr PL1 148 A3
Holman Ave TR14 138 C4
Holman Ct PL2 128 C8
Holman Rd PL14 113 E6
Holmans Bldgs PL1 127 D2
Holmans Mdw PL15 19 C1
Holman's Pl 1 TR13 98 C8
Holman's Terr TR16 80 B5
Holmbush Arch Rd PL25 115 B3
Holmbush Hill PL17 39 F7
Holmbush Ind Est PL25 115 B4
Holmbush Rd PL25 115 C4
Holmer Down PL6 125 D7
Holmes Ave PL3 129 B5
Holmwood Ave PL9 135 E5
Holne Chase PL6 125 B7
Holnicote Rd EX23 104 E5
Holt Cres TR7 110 D5
Holtwood Rd PL6 125 D6
Holwell Cl PL9 136 A5
Holy Cross RC Prim Sch
PL4 149 A3
Holyrood Pl PL1 148 C2
Holyway Cross PL15 18 A1
Holywell Ct TR3 82 B8
Holywell Rd
Cubert TR8 55 D8
Holywell TR8 43 C1
Liskeard PL14 113 E6
Newquay TR7 110 F6
Playing Place TR3 82 B8
Home Farm Rd PL9 135 E8
Homefield Pk PL31 109 F3
Home Park Ave PL3 128 E6
Home Park (Plymouth Argyle
Fc) PL2 128 C5
Home Park Rd PL12 123 A3
Home Pk
Landrake PL12 53 C3
Plymouth PL2 127 F4
Homer Park La S PL9 135 C5
Homer Park Rd PL28 20 F2
Homer Pk
Plymouth PL9 135 C5
Saltash PL12 122 D3
Homer Rise PL9 136 B7
Homer Water Pk PL26 58 B4
Homestead Ct TR11 144 F6
Home Sweet Home Terr
PL4 149 C2
Homeyard Homes The
TR2 83 F6
Honcray PL9 135 D8
Honey's Hill PL30 47 E7
Honey St PL31 109 E4
Honeysuckle Cl
Plymouth PL6 125 E7
Saltash PL12 122 D4
Honicknowle PL5 124 B2
Honicknowle Gn PL5 124 B2
Honicknowle La PL5 124 B1
Honicombe Cnr PL17 40 E5
Honicombe Manor Holiday
Village PL17 40 E5
Honicombe Pk PL17 40 E5
Honiton Cl PL5 124 B3
Honiton Wlk PL5 124 B4
Hood Hill TR14 79 A6
Hooe Hill PL9 135 C5
Hooe La PL9 135 D3
Hooe Manor PL9 135 C5
Hooe Prim Sch PL9 135 B5
Hooe Rd PL9 135 C5
Hooksbury Ave PL7 131 B3
Hooper Ct PL14 113 C8
Hooper La TR14 138 D2
Hoopers Cl PL12 53 C3
Hoopers La PL18 40 F6
Hooper St PL11 127 C3
Hope Terr TR7 110 D6
Hopton Cl PL6 128 F8
Hornapark Cl PL16 19 F3
Hornbrook Gdns PL6 124 D6
Hornby Ct PL1 148 A3
Hornby St 2 PL2 127 F4
Hornchurch La PL5 123 E4
Hornchurch Rd PL5 123 E5
Horn Cross PL9 135 E7
Horn Cross Rd PL9 135 F7
Hornick Hill PL26 58 E4
Horn La
Liskeard PL14 113 B6
Plymouth PL9 135 F7
Horn Lane Flats 4 PL9 135 F7
Horrabridge Com Prim Sch
PL20 42 C4
Horse & Jockey La 2
TR13 146 C5
Horsepool La PL11 65 B6
Horsepool Rd
Connor Downs TR27 78 E6
Sheviock PL11 65 B6
Horseshoe Cl PL26 47 A3
Horsewhim Dr PL17 39 E6
Horse Whim Dr PL25 115 B5
Horsham La
Plymouth, Honicknowle
PL5 124 C2
Plymouth, Tamerton Foliot
PL5 124 C7
Horsley Rise PL25 114 D3
Horswell Cl PL7 131 B5
Horton Cross EX22 3 F3
Hosford Cl PL9 136 A4
Hosken's Mdw TR19 97 A6
Hosking's Row TR15 140 B4
Hospital Rd
Plymouth PL4 149 B4
Stratton EX23 4 D1
Hotham Pl PL1 148 A4
Houldsworth Rd PL9 135 C7
Houndiscombe Rd PL4 128 E4
Hounster Dr PL10 132 D4
Hounster Hill PL10 132 D4
Housel Bay Rd TR12 102 F2
Housman Cl PL5 124 D3
Howard Cl
Plymouth PL5 123 F2
Saltash PL12 122 D3
Tavistock PL19 147 A5
Howard La EX23 7 C8
Howard Rd PL9 135 E8
Howards Way EX23 104 D5
Howe Downs TR14 79 A2
Howell's Rd 10 EX23 4 E1
Howeson La PL6 125 A4
How St PL4 149 A2
HTP Apartments TR1 137 E4
Hudson Cross EX22 5 E4
Hudson Rd PL27 31 F3
Hughville St TR14 138 D4
Hugus Rd TR3 69 D3
Hull's La TR11 145 C3
Humber Cl PL3 129 D6
Humphrey's Cl PL14 37 F3
Humphry Davy La TR27 142 D5
Humphry Davy Sch TR18 143 E6
Hungerford Rd PL2 128 B5
Hunkin Cl TR1 137 C5
Hunter Cl PL6 124 F2
Huntersfield TR14 138 F7
Hunters's Oak PL20 41 D2
Huntfield Gdns 15 EX23 4 E1
Huntingdon Gdns PL5 124 D4
Huntley Pl PL3 129 C4
Hunts Crossing Sta★
PL15 18 E4
Hurdon Rd PL15 106 D2
Hurdon Way PL15 106 C3
Hurdwick Rd PL19 147 A5
Hurland Rd TR1 137 D3
Hurlers The★ PL14 38 A6
Hurrabrook Cl PL6 125 E2
Hurrabrook Gdns PL6 125 E2
Hurrell Cl PL6 124 D6
Hurrell Ct PL3 129 C5
Hursley Bsns Pk PL6 121 D1
Hurst Cl PL9 135 F5
Hustyns PL27 33 D3
Hutchings Cl PL6 124 D6
Huthnance Cl TR1 137 F5
Hutton Hts TR1 69 F3
Huxham Cl PL6 129 A8
Huxley Cl PL7 130 F7
Hyde Park Jun & Inf Schs
PL3 128 E5
Hyde Park Rd PL3 128 E5

I

Idless La TR4 69 F6
Idless Wood Forest Walk★
TR4 70 B6
Ilbert Cotts PL7 130 E4
Ilbert St PL1 148 B4
Illogan Downs TR15 139 B8
Illogan Pk 8 TR16 67 E4
Illogan Sch TR16 67 D5
Imperial Ct TR11 145 D3
Ince Cl PL11 126 F4
Inchkeith Rd PL6 124 F7
Indian Queens Com Prim Sch
TR9 45 E1
Indian Queens Ind Est
TR9 45 F2
Industrial Est The TR6 55 B4
Infirmary Hill TR1 137 C4
Ingra Rd PL3 129 A6
Ingra Tor Cl 2 PL20 42 C3
Ingra Wlk PL6 125 B8
Innes Ho PL1 148 B3
Inney Cl PL17 39 F4
Inny Vale Holiday Village
PL32 16 A5
Inow Terr TR11 93 A2
Institute Hill TR13 98 B8
Instow Wlk PL5 124 A3
Inswell Ct PL19 147 A6
Insworke Cl PL10 133 A6
Insworke Cres PL10 132 F6
Insworke Pl PL10 133 A6
Inverdene PL3 128 D5
Ipswich Cl PL5 124 C4
Iron Mine La PL20 42 E3
Isacombe Oaks PL17 39 F6
Island Cres TR7 110 E6
Island Ct PL13 117 D2
Island Lanes PL31 109 F1
Island Point TR8 44 C6
Island Rd 4 TR26 141 B6
Island Sq 8 TR26 141 B6
Islington Wharf TR10 144 D8
Ivanhoe 6 TR7 110 F6
Ivanhoe Rd PL5 123 D2
Ivey Terr PL14 113 D7
Ivy Cotts PL18 40 F6
Ivydale PL15 106 B6
Ivydale Rd PL4 128 F4
Ivydene Flats TR7 111 D7
Ivy La TR18 143 C5
Ivyleaf Holiday Pk EX23 4 F3

J

Jack Bice Cl PL14 113 E5
Jackett's Steps 6 TR11 145 C2
Jack La TR18 143 C2
Jackman's Mdw PL10 133 A3
Jacks Cl TR10 144 D7
Jack's La PL11 132 B8
Jackson Cl PL5 127 F8
Jackson Pl PL2 127 F4
Jackson Way PL12 122 E3
Jack Stephens Est TR18 143 D6
Jacob's Ladder TR11 145 B4
Jacobstow Com Prim Sch
EX23 11 A6
Jago Ave PL11 127 B3
Jago Cl PL31 109 B3
Jago's Slip TR11 145 B5
Jake's La 1 TR4 69 A3
Jamaica Pl 14 TR18 143 C7
Jamaica Terr 13 TR18 143 C7
James Cl PL9 136 B6
James Pl
Plymouth PL4 148 C4
Truro TR1 137 D4
James Rd PL19 147 E2
James's Cross EX23 2 C2
James St
Plymouth, Mount Wise
PL1 127 E1
Plymouth PL4 148 C4

Jane's Ct 9 TR11 145 B5
Jasmine Gdns
Plymouth, Chaddlewood PL7 131 B5
Plymouth, Glenholt PL6 125 E6
Jasmine Way PL28 31 F7
Jasper Parc PL14 37 F3
Jays Cross PL15 19 C6
Jean Cres PL3 129 B6
Jeanne Rees Ct 9 PL14 113 B5
Jedburgh Cres PL2 128 A8
Jeffery Cl PL6 124 D6
Jelbert Way TR18 88 E6
Jellicoe Rd PL5 124 E1
Jenkins Cl PL9 136 A5
Jenkins Ct TR7 110 E6
Jenkins Terr 5 TR15 140 C5
Jenner Parc TR9 45 D6
Jennings Rd TR10 144 A6
Jennings St TR18 143 E5
Jenns Cross EX22 5 F7
Jennycliff La PL9 135 A6
Jennys Combe Cl PL9 135 F4
Jephson Rd PL4 129 B3
Jericho La TR27 142 D1
Jeryon Cl PL25 114 E6
Jessops PL7 130 D7
Jethan Dr TR14 138 B4
Jetty St PL26 73 C3
Jewell's Terr TR16 80 B5
Jinkin Ave PL4 149 B4
John Ellis Ct TR27 142 C5
John Kitto Com Coll The PL5 124 B1
John La PL4 148 C4
John's Cnr TR20 89 F5
Johnson Cl 2 PL20 41 B1
Johnson Pk PL18 41 A3
John Sparke Ho 17 PL1 149 A2
Johns Pk TR15 140 B6
John St
Plymouth PL1 127 E3
Truro TR1 137 C4
Jon Davey Dr TR16 140 C7
Jopes Cl 2 PL14 38 A3
Jordan La PL20 42 C5
Jorys Mdw PL30 23 E3
Joseph's Ct 27 TR6 55 A5
Joseph's La TR18 143 C8
Jubilee Bglws 20 TR18 143 C1
Jubilee Cl
Cubert TR4 55 D8
Duloe PL14 51 A1
Kilkhampton EX23 5 A6
Saltash PL12 122 D2
Jubilee Cotts
Landrake PL12 53 C3
Saltash PL12 122 C1
Jubilee Ct 15 TR26 77 A6
Jubilee Hill PL13 62 D5
Jubilee Mdw PL25 115 C5
Jubilee Pl
Camborne TR14 138 E3
Plymouth PL3 129 C4
Jubilee Rd
Falmouth TR11 145 A5
Pensilva PL14 38 D4
Plymouth PL5 123 F3
Threemilestone TR3 69 C3
Wadebridge PL27 108 C5
Jubilee St TR7 110 D6
Jubilee Terr
Bodmin PL31 109 B5
Goonhavern TR4 55 D5
Helston TR13 146 C4
Plymouth PL4 129 B2
Julian St PL4 149 C2
Julian Wlk PL6 125 E6
Juliot Well Holiday Pk PL32 105 A2
Jump Cl PL6 121 C1
Juniper Way PL7 131 B5

K

Kailem Cl TR9 45 D5
Karenza Ct TR26 141 E2
Kathleaven St PL5 123 D1
Kay Cl PL7 130 F7
Kay Cres PL31 109 B3
Kay Gdns PL27 108 E5
Kays Mews 7 PL34 14 C7
Kea Com Prim Sch TR3 70 A1
Keason Est PL14 39 A2
Keason Hill PL12 53 C8
Keast Cl 2 TR9 45 E1
Keat St PL2 127 E4
Kedlestone Ave PL5 124 A3
Keeble Pk TR3 81 E6
Keep The PL12 122 C2
Kehelland Village Sch TR14 66 F1
Keigwen Pl TR19 88 C1
Kel Avon Cl TR1 137 F5
Kellaway Pk TR13 146 D6
Kelley Rd TR11 144 E5
Kelliwith TR3 82 B6
Kellow Hill PL13 62 D2
Kellow Pk PL11 65 A7
Kellow Rd PL26 58 C8
Kelly Cl PL5 127 C7
Kelly Coll PL19 147 D7
Kelly Pk PL30 34 C8
Kelvin Ave PL4 149 C4
Kelwyn Ct TR26 141 C2
Kemp Cl TR1 137 D4
Kempe Cl PL2 127 F6
Kemp's Cl 7 TR5 54 C1
Kempton Terr PL11 127 B2
Kemyell Pl PL2 127 E4
Kendal Gn TR2 57 C1
Kendal Pl PL5 124 E4
Kenidjack Cl TR26 141 E1
Kenilworth Rd PL2 128 B7
Kenilworth Way PL26 58 E5
Kenley Gdns PL5 123 F4
Kenmare Dr PL7 131 A5
Kennall Pk TR3 81 B4
Kennall Vale TR3 81 B4
Kennall Vale Sch TR3 81 B4
Kenna Pk TR1 69 F3
Kenn Cl PL5 124 B3
Kennedy Cl TR15 139 B8
Kennel Hill PL7 130 D4
Kennel Hill Cl PL7 130 C4
Kennerley Terr 16 TR2 95 A6
Kennet Cl PL3 129 B6
Kenneth Launder Ct 10 PL14 113 B5
Kensa Way TR27 78 E6
Kensey Pl 3 PL15 106 C6
Kensey Valley Mdw PL15 106 D6
Kensey View PL15 106 D5
Kensington Pl 8 PL4 128 F4
Kensington Rd PL4 149 B4
Kenstella Rd TR18 143 C2
Kent Ave PL25 115 D3
Kent Cl PL26 58 C8
Kent Rd PL2 127 F5
Kenwyn Church Rd TR1 137 B6
Kenwyn Cl
Bude EX23 104 D7
Truro TR1 137 B6
Kenwyn Hill TR1 137 B6
Kenwyn Mews TR1 137 C4
Kenwyn Pk
St Kew Highway PL30 23 B2
Truro TR1 137 B6
Kenwyn Rd
Truro TR1 137 C5
Truro TR4, TR1 137 A7
Kenwyn St TR1 137 C4
Kenython La TR19 86 F7
Keppel Pl PL2 127 F4
Keppel St PL2 127 F4
Keppel Terr 8 PL2 127 F4
Kerensa Gdns TR5 68 D8
Kerensa Gn TR11 144 E5
Kergilliack Rd TR11 144 D5
Kerhuon Ct PL31 109 D5
Kerley Gr TR1 69 F3
Kerley Hill TR4 69 A3
Kerley Vale TR4 69 A3
Kernick Bsns Pk TR10 144 A6
Kernick Gdns TR10 144 A6
Kernick Rd TR10 144 B7
Kernick Road Ind Est TR10 144 A7
Kernick Way TR27 142 E8
Kernow Cl
Bodmin PL31 109 F5
Torpoint PL11 126 E3
Wadebridge PL27 108 B5
Kernow Cres EX23 104 E4
Kernow Ct
Newquay TR7 110 E6
Torpoint PL11 126 E3
Kernow Mill* PL12 52 E1
Kernyk Lowen TR14 138 F5
Kerris Gr TR1 137 B5
Ker St Ope PL1 127 E2
Kersbrook Cross PL17 27 F2
Kersey Cl TR11 145 C7
Kersey Rd TR11 145 B7
Ker St PL1 127 E1
Keryor Cl PL25 114 F3
Kestell Parc PL31 109 E2
Kestle Dr TR1 69 F3
Kestral Units PL5 124 A1
Kestral Way 10 TR16 67 E4
Kestrel Cl
Plymouth PL6 125 D8
7 Porthleven TR13 98 B8
Keswick Cres PL6 125 D2
Keveral Gdns PL11 64 B5
Keveral La PL11 64 B5
Kew Cl TR7 111 A4
Kew Noweth TR14 138 D2
Kew Pendra TR19 97 A6
Kew Pendra Cl TR19 97 A6
Kew Vean TR26 141 C3
Keyes Cl PL1 127 F2
Keyham Barton RC Prim Sch PL2 127 E6
Keyham Ct PL2 127 E6
Keyham Rd PL2 127 E4
Keyham St PL5 127 E8
Keyham Sta PL2 127 E6
Khyber Cl PL11 127 A3
Kibbiscombe Terr PL14 63 A8
Kidwelly Cl PL7 131 C4
Kiel Pl PL3 129 D5
Kilhallon PL24 60 C5
Kilhallon Woodlands PL24 60 C5
Kilkhampton Jun & Inf Sch EX23 5 A6
Killarney Springs Leisure Pk* EX23 3 B1
Killatree Cross EX22 8 F7
Killerton Rd EX23 104 E5
Killicourt TR3 82 A7
Killiers Ct TR15 139 C7
Killiersfield TR15 139 C6
Killigrew Ave PL12 122 D1
Killigrew Gdns TR4 70 D8
Killigrew Pl 9 TR11 145 A4
Killigrew Rd PL14 113 D6
Killigrew St TR11 145 A4
Killivose Gdns TR14 138 D1
Killivose Rd TR14 138 D1
Killyvarder Way PL25 115 B6
Kilmar Cl PL14 37 F3
Kilmar Rd PL14 113 E6
Kilmar Way PL14 37 F3
Kilminorth Woods (Nature Reserve)* PL13 117 A4
Kilna La PL12 53 A2
Kiln Cl
Cawsand PL10 133 A1
Mevagissey PL26 73 C4
Plymouth PL5 127 C8
Kiln Mdws TR12 92 C1
Kilworthy Hill PL19 147 C6
Kilworthy Rd PL19 147 C6
Kimber Ct TR11 145 B2
Kimberley Ct TR7 110 D6
Kimberley Foster Cl PL11 65 B5
Kimberley Park Rd TR11 145 A4
Kimberley Pk PL14 38 A3
Kimberley Pl TR11 145 A4
Kimberly Cl TR7 110 D6
Kimberly Dr PL6 125 B1
Kiming EX23 104 E4
King Arthurs Terr 5 PL34 14 C7
King Charles Prim Sch TR11 145 A3
King Edward Cres TR7 110 D7
King Edward Rd PL12 122 F2
Kingfisher Cl PL6 125 E6
Kingfisher Dr PL25 115 A4
Kingfisher Way PL9 135 C7
King George V Memorial Wlk TR27 142 C6
King's Ave
Falmouth TR11 144 F4
St Austell PL25 114 D3
Kingsbury Ho TR11 145 A6
Kings Cl PL6 125 E6
Kings Cross EX39 2 E5
Kings Ct PL1 128 A3
King's Hill EX23 104 E3
Kings Hill Cl EX23 104 E4
King's Hill Ind Est EX23 104 F3
Kings Hill Mdw EX23 104 E3
Kingsland Gardens Cl PL3 128 E6
Kingsley Ave PL11 127 B2
Kingsley Cl TR1 69 E3
Kingsley Cove TR4 68 A7
Kingsley Ct TR9 57 E8
Kingsley Meade TR8 111 B5
Kingsley Rd PL4 128 E4
Kingsley Terr TR16 67 C6
Kingsley Way TR13 146 C5
Kingsmill Rd PL12 122 C5
Kings Pippin PL26 58 E5
Kings Rd
Marazion TR17 89 B5
Plymouth, Devonport PL1 127 F2
Plymouth, West Park PL5 123 F3
4 St Mawes TR2 95 A6
King's Rd
Camborne TR14 138 D4
Penzance TR18 143 D5
Plymouth PL1 128 A2
Kings Sch PL3 128 E6
King's St PL22 112 C2
King St
Bude EX23 104 E5
Gunnislake PL18 41 A6
Millbrook PL10 132 E5
Newquay TR7 110 D6
Plymouth PL1 148 B3
Redruth TR15 140 B5
Tavistock PL19 147 B6
Torpoint PL11 127 C3
Truro TR1 137 D4
King's Tamerton Rd PL5 123 F2
Kingston Cl PL7 131 A5
Kingston Dr PL7 131 B5
Kingston Rd PL17 28 E1
Kingsway PL10 133 B2
Kingsway Gdns PL6 124 F3
Kingswear Cres PL6 125 B1
King's Wood* PL26 73 B7
Kingswood Est PL14 38 C1
Kingswood Park Ave PL3 128 D6
Kingswood Rd PL18 41 A6
Kinnard Cres PL6 124 F7
Kinross Ave PL4 129 A4
Kinsale Rd PL5 123 F3
Kinsman Est PL31 109 C3
Kinterbury Rd PL5 127 B8
Kinterbury St PL1 149 A2
Kinterbury Terr PL5 127 B8
Kinver Cl PL6 125 D4
Kipling Gdns PL5 124 D2
Kirby Rd TR1 137 A4
Kirkby Pl PL4 148 C4
Kirkby Terr PL4 148 C4
Kirkdale Gdns PL2 128 B7
Kirkella Rd PL20 42 D2
Kirkland Cl PL6 125 C7
Kirkstall Cl PL2 128 A8
Kirkwall Rd PL5 124 E3
Kirland Bower PL30 48 B7
Kirland Rd PL30 109 B2
Kirton Pl PL3 129 B5
Kit Hill Cres PL5 127 C8
Kit Hill Ctry Pk* PL17 40 A6
Kitley Way PL5 123 D1
Kitter Dr PL9 136 A5
Kittiwake Cl TR27 77 E3
Kitts Ct 17 TR18 143 E5
Kleinfontein Terr PL14 38 D4
Knapmedown PL15 11 B1
Knapps Cl PL9 136 C6
Knave-Go-By TR14 79 D5
Kneele Gdns PL3 128 E8
Knighton Rd PL4 149 C3
Knighton Terr 3 PL20 42 C5
Knightor Cl PL26 59 E6
Knights Cl 1 PL34 14 C7
Knights Ct PL22 112 B3
Knights Hill TR1 137 B6
Knight's Mdws TR3 81 F7
Knights Way TR15 140 D7
Knill Cl TR26 141 C2
Knill Cross PL10 132 E5
Knill Cross Cotts PL10 132 E5
Knoll Pk TR1 137 F4
Knoll The PL7 130 B6
Knowland Cl PL1 127 F3
Knowle Ave PL2 127 E6
Knowle Prim Sch PL5 124 A4
Knowle Terr PL20 42 E4
Koth Karrji PL30 23 E7
Kyl Cober Parc PL17 28 E1
Kynance Cl PL11 126 F4
Kynance Ho TR1 69 E4
Kynance Terr TR12 102 F2

L

Labernum Terr EX23 5 A6
Laburnum Cl TR11 144 F5
Laburnum Cotts PL19 147 C6
Laburnum Dr TR11 144 F5
Lacey Cl TR14 79 E5
Ladock CE Sch TR2 57 C2
Ladock Rd
Ladock TR2 57 C1
Probus TR2 71 C7
Ladycross PL15 18 F7
Lady Modifords CE Prim Sch PL20 42 E4
Ladysmith Ct PL4 149 C4
Ladysmith Rd PL4 129 B3
Lady St TR13 146 B5
Ladywell PL28 107 D5
Ladywell Pl PL4 149 B3
Laflouder Fields TR12 99 A2
Laflouder La TR12 99 A2
Lafrowda Cl TR19 86 E6
Lafrowda Terr TR19 86 F6
Laguna Ct TR15 140 B5
Laira Ave PL3 129 D4
Laira Bridge Rd PL4 129 B1
Laira Gdns PL3 129 C4
Laira Green Prim Sch PL3 129 C4
Laira Park Cres PL4 129 B4
Laira Park Pl PL4 129 B4
Laira Park Rd PL4 129 B4
Laira Pl PL4 149 C2
Laira St PL4 149 C3
Laity La TR26 77 C4
Laity Rd TR14 79 E4
Laity Wlk PL6 124 D6
Lake La
Dousland PL20 42 E3
Liskeard PL14 113 D5
Lake Mews PL10 132 E5
Lake Rd PL9 135 B6
Lakeside PL19 147 B6
Lakeside Dr PL5 123 E5
Lake View PL12 53 C8
Lake View Cl PL5 124 B6
Lakeview Dr PL5 124 B5
Lalebrick Rd PL9 135 B5
Lamanva Cl 16 TR16 67 E4
Lamanva Rd 17 TR16 67 E4
Lambert Rd PL5 124 B6
Lambert Terr 4 TR11 145 A5
Lambhay Hill PL1 149 A1
Lambhay St PL1 149 A1
Lambourne Ave 7 TR5 54 D1
Lamb Pk 5 PL24 60 C4
Lambs La TR11 144 E5
Lamellyn Dr TR1 69 F3
Lamellyn Rd PL24 60 B4
Lamerhooe Cross PL19 29 C1
Lamerhooe Dr
Horsebridge PL19 29 C1
Luckett PL19 40 C8
Lamerton Cl PL5 124 B3
Lametton Gn PL14 51 B4
Lamledra Hill PL26 85 D5
Lamorak Cl PL26 73 B3
Lamorna Ct TR16 67 D6
Lamorna Dr 11 PL17 39 F4
Lamorna Parc 12 PL17 39 F4
Lamorna Pk
St Austell PL25 114 E7
Torpoint PL11 126 E4
Lamorne Cl 4 TR6 55 A4
Lampen Rd PL14 36 F2
Lampen Terr PL14 36 F2
Lana Cotts EX22 13 C7
Lanadwell St PL28 107 D5
Lanaton Rd TR10 144 A8
Lancamshire La TR20 89 F5
Lancaster Cres PL27 31 F3
Lancaster Gdns PL5 124 D4
Lanchard La PL14 113 B5
Lanchard Rd PL14 113 B5
Lanchard Rise PL14 113 B5
Landaviddy La PL13 62 D2
Lander Ct TR1 137 D3
Lander Rd PL12 122 F3
Landeryon Gdns TR18 143 D5
Landithy TR20 143 A8
Landlake Cross PL15 28 A8
Landlake Rd PL15 106 B2
Landrake Cl PL5 127 C8
Landreath Pl PL24 60 B5
Landrew Rd PL25 114 F6
Lands End Rd TR19 97 A6
Land's End (St Just) Aerodrome TR19 86 F3
Lands Pk PL9 135 F7
Landulph Cross PL12 118 F1
Landulph Gdns PL5 127 C8
Landulph Prim Sch PL12 118 F1
Lane End Cross PL19 29 D2
Lanepark La EX39 2 D5
Lane Reddin Terr 21 TR18 143 C2
Lane The PL7 130 D6
Langage Cross PL7 131 F6
Langage Ind Est PL7 131 D4
Langage Pk PL7 131 C4
Langage Science Pk PL7 131 D5
Langarth Cl TR3 69 D4
Langdale Cl PL6 125 D1
Langdale Gdns PL6 125 D1
Langdon Cross PL15 18 D8
Langdon Ct PL9 136 B6
Langdon Down Way PL11 126 E3
Langerwell Cl PL12 122 C3
Langerwell La PL12 122 C3
Langfords Mdw 4 PL35 9 C1
Lang Gdns PL18 41 A3
Lang Gr
Plymouth PL9 136 C7
Tavistock PL19 147 D5
Langham Pl PL4 149 C3
Langhill Rd PL3 128 D5
Langley Cl PL6 125 A7
Langley Cres PL6 124 F7
Langley Jun & Inf Schs PL6 125 A6
Langman Ct 13 PL20 41 B1
Langmead Cl PL6 129 C8
Langmead Rd PL6 129 C8
Langmore Cl PL6 129 A7
Langorran Rd TR14 138 B3
Lang Rd PL14 113 B4
Langreek Bglws PL13 62 C2
Langreek Rd PL13 62 C2
Langstone Rd PL2 128 C7
Langstone Terr PL2 128 C7
Langton Rd
Falmouth TR11 145 A6
8 Yelverton PL20 42 C3
Langton Terr 8 TR11 145 A5
Langurroc Rd TR8 110 A3
Langurtho Rd PL23 116 B4
Langweath Est TR12 99 D7
Langweath Gdns TR27 77 E3
Langweath La TR12 99 D7
Langwedh TR16 67 D4
Lanhenvor Ave TR7 110 E5
Lanherne Ave TR8 45 A8
Lanheverne Parc 4 TR12 101 C4
Lanhydrock Ho & Gdns* PL30 48 D6
Lanhydrock Rd PL4 129 B2
Lanhydrock View PL31 109 D3
Lanivet Com Prim Sch PL30 47 E7
Lanjowan TR13 146 B6
Lankelly Cl PL23 116 B4
Lankelly La PL23 116 A4
Lanlivery Com Prim Sch PL30 48 D2
Lanlovie Mdw TR8 55 D8
Lanmoor Est TR16 80 D6
Lannarth Glas TR16 140 E1
Lanner Gn TR16 140 E1
Lanner Hill
Redruth, Pennance TR16 140 E1
Redruth TR15 140 D2
Lanner Moor Terr TR16 80 E6
Lanner Prim Sch TR16 80 D6
Lanner Sq TR16 80 D6
Lannoweth Rd TR18 143 F6
Lanoweth TR10 81 D2
Lanreath CE Prim Sch PL13 62 A8
Lanreath Farm & Folk Mus* PL13 62 B8
Lansallos St PL13 62 D1
Lansdown Cl EX23 104 D5
Lansdowne TR26 141 B4
Lansdowne Cl TR18 143 C5
Lansdowne Ct TR18 143 B5
Lansdowne Pk TR16 68 C3
Lansdowne Pl TR18 143 C4
Lansdowne Rd
Callington PL17 39 E4
Falmouth TR11 145 C3
Penzance TR18 143 C5
Plymouth PL6 124 F2
Lansdown Rd
Bude EX23 104 D5
Wadebridge PL27 108 B5
Lantallack Cross PL12 53 A3
Lanuthnoe Est TR27 77 F1

Lan–Lyn 167

Lanwithan Cl PL22 . . . . . . 112 D2
Lanwithan Rd PL22. . . . . . 112 E1
Lanxon Cres PL30. . . . . 48 C2
Lanyon Ct PL14 . . . . 37 F3
Lanyon Rd TR3 . . . . 82 B8
Lappa Valley Steam Railway★ TR8 . . . . 56 C7
Lapthorn Cl PL9 . . . . 135 C7
Larch Cl PL12. . . . . 122 C3
Larch Dr PL6 . . . . 125 E7
Larcombe Rd PL25 . . . . . . 115 A6
Laregan Hill TR18 . . . . 143 C3
Lariggan Cres TR18 . . . . . 143 D4
Lariggan Rd TR18 . . . . 143 D4
Larkfield Cl PL26. . . . . 58 E5
Larkhall Rise PL3 . . . . 129 B5
Larkham Cl PL7 . . . . 130 C6
Larkham La PL7 . . . . 130 C6
Lark Hill PL2. . . . . 128 A6
Latham Cl PL6 . . . . 129 A7
Latimer Cl PL7. . . . . 131 B5
Latimer Wlk PL6 . . . . 124 E7
Launcells Cross EX23 . . . . . .5 B1
Launceston Castle★ PL15 . . . . 106 C6
Launceston Cl
Bodmin PL31 . . . . 109 F4
Plymouth PL6. . . . . 125 B7
Launceston Coll PL15 . . . 106 C4
Launceston Com Prim Sch PL15 . . . . 106 C5
Launceston Hospl PL15 . 106 C4
Launceston Rd
Bodmin PL31 . . . . 35 B1
Kelly Bray PL17 . . . . 39 E6
Launceston Ret Pk PL15 106 C4
Launceston Sta★ PL15 . . 106 B6
Launceston Steam Rly★ PL15 . . . . 18 E3
Laura Cl PL34. . . . . 14 D7
Laura Dr PL25 . . . . 115 A5
Laurel Ct PL2. . . . . 128 A7
Laurel Dene PL2 . . . . 128 A7
Laurel Dr PL6. . . . . 125 E5
Laurel Rd PL2 . . . . 128 A7
Laurels The PL18 . . . . 40 E6
La Vague TR3. . . . . 82 C5
Lavington Cl PL7. . . . . 131 B5
Lavinia Dr PL7 . . . . 130 C5
Lavorrick Orchs PL26 . . . . 73 C4
Lawn Cl 2 PL7 . . . . 131 C5
Lawn Steps TR11. . . . . 145 B4
Lawns The
Plymouth PL5. . . . . 124 E1
Torpoint PL11 . . . . 127 A4
Lawn The
Par PL24 . . . . 60 B5
Tavistock PL19. . . . . 147 D6
Lawrence House Mus★ PL15. . . . . 106 C6
Lawrence Rd
Plymouth PL9. . . . . 135 A6
St Agnes TR5 . . . . 54 C1
Lawry Cl 6 PL14. . . . . 113 B5
Lawson Gr PL9. . . . . 135 C7
Lawton Cl TR7 . . . . 110 B5
Law Wlk PL6. . . . . 124 D6
Leader Rd TR7. . . . . 111 E7
Leafield PL31 . . . . 35 B2
Leander Way PL5 . . . . 124 D2
Leanway PL12 . . . . 122 E2
Leap Pk TR3. . . . . 69 C3
Leas The TR1 . . . . 137 E5
Leat Cl PL20 . . . . 42 E3
Leatfield PL26 . . . . 73 C3
Leatfield Dr PL6 . . . . 124 F4
Leatherby Cl PL6. . . . . 124 E7
Leather Tor Cl 4 PL20 . . . 42 C3
Leat Rd
Lifton PL16. . . . . 19 F3
Pendeen TR19 . . . . 75 A1
Leatside PL6. . . . . 121 C1
Leats The TR1 . . . . 137 C4
Leat The 9 EX23. . . . . .4 E1
Leat View PL12 . . . . 122 B3
Leat Wlk
Plymouth PL3. . . . . 128 E6
Roborough PL6 . . . . 121 D1
Saltash PL12 . . . . 122 D4
Leaves Yd PL3 . . . . 129 B7
Lea Way EX23. . . . . 104 F6
Leburnick Cross PL15 . . . . 28 D8
Ledgate La PL7 . . . . 131 F8
Ledra Cl TR12. . . . . 103 A4
Ledrah Gdns PL25. . . . . . . 114 B3
Ledrah Rd PL25. . . . . 114 B3
Ledrak Parc TR13 . . . . 146 B8
Leedstown Com Prim Sch TR27. . . . . 78 E1
Leeside Ct 7 PL2 . . . . 128 A4
Lefra Orch TR19 . . . . 97 B6
Legendry Land's End★ TR19. . . . . 96 A5
Leggos Ct 10 TR15 . . . . . . 140 B5
Legion La 3 PL24. . . . . 60 D5
Legis Wlk PL6 . . . . 125 B8
Leigham Ct PL1. . . . . 148 B2
Leigham Manor Dr PL6. . 129 F8
Leigham Prim Sch PL6. . 125 E1
Leigham St PL1. . . . . 148 B1
Leigham Terrace La PL1. 148 B2
Leigh Ct PL6. . . . . 129 A8
Leigh La
Hatt PL12. . . . . 53 D6
Roborough PL6 . . . . 121 D2
Leighton Rd PL3 . . . . 128 F8
Lelant Mdws TR26 . . . . 77 E4
Lelant Saltings Sta TR26. . 77 E3
Lelant Sta TR26. . . . . 77 E4
Lemellen Gdns PL30 . . . . . 23 B2
Lemin Parc TR27. . . . . 78 E3
Lemin's Ct TR15 . . . . 140 B5
Lemon Hill TR11 . . . . 82 A3
Lemon Hill Gdns TR11. . . . 82 A3
Lemon Mews Rd TR1. . . . 137 D4
Lemon Quay TR1. . . . . 137 D4
Lemon Row TR1 . . . . 137 D3
Lemon St
St Keverne TR12 . . . . 101 D4
Truro TR1. . . . . 137 D4
Lemon Terr TR4 . . . . 81 D8
Lender La 5 TR12 . . . . 99 A2
Lendewedneck Com Prim Sch TR12 . . . . 102 F2
Lendra La PL17 . . . . 39 D4
Lerryn CE Prim Sch PL22. 61 D8
Lerryn View PL22 . . . . 61 C8
Lerwick Rd PL27 . . . . 31 F3
Lescudjack Cres TR18. . . . 143 F6
Lescudjack Rd TR18. . . . . 143 E6
Lescudjack Terr TR18 . . . 143 F6
Lesingey La TR20 . . . . 88 A5
Leskinnick Pl 15 TR18 . . . . 143 E6
Leskinnick St TR18. . . . . . 143 F6
Leskinnick Terr TR18. . . . 143 E6
Leslie Ct TR13 . . . . 146 B6
Lesnewth 18 PL24. . . . . 60 B4
Lester Cl PL3 . . . . 129 B6
Lestraynes La TR10 . . . . . . 92 E8
Lethlean Cl TR27. . . . . 142 D7
Lethlean La TR27 . . . . 142 D7
Lethlean Towans TR27 . . 142 D8
Levant Beam Engine★ TR19. . . . . 74 E1
Levant Cl TR19. . . . . 86 F8
Levant Rd TR19 . . . . 86 F8
Leven Cotts EX23 . . . . 104 D5
Leverlake Rd EX23 . . . . .6 F4
Levine View TR11 . . . . 144 E1
Lewannick Cl PL15 . . . . 27 B7
Lewannick Com Prim Sch PL15 . . . . 27 B7
Lewannick Rd TR8 . . . . 43 D1
Lewarne Cres TR7 . . . . . . 111 C7
Lewarne Rd TR7 . . . . 111 C8
Lewes Gdns PL5 . . . . 124 C4
Lewis Way PL25. . . . . 114 E6
Lewman Cl TR2. . . . . 71 C6
Lewman Rd TR2 . . . . 71 C6
Leworthy Cross EX22. . . . . . .8 E4
Ley La PL20. . . . . 119 D6
Leypark Ct PL6 . . . . 125 E2
Leypark Dr PL6 . . . . 125 E2
Leypark Wlk PL6. . . . . 125 E2
Leys La TR17 . . . . 89 B5
Libby Ct PL12. . . . . 122 C5
Liberator Row 4 PL27 . . . . 31 F3
Lidden Cl TR18 . . . . 143 C3
Lidden Cres TR18 . . . . 143 C3
Lidden Rd TR18. . . . . 143 C3
Liddicoat Rd PL22. . . . . . . 112 D3
Liddle Way PL7 . . . . 131 B6
Lifeboat Hill 32 TR26 . . . . 141 B6
Lifton Com Prim Sch PL16 . . . . 19 F4
Liftondown Cross PL16. . . 19 D4
Lifton Rd PL4. . . . . 149 C2
Lighterage Hill TR1 . . . . . 137 E2
Lighthouse Hill TR16 . . . . . 67 C6
Lighthouse La PL26 . . . . . . 85 C5
Lighthouse Rd TR12. . . . . . 102 F2
Lilac Cl PL9. . . . . 135 C5
Lily Way PL28. . . . . 31 F7
Limerick Pl PL4. . . . . 149 C3
Limes La PL14 . . . . 113 B5
Limes The PL6. . . . . 124 F2
Limetree Rd PL3 . . . . 128 D7
Lime Tree Way PL15 . . . . . . 27 D4
Lincoln Ave PL4 . . . . 149 C4
Lincoln Row 6 PL27 . . . . . 31 F3
Linden Ave TR7. . . . . 110 E5
Linden Cres TR7 . . . . 110 E5
Linden Terr PL4 . . . . 149 C3
Lingard Cl PL14. . . . . 113 A6
Lingfield Ave PL26 . . . . 58 E1
Linhay Cl PL25. . . . . 115 D6
Linkadells PL7. . . . . 130 D6
Link Cl TR11 . . . . 144 F4
Linketty La PL7 . . . . 130 C5
Linketty La E PL6 . . . . 125 A1
Linketty La W PL6. . . . . . . 128 F8
Link Rd PL15 . . . . 106 B3
Links The
Falmouth TR11. . . . . 144 F1
Praa Sands TR20. . . . . 90 C4
Links View EX23 . . . . 104 F6
Linley Cl TR3 . . . . 69 D3
Linnet Ct PL12 . . . . 122 C2
Linton Cl PL5 . . . . 124 C8
Linton La EX39. . . . . .2 E5
Linton Rd PL5 . . . . 124 C7
Linton Sq PL5 . . . . 124 C8
Lippell Dr PL9 . . . . 135 E6
Lipson Ave PL4 . . . . 149 C4
Lipson Com Coll PL4. . . . . 129 C4
Lipson Ct PL4. . . . . 149 B3
Lipson Rd PL4 . . . . 149 B4
Lipson Terr PL4. . . . . 149 C4
Lipson Vale PL4. . . . . 129 A4
Lipson Vale Prim Sch PL4 . . . . 129 A4
Lipstone Cres PL4 . . . . . . 149 C4
Lisbon Terr TR19 . . . . 97 A6
Liscawn Terr PL11 . . . . . . 127 B3
Liscombe Cl PL18 . . . . 41 A7
Lishaperhill Cross EX22 . . . .5 E2
Liskeard Bsns Pk PL14 . . 113 E6
Liskeard Com Hospl PL14 . . . . 113 E7
Liskeard & District Mus★ PL14 . . . . 113 C6
Liskeard Hill PL14. . . . . 36 F2
Liskeard Inf Sch PL14 . . . 113 B6
Liskeard Jun Sch PL14 . . 113 A6
Liskeard Rd
Callington PL17 . . . . 39 E4
Saltash PL12 . . . . 122 B3
Trematon PL12 . . . . 53 E3
Liskeard Sch & Com Coll PL14 . . . . 113 C7
Liskeard Sta PL14. . . . . . . 113 B4
Liskeard Town Mus★ PL14 . . . . 113 C6
Liskerrett Rd PL14 . . . . . . 113 D5
Liskey TR6 . . . . 55 A4
Liskey Hill TR6. . . . . 55 A4
Liskey Hill Cres 1 TR6 . . . 55 A4
Liskey Tourist Pk TR3 . . . . 69 C4
Lisson Gr PL4. . . . . 128 F4
Lister Cl PL7. . . . . 130 F6
Lister Hill 10 TR11 . . . . . . 145 A4
Lister St TR11. . . . . 145 A3
Listowel Dr PL13. . . . . 117 D4
Listry Rd TR7 . . . . 110 E5
Litchaton Cres PL7. . . . . . 130 B7
Litchaton Way PL7 . . . . . . 130 B7
Litchfield Cl PL7 . . . . 131 B6
Little Ash Gdns PL5 . . . . . 123 B1
Little Ash Rd PL5 . . . . 123 B1
Little Bodieve Holiday Pk PL27. . . . . 108 D7
Little Bridge Cross EX22. . . 8 A5
Littlebridge Mdw EX22 . . . . 8 A5
Little Bridge Pk PL27. . . . 108 D6
Little Butts PL9 . . . . 135 E6
Little Castle St 7 TR1. . . . 137 C4
Little Dean PL14 . . . . 113 A5
Little Dinas PL28. . . . . 107 E4
Little Dock La PL5 . . . . . . 124 B2
Little Down La PL6. . . . . . 121 E3
Little Down Pk TR7 . . . . . 111 A4
Little Fancy Cl PL6. . . . . . 125 C7
Little Gilly Hill 3 TR15 . . 140 C4
Little Gregwartha TR16. . . 80 A5
Little-in-sight 19 TR26 . . 141 A5
Little La
Hayle TR27. . . . . 142 E7
Kingsand PL10. . . . . 133 A2
Staddiscombe PL9. . . . . . . 135 D3
Little Laney PL13. . . . . 62 D1
Little Mdw
Bodmin PL31 . . . . 109 D5
Pyworthy EX22 . . . . 8 E5
Little Mill La TR27. . . . . 77 E2
Little Oaks TR10 . . . . 144 B6
Little Orch PL12 . . . . 53 C3
Little Point Cres PL10 . . . . 132 F5
Little Stark Cl PL26 . . . . . . 58 B4
Littleton Pl PL2 . . . . 127 F4
Little Treloweth TR15 . . . . 139 B6
Little Trelower Pk PL26 . . . 58 F1
Little Trelyn PL27 . . . . 21 E2
Little Trethewey Est TR19 96 E4
Little Trethiggey TR8. . . . . 111 F2
Little Treverrow PL27 . . . . 21 E2
Little Western Rly★ TR7. 110 F5
Little Woburn Cl PL15 . . . 106 C4
Littlewood Cl PL7 . . . . 131 A4
Lizard Cl PL6 . . . . 124 F7
Lizard Head La TR12 . . . . 102 E2
Lizard Lighthouse TR12 . 102 F1
Lizard Nature Reserve The★ TR12. . . . . 100 F2
Lizard Wlk PL6 . . . . 125 A7
Llawnroc Cl TR14 . . . . 138 E2
Llewellyn Cl PL32 . . . . 105 C3
Lloyds Rd TR12 . . . . 103 A2
Loatmead Cross EX22 . . . . . 3 E3
Lockeridge Rd PL20. . . . . . . 41 B1
Lockington Ave PL3. . . . . 128 F7
Locks Wlk PL1. . . . . 127 E1
Lockyer Ct PL1 . . . . 148 C2
Lockyer Mews PL19. . . . . 147 C6
Lockyer Rd PL3 . . . . 128 E5
Lockyers Quay PL4. . . . . . 149 B2
Lockyer St PL1. . . . . 148 C2
Lockyer Terr PL12 . . . . . . 123 A3
Lodenek Ave PL28 . . . . . . 107 D4
Lodge Dr TR1. . . . . 137 F6
Lodge Gdns PL6 . . . . 124 E3
Lodge Hill PL14. . . . . 113 A3
Lodge La PL8. . . . . 136 F5
Lodge Way TR9 . . . . 45 F2
Loe Bar Rd TR13 . . . . 98 C8
Loe Valley Rd TR13. . . . . . 146 B7
Lofoten Cl PL1. . . . . 127 E2
Loftus Gdns PL5 . . . . 123 C2
Logans Ct TR26 . . . . 141 D2
Loggans Cl TR27 . . . . 142 E8
Loggans Rd
Hayle TR27. . . . . 78 B6
Phillack TR27 . . . . 142 E8
Loggans Way TR27 . . . . . 142 E8
Loggans Wlk TR27 . . . . . . 142 E8
Lollabury Rd PL12. . . . . . . 122 E3
Lomond Hall TR26 . . . . . . 141 D1
Longacre
Harrowbarrow PL17 . . . . . . 40 C4
Plymouth PL7. . . . . 130 B7
Long Acre PL12. . . . . 122 B4
Long-A-Row Cl EX23. . . . . 10 C6
Long Barn The TR20 . . . . . 89 D8
Longbridge Cl PL6 . . . . . . 129 F6
Longbridge Rd
Plymouth, Laira PL3. . . . . . 129 C4
Plymouth, Longbridge PL6. 129 E7
Longbrook Barton PL7 . . 130 D5
Longbrook St PL7. . . . . . . 130 F4
Longcause PL7 . . . . 130 F4
Longcause Com Specl Sch PL7. . . . . 130 F4
Longcoombe La PL13 . . . . 62 D3
Long Cross PL29 . . . . 22 C6
Longcross Victorian Gardens★ PL29. . . . . 22 C6
Long Down Gdns PL6 . . . 125 E3
Longdowns Trad Est TR10. 81 A1
Longfield TR11 . . . . 144 E4
Longfield Cl 25 PL17 . . . . . 39 F4
Longfield Dr PL32. . . . . . . 105 C3
Longfield Pl PL4 . . . . 149 B4
Longfield Rd PL32 . . . . . . 105 C3
Longfield Villas PL9. . . . . . 135 D8
Longhouse La PL27 . . . . . . 21 E3
Long La
High Street PL26 . . . . 58 C4
Ludgvan TR20 . . . . 89 A7
St Erth TR20, TR27. . . . . 89 E8
Longlands PL9. . . . . 135 D8
Longlands La PL12 . . . . . . 122 B1
Long Lanes TR20. . . . . 89 F7
Long Ley PL3 . . . . 129 B6
Longman's La 3 PL17. . . . 39 E4
Long Mdw PL7. . . . . 130 D7
Longmeadow Cl PL7 . . . . 130 E7
Longmeadow Rd PL12. . . 122 E3
Long Moor TR12 . . . . 103 A5
Long Orch PL20. . . . . 41 B1
Long Park Cl PL9 . . . . 135 F5
Longpark Dr EX23. . . . . .6 F5
Long Park Dr PL6. . . . . 125 D7
Long Park Rd PL12. . . . . . . 122 D2
Longpark Way PL25 . . . . . 114 F5
Long Pk PL15 . . . . 18 D2
Long Rd PL12. . . . . 122 B4
Longrock Bsns Pk TR20 . . 88 F6
Longrock Ind Est TR20 . . . 88 F6
Long Row TR19 . . . . 97 F7
Long Rowden PL3. . . . . . . 128 E6
Long Steps PL23 . . . . 116 C4
Longstone Ave PL6 . . . . . 125 A6
Longstone Cl TR26 . . . . . . 141 E1
Longstone Hill TR26. . . . . 141 E1
Long Terrace Cl 5 PL7. . 131 C5
Longview Rd PL12 . . . . . . 122 D3
Longview Terr PL3. . . . . . 129 B7
Longwood Cl PL7 . . . . 131 A4
Longwool Mdw EX23 . . . . . . .7 B6
Looe Bay Holiday Pk PL13. . . . . 117 F8
Looe Com Sch PL13. . . . . 117 D6
Looe Hill
Looe PL13 . . . . 63 F5
Seaton PL13, PL11. . . . . 64 A5
Looe Prim Sch PL13 . . . . 117 D4
Looe St PL4 . . . . 149 A2
Looe Sta PL13 . . . . 117 C4
Lookout The 7 TR11. . . . . 145 B5
Looseleigh Cl PL6. . . . . . . 125 A4
Looseleigh La PL6 . . . . . . 124 F5
Looseleigh Pk PL6 . . . . . . 124 E5
Lopes Dr PL6 . . . . 121 C1
Lopes Rd
Dousland PL20. . . . . 42 E3
Plymouth PL2. . . . . 128 B6
Lopwell Cl PL6. . . . . 124 F5
Lord Louis Cres PL9. . . . . . 134 F6
Lords Mdw TR2. . . . . 71 F3
Lorrimore Ave PL2. . . . . . . 127 F5
Loscombe Ct TR16 . . . . 80 A5
Loscombe La TR16 . . . . 80 A5
Loscombe Rd TR16. . . . . . 139 E1
Lost Gdns of Heligan The★ PL26 . . . . 73 B5
Lostwithiel Mus★ PL22. . 112 C2
Lostwithiel Rd PL30, PL31 . 48 C7
Lostwithiel Sch PL22. . . . 112 C2
Lostwithiel St PL23 . . . . . 116 C4
Lostwithiel Sta PL22 . . . . 112 D2
Lostwood Rd PL25 . . . . . . 114 E4
Lotherton Cl PL7. . . . . 131 B3
Loughboro Rd PL5 . . . . . . 123 C1
Love La
Bodmin PL31 . . . . 109 F5
Hayle TR27. . . . . 142 E7
Mousehole TR19 . . . . 88 C1
Penryn TR10 . . . . 144 D8
Penzance TR18 . . . . 143 C4
Saltash PL12 . . . . 122 E2
24 St Ives TR26. . . . . 141 B6
Lovell Rd PL3. . . . . 128 F6
Lovely La PL12. . . . . 65 A8
Loveny Cl PL14 . . . . 36 F2
Loveny Rd PL14. . . . . 36 F2
Lovibond Wlk PL27. . . . . . 108 C5
Lowenac Cres TR27 . . . . . . 78 E6
Lowenac Gdns TR14. . . . . 138 C2
Lowen Ct 7 TR1. . . . . 137 D4
Lowenek Cl TR11 . . . . 144 E5
Lowenna Manor PL27 . . . . 21 E3
Lowen Way TR3. . . . . 69 C3
Lower Anderton Rd PL10 132 F5
Lower Barncoose TR15. . 139 F6
Lower Biteford Cross EX39 . 3 E6
Lower Bore St PL31 . . . . . 109 D5
Lower Boscaswell Parc TR19 . . . . 74 F1
Lower Broad La TR15, TR16 . . . . 139 C8
Lower Cardrew La TR15 . 140 B6
Lower Castle Rd TR2. . . . . 95 A5
Lower Chapel St PL13 . . . 117 D3
Lower Church St TR27. . . 142 D6
Lower Cleaverfield PL15. 106 C7
Lower Clicker Rd PL14 . . . 51 F4
Lower Compton Rd PL3 . 128 F5
Lower Coronation Terr 9 PL17. . . . . 39 F4
Lower Eastcliff TR4 . . . . . . 68 A7
Lower Elms PL27. . . . . 21 F3
Lower Fairfield PL12 . . . . . 65 A8
Lower Farm Rd PL7 . . . . . 131 A4
Lower Fore St PL12 . . . . . 123 A2
Lower Glen Pk PL14. . . . . . 38 D4
Lower Goongumpas La TR16 . . . . 68 F1
Lower Goonrea PL13. . . . . 117 B4
Lower Greenbanks PL27. . 21 E2
Lower Green St TR18. . . . 143 D1
Lower Gurnick Rd TR18 . 143 B3
Lower Hill TR13. . . . . 146 C6
Lower Hillcrest
Helston TR13 . . . . 146 C6
9 Perranporth TR6. . . . . . . 55 A4
Lower Hillside PL14. . . . . . 50 B6
Lower Hugus Rd TR3. . . . . 69 C3
Lower Kelly PL18 . . . . 41 A3
Lower La
Mawgan TR12 . . . . 99 D7
6 Plymouth PL1. . . . . 149 A2
Lower Lux St 5 PL14. . . . 113 C6
Lower Market St
Looe PL13 . . . . 117 D3
Penryn TR10 . . . . 144 C7
Lower Mdw 5 TR4. . . . . . . 69 A3
Lower Merritts Hill 22 TR16 . . . . 67 E4
Lower Middle Hill PL14. . . 38 E4
Lower Molinnis PL26. . . . . 47 D2
Lower Parc TR12. . . . . 92 C2
Lower Park Dr PL9. . . . . . 135 F4
Lower Pengegon TR14 . . . 138 F3
Lower Peverell Rd TR18 . 143 E7
Lower Pk TR2. . . . . 70 F5
Lower Polstain Rd TR3 . . . 69 D3
Lower Port View PL12. . . 122 F2
Lower Pumpfield Row TR15 . . . . 139 B6
Lower Rd PL11. . . . . 64 C4
Lower Redannick TR1. . . 137 C4
Lower Ridings PL7 . . . . . . 131 B7
Lower Rosewin Row 9 TR1 . . . . 137 D5
Lower Row PL10. . . . . 133 A2
Lower Rowes Terr PL26 . . 58 D5
Lower Saltram PL9. . . . . . 135 C7
Lower Sheffield TR19 . . . . 97 F7
Lowerside PL2. . . . . 128 A8
Lower Sq EX22. . . . . 11 E8
Lower St
Looe PL13 . . . . 117 D3
Plymouth PL4. . . . . 149 A3
Lower Tamar Terr PL18 . . 41 A7
Lower Terr TR3 . . . . 81 B4
Lower Town PL17 . . . . 28 E1
Lowertown Cl PL12 . . . . . . 53 C3
Lowertown La TR13 . . . . . 146 C7
Lower Tregongeeves PL26. . . . . 59 A1
Lower Tywarnhayle 18 TR6 . . . . 55 A5
Lower Well La TR13 . . . . . 146 C6
Lower Well Pk PL26 . . . . . . 73 C3
Lower Wesley Terr PL14. . 38 D4
Lower Woodside PL25. . . 114 A4
Lowery Cross PL20. . . . . . . 42 F4
Low Lee Rd TR19 . . . . 88 D1
Lowley Rd PL15 . . . . 18 E2
Lucas Cl PL31. . . . . 109 E3
Lucas La PL7 . . . . 130 D6
Lucas Terr PL4 . . . . 129 B2
Lucknow Rd PL31 . . . . 48 D8
Lucknow Rd S 3 PL31 . . . 48 D8
Ludgvan Com Prim Sch TR20. . . . . 89 B8
Ludlow Rd 2 PL3. . . . . . . 128 E6
Luffman Cl PL13 . . . . 62 D6
Lugger The TR2. . . . . 83 B2
Lukes Cl TR1 . . . . 137 F5
Luke's La TR20. . . . . 89 F6
Lulworth Dr PL6 . . . . 125 B7
Lundnant Cvn Site PL27 . 21 E6
Lundy Cl PL6 . . . . 124 F7
Lundy Dr EX23 . . . . 10 C6
Lundy Rd PL29. . . . . 22 E7
Lusart Dr TR12. . . . . 102 F2
Lusty Glaze Rd TR7 . . . . . 111 A7
Lutsford Cross EX39. . . . . . . 3 A6
Lutyens Fold PL19 . . . . 29 C6
Luxmore Cl PL6. . . . . 125 E1
Luxon Dr TR7 . . . . 110 F4
Luxstowe Dr 1 PL14 . . . . 113 C6
Luxstowe Gdns PL14 . . . . 113 C6
Luxulyan Rd PL24 . . . . 115 F7
Luxulyan Sch PL30. . . . . . . 48 A1
Luxulyan Sta PL30 . . . . 47 F1
Lych Cl PL9. . . . . 135 A6
Lychgate Dr TR1 . . . . 137 C6
Lydcott Cl PL13 . . . . 63 F8
Lydcott Cres PL13. . . . . 63 F8
Lydcot Wlk PL6 . . . . 125 A1
Lydford Park Rd PL3 . . . . 128 D5
Lyd Gdns PL19. . . . . 147 D5
Lydia Way PL4 . . . . 149 B4
Lympne Ave PL5 . . . . 123 F5
Lynbridge Ct 5 PL19. . . . 147 B5

Lyndhurst Ave PL25 ... 115 A4
Lyndhurst Cl PL2 ... 128 C6
Lyndhurst Rd PL2 ... 128 C6
Lyndon Ct PL12 ... 122 D4
Lyndrick Rd PL3 ... 128 E7
Lynes Cotts 2 PL14 ... 51 A7
Lynher Cl PL15 ... 27 B3
Lynher Ct PL12 ... 122 F1
Lynher Dr PL12 ... 122 F1
Lynher St PL5 ... 123 D2
Lynher View PL17 ... 38 E8
Lynher Way
28 Callington PL17 ... 39 F4
North Hill PL15 ... 27 A4
Lyn-Meynek TR15 ... 140 D4
Lynmouth Cl PL7 ... 130 C7
Lynstone Cotts EX23 ... 104 D3
Lynstone Rd EX23 ... 104 D4
Lyn Terr 7 TR18 ... 143 C1
Lynwood Ave PL7 ... 130 B6
Lynwood Cl PL31 ... 109 E4
Lynwood Cotts 1 TR19 ... 88 C1
Lynwood Flats TR13 ... 91 A1
Lyons Rd PL25 ... 115 B4
Lytton Pl PL25 ... 114 F4

M

Mabbots Ct TR18 ... 143 F6
Mabe Com Prim Sch
TR10 ... 81 C1
Mabena Cl PL30 ... 34 C8
MacAdam Rd PL4 ... 149 C1
MacAulay Cres PL5 ... 124 C1
Macey St PL11 ... 127 C3
Mackenzie Pl PL5 ... 123 C2
McLean Dr PL26 ... 58 D5
Madden Rd PL1 ... 127 F2
Maddever Cres PL14 ... 113 C5
Maddock Cl PL7 ... 131 A4
Maddock Dr PL7 ... 131 B4
Maddocks Cross EX22 ... 3 F2
Madeira Dr EX23 ... 6 F5
Madeira Rd
Falmouth TR11 ... 145 A1
Plymouth PL1 ... 149 A1
Madeira Villas 1 PL20 ... 42 C5
Madeira Wlk TR11 ... 145 A2
Madford La PL15 ... 106 C5
Madge Ct PL19 ... 147 B6
Madge La PL19 ... 147 B6
Madison Terr TR27 ... 142 E7
Madison Vean TR27 ... 142 E7
Madron Rd TR18 ... 143 C7
Maenporth Est TR11 ... 93 E4
Maenporth Rd TR11 ... 93 E4
Maen Valley Pk TR11 ... 93 E5
Maer Down Rd EX23 ... 104 C7
Maer La EX23 ... 104 D8
Magdalen Gdns PL7 ... 130 F3
Magnificent Music Machines
Mus★ PL14 ... 51 C3
Magnolia Cl 3 PL7 ... 131 B5
Magnolia Ct 3 PL9 ... 135 F7
Magor Ave TR14 ... 79 E5
Maida Vale Terr PL4 ... 128 F4
Maiden St 1 EX23 ... 4 E1
Maidenwell Rd PL7 ... 130 C5
Maidstone Pl PL5 ... 123 E4
Maine Gdns PL2 ... 127 F7
Main Rd
Crumplehorn PL13 ... 62 D2
Downderry PL11 ... 64 C5
Main St TR18 ... 143 C7
Mainstone Ave PL4 ... 149 C2
Maitland Dr PL3 ... 128 F8
Maker La PL10 ... 133 B4
Maker Rd PL11 ... 127 A2
Maker View PL3 ... 128 B4
Malabar Ho TR1 ... 69 F3
Malabar Rd TR1 ... 69 F3
Mallard Cl PL7 ... 130 F5
Mallets Ct PL27 ... 108 C6
Malmesbury Cl PL2 ... 128 B8
Malory Cl PL5 ... 124 D2
Malpas Ho TR1 ... 137 E4
Malpas Rd TR1 ... 137 E2
Malt House Ct TR27 ... 142 D6
Malt House Gdns 2
TR18 ... 143 C2
Malthouse La TR17 ... 89 C5
Malt House The 3 TR18 . 143 C2
Manaccan Prim Sch
TR12 ... 101 A8
Manadon Cl PL5 ... 124 E1
Manadon Dr PL5 ... 124 E1
Manadon Hill PL5, PL6 ... 124 E1
Manadon Vale Prim Sch
PL5 ... 128 E8
Manaton Cl TR13 ... 146 D8
Manby Gdns PL5 ... 123 F5
Mandalay Villas 8 TR9 ... 45 E1
Mandeley Cl PL33 ... 14 D2
Manely Way PL17 ... 40 C4
Manewas Way TR7 ... 111 B7
Manfield Way PL25 ... 115 C4
Manifold Gdns PL3 ... 129 D5
Manley Cl PL14 ... 113 B5
Manley Rd PL14 ... 113 B5
Manley Terr 5 PL14 ... 113 B5
Mannamead Ave PL3 ... 128 F5
Mannamead Ct 9 PL3 ... 128 F6
Mannamead Rd PL3 ... 128 F6
Man Of War View TR12 .. 102 F2
Manor Bourne Rd PL9 ... 135 C1
Manor Cl
Blisland PL30 ... 35 D8
Crackington Haven EX23 ... 10 C6
Falmouth TR11 ... 144 E5
Heamoor TR18 ... 143 D7
Helston TR13 ... 146 D8
St Austell PL25 ... 114 F5
Tavistock PL19 ... 147 A6
Manor Cotts TR11 ... 145 D3
Manor Cres TR11 ... 144 E5
Manor Ct 1 TR2 ... 95 A6
Manor Dr TR26 ... 141 C3
Manor Farm PL20 ... 42 E3
Manor Farm Cl 7 TR20 .. 89 E5
Manor Gdns
Camelford PL32 ... 105 D4
Horrabridge PL20 ... 42 B4
Millbrook PL10 ... 132 F6
Plymouth PL1 ... 148 B2
Redruth TR15 ... 140 B6
St Erth TR27 ... 142 A1
Truro TR1 ... 137 E5
Manor La PL3 ... 129 D5
Manor Park Cl PL7 ... 130 F5
Manor Park Dr PL7 ... 131 A4
Manor Pk
Dousland PL20 ... 42 E3
Duloe PL14 ... 51 A1
Saltash PL12 ... 122 D2
Manor Pl TR18 ... 143 D7
Manor Rd
Bude EX23 ... 104 E4
Camborne TR14 ... 138 C2
Carharrack TR16 ... 80 E8
Falmouth TR11 ... 144 E5
Newquay TR7 ... 110 D6
Plymouth PL9 ... 135 E8
Tavistock PL19 ... 147 B6
Manor St PL1 ... 148 A3
Manor View PL24 ... 60 B4
Manor Way
Heamoor TR18 ... 143 D7
Helston TR13 ... 146 D8
Manse Rd 6 TR3 ... 81 F7
Mansion Ho The PL1 ... 134 A8
Manson Pl PL26 ... 58 C8
Manston Cl PL5 ... 123 E5
Mantle Gdns PL5 ... 127 D8
Maple Ave
Camelford PL32 ... 105 E5
Torpoint PL11 ... 127 A3
Maple Cl
Bodmin PL31 ... 109 B4
23 Callington PL17 ... 39 F4
Plymouth PL6 ... 125 E6
5 St Columb Major TR9 ... 45 D6
St Dennis PL26 ... 58 B8
Tavistock PL19 ... 147 C3
Maple Ct 2 PL9 ... 135 F7
Maple Gr
Plymouth, Mutley PL4 ... 128 D4
Plymouth, Plympton PL7 .. 130 B5
Maple Way PL6 ... 125 E7
Marazion Mus★ TR17 ... 89 B5
Marazion Sch TR17 ... 89 C5
Marchant's Cross PL20 ... 42 F1
Marchant's Way PL20 ... 42 F2
Marconi Centre Mus The★
TR13 ... 98 F2
Marconi Cl TR13 ... 146 B6
Marcus Hill TR7 ... 110 E6
Marcwheal 6 TR19 ... 88 C1
Mardon Cl PL6 ... 125 D4
Marett Rd PL5 ... 123 F3
Margaret Ave PL25 ... 114 E3
Margaret Cnr PL31 ... 109 C4
Margaret Cres PL31 ... 109 C4
Margaret Gdns PL27 ... 108 D5
Margaret Pk PL3 ... 128 E8
Margaret Pl TR11 ... 144 F3
Margaret's La PL29 ... 22 D7
Margate La PL30 ... 35 C1
Marhamchurch CE Prim Sch
EX23 ... 7 B6
Maria's La TR19 ... 96 B7
Maribou Ct PL28 ... 31 F7
Marina Ct TR16 ... 67 C5
Marina Rd PL5 ... 123 F3
Marina Terr 7 PL4 ... 128 F4
Marine Cres 5 TR11 ... 145 C3
Marine Ct
Falmouth TR11 ... 145 D3
26 Perranporth TR6 ... 55 A5
Torpoint PL11 ... 127 B2
Marine Dr
Looe PL13 ... 117 D1
Torpoint PL11 ... 127 B2
Widemouth Bay EX23 ... 6 E5
Marine Par TR2 ... 95 A5
Marine Rd PL9 ... 135 B7
Marine Terr
Boscastle PL35 ... 9 C2
7 Penzance TR18 ... 143 E4
Maristow Ave PL2 ... 127 F5
Maristow Cl PL6 ... 124 F5
Maritime Mus★ TR18 ... 143 E5
Market Ave PL1 ... 148 B3
Market Cl PL1 ... 128 A1
Market Ct
Hayle TR27 ... 142 D6
9 Launceston PL15 ... 106 C6
Market Hill PL25 ... 114 C4
Market House Arc
3 Bodmin PL31 ... 109 E5
10 Launceston PL15 ... 106 C6
Market Inn PL24 ... 60 B5
Market Jew St TR18 ... 143 E5
Market Pl
Camelford PL32 ... 105 D4
Helston TR13 ... 146 B5
Marazion TR17 ... 89 B5
Padstow PL28 ... 107 D5
25 Penzance TR18 ... 143 E5
St Columb Major TR9 ... 45 E6
33 St Ives TR26 ... 141 B6
Week St Mary EX22 ... 11 E8
Market Rd
Plymouth PL7 ... 130 D5
Tavistock PL19 ... 147 C5
Market Sq
19 Callington PL17 ... 39 E4
Hayle TR27 ... 142 D6
Plymouth PL1 ... 148 C3
St Day TR16 ... 68 D1
St Just TR19 ... 86 F6
Market St
Bodmin PL31 ... 109 E5
Devoran TR3 ... 81 F6
Falmouth TR11 ... 145 B4
Fowey PL23 ... 116 D4
Hayle TR27 ... 142 D6
Kingsand PL10 ... 133 A1
11 Launceston PL15 ... 106 C6
Liskeard PL14 ... 113 C6
Plymouth PL1 ... 128 A1
6 St Austell PL25 ... 114 C3
St Just TR19 ... 86 F6
3 Stratton EX23 ... 4 E1
Tavistock PL19 ... 147 C5
Market Strand
Falmouth TR11 ... 145 B4
Padstow PL28 ... 107 D5
7 Redruth TR15 ... 140 B5
31 St Ives TR26 ... 141 B6
Market Way
Plymouth PL1 ... 148 C3
5 Redruth TR15 ... 140 B4
Marks Dr PL31 ... 109 E3
Mark's Way TR7 ... 110 D4
Markwell La PL12 ... 53 C1
Marlborough Ave TR11 ... 145 A3
Marlborough Cl
1 Falmouth TR11 ... 145 A3
Saltash PL12 ... 122 F1
Marlborough Cres TR11 . 145 A3
Marlborough Ct 5 TR11. 145 A3
Marlborough Gr 2 TR11 145 A3
Marlborough Prim Sch
PL1 ... 127 E2
Marlborough Rd
Falmouth TR11 ... 145 B3
Plymouth PL4 ... 149 A4
Marlborough Row PL1 ... 127 E2
Marlborough Sch TR11 ... 145 A3
Marlborough St PL1 ... 127 E2
Marlborough Way PL26 .. 58 E1
Marldon Cl PL5 ... 124 B3
Marlow Cres PL16 ... 29 F8
Marlow Gdns PL9 ... 135 F5
Marriotts Ave TR14 ... 138 B4
Marrowbone Slip PL4 ... 149 B2
Marryat Gdns PL5 ... 124 E1
Marshall Ave PL27 ... 108 D5
Marshall Cl
Roche PL26 ... 46 F3
Tavistock PL19 ... 147 D2
Marshallen Rd TR4 ... 68 C6
Marshall Rd
Bodmin, Nanstallon PL30 .. 34 C2
Bodmin PL31 ... 109 D3
Plymouth PL7 ... 130 A5
Tavistock PL19 ... 147 D2
Marshalls Way PL29 ... 22 D6
Marsh Cl PL6 ... 129 F6
Marshfield View PL11 ... 64 B5
Marsh La
Angarrack TR27 ... 142 F7
Calstock PL18 ... 41 A3
Hayle TR27 ... 142 E7
Marshlands PL27 ... 34 A6
Marsh Mills PL6 ... 129 F7
Marsh Mills Pk PL6 ... 129 F6
Marsh Mills Ret Pk PL6 . 129 E7
Marsh Mills Sta★ PL7 ... 130 A7
Marthus Ct 10 PL14 ... 113 C5
Martin Cl TR15 ... 140 D5
Martin Ho 11 TR15 ... 140 B4
Martin La
Plymouth, Barbican PL4 .. 149 A2
Plymouth, Millbay PL1 ... 148 B2
Martins Cl PL14 ... 113 E7
Martin's Ct 2 PL31 ... 109 D5
Martin's La TR15 ... 139 C8
Martin Sq 6 PL17 ... 39 F4
Martin St PL1 ... 148 B2
Martinvale Ave TR15 ... 140 E7
Martinvale Parc TR15 ... 140 E7
Martlesham Pl PL5 ... 123 F4
Martyn's Cl TR4 ... 55 D4
Mary Dean Ave PL5 ... 124 C7
Mary Dean Cl PL5 ... 124 C7
Mary Dean's CE Prim Sch
PL5 ... 124 C7
Maryland Gdns PL2 ... 127 F7
Mary Moon Cl PL12 ... 53 B7
Mary Newman's Cottage★
PL12 ... 123 A2
Mary Seacole Rd PL1 ... 148 A3
Marythorne Rd 15 PL20 ... 41 B1
Masefield Gdns PL5 ... 124 B1
Masons Row PL18 ... 40 F6
Masterman Rd PL2 ... 127 F4
Matela Cl 10 TR13 ... 98 C8
Matthews Way PL14 ... 51 F6
Maudlin Cl PL14 ... 113 D5
Maudlins La PL19 ... 147 A5
Maunsell Cl PL2 ... 127 F7
Mavisdale PL2 ... 127 F6
Mawes Ct PL18 ... 40 D5
Mawgan Cl TR12 ... 99 D6
Mawgan Cross TR12 ... 99 D7
Mawgan-in-Pydar Com Prim
Sch TR8 ... 45 A8
Mawgan Vu TR9 ... 57 E8
Mawnan CE Prim Sch
TR11 ... 93 D3
Maxwell Rd PL4 ... 135 B8
Maxworthy Cross PL15 ... 12 B4
Maybank Rd PL4 ... 149 C3
Maybrook Dr PL12 ... 122 D2
Mayers Way PL9 ... 135 D6
Mayfair Cres PL6 ... 125 B1
Mayfair Ho PL4 ... 149 A3
Mayfield Cl
Bodmin PL31 ... 35 B2
Port Isaac PL29 ... 22 D7
St Austell PL25 ... 115 A4
Mayfield Cres TR7 ... 110 E5
Mayfield Dr
Port Isaac PL29 ... 22 E7
Roche PL26 ... 47 A3
Mayfield Rd
Falmouth TR11 ... 144 F4
Newquay TR7 ... 110 E5
Port Isaac PL29 ... 22 D7
Mayflower Cl
19 Bere Alston PL20 ... 41 B1
Plymouth PL9 ... 135 F7
Mayflower Dr PL2 ... 128 B5
Mayflower St PL1 ... 148 C3
May Gdns TR16 ... 80 D6
May La PL13 ... 117 F5
Maymear Terr TR30 ... 23 E3
Mayna Parc PL15 ... 18 B8
Maynarde Cl PL7 ... 131 B5
Maynard Pk PL20 ... 41 B1
Mayne Cl PL15 ... 106 B7
Maynes Row TR14 ... 139 A5
Mayon Farm TR19 ... 96 B6
Mayon Green Cres TR19 .. 96 B7
May Terr PL4 ... 149 B3
Mead Cnr EX39 ... 2 D4
Meadfoot Terr 2 PL4 ... 128 F5
Mead Hos The TR18 ... 143 F8
Meadowbank TR11 ... 82 A3
Meadowbank Rd TR11 ... 145 A6
Meadow Brook PL19 ... 147 A4
Meadow Cl
Gloweth TR1 ... 69 E3
Newquay TR7 ... 111 A4
Plymouth PL7 ... 131 D4
Polruan PL23 ... 116 D2
Saltash PL12 ... 122 F3
St Austell PL25 ... 114 F6
St Stephen PL26 ... 58 B4
Meadow Ct
Mevagissey PL26 ... 73 C3
Padstow PL28 ... 107 B4
Stithians TR3 ... 80 E4
St Mabyn PL30 ... 34 C8
Meadow Dr
Bude EX23 ... 104 F6
Camborne TR14 ... 138 C4
Looe PL13 ... 117 D5
Par PL24 ... 115 F5
Saltash PL12 ... 122 D4
Meadowfield Pl PL7 ... 131 B3
Meadow Flats 27 TR26 ... 141 B6
Meadowhead PL27 ... 108 C4
Meadow La TR1 ... 137 D3
Meadowlands PL6 ... 125 D7
Meadow Pk
7 Liskeard PL14 ... 113 B5
Plymouth PL9 ... 135 C5
Trewoon PL25 ... 59 A3
Meadow Pl PL31 ... 109 D4
Meadow Plash PL30 ... 35 C8
Meadow Rd PL13 ... 62 A7
Meadow Rise
Foxhole PL26 ... 58 D6
1 Penwithick PL26 ... 59 D7
Plymouth PL7 ... 131 A4
12 St Columb Major TR9 ... 45 E6
Meadowside
Launceston PL15 ... 106 A4
Lewannick PL15 ... 27 A6
Newquay TR7 ... 111 A4
Plymouth PL9 ... 135 F7
St Austell PL25 ... 115 C6
Whitstone EX22 ... 12 B8
Meadowside Cl
Hayle TR27 ... 142 A3
St Kew Highway PL30 ... 23 B2
Meadowside Rd TR11 ... 144 F2
Meadow St PL26 ... 73 C3
Meadows The
St Dennis PL26 ... 58 C8
St Dominick PL12 ... 40 D2
St Teath PL30 ... 23 E7
Torpoint PL11 ... 126 E4
Meadowsweet Pk PL12 ... 122 C2
Meadow Terr PL14 ... 37 F3
Meadow The
Illogan TR16 ... 67 D4
Polgooth PL26 ... 59 A1
47 St Ives TR26 ... 141 B6
Truro TR1 ... 137 B5
Meadow View
Camborne TR14 ... 138 E1
8 Goldsithney TR20 ... 89 E5
St Minver PL27 ... 21 F3
Meadow View Rd PL7 ... 130 D5
Meadow Villas 8 TR18 .. 143 C1
Meadow Way
Plymouth PL7 ... 130 D7
St Issey PL27 ... 32 E6
Meadow Wlk PL23 ... 116 D2
Mead The PL7 ... 130 D7
Meadway
Looe PL13 ... 117 E4
Saltash PL12 ... 122 E1
St Austell PL25 ... 114 F5
Mearwood La TR11 ... 144 F4
Meaver Rd TR12 ... 99 B1
Meavy Ave PL5 ... 124 E2
Meavy Bourne PL20 ... 42 D2
Meavy CE Prim Sch PL20 . 42 F2
Meavy La PL20 ... 42 D2
Meavy Villas PL20 ... 42 D2
Meavy Way
Plymouth PL5 ... 124 E2
Tavistock PL19 ... 147 D5
Meddon Cross
Edistone EX39 ... 3 C5
Welcombe EX39 ... 3 C4
Medland Cres PL6 ... 124 D6
Medland Gdns PL25 ... 114 C4
Medlyn Ct TR13 ... 146 B5
Medrose St PL33 ... 14 E3
Medrose Terr 22 TR18 ... 143 E6
Medrow PL15 ... 27 A8
Medway Pl PL3 ... 129 D6
Melbourne Cotts PL1 ... 148 B3
Melbourne Gn 2 PL1 ... 148 B3
Melbourne Pl PL1 ... 148 B4
Melbourne Rd PL14 ... 113 B5
Melbourne St PL1 ... 148 B3
Melbourne Terr 17 TR18. 143 C7
Mellanear Cl TR27 ... 142 B4
Mellanear Ct TR27 ... 142 B4
Mellanear Rd TR27 ... 142 B3
Mellanvrane La TR7 ... 110 F4
Melliars Way EX23 ... 104 F6
Melrose Ave PL2 ... 128 C8
Melrose Terr 6 TR9 ... 45 E1
Melvill Cres TR11 ... 145 B3
Melvill Ct TR11 ... 145 B2
Melville Pl 1 PL2 ... 128 A5
Melville Rd
Plymouth PL2 ... 128 A5
Threemilestone TR3 ... 69 D3
Melville Terr PL22 ... 112 C2
Melville Terrace La PL2 . 128 A5
Melvill La TR11 ... 145 B2
Melvill Rd TR11 ... 145 C2
Memory La PL9 ... 135 E7
Menabilly Cl PL17 ... 39 E3
Menabilly Rd PL25 ... 114 E6
Menacuddle Hill PL25 ... 114 C4
Menacuddle La PL25 ... 114 C4
Menadue Ct TR27 ... 78 E3
Menage St TR13 ... 146 C5
Menague PL27 ... 21 E3
Menakarne TR16 ... 80 F8
Menallack Cheese Farm★
TR10 ... 93 A6
Mena Park Cl PL9 ... 136 B7
Mena Park Rd PL9 ... 136 B7
Meneage Cotts 3 TR13 . 146 C5
Meneage Ho 4 TR13 ... 146 C5
Meneage Parc TR13 ... 146 C5
Meneage Rd TR13 ... 146 C4
Meneage St TR13 ... 146 C5
Meneage Villas PL25 ... 114 B3
Menear Rd PL25 ... 115 A6
Menefreda Way PL27 ... 22 A4
Meneth TR12 ... 92 C1
Meneth Rd TR14 ... 138 F2
Menhaye Gdns TR15 ... 139 D7
Menhay View TR11 ... 144 C3
Menheniot Cres PL15 ... 18 D5
Menheniot Prim Sch
PL14 ... 52 A5
Menheniot Sta PL14 ... 51 F4
Menhinick Cl PL12 ... 53 C3
Menhyr Dr TR26 ... 141 C2
Menna La TR2 ... 57 E5
Mennaye Ct TR18 ... 143 D4
Mennaye Rd TR18 ... 143 D4
Merafield Cl PL7 ... 130 B5
Merafield Dr PL7 ... 130 C4
Merafield Farm Cotts
PL7 ... 130 B4
Merafield Rd PL7 ... 130 B4
Merafield Rise PL7 ... 130 C4
Merbein Cotts TR8 ... 44 E8
Merchants House (Mus)★
PL1 ... 148 C2
Merchants Quay PL15 ... 18 E2
Meredith Rd PL2 ... 128 C6
Meres Valley TR12 ... 99 A2
Meridian Ho PL4 ... 149 A3
Merlin Cl PL6 ... 125 E8
Merlins Way PL34 ... 14 D7
Mermaid Ct TR7 ... 111 C8
Merrick Ave TR1 ... 137 E6
Merrifield Cl TR1 ... 137 B5
Merrifield Cross EX22 ... 7 F4
Merrill Pl TR11 ... 145 A3
Merritts Hill TR16 ... 67 E4
Merritts Way TR15 ... 139 C7
Merrivale Rd
Plymouth, Ham PL2 ... 128 B7
Plymouth, Honicknowle
PL5 ... 124 B3
Merrivale View Rd PL20 .. 42 E3
Merrose Cvn Site TR2 ... 83 B4
Merry Mit Mdw TR11 ... 144 C3
Mersey Cl PL3 ... 129 D6
Merther Cl TR13 ... 91 B3
Messack Cl TR11 ... 144 E2

Metha Pk TR8 56 C7
Metha Rd TR8 56 C7
Methleigh Bottoms TR13 91 A1
Methleigh Parc TR13 91 A1
Mevagissey Aquarium★ PL26 73 C3
Mevagissey Com Prim Sch PL26 73 C4
Mevagissey Ho TR1 69 E4
Mevagissey Mus★ PL26 73 C3
Mews Ct PL14 51 F6
Mews The
Launceston PL15 106 A8
Par PL24 60 B5
3 Penzance TR18 143 E6
Plymouth, Devonport PL1 128 A3
Plymouth, Stonehouse PL1 148 A3
Mexico La TR27 142 C7
Mexico Terr TR27 142 C8
Michael Rd PL3 129 A5
Michaelstow Holiday Village PL30 23 F5
Michell Ave TR7 110 E6
Michell Ct TR7 110 D6
Michigan Way PL3 129 C6
Mid Churchway PL9 136 A7
Mid Cornwall Bsns Ctr PL25 115 E4
Middle Down Cl PL9 136 A5
Middlefield Rd PL6 124 D6
Middlefield Cl PL12 122 B2
Middlegates 5 TR5 54 D1
Middle Market St PL13 117 D3
Middle Rd TR15 140 E7
Middle Rosewin Row 8 TR1 137 D5
Middle Row TR13 90 E3
Middle St
Padstow PL28 107 D5
Port Isaac PL29 22 D7
Middle Stennack Cotts 13 TR26 141 A5
Middleton Cres TR7 110 F4
Middletons Row 6 TR15 140 C5
Middleton Wlk PL5 123 D4
Middleway PL24 60 B5
Middlewell Parc PL27 108 B4
Middle Wharf PL26 73 C3
Midella Rd PL20 42 D2
Mid Moor PL14 38 B6
Midway Dr TR1 137 E5
Midway Rd PL31 109 A5
Miers Cl PL5 127 C8
Miers Ct PL5 127 C8
Milch Pk PL12 122 C2
Mildmay St PL4 149 A4
Mile End TR12 102 F4
Milehouse Rd PL2 128 A5
Miles Mitchell Ave PL6 125 A1
Milestone Ct TR3 69 D4
Milford La PL5 124 B5
Military Rd
Millbrook PL10 132 C3
Plymouth PL3 129 E6
Rame PL10 64 C2
St Mawes TR2 95 B4
Milladon La PL12 64 D8
Mill Ball Hill EX23 10 B7
Millbank Mdw TR27 78 E1
Millbay Rd PL1 148 A2
Mill Bridge PL1 148 A3
Millbrook Bsns Ctr PL11 132 C6
Millbrook CE Prim Sch PL10 132 E5
Mill Cl
Porthleven TR13 91 A1
Wadebridge PL27 108 E5
Mill Cotts TR13 146 A6
Millendreath Holiday Village PL13 117 F5
Millenium Appartments TR10 81 D2
Millennium Way TR13 146 D8
Miller Bsns Pk PL14 113 B4
Miller Ct
Liskeard PL14 113 B4
Plymouth PL1 148 A2
Miller Way PL6 125 E3
Millet Cl TR17 89 D5
Millfield TR18 88 E6
Mill Flats TR13 146 B6
Mill Ford Sch PL5 123 F4
Mill Gdns PL22 112 C2
Millham La PL22 112 E3
Mill Hill
Crumplehorn PL13 62 D1
Lelant TR27 77 E3
Lostwithiel PL22 112 D2
St Just In R TR2 82 F3
Mill Hill Cotts PL19 30 B1
Millhouse Pk PL11 127 A2
Mill La
Camelford PL32 105 D5
Coad's Green PL15 27 C1
Grampound TR2 72 A7
Helston TR13 146 B6
20 Mousehole TR19 88 C1
Porthleven TR13 91 A1
St Breward PL30 24 B3
St Germans PL12 65 A8
Torpoint PL11 127 A2
Tregony TR2 71 F3
Truro TR3 137 C1
Millpond Ave TR27 142 B4
Millpool
Lostwithiel PL22 112 F3
Rilla Mill PL14 38 E8
Mill Pool 15 TR19 88 C1
Millpool Head PL10 132 E4
Millpool Rd PL10 133 A6
Mill Rd
Millbrook PL10 133 A5
Padstow PL28 107 D5
Penponds TR14 79 B5
Perranporth TR6 55 B4
Tideford PL12 52 F2
Mill Rd Est PL12 52 F2
Mill Sq PL28 107 D5
Mills Rd PL1 127 F2
Mills' St TR16 68 E1
Mill St PL31 109 E5
Milltown Gdns PL15 18 E6
Mill View Gdns PL10 132 F5
Mill View Rd PL10 132 F5
Millway Pl PL9 135 D8
Millwood Dr PL6 125 E1
Milne Pl PL1 127 F3
Milton Abbot Sch PL19 29 D5
Milton Cl PL5 124 D2
Milton Cres PL19 147 D5
Milton Ct
Plymouth, Cattedown PL4 149 C2
Plymouth, Prince Rock PL4 129 B1
Minack Theatre★ TR19 96 E2
Mine Hill PL14 51 F6
Mine La PL30 47 E7
Mineral Tramways Discovery Ctr★ TR15 139 B4
Miners Ct
Perranporth TR6 55 A4
Redruth TR15 140 C5
Miners Row TR15 140 C5
Miners Way PL14 113 D7
Minerva Cl PL7 131 A6
Minions Heritage Ctr★ PL14 38 B6
Minions Row PL14 38 B6
Minnie Pl TR11 145 B3
Minorca La PL26 47 D2
Minses Cl PL9 136 C7
Minster Ave EX23 104 F4
Minster Mdw TR12 101 A8
Minster Terr TR12 101 A8
Minton Cl PL25 115 A4
Mirador Pl PL4 129 C3
Mission The TR18 143 F4
Misterton Cl PL9 136 B8
Mitchell Cl
Lizard TR12 102 F2
Plymouth PL9 135 D5
Mitchell Ct 11 TR1 137 D5
Mitchell Hill TR1 137 D5
Mitchell Hill Terr 4 TR1 137 D5
Mitchell La
Camborne TR14 138 E3
Mitchell TR8 56 E5
Mitchell Mews 17 TR1 137 D4
Mitchell Rd
Camborne TR14 138 C3
St Austell PL25 114 F4
Mitchell's Boatyard PL26 73 C2
Mitchells Cnr 24 TR6 55 A5
Mithian Sch TR5 54 E1
Mitre Cl PL19 147 A3
Mitre Ct 15 PL1 149 A2
Modbury Cl PL5 124 B3
Modus La PL26 58 E1
Modyford Wlk PL20 41 F3
Mohun's Cl PL19 147 C4
Mohun's Pk PL19 147 C3
Molenick La PL12 52 E3
Molesworth Ct 4 PL27 108 B5
Molesworth Rd
Plymouth, Plympton PL7 130 C6
Plymouth, Stoke PL1, PL3 128 A3
Molesworth St
Tintagel PL34 14 C7
Wadebridge PL27 108 B5
Molesworth Terr PL10 132 F5
Molinnis PL26 47 C2
Molinnis Rd PL26 47 C2
Mollison Rd PL5 123 E2
Molyneaux Pl 10 PL1 127 F3
Monastery Cl TR12 101 D4
Mongleath Ave TR11 144 E3
Mongleath Cl TR11 144 E3
Mongleath Rd TR11 144 E3
Monica Wlk PL4 149 B4
Monkey Sanctuary The★ PL13 63 F5
Monks Hill PL15 28 C4
Monksmead PL19 147 A4
Monks Park Cotts PL15 106 D6
Monmouth Gdns PL5 124 C4
Monmouth La PL22 112 D2
Montacute Ave PL5 124 B2
Montague Ave TR15 140 A6
Monterey Cl EX23 104 E4
Monterey Gdns TR1 137 E5
Montgomery Cl PL12 122 D3
Montgomery Rd 2 PL26 59 D7
Montpelier Com Prim Sch PL2 128 B6
Montpelier Rd PL2 128 C7
Monument Rd TR13 146 B5
Monument St PL1 127 E1
Monument Way PL31 109 C4
Moon La PL4 149 A3
Moonrakers TR26 141 D2
Moonsfield 5 PL17 39 F4
Moon St PL4 149 A3
Moorcroft Cl PL9 136 A7
Moor Cross EX22 8 D3
Moor Cross Cotts EX23 4 C3
Moorfield PL16 19 F4
Moorfield Ave 4 PL6 129 C7
Moorfield Rd
Camborne TR15 139 C6
St Giles on t H PL15 13 F1
Moor La PL5 123 E1
Moorland Ave PL7 130 F6
Moorland Cl
Liskeard PL14 113 D7
Pendeen TR19 74 F1
Yelverton PL20 121 D8
Moorland Ct
1 St Austell PL25 114 C3
Yelverton PL20 42 C2
Moorland Dr PL7 130 E6
Moorland Gdns PL7 130 F6
Moorland Rd
Indian Queens TR9 45 F2
Launceston PL15 106 A4
Plymouth PL7 130 E5
St Austell PL25 114 C3
Tywardreath PL24 60 C4
Moorland Road Ind Est TR9 45 F2
Moorlands La PL12 122 C4
Moorlands Trad Est PL12 122 C4
Moorland View
Golberdon PL17 39 B6
Liskeard PL14 113 D7
Plymouth, Derriford PL6 125 A5
Plymouth, Plymstock PL9 136 B7
Saltash PL12 122 F4
Moorland Way PL18 40 F5
Moorlan Mdws PL26 47 A3
Moor Parc TR12 100 D6
Moor St TR14 138 D3
Moors The PL22 112 C1
Moorswater Ind Est PL14 51 A7
Moor The TR11 145 B4
Moor View
Bodmin PL31 109 F2
Plymouth, Keyham PL2 127 F5
Plymouth, Laira PL3 129 C4
Plymouth PL9 135 D7
Torpoint PL11 127 B3
Moorview Ct PL6 125 F5
Moorview Terr PL14 38 D7
Moor View Terr
Plymouth PL4 128 E4
Yelverton PL20 42 D2
Morcom Cl PL25 115 A5
Moresk Cl TR1 137 D5
Moresk Gdns TR1 137 D5
Moresk Rd TR1 137 D5
Moreton Ave PL6 124 F1
Morice Sq PL1 127 E2
Morice St PL1 127 E2
Morice Town Prim Sch PL2 127 E4
Morlaix Ave TR1 137 D3
Morlaix Dr PL6 125 B4
Morla La TR15 140 A6
Morleigh Cl PL25 114 F3
Morley Cl PL7 130 A5
Morley Ct PL1 148 B3
Morley Dr PL20 42 A2
Morley View Rd PL7 130 C6
Morrab Ct 8 TR7 110 F6
Morrab Pl 34 TR18 143 E5
Morrab Rd
Camborne TR14 138 C3
Penzance TR18 143 E5
Morrab Terr 35 TR18 143 E5
Morris Gdns TR7 110 D4
Morrish Pk PL9 135 F6
Morshead Rd PL6 124 F2
Mortain Rd PL12 122 D4
Mortimore Cl PL12 122 D2
Morvan Trad Est PL25 114 F3
Morven Rd PL25 114 F3
Morview Rd PL13 63 F8
Morwell Gdns PL2 128 A6
Morwellham Quay★ PL19 41 B4
Morwenna Gdns TR6 55 B5
Morwenna Rd EX23 2 D1
Morwenna Terr EX23 104 D6
Morweth Cotts PL11 64 C5
Morweth Ct PL11 64 C5
Moses Cl PL6 124 E7
Moses Ct PL6 124 E7
Mosquito Cres 3 PL27 31 F3
Moss Side Ind Est PL17 39 F4
Moss Terr PL23 116 D3
Mostyn Ave PL4 129 A4
Mote Pk PL12 122 C3
Mothecombe Wlk PL6 125 E1
Moulton Cl PL7 131 B5
Moulton Wlk PL7 131 B4
Mount Agar Rd TR3 81 F7
Mount Ambrose TR15 140 E7
Mountbatten Cl
Plymouth PL9 135 D6
St Columb Minor TR7 111 E7
Mountbatten Rd 5 PL26 59 D7
Mount Batten Waterside Pk★ PL9 134 F7
Mountbatten Way PL9 135 E6
Mount Bennett Rd 5 PL24 60 D5
Mount Bennett Terr 4 PL24 60 D5
Mount Camel PL32 105 C4
Mount Carbis Gdns TR15 140 C3
Mount Carbis Rd TR15 140 D3
Mount Charles Jun & Inf Sch PL25 114 F3
Mount Charles Rd PL25 114 F3
Mount Cres PL24 60 C4
Mount Edgcumbe Country Pk★ PL10 133 E6
Mount Edgcumbe Terr TR11 145 B4
Mountfield Terr 6 PL24 60 C4
Mount Folly TR27 142 C6
Mount Folly Sq PL31 109 E4
Mount Ford PL19 147 A5
Mount George Rd TR3 82 B7
Mount Gould Ave PL4 129 B2
Mount Gould Cres PL4 129 B3
Mount Gould Hospl PL4 129 B3
Mount Gould Rd PL4 129 B3
Mount Gould Way PL4 129 B3
Mount Hawke Chalet Pk TR4 68 B6
Mount Hawke Com Prim Sch TR4 68 C6
Mount Ho PL11 64 C5
Mount House Sch PL19 147 E7
Mountlea Dr 9 PL24 60 C4
Mount Lidden TR18 143 C4
Mount Pleasant
Bodmin PL31 109 E5
Boscastle PL35 9 D1
Falmouth TR11 144 E1
Hayle TR27 142 C6
Lelant TR26 77 E3
Millbrook PL10 132 E5
Newlyn TR18 143 C4
Par PL24 60 B6
Plymouth PL5 124 B2
39 St Ives TR26 141 B6
Mount Pleasant Cl TR14 138 E1
Mount Pleasant Gdns TR27 142 C6
Mount Pleasant Pl PL22 112 C3
Mount Pleasant Rd
Camborne TR14 138 D1
11 Porthleven TR13 98 B8
Threemilestone TR3 69 D3
Mount Pleasant Terr
Mousehole TR19 88 C1
Redruth TR15 140 E7
Mount Pleasure TR14 138 E1
Mount Prospect Terr TR18 143 C3
Mount Rd PL24 60 C4
Mount's Bay Holiday Flats TR18 88 E6
Mounts Bay Rd TR18 143 C4
Mount's Bay Sch & Com Sports Coll TR18 143 B7
Mounts Bay Terr TR13 90 E3
Mount's Bay Terr 21 TR13 98 C8
Mount's Rd 20 TR13 98 C8
Mount St
Mevagissey PL26 73 C3
Penzance TR18 143 E6
Plymouth, Mount Wise PL1 127 E1
Plymouth, Mutley PL4 149 A4
Mount Stamper Rd PL25 114 D7
Mountstephen Cl PL25 114 B3
Mount Stephens La TR11 144 F4
Mount Stone Rd PL1 134 A8
Mount Street Prim Sch PL4 149 A4
Mount Tamar Cl PL5 123 E2
Mount Tamar Sch PL5 123 E2
Mount Tavy Rd PL19 147 E6
Mount Terr 9 PL24 60 B4
Mount View
Lane TR8 111 B3
Madron TR20 88 A7
Mount View Cotts TR20 89 A7
Mount View Terr
5 Marazion TR17 89 C5
24 Newlyn TR18 143 C2
Mount Whistle Rd TR14 138 F7
Mount Wise
Launceston PL15 106 C5
Newquay TR7 110 D5
Mount Wise Com Prim Sch PL1 127 E1
Mount Wise Cotts TR7 110 E5
Mount Wise Ct PL1 127 F1
Mount Zion 52 TR26 141 B6
Mourne Villas PL9 135 F8
Mousehole Com Prim Sch TR19 88 C1
Mousehole La TR19 88 C1
Mowbray Mews PL32 10 B2
Mowhay Cl TR7 111 A4
Mowhay Cotts PL26 85 C5
Mowhay La 1 PL17 39 E4
Mowhay Mdw
St John PL11 132 B8
Wadebridge PL27 108 B4
Mowhay Rd
Plymouth PL5 123 F1
Plymouth PL5 124 A2
Mowie The 13 TR9 45 E2
Moyle Rd PL28 107 E4
Mudges Terr PL18 41 A6
Mudge Way PL7 130 E5
Mulberry Cl PL6 125 E7
Mulberry Ct 12 TR11 145 B5
Mulberry Gr PL19 147 C2
Mulberry Quay 11 TR11 145 B5
Mulberry Rd PL12 122 E1
Mulgrave St PL1 148 C2
Mullet Ave PL3 129 C4
Mullet Cl PL3 129 C4
Mullet Rd PL3 129 C4
Mullion Cl PL11 126 F4
Mullion Com Prim Sch TR12 99 A1
Mullion Cove TR12 102 B7
Mullion Cove Bglws TR12 98 F1
Mullion Rural Workshops TR12 99 A1
Mullion Sch TR12 99 B1
Mundys Field TR12 103 A5
Muralto Ho PL19 147 A4
Murdoch Cl
Redruth TR15 140 B6
Truro TR1 137 E6
Murdock Rd PL11 126 F3
Murray Villas TR19 86 E6
Murtons Terr TR16 80 E7
Mus of Witchcraft★ PL35 9 C2
Mutley Ct PL4 149 A4
Mutley Plain PL4 128 E4
Mutley Plain La PL4 128 E4
Mutley Rd PL3 128 E5
Mutton Hill TR27 78 D6
Mutton Row TR10 144 C8
Mylor Cl PL2 128 D8
Mylor Com Prim Sch TR11 82 A3
My Lords Rd TR9 57 E8
Myrtle Cl PL20 42 E3
Myrtle Ct PL26 73 C3
Myrtles Ct PL12 122 D4
Myrtleville PL2 128 A6
Mythyon Ct 4 TR18 143 C7

N

Nailzee Ho PL13 117 D2
Nailzee Point PL13 117 D2
Nalder's Ct 10 TR1 137 C4
Nampara Cl TR26 141 E2
Nampara Ct 7 TR6 55 A4
Nampara Way TR1 137 F4
Nancarrows PL12 122 C2
Nancealverne TR18 143 D6
Nancealverne Sch TR20 143 C6
Nancedden Farm TR20 89 A8
Nancegollan Ind Est TR13 91 B7
Nancemere Rd TR1 137 D6
Nancevallon TR14 139 B3
Nancherrow Hill TR19 86 F6
Nancherrow Row TR19 86 F6
Nancledra Sch TR 26 76 F3
Nangitha Cl TR11 144 C3
Nangitha Terr TR11 144 C3
Nanhayes Row TR8 56 B7
Nanjivey Pl 8 TR26 141 A5
Nanjivey Terr 9 TR26 141 A5
Nanpean Com Prim Sch PL26 58 D6
Nanpusker Cl TR27 142 E6
Nanpusker Rd TR27 78 C4
Nansalsa Ct TR7 111 A6
Nansavallon Rd TR1 69 F3
Nanscober Pl TR13 146 B8
Nanscothan 10 TR15 140 B4
Nans Kestenen TR13 146 B5
Nansloe Cl TR13 146 D4
Nansloe Com Prim Sch TR13 146 C4
Nansmellyon Rd TR12 99 A1
Nanstallon Com Prim Sch PL30 34 C1
Nanterrow La TR27 66 D1
Nanturras Parc TR20 89 F5
Nanturras Row TR20 89 E5
Napier St PL1 127 F3
Napier Terr PL4 128 E4
Narkurs Cross PL11 64 D7
Narrowcliff TR7 111 A7
Narrow La
Botusfleming PL12 122 C7
Summercourt TR8 57 C8
Nash Cl PL7 131 A5
Nathan Cl TR7 111 B5
National Marine Aquarium★ PL4 149 A2
National Maritime Mus (Cornwall)★ TR11 145 C3
National Seal Sanctuary The★ TR12 92 C1
National Seal Sanctuary Visitor Ctr★ TR12 92 C1
Navy Inn Ct 10 TR18 143 C1
Neal Cl PL7 131 B4
Neath Rd PL4 149 C4
Neeham Rd TR8 56 B7
Nelson Ave PL1 127 F3
Nelson Gdns 5 PL1 127 F3
Nelson St PL4 149 A4
Nelson Terr PL6 125 E6
Nepean St 1 PL2 127 F3
Neptune Ave PL27 31 F3
Neptune Pk PL9 135 B8
Neswick St PL1 148 B3
Neswick Street Ope PL1 148 A3
Nethercott Cross EX21 13 F7
Netherton Est PL20 42 A3
Netherton Rd PL28 107 D4
Nettell's Hill TR15 140 B5
Nettlehayes PL9 136 D7
Netton Cl PL9 136 B6
Nevada Cl PL3 129 D6
Nevada Pl 16 TR18 143 C7
Nevada St TR18 143 C7
Nevada Villas 8 PL24 60 C4
Newacott Cross EX22 7 F5

New Barn Hill PL7 130 F3
New Bglws PL30 36 B3
Newbridge Hill PL18 41 A6
Newbridge La TR1, TR3 69 F3
New Bridge St 9 TR1 137 D4
Newbridge Way TR1 69 F3
Newbury Cl PL5 124 B4
Newcastle Gdns PL5 124 B5
New Connection St 4
TR14 138 D3
New Cotts
Gunnislake PL18 41 A6
Kilkhampton EX23 5 A6
New Ct TR11 145 B4
New Cut TR15 140 B5
New Dairy La TR17 89 B6
New George St PL1 148 C3
Newham Est TR1 137 D3
Newham Ind Est TR1 137 D2
Newham La
Helston TR13 146 A7
Lostwithiel PL22 49 A1
Newham Rd TR1 137 E2
New Hill Est TR2 72 A7
New Hos TR14 139 B3
Newhouses PL17 38 E8
New La TR15 140 E7
New Launceston Rd
PL19 147 A5
Newlyn Art Gall★ TR18 143 C3
Newlyn Rd TR19 97 B6
Newlyn Sch TR18 143 C3
Newman Rd
Plymouth PL5 123 E2
Saltash PL12 122 F3
Newmills Cl TR1 137 B6
New Mills Farm Pk★
PL15 18 D4
New Mills La TR1, TR4 137 A6
Newmills Sta★ PL15 18 D4
New Molinnis PL26 47 C2
Newnham Ind Est PL7 130 F6
Newnham Rd PL7 130 F7
Newnham Way PL7 130 F6
New Northernmaye 2
PL15 106 C6
New Park Rd
Plymouth PL7 131 A4
Wadebridge PL27 108 C5
New Passage Hill PL1 127 E3
New Pk
Horrabridge PL20 42 C4
Wadebridge PL27 108 C4
Newport
Callington PL17 39 E4
St Germans PL12 65 A8
Newport Cl 8 PL17 39 F4
Newport Ind Est PL15 106 C6
New Portreath Rd
Illogan TR16 67 F5
Redruth TR16 140 A7
Newport Sq PL15 106 B7
Newport St
Millbrook PL10 132 E5
Plymouth PL1 128 A1
Newport Terr 3 PL17 39 F4
Newquay Airport TR8 44 F8
Newquay Hospl TR7 110 F5
Newquay Jun Sch TR7 110 F6
Newquay Rd
Goonhavern TR4 55 D4
St Columb Major TR9 45 D6
Truro TR1 137 F7
Newquay Sta TR7 110 F6
Newquay Tretherras Sch
TR7 111 B6
New Rd
Barripper TR14 79 B5
Bere Alston PL20 41 B2
Boscastle PL35 9 C2
Cadgwith TR12 103 A4
Callington PL17 39 E4
Camborne TR14 139 B3
Cawsand PL10 133 A1
Kingsand PL10 133 B2
Lifton PL16 19 F4
Liskeard PL14 113 B5
Newlyn TR18 143 C3
Perranporth TR6 55 B4
Port Isaac PL29 22 D7
Roborough PL6 121 D2
Saltash PL12 122 E3
St Columb Major TR9 45 E6
St Hilary TR20 89 F6
Stithians TR3 80 F3
St Just TR19 86 F6
Stratton EX23 4 D1
Summercourt TR8 57 D7
Tregony TR2 71 F3
Troon TR14 79 E4
New Road Cl PL10 133 A2
New Road Hill PL23 116 C4
New Road Terr PL12 53 C3
New Row
Gweek TR12 92 C1
Mylor Bridge TR11 82 A3
Nancledra TR 20 76 F2
Redruth TR16 139 D1
Summercourt TR8 57 B6
New St
Bugle PL26 47 C1
Falmouth TR11 145 B4
Millbrook PL10 132 E5
Padstow PL28 107 D5
Penryn TR10 144 D7
New St *continued*
Penzance TR18 143 E5
Plymouth PL1 149 A2
Troon TR14 79 E4
Newtake Rd PL19 147 E2
Newton Ave PL5 123 E2
Newton Ct
Dobwalls PL14 50 E8
Redruth TR15 140 B6
Newton Farm Cotts PL13 62 E3
Newton Gdns PL5 123 F2
Newton Pk 13 TR2 95 A6
Newton Rd
St Mawes TR2 95 A6
Troon TR14 79 E5
Newton's Margate Ind Est
PL31 35 B1
Newtown PL23 60 F3
Newtown La TR17, TR20 89 A7
New Town La TR18 143 E5
New Windsor Terr 11
TR11 145 A4
New Wood Cl PL6 125 E8
New Zealand Ho PL3 128 B4
Nicholas Ave TR16 80 A5
Nicholas Mdw PL17 40 E4
Nicholas Parc 3 TR18 143 C7
Nicholson Rd PL5 124 E2
Nicolls Flats PL15 106 B5
Nightingale Cl PL9 136 C8
Nine Oaks PL20 42 F3
No Go By Hill TR19 86 F7
No Mans' Land Rd TR11 93 D5
Nook The PL19 147 D6
Norfolk Cl PL3 129 C5
Norfolk Rd
Falmouth TR11 145 B4
Plymouth PL3 129 C4
Norman Cotts PL15 106 C7
Normandy Hill PL5 123 B2
Normandy Way
Bodmin PL31 109 F2
Camborne TR14 138 F3
Plymouth PL5 123 C2
Norman's Way PL30 23 E3
Northampton Cl PL5 124 B5
North Cl EX23 5 A6
North Cliff 12 TR19 88 C1
North Cnr 1 TR18 143 C2
North Cornwall Mus & Gall★
PL32 105 C4
Northcott Mouth Rd
EX23 104 F8
North Dimson PL18 40 F6
North Down Cres PL2 127 F6
North Down Gdns PL2 127 F6
North Down Rd PL2 128 B6
Northesk St PL2 128 A4
Northey Cl TR4 69 F6
Northey Rd PL31 109 D4
Northfield Cl TR16 68 E1
Northfield Dr TR1 137 D3
Northgate Pl 1 PL15 106 C6
North Grange Ind Est TR3 81 F6
North Hill
Blackwater TR4 68 E5
Carharrack TR16 80 F8
Chacewater TR4 68 F3
Plymouth PL4 149 A4
North Hill Pk PL25 114 D4
North Moor Cross EX22 3 F3
Northolt Ave PL5 123 D4
North Orchard Ct 1 TR20 89 E5
North Par
Camborne TR14 138 E3
Falmouth TR11 145 A6
Penzance TR18 143 E5
Portscatho TR2 83 B2
North Parade Rear TR14 138 D3
North Park Villas PL12 122 C4
North Petherwin Ind Est
PL15 18 A8
North Petherwin Prim Sch
PL15 12 B1
North Pl 15 TR26 141 B6
North Pool Cl TR15 139 C7
North Pool Rd TR15 139 C7
North Prospect Prim Sch
PL2 128 A7
North Prospect Rd PL2 128 A6
North Quay
Hayle TR27 142 B6
Padstow PL28 107 D6
Plymouth PL4 149 A2
North Quay Hill TR7 110 D7
North Quay Par PL28 107 E6
North Rd
Camborne TR14 138 D3
Goldsithney TR20 89 E5
Landrake PL12 53 C3
Lifton PL16 19 F4
Looe PL13 117 C3
Pentewan PL26 73 C6
Redruth TR16 140 E1
Saltash PL12 122 F3
St Teath PL30 23 E7
Torpoint PL11 127 B3
Whitemoor PL26 58 E8
Yelverton PL20 42 C3
North Rd E PL4 148 C4
North Rd W PL1 148 B4
North Roskear Mdw
TR14 138 E5
North Roskear Rd TR14 138 F5
North Row TR19 86 F6
North St
Fowey PL23 116 D4
Launceston PL15 106 A8
North St *continued*
Lostwithiel PL22 112 C2
Marazion TR17 89 B5
14 Mousehole TR19 88 C1
Plymouth PL4 149 A3
Redruth TR15 140 B6
St Austell PL25 114 C4
Tavistock PL19 147 C5
Tywardreath PL24 60 D5
North Terr
2 Penzance TR18 143 E4
12 St Ives TR26 141 B5
Whitemoor PL26 58 E8
Northumberland St PL5 127 E8
Northumberland Terr
PL1 148 B1
North View PL13 117 D4
North Way TR8 111 F4
North Weald Gdns PL5 123 E5
Norton Ave PL4 149 C4
Norton Ct 2 PL31 109 E5
Norwich Ave PL5 124 B5
Notre Dame Cl PL6 124 F5
Notre Dame Ho PL1 148 B3
Notre Dame RC Sch PL6 124 F5
Notter Mill Holiday Village
PL12 53 D4
Notte St PL1 148 C2
Novorossisk Rd PL6 125 E2
Noweth Pl TR11 144 E5
Nunnery Hill PL26 72 F7
Nurseries The TR11 144 D5
Nursery Cl
Plymouth PL5 124 B7
Truro TR1 137 D5
11 Tywardreath PL24 60 D5
Nut La TR27 77 E3
Nut Tree Hill PL12 65 B8

O

Oakapple Cl PL7 130 B7
Oak Apple Cl PL12 122 D4
Oak Ave PL12 40 A1
Oakcroft Rd PL2 128 B6
Oakdene Rise PL9 135 F6
Oakdene Villas 7 TR9 45 E1
Oak Dr
8 Liskeard PL14 113 B5
Plymouth PL6 124 F3
Oakey Orch PL17 40 D4
Oakfield PL15 27 D3
Oakfield Cl PL7 131 C6
Oakfield Pl PL4 129 B1
Oakfield Rd
Falmouth TR11 144 F5
Plymouth PL7 130 C6
Oakfield Terrace Rd PL4 129 B1
Oak Ford PL30 48 C7
Oakham Rd PL5 124 B5
Oakhill PL30 47 C6
Oak La
Truro TR1 69 E4
Whitstone EX22 7 F1
Oakland Pk TR11 144 D5
Oaklands PL19 147 D2
Oaklands Bsns Pk PL13 63 D8
Oaklands Cl PL6 125 C7
Oaklands Dr PL12 122 C3
Oaklands Gn PL12 122 D3
Oaklands Ind Est PL14 113 E6
Oaklands Rd PL14 113 E6
Oakleigh Terr TR7 110 F6
Oak Park Terr PL14 113 A6
Oak Pk PL30 23 E3
Oak Rd PL19 147 C2
Oakridge PL12 53 C7
Oak Ridge PL16 19 F4
Oaks The
Quintrell Downs TR8 111 F3
St Austell PL25 114 B3
Oak Tree Cl PL25 115 B3
Oaktree Ct PL6 124 F1
Oak Tree La PL19 147 C3
Oak Tree Pk PL6 125 D6
Oak Vale TR2 72 A7
Oak Way TR1 137 D5
Oakwood Cl PL6 125 D7
Oakwood Pk PL31 109 F4
Oakwood Rise PL32 105 E5
Oates Rd
Helston TR13 146 C6
Marazion TR17 89 C5
Plymouth PL2 128 B5
Observer Cl TR1 137 C3
Ocean Cres 22 TR13 98 C8
Ocean Ct
Plymouth PL1 133 F8
Porthtowan TR4 68 A7
Ocean St PL2 127 E6
Ocean View
Indian Queens TR9 45 E1
Polruan PL23 116 D2
Porthleven TR13 98 B8
Ocean View Rd EX23 104 D7
Ocean View Terr TR26 141 A6
Octagon St PL1 148 B3
Octagon The PL1 148 B2
Okehampton Cl PL7 131 B4
Old Bakehouse Flats The
TR18 143 F6
Old Barn Ct TR7 110 D4
Old Barns The TR14 66 F2
Old Boat Yard The PL28 107 E6
Old Boys School TR16 67 E5
Old Brewery Yd 4 TR18 143 E5
Old Bridge St TR1 137 D4
Old Butchers Shop The
TR20 89 B8
Old Cable La TR19 96 E3
Old Callywith Rd PL31 35 B2
Old Canal Cl EX23 7 B6
Old Carnon Hill TR3 81 F6
Old Chapel The TR4 68 F5
Old Chapel Way PL10 132 F6
Old Chough Flats TR7 111 B7
Old Church Rd TR11 93 E2
Old Church The TR18 143 D4
Old Coach Rd
Lanivet PL26, PL30 47 D6
Playing Place TR3 82 B8
Truro TR3 70 A1
Old Coastguard Cotts
PL11 65 A4
Old Coastguard Row
TR19 96 B7
Old Corn Mill The TR12 92 C1
Old Dairy The
Plymouth PL3 129 B6
Sancreed TR20 87 E4
Old Drovers Way EX23 4 E1
Old English Ind Est PL20 42 E3
Old Exeter Rd PL19 147 D7
Old Falmouth Rd TR1 137 C1
Old Farm Rd PL5 127 C8
Old Ferry Rd PL12 123 A3
Old Foundry Ct TR19 86 F6
Old Foundry The
Menheniot PL14 51 E6
Tavistock PL19 147 D6
Old George St PL1 148 C2
Old Grammar School Ct
PL22 112 C2
Old Greystone Hill PL15,
PL19 28 F6
Old Guildhall Mus★
PL13 117 D3
Old Hill
Falmouth TR11 144 F6
Grampound TR2 72 A7
Helston TR13 146 A6
Old Hill Cres TR11 144 F5
Old La PL26 46 F3
Old Laira Rd PL3 129 C4
Oldlands Cl PL6 125 B6
Old Launceston Rd PL19 147 B6
Old Laundry The PL1 148 A3
Old Lawn School La
PL25 114 B3
Old Market Pl PL31 109 C4
Old Mill Cl PL15 27 B3
Old Mill Ct PL7 130 E5
Old Mill Herbary The★
PL30 34 F6
Old Mill La
Camborne TR14 78 F6
Penponds TR14 79 A6
Old Mill The
3 Boscastle PL35 9 C2
Lerryn PL22 61 D8
Old Mine La PL18 40 E6
Old Nursery Cl TR13 91 A1
Old Orchard Cl EX23 7 B6
Old Orchard The PL22 112 C2
Old Park Rd PL3 128 D6
Old Paul Hill TR18 143 C2
Old Plymouth Rd PL3 129 E5
Old Portreath Rd
Illogan TR16 67 F5
Redruth TR15 67 F4
Old Post Office★ PL34 14 C7
Old Post Office Hill 8
EX23 4 E1
Old Pound PL26 58 E6
Old Priory PL7 130 D5
Old Priory Jun Sch PL7 130 D5
Old Quarry Rd PL20 42 A3
Old Quay La PL12 65 B8
Old Rd
Boscastle PL35 9 C2
Liskeard PL14 113 A6
Old Rectory Dr TR9 45 E6
Old Rectory Mews Cvn Pk
TR9 45 D6
Old Roselyon Cres PL24 60 B5
Old Roselyon Rd PL24 60 C4
Old Sandy La TR16 140 D3
Old School Cl PL27 21 F3
Old School Ct
Padstow PL28 107 D5
Wadebridge PL27 108 B5
Old School Ho The PL10 133 A1
Old Schoolhouse The
TR11 145 B4
Old School La PL30 34 D4
Old School Rd PL5 127 C8
Old School The 10 TR5 54 D1
Old Smithy Cl 4 TR17 89 C5
Old Smithy Cotts EX39 2 E4
Old Station Rd
Horrabridge PL20 42 C4
1 Liskeard PL14 51 A7
Old Station The PL20 42 B4
Old Tannery Bsns Pk The 4
PL4 149 A4
Old Town Hall The PL24 60 B5
Old Town St PL1 148 C3
Old Tram Rd TR3 82 A5
Old Vicarage Cl TR3 80 F4
Old Vicarage Gate TR27 142 A1
Old Vicarage Pl 11 PL25 114 C3
Old Vicarage The TR 26 76 E5
Old Warleigh La PL5 124 B7
Old Well Gdns TR10 144 C8
Old Wharf The PL9 135 C7
Old Woodlands Rd PL5 124 D3
Old Workhouses The
TR15 140 B8
Oliver Ct PL12 40 A1
Oliver's Terr TR13 146 C5
Olive Villas TR3 81 F6
Olivey Pl TR11 82 A3
Olivia Ct PL4 149 B4
Omaha Rd PL31 109 F3
Onslow Rd PL2 128 C7
Ope's Ct 13 TR11 145 B5
Opies La PL31 109 C5
Opie's Row TR16 80 B5
Opie's Terr TR16 80 A5
Orange La TR26 141 A6
Orchard Ave PL6 129 B7
Orchard Cl
Helston TR13 146 B7
3 Plymouth PL7 131 C5
Poughill EX23 4 D2
St Austell PL25 114 E4
St Giles on t H PL15 13 F1
St Mellion PL12 53 C8
Tavistock PL19 41 D8
Tideford PL12 52 F2
Truro TR1 69 F3
Orchard Cotts
Lamerton PL19 30 B3
St Austell PL25 114 F5
Orchard Cres PL9 135 C7
Orchard Ct
Lamerton PL19 30 A3
Penzance TR18 143 C5
Orchard Gr PL25 114 B4
Orchard Ho 11 TR18 143 C2
Orchard La
Helford TR12 93 B1
Plymouth PL7 130 E6
Orchard Pk PL26 47 C2
Orchard Pl 10 TR18 143 C2
Orchard Rd PL2 128 B7
Orchard Terr 20 TR18 143 C2
Orchard The
Gunnislake PL18 41 A6
Lerryn PL22 61 D8
Newquay TR7 111 B7
North Petherwin PL15 18 B8
St Erth TR27 77 E2
Orchardton Terr 2 PL9 135 F5
Orchard Vale TR11 145 C7
Orchard Way 6 TR20 89 E5
Orchard Wlk 13 PL27 108 B5
Ordnance St PL1 127 E2
Ordulf Rd PL19 147 A5
Oregon Way PL3 129 D6
Oreston Prim Sch PL9 135 C7
Oreston Rd PL9 135 C8
Orion Dr PL27 31 F3
Osborne Ct PL1 148 C2
Osborne Parc TR13 146 B7
Osborne Pl PL1 148 C2
Osborne Rd PL3 128 A3
Osborne Villas
10 Falmouth TR11 145 C3
2 Plymouth PL3 128 A3
Osprey Gdns PL9 136 C7
Otterham Com Prim Sch
PL32 10 C2
Otterham Pk PL32 16 A8
Ottery Cotts PL19 30 A2
Ottery Park Ind Est PL19 30 A2
Outland Rd PL2 128 C7
Overcliff PL29 22 D8
Overdale Rd PL2 128 A7
Overton Gdns 3 PL3 128 F5
Overtonn Villas PL15 106 C5
Owen Dr PL7 130 C7
Owen Sivell Cl PL14 113 E6
Oxford Ave PL3 128 E5
Oxford Gdns PL3 128 E5
Oxford Pl PL1 148 C3
Oxford St PL1 148 B3
Oxford Terr 4 PL1 148 B3
Oxland Rd TR16 67 E5

P

Paardeburg Rd 2 PL31 48 D8
Packet La TR20 89 F5
Packington St PL2 128 A4
Packsaddle TR10 81 D2
Packsaddle Cl TR10 81 D2
Paddock Cl
Plymouth PL9 135 E5
Saltash PL12 122 D4
Paddock The
Helston TR13 146 C7
Helston TR13 146 C8
Redruth TR15 140 D2
Sticker PL26 58 E1
Paddons Row PL19 147 C6
Padnover Terr 22 TR26 141 B5
Padstow Harbour Ind Est
PL28 107 E4
Padstow Mus★ PL28 107 D5
Padstow Sch PL28 107 C4
Padstow Workshop Units
PL28 107 B4
Page's Cross PL15 106 D4
Paiges Farm PL9 135 C1
Painton Water EX39 3 A8
Palace Rd PL25 114 D4
Palace St PL1 149 A2
Palm Ct TR1 137 D3
Palmers Terr PL34 14 C6
Palmerston St PL1 148 A4
Palmers Way PL27 108 D6

Pannier La TR26 . . . . 141 C2
Pannier Mkt PL19 . . . . 147 C5
Panson Cross PL15 . . . . 13 E3
Parade PL1 . . . . 149 A2
Parade Bsns Pk 4 PL19 . 147 B4
Parade Hill TR19 . . . . 88 D1
Parade Ope PL1 . . . . 149 A2
Parade Pass 23 TR18 . . . . 143 E5
Parade Rd PL5 . . . . 124 A3
Parade Sq PL22 . . . . 112 D2
Parade St TR18 . . . . 143 E5
Parade The
Helston TR13 . . . . 146 C5
Liskeard PL14 . . . . 113 C6
Lostwithiel PL22 . . . . 112 D2
Millbrook PL10 . . . . 132 E5
Milton Abbot PL19 . . . . 29 C6
Mousehole TR19 . . . . 88 D1
Truro TR1 . . . . 137 E4
Paradise Park & The World Parrot Trust* TR27 . . . . . 142 A4
Paradise Pk EX22 . . . . 7 F1
Paradise Pl PL1 . . . . 128 A2
Paradise Rd
Boscastle PL35 . . . . 9 C1
Plymouth PL1 . . . . 128 A2
Parc-Abnac TR20 . . . . 88 B7
Parc-An-Bal Ct TR14 . . . . 138 E4
Parc-An-Bre Dr PL26 . . . . 58 C8
Parc-an-Cady Est TR19 . . 97 A6
Parc-An-Challow TR10 . . 144 B8
Parc-An-Creet TR26 . . . . . 77 A7
Parc-An-Dillon Rd TR2 . . 83 B2
Parc-An-Dix La TR27 . . . 142 C7
Parc-An-Dower TR13 . . . 146 C6
Parcandowr TR2 . . . . 57 E1
Parc-An-Forth 6 TR26 . . 77 A6
Parc An Gate TR19 . . . . . . 88 C1
Parc-An-Gwarry 7 TR3 . . 81 F7
Parc-An-Ithan TR12 . . . . 102 F2
Parc-An-Maen 11 TR13 . . 98 C8
Parc An Manns TR11 . . . . . 93 D3
Parc-An-Peath TR19 . . . . . 97 A6
Parc-An-Stamps 4 TR26 77 A6
Parc An Yorth TR19 . . . . . . 86 F8
Parc-Askell Cl TR12 . . . . . 99 E5
Parc Bean Terr TR26 . . . . 141 A6
Parc Behan Ct TR2 . . . . . . 83 F6
Parc Bowen TR13 . . . . 92 A3
Parc-Bracket St TR14 . . 138 D3
Parc Brawse TR12 . . . . . . 102 F2
Parc Briwer TR10 . . . . . . 144 D7
Parc Eglos
Helston TR13 . . . . 146 B6
St Merryn PL28 . . . . 31 F8
Parc Eglos Sch TR13 . . . 146 C6
Parc Enys TR12 . . . . 99 B4
Parc Erissey Ind Est TR16 . 68 A3
Parc Fer Cl EX23 . . . . 4 E1
Parc Godrevy TR7 . . . . . . 110 C5
Parc Holland TR13 . . . . . . 146 D8
Parc Ledden TR13 . . . . . . 146 C6
Parc Letta TR18 . . . . 143 C7
Parc Mellan TR18 . . . . 143 D7
Parc Merys TR2 . . . . 83 B2
Parc Monga Rd TR11 . . . . . 92 F3
Parc Morrep TR20 . . . . 90 B3
Parc-n-Drea Cvn Pk TR12 99 B4
Parc Owles TR26 . . . . 141 D2
Parc Peneglos TR11 . . . . . . 82 A3
Parc Pennkarn PL33 . . . . . 14 E3
Parc Rowan TR9 . . . . 57 E8
Parc Shady TR26 . . . . 77 C1
Parc Stephney TR11 . . . . 144 C2
Parc Terr 19 TR18 . . . . . . 143 C1
Parc Trenance PL28 . . . . . . 31 F7
Parc Trethias PL28 . . . . 31 F7
Parc Vean PL30 . . . . 34 C1
Parc Venton Cl 2 TR14 . 138 F2
Parc Villas 17 TR18 . . . . . 143 C1
Parc Wartha Ave TR18 . . 143 D6
Parc Wartha Cres TR18 . . 143 D6
Par Gn PL24 . . . . 60 C4
Pargolla Rd TR7 . . . . 110 F6
Park 30 PL15 . . . . 106 A3
Parka Cl 12 TR9 . . . . 45 E2
Park-An-Bans TR14 . . . . 138 E1
Parkancreeg 9 TR3 . . . . . 81 F7
Park An Gonwyn TR26 . . . 141 E2
Park An Gorsaf TR14 . . . 138 D2
Park An Harvey TR13 . . . 146 C6
Park-an-Mengleth TR15 140 D4
Park-An-Pyth TR19 . . . . . . 75 A1
Park-An-Tansys TR14 . . . 138 F2
Parka Rd
Indian Queens TR9 . . . . . . 45 E1
8 St Columb Road TR9 . . . . 45 E2
Park Ave
Plymouth, Devonport PL1 . . . . 127 E3
Plymouth, Plymstock PL9 . 135 D7
St Ives TR26 . . . . 141 B5
Park Cl
Illogan TR15 . . . . 139 B8
Nancegollan TR13 . . . . 91 B7
Plymouth PL7 . . . . 130 B7
Park Cnr TR18 . . . . 143 E5
Park Cres
Falmouth TR11 . . . . 145 A4
Helston TR13 . . . . 146 B5
Plymouth PL9 . . . . 135 C7
Ponsanooth TR3 . . . . 81 B4
Park Ct
Chillaton PL16 . . . . 29 F8
28 Penzance TR18 . . . . 143 E5
Park Dr PL31 . . . . 109 B4
Parkenbutts TR7 . . . . 111 D7
Parkengear Vean TR2 . . . . 71 D6
Parkengue TR10 . . . . 144 A7
Parkenhead La PL28 . . . . . 20 F2
Park Enskellaw 6 TR12 . . 99 A2
Park-en-Vine PL27 . . . . . . 32 D6
Parker Cl PL7 . . . . 130 B5
Parker Rd PL2 . . . . 128 B6
Parker's Gn PL18 . . . . 40 F6
Parkesway PL12 . . . . 122 D2
Park Fenton PL14 . . . . . . 113 D5
Parkfield Dr PL6 . . . . 125 F1
Park Gwyn PL26 . . . . 58 B4
Park Hill TR11 . . . . 145 A4
Park Ho PL25 . . . . 114 B3
Park Holly TR14 . . . . 138 B3
Parkins Terr 7 TR1 . . . . 137 D5
Park La
8 Bere Alston PL20 . . . . . . 41 B1
Bugle PL26 . . . . 47 C1
Camborne TR14 . . . . 138 E2
Falmouth TR11 . . . . 145 A4
Plymouth PL9 . . . . 135 C7
Parklands PL26 . . . . 58 C7
Parklands Cl TR7 . . . . 111 D6
Park Leder TR16 . . . . 68 C3
Park Leven TR16 . . . . 139 C8
Park Lowen TR26 . . . . 141 C2
Parknoweth TR12 . . . . 99 A4
Parknoweth Cl TR8 . . . . . . 56 B6
Park Pl
Grampound Road TR2 . . . . . 57 E1
Wadebridge PL27 . . . . 108 B5
Park Place La 12 PL3 . . . . 128 A4
Park Rd
Camborne TR14 . . . . 138 E4
Fowey PL23 . . . . 116 C4
Illogan TR15 . . . . 139 B7
Lifton PL16 . . . . 19 F3
Liskeard PL14 . . . . 113 C6
18 Newlyn TR18 . . . . 143 C1
Plymouth PL3 . . . . 129 A6
Ponsanooth TR3 . . . . 81 B4
Redruth TR15 . . . . 140 C4
St Austell PL25 . . . . 114 C3
St Dominick PL12 . . . . 40 D2
Torpoint PL11 . . . . 127 B3
Wadebridge PL27 . . . . 108 B5
Whitemoor PL26 . . . . 58 E8
Park Rd Hos PL22 . . . . 112 C2
Park Rise TR11 . . . . 145 A4
Parkryn Rd 4 TR19 . . . . . . 88 C1
Parkside PL2 . . . . 127 F5
Parkside Com Tech Coll PL1 . . . . 127 E3
Park St PL3 . . . . 128 A4
Park Stenak TR16 . . . . 80 F8
Parkstone La PL7 . . . . 130 F6
Park Street Ope PL3 . . . . 128 A4
Park Terr
Falmouth TR11 . . . . 145 A4
Truro TR1 . . . . 70 D1
Park The
Penryn TR10 . . . . 144 B7
Tregony TR2 . . . . 71 F4
Parkvedras Ho 5 TR1 . . . 137 B4
Parkvedras Terr 4 TR1 . 137 B4
Parkventon PL26 . . . . 47 C2
Park View
Lifton PL16 . . . . 19 F4
Liskeard PL14 . . . . 113 C6
Perranarworthal TR3 . . . . . 81 E6
Plymouth PL4 . . . . 149 C3
Summercourt TR8 . . . . 57 B7
Truro TR1 . . . . 137 C3
Parkview Apartments TR7 . . . . 110 F5
Park View Cl TR3 . . . . 82 A7
Park View Rd TR13 . . . . . 146 B5
Park View Terr PL27 . . . . 108 B5
Park Villas TR3 . . . . 81 B4
Park Way PL25 . . . . 114 F5
Parkway Ct PL6 . . . . 129 E7
Parkway Ind Est The PL6 . . . . 129 E7
Parkway The PL3, PL5, PL6 . . . . 124 B1
Park Wise TR10 . . . . 144 C8
Parkwood Cl PL6 . . . . 121 B2
Parkwood Ct PL19 . . . . . . 147 D6
Parkwood Rd
Tavistock PL19 . . . . 147 D6
Tavistock PL19 . . . . 147 E7
Park Wood Rise PL16 . . . . 19 F4
Parkwoon Cl PL26 . . . . 46 F3
Par La PL24 . . . . 60 B4
Par Moor Rd
Par PL24, PL25 . . . . 60 B3
St Austell PL24, PL25 . . . . 115 F4
Parnell Cl PL6 . . . . 129 A8
Parr La PL4 . . . . 149 B2
Parr St PL4 . . . . 149 B2
Parsonage Ct PL16 . . . . . . 19 F4
Parsons Cl PL9 . . . . 136 A4
Parsons Gn PL17 . . . . 39 E6
Par Sta PL24 . . . . 60 C5
Partwayes PL19 . . . . 30 A3
Pascoe Cl TR3 . . . . 69 D4
Pasley St E PL2 . . . . 127 F4
Pasley St PL2 . . . . 127 E4
Passage Hill TR11 . . . . 82 A3
Passage La PL23 . . . . 116 B5
Passage St PL23 . . . . 116 D5
Passmore Cl
Blackwater TR4 . . . . 68 E5
Liskeard PL14 . . . . 113 D6
Pathfields EX23 . . . . 104 E5
Pathway Fields The TR27 . . . . 142 C5
Patna Pl PL1 . . . . 148 B4
Pato Point PL11 . . . . 127 A5
Patterdale Cl PL6 . . . . . . 125 D3
Patterdale Wlk PL6 . . . . . 125 D3
Pattinson Cl PL6 . . . . 125 E2
Pattinson Ct PL6 . . . . 125 E2
Pattinson Dr PL6 . . . . 125 F2
Paull Rd PL31 . . . . 109 B4
Paulls Row 4 TR15 . . . . . 140 C5
Paul's Row TR1 . . . . 137 D5
Paul's Terr TR1 . . . . 137 D5
Paviland Grange 6 PL1 . 128 A3
Pavilion Pk TR14 . . . . 138 F4
Pavlova Cl PL14 . . . . 113 C5
Pavlova Ct 6 PL14 . . . . . 113 C5
Paynter's Cross PL12 . . . . . 53 E7
Paynter's Cross Cotts PL12 . . . . 53 E7
Paynters La TR16 . . . . 67 E4
Paynter's Lane End Est TR16 . . . . 67 D4
Paynter Wlk 5 PL7 . . . . . 131 B5
Peacock Ave PL11 . . . . . . 127 A3
Peacock Cl PL7 . . . . 130 F7
Peacock La PL4 . . . . 149 A2
Pearce's La 12 TR26 . . . . 141 A5
Pearce's Row 3 PL24 . . . . 60 C4
Pearn Cotts 2 PL3 . . . . . . 128 F6
Pearn Gdns PL3 . . . . 129 A7
Pearn Rd PL3 . . . . 129 A7
Pearn Ridge PL3 . . . . 129 A7
Pearson Ave 3 PL4 . . . . . 128 F4
Pearson Rd PL4 . . . . 128 F4
Pebble Ct TR7 . . . . 111 C7
Pedlars Cl PL15 . . . . 18 B8
Pedna Carne Mobile Home Pk TR9 . . . . 57 E8
Pednandrea TR19 . . . . 86 E6
Pedn-mên-du TR19 . . . . . . 96 A7
Pedn-Moran TR2 . . . . 95 B6
Pednolva Wlk TR26 . . . . . 141 B5
Pedn-y-ke 1 TR12 . . . . . . 99 A1
Peek Moor Cross EX22 . . . 13 E4
Peeks Ave PL9 . . . . 135 F7
Peel St PL1 . . . . 128 A1
Peguarra Cl PL28 . . . . 20 E1
Peguarra Ct PL28 . . . . 20 E1
Pelean Cross TR3 . . . . 81 B5
Pelham Ct 11 TR11 . . . . . 145 C3
Pellew Cl
7 Falmouth TR11 . . . . 145 A5
Padstow PL28 . . . . 107 C5
Pellew Cres TR13 . . . . . . 146 C4
Pellew Pl PL2 . . . . 127 F4
Pellew Rd TR11 . . . . 145 A5
Pellor Fields TR13 . . . . 90 F3
Pelynt Prim Sch PL13 . . . . 62 D6
Pembrey Wlk PL5 . . . . 123 E4
Pembroke Cl 7 PL24 . . . . . 60 C4
Pembroke La PL1 . . . . 127 E1
Pembroke Rd TR7 . . . . . . 111 E7
Pembroke St
Plymouth PL1 . . . . 127 E1
Plymouth PL1 . . . . 127 F1
Pemros Rd PL5 . . . . 123 C1
Penair Cres TR1 . . . . 137 F6
Penair Sch TR1 . . . . 70 D4
Penair View TR1 . . . . 137 F4
Penally Ct PL35 . . . . 9 D2
Penally Hill PL35 . . . . 9 D2
Penally Terr PL35 . . . . 9 C2
Penalverne Ave TR18 . . . 143 D5
Penalverne Cres TR18 . . . 143 D5
Penalverne Dr TR18 . . . . 143 D5
Penalverne Pl TR18 . . . . . 143 D5
Penameyne Ct 5 TR26 . . 141 B6
Pen-An-Gwel TR26 . . . . . 141 A4
Penare Gdns 2 TR18 . . . 143 E6
Penare Rd TR18 . . . . 143 E6
Penare Terr TR18 . . . . 143 E6
Penarrow Cl TR11 . . . . . . 144 E2
Penarrow Rd TR11 . . . . . . 145 C8
Penarth PL13 . . . . 117 B3
Penarth Rd TR11 . . . . 145 A5
Penarwyn Cres TR18 . . . . 143 B7
Penarwyn Rd PL24 . . . . . . 60 B4
Penarwyn Woods 6 PL24 60 B4
Penbeagle Cl 17 TR26 . . . . 77 A6
Penbeagle Cres 8 TR26 . . 77 A6
Penbeagle Ind Est TR26 . . 77 A6
Penbeagle La TR26 . . . . . . 77 A6
Penbeagle Terr 7 TR26 . . 77 A6
Penbeagle Way TR26 . . . . 141 A4
Penberthy Cross TR27 . . . . 89 F7
Penberthy Rd
Helston TR13 . . . . 146 C5
Portreath TR16 . . . . 67 D6
Penbothidno TR11 . . . . 92 F3
Pen Brea Cl TR2 . . . . 95 B6
Penbrea Rd TR18 . . . . 143 E7
Penbugle La PL31 . . . . . . 109 E7
Pencair Ave PL11 . . . . 126 E2
Pencalenick Sch TR1 . . . . . 70 E4
Pencantol TR4 . . . . 81 C7
Pencarn Parc TR16 . . . . . . 80 A5
Pencarrick Cl TR1 . . . . . . 137 B6
Pencarrow* PL30 . . . . 34 D6
Pencarrow Cl PL17 . . . . 39 E3
Pencarrow Rd 13 TR16 . . . 67 E4
Pencavo Hill PL12 . . . . 53 A3
Pencoys Prim Sch TR16 . . 80 A5
Pencreber Rd 3 PL20 . . . . 42 C4
Pendale Sq TR1 . . . . 137 B4
Pendarves
St Merryn PL28 . . . . 31 F7
Tresillian TR2 . . . . 70 F5
Pendarves Flats TR18 . . . 143 D6
Pendarves Rd
Camborne TR14 . . . . 138 C1
Pendarves Rd *continued*
Falmouth TR11 . . . . 144 F6
Penzance TR18 . . . . 143 D6
Truro TR1 . . . . 137 C6
Pendarves St
Camborne, Beacon TR14 . . 138 F1
Troon TR14 . . . . 79 E4
Pendarves View TR14 . . . 138 C1
Pendean Ave PL14 . . . . . . 113 B6
Pendean Cl PL14 . . . . 113 B6
Pendean Ct PL14 . . . . 113 B6
Pendean Dr PL14 . . . . 113 B6
Pendeen Cl
Plymouth PL6 . . . . 124 F6
Threemilestone TR3 . . . . . . 69 D3
Pendeen Cres
Plymouth PL6 . . . . 125 A6
Threemilestone TR3 . . . . . . 69 D3
Pendeen Ho TR1 . . . . 69 E4
Pendeen Lighthouse Mus* TR19 . . . . 75 A1
Pendeen Pk TR13 . . . . 146 C8
Pendeen Pl TR7 . . . . 110 F6
Pendeen Prim Sch TR19 . . 75 A1
Pendeen Rd
Porthleven TR13 . . . . 91 B1
Threemilestone TR3 . . . . . . 69 D3
Truro TR1 . . . . 137 E3
Pendennis Castle* TR11 145 E2
Pendennis Cl
Penzance TR18 . . . . 143 E7
Plymouth PL3 . . . . 128 F8
Torpoint PL11 . . . . 126 F3
Pendennis Ct TR11 . . . . . . 145 D3
Pendennis Pl TR18 . . . . . . 143 F7
Pendennis Rd
Falmouth TR11 . . . . 145 D3
Looe PL13 . . . . 117 D5
Penzance TR18 . . . . 143 E7
Pendennis Rise TR11 . . . . 145 D3
Pender's La TR15 . . . . 140 B5
Pendilly Ave PL11 . . . . . . 126 F2
Pendilly Dr PL25 . . . . 114 E7
Pendinnes Gdns PL15 . . . 106 B8
Pendour Pk PL22 . . . . 112 E2
Pendower Ct TR2 . . . . 83 D5
Pendower Rd
Looe PL13 . . . . 117 E4
Veryan TR2 . . . . 83 F6
Pendower Terr TR14 . . . . 138 E1
Pendragon Cres TR7 . . . . 111 A4
Pendragon Ho TR11 . . . . . 145 D3
Pendragon Rd PL14 . . . . . 113 D6
Pendra Loweth TR11 . . . . 144 D1
Pendray Gdns PL14 . . . . . . 50 E7
Pendrea Cl TR18 . . . . 143 F7
Pendrea Pk TR14 . . . . 138 F5
Pendrea Pl TR18 . . . . 143 F7
Pendrea Rd TR18 . . . . 143 F7
Pendrea Wood TR1 . . . . 69 F3
Pendrim Rd PL13 . . . . 117 D4
Pendruccombe Ct PL15 . 106 D5
Pen-Eglos 8 TR2 . . . . 95 A6
Penforth TR14 . . . . 138 E2
Penganne Cl TR7 . . . . 110 D4
Pengarrock Hill TR12 . . . 101 D5
Pengarth 1 TR5 . . . . 54 D1
Pengarth Cl TR1 . . . . 137 C2
Pengarth Rd TR11 . . . . . . 145 A3
Pengarth Rise TR11 . . . . . 145 A3
Pengegon Moor TR14 . . . . 138 F2
Pengegon Parc TR14 . . . . 138 F2
Pengegon Way TR14 . . . . 138 F2
Pengelly
24 Callington PL17 . . . . 39 F4
Delabole PL33 . . . . 14 E2
Pengelly Cl PL11 . . . . 126 F5
Pengelly Cross
Godolphin Cross TR27 . . . . 90 F7
Wadebridge PL27 . . . . 108 C1
Pengelly Hill PL11 . . . . . . 127 A5
Pengelly Pk PL11 . . . . 126 F5
Pengelly Pl TR11 . . . . 144 E5
Pengellys Row TR14 . . . . 139 A5
Pengelly Way TR3 . . . . 69 D3
Pengeron Ave 1 TR14 . . . 138 F7
Pengersick Est TR20 . . . . . 90 C3
Pengersick La TR20 . . . . . . 90 C3
Pengersick Parc TR20 . . . . 90 C3
Pengliddon PL27 . . . . 33 B7
Pengover Cl PL14 . . . . 113 D6
Pengover Gn PL14 . . . . 51 E8
Pengover Hts PL14 . . . . . . 113 D6
Pengover Parc TR15 . . . . 140 C6
Pengover Pk PL14 . . . . . . 113 D6
Pengover Rd PL14 . . . . . . 113 E6
Pengrowyn PL26 . . . . 59 D6
Pengwarras Rd TR14 . . . . 138 C3
Pengweal 16 TR18 . . . . . . 143 C2
Penhale 1 TR6 . . . . 55 A5
Penhale Cl PL14 . . . . 37 F3
Penhale Cotts TR3 . . . . 82 D6
Penhale Est TR15 . . . . 140 B6
Penhale Gdns TR9 . . . . 57 D8
Penhale Mdw PL14 . . . . 37 F3
Penhale Rd
Barripper TR14 . . . . 79 A4
Carnhell Green TR14 . . . . . 78 F4
Falmouth TR11 . . . . 144 F1
Penwithick PL26 . . . . 59 D7
Penhaligon Cl TR15 . . . . . 140 D4
Penhaligon Ct TR1 . . . . . . 137 E5
Penhaligon Way PL25 . . . 114 F4
Penhall La TR4 . . . . 68 C6
Penhallow TR15 . . . . 139 B8
Penhallow Cl
Mount Hawke TR4 . . . . 68 C6
Veryan TR2 . . . . 83 C5
Penhallow Ct TR7 . . . . 111 C7
Penhallow Parc PL33 . . . . . 14 D2
Penhallow Rd TR7 . . . . . . 111 C7
Penhalls Way TR3 . . . . 82 B8
Penhalt Farm Holiday Pk EX23 . . . . 6 E3
Penhaven Cl TR8 . . . . 56 B7
Penhaven Ct TR7 . . . . 110 E6
Penhellaz Hill TR13 . . . . . 146 B6
Penhellaz Rd TR13 . . . . . . 146 B6
Penhole Cl PL15 . . . . 27 D3
Penina Ave TR7 . . . . 110 F4
Peninsula Medical Sch PL6 . . . . 125 C3
Peninsular Pk PL12 . . . . . 122 C4
Penjerrick Gdns* TR11 . . . 93 D5
Penjerrick Hill
Budock Water TR11 . . . . . . 144 C1
Falmouth TR11 . . . . 93 E5
Penkenna Cl EX23 . . . . 10 C6
Penkernick Cl TR18 . . . . . 143 B1
Penkernick Way TR9 . . . . . 45 E6
Penknight La PL22 . . . . . . 112 A2
Penlean Cl TR15 . . . . 140 D7
Penlea Rd TR10 . . . . 144 B8
Penlee Apartments PL23 116 C3
Penlee Cl
13 Callington PL17 . . . . 39 F4
Praa Sands TR20 . . . . 90 C3
Tregony TR2 . . . . 71 F4
Penlee Cotts PL10 . . . . 64 C2
Penlee Cvn Site TR19 . . . . 88 D1
Penlee Gdns PL3 . . . . 128 A4
Penlee Ho TR1 . . . . 69 E4
Penlee House Gall & Mus* TR18 . . . . 143 E5
Penlee Manor Dr TR18 . . 143 E4
Penlee Pk PL11 . . . . 126 E4
Penlee Pl 4 PL4 . . . . 128 F4
Penlee Rd PL3 . . . . 128 A4
Penlee St 11 TR18 . . . . . . 143 E6
Penlee View Terr 3 TR18 . . . . 143 E4
Penlee Villas TR3 . . . . 82 B8
Penlee Way PL3 . . . . 128 B4
Penlu TR14 . . . . 138 F5
Penlu Ho TR14 . . . . 138 F5
Penluke Cl TR16 . . . . 80 A5
Penlyne Woodland Trail* PL22 . . . . 112 E5
Penmare Cl TR27 . . . . 142 E7
Penmare Ct TR27 . . . . 142 E7
Penmare Terr TR27 . . . . . 142 E7
Penmayne Parc TR16 . . . . 140 F1
Penmayne Villas PL27 . . . . 21 E3
Penmead Rd PL33 . . . . 14 E2
Penmelen PL32 . . . . 105 C4
Penmeneth TR13 . . . . 146 F8
Penmenner Est 7 TR12 . . 101 C4
Penmenner Rd TR12 . . . . 102 F2
Penmere Cl
Helston TR13 . . . . 146 B7
Penzance TR18 . . . . 143 E7
Penmere Cres TR11 . . . . . 144 F3
Penmere Ct 4 TR11 . . . . . 145 A3
Penmere Dr TR7 . . . . 110 C5
Penmere Hill 7 TR11 . . . 145 A3
Penmere Pl
3 Falmouth TR11 . . . . 145 A3
Penzance TR18 . . . . 143 E7
Penmere Rd
Penzance TR18 . . . . 143 E7
St Austell PL25 . . . . 115 A4
Penmere Sta TR11 . . . . . . 144 F3
Penmerrin Ct TR7 . . . . 110 E5
Penmeva View PL26 . . . . . . 73 C3
Penmorvah TR11 . . . . 82 A2
Penmorvah Pl TR14 . . . . . 138 E2
Penmorvah Rd TR1 . . . . . 137 F6
Pennance Hill TR11 . . . . . . 93 F5
Pennance Ho TR11 . . . . . . 145 A2
Pennance La TR16 . . . . . . 140 F1
Pennance Parc TR16 . . . . 140 F1
Pennance Rd
Falmouth TR11 . . . . 145 A2
Lanner TR16 . . . . 80 E7
Redruth TR16 . . . . 140 F1
Pennance Terr TR16 . . . . 140 F1
Penn An Drea TR13 . . . . . 146 D8
Pennant Farm PL29 . . . . . . 22 E6
Pennard Villas PL27 . . . . . . 33 B5
Pennor Dr PL25 . . . . 114 D3
Pennoweth Prim Sch TR15 . . . . 140 C5
Pennycomequick Hill PL1, PL3 . . . . 148 B4
Pennycross Cl PL2 . . . . . . 128 D8
Pennycross Park Rd PL2 128 C7
Pennycross Prim Sch PL2 . . . . 128 C8
Pennygillam Ind Est PL15 . . . . 106 A4
Pennygillam Way PL15 . . . 18 E2
Pennys La PL24 . . . . 115 F5
Penny's La PL9 . . . . 136 D6
Penoweth TR11 . . . . 82 A2
Penpol Ave TR27 . . . . 142 C5
Penpol Hill
Crantock TR8 . . . . 110 B4
Devoran TR3 . . . . 82 B6
Penpol Rd TR27 . . . . 142 B5
Penpol Sch TR27 . . . . 142 C5
Penpol Terr TR27 . . . . 142 B5
Penpol Vean TR27 . . . . . . 142 C5
Penponds Rd TR13 . . . . 91 A1

Penponds Sch TR14 79 B5
Penpons Cl TR18 143 C4
Penpont Rd TR15 140 D6
Penpont View PL15 26 C7
Pen Porth Ave TR26 77 A7
Penquite Dr PL31 109 F5
Penrice Com Coll PL25 115 A3
Penrice Hospl (Maternity & Gastric) PL26 114 F1
Penrice Parc PL25 115 A3
Penrith Cl PL6 125 D3
Penrith Gdns PL6 125 D3
Penrith Wlk PL6 125 D3
Penrose Ct
 Penzance TR18 143 F6
 2 South Tehidy TR14 138 F7
Penrose Parc TR13 91 B1
Penrose Rd
 Falmouth TR11 145 A4
 Helston TR13 146 C6
Penrose St PL1 148 B3
Penrose Terr TR18 143 F6
Penrose Villas 5 PL4 128 F4
Penrose Walks★ TR12, TR13 98 D8
Penruan La TR2 95 B6
Penryn Coll TR10 144 B7
Penryn Com Inf Sch TR10 144 B7
Penryn Jun Sch TR10 144 B8
Penryn St TR15 140 B4
Penryn Sta TR10 144 B8
Pensans Prim Sch (Inf) TR18 143 E7
Pensans Prim Sch (Jun) TR18 143 D6
Penscombe Cross PL15 28 C6
Penscott La PL26 114 C1
Pensilva TR6 55 A4
Pensilva Prim Sch PL14 38 E5
Pensilva Rd TR1 137 E6
Pensilva Rural Workshops PL14 38 E4
Penstowe Pk Holiday Village EX23 4 F6
Penstowe Rd EX23 5 A6
Penstrasse Pl 1 PL24 60 D5
Penstraze Bsns Ctr TR4 69 A5
Penstraze La PL26 47 A4
Pensylva PL25 114 E3
Pentalek Rd TR14 138 D1
Pentamar St PL2 127 E4
Pentargon Rd 1 PL35 9 C1
Pentewan Hill PL26 73 D6
Pentewan Rd PL25, PL26 59 C1
Pentidna La TR27 66 B2
Pentillie PL26 73 C4
Pentillie Cres PL4 128 D4
Pentillie Gdns
 14 Callington PL17 39 E4
 St Austell PL25 114 F6
Pentillie Rd
 Bere Alston PL20 41 B1
 Plymouth PL4 128 E4
Pentillie Way PL26 73 C4
Pentire Ave TR7 110 A5
Pentire Cres TR7 110 B5
Pentire Ct TR7 110 B6
Pentire Gn TR8 43 D3
Pentire Hts TR7 110 A5
Pentire Rd
 Newquay TR7 110 C5
 Penryn TR10 144 B8
 Torpoint PL11 126 F3
Pentland Cl PL6 124 F7
Pen Tor PL30 35 C8
Pentor Ct PL30 35 C8
Pentour 3 PL24 60 B4
Pentowan Ct TR26 141 E2
Pentowan Rd TR27 142 E8
Pentreath Cl
 Fowey PL23 116 B5
 Lanner TR16 80 E7
 Penzance TR18 143 D7
Pentreath La
 Lizard TR12 102 F2
 Praa Sands TR20 90 B3
Pentreath Terr TR16 80 E7
Pentre Ct EX23 4 D4
Pentrevah Ct TR7 110 D6
Pentrevah Rd 8 PL26 59 D7
Pen-Tye TR27 78 E3
Pentyre Ct PL4 149 C4
Pentyre Terr PL4 149 C4
Penvale 4 PL14 38 E4
Penvale Cl TR14 79 B5
Penvale Cres TR10 144 B8
Penvale Ct 8 TR11 145 A4
Penvale Dr TR10 144 B8
Penvean Cl TR10 93 C8
Penvean La TR11 144 E5
Penvenen 2 TR6 55 A5
Penventinnie La TR1 69 E4
Penventinue La PL23 116 B7
Penventon Terr
 Four Lanes TR16 80 B6
 Redruth TR15 140 A4
Penventon View TR13 146 B5
Penview Cres TR13 146 B5
Penvorder Cotts PL30 24 B2
Penvorder La PL30 24 B2
Penware Parc TR14 138 C1
Penwarne Cl TR14 138 F7
Penwarne La PL26 73 C3
Penwarne Rd TR11 93 D5
Penwartha TR12 101 B2
Penwartha Cl
 Constantine TR11 92 F3
 St Columb Minor TR7 111 D7
Penwartha Ct TR11 92 F3
Penwartha Rd
 15 Illogan TR16 67 E4
 Perranporth TR6 55 B4
Penwartha Vean 14 TR16 67 E4
Penwerris Ct TR11 145 A6
Penwerris Farm TR11 144 F5
Penwerris La TR11 145 A6
Penwerris Rd TR1 69 F3
Penwerris Rise TR20 90 B3
Penwerris Terr 10 TR11 145 A5
Penwethers La TR1 69 F3
Penwinnick Cl 9 TR5 54 C1
Penwinnick Parc 4 TR5 54 D1
Penwinnick Rd
 St Agnes TR5 68 D8
 St Austell PL25 114 B3
Penwith Bsns Ctr TR20 88 F6
Penwith Cl TR26 141 A4
Penwith Coll TR18 143 D7
Penwithhick Rd PL26 59 D7
Penwithian Cl TR27 142 E6
Penwithick Pk 6 PL26 59 D7
Penwith Rd TR26 141 A4
Penwith St 12 TR18 143 E6
Penworth Cl PL15 106 C5
Penwyth TR12 92 C1
Pen y Bryn PL27 108 D6
Penzance Rd
 Helston TR13 146 A6
 St Buryan TR19 97 C7
Pepo La TR2 72 A7
Pepper Cl PL12 40 C2
Pepper La PL9 136 D7
Peppers Ct PL12 40 C2
Peppers Hill Cl PL15 18 F7
Peppers Park Rd PL14 113 E6
Pepper St PL19 147 C6
Pepys Pl PL5 124 E1
Percuil View TR2 95 B6
Percy Davy Cl TR6 55 A5
Percy St PL5 123 D1
Percy Terr PL4 129 A4
Pergolla Ct 9 TR7 110 F6
Perhaver Pk PL26 85 D5
Perhaver Way PL26 85 D5
Periwinkle Dr PL7 131 C5
Per Kithen TR12 102 F2
Permarin Rd TR10 144 C8
Perran-ar-worthal Com Prim Sch TR3 81 D6
Perran Cl TR3 81 F6
Perrancombe Garden Ct TR6 55 A4
Perran Crossroads TR20 89 E5
Perranporth Cl PL5 123 E4
Perranporth Com Prim Sch TR6 55 A4
Perran Sands Holiday Ctr TR6 55 B6
Perran View Holiday Pk TR5 54 E2
Perranwell Rd TR4 55 D4
Perranwell Sta TR3 81 E6
Perranzabuloe Mus★ TR6 55 A5
Perryman Cl PL7 130 E7
Perseverance Cotts 1 PL7 130 E7
Peryn Rd PL19 147 A5
Peter Hopper's Hill PL5 120 C2
Peter's Cl PL9 136 C7
Petersfield Cl PL3 129 B6
Peters Hill PL26 58 E4
Peters Park Cl PL5 123 E1
Peter's Park La PL5 123 E1
Peters Row TR19 75 A1
Petes Pl 24 TR26 141 B5
Petherick Creek Holiday Bglws PL27 32 C7
Petherick Rd EX23 104 E7
Pethericks Mill EX23 104 E4
Pethick Cl PL6 124 D6
Pethill Cl PL6 125 F2
Pethybridge Dr PL31 109 B3
Peverell Park Rd PL3 128 D6
Peverell Rd
 Penzance TR18 143 E7
 7 Porthleven TR13 98 C8
Peverell Terr
 Plymouth PL3 128 D5
 Porthleven TR13 98 B8
Pew Tor Cl
 Tavistock PL19 147 E5
 3 Yelverton PL20 42 C3
Phernyssick Rd PL25 114 F6
Philgray Cl TR27 142 E7
Philip Cl PL9 136 A6
Philip Gdns PL9 135 F6
Phillack Hill TR27 142 D7
Phillimore St 3 PL2 127 F4
Phoenix Bsns Pk PL6 125 F4
Phoenix Cl 8 PL20 42 C4
Phoenix St PL1 148 A2
Piala Pl TR27 142 E7
Piazza 14 TR26 141 B6
Piazza The 5 PL31 109 E5
Pickard Way EX23 104 D7
Pickering Villas TR4 69 A3
Picketts Yd TR10 144 D7
Pick Pie Dr PL6 125 E8
Pier La PL10 133 A1
Pier St PL1 148 B1
Pigmeadow La PL14 113 C6
Pike Rd PL3 129 D5
Pikes Hill PL23 116 C4
Pike's Hill TR11 145 B3
Pike St PL14 113 C6
Pilchard Works The★ TR18 143 C3
Pilgrim Cl PL2 128 B6
Pilgrim Ct 11 PL20 41 B1
Pilgrim Dr PL20 41 B1
Pilgrim Prim Sch PL1 148 B3
Pilgrims Way TR27 78 C1
Pillars Cl TR8 56 F5
Pillars Rd
 Flushing TR11 145 B8
 Mylor Bridge TR11 82 A2
Pillar Wlk PL6 124 E7
Pill La PL12 122 E4
Pillmere Dr PL12 122 D4
Pilot Cotts PL28 21 B4
Pinch Hill EX23 7 B7
Pinder Ct PL19 147 B5
Pine Cl TR13 146 D5
Pine Ct
 Par PL24 115 F6
 Perranarworthal TR3 81 D6
Pine Green Cvn Pk PL14 50 C7
Pine Lodge Gdns★ PL25 115 D4
Pine Rd TR18 143 B4
Pine Trees Camp Site★ TR12 99 F5
Pine View
 Gunnislake PL18 41 A6
 St Dennis PL26 46 D1
Pinewood Cl PL7 130 F6
Pinewood Dr PL6 125 E7
Pinewood Flats PL27 21 D5
Pinkhams Cotts PL12 122 B6
Pink Moors TR16 68 D1
Pin La PL1 149 A2
Pinnacle Quay PL4 149 B2
Pinsla Garden & Nursery★ PL30 35 E1
Pinslow Cross PL15 19 C8
Pintail Ave TR27 77 E3
Pipers Cl PL15 18 E2
Piran Hts EX23 104 C2
Pitick Terr TR11 145 B6
Pitland Cnr PL19 30 D4
Pit Mdw TR11 144 E3
Pits La PL10 64 B2
Pityme PL27 21 F3
Pityme Bsns Ctr PL27 21 F3
Pityme Farm Rd PL27 21 F3
Pityme Ind Est PL27 21 F3
Pixon La PL19 147 B4
Pixon Trad Ctr 2 PL19 147 B4
Place de Brest PL1 148 C3
Place Parc TR7 111 D7
Place Rd PL23 116 C4
Place Stables PL23 116 C4
Place View PL23 116 C4
Place View Rd 15 TR2 95 A6
Plaidy La PL13 117 E4
Plaidy Park Rd PL13 117 E4
Plain-An-Gwarry TR15 140 B5
Plaistow Cl PL5 123 E2
Plaistow Cres PL5 123 E2
Plaistow Hill Inf Sch PL5 123 E2
Planet Pk PL33 14 D2
Plantation La TR27 142 B5
Plas Newydd Ave PL31 109 E3
Platt The PL27 108 C5
Playingfield La TR7 110 D5
Pleasant Pl 15 TR18 143 C7
Pleasant Terr TR19 86 E6
Pleasure Hill Cl PL9 135 D8
Plestin Cl PL15 106 C7
Pleyber Christ Way PL22 112 C2
Pleydon Cl PL13 62 E2
Plintona View PL7 130 E7
Plougastel Dr PL12 122 E3
Plough Ct TR10 81 C2
Plough Gn PL12 122 C3
Plumer Rd PL6 124 F2
Plymbridge Gdns PL7 130 C7
Plymbridge La PL6 125 B4
Plymbridge Rd
 Plymouth, Eggbuckland PL6 125 C1
 Plymouth, Estover PL6 125 E5
 Plymouth, Mainstone PL6 125 F2
 Plymouth, Plympton PL7 130 C7
Plym Cres PL19 147 D5
Plymouth City Airport PL6 125 C5
Plymouth Coll PL4 128 E4
Plymouth Coll Inf Sch PL3 128 F5
Plymouth Coll of Art & Design PL4 149 A3
Plymouth Coll of Art & Design (Sutton Annexe) PL4 149 A3
Plymouth Coll of F Ed PL1 128 A2
Plymouth Coll of F Ed (Annexe) PL1 148 C4
Plymouth Coll Prep Sch PL3 128 E6
Plymouth Discovery Ctr★ PL3 129 F6
Plymouth Dome Discovery Ctr★ PL1 148 C1
Plymouth High Sch for Girls PL4 149 A4
Plymouth Medical & Tech Pk PL6 125 A3
Plymouth Nuffield Hospl The PL6 125 B4
Plymouth Pavilions PL1 148 B2
Plymouth Rd
 Liskeard PL14 113 D5
 Plymouth PL7 130 B6
 Tavistock PL19 147 B4
Plymouth Road Ind Est PL19 147 C3
Plymouth Ski Ctr★ PL6 129 E7
Plymouth Sound Camping Site PL9 135 C1
Plymouth Sta PL4 148 C4
Plymouth Trade Pk PL4 149 C1
Plympton Hill PL7 130 F3
Plympton Hospl PL7 130 D5
Plympton St Mary CE Inf Sch PL7 130 D5
Plympton St Maurice Prim Sch PL7 130 F3
Plym St PL4 149 A3
Plymstock Rd PL9 135 D7
Plymstock Sch PL9 135 F8
Plymtree Dr PL7 130 C7
Plym Valley Rly★ PL7 130 A7
Plym View Prim Sch PL3 129 D6
Poad's Trust PL14 51 F5
Pochin Ho PL25 114 F7
Pocklington Rise PL7 130 E5
Pocohontas Cres 4 TR9 45 E1
Pode Dr PL7 131 B4
Point Curlew Country Holiday Est PL28 31 F6
Point Neptune PL23 116 B3
Point Rd TR3 82 A6
Polapit Tamar PL15 19 A8
Polbathic Rd TR15 140 C6
Polbreen Ave TR5 54 C1
Polbreen La TR5 54 C1
Poldark Gdns 7 PL24 60 B4
Poldark Mine Heritage Complex★ TR13 92 A6
Poldark Rd 12 TR16 67 E4
Poldhu Cl TR26 141 D1
Poldhu Rd
 Liskeard PL14 113 D6
 Mullion TR12 99 A2
Poldice La TR16 68 E1
Poldice Terr TR16 68 E1
Poldrea PL24 60 D5
Poldrissick Hill PL12 53 C2
Poldrissick La PL12 53 C2
Poldue Cl TR15 140 D6
Polean La PL13 117 B4
Polean Trad Est PL13 117 B4
Polecoverack La TR12 101 C1
Polgarth
 1 Camborne TR15 139 C6
 Newlyn TR18 143 B3
Polgarth Cl TR26 141 D1
Polgaver Ho PL25 115 E3
Polgine Cl TR14 79 E5
Polgine La TR14 79 E5
Polglase Wlk TR4 70 D8
Polglaze Cl TR18 143 D7
Polglist PL26 58 D5
Polgoon Cl TR18 143 C5
Polgooth Cl TR15 140 D6
Polgover Way 5 PL24 60 B4
Polgrain Rd TR14 138 F6
Polgrean Pl PL24 60 B5
Polhigey Terr TR16 80 C2
Polhorman La TR12 99 A2
Police Ho TR11 145 B4
Polisken Way TR4 56 D1
Polkerris Pk PL24 60 C4
Polkerris Rd TR16 80 F8
Polkirt Hill
 Gorran Haven PL26 73 B1
 Mevagissey PL26 73 C3
Polkirt Hts PL26 73 C3
Polkyth Par PL25 114 E4
Polkyth Rd PL25 114 F4
Pollard Cl
 Plymouth PL9 135 B5
 Saltash PL12 122 B2
Pollard Rd 7 PL17 39 F4
Pollards Cl
 Goonhavern TR4 55 D4
 Pensilva PL14 38 E4
Pollards Way PL12 122 E3
Polmark Dr PL28 20 D2
Polmarth Cl PL25 114 F6
Polmassick Vineyard★ PL26 72 E4
Polmear Ct 9 PL27 108 B5
Polmear Hill PL24 60 E4
Polmear Parc PL24 60 D4
Polmear Rd
 St Austell PL25 114 F3
 Tywardreath PL24 60 D4
Polmeere Ho TR18 143 E7
Polmeere Rd TR18 143 E7
Polmena La PL22 112 E1
Polmennor Dr TR26 141 D1
Polmennor Rd
 Falmouth TR11 144 F1
 Heamoor TR18 143 C8
Polmenor Downs N TR14, TR27 78 F5
Polmenor Downs S TR14 78 F4
Polmeor Cl TR26 141 D1
Polmewan Flats PL26 59 A1
Polmorla Mews 10 PL27 108 B5
Polmorla Rd PL27 108 B5
Polmorla Wlk PL27 108 C5
Polmor Rd TR20 89 B8
Polpeor Row TR27 77 A3
Polperro Heritage Mus★ PL13 62 E2
Polperro Model Village★ PL13 62 D1
Polperro Prim Sch PL13 62 E2
Polperro Rd PL13 117 B4
Polpey La PL24 60 D5
Polruan Cl TR26 77 C4
Polruan Com Prim Sch PL23 116 D2
Polruan Ct TR1 137 E2
Polruan Rd
 Redruth TR15 140 D6
 Truro TR1 137 E2
Polruan Terr PL1 148 A3
Polscoe Rd PL22 112 F3
Polsethow TR10 144 B7
Polstain Cres TR3 69 D3
Polstain Rd TR3 69 D3
Polstain Villas TR3 69 D3
Polsue Way TR2 70 F5
Poltair Ave PL25 114 E4
Poltair Cl TR18 143 C7
Poltair Cres PL25 114 D4
Poltair Ct PL25 114 E4
Poltair Dr TR10 144 B7
Poltair Hospl TR20 143 B8
Poltair Rd
 Penryn TR10 144 B7
 St Austell PL25 114 D4
Poltair Sch PL25 114 D4
Poltair Terr 7 TR18 143 C7
Poltamar PL15 106 D5
Poltesco La TR12 103 B5
Poltisco Cl TR1 137 E3
Poltisco Wharf TR1 137 E4
Poltisko Rd TR10 144 B7
Poltisko Terr TR10 144 B7
Poltreen Cl TR26 141 D1
Polurrian Rd TR12 99 A1
Polvarth Est TR2 95 B6
Polvarth Rd TR2 95 A6
Polvean Cross PL14 51 A1
Polvean Terr PL14 51 A1
Polvella Cl TR7 110 B5
Polvellan Manor PL13 117 C4
Polvellan Terr PL13 117 C4
Polvelyn Parc TR27 142 E7
Polventon Cl
 Falmouth TR11 144 E4
 Heamoor TR18 143 C7
Polventon Parc 6 TR12 101 C4
Polvillion Rd PL23 116 B4
Polweath Cl TR18 143 E7
Polweath Rd TR18 143 E7
Polwhaveral Terr 6 TR11 145 A5
Polwheal Rd TR14 138 F6
Polwhele House Sch TR4 70 C6
Polwhele Rd
 Newquay TR7 111 A3
 Truro TR1 137 F6
Polwithen Ct TR26 141 C2
Polwithen Dr TR26 141 C1
Polwithen Gdns TR26 141 C1
Polwithen Rd
 Falmouth TR11 145 A4
 Penryn TR10 144 B7
 Penzance TR18 143 D5
Polwrath Terr PL14 38 A3
Polwyn Cl TR18 143 B7
Polyear Cl PL26 59 A1
Polyne Cotts PL13 62 F3
Polzeath Ct PL27 21 D6
Polzeath Gdns PL2 128 D8
Pomphlett Cl PL9 135 D8
Pomphlett Farm Ind Est PL9 129 E1
Pomphlett Gdns PL9 135 D8
Pomphlett Prim Sch PL9 135 E8
Pomphlett Rd PL9 135 E8
Ponchin Dr PL25 114 E7
Pondbridge Hill 1 PL14 113 C5
Pondfield Rd PL12 122 B3
Pondhu Cres PL25 114 B3
Pondhu Prim Sch PL25 114 B2
Pondhu Rd PL25 114 C3
Pond La TR15 140 A6
Pond Lanes End TR15 140 B6
Ponds Hill TR19 75 B1
Pond View Terr PL26 58 D5
Pond Wlk TR27 142 D7
Poniou La TR20 88 F6
Poniou Rd TR20 88 F6
Poniou Way TR20 88 F6
Ponsandane Farm Mews TR18 143 F7
Ponsharden Cotts TR11 144 F6
Ponsharden Ind Est TR11 144 E6
Ponsmere Ct 9 TR6 55 A5
Ponsmere Rd TR6 55 A5
Ponsonby Rd PL3 128 B4
Ponstantual Hill TR12 99 D7
Ponsvale TR3 81 B4
Pontsmill Rd PL24 60 C6
Pool Bsns & Enterprise Coll TR15 139 B6
Poole Park Rd PL5 127 C8
Pool Hall PL14 51 F5
Pool Ind Est TR15 139 C5
Pool's Ct TR27 142 D6
Pool St PL31 109 E5
Poplar Cl PL7 131 B5
Poplars Ct 16 TR6 55 A5
Poplar Terr TR11 145 B7
Popplestone Pk PL8 136 F5
Porcupine Rd PL24 60 C6

Pordenack Cl TR26 141 E2
Porfell Animal Land★ PL14 50 A2
Porhan Gn TR11 144 E6
Pork St TR12 100 D6
Porsham Cl PL6 121 B1
Porsham La PL5 124 E8
Porspoder Pl PL10 133 A2
Portbigham PL13 117 C3
Portbyhan Rd PL13 117 C3
Porteath Bee Ctr★ PL27 22 A6
Porteous Cl PL1 127 F3
Porter Way PL12 122 C3
Porth Beach Rd TR7 111 B8
Porth Bean Ct TR7 111 C7
Porth Bean Rd TR7 111 C7
Porthcollum La TR27 78 A1
Porthcurno Telegraph Mus★ TR19 96 E3
Portheast Cl PL26 85 C5
Portheast Way PL26 85 C5
Porthellow Vineyard★ TR12 101 D5
Portherras Cross TR19 75 A1
Portherras Terr TR19 75 A1
Portherras Villas TR19 75 A1
Porthgwidden TR3 82 C4
Porthgwidden Studios TR26 141 C6
Porthia Cl TR26 141 A4
Porthia Cres TR26 141 A4
Porthia Rd [12] TR26 77 A6
Porthilly Cvn Site PL27 21 D2
Porthilly La PL27 21 D2
Porthilly View PL28 107 E4
Porthkerris Water Sports Ctr★ TR12 101 E5
Porthleven Rd TR13 146 A5
Porthleven Sch TR13 91 B1
Porthmellon Gdns PL17 39 F4
Porthmeor Ct [51] TR26 141 B6
Porthmeor Hill TR26 141 A6
Porthmeor Rd
St Austell PL25 115 B3
[6] St Ives TR26 141 B6
Porthmeor Sq [21] TR26 141 B6
Porthmeor Studios [50] TR26 141 B6
Porthminster Terr [23] TR26 141 B5
Porth Par TR7 111 C8
Porthpean Beach Rd PL26 59 E1
Porthpean Rd PL25, PL26 114 F2
Porthrepta Rd TR26 141 E1
Porth Sawle Flats TR2 83 B2
Porth View TR2 95 B6
Porth Way TR7 111 B7
Port Isaac Com Prim Sch PL29 22 E7
Port La PL15 27 B2
Portland Cl PL14 113 D7
Portland Ct [9] PL1 127 F3
Portland Gdns TR11 144 F4
Portland Pl [23] TR19 88 C1
Portland Rd PL1 127 F3
Portland Sq PL4 148 C4
Portland Terr PL14 113 C7
Portland Villas PL4 148 C4
Portmellon Pk PL26 73 C3
Portreath Com Prim Sch TR16 67 D6
Portuan Rd PL13 117 D1
Portway Cl PL9 136 D7
Posses La TR18 88 E6
Possession La PL12 53 C3
Post Box Row TR14 139 B3
Post Office Row PL26 58 D7
Potters La PL35 9 C1
Potters Way PL7 130 D5
Pottery Est PL10 132 E6
Pottery Rd PL1 127 D3
Poughill Rd EX23 104 F7
Poultney Cl PL7 131 A5
Pounda PL14 51 B4
Pound Dean PL14 113 A5
Poundfield Cl [2] EX23 4 D1
Poundfield Hill [1] EX23 4 D1
Poundfield La EX23 4 D1
Pound Hill PL12 53 C3
Pound La
Bodmin PL31 109 E5
Stoke Climsland PL17 28 E1
Threemilestone TR3 69 E1
Pound Pk PL14 51 F5
Pound Rd PL20 42 B3
Pound's Cross PL6 120 E5
Pounds Park Rd
[1] Bere Alston PL20 41 B1
Plymouth PL3 128 D7
Pounds Pk PL12 122 F3
Pound St
Liskeard PL14 113 C6
Plymouth PL1 134 A8
Poundstock Cl PL30 35 F3
Powderham Rd PL3 128 F7
Powis Gdns PL5 124 B2
Powisland Dr PL6 125 A5
Praa Sands Holiday Village TR20 90 B3
Praed Pl TR26 77 E4
Praed's La TR17 89 C5
Pras Coth TR16 68 C3
Praze-An-Creet TR26 77 A7
Praze-An-Cronor TR9 45 E5
Prazegooth La TR12 103 A4
Praze Mdw TR10 144 C8
Praze Rd
Leedstown TR27 78 E1
Praze Rd *continued*
Newquay TR7 111 B7
Porthleven TR13 91 B1
Praze-an-Beeble TR14 79 A2
Praze The TR10 144 C8
Predannack Rd [4] TR12 99 A1
Preeze Cross PL30 35 E6
Prestonbury Cl PL6 125 B7
Prevenna Rd [2] TR19 88 C1
Prideaux Cl PL12 122 C5
Prideaux Place★ PL28 107 C6
Prideaux Rd PL24 60 B6
Pridham La PL2 128 D7
Pridmouth Rd PL25 114 E6
Priestacott Pk EX23 5 A6
Priesthood Terr PL10 132 E5
Priestley Ave PL5 123 E2
Primitive Row TR14 139 A5
Primrose Cl
Camborne TR14 138 B4
[9] Goldsithney TR20 89 E5
Roche PL26 47 A3
Torpoint PL11 126 E4
Primrose Cotts TR2 71 C6
Primrose Ct TR26 141 B4
Primrose Dr PL28 31 F7
Primrose Gdns
Illogan TR16 67 D4
Tavistock PL19 147 E4
Primrose Hill TR20 89 E5
Primrose La [4] TR20 89 E5
Primrose Rd EX23 104 F5
Primrose Terr
Newlyn TR18 143 D1
Portreath TR16 67 D6
Tresillian TR2 70 F5
Primrose Valley TR26 141 C4
Primrose Way PL15 27 A6
Primrose Wlk PL12 122 D4
Prince Charles Cl PL15 106 C7
Prince Charles Ho PL25 114 E5
Prince Charles Pk PL25 114 E5
Prince Charles Rd PL25 114 E5
Prince Maurice Ct PL4 149 B3
Prince Maurice Rd PL4 128 F4
Prince of Wales Quarry Trail★ PL34 14 E5
Prince Philip Rd PL15 106 C7
Prince Rock Prim Sch PL4 129 B2
Princes Rd PL6 125 E6
Princes Row PL14 38 B6
Princess Ave
Plymouth, Plymstock PL9 135 E6
Plymouth, West Park PL5 124 A3
Princess Cres PL9 135 E6
Princess Ct [12] TR18 143 E5
Princess Parc TR9 45 E1
Princes Sq PL13 117 C3
Princess Rd PL14 38 E4
Princess St
Plymouth PL1 148 C2
St Just TR19 86 E6
Princess Street Ope PL1 148 C2
Princes St
Bude EX23 104 D6
Looe PL13 117 C3
Penzance TR18 143 E5
Plymouth PL1 127 E2
Prince's St TR1 137 D4
Princess Terr [8] PL14 38 E4
Princess Villas PL17 28 B1
Princess Way PL1 148 C2
Prior's Barn PL31 109 F4
Priors Cl [10] TR26 77 A6
Priors Row TR13 90 E3
Priory Cl
Par PL24 60 C5
Tavistock PL19 147 D3
Priory Cotts PL15 106 B6
Priory Dr PL7 130 D5
Priory Gdns PL19 147 D3
Priory La PL15 106 B7
Priory Lawn Terr PL3 129 A6
Priory Mill PL7 130 D5
Priory Park Rd PL15 106 B6
Priory Rd
Bodmin PL31 109 F4
Plymouth PL3 129 A6
St Austell PL25 114 C4
St Columb Minor TR7, TR8 111 E7
Priory Ridge PL7 130 D5
Prislow Cl TR11 144 E2
Prislow Fields TR11 144 E2
Prislow La TR11 144 E2
Probus Com Prim Sch TR2 71 C6
Probus Gdns★ TR2 71 D6
Promenade The PL1 148 C1
Prospect Bldgs TR7 110 E6
Prospect Cl TR27 142 D6
Prospect Gdns TR1 137 E6
Prospect La PL12 122 C3
Prospect Pl
Ashton TR13 90 E3
[3] Falmouth TR11 145 B5
Hayle TR27 142 D6
Helston TR13 146 C5
Mevagissey PL26 73 C4
[26] Penzance TR18 143 E6
Plymouth PL1 148 B2
[8] Porthleven TR13 98 B8
[3] Truro TR1 137 D5
Prospect Row
Ashton TR13 90 E3
Plymouth PL1 127 E1
Prospect St PL4 149 A3
Prospect Terr
Bodmin PL31 109 E4
Gunnislake PL18 41 A6
Gunnislake, St Ann's Chapel PL18 40 E5
Mevagissey PL26 73 C4
Prospect Wlk PL12 122 C3
Prosper Cl PL26 47 A2
Prosper Hill TR27 66 B1
Prosper Rd PL26 47 A2
Prouse Cres PL2 128 C8
Prouse Rise PL12 122 E2
Prouts Ct [4] PL15 106 C6
Prout's La TR27 78 D6
Prouts Mews [5] PL15 106 C6
Prouts Way PL15 18 C2
Providence Pl
Calstock PL18 41 A3
Plymouth PL1 128 A3
Providence St PL4 149 A4
Provis Rd TR18 143 C4
Prynne Cl PL1 148 B3
Puckator La PL14 38 A2
Puggis Hill TR14 138 A5
Pulla Cross TR4 81 B6
Putnam Cl PL14 113 D5
Pydar Cl TR7 111 B5
Pydar Mews [8] TR1 137 C4
Pydar St TR1 137 C5
Pym St
Plymouth PL1 127 F3
Tavistock PL19 147 C6
Pyramid Cl PL25 58 F4
Pyworthy CE Prim Sch EX22 8 E5

Q

Quakers Rd TR4, TR3 81 B6
Quant Pk PL19 147 C6
Quarry Cl EX23 104 E7
Quarry Cnr PL20 41 C2
Quarry Cotts
Plymouth, Honicknowle PL5 124 B2
Plymouth PL1 148 A3
Quarry Cres PL15 106 A3
Quarry Ct TR11 145 B4
Quarryfield Camping Site TR8 110 A4
Quarry Gdns TR18 143 D5
Quarry Hill
Falmouth TR11 145 B4
Gulval TR18 88 E7
Quarry House Flats TR1 137 E3
Quarry La
Gunnislake PL18 40 F6
Landrake PL12 53 D3
Launceston PL15 18 E2
Sheffield TR19 97 F7
St Germans PL12 65 A8
Quarrymans Cotts PL27 33 B7
Quarry Park Ave PL9 135 D7
Quarry Park Rd
Newquay TR7 110 F5
Plymouth, Peverell PL3 128 D5
Plymouth, Plymstock PL9 135 D7
Quarry Park Terr PL31 109 C4
Quarry Rd
Pensilva PL14 38 E4
Perranporth TR6 55 B4
Quarry St
St Germans PL12 65 A8
Torpoint PL11 127 C3
Quarterdeck The PL1 134 A8
Quay Hill
Falmouth TR11 145 C4
Penryn TR10 144 D7
Quay La PL12 53 D1
Quay Mews [8] TR1 137 D4
Quay Rd
Crumplehorn PL13 62 D1
Devoran TR3 81 F6
Landrake PL12 53 A2
Looe PL13 117 C3
Mylor Bridge TR11 82 B4
Plymouth PL1 149 A2
St Agnes TR5 54 D2
St Austell PL25 115 B2
St Germans PL12 65 B8
Tideford PL12 52 F2
Quayside [6] PL19 147 B5
Quay St
Falmouth TR11 145 C4
Looe PL13 117 C3
Lostwithiel PL22 112 C2
[11] Mousehole TR19 88 C1
Penzance TR18 143 F4
St Ives TR26 141 C6
Truro TR1 137 D4
Quay The
Pentewan PL26 73 C6
Penzance TR18 143 F5
Plymouth PL9 135 C7
Polruan PL23 116 D3
Portscatho TR2 83 B2
St Germans PL12 65 B8
St Mawes TR2 95 A6
Queen Anne Gdns TR11 144 E3
Queen Anne's Quay PL4 149 B2
Queen Elizabeth Rd PL15 106 C7
Queen Mary Ct TR11 145 B2
Queen Mary Rd TR11 145 B2
Queens Cl
[5] Indian Queens TR9 45 E1
Plymouth PL6 125 E6
Queen's Cres PL31 109 B3
Queen's Ct [6] TR18 143 E4
Queen's Gate
Plymouth, Lipson PL4 149 B4
Plymouth, Stoke PL3 148 A4
Queen's Gate Mews PL4 149 B4
Queen's Gate Villas PL4 149 B4
Queen's Gate Villas Rd PL4 149 B4
Queens Pk PL27 108 C4
Queens Rd
Plymouth PL5 123 F3
St Austell PL25 114 E3
Queen's Rd PL4 149 B4
Queen's Sq [24] TR18 143 E5
Queen St
Bude EX23 104 D6
Goldsithney TR20 89 E5
Lostwithiel PL22 112 C2
Penzance TR18 143 E5
Plymouth PL1 127 D2
St Just TR19 86 E6
Queen's Way
[2] Goldsithney TR20 89 E5
Hayle TR27 142 C5
Queen Terr PL17 40 C4
Quenchwell Rd TR3 81 F7
Quethiock Prim Sch PL14 52 C7
Quillet Rd TR18 143 B3
Quilver Cl PL26 85 D5
Quimperle Way PL14 113 E6
Quintrell Cl TR8 44 E3
Quintrell Downs Sta TR8 111 F3
Quintrell Gdns TR8 44 E3
Quintrell Rd TR7, TR8 111 E5

R

Rabys Row TR16 140 F8
Race Hill
Launceston PL15 106 C5
Truro TR4 81 C8
Race Hill Terr PL15 106 C5
Rachel's Way [17] TR9 45 E6
Radcliffe Cl PL6 124 E6
Radford Ave PL4 129 B1
Radford La PL10 132 D4
Radford Park Dr PL9 135 D6
Radford Park Rd PL9 135 D6
Radford Rd PL1 148 B1
Radford View PL9 135 D6
Radiant Ho PL1 148 B2
Radland Cross PL12 40 C3
Radnor Cl PL31 109 F4
Radnor Hall PL4 149 A3
Radnor Pl PL4 149 A3
Radnor Rd
Redruth, North Country TR16 140 C8
Redruth, Scorrier TR16 68 D3
Radnor St PL4 149 A3
Raginnis Hill [25] TR19 88 C1
Raglan Ct PL1 127 F2
Raglan Gdns PL1 127 F2
Raglan Rd PL1 127 F2
Railway Cotts
Camborne TR14 139 A3
Falmouth TR11 145 D3
[6] Plymouth, Ford PL2 127 F5
Plymouth, Plymstock PL9 135 D7
Tavistock PL19 147 B6
Railway Cres PL14 38 A4
Railway Terr
Bodmin PL31 109 D5
Carharrack TR16 80 F8
Railway Villas TR15 139 F6
Rainham Cl TR15 139 C8
Rainyfields PL28 107 D5
Rainy Fields Cl PL28 107 D5
Raleigh Cl PL28 107 C4
Raleigh Ct PL7 131 B6
Raleigh Pl [13] TR11 145 A4
Raleigh Rd PL28 107 C5
Raleigh St PL1 148 B3
Ralph's Ct PL19 147 B5
Ramage Cl PL6 125 F3
Rame Croft TR10 80 E1
Ramehead Cotts PL10 64 B1
Ramehead La PL10 64 B1
Rame La
Cawsand PL10 132 F1
Rame PL10 64 B2
Rame Terr TR10 80 E1
Rame View PL13 117 E5
Ramillies Ave PL5 124 A4
Ramoth Way TR6 55 B5
Ramsey Gdns PL5 124 D1
Ranch View PL15 106 A5
Randwick Park Rd PL9 135 D7
Ranelagh Ct TR7 111 C7
Ranelagh Mews PL31 109 D5
Ranelagh Rd PL25 114 F4
Ransum Way PL19 147 B4
Raphael Cl PL9 136 B5
Raphael Dr PL9 136 A6
Raphael Rd PL13 62 C1
Rapson Rd PL14 113 D6
Rashleigh Ave
Plymouth PL7 130 F7
Saltash PL12 122 D1
Rashleigh Ct PL25 115 C3
Rashleigh La PL23 116 A4
Rashleigh Mews PL25 115 A3
Rashleigh Pl PL25 114 F4
Rashleigh Vale TR1 137 E4
Ratcliffes La TR13 146 A5
Rattle St PL26 85 D5
Rawley Ct TR7 110 E5
Rawley La TR7 110 E5
Rawlin Cl PL6 129 C8
Rawlings La PL23 116 D5
Raymond Rd TR15 140 C4
Raymond Way PL7 130 D6
Raynham Rd PL3 128 B4
Read Cl TR10 144 B7
Reading Wlk PL5 124 C4
Readymoney Rd PL23 116 B3
Reawla La TR27 78 E3
Rebecca Cl PL24 60 B6
Recreation Rd PL2 128 C7
Recreation Road Ind Est PL2 128 C7
Rectory Gdns
Camborne TR14 138 C2
Lanreath PL13 62 B8
St Stephen PL26 58 B4
Rectory Rd
Camborne TR14 138 C2
Lanivet PL30 47 F6
Plymouth PL1 128 A2
St Buryan TR19 97 B6
St Dennis PL26 46 B1
St Stephen PL26 58 B4
Rectory The TR1 137 C5
Redannack [2] TR12 99 A2
Redannack N [1] TR12 99 A2
Redannick Cres TR1 137 B3
Redannick La TR1 137 B4
Redbrooke Rd TR14 138 E2
Redbrooke Terr TR14 138 E2
Reddicliff Cl PL9 135 E5
Reddicliff Rd PL9 135 D5
Reddington Rd PL3 129 B7
Redfern Ct [2] TR26 141 B5
Redhill Cl PL5 123 E4
Redinnick Gdns [4] TR18 143 E4
Redinnick Pl TR18 143 D4
Redinnick Terr [1] TR18 143 E4
Red La
Bugle PL26 47 C2
Rosudgeon TR20 89 F5
Redmoor Cl
Kelly Bray PL17 39 E6
Tavistock PL19 147 A7
Redmoor Rd PL17 39 E6
Redruth Cl PL5 124 A5
Redruth Highway TR15 140 E7
Redruth Rd TR13 146 D7
Redruth Sch TR15 140 A4
Redruth Sta TR15 140 C5
Redruth Tech Coll TR15 140 A5
Redvale Rd PL30 23 E3
Redvers Gr PL7 130 E4
Redvers Hts TR15 140 B3
Redwing Dr PL6 125 D8
Redwood Cl EX23 104 E5
Redwood Dr PL7 131 B5
Redwood Gr EX23 104 E5
Reeds Pk PL22 112 D2
Reeds Way TR7 110 D5
Reen Hill TR6 55 B4
Reen La TR6 55 B5
Reens Cres TR18 143 D7
Reens Rd TR18 143 C7
Reeves Cl TR13 91 B1
Regal Ct PL12 122 F2
Regan Ct TR10 144 A7
Regency Ho PL25 115 E3
Regent Bldgs [36] TR18 143 E5
Regent Ct PL4 149 A3
Regent Sq [21] TR18 143 E5
Regent St PL4 149 A3
Regent Terr
Penzance TR18 143 E4
St Just TR19 86 E6
Reigate Rd PL9 135 E8
Relistian La TR27 78 E3
Relistian Pk TR27 78 E3
Relubbus Hill TR20 90 A6
Relubbus La TR20 90 A6
Rendlesham Gdns PL6 125 E3
Rendle St
Delabole PL33 14 E3
Plymouth PL1 148 B3
Renney Rd PL9 135 C1
Rennie Ave PL5 123 C1
Renoir Cl PL9 136 A6
Renown St PL2 127 E6
Reperry Cross PL30 47 F6
Reppersfield Row TR13 90 F3
Rescorla Ct TR27 142 C5
Research Way PL6 125 C4
Reservoir Cres PL9 136 B7
Reservoir La [1] PL3 128 F6
Reservoir Rd
Plymouth, Hartley PL3 128 F6
Plymouth, Plymstock PL9 136 B7
Reservoir Way PL9 136 B7
Reskadinnick Rd TR14 138 B4
Resolution Ho PL4 149 B3
Respryn Cl PL14 113 D6
Respryn Rd PL31 48 D8
Restormel Castle★ PL22 112 C5
Restormel Ind Est PL22 112 D2
Restormel Rd
Looe PL13 117 D4
Lostwithiel PL22 112 C4
Newlyn TR18 143 C3
Plymouth PL4 148 C4
Restormel Terr
Falmouth TR11 145 B3
Plymouth PL4 148 C4

Restronguet Hill TR11 82 B4
Resugga Green Residential Homes Pk PL26 59 D7
Reswythen Wlk [4] TR14 138 F7
Retallack Gdns [3] TR20 89 E5
Retallick Mdws PL25 115 B5
Retanna Cvn Pk TR13 92 D7
Retanning La PL26 58 E1
Retreat The
[8] Chacewater TR4 69 A3
Plymouth PL3 129 B7
St Columb Major TR9 45 E6
Revell Park Rd PL7 130 D6
Revel Rd PL3 129 A6
Reynolds Gr PL5 127 C8
Reynolds Rd PL7 130 C6
Rheola Gdns PL6 125 D3
Rhind St PL31 109 E5
Rhodes Cl PL7 130 E7
Rhubarb Hill TR8 43 B1
Rhude Cross EX23 5 B3
Rialton Hts TR7 111 E7
Rialton Rd TR7, TR8 111 E6
Ribble Gdns PL3 129 D7
Rice La PL26 85 C5
Richard Lander Sch TR1 69 F3
Richards Cres TR1 69 F3
Richards La TR16 67 E4
Richards Row PL3 128 F7
Richards Terr PL10 132 E5
Richmond Hill TR1 137 B4
Richmond Pl
[40] St Ives TR26 141 B6
[3] Truro TR1 137 B4
Richmond Rd
Pelynt PL13 62 D6
Plymouth PL6 125 A2
Richmond St
Heamoor TR18 143 C7
Penzance TR18 143 E6
Richmond Terr
Buckland Monachorum PL20 41 F3
Truro TR1 137 B4
Richmond Way TR26 141 D1
Richmond Wlk PL1 127 F1
Ricketts Rd PL26 59 A1
Rick Mdw PL15 18 E6
Ride The PL7, PL9 129 D2
Ridge Cross PL9 136 A3
Ridgegrove Hill PL15 106 D6
Ridgegrove La PL15 106 C7
Ridge Ho PL4 129 A4
Ridgeo Mill TR18 143 F8
Ridge Park Ave PL4 128 D4
Ridge Park Rd PL7 130 F5
Ridge Pk PL7 130 E5
Ridge Rd PL7 130 E3
Ridgevale Cl TR18 143 F8
Ridgevale La TR18 143 F8
Ridgeway
[28] Perranporth TR6 55 A5
Plymouth, Plympton PL7 130 D5
Plymouth, Plympton St Maurice PL7 130 F5
Probus TR2 71 C6
Saltash PL12 122 D1
Ridgeway Sch PL7 130 E5
Ridgewell Terr TR9 57 E8
Ridgewood Cl PL26 114 F1
Riga Terr PL3 129 C4
Rigdale Cl PL6 129 A7
Ringmore Way PL5 124 B3
Ringway Flats [8] PL31 109 D5
Ringwell Valley Holiday Pk TR3 81 F7
Rinsey La TR13 90 D2
Risdon Ave PL4 129 B1
Rivendell PL27 108 C4
River Ct
Saltash PL12 122 D5
Tavistock PL19 147 D6
Riverford Cl PL6 125 D7
Riversdale Pl [8] PL27 108 B5
Riverside
Angarrack TR27 78 C4
[3] Chacewater TR4 69 A3
Lanivet PL30 47 E7
Launceston PL15 106 B7
Lelant TR26 77 E4
Padstow PL28 107 E5
Riverside Ave TR7 110 A5
Riverside Bsns Pk PL1 127 E3
Riverside Cl [1] PL20 42 C4
Riverside Cott PL12 122 C1
Riverside Cres TR7 110 A5
Riverside Ct PL22 112 C2
Riverside Ho TR1 137 D1
Riverside Holiday Pk TR8 111 B1
Riverside Mews
Angarrack TR27 78 C5
Saltash PL12 123 A3
Riverside Pl PL1 127 D2
Riverside View TR1 137 E3
Riverside Wlk PL5 124 B6
River St
Mevagissey PL26 73 C3
Portscatho TR2 83 B2
Truro TR1 137 C4
Rivers The PL12 122 E1
Riverview TR11 145 A6
River View
Flushing TR11 145 B7
Gunnislake PL18 40 E5
River View *continued*
Lerryn PL22 61 C7
Plymouth PL4 129 B1
Saltash PL12 122 F3
Tresillian TR2 70 E4
River View La PL4 129 B1
River Wlk PL25 114 B3
Riviera Apartments TR26 141 D2
Riviera Est TR1 70 D1
Riviera La TR2 95 A6
Riviere Chalet Camp TR27 142 A7
Riviere Sands Holiday Park TR27 142 B8
Riviere Towans TR27 142 B7
Roach's Ct TR26 141 E1
Roach's Row TR15 140 B5
Robartes Ct [13] TR1 137 C4
Robartes Gardens Flats PL25 114 E4
Robartes Gdns PL25 114 E4
Robartes Jun Sch PL31 109 D4
Robartes Pl PL25 114 E5
Robartes Rd
Bodmin PL31 109 D4
Newquay TR7 110 F5
St Dennis PL26 58 C8
Robartes Terr
[3] Illogan TR16 67 E4
Lostwithiel PL22 112 C3
Robert Adams Cl PL7 130 B5
Robert Eliot Ct PL25 114 B3
Robert Hichens Rd TR11 145 A5
Roberts Ave PL11 127 B3
Roberts Rd PL5 127 D8
Robin Dr PL15 106 E4
Robins Cl [13] PL24 60 B4
Robins Way PL9 135 E8
Roborough Ave PL6 125 B5
Roborough Cl PL6 125 B5
Roborough Down La PL6 121 F5
Roborough La PL5 124 D8
Robyns Cl PL7 131 B5
Roche Com Prim Sch PL26 46 F2
Roche Rd
Bugle PL26 47 C2
Stenalees PL26 59 C7
Roche Rural Workshops PL26 47 A4
Roche Sta PL26 47 A4
Rochester Rd [3] PL4 128 E4
Rochford Cres PL5 123 F5
Rock Cl [1] TR14 138 F2
Rock Close Ho TR27 142 A1
Rockfield Ave PL6 124 F6
Rock Gdns PL9 129 D1
Rockhaven Gdns PL27 21 F3
Rockhead St PL33 14 E3
Rock Hill PL5 124 C7
Rockingham Rd PL3 129 A5
Rock La PL31 109 C4
Rock Rd
Newlyn TR18 143 C3
St Minver PL27 21 E2
Rock Terr
Heamoor TR18 143 C7
Plymouth PL7 130 D4
Rock Twrs PL13 117 D2
Rock View Parc PL26 47 A3
Rock Villas PL27 21 D2
Rockville Pk PL9 135 E8
Rockwood Rd PL6 125 E8
Rocky Hill PL19 147 B5
Rocky La
Praa Sands TR20 90 C6
St Agnes TR5 54 C2
Veryan TR2 83 D5
Rocky Park Ave PL9 135 E8
Rocky Park Rd PL9 135 E8
Rodda Cl PL18 41 A7
Rodda's Rd TR4 68 C6
Roddick Way [8] PL7 131 C5
Rodings The PL14 51 F5
Rodney St PL5 127 D8
Rodwell Cl TR15 140 D5
Rodwill Cl TR27 78 E1
Roebuck Villas TR11 145 D3
Roekindale Cl TR15 139 D6
Roeselare Ave PL11 127 A3
Roeselare Cl PL11 127 A3
Rogate Dr PL6 125 D4
Rogate Wlk PL6 125 D4
Rogers Dr PL12 122 D4
Roland Bailey Gdns PL19 147 A6
Rollis Park Cl PL9 135 C8
Rollis Park Rd PL9 135 C8
Rolston Cl PL6 124 D6
Roma Cl TR7 111 C7
Roma Ct TR27 142 B5
Roman Bridge PL13 62 D1
Roman Dr PL31 109 F2
Roman Rd PL5 123 E2
Roman Way PL5 123 E2
Romilly Gdns PL7 130 B5
Romney Cl PL5 124 B1
Ronald Terr PL2 127 F5
Ronsdale Cl PL9 135 D8
Roope Cl PL5 127 C7
Ropehaven Cl PL25 114 E6
Ropehaven Rd PL25 114 E6
Roper Ave PL9 135 D8
Ropewalk Ct [2] TR11 145 C3
Ropewalk Rd TR3 137 C1
Ropewalk The TR18 143 C4
Rope Wlk
Mount Hawke TR4 68 C6
Padstow PL28 107 D5
Rope Wlk The
[3] St Ives TR26 141 B6
[9] St Mawes TR2 95 A6
Rorkes Cl PL5 123 E2
Roscadghill Parc [1] TR18 143 C7
Roscadghill Rd TR18 143 C6
Roscarrack TR15 139 B8
Roscarrack Cl TR11 144 E2
Roscarrack Rd TR11 144 D1
Roscarrick Villas TR11 93 D3
Roscarrock Hill PL29 22 D7
Roseacre Dr [8] TR15 140 C5
Roseannon TR11 93 D3
Rosebery Ave PL4 149 C4
Rosebery La PL4 149 C4
Rosebery Rd PL4 149 C4
Roseclave Cl PL7 131 C6
Rosecott Pk EX23 5 A6
Rose Cotts
Camborne TR14 138 E3
Plymouth PL6 129 B8
Stithians TR3 80 F3
Rosecraddoc Holiday Village PL14 38 B2
Rosecraddoc Lodge Holiday Bglws PL14 38 B2
Rosecraddoc View PL14 38 A2
Rosedale Ave PL2 128 D7
Rosedale Gdns PL31 35 B2
Rosedale Rd TR1 137 C5
Rosedene Farm TR3 69 C4
Rosedown Ave PL2 128 A7
Rose Eglos TR11 144 C2
Rose Eglos Cl TR11 144 C2
Rose Gdns PL6 125 E6
Rosehill
Ladock TR2 57 C1
Lanivet PL30 47 C6
Marazion TR17 89 B5
Mylor Bridge TR11 82 A2
Rose Hill
Altarnun PL15 26 C8
Fowey PL23 116 C4
Porthtowan TR4 68 A6
Port Isaac PL29 22 D7
Redruth TR15 140 B5
Sticker PL26 58 F1
Rose Hill Cl PL22 112 C2
Rosehill Gdns TR18 143 B6
Rosehill Mdw TR18 143 B6
Rose Hill Rd PL24 60 B5
Rose Hill Terr PL17 41 A3
Rose Hill Touring Pk TR4 68 A6
Rosehip Cl PL6 125 E7
Rose In The Bush Pk TR12 99 B8
Rose La [23] TR26 141 B6
Roseland Com Sch The TR2 72 A4
Roseland Cres
[6] Chacewater TR4 69 A3
Tregony TR2 71 F3
Roseland Flats TR2 82 E1
Roseland Gdns
Bodmin PL31 109 E6
Redruth TR15 140 D6
Veryan TR2 83 F6
Roseland Pk TR14 138 D4
Roselands Rd PL31 109 F6
Roseland Terr TR4 55 F2
Roselidden Parc TR13 146 B7
Roseline Est TR13 80 D1
Roselyon Pl PL24 60 C5
Roselyon Prep Sch PL24 60 C4
Rose Mdw TR3 80 F3
Rose Mdws TR4 55 D4
Rosemellen Terr PL14 113 B4
Rosemellin TR14 138 E4
Rosemellin Com Prim Sch TR14 138 E4
Rosemorran [28] TR26 141 B5
Rosemullion [4] TR6 55 A5
Rosemullion Gdns [3] TR14 138 F7
Rose Mullion Gdns PL17 39 F5
Rosemullion Ho TR1 69 E4
Rosemundy TR5 54 D1
Rosenannon La TR15 139 B8
Rosenannon Rd TR15 139 B8
Rose Row TR15 140 B5
Rose Terr
Gunnislake PL18 40 E5
Mitchell TR8 56 F5
[23] Penzance TR18 143 E6
Rosevale TR18 143 D4
Rosevale Cres TR14 138 C4
Rosevale Gdns PL30 59 F8
Rosevallley TR3 69 C3
Rose Valley TR19 75 B2
Rosevallon La PL31 109 C5
Rosevean Ave TR14 138 E3
Rosevean Cl TR14 138 E3
Rosevean Ct [8] PL3 128 F6
Rosevean Gdns PL3 128 F6
Rosevean Ho [7] PL3 128 F6
Rosevean Rd TR18 143 E6
Rosevean Terr TR18 143 E6
Roseveare Cl PL9 136 A8
Roseveare Dr PL26 46 D1
Roseveare Mobile Home Pk PL26 46 D1
Rosevear Rd PL26 47 C1
Rosewall Cotts [16] TR26 141 A5
Rosewall Terr [17] TR26 141 A5
Rosewarne TR13 91 A1
Rosewarne Cl TR14 138 D4
Rosewarne Farm Cvn Pk TR14 138 D4
Rosewarne Gdns TR14 138 D3
Rosewarne Manor Holiday Village TR27 78 F5
Rosewarne Mdws TR14 138 D5
Rosewarne Mews TR14 138 D4
Rosewarne Pk TR14 138 E4
Rosewarne Rd
[1] Camborne TR14 138 D3
Carnhell Green TR27 78 F4
Rosewarne Terr TR14 138 D5
Rosewarne (Trng Ctr) TR14 138 D5
Rosewater Cvn Pk PL30 23 D7
Rosewin Mews [3] TR9 45 E6
Rosewin Row
[2] St Columb Major TR9 45 E6
Truro TR1 137 D5
Rosewithian Cl TR27 78 E6
Rosewood Cl PL9 135 F5
Roseworthy Hill TR14 78 F6
Rosina Way PL26 59 D7
Roskear TR14 138 E4
Roskear Croft TR14 138 E6
Roskear Fields TR14 138 E4
Roskear Parc TR14 138 F5
Roskear Rd TR14 138 E3
Roskear Sch TR14 138 F3
Roskilling TR13 146 D7
Roskilling Wartha TR13 146 D7
Roskilly Cotts TR19 88 C2
Roskilly's Open Farm* TR12 101 D3
Roskrow Cl TR16 80 A5
Roskruge Cl TR13 146 D8
Ros Lyn TR26 141 C1
Roslyn Cl
St Austell PL25 114 F5
[2] St Austell PL25 115 A5
Rosparc TR2 71 D6
Rosparvah Gdns TR18 143 C7
Rospeath Cres PL2 128 D8
Rospeath La TR20 89 C7
Rossett Gdns PL31 35 B1
Rossiter Ho TR19 96 B6
Rosslyn Park Rd PL3 128 D5
Ross St PL2 127 E4
Rossventon TR4 69 A1
Rostalek PL30 24 B2
Rothbury Cl PL6 125 E4
Rothbury Gdns PL6 125 D4
Rothesay Gdns PL5 124 D3
Rougemont Cl PL3 129 B7
Rough La TR3 81 B4
Rough St TR16 80 D6
Roughtor Dr PL32 105 C3
Roughtor Rd PL32 15 D1
Roughtor View PL33 14 D2
Roundhayes Farm Cotts EX23 10 C5
Round Ring TR10 144 D8
Round's La PL34 14 D7
Rous Rd PL12 40 C2
Rowan Cl
Bodmin PL31 109 B4
Plymouth PL7 131 B5
Tavistock PL19 147 C3
Rowan Ct PL12 122 C2
Rowans The
Bude EX23 104 E4
Lifton PL16 19 F4
St Mellion PL12 53 C8
Rowan Way PL6 125 E7
Rowden St PL3 128 E5
Rowdown Cl PL7 131 D4
Rowe's La TR13 146 E8
Rowe St PL11 127 B3
Rowes Terr PL26 58 D5
Row La PL5 123 E2
Rowland Cl PL9 135 E5
Rowse Gdns PL18 41 A3
Row The
Pillaton PL12 53 B7
Portloe TR2 84 A4
Royal Cornwall Hospl TR1 69 E4
Royal Cornwall Mus* TR1 137 C4
Royale Ct TR18 143 F6
Royal Eye Infmy PL4 128 E4
Royalist Ct [14] TR11 145 C3
Royal Navy Ave PL2 127 F6
Royal Par PL1 148 C2
Royal Talbot PL22 112 C2
Royal William Rd PL1 134 A8
Roydon Cl PL15 106 B8
Roydon La PL15 106 B8
Roydon Rd PL15 106 B8
Royffe Way PL31 109 F3
Ruby Terr TR13 92 B8
Rudyerd Wlk PL3 129 D6
Rufford Cl PL2 128 A7
Rule Cross EX23 2 E2
Ruminella View TR12 103 A4
Rumours Apartments TR7 111 B7
Rundle Ct PL14 113 B4
Rundles Ct TR1 137 E3
Runnymede Ct PL6 125 E2
Rush Park Terr PL18 40 F7
Ruskin Cres PL5 124 D2
Ruskin Ct TR9 45 D5
Russell Ave PL3 128 F7
Russell Cl
Gunnislake PL18 41 A7
Plymouth PL9 136 B7
Russell Cl *continued*
Saltash PL12 122 C3
Russell Court Gdns PL19 147 B6
Russell Ct
Plymouth PL1 148 C2
Saltash PL12 122 C3
Tavistock PL19 147 B6
Russell Mews PL31 109 C5
Russell Pl PL1 148 B4
Russell St
[7] Liskeard PL14 113 C5
Tavistock PL19 147 C5
Russell Way [4] TR10 144 C7
Russet Wood PL5 123 F4
Rutger Pl PL1 148 A4
Ruthern Valley PL30 34 A1
Ruthven Cl PL6 128 F8
Ruthy's La PL28 107 D5
Rutland Rd PL4 128 F4
Rydal Cl PL6 125 D2
Ryder Rd PL2 127 F4
Rydon La EX22 8 F7
Rye Hill
Ponsanooth TR3 81 B4
Saltash PL12 122 C2
Rylands Terr PL30 24 B3

S

Saffron Cl PL23 116 C4
Sail Loft Flats [2] TR26 141 B6
St Agnes Mus* TR5 54 C1
St Agnes Sch TR5 54 C1
St Albans Pk PL20 42 D2
St Ambrusca Rd TR8 110 A3
St Andrew's CE Prim Sch
Buckland Monachorum PL20 41 F3
Plymouth PL1 148 B2
St Andrews Cl
[12] Bere Alston PL20 41 B1
Ponsanooth TR3 81 B4
Saltash PL12 122 C2
St Andrew's Cl PL18 41 A3
St Andrew's Cross [1] PL1 149 A2
St Andrew's Pl PL10 133 A1
St Andrews Rd PL19 147 D2
St Andrew's Rd
Par PL24 60 C5
[12] Stratton EX23 4 D1
St Andrew's St
Cawsand PL10 133 A1
[1] St Ives TR26 141 B5
St Andrew St
Millbrook PL10 132 E5
Plymouth PL1 148 C2
St Andrews Terr TR3 81 B4
St Andrew's Terr PL24 60 C5
St Annes TR11 93 D3
St Annes Cl
Lelant TR26 77 E4
Whitstone EX22 7 F1
St Annes Rd [17] PL24 60 B4
St Anne's Rd
Newquay TR7 111 A7
Plymouth PL6 125 D6
Saltash PL12 122 E3
[3] Trewoon PL25 59 A3
St Ann's Hill EX23 104 F3
St Anta Rd TR26 141 E1
St Anthony Way TR11 145 A2
St Aubyn Ave PL2 127 F5
St Aubyn Cres TR7 111 A6
St Aubyn Est TR14 79 B2
St Aubyn Rd PL1 127 E3
St Aubyns TR20 89 E5
St Aubyn's Rd TR1 137 D3
St Aubyn St PL1 127 E2
St Aubyn's Vean TR1 137 D3
St Austell Bay Bsns Pk PL25 115 E4
St Austell Com Hospl PL26 114 F1
St Austell Hospl PL25 114 A3
St Austell Rd PL24 115 F5
St Austell Row [2] TR2 95 A6
St Austell St
Summercourt TR8 57 C6
Truro TR1 137 D4
St Austell Sta PL25 114 D4
St Barnabas Ct PL1 148 A4
St Barnabas Hospl PL12 122 F2
St Barnabas Terr PL1 148 A4
St Benedicts Cl [13] PL24 60 D5
St Benets Cl PL30 47 E6
St Blazey Rd PL24 60 C4
St Boniface Cl PL2 128 C7
St Boniface Dr PL2 128 C7
St Boniface's RC Coll PL5 124 E1
St Breaca Cl TR13 91 A3
St Breock Prim Sch PL27 108 B5
St Breward Prim Sch PL30 24 B3
St Bridget Ave PL6 124 F1
St Budeaux Ferry Rd Sta PL5 127 D8
St Budeaux Foundation CE Jun Sch PL5 123 F2
St Budeaux Victoria Rd Sta PL5 123 D1
St Buryan Hill TR19 96 F4
St Buryan Prim Sch TR19 97 B6
St Cadocs PL28 31 F7
St Carantoc Way TR8 43 D3

St Catherine's Castle★ PL23 116 B2
St Catherine's CE Prim Sch PL15 106 A4
St Catherines Ct PL23 116 C3
St Clare Flats TR18 143 D6
St Clare St TR18 143 D6
St Cleer Dr PL27 108 D6
St Cleer Prim Sch PL14 38 A3
St Cleer Rd PL14 113 C7
St Clement's Cl TR1 137 E4
St Clement's Hill TR1 137 E4
St Clements Parc TR1 137 E4
St Clement St TR1 137 D5
St Clements Terr 26 TR19 88 C1
St Clement's Terr 3 TR1 137 D5
St Clement Vean TR1 137 F6
St Columb Bsns Ctr TR9 45 E6
St Columb Major Bsns Pk TR9 45 E5
St Columb Major Com Prim Sch TR9 45 D6
St Columb Major Ind Est TR9 45 D5
St Columb Minor Sch TR7 111 D7
St Columb Road Ind Workshops TR9 45 D2
St Columb Road Sta TR9 45 D2
St Crewenna Terr TR27 78 E1
St Cuthbert Cl PL15 106 B7
St Cuthbert's Rd TR7 110 D6
St Cyriac PL30 47 F1
St Davids Cl EX23 4 C8
St David's Rd PL19 147 E5
St Day & Carharrack Com Sch TR16 68 E1
St Day Rd
 Redruth TR15 140 C5
 Redruth TR16 140 E5
St Dennis Com Prim Sch PL26 58 C8
St Dominic Cl PL31 109 E5
St Dominick CE Sch PL12 40 D2
St Dominic Pk PL17 40 C4
St Dominic Sq 4 TR1 137 C4
St Dominic St
 9 Penzance TR18 143 E6
 5 Truro TR1 137 C4
St Dunstan's Abbey Plymouth Coll Jun Sch PL1 148 A3
St Dunstan's Terr PL4 149 C3
St Edmunds La PL28 107 D5
St Edward Gdns PL6 125 B1
St Edward's CE Prim Sch PL6 125 C1
St Eia St TR26 141 C6
St Elizabeth Cl PL7 130 F3
St Elvan Cres TR13 91 A1
St Elwyns Rise TR27 142 B6
St Enodoc Cl PL27 108 D6
St Erme with Trispen Com Prim Sch TR4 70 D8
St Erth Com Prim Sch TR27 142 A1
St Erth Hill TR27 77 F1
St Erth Ind Est TR27 77 E2
St Erth Rd PL2 128 D7
St Erth Sta TR27 77 E2
St Eval Pl PL5 123 E4
St Fimbarrus Rd PL23 116 C3
St Francis CE Prim Sch TR11 144 E3
St Francis Ct PL5 124 B3
St Francis Rd TR9 45 E2
St Francis St 6 TR18 143 E6
St Gabriel's Ave PL3 128 D5
St George's Arc TR11 145 B4
St George's Ave PL2 128 C7
St George's CE Prim Sch PL1 148 A1
St George's Cres PL31 109 C4
St Georges Ct
 Looe PL13 117 D2
 1 Plymouth PL2 127 F4
St George's Hill TR6 55 A4
St Georges Hill Cl 13 TR6 55 A4
St George's Pk PL22 112 C3
St Georges Rd
 Nanpean PL26 58 D6
 Saltash PL12 122 D3
St George's Rd
 Hayle TR27 142 C5
 Looe PL13 117 D4
 Newquay TR7 110 D5
 Saltash PL12 122 E3
 Truro TR1 137 B5
St George's Terr
 Perranporth TR6 54 F4
 Plymouth PL2 127 F4
St Germans Prim Sch PL12 65 A8
St Germans Rd PL17 39 F3
St Germans Sta PL12 65 B8
St Giles Dr PL27 108 C6
St Giles Mews PL27 108 C6
St Giles on the Heath Com Sch PL15 13 F1
St Gluvias Parc TR10 144 D8
St Gluvias St TR10 144 D7
St Golder Rd TR18 143 B3
St Grace's Ct TR2 71 C6
St Helens Wlk PL5 124 C5
St Henry St 4 TR18 143 E6
St Hilary Sch TR20 89 F6
St Hilary Terr PL4 149 C3
St Ive Rd PL14 38 E4
St Ives Bay Chalet & Cvn Pk TR27 78 B6
St Ives Bay Holiday Pk TR27 78 B6
St Ives Holiday Village TR20, TR26 77 C3
St Ives Jun & Inf Schs TR26 141 A5
St Ives La TR27 66 B1
St Ives Museum★ TR26 141 C6
St Ives Mushroom Farm TR26 77 A5
St Ives Rd
 Carbis Bay TR26 141 D1
 Pendeen TR19 75 A1
St Ives Sch TR26 141 B3
St Ives Sta TR26 141 B5
St James Ct
 Delabole PL33 14 E2
 Plymouth PL1 148 B2
 Torpoint PL11 127 B3
St James Mews PL1 148 B2
St James Pl TR13 146 B6
St James' Pl E PL1 148 B2
St James' Pl W PL1 148 B2
St James Rd PL11 127 B2
St James' St TR18 143 E5
St James's Terr TR10 144 B7
St James View TR9 57 D8
St Johns PL19 147 C5
St Johns Ave PL19 147 C5
St John's Bridge Rd PL4 149 B2
St Johns Cl PL6 125 D4
St John's Cl
 Helston TR13 146 A6
 Millbrook PL10 132 E5
St Johns Ct 7 TR18 143 E5
St John's Ct
 7 Falmouth TR11 145 A4
 Hayle TR27 142 D6
St John's Dr PL9 135 B6
St Johns Gdns TR11 145 B6
St Johns La PL11 132 B8
St John's RC Prim Sch TR14 138 E2
St Johns Rd
 Launceston PL15 106 B4
 Plymouth PL4 149 C2
St John's Rd
 Helston TR13 146 B6
 Horrabridge PL20 42 C4
 Millbrook PL10 132 F5
 Newquay TR7 110 D5
 Plymouth PL4 149 B2
 Plymouth, Turnchapel PL9 135 A6
St John's St
 Hayle TR27 142 D6
 Plymouth PL4 149 B2
St John's Terr
 Devoran TR3 81 F6
 Pendeen TR19 75 A1
 5 Penzance TR18 143 E6
St Johns Wlk TR26 77 A7
St Joseph's Cl PL6 124 F1
St Joseph's RC Prim Sch PL1 127 E2
St Joseph's Rd PL15 106 B8
St Joseph's Sch PL15 106 B7
St Jude's Rd PL4 149 B2
St Julian's Cotts PL10 133 E7
St Julitta PL30 48 A1
St Just Prim Sch TR19 86 E6
St Keri Ct PL15 18 A5
St Keverne Com Prim Sch TR12 101 D4
St Keverne Pl PL2 128 D8
St Keverne Rural Workshops TR12 101 C3
St Kew Com Prim Sch PL30 22 F3
St Keyne Cl TR1 137 C6
St Keyne Sta PL14 51 C3
St Lawrence Mews PL4 149 A4
St Lawrence Rd
 Bodmin PL30, PL31 109 A4
 Plymouth PL4 149 A4
St Leonards PL31 109 C5
St Leonard's Rd
 Launceston PL15 106 B8
 Plymouth PL4 149 C2
St Leonards Terr PL31 109 C5
St Leo Pl PL2 127 E4
St Levan Cl 8 TR17 89 C5
St Levan Com Prim Sch TR19 96 E5
St Levan Rd
 7 Marazion TR17 89 C5
 Plymouth PL2 127 F5
St Mabyn CE Sch PL30 34 D8
St Mabyn Holiday Pk PL30 34 E8
St Madderns CE Sch TR20 143 A8
St Margarets Holiday Pk PL26 59 A1
St Margarets La PL26 59 A1
St Margarets Rd PL7 130 B7
St Mark's Prim Sch EX23 2 E2
St Marks Rd PL6 125 D5
St Marnarch's PL13 62 B8
St Marnarch's Rd PL13 62 B8
St Martin-in-Meneage Com Prim Sch TR12 100 D6
St Martin's Ave PL3 128 D7
St Martin's CE Prim Sch PL14 113 D5
St Martins Cl
 Lewannick PL15 27 B7
St Martins Cl *continued*
 Looe PL13 117 D5
St Martin's Cl 2 TR14 138 C2
St Martin's Cres TR14 138 C3
St Martins Rd EX23 7 B8
St Martin's Rd PL13 117 D6
St Martin's Terr TR14 138 C4
St Marwenne Cl EX23 7 B6
St Maryhaye PL19 147 A5
St Mary's PL13 117 D3
St Mary's CE Prim Sch TR18 143 E4
St Mary's CE Sch TR1 137 C6
St Marys Cl PL7 130 D5
St Mary's Cl PL31 109 C4
St Mary's Cres PL31 109 C4
St Marys Ct PL7 130 D5
St Mary's Ct TR7 110 D5
St Mary's Gdns PL31 109 C4
St Mary's RC Prim Sch
 Bodmin PL31 109 C4
 Falmouth TR11 144 E3
St Mary's RC Sch TR18 143 E7
St Marys Rd PL24 60 B4
St Mary's Rd
 Bodmin PL31 109 B3
 Launceston PL15 106 C8
 Newquay TR7 110 D5
 Plymouth PL7 130 C6
St Mary's St
 Penzance TR18 143 E6
 12 Truro TR1 137 D4
St Mary's Street Mews 10 TR1 137 D4
St Mary St PL1 148 A2
St Mary's Terr TR18 143 E5
St Mary's Terr 4 TR1 137 C5
St Matthews Hill PL27 108 D5
St Maurice Ct PL7 130 F4
St Maurice Mews PL7 130 E4
St Maurice Rd PL7 130 F3
St Maurice View PL7 131 B4
St Mawes Castle★ TR2 95 A5
St Mawes Com Prim Sch TR2 95 A6
St Mawes Terr 8 PL2 127 F5
St Mawgan Cl PL31 109 F5
St Mellans Terr 5 TR12 99 A1
St Mellion CE School PL12 53 D8
St Meriadoc CE Inf Sch TR14 138 C2
St Meriadoc CE Jun Sch TR14 138 B2
St Meriadoc Rd TR14 138 C3
St Merryn Airfield PL28 31 F6
St Merryn Holiday Village PL28 31 F7
St Merryn Sch PL28 31 E8
St Mewan Com Prim Sch PL26 59 A2
St Mewan La PL25, PL26 59 A3
St Michael Ave PL2 127 F5
St Michael CE Prim Sch TR13 146 C5
St Michaels Cl PL15 19 C1
St Michael's Cl
 Hayle TR27 142 B4
 Plymouth PL1 127 E1
St Michael's Cotts 11 TR18 143 E5
St Michaels Ct
 Mawnan Smith TR11 93 D3
 18 Penzance TR18 143 E5
St Michael's Ct 7 PL1 127 F3
St Michael's Hospl TR27 142 B4
St Michael's Mount★ TR17 89 B4
St Michael's RC Small Sch TR1 137 C4
St Michael's Rd
 Newquay TR7 110 D5
 Perranporth TR6 55 A4
 Ponsanooth TR3 81 C4
 9 Stratton EX23 4 D1
St Michael's St TR18 143 E6
St Michael's Terr
 Penzance TR18 143 D6
 8 Plymouth, Devonport PL1 127 F3
 Plymouth PL4 148 C4
St Minver House Holiday Est PL27 22 A3
St Minver Sch PL27 21 F3
St Modwen Rd PL6 129 F7
St Moritz Ct PL27 21 D5
St Moritz Villas PL27 21 D5
St Nazaire App PL1 127 F2
St Nazaire Cl PL1 127 E2
St Neot Com Prim Sch PL14 36 F2
St Newlyn East Prim Sch TR8 56 B7
St Nicholas' CE Sch PL11 64 C4
St Nicholas Cl TR27 78 C6
St Nicholas Ct 1 TR26 141 B6
St Nicholas Pk PL22 112 B3
St Nicholas St
 Bodmin PL31 109 E4
 14 Truro TR1 137 D4
St Nonna's Cl PL15 26 C8
St Olaf's Rd 13 EX23 4 D1
St Pancras Ave PL2 128 D8
St Paternus Cl PL15 27 E8
St Pauls Cl PL3 129 C5
St Paul's RC Prim Sch PL5 123 D1
St Paul St PL1 134 A8
St Peter Cl PL7 130 F4
St Peter's CE Jun Sch PL19 147 D5
St Peters CE Prim Sch PL1 148 B3
St Peters Ct PL1 148 A3
St Peter's Hill TR18 143 C1
St Peter's RC Prim Sch PL5 124 B5
St Peters Rd
 Plymouth PL5 124 C2
 11 Stratton EX23 4 D1
St Peter's Rd TR11 145 B7
St Peters St 16 TR26 141 B6
St Peters Way TR13 98 C8
St Petroc's CE Prim Sch PL31 109 E4
St Petroc's Cl PL31 109 E4
St Petrocs Mdw PL28 107 C5
St Petroc's Sch EX23 104 D7
St Petry TR20 89 E5
St Philip St 8 TR18 143 E6
St Piran Cl PL31 109 B4
St Pirans Cl 2 TR1 137 D4
St Piran's Cl PL25 114 F6
St Pirans Ct
 Camborne TR14 138 D3
 13 Penzance TR18 143 E5
 Tintagel PL34 14 E8
St Piran's Hill TR3 81 D6
St Pirans Ho 15 TR6 55 A5
St Pirans Par 10 TR6 55 A5
St Pirans Parc 14 TR13 98 C8
St Piran's Prep Sch TR27 142 B4
St Pirans Rd TR6 55 A5
St Piran's Rd TR7 110 D6
St Pirans Way TR20 89 D4
St Pol-de-Leon View TR19 88 C2
St Rumon's CE Inf Sch PL19 147 C6
St Sampsons Cl 6 PL24 60 D5
St Sampson's Terr PL23 61 B5
St Saviour's Hill PL23 116 D2
St Saviour's La PL28 107 D6
St Simon's La PL4 129 B3
St Smithwick Way TR11 145 C3
St Stephen Churchtown Com Prim Sch PL26 58 B4
St Stephen Rd PL7 130 F3
St Stephens Com Prim Sch
 Launceston PL15 106 B8
 Saltash PL12 122 E2
St Stephens Ct PL15 106 B7
St Stephen's Hill
 Launceston PL15 106 B7
 Saltash PL12 122 C1
St Stephen's Pl PL7 130 E5
St Stephens Rd PL26 58 E1
St Stephen's Rd PL12 122 E2
St Stephen St PL1 127 F1
St Sulien
 Luxulyan PL30 48 A1
 Luxulyan PL30 60 A8
St Teresa Ho PL4 149 A3
St Therese Cl 20 PL17 39 F4
St Therese's Ct PL1 127 F2
St Thomas Cl
 Plymouth PL7 130 F3
 Truro TR1 69 F3
St Thomas Hill PL15 106 B6
St Thomas Rd PL15 106 B6
St Thomas' Rd TR7 110 F5
St Thomas St TR10 144 D7
St Tinney Farm PL32 10 D1
St Treath Com Prim Sch PL30 23 E7
St Tudy CE Prim Sch PL30 23 E3
St Uny CE Sch TR26 141 D1
St Uny Cl TR26 77 E3
St Uny Cres TR15 139 F5
St Vincent St PL2 127 E4
St Warren St 7 TR18 143 E6
St Wenn Sch PL30 46 D7
St Winnolls Pk PL13 117 D4
St Winnow Barton Farm Mus★ PL22 61 A8
St Winnow CE Sch PL22 112 F2
Salamanca St PL11 127 B3
Salcombe Rd PL4 149 C4
Salisbury Ope PL3 128 B5
Salisbury Rd
 Plymouth PL4 149 C4
 Truro TR1 137 B4
Salisbury Road Jun Sch PL4 149 C3
Salmon Row 3 TR1 137 D4
Saltash Bsns Pk PL12 122 C4
Saltash Com Sch PL12 122 E1
Saltash Ind Est PL12 122 D4
Saltash Parkway Ind Est PL12 122 B4
Saltash Rd
 Callington PL17 39 F4
 Plymouth, Keyham PL2 127 E6
 Plymouth PL3 148 C4
Saltash Sta PL12 123 A2
Saltbox Cl TR11 82 A2
Saltbox Rd TR11 82 A2
Saltburn Rd PL5 123 C1
Salt Cellar Hill 10 TR13 98 B8
Saltings Cl TR26 77 E3
Saltings Reach TR26 77 E3
Saltings The TR26 77 E4
Salt Mill PL12 122 F4
Saltponds 27 TR19 88 C1
Saltram House★ PL7 130 A4
Saltram Terr PL7 130 E5
Salts Mdw PL14 50 B6
Sampford Gdns PL20 42 D5
Sampford Terr 6 PL20 42 C5
Sampson Cl PL18 40 D6
Sampson Gdns TR3 81 B4
Sampson's Ct TR27 78 D6
Sampson Way TR3 69 D3
Sampys Hill TR11 93 D3
Samuel Bone Cl PL14 113 D6
Sanctuary Cl TR14 138 C2
Sanctuary La
 Helston TR13 146 C6
 12 Stratton EX23 4 E1
Sanctuary Lane Flats TR13 146 C6
Sandbank Holiday Flats TR27 66 B1
Sand Bay TR11 145 C2
Sand-Bay Holiday Flats 6 TR6 55 A5
Sandercock Cl PL17 39 F7
Sandfield Cres 3 TR14 138 C2
Sandford Rd PL9 135 F8
Sand Hill PL18 41 A6
Sand Hill Pk PL18 40 F5
Sandhole Cross EX39 2 D8
Sandhurst Terr 1 TR1 137 C5
Sand La PL18 41 A3
Sandon Wlk PL6 125 A1
Sandows La 15 TR26 141 A5
Sandplace Rd
 Looe PL13 117 C6
 Looe, Sandplace PL13 63 B7
Sandplace Sta PL13 63 B8
Sandra Way PL31 109 C5
Sandyacres
 Hayle TR27 78 B6
 Phillack TR27 142 E8
Sandy Cl PL14 51 B3
Sandy Cove TR4 68 A7
Sandy Cove Bglws TR20 90 B3
Sandy Cove Travel Lodge TR4 68 A6
Sandy Ct TR8 31 B2
Sandy Hill PL25 114 F4
Sandy Hill Com Prim Sch PL25 114 F4
Sandyhills PL27 21 E2
Sandy La
 Harlyn PL28 20 D2
 Redruth TR15, TR16 140 D5
 Trevone PL28 20 F2
Sandylake La PL22 112 F3
Sandymoor TR14 139 B3
Sandymouth Bay Holiday Pk EX23 4 C5
Sandy Rd
 Plymouth PL7 131 C4
 Porthtowan TR4 68 A7
Sango Ct PL10 132 F6
Sango Rd PL11 127 A2
Saracen Cl TR10 144 C7
Saracen Cres TR10 144 C7
Saracen Ho 5 TR10 144 C7
Saracen Pl TR10 144 C7
Saracen Way TR10 144 C7
Sarah Cl PL20 41 B1
Sarahs Cl PL28 107 D4
Sarah's Ct PL28 107 D4
Sarah's Gate PL27 32 C7
Sarah's La PL28 107 D4
Sarah's Mdw PL28 107 D4
Sarah's View PL28 107 D4
Sargents Mdw EX23 2 D1
Sarum Cl PL3 128 F7
Saunders La PL11 65 A5
Saunders Wlk PL6 124 D6
Savage Rd PL5 127 D7
Savery Terr PL4 129 A4
Savoy Bldg 3 PL25 114 C3
Sawles Rd
 St Austell PL25 114 B2
 St Austell PL25 114 D2
Sawmills La TR16 68 D3
Sawrey St PL1 148 A2
Sawyers Ct TR13 92 A6
Scarletts Well Pk PL31 109 C6
Scarletts Well Rd PL31 109 C5
Scarlett's Well Rd PL31 109 B5
Scarne Ind Est PL15 106 C3
Scholars Cl PL14 38 F2
Scholar's La TR13 91 C3
School Cl
 Par PL24 60 B4
 Plymouth PL7 130 D7
 St Columb Minor TR7 111 E6
 Tavistock PL19 147 D5
School Dr PL6 125 D7
School Hill
 Golant PL23 61 B5
 Herodsfoot PL14 50 E3
 Lanjeth PL26 58 E4
 Mevagissey PL26 73 C4
 Padstow PL28 107 D5
 Perranarworthal TR3 81 D6
 Shortlanesend TR4 69 F6
 South Petherwin PL15 27 E8
 St Buryan TR19 96 E5
 St Keverne, Porthallow TR12 101 D6
 St Keverne TR12 101 D4
 St Neot PL14 36 F2

School La
Budock Water TR11 144 C3
Gulval TR18 88 E6
Jacobstow EX23 11 A6
Marazion TR17 89 C5
Plymouth PL7 130 E4
Polruan PL23 116 D2
Redruth TR15 140 D5
St Austell PL25 115 C6
St Erth TR27 142 A1
St Hilary TR20 89 F6
Troon TR14 79 E4
Truro TR1 137 C3
School Rd
Breage TR13 90 F3
Landrake PL12 53 C3
Pensilva PL14 38 E5
Summercourt TR8 57 B7
Tavistock PL19 147 D2
School Wlk PL27 108 D6
Sclerder La PL13 62 E4
Scoble's Terr TR1 70 D1
Sconner Rd PL11 127 A3
Scoria Cl TR16 68 D3
Scorrier House Workshops TR16 68 D2
Scorrier St TR16 68 E1
Scott Ave PL5 127 C8
Scott Bsns Pk PL2 128 A6
Scott Cl 2 PL14 38 E4
Scott Hospl PL2 128 A6
Scott Rd
Plymouth PL2 128 A6
Plymouth PL2 128 B6
Scowbuds TR14 138 F5
Scrations La PL22 112 C2
Screech Owl Sanctuary* TR9 46 A3
Seabank TR11 145 B2
Seacroft Rd PL5 123 C2
Sea Front Ct PL13 117 D3
Seagull Tourist Pk PL28 31 F6
Seaholme Ct TR11 145 A5
Sea La TR27 142 D6
Seapoint Ho TR7 110 E6
Sea Rd PL25 115 D2
Seaspray Leisure Flats TR4 68 A7
Seaton Ave PL4 128 E4
Seaton Beach Flats PL11 64 B5
Seaton Bsns Pk PL6 125 B3
Seaton La PL4 128 E4
Seaton Pk PL11 64 B5
Seaton Pl PL2 127 F5
Seaton Valley Countryside Pk* PL13, PL11 64 B6
Seaton Way PL20 42 A2
Sea Urchin TR26 141 E2
Sea View
Crackington Haven EX23 10 C6
Gunnislake PL18 40 E5
Sea View Ave PL4 149 C4
Seaview Cotts 10 TR11 145 B5
Sea View Cotts PL26 73 C3
Sea View Cres 11 TR2 95 A6
Sea View Ct TR11 145 B3
Sea View Pl TR26 141 C6
Sea View Rd
Falmouth TR11 145 B2
12 St Mawes TR2 95 A6
Seaview Terr TR8 57 E6
Sea View Terr
Camborne TR14 138 E2
Carn Towan TR19 96 C7
Helston TR13 146 B6
6 Newlyn TR18 143 C1
Par PL24 60 B6
Penwithick PL26 59 D7
Plymouth PL4 149 B4
Redruth TR15 140 C5
20 St Ives TR26 141 B5
Seawell Rd EX23 104 F7
Second Ave
Plymouth, Billacombe PL9 130 A1
Plymouth, Devonport PL1 128 A2
Plymouth, Weston Mill PL2 127 E7
Sedley Way PL5 124 D3
Sefton Ave PL4 129 B3
Sefton Cl PL4 149 C4
Segrave Rd PL2 128 B6
Seiners Ct 10 TR6 55 A4
Selkirk Ho 5 PL9 135 F7
Selkirk Pl PL5 124 E2
Selsden Cl PL9 136 C6
Sendall's Way PL6 124 F4
Seneschall Pk TR13 146 D8
Sennen Cl PL11 126 F4
Sennen Hts TR19 96 B7
Sennen Pl PL2 127 E5
Sennen Sch TR19 96 C7
Sentry Cl PL27 32 D6
Sergeants Hill TR4 68 F3
Serpell Cl PL6 124 E6
Serpells Mdw PL15 17 F1
Sethnoe Way TR13 91 A3
Seton Gdns TR14 138 B4
Setons The 6 TR14 138 F7
Seven Stars La PL5 124 C6
Seven Trees Ct PL4 149 B4
Severn Pl PL3 129 C5
Sewell Ct PL3 128 E5
Seymour Ave
Newquay TR7 110 E6
Plymouth PL4 149 B4
Seymour Cl TR3 69 C3
Seymour Dr PL3 128 F5
Seymour Mews PL4 149 C4
Seymour Pk PL3 129 A5
Seymour Pl PL1 148 A4
Seymour Rd
Plymouth, Mannamead PL3 128 F5
Plymouth, Plympton PL7 130 C6
Seymour St PL4 149 A3
Shackleton Cres 9 PL27 31 F3
Shackleton Ct PL5 124 E1
Shackleton Dr TR7 111 B5
Shaft Downs La TR27 78 F3
Shaftesbury Cotts PL4 149 A4
Shaftesbury Ct 3 PL4 149 A4
Shakespeare Rd PL5 124 C2
Shaldon Cres PL5 124 B3
Shallowford Cl PL6 129 C8
Shallowford Rd PL6 129 C8
Shapleys Gdns PL9 136 A5
Shapters Rd PL4 149 C2
Shapters Way PL4 135 B8
Sharaman Cl PL25 115 A5
Sharlands Rd EX23 7 B6
Sharon Way PL6 125 A5
Sharpitor Row PL20 42 E4
Sharrose Rd PL9 135 B5
Shaw Way PL9 135 A7
Shearwood Cl PL7 130 C6
Sheep Fair Mdw 14 PL17 39 F4
Sheepstor Rd PL6 125 D1
Sheila's Ct TR26 141 D1
Shelburne Ct TR11 144 F3
Shelburne Rd TR11 144 F3
Shell Cl PL6 125 E1
Shelley Ave PL19 147 D5
Shelley Rd PL25 115 A4
Shelley Way PL5 123 D1
Shepherd's La PL4 149 B2
Sherborne Cl PL9 136 C6
Sherford Cres
Plymouth, Elburton PL9 136 C7
Plymouth, West Park PL5 124 A3
Sherford Rd PL9 136 D7
Sherford Wlk PL9 136 E7
Sheridan Rd PL5 124 C1
Sherrell Pk PL20 41 B1
Sherril Cl PL9 135 F4
Sherwell La PL4 149 A4
Sherwood Dr PL31 109 C5
Sheviock La PL11 65 B5
Shilla Pk PL32 24 A8
Shilson Terr PL15 106 C5
Shipley Wlk PL6 125 A1
Shirburn Rd PL6 129 B8
Shire Horse Farm & Carriage Mus The* TR16 79 F5
Shires Way PL26 46 F3
Shirley Gdns PL5 124 C1
Shoemaker's La PL12 122 E2
Shoemakers Row PL13 63 B7
Shoot Row TR15 140 C5
Shop Hill 3 TR17 89 C5
Shop Pk PL14 38 A2
Shoreline TR7 111 B8
Shores La PL27 21 E3
Shortacross PL14 38 A2
Short Cotts PL11 127 A3
Short Cross Mews TR4 68 C6
Short Cross Rd TR4 68 C6
Shortlands EX22 8 E5
Shortlanesend Com Prim Sch TR4 69 F6
Short Park Rd PL3 128 D5
Shortwood Cres PL9 136 A7
Shrewsbury Rd PL5 124 C4
Shrubberies Hill TR13 98 C8
Shute Hill
Breage TR13 90 F3
Carharrack TR16 80 E8
Helston TR13 146 C6
Lostwithiel PL22 112 C2
Mawnan Smith TR11 93 D3
Pelynt PL13 62 D5
Shute La
Penryn TR10 144 C8
Pensilva PL14 38 E4
6 Porthleven TR13 98 B8
Shute Mdw TR10 144 C7
Shute Park Rd PL9 135 F6
Shutta Rd PL13 117 C4
Sidings The
Bugle PL26 47 C2
Delabole PL33 14 E2
Sidney Terr 7 TR15 140 C5
Silvanus Jenkin Ave PL14 113 E5
Silver Birch Cl PL6 125 C7
Silver Ct 1 TR15 140 B4
Silverdale Ct TR7 110 E6
Silverdale Rd TR11 145 A2
Silver Hill TR3 81 D6
Silvershell Rd PL29 22 D7
Silvershell View PL29 22 D7
Silver St
Bere Ferrers PL20 120 A3
Saltash PL12 123 A2
Silver Terr PL10 133 A6
Silverton Cl EX23 104 E5
Silverton Rd EX23 104 E5
Silver Way TR3 69 C3
Simms Terr PL18 41 A6
Simon Cl PL9 135 E6
Simpsons Ct 30 TR18 143 E5
Singlerose Rd PL26 59 C7
Sir James Smith's Com Sch PL32 105 C4
Sir John Hunt Com Coll (Southway Campus) PL6 124 F6
Sir John Hunt Com Sports Coll PL5 124 D4
Sir Robert Geffery's CE Prim Sch PL12 53 C3
Sir Williams Morles Almshouses PL12 65 A8
Sithney Common Hill TR13 91 C2
Sithney Com Prim Sch TR13 91 B5
Sithney Old Hill TR13 146 A6
Sithney St PL5 123 C1
Six Turnings TR11 82 A2
Skardale Gdns PL6 129 D8
Skardon Pl PL4 149 A4
Skerries Rd PL6 124 F7
Skidden Hill 18 TR26 141 B5
Skinnard La PL18 40 F5
Skitches Cnr EX23 4 D1
Skyburriowe La TR12 99 C6
Skylark Rise PL6 125 E8
Slade Cl PL9 136 A5
Slade Park Rd PL14 38 E5
Slades La 2 TR10 144 C7
Slades Rd PL25 114 E5
Slatelands Cl PL7 131 B3
Slipway PL27 21 D2
Slipway Quay PL12 119 B2
Smallack Cl PL6 124 F2
Smallack Dr PL6 124 F2
Smallridge Cl PL9 135 F5
Smallridge La EX23 4 F1
Smeaton Sq PL3 129 D6
Smithfield Ct TR8 111 B3
Smithfield Dr PL12 122 B3
Smithick Hill TR11 145 B4
Smith's Cotts PL14 113 C6
Smiths Way PL12 122 B3
Smithy Cl PL12 122 C4
Smithy Ct PL32 105 D3
Smithy La TR3 81 F7
Smugglers Row 8 TR11 145 B5
Snell Dr PL12 122 B3
Snowdrop Cres PL15 106 E4
Snow's Pas TR11 145 B4
Socotra Dr 7 PL25 59 A3
Solar Row 6 TR1 137 D5
Somer Ct TR11 145 B4
Somerset Cotts 10 PL3 128 A4
Somerset Pl PL3 128 A4
Somerset Place La 11 PL3 128 A4
Somerville Rd TR6 55 A4
Sona Merg Cl TR18 143 C7
Soper's Hill PL5 120 E1
South Albany Rd TR15 140 C3
Southbourne Cl PL26 58 E6
Southbourne Rd PL25 114 E2
Southcliff TR11 145 C2
South Cliff 18 TR19 88 C1
South Coombe La PL17 39 F8
Southcott Mdws EX23 11 A6
Southdown Cl PL26 58 E1
Southdown Cotts PL10 133 B6
Southdown Rd
Millbrook PL10 133 A6
Sticker PL26 58 E1
South Down Rd PL2 128 B6
South Downs TR15 140 D2
Southdown Terr PL10 133 A6
South Dr
Redruth TR15 140 D2
South Tehidy TR14 138 E8
South East Cornwall Discovery Ctr* PL13 117 C4
Southella Rd PL20 42 D2
Southern Cl PL2 127 F7
Southernhaye PL15 106 C5
Southern Rd PL17 39 F4
Southern Terr PL4 128 F4
Southernway PL9 136 A8
Southern Way PL27 108 C5
Southfield PL12 122 C3
Southfield Rd EX23 104 E5
Southfields EX22 8 A5
Southfields Pl 3 TR26 141 A5
Southgate Ave PL9 135 E4
Southgate Cl PL9 135 E4
Southgate Pl PL15 106 C5
Southgate St
Launceston PL15 106 C5
Redruth TR15 140 C3
South Harbour TR10 144 D7
South Hill
Plymouth, Hooe PL9 135 C5
Plymouth, Stoke PL1 128 A3
South Hill Rd PL17 39 E5
Southlea Terr TR3 80 F3
Southleigh Ho 15 TR1 137 C4
Southleigh Mews 14 TR1 137 C4
South Milton St PL4 149 C2
South Par 33 TR18 143 E5
South Park Cl TR15 140 A4
Southpark Rd PL24 60 C5
South Petherwin Com Prim Sch PL15 27 E8
South Pk
Jacobstow EX23 11 A6
Redruth TR15 139 F6
16 St Columb Major TR9 45 E6
South Pl TR19 86 E6
South Place Folly 5 TR18 143 E4
South Place Gdns TR19 86 E6
South Quay PL28 107 D5
South Quay Hill TR7 110 D6
South Rd
Goldsithney TR20 89 E5
Stithians TR3 80 F3
South Roskear Terr TR14 138 F4
Southside Ope 14 PL1 149 A2
Southside St PL1 149 A2
South St
Fowey PL23 116 D4
Grampound Road TR2 57 E1
Lostwithiel PL22 112 C2
St Austell PL25 114 C3
South Terr
Camborne TR14 138 D2
12 Penzance TR18 143 E4
South Towan TR4 68 A6
South Trelawny Prim Sch PL2 128 A8
Southview PL10 133 A6
South View
9 Horrabridge PL20 42 C4
Liskeard PL14 113 D7
Penryn TR10 144 C8
Plymouth, Crownhill PL5 124 E2
Plymouth, Elburton PL9 136 B6
Porthleven TR13 91 A1
South View Cl PL7 130 D7
Southview Dr PL31 109 E5
South View Parc TR4 68 A6
South View Pk PL7 130 D7
Southview Rd 15 PL24 60 B4
Southview Terr 8 TR19 88 C1
South View Terr
Blackwater TR4 68 E5
Nancegollan TR13 91 B7
Plymouth PL4 149 C3
Southway PL28 20 F2
South Way TR8 111 F3
Southway Dr PL6 124 E6
Southway La
Plymouth, Southway PL6 125 B6
Plymouth, Tamerton Foliot PL6 124 C6
Southway Prim Sch PL6 124 E6
Southwell Rd PL6 124 E1
Sovereign Ct PL7 130 C5
Spargo Ct TR10 93 C8
Sparkatown La PL20 42 E3
Sparke Cl PL7 131 B4
Sparkwell All Saints Prim Sch PL7 131 F8
Spar La TR15 67 D4
Sparnon Cl
Redruth TR15 140 C4
St Austell PL25 114 B4
Sparnon Cross TR13 90 F5
Sparnon Ct TR15 140 C4
Sparnon Hill 1 TR15 140 C4
Sparnon Terr 2 TR15 140 C4
Sparry La TR16 80 F8
Spaven Mor TR14 138 F5
Speares The PL12 122 B2
Spear's Terr TR11 144 F1
Speech La TR3 81 C4
Speedwell Cl
Bude EX23 104 F5
Millbrook PL10 132 F5
Speedwell Cres PL6 129 B7
Speedwell Wlk PL6 129 B7
Spencer Gdns PL12 122 F1
Spencer Rd PL9 135 E8
Spernen Cl TR26 141 C2
Spernen Wyn Rd TR11 145 B2
Spicers La 11 EX23 4 E1
Spindrift TR8 44 C6
Spinnaker Quay PL9 134 F7
Spinnakers TR7 110 A5
Spinney The PL7 131 A4
Spire Ct PL3 129 B5
Spire Hill Pk PL12 122 C2
Spires The TR1 137 C6
Spirit of The West (American Theme Pk)* TR9 46 A8
Spitfire Row PL27 31 F3
Sportsmans PL32 105 C3
Sportsmans Rd PL32 105 C3
Springfield
Horrabridge PL20 42 C4
Portscatho TR2 83 B2
Springfield Ave PL9 136 B6
Springfield Bsns Pk PL15 18 E2
Springfield Cl
Dobwalls PL14 50 E7
Lostwithiel PL22 112 D2
Phillack TR27 142 D7
Plymouth PL9 136 B7
Polgooth PL26 59 A1
St Austell PL25 114 F5
Springfield Dr PL3 128 A4
Springfield Gate PL13 117 D5
Springfield La PL9 136 B7
Springfield Pk
Barripper TR14 79 B5
Mylor Bridge TR11 82 A3
Widegates PL13 63 E7
Springfield Pl 15 TR9 45 E6
Springfield Rd
Falmouth TR11 144 E5
Goldsithney TR20 89 E5
Liskeard PL14 113 E6
Looe PL13 117 D5
Newquay TR7 110 F6
Plymouth PL9 136 B6
Springfield Rise PL9 136 B7
Springfields PL26 47 C2
Springfields Fun Pk & Pony Ctr* TR9 45 E4
Springfield Way
Roche PL26 46 F3
St Day TR16 68 D1
Threemilestone TR3 69 C3
Springhill PL2 128 C8
Spring Hill PL19 147 B5
Springhill Gn PL2 128 C8
Spring Pk PL6 125 E7
Springwell View PL31 109 F5
Springwood Cl PL7 131 A3
Spruce Gdns PL7 131 B5
Spurway Rd PL14 113 D5
Square The
16 Bere Alston PL20 41 B1
Cawsand PL10 133 A1
2 Chacewater TR4 69 A3
Grampound Road TR2 57 E1
Gunnislake PL18 41 A6
Gunnislake, St Ann's Chapel PL18 40 E5
Kilkhampton EX23 5 A6
Landrake PL12 53 C3
Leedstown TR27 78 E1
Lizard TR12 102 F2
Ludgvan TR20 89 A8
Manaccan TR12 101 A7
Marazion TR17 89 B5
Pendeen TR19 75 A1
Penryn TR10 144 D7
Pentewan PL26 73 C6
Plymouth, Stonehouse PL1 128 A2
Portreath TR16 67 C6
Portscatho TR2 83 B2
Praze-an-Beeble TR14 79 B2
Probus TR2 71 C6
Redruth TR16 80 B5
Saltash PL12 122 C3
St Keverne TR12 101 D4
3 St Mawes TR2 95 A6
St Stephen PL26 58 B4
St Teath PL30 23 E7
Tregony TR2 71 F3
Veryan TR2 83 F6
Week St Mary EX22 11 E8
Squire La TR16 80 F8
Squires La TR13 91 C2
Stable Ct PL27 108 C6
Stable Hobba Ind Est TR18 143 B3
Stables The TR14 67 B4
Staddiscombe Rd PL9 135 F4
Staddon Cres PL9 135 E6
Staddon Gn PL9 135 D6
Staddon La PL9 135 B4
Staddon Park Rd PL9 135 E6
Staddon Terrace La PL1 148 B4
Stafford Cl TR7 111 D6
Staggy La TR3 81 F7
Stag La
Plymouth, Elburton PL9 136 B8
Plymouth, Plympton PL9 130 B1
Stamford Cl PL9 135 A6
Stamford Fort Cotts PL9 135 A6
Stamford Hill EX23 4 D1
Stamford La PL9 135 A6
Stamps Hill
Fraddon PL26 57 F8
Indian Queens TR9 45 F1
Stamps La TR15 139 D6
Stamps The PL17 40 D5
Stanborough Cross PL9 136 C7
Stanborough Rd PL9 136 B7
Stanbury Ave PL6 124 F1
Stanbury Cl PL15 13 F1
Stanbury Cross EX23 2 C1
Standarhay Cl PL9 136 C7
Standarhay Villas PL9 136 C7
Stanford Cl 5 TR18 143 D5
Stanford Mews TR9 45 E6
Stanford Terr TR18 143 D5
Stangray Ave PL4 128 D4
Stanharver Cl TR7 111 E6
Stanhope Rd PL5 123 C1
Stanley Ct 4 PL31 109 D5
Stanley Pl PL4 129 B2
Stanley Terr 1 TR15 140 B5
Stanley Way TR15 140 C6
Stannary Bridge Rd PL19 147 D6
Stannary Rd PL26 59 C8
Stantons Row PL14 38 A3
Stanways Rd TR7 111 D7
Staple Cl PL6 121 C1
Stapleford Gdns PL5 123 F5
Stapleton Rd EX23 104 F4
Star Pk PL18 41 A6
Statham Rd PL31 109 D4
Station App
3 Newquay TR7 110 F6
3 St Columb Road TR9 45 E2
St Erth TR27 77 E2
Station Hill
Hayle TR27 142 B5
Lelant TR26 77 E4
Praze-an-Beeble TR14 79 B2
Redruth TR15 140 B4
Station La PL18 41 A3
Station Par TR7 110 F6
Station Rd
Bere Alston PL20 41 B1
Bere Ferrers PL20 119 E3
Bugle PL26 47 C2
Camborne TR15 139 C5
Carnhell Green TR14 78 F4
Chacewater TR4 68 F4
Fowey PL23 116 D5

Station Rd *continued*
Grampound Road TR2 ..... 57 E1
Gunnislake PL18 ..... 40 F6
Helston TR13 ..... 146 C7
Horrabridge PL20 ..... 42 C4
Kelly Bray PL17 ..... 39 F6
Launceston PL15 ..... 106 C6
Liskeard PL14 ..... 113 B4
Looe PL13 ..... 117 C4
Mary Tavy PL19 ..... 30 F5
North Brentor PL19 ..... 30 E8
Padstow PL28 ..... 107 D5
Par PL24 ..... 60 C5
Penryn TR10 ..... 144 B8
Penzance TR18 ..... 143 F6
Perranarworthal TR3 ..... 81 E6
Perranporth TR6 ..... 55 B5
Plymouth, Elburton PL9 ..... 136 C7
Plymouth, Keyham PL2 ..... 127 E5
Plymouth, Plympton PL7 ..... 130 E5
Plymouth, Tamerton Foliot PL5 ..... 124 A6
Redruth TR15 ..... 140 C5
Saltash PL12 ..... 123 A2
St Columb Major TR9 ..... 45 E5
1 St Columb Road TR9 ..... 45 E2
St Mabyn PL30 ..... 34 C8
St Newlyn East TR8 ..... 56 B7
Truro TR1 ..... 137 B4
Yelverton PL20 ..... 42 D2
Station View PL19 ..... 30 E8
Station Yd 6 PL31 ..... 109 D5
Steamers Hill TR27 ..... 78 C5
Steamers Mdw TR27 ..... 78 C5
Steeple Cl
Plymouth PL9 ..... 135 F4
St Ives TR26 ..... 141 B3
Steeple La TR26 ..... 141 B3
Steeple View Ct TR26 ..... 141 C1
Steer Park Rd PL7 ..... 131 C5
Steer Point Cotts PL8 ..... 136 F2
Stefan Cl PL9 ..... 135 B5
Stenalees Hill PL26 ..... 59 C7
Stenlake Pl PL4 ..... 129 B2
Stenlake Terr PL4 ..... 129 B2
Stennack Gdns 14 TR26 ..... 141 A5
Stennack Parc TR19 ..... 86 F8
Stennack Rd PL25 ..... 115 B4
Stennack The TR26 ..... 141 B5
Stentaway Cl PL9 ..... 135 F8
Stentaway Dr PL9 ..... 136 A8
Stentaway Rd PL9 ..... 135 F8
Stephens Rd PL14 ..... 113 E7
Stephney Cl TR11 ..... 144 C2
Steppy Downs Rd TR27 ..... 78 A1
Stewarts Rd EX22 ..... 11 E8
Stiles The TR8 ..... 56 B7
Stillman Ct 7 PL4 ..... 149 A2
Stillman St PL4 ..... 149 A2
Stippy Stappy 11 TR5 ..... 54 D1
Stirling Ct PL5 ..... 123 C1
Stirling Rd PL5 ..... 123 C1
Stithians Com Prim Sch TR3 ..... 80 F4
Stithians Row TR16 ..... 80 B5
Stockadon Farm Barns PL12 ..... 118 B4
Stoggy La PL7 ..... 131 A6
Stoke Climsland Sch PL17 ..... 28 D1
Stoke Damerel Bsns Ctr 9 PL3 ..... 128 A4
Stoke Damerel Com Coll PL3 ..... 128 B4
Stoke Damerel Prim Sch PL1 ..... 128 A3
Stoke Hill La PL20 ..... 42 B2
Stoke Rd
Bray Shop PL17 ..... 28 A1
Kelly Bray PL17 ..... 39 E6
Linkinhorne PL17 ..... 39 A8
Plymouth PL1 ..... 148 A3
Stokesay Ave PL6 ..... 125 A5
Stokes La PL1 ..... 149 A2
Stokes Rd TR1 ..... 137 C5
Stoke Terr PL17 ..... 39 E6
Stokingway Cl PL9 ..... 135 E5
Stonebarton Cl PL7 ..... 130 C6
Stonebarton Rd PL7 ..... 130 C6
Stone Chair La TR19 ..... 96 B7
Stone Cross PL16 ..... 19 F5
Stonehall Flats PL1 ..... 128 A1
Stone Hill EX23 ..... 4 E2
Stonehouse Bridge PL1 ..... 128 A1
Stonehouse St PL1 ..... 148 A2
Stonerock Flats PL13 ..... 117 C1
Stones Ct 30 TR26 ..... 141 B5
Stonewood Ct 4 TR9 ..... 45 E6
Stoney Hill PL25 ..... 59 A4
Stoney La
Polgooth PL26 ..... 59 A1
St Austell PL25 ..... 114 C4
Stoney Lands PL12 ..... 53 C3
Stony La
Bodmin PL31 ..... 34 D1
Gunnislake PL18 ..... 40 F5
Stopford Pl PL1 ..... 127 F3
Stott Cl PL3 ..... 129 D5
Stour Cl PL3 ..... 129 D6
Stourscombe PL15 ..... 106 F3
Stourscombe Wood PL15 ..... 106 F4
Stowe Gdns PL5 ..... 124 B2
Stowford Cl PL20 ..... 42 E3
Stowford Cross EX22 ..... 5 F8
Stracey Rd TR11 ..... 145 B2
Strafford Cl EX23 ..... 104 C3
Strand TR18 ..... 143 C2
Strand St
Padstow PL28 ..... 107 D5
Plymouth PL1 ..... 134 A8
Strand The
Bude EX23 ..... 104 D5
Falmouth TR11 ..... 145 C2
Padstow PL28 ..... 107 D5
Strangways Terr TR1 ..... 137 D3
Strangways Villas TR1 ..... 137 D3
Stratton Hospl EX23 ..... 4 D1
Stratton Pl TR11 ..... 145 A6
Stratton Prim Sch EX23 ..... 4 D1
Stratton Rd
Bude EX23 ..... 104 F4
Stratton EX23 ..... 4 D1
Stratton Terr
Falmouth TR11 ..... 145 A6
Truro TR1 ..... 137 B4
Stratton Wlk PL2 ..... 128 D8
Strawberry Cl TR15 ..... 140 B6
Strawberry Cres TR15 ..... 140 B6
Strawberry Fields TR16 ..... 140 E1
Strawberry Gdns TR16 ..... 140 E1
Strawberry La
Hayle TR27 ..... 142 D4
Lelant TR26 ..... 77 E4
Redruth TR15 ..... 140 B6
Stray Park Ct TR14 ..... 138 F2
Stray Park Rd TR14 ..... 138 E2
Stray Park Way TR14 ..... 138 F2
Street-An-Garrow 17 TR26 ..... 141 B5
Street-An-Pol 3 TR26 ..... 141 B5
Stretyn 5 TR3 ..... 81 F7
Strickland Cotts 6 TR18 ..... 143 C2
Stringers Hill TR20 ..... 88 A5
Strode Rd PL7 ..... 130 F6
Stroma Cl PL6 ..... 124 F7
Stroud Park Rd PL2 ..... 128 C7
Stuart Rd PL3 ..... 148 A4
Stuart Road Prim Sch PL1 ..... 148 A4
Stuarts Way PL12 ..... 53 E5
Stucley Rd EX23 ..... 4 D1
Sturdee Rd PL2 ..... 128 A5
Stursdon Cross EX23 ..... 5 A8
Sugar Mill Bsns Pk PL9 ..... 129 C1
Summercourt TR10 ..... 144 D7
Summercourt Com Prim Sch TR8 ..... 57 C7
Summerfield Cl PL26 ..... 73 B3
Summerfields PL12 ..... 122 D1
Summerheath TR10 ..... 81 C1
Summerhill Rd PL15 ..... 106 A5
Summer La PL13 ..... 62 D6
Summerlands Cl PL7 ..... 131 C5
Summerlands Gdns PL7 ..... 131 C5
Summerlane Pk PL13 ..... 62 D6
Summerleaze Ave EX23 ..... 104 D7
Summerleaze Cres EX23 ..... 104 D6
Summer Lodge Holiday Village TR8 ..... 45 B2
Summers Cl PL6 ..... 129 B7
Summers St PL22 ..... 112 C2
Summerville Cross EX39 ..... 3 C6
Suncrest PL14 ..... 38 A4
Suncrest Est TR9 ..... 45 E1
Sunderland Cl PL9 ..... 135 A6
Sunderland Rd PL27 ..... 31 F3
Sun Girt La PL14 ..... 113 C5
Sunland Holiday Est TR16 ..... 67 C5
Sunley Orford Ho 6 TR1 ..... 137 D4
Sunningdale TR1 ..... 137 A4
Sunningdale Rd PL12 ..... 122 C2
Sunnybank 23 TR13 ..... 98 C8
Sunny Bank
Bodmin PL30 ..... 48 E8
Liskeard PL14 ..... 113 A4
Sunnybanks PL12 ..... 53 E4
Sunny Cnr
Goldsithney TR20 ..... 89 F5
Truro TR4 ..... 81 B7
Sunny Corner La TR19 ..... 96 C7
Sunnycroft PL13 ..... 117 C3
Sunny Dene PL5 ..... 123 D1
Sunnyside
Carnkie TR13 ..... 80 D1
Crantock TR8 ..... 110 A3
Menheniot PL14 ..... 51 F5
Menheniot PL14 ..... 52 B5
2 Perranporth TR6 ..... 55 A4
Portscatho TR2 ..... 83 B2
7 Redruth TR15 ..... 140 B4
Sunnyside Mdw PL32 ..... 105 D4
Sunnyside Parc TR15 ..... 139 C8
Sunnyside Rd PL4 ..... 129 B2
Sunny Terr TR18 ..... 143 B2
Sunnyvale Cl TR16 ..... 67 C6
Sunnyvale Rd TR16 ..... 67 D6
Sunrising Est PL13 ..... 117 D5
Sunset Dr 8 TR13 ..... 98 C8
Sunset Gdns 9 TR13 ..... 98 C8
Sunshine Terr PL19 ..... 147 D6
Sun Valley Pk TR9 ..... 45 E6
Sunway Cl PL19 ..... 147 A6
Sunwell La
Antony PL11 ..... 65 E4
St John PL11 ..... 132 A8
Surf View TR7 ..... 110 A6
Sussex Pl PL1 ..... 148 C2
Sussex Rd PL2 ..... 127 F5
Sussex St PL1 ..... 148 C2
Sussex Terr 5 PL2 ..... 127 F5
Sutherland Rd PL4 ..... 149 A4
Sutton Ct PL1 ..... 127 F1
Sutton Mews 22 PL4 ..... 149 A2
Sutton Pl PL4 ..... 149 B2
Sutton Rd PL4 ..... 149 B2
Sutton Wharf PL4 ..... 149 A2
Swaindale Rd 3 PL3 ..... 128 E6
Swale Cl PL3 ..... 129 B6
Swallow Cl EX23 ..... 104 D5
Swallowfield Cl PL24 ..... 60 D5
Swallow Ho 13 TR11 ..... 145 C3
Swallows End PL9 ..... 135 E8
Swan Cl PL10 ..... 133 A6
Swan Gdns PL7 ..... 130 F5
Swanpool Ct TR11 ..... 145 A1
Swanpool Hill TR11 ..... 145 A2
Swanpool Rd TR11 ..... 144 F1
Swanpool St TR11 ..... 145 C3
Swanvale Rd TR11 ..... 144 F3
Sweet Briar Cres TR7 ..... 111 A4
Swift Gdns PL5 ..... 124 C2
Swinburne Gdns PL5 ..... 124 C1
Swingate Cross EX22 ..... 13 E8
Sycamore Ave
Plymouth PL4 ..... 149 C2
St Austell PL25 ..... 114 E5
Tavistock PL19 ..... 147 C2
Sycamore Cl
Bodmin PL31 ..... 109 B4
Polgooth PL26 ..... 59 A1
Praze-an-Beeble TR14 ..... 79 B2
Rock PL27 ..... 21 E3
Sycamore Dr
Illogan TR15 ..... 139 D7
Plymouth PL6 ..... 125 C7
Redruth TR15 ..... 140 D5
Torpoint PL11 ..... 127 A3
Sycamore Gdns TR8 ..... 57 B7
Sycamore Rd PL12 ..... 122 B3
Sycamores The PL25 ..... 114 C4
Sycamore Way PL6 ..... 125 E6
Sydenham Cross PL19 ..... 29 C2
Sydney Cl
Plymouth PL7 ..... 130 E4
St Austell PL25 ..... 114 C3
Sydney Rd
Newquay TR7 ..... 110 D6
Torpoint PL11 ..... 127 B3
Sydney St PL1 ..... 148 B4
Sylvan Cl PL25 ..... 114 E6
Sylvan Ct PL1 ..... 128 A3
Sylverton Pl 12 TR18 ..... 143 C7
Symons Cl
Blackwater TR4 ..... 68 E5
St Austell PL25 ..... 115 A5
Symons Hill TR11 ..... 145 A5
Symons Rd PL12 ..... 122 F2
Symons Row PL14 ..... 37 F3
Symons Terr TR15 ..... 140 B5
Syra Cl PL30 ..... 23 B2

T

Tabernacle St TR1 ..... 137 D4
Tackbear Rd EX22, EX23 ..... 7 E4
Tailyour Rd PL6 ..... 124 F2
Talbot Gdns PL5 ..... 127 D7
Talexandra Terr PL15 ..... 106 D5
Talgos Cl TR16 ..... 140 E8
Talland Ct 29 TR26 ..... 141 B5
Talland Hill PL13 ..... 62 E2
Talland Rd TR26 ..... 141 B5
Talmena Ave PL27 ..... 108 A5
Talveneth
Camborne TR14 ..... 138 F3
Pendeen TR19 ..... 75 A1
Redruth TR15 ..... 140 C6
Talvenydh Ct PL31 ..... 109 D5
Tamar Ave
Plymouth PL2 ..... 127 E5
Tavistock PL19 ..... 147 D5
Tamar Bridge PL5 ..... 123 A2
Tamar Cl
18 Bere Alston PL20 ..... 41 B1
29 Callington PL17 ..... 39 F4
Tamar Ho PL1 ..... 127 E1
Tamarisk La TR7 ..... 111 A4
Tamar Otter Sanctuary★ PL15 ..... 18 B8
Tamar Pk Cvn Site PL18 ..... 40 D6
Tamar Science Pk PL6 ..... 125 C4
Tamarside Com Coll PL5 ..... 123 E1
Tamar St
Plymouth PL1 ..... 127 E3
Saltash PL12 ..... 123 A2
Torpoint PL11 ..... 127 C3
Tamar Terr
Calstock PL17 ..... 41 A3
Horsebridge PL19 ..... 29 C1
Launceston PL15 ..... 106 D5
Saltash PL12 ..... 123 A2
Tamar Units PL15 ..... 18 E2
Tamar Valley Donkey Pk★ PL18 ..... 40 D5
Tamar View
Launceston PL15 ..... 106 D5
Milton Abbot PL19 ..... 29 C6
St Dominick PL12 ..... 40 D2
Tamar View Ind Est PL12 ..... 122 D5
Tamar Villas PL9 ..... 135 D7
Tamar Way PL18 ..... 41 A6
Tamar Wharf PL1 ..... 127 D3
Tamblin Ave PL14 ..... 50 E7
Tamerton Ave PL5 ..... 123 D1
Tamerton Cl PL5 ..... 124 A6
Tamerton Foliot Rd PL6 ..... 124 D5
Tamerton Rd PL6 ..... 121 B2
Tamerton Vale Prim Sch PL6 ..... 124 C6
Tangmere Ave PL5 ..... 123 E5
Tangye Cl TR16 ..... 67 E5
Tangye Rd TR15 ..... 139 C6
Tanhouse Rd PL22 ..... 112 C2
Tanwood View PL31 ..... 109 C5
Tapson Dr PL9 ..... 135 A6
Taranto Rd TR13 ..... 146 D4
Taroveor Rd TR18 ..... 143 E6
Taroveor Terr 3 TR18 ..... 143 E5
Tarr PL22 ..... 49 E3
Tarrandean La TR3 ..... 81 E6
Tarten Cross PL12 ..... 53 B4
Tate Gallery★ TR26 ..... 141 B6
Taunton Ave PL5 ..... 124 B5
Taunton Pl PL5 ..... 124 B5
Tavern Barn PL23 ..... 116 C5
Tavistock Coll PL19 ..... 147 A3
Tavistock Com Prim Sch PL19 ..... 147 B4
Tavistock Cross PL20 ..... 41 C2
Tavistock Hospl PL19 ..... 147 B5
Tavistock Mus★ PL19 ..... 147 C6
Tavistock Pl PL4 ..... 149 A3
Tavistock Rd
Callington PL17 ..... 39 F4
Launceston PL15 ..... 106 D5
Launceston, Stourscombe PL15 ..... 106 E3
Plymouth, Manadon PL5 ..... 124 E1
Plymouth PL6 ..... 125 B5
Yelverton PL20 ..... 42 C3
Tavy Pl PL4 ..... 128 F4
Tavy Rd
Saltash PL12 ..... 123 A3
Tavistock PL19 ..... 147 D5
Taw Cl PL3 ..... 129 D6
Tayberry Dr TR16 ..... 140 F1
Tay Gdns PL3 ..... 129 D7
Taylor Cl PL12 ..... 122 C3
Taylor Rd PL12 ..... 122 C4
Taylor's Cross EX23 ..... 5 B7
Taylor Sq PL19 ..... 147 B6
Teachers Cl PL9 ..... 135 F6
Teats Hill Flats PL4 ..... 149 B1
Teats Hill Rd PL4 ..... 149 B1
Tedder Rd 4 PL26 ..... 59 D7
Tees Cl PL3 ..... 129 C7
Teetotal St TR26 ..... 141 C6
Tehidy Cl TR14 ..... 138 F7
Tehidy Copse TR14 ..... 67 B4
Tehidy Country Park★ TR14 ..... 67 B4
Tehidy Gdns TR14 ..... 138 F7
Tehidy Rd
Camborne TR14 ..... 138 D4
Tywardreath PL24 ..... 60 D5
Tehidy Terr TR11 ..... 145 A6
Teign Rd PL3 ..... 129 B6
Telcarne Cl TR27 ..... 78 D6
Telegraph Hill TR16 ..... 68 E1
Telegraph St TR16 ..... 68 D1
Telegraph Wharf PL1 ..... 134 A8
Telephone La PL26 ..... 59 C8
Telford Cres PL5 ..... 123 F2
Temeraire Rd PL5 ..... 124 D2
Tenacres La PL14 ..... 38 E4
Tenby Rd PL5 ..... 123 C1
Tencreek Ave TR18 ..... 143 E5
Tencreek Cvn And Camping Pk PL13 ..... 63 A3
Tenderah Ct TR13 ..... 146 C7
Tenderah Rd TR13 ..... 146 C6
Tennyson Gdns PL5 ..... 124 B1
Tern Gdns PL7 ..... 130 F5
Terrace The
Chacewater TR4 ..... 68 F3
Crafthole PL11 ..... 65 B5
Dobwalls PL14 ..... 50 D7
Downderry PL11 ..... 64 C5
East Portholland PL26 ..... 84 E5
Harrowbarrow PL17 ..... 40 D5
Penryn TR10 ..... 144 C7
Pentewan PL26 ..... 73 D6
Port Isaac PL29 ..... 22 E7
Portwrinkle PL11 ..... 65 A4
Rock PL27 ..... 21 D2
St Ives TR26 ..... 141 B5
Yeolmbridge PL15 ..... 18 E6
Terra Nova Gn PL2 ..... 128 B5
Terras Hill PL22 ..... 112 C3
Terras Rd PL26 ..... 58 A4
Tethadene PL30 ..... 23 E7
Tewington Pl PL25 ..... 114 B4
Tewkesbury Cl PL2 ..... 128 A8
Thackeray Gdns PL5 ..... 124 B1
Thames Gdns PL3 ..... 129 D5
Thanckes Cl PL11 ..... 127 A3
Thanckes Dr PL11 ..... 127 A4
Theatre Ope PL1 ..... 127 F1
Theatre Royal Plymouth PL1 ..... 148 C2
Therlow Rd PL3 ..... 129 B6
Thetford Gdns PL6 ..... 129 D8
Theydon Rd TR11 ..... 144 F3
Third Ave
Plymouth, Billacombe PL9 ..... 130 A1
Plymouth, Camels Head PL2 ..... 127 E7
Plymouth, Stoke PL1 ..... 128 A2
Thirlmere Gdns PL6 ..... 124 F4
Thistle Cl PL6 ..... 125 E7
Thomas Bullock Cl PL30 ..... 48 C2
Thomas Johnson Ct 6 TR1 ..... 137 C4
Thomas St 4 TR13 ..... 98 C8
Thomas Terr 5 TR13 ..... 98 C8
Thornberry Terr TR18 ..... 143 F6
Thornbury Park Ave PL3 ..... 128 D6
Thornbury Prim Sch PL6 ..... 125 D4
Thornbury Rd PL6 ..... 125 E4
Thorn Cl PL15 ..... 26 C7
Thorndon Cross EX22 ..... 8 F5
Thorne Cross EX23 ..... 4 F2
Thornhill Rd PL3 ..... 128 E6
Thornhill Way PL3 ..... 128 E6
Thorn La PL12 ..... 122 C3
Thorn Moor Cross PL15 ..... 19 F7
Thornpark Rd PL25 ..... 114 E5
Thorn Pk PL3 ..... 128 F5
Thorn Terr PL14 ..... 113 B5
Thornton Ave PL4 ..... 149 B4
Thornton Cl PL26 ..... 46 F3
Thornville Terr PL9 ..... 135 C7
Thornwell La PL12 ..... 53 E2
Thornyville Cl PL9 ..... 135 C8
Thornyville Dr PL9 ..... 135 D8
Thornyville Villas PL9 ..... 135 C8
Three Corners Cl PL32 ..... 105 B2
Three Cross TR13 ..... 91 F5
Three Holes Cross PL27 ..... 34 A8
Threemilestone Ind Est TR4 ..... 69 C3
Threemilestone Ret Pk TR3 ..... 69 C4
Threemilestone Sch TR3 ..... 69 D3
Thurlestone Wlk PL6 ..... 129 D8
Tiddy Brook Rd
Tavistock PL19 ..... 147 E2
Whitchurch PL19 ..... 147 E2
Tiddy Cl
St Germans PL12 ..... 65 B8
Tavistock PL19 ..... 147 B3
Tideford Cross La PL12 ..... 52 F3
Tideford Dr
Landrake PL12 ..... 53 A2
St Germans PL12 ..... 65 B8
Tideford Rd PL12 ..... 53 C3
Tidemill Ho TR11 ..... 145 C3
Tides Reach TR7 ..... 111 B7
Tillard Cl PL7 ..... 131 C5
Tillie St 5 PL17 ..... 39 E4
Tilly Cl PL9 ..... 135 F4
Timber Cl PL25 ..... 114 B4
Tincombe PL12 ..... 122 C2
Tincroft Rd TR15 ..... 139 B4
Tin La PL4 ..... 149 A2
Tinners Dr PL27 ..... 21 D6
Tinners Way
Callington PL17 ..... 39 F5
New Polzeath PL27 ..... 21 D6
16 St Ives TR26 ..... 77 A6
Tinners Wlk TR11 ..... 145 D3
Tinney Dr TR1 ..... 137 F5
Tintagel Castle★ PL34 ..... 14 B8
Tintagel Cres PL2 ..... 128 C8
Tintagel Hotel 8 PL34 ..... 14 C7
Tintagel Hts PL34 ..... 14 D6
Tintagel Prim Sch PL34 ..... 14 C6
Tintagel Rd PL35 ..... 9 C1
Tintagel Terr PL29 ..... 22 D7
Tintagel Toy Mus★ PL34 ..... 14 C7
Tintagel Visitor Ctr★ PL34 ..... 14 C7
Tintern Ave PL4 ..... 149 C2
Tiny Mdws
Launceston PL15 ..... 18 E1
South Petherwin PL15 ..... 27 F8
Tipple Cross PL15 ..... 19 C6
Tithe Rd PL7 ..... 130 B7
Tiverton Cl PL6 ..... 125 B8
Tobruk Rd PL12 ..... 122 E3
Toby Way TR7 ..... 110 D7
Toddington Lea PL26 ..... 58 E5
Tolcarne Cl PL25 ..... 114 E3
Tolcarne Mews 7 TR7 ..... 110 F6
Tolcarne Rd
Camborne TR14 ..... 79 D5
Newquay TR7 ..... 110 F6
St Day TR16 ..... 68 D1
Tolcarne St TR14 ..... 138 D2
Tolcarne Terr TR18 ..... 143 C3
Tolgarrick Rd TR14 ..... 138 F5
Tolgus Hill TR15 ..... 140 A5
Tolgus Pl TR15 ..... 140 A6
Tolgus Tin★ TR16 ..... 67 F5
Tolgus Vean TR15 ..... 140 A5
Tolgus Wartha TR15 ..... 140 A6
Tollgate Cl PL14 ..... 113 B4
Tollox Pl PL3 ..... 129 B4
Tollyfrank Hill TR2 ..... 83 F6
Tolpedn Flats TR26 ..... 141 E2
Tolponds Rd TR13 ..... 91 A1
Tolroy Holiday Village TR27 ..... 142 C2
Tolroy Rd TR27 ..... 142 D1
Tolskithy La TR15 ..... 139 E6
Tolticken Hill TR16 ..... 67 E6
Toltuff Cres TR18 ..... 143 C4
Toltuff Rd TR18 ..... 143 C4
Tolvaddon Energy Pk TR14 ..... 138 F7
Tolvaddon Rd TR15 ..... 139 A5
Tolvan Cross TR12 ..... 92 C2
Tolver Pl TR18 ..... 143 E6
Tolver Rd TR18 ..... 143 E6
Tolverth Terr TR20 ..... 88 F6
Tolview Terr TR27 ..... 142 B4
Tom Lyon Rd PL14 ..... 113 E5
Tom Nicolls Cl 7 PL14 ..... 38 A3
Top Hill TR2 ..... 57 E1
Top Of The Town Ctyd PL12 ..... 122 F2

Top Rd PL11 ... 64 C5
Torbridge Cl PL12 ... 122 D2
Torbridge Rd
6 Horrabridge PL20 ... 42 C4
Plymouth PL7 ... 130 E6
Torbryan Cl PL6 ... 129 E8
Tor Cl
Plymouth, Hartley PL3 ... 128 E7
Porthleven TR13 ... 91 B1
Tor Cres PL3 ... 128 E7
Tor La PL12 ... 122 B1
Torland Rd PL3 ... 128 E7
Torleven Rd TR13 ... 91 B2
Torpoint Com Sch PL11 . 127 A4
Torpoint Inf Sch PL11 ... 127 B3
Tor Rd
Newquay TR7 ... 110 E6
Plymouth PL3 ... 128 E7
Torridge Cl PL7 ... 131 A6
Torridge Rd PL7 ... 130 F6
Torridge Way PL3 ... 129 C5
Torr La PL3 ... 128 E7
Torr Rd PL3 ... 128 E7
Torr View Ave PL3 ... 128 D7
Tors View Cl PL17 ... 39 F4
Torver Cl PL6 ... 125 D2
Tor View
Bugle PL26 ... 47 C2
Camelford PL32 ... 105 C2
7 Horrabridge PL20 ... 42 C4
Tregadillett PL15 ... 18 C2
Torwood Cl PL31 ... 109 D4
Tory Brook Ave PL7 ... 130 E6
Tory Brook Ct PL7 ... 130 E6
Tory Way PL7 ... 130 D6
Tosberry Cross EX39 ... 3 B8
Tothill Ave PL4 ... 149 B3
Tothill Rd PL4 ... 149 B3
Totnes Cl PL7 ... 131 B4
Towan Blystra Rd TR7 ... 111 A5
Towan Ct PL28 ... 31 E8
Towan Rd
Pentewan PL26 ... 73 D8
Porthtowan TR4 ... 68 A7
Towednack Rd TR26 ... 77 A6
Tower Cl
Pelynt PL13 ... 62 D6
Sennen TR19 ... 96 B6
Tower Ct PL12 ... 122 C2
Towerfield Dr PL6 ... 125 C8
Tower Hill
Looe PL13 ... 117 D3
Wadebridge PL27 ... 108 E5
Tower Hill Rd PL15 ... 13 F1
Tower Mdws TR19 ... 97 A6
Tower Park Est PL13 ... 62 D6
Tower Park Rd PL13 ... 62 C6
Tower Pk
Fowey PL23 ... 116 B3
Lanivet PL30 ... 47 E7
Pelynt PL13 ... 62 D6
Tower Pk Cvn & Camping Pk
TR19 ... 97 A7
Tower Rd
Newquay TR7 ... 110 D6
St Erme TR4 ... 70 D8
Towers Cl PL6 ... 125 F2
Tower St PL15 ... 106 C6
Tower View PL12 ... 122 D1
Town Arms Pas PL31 ... 109 E5
Town End PL31 ... 109 C5
Town Farm TR15 ... 140 C3
Town Farm Cl 5 PL20 ... 42 C4
Townfield TR15 ... 139 C6
Town Hill TR5 ... 54 D1
Town Mill Gdns PL19 ... 147 C6
Town Mills PL15 ... 106 B7
Town Mills Flats PL15 ... 106 B7
Town Quay TR1 ... 137 D4
Townsend
Polruan PL23 ... 116 D2
14 Stratton EX23 ... 4 E1
Townshend Ave PL2 ... 127 E5
Townswell Cl PL12 ... 53 E2
Townswell La PL12 ... 53 E2
Traboe Cross TR12 ... 100 D3
Tracey Ct PL1 ... 148 B3
Trafalgar Cl PL5 ... 127 D8
Trafalgar Ct TR18 ... 143 F6
Trafalgar Pl 3 PL1 ... 127 F3
Trafalgar Place La PL1 ... 127 F3
Trafalgar Sq TR1 ... 137 D4
Trafalgar St PL4 ... 149 A3
Traine Brake PL9 ... 136 C1
Traine Rd PL9 ... 136 B1
Traly Cl EX23 ... 104 F4
Tram La TR16 ... 140 E1
Tramway Rd PL6 ... 125 E7
Trannack Com Prim Sch
TR13 ... 91 E5
Trannack Mill Ind Est
TR13 ... 91 E5
Trannack Terr TR18 ... 143 E7
Tranquil La PL31 ... 109 C5
Transit Way PL5 ... 124 C3
Trasdeves Orch 16 PL17 ... 39 F4
Travellers Rest Pk TR12 ... 99 B8
Travers Cl PL14 ... 113 A6
Treago Gdns PL6 ... 125 C8
Trease TR19 ... 75 A1
Treassowe Rd TR18 ... 143 E6
Treassowe Riding TR20 ... 88 F8
Treator Cotts PL28 ... 107 A5
Trebah Gdns★ TR11 ... 93 C2
Treban Rd TR18 ... 143 C4
Trebartha Cl PL17 ... 39 E3
Trebartha Rd TR1 ... 137 F5
Trebarthen Terr TR4 ... 55 D5
Trebarva Cl TR15 ... 140 A6
Trebarvah La TR20 ... 89 E4
Trebarvah Rd TR11 ... 92 E4
Trebarwith Cres TR7 ... 110 E6
Trebarwith Rd PL33 ... 14 D4
Treberran Gdns TR14 ... 138 F6
Treboul Cross PL12 ... 64 F8
Treboul Way PL12 ... 65 B8
Treburdon Dr PL26 ... 46 F3
Treburgie Water PL14 ... 50 D7
Treburley Cl PL15 ... 28 C4
Treburley Ind Est PL15 ... 28 C4
Trebyhan Parc TR3 ... 80 F3
Treby Rd PL7 ... 130 F4
Trecarn Cl PL15 ... 106 B5
Trecarne
Falmouth TR11 ... 144 E5
Tremar PL14 ... 38 A3
Trecarne Cl
Polgooth PL26 ... 59 A1
St Austell PL25 ... 115 B5
Truro TR1 ... 137 E5
Trecarne Gdns PL33 ... 14 E3
Trecarne View PL14 ... 37 F3
Trecarrack Rd TR14 ... 138 F3
Trecarrell PL15 ... 106 C4
Trecarrell Cl PL15 ... 106 D4
Trecerus Ind Est PL28 ... 107 B4
Tredanek Cl PL31 ... 109 B5
Tredarrup Cross PL15 ... 11 A1
Tredarvah Dr TR18 ... 143 C5
Tredarvah Rd TR18 ... 143 C5
Tredaula Manor Cvn Pk
PL15 ... 26 D7
Tredavoe La TR18 ... 143 B1
Tredenham Cl 4 PL24 ... 60 C4
Tredenham Rd TR2 ... 95 B6
Tredethy Rd PL30 ... 34 F6
Tredinnick Cotts TR 20 ... 76 A1
Tredinnick La PL12 ... 53 B2
Tredinnick Lane-End
PL13 ... 64 A8
Tredinnick Way 12 TR6 ... 55 A4
Tredinnick Wood Cl
TR13 ... 146 D8
Tredour Rd TR7 ... 110 E4
Tredova Cres TR11 ... 145 B2
Tredragon Cl TR8 ... 31 C2
Tredragon Rd TR8 ... 31 C2
Tredrea Gdns TR3 ... 81 D5
Tredrea La TR27 ... 77 E2
Tredrea Manor TR3 ... 81 D5
Tredrizzick Cl PL27 ... 21 F3
Tredruston Rd PL27 ... 33 B6
Tredydan Rd PL15 ... 106 B6
Tredynas Rd TR11 ... 145 D3
Tredyson Pl TR11 ... 145 A3
Tre-El- Verne Cl TR1 ... 137 A4
Treen Cotts TR26 ... 75 F4
Treen Flats TR14 ... 138 F3
Treen Hill TR19 ... 96 F4
Treetop Cl PL12 ... 122 D4
Treetops Hill PL13 ... 117 A3
Treeve Farm Ind Units
TR27 ... 78 C6
Treeve La TR27 ... 78 C6
Treffry Ct TR7 ... 110 D6
Treffry La PL30 ... 48 C6
Treffry Rd TR1 ... 137 E7
Treffry Way 12 PL24 ... 60 B4
Trefinnick Rd PL17 ... 39 B8
Trefleur Cl 3 PL35 ... 9 C1
Trefloyd Cl PL17 ... 39 E6
Treforda Rd TR7 ... 110 F4
Treforest Rd PL27 ... 108 A6
Treforthlan 7 TR16 ... 67 E4
Treforthlan Cl 6 TR16 ... 67 E4
Trefrew Rd PL32 ... 105 D5
Trefusis Cl TR1 ... 137 F5
Trefusis Ct TR11 ... 145 A6
Trefusis Gdns PL3 ... 129 A4
Trefusis Rd
Falmouth TR11 ... 144 E2
Flushing TR11 ... 145 C6
Redruth TR15 ... 140 C4
Trefusis Terr
Millbrook PL10 ... 132 E6
Redruth TR15 ... 140 C5
Tregadillett Com Prim Sch
PL15 ... 18 C2
Tregaer TR11 ... 145 C3
Tregainlands Pk PL30 ... 34 D3
Tregalister Gdns PL12 ... 65 B8
Tregaller La PL15 ... 18 E1
Treganoon Rd TR15 ... 140 D7
Tregargus View PL26 ... 58 B4
Tregarland Cl
Camborne TR14 ... 138 E2
Coad's Green PL15 ... 27 D4
Tregarne Terr PL25 ... 114 C4
Tregarrian Rd TR14 ... 138 F7
Tregarrick PL13 ... 117 B3
Tregarrick Cl TR13 ... 146 B7
Tregarrick Ct PL13 ... 117 B3
Tregarrick La PL13 ... 62 D6
Tregarrick Rd PL26 ... 46 F3
Tregarrick Way PL13 ... 62 D6
Tregarth 12 PL26 ... 59 D7
Tregartha Way PL14 ... 113 D6
Tregarthen 2 TR26 ... 141 A5
Tregarth Pl TR18 ... 143 C4
Tregassack Rd TR20 ... 88 F7
Tregassick Rd TR2 ... 83 B1
Tregatillian Cvn Pk TR9 ... 45 F6
Tregavarras Row PL26 ... 85 A5
Tregavethan View TR3 ... 69 C4
Tregay La PL14 ... 113 C7
Tregea Hill TR16 ... 67 C6
Tregear Cl TR12 ... 99 D6
Tregear Gdns TR1 ... 137 C4
Tregease Rd TR5 ... 54 C1
Tregea Terr TR16 ... 67 C6
Tregellas Rd TR12 ... 99 B1
Tregellast Cl TR12 ... 101 D4
Tregellast Parc TR12 ... 101 D4
Tregellast Rd TR12 ... 101 D3
Tregembo Hill TR20 ... 90 A7
Tregender La TR20 ... 89 B8
Tregender Rd TR20 ... 89 B8
Tregenna Cl
Plymouth PL7 ... 131 C4
Wainhouse Corner EX23 ... 10 F6
Tregenna Ct
Camborne TR14 ... 138 C2
Falmouth TR11 ... 145 C3
Tregenna Fields TR14 ... 138 C2
Tregenna Hill 16 TR26 ... 141 B5
Tregenna La TR14 ... 138 C2
Tregenna Parc TR26 ... 141 C3
Tregenna Pl 4 TR26 ... 141 B5
Tregenna Rd PL30 ... 35 C8
Tregenna Terr TR26 ... 141 B5
Tregenver Rd TR11 ... 144 F4
Tregenver Terr TR11 ... 144 F4
Tregenver Villas TR11 ... 144 F4
Tregeseal Hill TR19 ... 86 F7
Tregeseal Row TR19 ... 86 F6
Tregeseal Terr TR19 ... 86 F6
Tregew Cl TR11 ... 145 B7
Tregew Rd
Flushing TR11 ... 145 B8
Penryn TR10, TR11 ... 81 F2
Treggodick Cotts TR20 ... 143 A8
Tregian Cl TR1 ... 137 F5
Tregidden Hill TR12 ... 100 F5
Tregie TR18 ... 143 B3
Tregiskey Cotts PL26 ... 73 C5
Tregisky La TR12 ... 101 C1
Treglenwith Rd TR14 ... 138 C4
Treglisson Rural Workshops
TR27 ... 78 C3
Treglyn Cl TR18 ... 143 B1
Treglyn Farm Cotts PL27 . 22 B3
Tregoddick Cl TR20 ... 88 B7
Tregolds La PL28 ... 31 F7
Tregolls Cl TR1 ... 137 E5
Tregolls Rd TR1 ... 137 E5
Tregolls Sch TR1 ... 137 F5
Tregoney Hill PL26 ... 73 C3
Tregongeeves La PL26 ... 59 A2
Tregonhay PL14 ... 38 C7
Tregonhayne Ct TR2 ... 72 A4
Tregoniggie Ind Est
TR11 ... 144 D4
Tregoning Rd PL11 ... 126 F2
Tregonissey Cl PL25 ... 114 D5
Tregonissey Rd PL25 ... 114 E5
Tregonissy La End PL25 . 114 E6
Tregonning Cl TR13 ... 90 E3
Tregonning Ct 8 TR6 ... 55 A5
Tregonning Parc 9
TR12 ... 101 C4
Tregonning Rd TR3 ... 80 F3
Tregonning Terr TR13 ... 90 F5
Tregonning View 17 TR13 98 C8
Tregony Com Prim Sch
TR2 ... 71 F4
Tregony Hill TR2 ... 71 F3
Tregony Rd TR2 ... 71 D6
Tregony Rural Workshops
TR2 ... 71 E3
Tregorrick Rd PL26 ... 114 E1
Tregos Rd TR26 ... 141 C2
Tregoss Rd TR7 ... 110 F6
Tregothnan Rd
Falmouth TR11 ... 145 A5
Truro TR1 ... 137 E3
Tregowris Court Cotts
TR12 ... 101 B5
Tregrea TR14 ... 138 E1
Tregrehan Gdns★ PL24 ... 115 E6
Treguddock Dr PL27 ... 108 D5
Tregullan TR15 ... 139 C8
Tregullan View PL31 ... 109 D3
Tregullow Rd TR11 ... 144 F5
Tregundy Cl 21 TR6 ... 55 A5
Tregundy Ct 20 TR6 ... 55 A5
Tregundy La TR6 ... 55 A5
Tregundy Rd TR6 ... 55 A5
Tregunna Cl TR13 ... 91 B1
Tregunnel Cvn Pk TR7 ... 110 D5
Tregunnel Hill TR7 ... 110 D4
Tregunnick La PL11 ... 64 B6
Tregunnus La PL11 ... 64 D5
Tregunter Mews TR11 ... 145 D3
Tregurra La TR1 ... 137 E6
Tregurrian Hill TR8 ... 44 D8
Tregurtha Farm Cotts
TR17 ... 89 D6
Tregurtha View TR20 ... 89 E5
Tregurthen Cl TR14 ... 138 C2
Tregurthen Rd TR14 ... 138 C2
Tregustick Holiday Pk
TR8 ... 44 D6
Treguth Cl TR8 ... 43 B1
Tregwary Rd TR26 ... 141 A5
Tregye Campus (Truro Coll)
TR3 ... 82 A7
Tregye Rd TR3 ... 82 A7
Trehaddle TR4 ... 81 B7
Trehane Rd TR14 ... 138 B3
Trehannick Cl PL30 ... 23 E7
Trehaverne Cl TR1 ... 137 C5
Trehaverne La TR1 ... 137 C5
Trehaverne Terr 3 TR1 . 137 C5
Trehaverne Vean TR1 ... 137 C5
Trehawke La PL14 ... 38 C1
Trehayes Mdw TR27 ... 77 E2
Trehayes Parc TR27 ... 142 E7
Trehaze-Na Cl PL32 ... 10 C3
Treheath Rd PL14 ... 50 E7
Trehill Cross PL12 ... 40 C2
Trehill La PL10 ... 64 B2
Trehunsey Cl TR11 ... 93 E2
Trehurst TR18 ... 143 D4
Trekeen Rd TR10 ... 144 B8
Trekenner Com Prim Sch
PL15 ... 28 C5
Trekenning Rd TR9 ... 45 D5
Trekestle Cvn Pk PL15 ... 18 C2
Trekestle Pk PL15 ... 18 C2
Trekye Cl TR16 ... 80 B5
Trelake Rd PL25 ... 114 B4
Trelan TR14 ... 138 F3
Trelander Barton TR1 ... 137 E5
Trelander E TR1 ... 137 F4
Trelander Highway TR1 . 137 E4
Trelander N TR1 ... 137 F4
Trelander S TR1 ... 137 F4
Trelander Vean TR1 ... 137 F4
Trelantis Est PL28 ... 31 F8
Trelaske La PL13 ... 62 F4
Trelavour Prazey PL26 ... 58 B8
Trelavour Rd PL26 ... 58 C8
Trelavour Sq PL26 ... 58 C8
Trelawne Cl 10 TR3 ... 81 F7
Trelawne Cottage Gdns
PL13 ... 62 E4
Trelawne Gdns PL13 ... 62 E5
Trelawne Rd TR3 ... 81 F7
Trelawney Apartments
TR7 ... 110 F6
Trelawney Ave
Falmouth TR11 ... 145 B3
Plymouth PL5 ... 123 D1
Poughill EX23 ... 4 C3
Redruth TR15 ... 140 E7
St Ives TR26 ... 141 A5
Trelawney Cl
Bodmin PL31 ... 109 C4
Maenporth TR11 ... 93 E3
Torpoint PL11 ... 126 E3
Warbstow Cross PL15 ... 11 B1
Trelawney Cotts PL15 ... 106 D5
Trelawney Ct PL27 ... 21 E3
Trelawney Est
Madron TR20 ... 143 A8
Ponsanooth TR4 ... 81 B7
Trelawney Gdns PL14 ... 38 D4
Trelawney Hts 19 PL17 ... 39 F4
Trelawney Parc
St Columb Major TR9 ... 45 D5
Warbstow Cross PL15 ... 11 B1
Trelawney Pl
Hayle TR27 ... 142 C6
Penryn TR10 ... 144 C8
Plymouth PL5 ... 123 D1
Trelawney Rd
Bodmin PL31 ... 109 C3
Callington PL17 ... 39 F4
Camborne TR14 ... 138 D3
Chacewater TR4 ... 69 A3
Helston TR13 ... 146 C5
Newquay TR7 ... 110 E5
Padstow PL28 ... 107 D4
Plymouth PL3 ... 128 D5
Ponsanooth TR3 ... 81 B4
Saltash PL12 ... 122 E2
St Austell PL25 ... 114 E5
St Ives TR26 ... 141 A5
St Mawes TR2 ... 95 A6
Truro TR1 ... 137 B5
Trelawney Rise
18 Callington PL17 ... 39 F4
Torpoint PL11 ... 126 E3
Trelawney Terr
Cury TR12 ... 99 B4
Looe PL13 ... 117 C4
Trelawney Way
Hayle TR27 ... 142 C6
Torpoint PL11 ... 126 E3
Trelawny Ct TR14 ... 138 C3
Trelawny Rd
Falmouth TR11 ... 145 B4
Menheniot PL14 ... 52 A6
Plymouth PL7 ... 130 C6
St Agnes TR5 ... 54 C1
Tavistock PL19 ... 147 C6
Treleaver Way TR1 ... 69 F3
Trelee Cl TR27 ... 142 E7
Treleigh Ave TR15 ... 140 B6
Treleigh Com Prim Sch
TR16 ... 140 C8
Treleigh Ind Est TR16 ... 140 C7
Treleigh Terr TR15 ... 140 A5
Trelevan Cl PL25 ... 114 C3
Treleven Rd EX23 ... 104 F4
Treliddon La PL11 ... 64 C5
Treliever Cross TR10 ... 81 C1
Treliever Rd
Mabe Burnthouse TR10 ... 81 C1
Penryn TR10 ... 144 B8
Treligga Downs Rd PL33 . 14 D2
Trelil Cvn Site TR13 ... 146 E7
Trelil La TR11 ... 144 C2
Trelindon PL15 ... 27 E8
Trelinnoe Cl PL15 ... 27 E8
Trelinnoe Gdns PL15 ... 27 E8
Treliske Ind Est TR1 ... 69 E4
Treliske La TR1, TR4 ... 69 F4
Treliske Prep Sch TR1 ... 69 F4
Treliske Rd TR15 ... 140 D6
Trelispen Park Dr PL26 ... 85 C5
Trelispen Pk PL26 ... 85 C5
Trelissick Fields TR27 ... 142 B3
Trelissick Gdns
Callington PL17 ... 39 E3
Feock TR3 ... 82 D6
Trelissick Rd
Falmouth TR11 ... 144 F5
Hayle TR27 ... 142 B3
Trelissick Woodland Wlk★
TR3 ... 82 D6
Treloan La TR2 ... 83 B1
Treloar Terr PL15 ... 106 B6
Treloggan Ind Est TR7 ... 111 B4
Treloggan La TR7 ... 111 A5
Treloggan Rd TR7 ... 111 A4
Trelorrin Gdns PL3 ... 128 E5
Trelowarren★ TR12 ... 99 F6
Trelowarren Ct 13 PL17 ... 39 E4
Trelowarren St TR14 ... 138 D3
Treloweck TR14 ... 79 A4
Treloweth Cl
Plymouth PL2 ... 128 D8
St Erth TR27 ... 77 E2
Treloweth Com Prim Sch
TR15 ... 139 D6
Treloweth Gdns TR15 ... 139 C6
Treloweth La TR27 ... 77 E2
Treloweth Rd TR15 ... 139 C6
Treloweth Terr TR15 ... 139 B7
Treloweth Way TR15 ... 139 C7
Trelowth Rd PL26 ... 59 A1
Treloyhan Cl TR26 ... 141 C3
Treloyhan Park Rd TR26 . 141 C3
Trelyn PL27 ... 21 E3
Trelyn Rd TR12 ... 101 D4
Trelyon Ave TR26 ... 141 C4
Trelyon Cl TR19 ... 97 B6
Tremabe La PL14 ... 50 E7
Tremabe Pk PL14 ... 50 E7
Tremadart Cl PL14 ... 51 A1
Tremadart Farm Barns
PL14 ... 51 A1
Tremaddock Cotts PL14 .. 36 F3
Tremaddock Council Hos
PL14 ... 36 F3
Tremaine Cl TR18 ... 143 C7
Tremalic PL13 ... 117 B3
Tremall Parc TR3 ... 80 F3
Tremanor Way TR11 ... 144 D5
Tremar Cl PL14 ... 38 A2
Tremar La
St Cleer PL14 ... 37 F3
Tremar PL14 ... 38 A3
Tremarle Home Pk TR14 138 F5
Tremarne Cl TR3 ... 82 C5
Tremar Rd TR26 ... 77 A7
Tremarren Rd PL27 ... 108 B5
Trematon Cl PL11 ... 126 E4
Trematon Terr PL4 ... 128 E4
Tremayne Cl TR3 ... 81 F6
Tremayne Ho PL31 ... 109 B4
Tremayne Pk TR14 ... 138 F2
Tremayne Rd
Carharrack TR16 ... 80 F8
St Austell PL25 ... 114 E4
Truro TR1 ... 137 C5
Tremayne Rise PL19 ... 147 B5
Tremayne Terr PL13 ... 63 F8
Trembath Cres TR7 ... 110 E5
Trembear Rd PL25 ... 114 A4
Trembel Rd TR12 ... 99 B2
Trembrase TR19 ... 96 C7
Tremeadow Terr
Hayle TR27 ... 142 B4
Liskeard PL14 ... 113 D7
Tremear Gn 6 TR9 ... 45 E2
Tremearne Rd 16 TR13 ... 98 C8
Tremeddan Ct 2 PL14 ... 113 C6
Tremeddan La PL14 ... 113 C6
Tremeddan Terr PL14 ... 113 B4
Tremeer La PL30 ... 23 E3
Tremellin La TR27 ... 77 F1
Tremena Gdns PL25 ... 114 C4
Tremena Rd PL25 ... 114 C4
Tremenheere Ave TR13 . 146 D8
Tremenheere Rd TR18 ... 143 E6
Tremenva Ct 1 TR13 ... 146 C5
Tremewan 1 PL25 ... 59 A3
Tremodrett Rd PL26 ... 46 F3
Tremoh Ct TR2 ... 71 C6
Tremollett Cotts PL17 ... 28 B1
Tremore Rd TR15 ... 140 D6
Tremorva TR27 ... 142 C6
Tremorvah Barton TR1 ... 137 E5
Tremorvah Cres TR1 ... 137 E5
Tremorvah Ct
Falmouth TR11 ... 144 F1
Truro TR1 ... 137 E5
Tremorvah Pk TR11 ... 144 F1
Tremorvah Wood La
TR1 ... 137 E5
Tremough Barton Cotts
TR10 ... 81 C1
Tremoughdale TR10 ... 144 B8
Trenale La PL34 ... 14 D7
Trenalt Terr TR1 ... 137 B5
Trenance Ave TR7 ... 110 F5
Trenance Cl TR13 ... 146 B7
Trenance Ct TR7 ... 110 E4
Trenance Cvn Pk TR7 ... 110 F5
Trenance Hill PL25 ... 114 A5
Trenance Inf Sch TR7 ... 110 E5
Trenance La
3 Mullion TR12 ... 99 A1
Newquay TR7 ... 110 E4

Trenance Leisure Pk★
TR7 . . . . 111 A5
Trenance Pl PL25 . . . . 114 B4
Trenance Rd
Camborne TR14 . . . . 138 E4
Newquay TR7 . . . . 110 E5
St Austell PL25 . . . . 114 B4
Trenant TR16 . . . . 68 D1
Trenant Cl PL27 . . . . 21 E5
Trenant Cross PL14 . . . . 63 A6
Trenant Ind Est PL27 . . . . 108 D6
Trenant Rd
Looe PL13 . . . . 117 D5
2 Tywardreath PL24 . . . . 60 D5
Trenant Vale PL27 . . . . 108 D6
Trenarren View PL25 . . . . 115 A6
Trenarth TR10 . . . . 144 C8
Trenarth Rd TR7 . . . . 110 E5
Trenawin La TR27 . . . . 78 E5
Trencher La PL10 . . . . 132 D2
Trencreek Cl TR4 . . . . 56 D1
Trencreek La TR8 . . . . 111 B4
Trencreek Rd TR7, TR8 . . 111 B4
Trencrom La TR26 . . . . 141 D1
Trencrom Row TR20 . . . . 77 B3
Trendeal Gdns 1 TR18 . . 143 E5
Trendlewood Rd PL6 . . . . 125 D7
Trendreath Cl TR26 . . . . 77 E3
Treneague Pk PL27 . . . . 108 B4
Trenear Cl TR15 . . . . 140 D6
Treneere La TR18 . . . . 143 D7
Treneere Rd TR18 . . . . 143 D6
Treneglos TR4 . . . . 81 C7
Treneglos Terr
Gulval TR18 . . . . 88 E6
Newlyn TR18 . . . . 143 C3
Trenerry Cl TR1 . . . . 137 D6
Trenerth Rd TR27 . . . . 78 E2
Trenethick Ave TR13 . . . . 146 D8
Trenethick Bsns Pk
TR13 . . . . 146 C8
Trenethick Cl TR13 . . . . 146 D7
Trenethick Farm TR13 . . . . 146 B8
Trenethick Parc TR13 . . . . 146 D8
Trengove PL26 . . . . 47 C1
Trengove Cross TR11 . . . . 92 D5
Trengrouse Ave PL11 . . . . 126 F3
Trengrouse Way TR13 . . . . 146 C5
Trengwainton Gdns★
TR20 . . . . 88 A6
Trenhaile Terr TR1 . . . . 70 D1
Trenhayle La TR27 . . . . 142 B2
Treningle View PL31 . . . . 109 C3
Treninnick Hill TR7 . . . . 110 F5
Treninnow & Wiggle Chalets
PL10 . . . . 132 C2
Trenithick Mdw TR4 . . . . 68 C6
Trenithon La TR8 . . . . 57 C6
Trennance Ct 6 TR12 . . . . 99 A1
Trennick La TR1 . . . . 137 E3
Trennick Row TR1 . . . . 137 E3
Trennick Villas Ct TR1 . . 137 E3
Trenode CE Sch PL13 . . . . 51 F1
Trenouth Cl 5 PL14 . . . . 38 A3
Trenovissick Rd PL24 . . . . 60 B4
Trenowah Rd PL25 . . . . 115 C5
Trenoweth Ave TR14 . . . . 138 B3
Trenoweth Cres TR18 . . . . 143 B4
Trenoweth Ct TR12 . . . . 102 F2
Trenoweth Est TR15 . . . . 140 A8
Trenoweth La TR10 . . . . 93 B8
Trenoweth Mdw TR12 . . . . 102 F2
Trenoweth Rd
Falmouth TR11 . . . . 144 F2
Penzance TR18 . . . . 143 B5
Trenoweth Terr TR10 . . . . 93 B8
Trenoweth Vean TR10 . . . . 81 B1
Trenowth Terr TR2 . . . . 57 E1
Trent Cl PL3 . . . . 129 B6
Trentham Cl PL6 . . . . 125 B6
Trentworthy Cross EX22 . . . . 3 E2
Trenwith La TR26 . . . . 141 A4
Trenwith Pl 14 TR26 . . . . 141 B5
Trenwith Rd TR14 . . . . 138 B3
Trenwith Sq TR26 . . . . 141 A5
Trenwith Terr 11 TR26 . . 141 B5
Trenython Rd 10 PL24 . . . . 60 B4
Treore Cl PL30 . . . . 23 A6
Treovis Cross PL14 . . . . 38 C8
Tre-Pol PL26 . . . . 58 F1
Treraven La PL27 . . . . 108 C3
Trerew Rd TR18 . . . . 143 C4
Trerice★ TR8 . . . . 44 D1
Trerice Ct 15 PL17 . . . . 39 E4
Trerice Dr TR7 . . . . 111 B5
Trerice Fields TR14 . . . . 79 B2
Trerice Holdings TR8 . . . . 44 C1
Trerice Pl TR26 . . . . 141 A5
Trerice Rd 6 TR26 . . . . 141 A5
Trerice Terr PL26 . . . . 58 A8
Trerieve PL11 . . . . 64 C5
Trerise Rd TR14 . . . . 138 C3
Treroosel Rd PL30 . . . . 23 D8
Treruffe Hill TR15 . . . . 140 B4
Treruffe Terr 9 TR15 . . . . 140 B4
Treryn Cl PL24 . . . . 60 B5
Tresaderns Rd TR15 . . . . 140 A6
Tresahar Rd TR11 . . . . 145 A3
Tresamble Hill TR4, TR3 . . 81 B6
Tresavean Est TR16 . . . . 80 E6
Tresavean Hill TR16 . . . . 80 E6
Tresavean Terr TR16 . . . . 80 E6
Tresawla Ct TR14 . . . . 138 F6
Tresawle Rd TR11 . . . . 145 A6
Tresawls Ave TR1 . . . . 69 F3
Tresawls Rd TR1, TR4 . . . . 69 E4
Tresawna Terr TR11 . . . . 145 B4
Trescobeas Rd TR11 . . . . 144 E5
Trescoe Rd TR20 . . . . 88 F6
Trescol Vean Sch TR3 . . . . 69 C2
Tresco Pl TR11 . . . . 144 F4
Trescore PL28 . . . . 31 F7
Trescowe Rd TR20 . . . . 89 F5
Tresdale Parc TR27 . . . . 78 D6
Treseder's Gdns TR1 . . . . 137 D5
Tresevern Hill TR3 . . . . 80 D4
Tresidder Cl TR11 . . . . 144 E4
Tresillian Ho TR1 . . . . 69 E4
Tresillian Rd TR11 . . . . 144 F6
Tresillian St PL4 . . . . 149 C2
Tresithney Rd TR16 . . . . 80 F8
Treskerby TR16 . . . . 140 F7
Treskewes Est 1 TR12 . . 101 C4
Treskilling PL30 . . . . 59 F8
Treslothan Rd TR14 . . . . 79 D4
Tresluggan Rd PL5 . . . . 123 D1
Tresooth Cl TR10 . . . . 144 D7
Tresooth La TR10 . . . . 144 C8
Tresooth Terr TR10 . . . . 144 D7
Tresowgar La TR2 . . . . 71 B6
Tresprison Ct TR13 . . . . 146 E5
Tressa Dowr La TR1 . . . . 137 F5
Treswithian Barns TR14 . 138 A3
Treswithian Park Rd
TR14 . . . . 138 B3
Treswithian Rd TR14 . . . . 138 B3
Tretawn Cl PL30 . . . . 23 B2
Trethannas Gdns TR14 . . . . 79 B2
Trethellan Hill TR7 . . . . 110 C5
Trethern Cl TR14 . . . . 79 E4
Tretherras Cl TR7 . . . . 111 A6
Tretherras Rd TR7 . . . . 111 A6
Trethevy Cl PL14 . . . . 37 F3
Trethevy Quoit★ PL14 . . . . 38 A3
Trethewey Cl 10 TR9 . . . . 45 E6
Trethewey Way TR7 . . . . 110 D5
Trethew Gdns TR14 . . . . 138 E4
Trethiggey Cres TR8 . . . . 111 F3
Trethiggey Touring Pk
TR8 . . . . 111 F2
Trethill La PL11 . . . . 65 C5
Trethorne Leisure Farm★
PL15 . . . . 18 B2
Trethorns Ct TR20 . . . . 89 A8
Trethosa Rd PL26 . . . . 58 B4
Trethowan Hts TR1 . . . . 69 F3
Trethurffe Terr TR9 . . . . 45 E5
Trethurffe Villas TR2 . . . . 57 C1
Trethurgy Gdns 17 PL17 . . 39 E4
Tretoil View PL31 . . . . 109 E2
Tretorvic TR18 . . . . 143 C8
Tretower Cl PL6 . . . . 124 F5
Trevadlock Hall Pk PL15 . . 27 A6
Trevail Cotts TR8 . . . . 43 D1
Trevail Way PL25 . . . . 114 E4
Trevale TR18 . . . . 143 C5
Trevalga Cl 5 TR6 . . . . 55 A4
Trevallack Parc 3 TR12 . 101 C4
Trevallack View 2 TR12 . 101 C4
Trevallion Pk TR3 . . . . 82 B5
Trevallyn Rd PL15 . . . . 106 B4
Trevance TR10 . . . . 144 A8
Trevance Pk PL24 . . . . 60 D5
Trevanion Cl PL27 . . . . 108 B4
Trevanion Ct
Mawnan Smith TR11 . . . . 93 D3
1 Newquay TR7 . . . . 110 F6
Truro TR1 . . . . 69 F3
Trevanion La PL25 . . . . 59 A3
Trevanion Pk PL27 . . . . 108 C4
Trevanion Rd
Liskeard PL14 . . . . 113 D5
St Austell PL25 . . . . 114 D2
2 Trewoon PL25 . . . . 59 A3
Wadebridge PL27 . . . . 108 B4
Trevanion Terr PL27 . . . . 108 C4
Trevannion Cl PL6 . . . . 129 A8
Trevanson Rd PL27 . . . . 108 A6
Trevanson St PL27 . . . . 108 B6
Trevarner Way PL27 . . . . 108 D6
Trevarno Cl PL25 . . . . 59 A3
Trevarnon Cl TR27 . . . . 78 D6
Trevarnon La TR27 . . . . 78 D6
Trevarrack Cl TR18 . . . . 143 F8
Trevarrack La TR18 . . . . 143 F8
Trevarrack Pl TR18 . . . . 143 F8
Trevarrack Rd TR18 . . . . 143 F8
Trevarrack Row TR18 . . . . 88 E6
Trevarren Ave TR16 . . . . 80 A5
Trevarrian Hill TR8 . . . . 44 D8
Trevarrian Holiday Pk
TR8 . . . . 44 E8
Trevarrick Ct TR26 . . . . 141 C1
Trevarrick Dr PL25 . . . . 114 B4
Trevarrick Rd PL25 . . . . 114 B3
Trevarth Est PL26 . . . . 73 C4
Trevarthian Ho TR17 . . . . 89 B5
Trevarthian Rd
St Austell PL25 . . . . 114 C4
St Austell PL25 . . . . 114 D4
Trevarth Rd TR11 . . . . 144 F5
Trevarth Terr TR16 . . . . 80 E7
Trevarweneth Rd 8 PL24 . 60 B4
Trevassack Ct TR27 . . . . 142 D6
Trevassack Hill TR27 . . . . 142 E6
Trevassack Parc TR27 . . . . 142 E6
Trevaunance Cl TR5 . . . . 54 C2
Trevaunance Cove Heritage
Trail★ TR5 . . . . 54 D2
Trevaunance Rd TR5 . . . . 54 C2
Trevaylor Camping & Cvn
Site TR19 . . . . 86 F7
Trevaylor Cl TR1 . . . . 137 E6
Trevaylor Rd TR11 . . . . 144 F5
Trevean Cl TR14 . . . . 138 B3
Trevean Gdns 3 TR18 . . . . 143 D5
Trevean La TR20 . . . . 89 F4
Trevean Rd
Penzance TR18 . . . . 143 D5
Truro TR1 . . . . 69 F3
Trevean Way
Newquay TR7 . . . . 110 C5
Rosudgeon TR20 . . . . 89 F4
Trevear Cl PL25 . . . . 114 D3
Trevear Rd PL26 . . . . 58 B4
Trevecca Cotts PL14 . . . . 113 C8
Treveglos TR27 . . . . 142 B6
Treveglos Rd TR11 . . . . 144 E1
Trevelga Ct TR7 . . . . 111 A7
Trevelgue Ct TR8 . . . . 44 C6
Trevelgue Cvn & Camping Pk
TR8 . . . . 44 D6
Trevelgue Rd TR7, TR8 . . . . 44 C6
Trevellan Rd TR11 . . . . 82 A3
Trevella Rd EX23 . . . . 104 E7
Trevella Vean TR4 . . . . 70 D8
Trevelthan Rd 18 TR16 . . . . 67 E4
Trevelva Rd TR1 . . . . 137 E2
Trevelveth Rd TR8 . . . . 110 B3
Trevelyan Cl 10 TR20 . . . . 89 E5
Trevelyan Rd TR15, TR16 . . 67 E4
Trevelyan Way 5 TR20 . . . . 89 E5
Trevemper Rd TR7, TR8 . . 110 F3
Trevena Cl TR18 . . . . 143 C4
Trevena Cross TR13 . . . . 90 F3
Trevena Dr 10 PL34 . . . . 14 C7
Trevena Gdns TR11 . . . . 93 D3
Trevena Lodge 6 PL34 . . . . 14 C7
Trevena Rd TR18 . . . . 143 C4
Trevena Terr TR7 . . . . 110 D6
Trevendon PL17 . . . . 28 D1
Treveneague Gdns PL2 . . 128 D8
Trevenen Rd TR13 . . . . 146 C5
Treveneth Cres TR18 . . . . 143 C1
Treveneth Pl 1 TR18 . . . . 143 C1
Treven La TR27 . . . . 78 B1
Trevenna Cross TR8 . . . . 45 A8
Trevenner Ho 8 TR15 . . . . 140 B5
Trevenner La TR17 . . . . 89 C5
Trevenner Mews 6
TR15 . . . . 140 B5
Trevenner Sq TR17 . . . . 89 C5
Treven Noweth TR16 . . . . 68 C3
Trevenson Ct TR15 . . . . 139 B6
Trevenson La
Camborne, Pool TR15 . . . . 139 A6
Camborne TR14 . . . . 138 D2
Trevenson Rd
Camborne TR15 . . . . 139 B5
Newquay TR7 . . . . 111 B6
Trevenson St TR14 . . . . 138 D2
Treventon Cl
Falmouth TR11 . . . . 144 E4
Portscatho TR2 . . . . 83 B2
Treventon Rd TR2 . . . . 83 B2
Treventon Rise 11 TR9 . . . . 45 E6
Treverbyn Cl
Liskeard PL14 . . . . 113 E6
Plymouth PL7 . . . . 130 D6
Treverbyn Com Prim Sch
PL26 . . . . 59 C8
Treverbyn Gdns PL25 . . . . 114 F4
Treverbyn Rd
Falmouth TR11 . . . . 144 E1
Padstow PL28 . . . . 107 E4
Plymouth PL7 . . . . 130 D6
St Austell PL25 . . . . 114 E7
Stenalees PL26 . . . . 59 C8
St Ives TR26 . . . . 141 A5
Truro TR1 . . . . 137 E6
Treverbyn Rise TR10 . . . . 144 A8
Trevere Cl TR27 . . . . 78 C6
Treverno Rd TR14 . . . . 138 E6
Treveryn Parc TR11 . . . . 144 C2
Trevessa Cl PL2 . . . . 128 D8
Trevethan Cl TR11 . . . . 145 A4
Trevethan Ct 2 TR11 . . . . 145 A5
Trevethan Gdns 2 TR11 . 145 A4
Trevethan Hill 1 TR11 . . . . 145 B5
Trevethan Pk PL20 . . . . 119 F4
Trevethan Rd TR11 . . . . 145 A4
Trevethan Rise TR11 . . . . 145 A4
Trevethenick Rd TR1 . . . . 137 E3
Treveth La TR13 . . . . 146 D8
Treveth Tean TR9 . . . . 57 E8
Treveth Ylyn TR14 . . . . 138 F5
Trevia La PL32 . . . . 105 B4
Trevian Cl 6 TR6 . . . . 55 A4
Trevia Pk Terr PL32 . . . . 105 C3
Treviglas Cl TR7 . . . . 111 D7
Treviglas Com Coll TR7 . . 111 D7
Treviglas La TR2 . . . . 71 C6
Treviglas Rise TR2 . . . . 71 C6
Trevilledor Cvn Pk PL27 . . 32 A2
Trevilley La PL30, PL33 . . . . 23 E8
Trevillick La PL30 . . . . 23 F6
Trevilling Rd PL27 . . . . 108 B6
Trevillis Pk PL14 . . . . 113 B4
Trevilson Cl TR8 . . . . 56 C7
Trevince Parc TR16 . . . . 80 F8
Trevingey Cl TR15 . . . . 140 A3
Trevingey Cres TR15 . . . . 140 A3
Trevingey Parc TR15 . . . . 140 A4
Trevingey Rd TR15 . . . . 140 A3
Trevisker Com Prim Sch
PL27 . . . . 31 F3
Treviskey Hill TR2 . . . . 84 B3
Trevissome Ct TR11 . . . . 144 F6
Trevithick PL28 . . . . 31 F8
Trevithick Ave PL11 . . . . 126 F4
Trevithick Cl
Newquay TR7 . . . . 110 F4
St Merryn PL28 . . . . 31 F8
Truro TR1 . . . . 137 E6
Trevithick Cres TR27 . . . . 142 D5
Trevithick Ct
3 Camborne, Illogan Highway
TR15 . . . . 139 C6
Camborne TR14 . . . . 138 C3
Truro TR1 . . . . 137 E6
Trevithick Prim Sch
TR14 . . . . 138 D1
Trevithick Rd
Camborne, Illogan Highway
TR15 . . . . 139 C6
Camborne TR14 . . . . 138 D3
Chacewater TR4 . . . . 69 A3
Falmouth TR11 . . . . 144 E5
Plymouth PL5 . . . . 123 E2
St Austell PL25 . . . . 114 E3
Truro TR1 . . . . 137 E5
Trevoarn TR27 . . . . 142 B5
Trevol Bsns Pk PL11 . . . . 126 D3
Trevollard PL13 . . . . 61 F7
Trevollard La PL12 . . . . 53 D1
Trevol Pl PL11 . . . . 126 E3
Trevol Rd PL11 . . . . 126 E3
Trevone Cres PL25 . . . . 114 A4
Trevone Gdns PL2 . . . . 128 D8
Trevone Rd PL28 . . . . 20 F2
Trevoney TR11 . . . . 144 C2
Trevor Cl PL28 . . . . 20 C1
Trevorder Cl PL11 . . . . 126 F2
Trevorder Dr PL25 . . . . 114 E7
Trevorder Rd PL11 . . . . 126 F2
Trevorgans Cross TR19 . . . . 96 F8
Trevose Ave TR7 . . . . 110 C6
Trevose Cl TR5 . . . . 54 C1
Trevose Ho TR1 . . . . 69 E4
Trevose Rd TR1 . . . . 69 F4
Trevose Way PL3 . . . . 129 C6
Trevowah Mdws TR8 . . . . 110 A3
Trevowah Rd TR8 . . . . 43 D3
Trevozah Cross PL15 . . . . 28 B8
Trevu Ho TR14 . . . . 138 E1
Trevu Rd TR14 . . . . 138 E2
Trevurvas La TR13 . . . . 90 C3
Trewall Hill PL11 . . . . 64 D5
Trewan Hall TR9 . . . . 45 E7
Trewans Terr TR15 . . . . 140 A6
Trewardreva Cross TR11 . 92 E4
Trewarlett Cross PL15 . . . . 28 A7
Trewarne La TR8 . . . . 111 F3
Trewartha Cl TR26 . . . . 141 D1
Trewartha Ct 4 PL14 . . . . 113 C6
Trewartha Est TR26 . . . . 141 D1
Trewartha Flats TR26 . . . . 141 D1
Trewartha Rd TR20 . . . . 90 C3
Trewartha Terr 13 TR18 . 143 E6
Trewarton Rd TR10 . . . . 81 D2
Trewarveneth Farm Cotts
TR18 . . . . 88 C2
Trewarveneth St TR18 . . 143 C2
Trewassa Flats PL32 . . . . 15 F5
Trewavas Cres TR13 . . . . 146 C5
Trewavas Rd TR18 . . . . 143 C1
Treweath Rd TR18 . . . . 143 D7
Treweege Row TR3 . . . . 80 E4
Treweeks Rd TR19 . . . . 75 A1
Treweese Cross PL14 . . . . 52 B7
Treweese Rd
Menheniot PL14 . . . . 52 B7
Quethiock PL14 . . . . 52 B8
Trewellard Hill TR19 . . . . 87 A8
Trewellard Ind Est TR19 . . 86 F8
Trewellard Rd TR19 . . . . 86 F8
Trewelloe Rd TR20 . . . . 90 C3
Trewelm La TR16 . . . . 68 E1
Trewen Rd TR11 . . . . 144 C2
Trewen Terr TR11 . . . . 144 C2
Trewern La TR20 . . . . 87 E6
Trewetha Farm Lodges
PL29 . . . . 22 E7
Trewetha La PL29 . . . . 22 D7
Trewey Hill TR 26 . . . . 76 B4
Trewhella La TR20 . . . . 89 F7
Trewhella Terr TR20 . . . . 90 A6
Trewhiddle Rd PL25 . . . . 114 C2
Trewidden Cl TR1 . . . . 137 E5
Trewidden Ct TR1 . . . . 137 E5
Trewidden Gdns★ TR20 . . 88 A4
Trewidden Rd TR26 . . . . 141 B5
Trewidland Com Prim Sch
PL14 . . . . 51 C3
Trewince TR11 . . . . 93 B3
Trewince La
Grampound Road TR2 . . . . 57 E1
Lostwithiel PL22 . . . . 112 C3
Porth Navas TR11 . . . . 93 B3
Trewince Manor TR2 . . . . 95 C6
Trewince Terr 2 TR18 . . 143 C1
Trewince Villas PL27 . . . . 32 E6
Trewinnard Ct TR1 . . . . 137 B6
Trewinnard Gr TR1 . . . . 137 B6
Trewinnard La TR27 . . . . 77 E1
Trewinnard Rd TR3 . . . . 81 D5
Trewinnick Council Hos
PL27 . . . . 32 A5
Trewinnick Rd PL27 . . . . 32 A5
Trewinnow Cross PL15 . . . . 27 D6
Trewint Cres PL13 . . . . 117 D4
Trewint Est PL14 . . . . 52 A5
Trewint La
Landrake PL12 . . . . 53 B2
Rock PL27 . . . . 21 D3
Trewint Rd PL14 . . . . 52 A6
Trewirgie Gdns TR15 . . . . 140 B4
Trewirgie Hill TR15 . . . . 140 B3
Trewirgie Inf Sch TR15 . . 140 B4
Trewirgie Jun Sch TR15 . 140 B4
Trewirgie Rd TR15 . . . . 140 B4
Trewirgie Vean TR15 . . . . 140 B4
Trewiston La PL27 . . . . 21 E3
Trewithan Parc PL22 . . . . 112 D2
Trewithen Gdns★ TR2 . . . . 71 E6
Trewithen Parc TR8 . . . . 56 B7
Trewithen Rd TR18 . . . . 143 D5
Trewithen Terr TR13 . . . . 90 D5
Trewithy Ct PL6 . . . . 124 F1
Trewithy Dr PL6 . . . . 124 F1
Trewollock Cl PL26 . . . . 85 C5
Trewollock La PL26 . . . . 85 C5
Trewoolsta Terr 6 PL14 . . 38 E4
Trewoon Rd TR12 . . . . 99 B2
Treworden Cl EX23 . . . . 4 E1
Treworder La PL27 . . . . 108 F5
Treworder Rd TR1 . . . . 137 B3
Treworgan Ct TR4 . . . . 56 D1
Treworgan View TR4 . . . . 56 D1
Treworlis Cl TR13 . . . . 146 D8
Treworthal Rd TR3 . . . . 81 D5
Treworvenneth Dr 9
TR17 . . . . 89 C5
Trewrickle La PL11 . . . . 65 A5
Trewyn Flats 41 TR26 . . . . 141 B6
Treyarnon Bay YH★ PL28 . 20 B1
Treyew Pl TR16 . . . . 80 F8
Treyew Prim Sch TR1 . . . . 137 A4
Treyew Rd TR1 . . . . 137 B3
Trezaise Ave PL26 . . . . 47 A2
Trezaise Cl PL26 . . . . 47 A2
Trezaise Rd PL26 . . . . 46 F2
Trezaise Sq PL26 . . . . 47 A2
Treza Rd TR13 . . . . 91 A1
Trezela Rd TR18 . . . . 143 D6
Trinity Cl
Bere Alston PL20 . . . . 41 B1
Carnkie TR16 . . . . 80 C2
Trinity House National
Lighthouse Ctr★ TR18 . . 143 F5
Trinity Praze TR16 . . . . 80 C2
Trinity St PL25 . . . . 114 C3
Trinity Way PL19 . . . . 147 A4
Tripp Hill PL14 . . . . 36 F2
Trispen Hill TR4 . . . . 56 D1
Tristan Rd TR1 . . . . 137 F5
Trolver Hill TR3 . . . . 82 B6
Trolvus Vean TR10 . . . . 81 A1
Troon Com Prim Sch
TR14 . . . . 79 E4
Troon Moor TR14 . . . . 79 E4
Troon Row TR13 . . . . 90 F3
Troubridge Rd TR13 . . . . 146 C4
Trowbridge Cl PL5 . . . . 124 C4
Troy Ct PL23 . . . . 116 C4
Truck Hill TR2 . . . . 71 B6
Trunglemoor Cotts TR19 . 88 C2
Trungle Parc TR19 . . . . 88 C2
Trungle Terr TR19 . . . . 88 C2
Truro Coll TR1 . . . . 69 E3
Truro Dr PL5 . . . . 124 A5
Truro High Sch for Girls
TR1 . . . . 137 C3
Truro Hill TR10 . . . . 144 C8
Truro La TR10 . . . . 144 C8
Truro Rd
Lanivet PL30 . . . . 47 F7
St Austell PL25 . . . . 114 A2
St Austell PL25 . . . . 114 B3
Truro Sch TR1 . . . . 137 E3
Truro Sta TR1 . . . . 137 B4
Truro Vean Terr TR1 . . . . 137 D5
Truthwall La TR19 . . . . 86 F7
Tryelyn PL31 . . . . 109 F2
Tryhornek TR26 . . . . 77 D4
Trythall Com Prim Sch TR
20 . . . . 76 B1
Trythogga Hill TR18 . . . . 143 F8
Trythogga Rd TR18 . . . . 143 F8
Tubbon Hill TR3 . . . . 81 A4
Tucker Cl PL5 . . . . 127 F8
Tuckers Cl TR8 . . . . 111 B4
Tuckingmill Terr TR13 . . . . 91 E4
Tudor Cl PL9 . . . . 135 E5
Tudor Ct PL12 . . . . 123 A2
Tudor Lodge Holiday Pk
TR20 . . . . 89 C7
Tuke Cl TR11 . . . . 144 E5
Turbill Gdns 4 PL7 . . . . 131 B5
Turfdown Rd PL30 . . . . 48 E8
Turf St PL31 . . . . 109 E5
Turnavean Rd PL25 . . . . 114 A5
Turnaware Rd TR11 . . . . 144 E2
Turnpike TR13 . . . . 146 C7
Turnpike Hill 2 TR17 . . . . 89 C5
Turnpike Pl PL14 . . . . 113 B4
Turnpike Rd
Connor Downs TR27 . . . . 78 D6
Marazion TR17 . . . . 89 C5
Turnpike The TR19 . . . . 86 F6
Turnquay PL9 . . . . 135 C7
Turret Gr PL4 . . . . 128 F4
Tuxton Cl PL7 . . . . 131 C3
Twelvewoods Cl PL14 . . . . 50 E8
Twelvewoods Pl PL14 . . . . 50 E8
Twinbrook Pk TR11 . . . . 93 B3
Two Chimneys Cvn Pk
TR20 . . . . 90 B3
Two Hills Pk PL12 . . . . 122 C2
Two Trees PL27 . . . . 108 B4
Two Trees Rd PL22 . . . . 112 F1
Tyacke Rd TR13 . . . . 146 B5
Tybesta TR2 . . . . 72 A7
Tye Hill Cl PL25 . . . . 59 A3
Tyland Rd PL32 . . . . 105 F4
Tylney Cl PL6 . . . . 125 B6
Tynance Ct PL26 . . . . 58 C8

Tyndale Cl PL5 124 B1
Tyringham Pl TR26 77 E4
Tyringham Rd TR26 77 E4
Tyringham Row TR26 77 E4
Tyshute La PL26 59 A1
Tything Wlk 4 PL3 128 E6
Tywardreath Highway
PL24 60 C6
Tywardreath Hill PL24 60 D4
Tywardreath Sch PL24 60 D5
Tywarnhale Way TR4 68 A6
Tywarnhayle Rd TR6 55 A5
Tywarnhayle Sq 23 TR6 55 A5

U

Uglow Cl TR14 138 C3
Ulalia Rd TR7 110 F6
Ullswater Cres PL6 124 E4
Umfulla Pl 13 TR26 141 B5
Under Chapel Yd TR18 143 F4
Undercliff TR27 142 D7
Undercliff Rd PL9 135 B7
Underhayes La PL15 106 A8
Underhill Rd PL3 128 A4
Underhill Villas 1 PL3 128 A3
Under La PL15 18 C3
Underlane
Boyton PL15 13 A3
Marhamchurch EX23 7 B6
Plymouth, Plympton PL7 130 C5
Plymouth, Plymstock PL9 135 E6
Under Rd
Boscastle PL35 9 C1
Bridgerule EX22 8 A5
Gunnislake PL18 41 A6
Underways PL20 41 B1
Underwood Rd PL7 130 D4
Unicorn Cl PL7 130 B6
Union Cnr TR11 144 D5
Union Hill
St Columb Major TR9 45 E6
6 Stratton EX23 4 D1
Truro TR1 70 D5
Union Pl
Fowey PL23 116 D4
Plymouth PL1 148 A2
Truro TR1 137 D5
Union Rd TR11 144 D6
Union Sq TR9 45 E6
Union St
Camborne TR14 138 D2
27 Penzance TR18 143 E5
Plymouth PL1 148 A2
Truro TR1 137 C5
United Downs Ind Pk
TR16 81 A8
United Rd TR16 80 F8
Unit Hos PL27 33 B5
Unity Cl PL6 125 D5
Unity Rd TR13 98 C8
University College Falmouth (Tremough Campus)
TR10 144 A8
University College Falmouth (Woodlane Campus)
TR11 145 B3
University Coll Falmouth (Annexe) TR11 145 B4
Univ of Plymouth PL1,
PL4 148 C3
Univ of Plymouth Bsns Sch
PL4 148 C4
Univ of Plymouth (Cookworthy Bldg)
PL4 149 A3
Univ of Plymouth The Hoe
Ctr PL1 148 C2
Upcott Cross EX39 2 F5
Upland Cl TR1 137 F6
Upland Cres TR1 137 E6
Upland Dr PL6 125 A5
Uplands
Lostwithiel PL22 112 B2
Saltash PL12 122 E1
Tavistock PL19 147 A4
Uplands Vean TR1 137 F5
Upper Castle Rd TR2 95 A6
Upper Chapel PL15 106 A4
Upper Dobbin Cl PL28 20 F2
Upper Dobbin La PL28 20 F2
Upper Eastcliffe Rd PL24 60 D4
Upper Hillcrest 8 TR6 55 A4
Upper Knollys Terrace La
PL3 128 C4
Upper Lemon Villas TR1 137 C3
Upper Ridings PL7 131 B7
Upper School La TR1 137 C3
Upperton La PL6 121 F3
Upper Tredrea TR3 81 D5
Upton Cl PL3 129 B7
Upton Cross EX23 104 C2
Upton Cross Prim Sch
PL14 38 C7
Upton Mdws EX23 104 C3
Upton Terr EX23 104 C2
Urban Terr PL17 39 F5
Uxbridge Dr PL5 123 E4
Uzella Pk PL22 112 C2

V

Vaagso Cl PL1 127 E2
Valency Row PL35 9 C2
Valentine Row 4 PL17 39 E4
Valiant Ave PL5 124 A4
Vallard's La PL12 53 E4
Valletort Flats PL1 128 A2
Valletort Ho PL1 148 C3
Valletort La PL1 128 A3
Valletort Pl PL1 128 A2
Valletort Rd PL1, PL3 128 A3
Valletort Terr PL1 148 A4
Valley Bglws PL13 117 F5
Valley Cl
Goonhavern TR4 55 C3
Truro TR1 69 F3
Valley Gdns 20 TR16 67 E4
Valley La TR3 81 F7
Valley Park La PL26 73 C3
Valley Rd
Bude EX23 104 E5
Carbis Bay TR26 141 C2
Mevagissey PL26 73 C4
Plymouth PL7 130 B5
Saltash PL12 122 E2
Valley The TR19 96 E3
Valley View
Bodmin PL31 109 E3
19 Illogan TR16 67 E4
Plymouth PL6 125 D7
Redruth TR16 140 E1
St Keyne PL14 51 A4
St Teath PL30 23 E7
Wadebridge PL27 108 C4
Valley View Cl PL3 129 B6
Valley View Dr TR1 69 F3
Valley View Pk PL31 34 D2
Valley View Rd PL3 129 B7
Valley View Terr TR3 81 B5
Valley Wlk PL6 125 E6
Vanguard Cl PL5 124 D1
Vapron Rd PL3 128 F6
Varfell La TR20 89 A7
Varley La PL14 113 B5
Varley Terr 1 PL14 113 B5
Vauban Pl PL2 127 F4
Vaughan Cl PL2 128 C7
Vauxhall Ct 10 PL4 149 A2
Vauxhall St PL4 149 A2
Vauxhall Street Flats 19
PL4 149 A2
Vean Rd TR14 138 E2
Vean Terr TR14 138 E2
Vear Ho TR14 138 D2
Vellan Cl TR14 79 B5
Vellandrucia TR3 80 F3
Vellanhoggan Mews TR18 88 E6
Vellan Parc Ave TR27 78 C5
Vellan Vrane TR27 78 C5
Venetian Views TR9 57 D8
Venland Cl 9 PL14 38 A3
Venn Cl 6 PL3 128 E6
Venn Cres PL3 128 E6
Venn Ct PL3 128 E6
Venn Gdns PL3 128 E7
Venn Gr PL3 128 E6
Venn Hill PL19 29 C6
Venn La PL2, PL3 128 C6
Venn Way PL3 128 E7
Venslooe Hill PL14 113 B7
Ventnor Terr TR26 141 A6
Venton Cl PL15 18 B8
Venton East Sq TR19 86 F6
Venton Lace Rd TR2 57 E1
Ventonleague Hill TR27 142 E7
Ventonleague Row TR27 142 E7
Ventonraze TR16 67 E4
Ventonraze Terr 2 TR16 67 E4
Venton Rd
Falmouth TR11 144 E4
St Ives TR26 141 C3
Ventonvaise 5 TR6 55 A5
Veor Rd TR7 111 C7
Verdun Terr PL14 113 B5
Vermont Gdns PL2 127 F7
Verna Pl PL5 123 D2
Verna Rd PL5 123 E2
Vernigo Cross PL12 40 B1
Vernon Pl TR11 145 B4
Vernon Villas PL24 60 B4
Veryan CE Sch TR2 83 F6
Viaduct Hill TR27 142 E6
Viaduct La TR14 138 A1
Vicarage Cl
Budock Water TR11 144 C3
Menheniot PL14 51 F5
Vicarage Gdns
Milton Abbot PL19 29 C6
Plymouth PL5 123 B1
Vicarage Hill
Budock Water TR11 144 C3
Mevagissey PL26 73 C4
10 St Austell PL25 114 C3
St Day TR16 68 E1
9 Tintagel PL34 14 C7
Vicarage La
Lelant TR26 77 E4
Manaccan TR12 101 A8
Poundstock EX23 6 F2
Vicarage Mdw PL23 116 C4
Vicarage Rd
Bude EX23 104 D5
Plymouth PL7 130 C6
Porthleven TR13 91 A1
St Agnes TR5 54 D1
Torpoint PL11 127 B2
Tywardreath PL24 60 D5
Vicarage Row TR13 90 F3
Vicarage Terr TR11 92 F4
Victoria Ave PL1 148 A4
Victoria Bsns Pk PL26 47 A4
Victoria Cl PL14 113 C6
Victoria Cotts
Budock Water TR11 144 C3
Falmouth TR11 145 B3
Plymouth PL6 129 B8
Victoria Ct 16 TR18 143 E6
Victoria Gdns
2 St Columb Road TR9 45 E2
Threemilestone TR3 69 D3
Victoria La PL12 122 F2
Victoria Mews 18 TR18 143 E6
Victoria Pk PL27 108 D6
Victoria Pl
31 Penzance TR18 143 E5
Plymouth, Devonport PL2 127 F4
Plymouth PL1 148 A2
Ponsanooth TR3 81 B4
9 St Austell PL25 114 C3
12 St Ives TR26 141 B6
Victoria Quay
5 Falmouth TR11 145 B5
Truro TR1 70 D1
Victoria Rd
Bude EX23 104 D7
Camelford PL32 105 E4
Plymouth PL5 123 D2
Roche PL26 46 F3
Saltash PL12 122 F2
St Austell PL25 114 F3
11 St Ives TR26 141 B6
Threemilestone TR3 69 D3
Victoria Road Prim Sch
PL5 123 D1
Victoria Row TR19 86 E6
Victoria Sq
Bodmin PL31 109 F3
17 Penzance TR18 143 E6
Truro TR1 137 C4
Victoria St
Camborne TR14 138 D2
St Columb Major TR9 45 E6
Torpoint PL11 127 B3
Victoria Terr
4 Liskeard PL14 113 B5
Nanpean PL26 58 D6
Plymouth PL4 148 C4
Portscatho TR2 83 B2
St Breward PL30 24 B3
Victory Rd EX22 13 A8
Victory St PL2 127 E6
Vigo Bridge Rd PL19 147 C6
Vigo Mews PL19 147 C6
Village Dr PL6 121 C1
Village Farm Cl EX23 7 B6
Village The
Buckland Monachorum
PL20 41 F3
Duloe PL14 51 A1
Villa Marina TR17 89 B5
Villiers Cl PL9 135 D7
Vincent Way PL12 122 F2
Vine Cres PL2 128 B6
Vinefield Ct TR11 145 B7
Vine Gdns PL2 128 B6
Vine Pl 10 PL24 60 D5
Vinery La PL7, PL9 130 E1
Vineyard The TR3 80 F3
Vingoe's La TR20 88 B7
Vinstone Way PL5 123 D1
Violet Dr PL6 125 E8
Violet La PL19 147 E6
Virgin Hill TR17 89 C6
Virginia Gdns PL2 127 F7
Virgin Pl 16 TR19 88 C1
Virgin St 26 TR26 141 B6
Visicks Works TR3 81 E6
Vivian Cl TR7 110 E5
Vivian Ct TR1 137 D3
Vivian Pk TR14 138 F2
Vivian Rd PL31 109 B4
Vixen Tor Cl PL20 42 C3
Vogue Hill TR16 68 D1
Vogue Terr TR16 68 D1
Vorfield Cl TR15 140 B6
Vosporth Hill TR8 110 A3
Voss Rd PL12 53 E1
Vounder Glaze TR19 86 E6
Voundervour La 20 TR18 143 E5
Vyvyan Dr TR8 44 E3
Vyvyan Pl TR13 146 C5
Vyvyan St TR14 138 D3
Vyvyan's Terr TR14 79 B2

W

Waddon Cl PL7 130 E7
Wadebridge Com Prim Sch
PL27 108 C6
Wadebridge Rd
St Mabyn PL30 34 C8
St Tudy PL30 23 E3
Wadebridge Sch PL27 108 D6
Wadeland Terr 3 PL14 51 A7
Wadham Cl 4 PL14 113 C5
Wadham Dr PL14 113 D5
Wadham Ho 5 PL14 113 C5
Wadham Rd PL14 113 D5
Wadham Terr 6 PL2 128 A5
Wagg La TR2 71 C6
Waggon Hill PL7 131 A4
Wain Pk PL7 130 F4
Wainsway TR6 55 A4
Wainways EX23 10 F6
Wakefield Ave PL5 123 E1
Wake St PL4 148 B4
Walcot Cl PL6 125 E3
Waldon Cl PL7 131 B6
Walker Lines Ind Est 4
PL31 48 D8
Walker Terr PL1 148 B1
Walkham Bsns Pk PL5 124 B1
Walkham Cl PL19 147 D5
Walkham Mdws PL20 42 C4
Walkhampton Rd PL20 42 C4
Walkhampton Wlk PL6 125 E1
Walkham Terr 4 PL20 42 C5
Walk Terr PL23 116 C2
Walk The PL15 106 C6
Wallace Mews 1 PL31 109 D5
Wallace Rd
Bodmin PL31 109 D5
Plymouth PL7 131 A4
Walled Gdn The TR10 144 A6
Wall Gdns TR27 78 E3
Wallpark Cl PL7 130 F7
Wall Rd TR27 78 E3
Wallsend Ind Est PL4 149 C1
Wall Vean TR27 78 E3
Walnut Cl PL7 131 B5
Walnut Dr PL7 131 C5
Walnut Gdns PL7 131 C5
Walreddon Cl PL19 147 B4
Walsingham Ct PL7 131 B6
Walsingham Pl 15 TR1 137 D4
Walters La PL15 18 D5
Walters Rd PL5 123 C2
Waltham Pl PL2 128 A8
Walton Cres PL5 124 C1
Wandle Pl PL3 129 D5
Wansford Mdws PL26 85 C5
Wanstead Gr PL5 124 A2
Wantage Gdns PL1 148 A3
Warbstow Com Prim Sch
PL15 11 B1
Warburton Gdns PL5 123 C1
Ward Cl 4 EX23 4 D1
Wardlow Cl PL6 128 F8
Wardlow Gdns PL6 128 F8
Wardour Wlk PL6 125 B7
Ward Pl PL3 129 B5
Warfelton Cres PL12 122 E2
Warfelton Gdns PL12 122 E2
Warfelton Terr PL12 122 E2
Waring Rd PL6 124 D7
Warleigh Ave PL2 127 E5
Warleigh Cres PL6 124 F5
Warleigh La PL2 127 E5
Warleigh Rd 2 PL4 128 E4
Warmwell Rd PL5 123 E4
Warne Cl TR2 71 F3
Warran La PL19 147 C3
Warraton Cl PL12 122 D3
Warraton Gn PL12 122 D3
Warraton La PL12 122 D3
Warraton Rd PL12 122 D3
Warren TR26 141 B5
Warren Cl 18 TR13 98 C8
Warren La PL5 124 A8
Warren Pk PL6 125 D7
Warren Rd TR9 45 F2
Warrens Field PL32 105 D5
Warren St PL2 127 E4
Warren The PL13 62 E1
Warspite Gdns PL5 124 D2
Warton Cl PL5 124 D3
Warwick Ave
Illogan TR16 67 D4
Plymouth PL5 124 D3
Warwick Cl PL28 31 F8
Warwick Cres 5 PL27 31 F3
Warwick Dr PL25 115 B5
Warwick Orchard Cl PL5 124 B3
Warwick Rd EX23 104 E4
Wasdale Cl PL6 125 D2
Wasdale Gdns PL6 125 D2
Washbourne Cl PL1 127 E3
Watergate Bay Holiday Pk
TR8 44 E8
Watergate La PL30 34 C8
Watergate Rd TR8 44 C6
Watering Hill Cl PL25 114 E3
Waterings Rd TR11 82 A2
Water La
Crantock TR8 110 A3
Delabole PL33 14 E3
Golant PL23 61 B5
Hayle TR27 142 B3
St Agnes TR5 54 D1
Waterloo TR1 137 E4
Waterloo Cl
Plymouth PL1 128 A2
St Mawes TR2 95 A6
Waterloo Ct PL1 128 A2
Waterloo Pl★ TR11 145 B4
Waterloo Rd TR11 145 B4
Waterloo St
Plymouth PL4 149 A4
Plymouth, Stoke PL1 128 A3
Waterloo Yard Flats PL1 128 A2
Water-Ma-Trout TR13 146 C8
Waters Ct TR15 140 E7
Waters Edge TR7 110 A6
Water's Edge PL28 107 E6
Watersedge Cl PL25 114 B4
Watersmead Parc TR11 144 C3
Watery La
Bodmin PL31 109 D5
Milton Combe PL6 120 D6
Watson Gdns PL4 149 B3
Watson Pl PL4 149 B2
Watts Park Rd PL2 128 C7
Watts Rd PL19 147 B5
Watts' Rd PL4 149 C3
Waveney Gdns PL5 124 C3
Waverley Rd PL5 123 D2
Wavish Pk PL11 126 E3
Waycott Wlk PL6 124 D6
Way Cross PL15 27 B3
Wayfield Rd TR11 82 B2
Wayside Ct TR7 111 A4
Wayside Folk Mus★ TR
26 76 B5
Wearde Rd PL12 122 E1
Webber Hill TR11 145 B4
Webber St TR11 145 B4
Webbs Ct 9 PL14 113 C6
Webb St PL23 116 D4
Wedgewood Rd PL25 115 A4
Weeks Rise PL32 105 B2
Weeks Row PL18 41 A6
Weekstone Cross EX22 8 C8
Weeth Cl TR14 138 C3
Weeth Com Prim Sch
TR14 138 C4
Weethes Cotts 6 TR18 143 D5
Weeth La TR14 138 C3
Weeth Rd TR14 138 C4
Weir Cl PL6 125 F2
Weir Gdns PL6 125 F2
Weir Rd PL6 125 F2
Welbeck Ave PL4 148 C4
Welcombe Cross EX39 3 B4
Welcome Cl TR4 56 D1
Welland Gdns PL3 129 C5
Weller Ct TR11 145 B3
Wellfield Cl
Coad's Green PL15 27 D3
Plymouth PL7 131 C5
Well Gdns PL1 148 B3
Wellhay Cl PL9 136 C6
Wellhouse The 8 PL14 113 C6
Wellington Cl TR14 138 C3
Wellington Gdns TR11 145 B4
Wellington Pl
Falmouth TR11 145 B4
Penzance TR18 143 D5
Wadebridge PL27 108 C4
Wellington Plantation
TR3 82 B7
Wellington Rd
Camborne TR14 138 D3
Porthleven TR13 91 B1
St Dennis PL26 58 C8
2 St Eval PL27 31 F3
Wellington St
Plymouth PL4 149 A4
Plymouth, Stoke PL1 128 A3
Torpoint PL11 127 B3
Wellington Terr
Falmouth TR11 145 B4
Porthleven TR13 91 B1
Portscatho TR2 83 B2
2 Truro TR1 137 C4
Well La
Constantine TR11 92 F4
Falmouth TR11 145 B4
Goldsithney TR20 89 F5
Lamorna TR19 97 E5
Liskeard PL14 113 C6
Looe PL13 117 C3
St Cleer PL14 37 F3
St Keverne TR12 101 D4
Tregony TR2 71 F3
Tremar PL14 38 A3
Welcombe EX39 2 E5
Well Mdw PL15 18 A5
Wellpark Rd PL18 40 F5
Well Park Rd PL11 127 B3
Wellsbourne Pk PL3 129 A6
Wells Ct PL10 132 E4
Well St
Callington PL17 39 E4
Delabole PL33 14 E3
Tregony TR2 71 F3
Tywardreath PL24 60 D5
Well Way TR7 111 C7
Welman Rd PL10 132 F6
Welsby Terr PL14 37 F3
Welsford Ave PL2 127 F5
Welway TR6 55 A4
Wembury Park Rd PL3 128 D6
Wembury Rd PL9 136 A4
Wendron CE Prim Sch
TR13 91 F5
Wendron St TR13 146 C6
Wenlock Gdns PL2 128 B8
Wensum Cl PL7 131 A4
Wentwood Gdns PL6 125 E3
Wentwood Pl PL6 125 E3
Wentworth Cl
Lynstone EX23 104 C3
Polzeath PL27 21 D5
Redruth TR15 140 C3
Wentworth Pl PL4 129 B2
Wentworth Way PL12 122 C2
Werrington Dr PL17 39 E4
Werrington Sch PL15 18 F7
Wesley Ave PL3 128 E5
Wesley Cl
Kelly Bray PL17 39 F6
Stenalees PL26 59 C8
Wesley Cottage★ PL15 26 B7
Wesley Ct
Penryn TR10 144 C8
Pensilva PL14 38 D4
25 Porthleven TR13 98 C8
Torpoint PL11 127 C3
Wesley La PL12 122 F2
Wesley Pl
5 Newlyn TR18 143 C2
Plymouth, Mutley PL3 128 E5
1 Plymouth, Stoke PL2 128 A4

Wesley Pl *continued*
St Austell PL25 . . . . 114 F3
7 St Ives TR26. . . . . 141 B5
Wesley Rd
Cubert TR8. . . . . 55 D8
Pensilva PL14 . . . . 38 D4
Saltash PL12 . . . . 122 F2
Wesley St
Camborne TR14. . . . . 138 E3
11 Heamoor TR18 . . . . 143 C7
Redruth TR15. . . . . 140 C5
Wesley Terr
Bugle PL26. . . . . 47 C2
Looe PL13 . . . . 117 D4
Wesley Way PL15 . . . . 26 B7
Wesley Yd TR7. . . . . 110 D6
West Ave 4 PL19 . . . . 147 B5
West Beach Rd TR4 . . . . . . 68 A6
West Beckon Cl EX23 . . . . . 2 D1
Westborne Hts TR15 . . . . 140 B3
Westborne Rd TR14. . . . . 138 B4
Westbourne Dr PL25 . . . . 114 B3
Westbourne La PL14 . . . . 113 B6
Westbourne Rd PL3. . . . . 128 D5
Westbourne Terr
Fraddon TR9 . . . . 57 D8
Saltash PL12 . . . . 122 F3
Westbridge Cotts PL19 . . 147 B4
Westbridge Ind Est 3
PL19 . . . . 147 B4
Westbridge Rd PL25 . . . . . 59 A3
West Bridge Rd PL15. . . . 106 B7
Westbury Cl PL5 . . . . 124 B4
Westby Rd EX23 . . . . 104 E5
West Camps Bay PL11. . . . 64 C4
West Charles St TR14 . . . 138 D2
West Cl TR13 . . . . 146 D7
West Cliff TR4 . . . . 68 A6
Westcliff Flats EX23. . . . . 104 D6
West Cnr 1 TR3. . . . . 81 F7
Westcombe Cres PL9 . . . 135 D5
West Cornwall Hospl
TR18. . . . . 143 D6
Westcott PL27 . . . . 108 A6
Westcott Cl PL6. . . . . 129 A8
Westcountry Cl PL2 . . . . . 127 F7
Westcove Ho 2 TR7 . . . . 110 F6
Westcroft Rd PL5 . . . . . . 123 D1
West Ct TR7 . . . . 110 C6
West Devon Bsns Pk
PL19 . . . . 147 B3
West Down Ct PL13 . . . . 117 C4
Westdown Rd PL33 . . . . . 14 D2
West Down Rd PL2. . . . . 128 B6
Westella Rd PL20 . . . . 42 D2
West End
Goldsithney TR20. . . . . 89 E5
Marazion TR17. . . . . 89 B5
Pentewan PL26 . . . . 73 C6
15 Porthleven TR13. . . . . . 98 B8
Redruth TR15. . . . . 140 B4
St Day TR16. . . . . 68 D1
West End Cl TR10 . . . . . . 144 C8
West End Cotts PL11 . . . . . 64 B8
West End Ct 2 TR15 . . . . 140 B4
West End Ind Est TR10 . . 144 B8
West End Sq 7 PL17 . . . . . 39 E4
Westend Terr TR10 . . . . . 144 C8
Westeria Terr PL2 . . . . . . 128 C7
Westerlands Rd PL27. . . . 108 B6
Western App PL1 . . . . 148 B2
Western Ave 5 PL14. . . . . . 51 A7
Western College Rd PL4. 128 F5
Western Dr PL3. . . . . 129 B4
Western Pl TR10. . . . . . . 144 B8
Western Promenade Rd
TR18 . . . . 143 E4
Western Rd PL15 . . . . 106 B5
Western Terr
Bodmin PL31 . . . . 109 C4
Falmouth TR11. . . . . 145 A3
Launceston PL15 . . . . 106 B5
Western Wood Way PL7 131 D5
West Fairholme Rd EX23 104 E7
Westfield PL7 . . . . 131 A6
Westfield Ave PL9 . . . . . . 135 C6
Westgate Mews PL15 . . . 106 C5
Westgate St PL15 . . . . . . 106 C5
Westground Way PL34 . . . 14 D7
Westhampnett Pl PL5 . . . 123 F4
Westhaul Pk PL25. . . . . . . 115 E4
Westhays Cl PL9 . . . . 135 F4
Westhead Rd PL10 . . . . 64 B2
Westheath Ave PL30,
PL31. . . . . 109 B3
Westheath Rd PL31 . . . . . 109 B3
West Hill
St Austell PL25 . . . . 114 C3
Wadebridge PL27 . . . . 108 A6
West Hill Ct 16 PL25. . . . . 114 C3
West Hill Rd PL4. . . . . 128 F4
West Hoe Rd PL1 . . . . 148 B1
West Kitty TR5. . . . . 54 C1
West La
Crafthole PL11. . . . . 65 B5
Delabole PL33 . . . . 14 E2
Landrake PL12. . . . . 53 B3
Westlake Cl PL11 . . . . 126 F3
West Looe Hill PL13. . . . . 117 B3
West Looe Sq PL13. . . . . . 117 C3
West Malling Ave PL5 . . . 123 E5
Westmoor Cl PL7 . . . . 131 C6
Westmoor Cres TR3. . . . . . 81 D6
Westmoor Pk PL19. . . . . . 147 C4
Weston Mill Com Prim Sch
PL2 . . . . 127 E7
Weston Mill Dr PL5 . . . . . 127 F8
Weston Mill Hill PL5 . . . . 123 F1
Weston Mill La PL5 . . . . . 124 A1
Weston Mill Rd PL5 . . . . . 123 E1
Weston Park Rd PL3 . . . . 128 D6
Westover Rd PL17 . . . . 39 E4
West Park Dr PL7 . . . . 131 C5
West Park Est PL27 . . . . . 108 D5
West Park Hill PL7 . . . . . . 131 B7
West Park Prim Sch PL5 124 A2
Westpark Rd PL27 . . . . . . 108 E4
West Park Rd EX23. . . . . . 104 D7
West Pentire Rd TR8 . . . . . 43 D3
West Pk
Perranarworthal TR3. . . . . . 81 D6
Redruth TR15. . . . . 139 F6
13 St Columb Major TR9 . . . 45 E6
Tideford PL12 . . . . 52 F2
Trewidland PL14 . . . . 51 C3
West Pl
Falmouth TR11. . . . . 145 A3
45 St Ives TR26. . . . . 141 B6
St Just TR19 . . . . 86 E6
West Point TR8 . . . . 111 C4
West Porthmear Cotts
PL25. . . . . 115 B2
West Porthmear Ct PL25 115 B2
West Rd
Looe PL13 . . . . 117 C4
Quintrell Downs TR8 . . . . . 111 E3
West Rise TR11 . . . . 144 F3
West St
Grimscott EX23 . . . . 5 B1
Liskeard PL14 . . . . 113 B6
Millbrook PL10. . . . . 132 E5
Penryn TR10 . . . . 144 C8
Polruan PL23. . . . . 116 C2
St Columb Major TR9. . . . . . 45 E6
Tavistock PL19. . . . . 147 B5
West Tehidy TR14. . . . . . . 138 F7
West Terr
Hayle TR27. . . . . 142 B6
Newlyn TR18 . . . . 143 C3
West Tolgus TR15. . . . . . . 139 D8
West Trevingey TR15. . . . . 140 A3
West Trewirgie Rd TR15. 140 B4
Westview TR6 . . . . 55 B5
West View
Porthleven TR13 . . . . 91 A1
Tavistock PL19. . . . . 147 E2
Trevone PL28. . . . . 20 E2
West View Rd 5 PL20. . . . . 41 B1
West Villas TR8. . . . . 57 B7
Westward PL27 . . . . 21 D5
Westward Rd TR26. . . . . . 141 A6
Westway PL9 . . . . 135 B5
West Week Cl EX22 . . . . . . 11 E8
West Wharf PL26 . . . . 73 C3
Westwinds PL32 . . . . 16 A8
Westwood PL14. . . . . 113 B6
Westwood Ave PL6 . . . . . 125 C6
Wetherham La PL30. . . . . . . 23 E3
Wetherham Manor Gardens*
PL30 . . . . 23 D2
Wharf Rd
Penzance TR18 . . . . 143 F5
St Ives TR26 . . . . 141 B6
Wharfside 8 TR18 . . . . . . 143 E5
Wharfside Village 9
TR18 . . . . 143 E5
Wharf The
22 Mousehole TR19. . . . . . . 88 C1
St Ives TR26 . . . . 141 B6
Wheal Agar
Camborne, Illogan Highway
TR15 . . . . 139 C6
5 Camborne TR14 . . . . . . 138 F7
Wheal Alfred Rd TR27 . . . 142 F5
Wheal-An-Wens TR17 . . . 89 C5
Whealbrake Lodge PL26. . 58 D6
Wheal Bull PL26 . . . . 58 D5
Wheal Busy La TR4. . . . . . 68 F3
Wheal Catherine Cl TR6 . . 55 B5
Wheal Damsel Rd TR16. . . 80 E8
Wheal Dance TR16. . . . . . 140 D3
Wheal Dream TR26 . . . . . 141 C6
Wheal Eliza Cl PL25 . . . . . 115 B5
Wheal Fortune La TR15 . 139 D6
Wheal Friendly La TR5 . . . 54 C2
Wheal Gerry TR14. . . . . . . 138 E4
Wheal Golden Dr TR8 . . . . 43 C1
Wheal Gorland Rd TR16 . . . 68 D1
Wheal Harmony Terr
TR15 . . . . 140 B7
Wheal Jane Mdws TR3 . . . 69 C3
Wheal Jewel (Gipsy Site)
TR16 . . . . 68 E1
Wheal Kitty TR5 . . . . 54 D1
Wheal Kitty La TR5. . . . . . . 54 D2
Wheal Kitty Workshops
TR5. . . . . 54 D2
Wheal Leisure TR6. . . . . . . 55 A5
Wheal Leisure Cl 25 TR6. . 55 A5
Wheal Margery TR26 . . . . 141 C3
Wheal Maria Cotts PL19. . 29 D1
Wheal Martyn Mus* PL26 59 B6
Wheal Northey PL25 . . . . 115 B5
Wheal Oak TR13 . . . . 146 D8
Wheal Quoit Ave TR5. . . . . 54 C1
Wheal Ramoth 3 TR6. . . . . 55 A5
Wheal Regent Pk PL25 . . 115 D3
Wheal Rodney Cvn Pk
TR17 . . . . 89 C6
Wheal Rodney Holiday Bglws
TR17 . . . . 89 C6
Wheal Rose 19 TR13 . . . . . 98 C8
Wheal Silver TR15 . . . . . . 140 B5
Wheal Speed Rd TR26. . . 141 C2
Wheal Tehidy La TR15. . . . 139 E6
Wheal Trefusis TR15 . . . . 140 D2
Wheal Trelawney TR16. . 140 D3
Wheal Venture Rd TR26 . 141 C3
Wheal View PL26 . . . . 58 B4
Wheal Virgin Ho TR26 . . . . 77 A6
Wheal Vor TR15 . . . . 140 D3
Wheal Vyvyan TR11 . . . . . . 92 F4
Wheal Whidden TR26 . . . 141 C2
Wheatfield Cres TR7 . . . . 111 A4
Wheatridge PL7 . . . . 130 B7
Wheel Ayr Terr TR26 . . . . 141 A6
Wheeler Higman Cl PL26 . 59 C7
Wheelgate House Sch
TR8. . . . . 43 D2
Wheelwright Ct PL20. . . . . 42 E4
Wherry Pl PL23 . . . . 116 D2
Wherry Way PL14. . . . . 50 E7
Whieldon Rd PL25 . . . . . . 115 A4
Whimple St PL1 . . . . 148 C2
Whin Bank Rd PL5 . . . . . . 124 E2
Whipsiderry Cl TR7 . . . . . . 44 C6
Whistley Down PL20 . . . . . 42 B2
Whitby Cres PL6 . . . . 125 A1
Whitby Rd PL6. . . . . 125 A1
Whitchurch Com Prim Sch
PL19 . . . . 147 D2
Whitchurch Rd
Horrabridge PL20 . . . . 42 C5
Tavistock PL19. . . . . 147 C3
Whitcross Hill TR15 . . . . . 139 C3
White Acres Holiday Pk
TR8 . . . . 45 B3
Whitebarrow Cotts PL14. . 37 A4
Whitecroft Way EX23. . . . . . 5 A6
Whitecross
Blisland PL30. . . . . 35 D7
Bodinnick PL23 . . . . 116 F6
White Cross
Cury TR12 . . . . 99 B4
Redruth TR16. . . . . 68 D3
White Cross Ct PL4 . . . . . 149 A3
Whitecross Ind Est TR8. . . 45 B2
Whitefield Terr PL4 . . . . . 149 B4
Whiteford Cl 18 PL17. . . . . 39 E4
Whiteford Rd PL3. . . . . . . 128 E6
Whitefriars La PL4 . . . . . . 149 B3
Whitegate PL26. . . . . 58 B8
Whitegate Mdws PL26. . . . 58 B8
Whitegate Rd TR7 . . . . . . 111 A6
Whitegate Sh Complex
TR7. . . . . 111 A7
Whitehall Bglws PL30 . . . . 23 B2
Whitehall Dr
9 Bere Alston PL20 . . . . . . 41 B1
Plymouth PL9. . . . . 136 B7
Whitehall Est PL30. . . . . . . 23 B2
White Hart Arc The
PL15. . . . . 106 C5
Whitehill Cross PL15 . . . . . 19 C6
Whitehill Terr TR13 . . . . . 146 C4
White Horse
Crowntown TR13 . . . . 91 A6
Nancegollan TR13 . . . . 91 A6
White House Cl TR26. . . . 141 C2
White La PL1 . . . . 149 A2
White Lady Rd PL9. . . . . . 135 D5
White Lodge EX23 . . . . 10 C7
Whitemoor Com Prim Sch
PL26 . . . . 58 E8
Whiterock Cl PL27 . . . . . . 108 B5
Whiterock Rd PL27. . . . . . 108 B5
Whiterocks Pk PL18. . . . . . 40 D6
Whiterock Terr PL27 . . . . 108 B5
White's Cl 3 TR5. . . . . 54 C1
White Smock Mdw 7 PL35 9 C1
Whitestone Cres PL31. . . . 109 C3
Whitestone Rd PL31. . . . . 109 C3
White Walls Ct 16 TR6. . . . 55 A4
Whitewater Ct PL7 . . . . . . 130 E6
Whitham Pk PL19. . . . . . . 147 C4
Whitleigh Ave PL5 . . . . . . 124 E2
Whitleigh Com Prim Sch
PL5 . . . . 124 D4
Whitleigh Cotts PL5. . . . . . 124 E2
Whitleigh Ct PL5. . . . . 124 D4
Whitleigh Gn PL5 . . . . 124 C4
Whitleigh Villas PL5 . . . . . 124 E2
Whitleigh Way PL5. . . . . . . 124 C4
Whitley Cl TR1. . . . . 137 D4
Whitley Grange PL14. . . . . 113 A6
Whitlieburn Terr PL13. . . . 117 C3
Whitpot Hill PL12 . . . . 64 F8
Whitsam Cross PL20 . . . . . 41 A1
Whitsand Bay Holiday Pk
PL10. . . . . 132 B3
Whitsand Bay View PL11 . 65 A4
Whitson Cross PL5. . . . . . 124 C7
Whitsoncross La PL5. . . . . 124 C7
Whitstone Com Prim Sch
EX22 . . . . 7 F1
Whitstone Head Sch EX22 . . 7 F1
Whittington St PL3. . . . . . 148 B4
Whitworth Cl TR5. . . . . 54 C1
Whity Cross PL12 . . . . 122 A4
Widegate Nursery PL9 . . 136 D8
Widemouth Bay Cvn Pk
EX23 . . . . 6 E3
Widemouth Bay Holiday
Village EX23 . . . . 6 F4
Widewell La PL6. . . . . 125 C7
Widewell Prim Sch PL6 . 125 B7
Widewell Rd PL6. . . . . 125 B7
Widey Court Prim Sch
PL6 . . . . 124 F1
Widey Cross PL6. . . . . 124 F1
Widey Ct PL6 . . . . 124 F1
Widey La PL6 . . . . 124 F1
Widey View PL3 . . . . 128 F6
Wilcove La PL11 . . . . 126 E5
Wildebeest Rd 7 PL27 . . . 31 F3
Wilderness Rd PL3. . . . . . 128 E5
Wilderness Trail* PL30. . . 48 C5
Wildflower La TR7 . . . . . . 111 A6
Wilkes Wlk TR1. . . . . 137 D4
Wilkinson Rd PL5 . . . . 127 D8
Willapark View PL35 . . . . . . 9 C1
Willas Rd PL16. . . . . 19 F4
William Edwards Cl
EX23 . . . . 104 E6
William Evans Cl PL6. . . . 124 D5
William Laundry Cl PL14 . 52 A5
William Prance Rd PL6. . 125 A3
Williams Ave PL4 . . . . 129 B1
Williams Ho PL31 . . . . 109 B4
William St
Camborne TR14 . . . . 138 D2
Truro TR1. . . . . 137 D4
William Young Mews
PL14. . . . . 113 E5
Willis Vean TR12. . . . . 99 A1
Willkinson Cl PL17 . . . . 39 E6
Willoughby Pl PL17 . . . . . . 39 E4
Willowby Pk PL20. . . . . 42 D2
Willow Cl
22 Callington PL17 . . . . 39 F4
Mylor Bridge TR11. . . . . 82 A3
Plymouth PL3. . . . . 129 E5
Quintrell Downs TR8 . . . . . . 44 E3
Willow Cotts PL7 . . . . 130 D4
Willow Ct PL6 . . . . 129 E7
Willow Dr TR14 . . . . 138 B4
Willowfield TR18. . . . . 143 C5
Willow Gn PL12. . . . . 122 D2
Willow Rd PL19 . . . . 147 C3
Willows The
Bugle PL26. . . . . 47 C1
Whipsiderry TR7 . . . . 44 C6
Willow Way PL14 . . . . 113 B5
Willow Wlk PL6. . . . . 125 D5
Wills Cl PL6 . . . . 124 E7
Wills La 53 TR26 . . . . 141 B6
Wills Moor PL26 . . . . 85 C5
Will's Row TR15 . . . . 139 C8
Wilminstone Ind Est
PL19 . . . . 147 E7
Wilmot Gdns PL5 . . . . 124 D3
Wilsey View PL15 . . . . 17 B7
Wilson Cres PL2 . . . . 128 B5
Wilson Way
Camborne TR15 . . . . 139 D5
14 Par PL24. . . . . 60 B4
Wilsworthy Cross EX22 . . . 12 C7
Wilton Rd PL1 . . . . 128 A3
Wilton St PL1. . . . . 148 A4
Wilton Terr PL13. . . . . 62 D6
Wiltshire Cl PL4 . . . . 128 F4
Winchester Gdns PL5 . . . 124 A5
Windermere Cres PL6. . . 124 F4
Winding Terr TR10. . . . . . . 81 A1
Windmill PL23 . . . . 116 C4
Windmill Hill
Launceston PL15. . . . . 106 C5
Saltash PL12 . . . . 122 E2
St Just In R TR2. . . . . 82 F2
Windmill Hill Terr PL15 . 106 C5
Windmill Ho PL23. . . . . . . 116 C4
Windmill Ind Est PL23. . . 116 C4
Windmill La PL15 . . . . 106 C5
Windsor Ct
Falmouth TR11. . . . . 145 B4
Newquay TR7. . . . . 110 D5
Windsor Dr PL25. . . . . 115 C3
Windsor Gr PL31. . . . . 109 F5
Windsor Hill 8 TR26. . . . . 141 B5
Windsor Ho 9 PL31. . . . . . 109 E5
Windsor La
Kelly Bray PL17 . . . . 39 F6
Saltash PL12 . . . . 122 E2
Windsor Mews PL31 . . . . 109 E5
Windsor Pl
Liskeard PL14 . . . . 113 C5
29 Penzance TR18. . . . . . . 143 E6
Plymouth PL1. . . . . 148 C2
Windsor Rd PL3 . . . . 129 B7
Windsor Terr
Falmouth TR11. . . . . 145 B4
Penzance TR18 . . . . 143 D6
4 St Ives TR26. . . . . 141 A5
Windsor Villas PL1. . . . . . 148 C2
Windsworth PL24 . . . . 115 F7
Windy Ridge PL26. . . . . 46 D1
Wingfield PL31 . . . . 35 B2
Wingfield Mans PL3. . . . . 128 A3
Wingfield Rd PL3 . . . . 148 A4
Wingfield Way PL3. . . . . . 148 A4
Winifred Baker Ct 5
PL4. . . . . 149 A4
Winnard's Perch TR9 . . . . 32 D1
Winnicott Cl PL6. . . . . 124 E7
Winnow Cl PL9 . . . . 135 F4
Winns Row TR13. . . . . 146 C6
Winsbury Ct PL6. . . . . 125 A1
Winsor Cotts PL15 . . . . . . 106 B7
Winsor Est PL13 . . . . 62 D5
Winstanley Wlk PL3. . . . . 129 D6
Winston Ave PL4. . . . . 148 C4
Winstowe Terr TR8 . . . . . 110 A3
Winwell Field PL27. . . . . . 108 D6
Witham Gdns PL3 . . . . . . 129 C5
Withnoe La PL10. . . . . 132 B6
Withnoe Terr PL10. . . . . . . 65 E3
Wixenford Ct PL9 . . . . 135 F8
Woburn Rd PL15. . . . . 106 B4
Woburn Terr PL9 . . . . 135 C7
Wodehouse Terr TR11. . . 145 B4
Wolcocke Cl TR17. . . . . 89 D5
Wollaton Gr PL5 . . . . 123 F3
Wolrige Ave PL7. . . . . 131 B5
Wolrige Way PL7 . . . . 131 A5
Wolsdon Pl PL1. . . . . 148 A3
Wolsdon St PL1. . . . . 148 B3
Wolseley Bsns Pk 2
PL2 . . . . 128 A5
Wolseley Cl PL2 . . . . 128 A5
Wolseley Rd
Plymouth, Camels Head
PL5 . . . . 127 F6
Plymouth, St Budeaux PL5 123 C1
Wolseley Road Flats PL2 127 F6
Wolverwood Cl PL7 . . . . . 131 C3
Wolverwood La PL7. . . . . 131 B3
Wombwell Cres PL2. . . . . 127 E7
Wood Acre PL12 . . . . 122 B4
Wooda La PL15 . . . . 106 B6
Wooda Rd PL15. . . . . 106 C6
Woodbine Cotts PL7 . . . . 130 E4
Woodbine La TR16. . . . . . . 67 D4
Woodbury Gdns PL5 . . . . 124 A3
Woodchurch PL20 . . . . 42 B3
Wood Cl PL12. . . . . 122 B3
Woodcock Cl PL10 . . . . . . 133 A6
Wood Dr PL12 . . . . 53 C8
Woodend Rd PL6 . . . . 125 D7
Woodfield Prim Sch PL5 124 C5
Woodfield Rd EX23 . . . . . 104 E7
Woodford Ave PL7 . . . . . . 130 A7
Woodford Cl PL7 . . . . 130 A7
Woodford Cres PL7 . . . . . 130 A6
Woodford Cross EX23 . . . . . 2 C1
Woodford Gn PL7. . . . . . . 130 B6
Woodford Inf Sch PL7. . . 130 B6
Woodford Jun Sch PL7. . . 130 B7
Woodford Rd PL6 . . . . 125 D6
Woodgate Rd PL14. . . . . . 113 A5
Woodgrove Pk PL26. . . . . . 59 A1
Woodhey Rd PL2. . . . . 128 A7
Wood La
Landrake PL12. . . . . 53 D2
Truro TR1. . . . . 137 D3
Tywardreath PL24 . . . . 60 D5
Woodland Ave
Penryn TR10 . . . . 144 B6
Plymouth PL9. . . . . 136 A8
12 Tywardreath PL24 . . . . . 60 D5
Woodland Cl
Gunnislake PL18 . . . . 40 F6
Lanivet PL30 . . . . 47 E7
St Austell PL25 . . . . 114 E3
Woodland Ct TR1 . . . . 137 E5
Woodland Dr PL7 . . . . 130 B4
Woodland Glade PL30. . . . 47 F7
Woodland Hts TR1 . . . . . . 137 E5
Woodland Rd
Plymouth PL7. . . . . 130 C6
St Austell PL25 . . . . 114 E3
Woodland Rise
Penryn TR10 . . . . 144 B7
Rilla Mill PL17 . . . . 38 E8
Woodlands
Dousland PL20. . . . . 42 E3
4 Mullion TR12. . . . . 99 A2
10 Par PL24. . . . . 60 C4
Plymouth PL9. . . . . 135 F6
Woodlands Ct PL5 . . . . . . 124 A3
Woodlands End PL6. . . . . 125 D5
Woodlands La PL6 . . . . . . 125 F1
Woodlands Sch PL5. . . . . 124 B4
Woodlands Terr 3 TR16 140 F1
Woodlands The TR14. . . . . 67 B4
Woodlands View PL13. . . 117 B4
Woodland Terr
Plymouth PL4. . . . . 149 B4
4 St Columb Road TR9. . . . 45 E2
Woodland Terr La PL4 . . 149 B4
Woodland View
Coombe PL26. . . . . 58 C2
Lanivet PL30 . . . . 47 E6
Woodland Way
Gunnislake PL18 . . . . 41 A7
Torpoint PL11 . . . . 126 F3
Woodlane TR11. . . . . 145 B3
Woodlane Cl TR11 . . . . . . 145 B3
Woodlane Cres TR11 . . . . 145 B3
Woodlane Dr TR11 . . . . . . 145 B3
Woodley Cl 8 EX23. . . . . 4 D1
Woodman's Cnr PL20 . . . . 42 D3
Woodovis Cvn Pk PL19 . . . 29 F1
Woodridge Cl TR27 . . . . . . 78 E1
Woods-Browning Ind Est
PL31 . . . . 109 F2
Woodside
Crapstone PL20. . . . . 42 B2
Penryn TR10 . . . . 144 B7
Plymouth PL4. . . . . 149 B4
Woodside Ave PL9 . . . . . . 135 C6
Woodside Ct PL7 . . . . 130 E4
Woodside La PL4 . . . . 149 B4
Woodstock Gdns PL5 . . . 123 D1
Woodvale Terr PL15 . . . . 106 C5
Wood View TR10. . . . . 144 B7
Woodview Pk PL9. . . . . . . 136 A6
Woodville Cl PL2 . . . . 127 F7
Woodville Rd
Morwenstow EX23. . . . . 2 C1
Plymouth PL2. . . . . 127 F6
Woodford EX23 . . . . 4 D8
Woodway
Penryn TR10 . . . . 144 B7
Plymouth PL9. . . . . 136 A7
Woolacombe Cross PL20 . 41 C1
Woolacombe Rd PL20. . . . 41 C1
Woollcombe Ave PL7 . . . 130 F4

Woolster Ct **8** PL4......149 A2
Woolwell Cres PL6......125 C8
Woolwell Dr PL6.......125 C7
Woolwell Rd PL6.......125 D7
Woon La **3** TR3.........81 F7
Worcester Rd PL25....115 A4
Wordsworth Cres PL2...127 F7
Wordsworth Rd PL2,....127 F7
World in Miniature★ TR4. 55 E4
Wotton Cross PL12......53 B4
Wreford Cl **11** TR9.......45 D6
Wren Gdns PL7........130 C6
Wren Ind Est TR1........69 E4
Wrens Gate PL9.......135 E8

Wrey Ave PL14..........113 C7
Wright Cl PL1..........127 E3
Wyatts La PL19.........147 B6
Wych Hazel Way TR7....110 F4
Wycliffe Rd PL3........129 B4
Wye Gdns PL3..........129 D7
Wykeham Dr PL2.......128 A7
Wyndham La PL1......148 A3
Wyndham Mews PL1....148 A3
Wyndham Pl PL1......148 A3
Wyndham St E PL1......148 B3
Wyndham St W PL1.....148 B3
Wyndham Sq PL1......148 A3
Wyndhurst Orch PL27...108 B6
Wythburn Gdns PL6.....125 D3

Y

Yardley Gdns PL6.......125 E3
Yarg Cheese Farm★ PL14. 38 D8
Yarrow Mead PL9.......136 D7
Yealmpstone Cl PL7.....131 B4
Yealmpstone Dr PL7....131 B3
Yealmpstone Farm Prim Sch
  PL7..................131 B3
Yeats Cl PL5............124 C2
Yellow Tor Ct PL12......122 C2
Yellow Tor La PL12......122 C2
Yellow Tor Rd PL12......122 B2
Yellow-wort TR16.......80 C3
Yelverton Bsns
  Pk PL20...............42 B2

Yelverton Cl PL5........123 E4
Yelverton Paperweight
  Mus★ PL20............42 C2
Yelverton Terr
  Tavistock PL19..........147 D6
  Yelverton PL20..........42 D2
Yeo Cl PL3............129 B5
Yeoland La PL20........42 C1
Yeoland Lane Cvn Pk
  PL20..................42 C1
Yeomadon Cross EX22....8 E4
Yeomans Cl PL14.......113 D5
Yeomans Way PL7......131 A4
Yewdale Gdns PL6......125 D2
Yew Tree Ct TR1.......137 F6
Yonder St PL9.........135 B6
York Pl PL2............127 F4

York Rd
  Plymouth PL5..........127 E8
  Torpoint PL11..........127 B3
York St
  Penzance TR18.........143 D6
  Plymouth PL1..........127 E2
York Terr **7** PL2......127 F5
Youldon Way PL20.......42 C4

Z

Zaggy La PL17..........39 E4
Zion St PL1.............148 C2
Zodiac Ho TR19.........96 E3

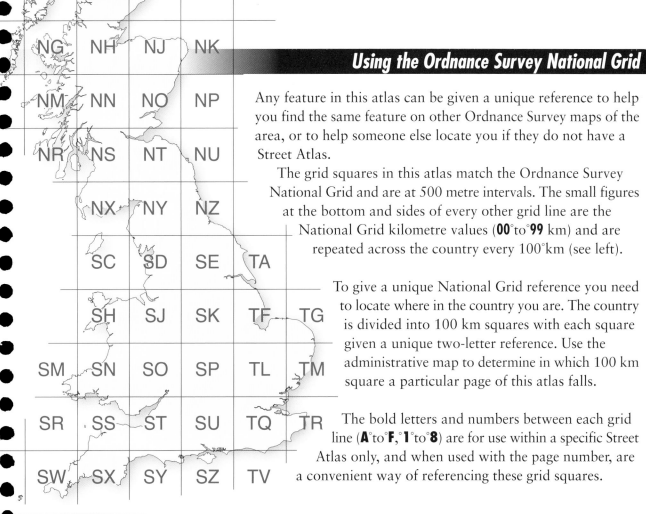

Any feature in this atlas can be given a unique reference to help you find the same feature on other Ordnance Survey maps of the area, or to help someone else locate you if they do not have a Street Atlas.

The grid squares in this atlas match the Ordnance Survey National Grid and are at 500 metre intervals. The small figures at the bottom and sides of every other grid line are the National Grid kilometre values (**00** to **99** km) and are repeated across the country every 100 km (see left).

To give a unique National Grid reference you need to locate where in the country you are. The country is divided into 100 km squares with each square given a unique two-letter reference. Use the administrative map to determine in which 100 km square a particular page of this atlas falls.

The bold letters and numbers between each grid line (**A** to **F**, **1** to **8**) are for use within a specific Street Atlas only, and when used with the page number, are a convenient way of referencing these grid squares.

Example   The railway bridge over DARLEY GREEN RD in grid square B1

Step 1: Identify the two-letter reference, in this example the page is in **SP**

Step 2: Identify the 1 km square in which the railway bridge falls. Use the figures in the southwest corner of this square: Eastings **17**, Northings **74**. This gives a unique reference: **SP 17 74**, accurate to 1 km.

Step 3: To give a more precise reference accurate to 100 m you need to estimate how many tenths along and how many tenths up this 1 km square the feature is (to help with this the 1 km square is divided into four 500 m squares). This makes the bridge about **8** tenths along and about **1** tenth up from the southwest corner.

This gives a unique reference: **SP 178 741**, accurate to 100 m.

Eastings (read from left to right along the bottom) come before Northings (read from bottom to top). If you have trouble remembering say to yourself Along the hall, THEN up the stairs !

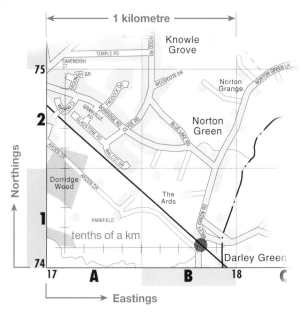

PHILIP'S MAPS

the Gold Standard for drivers

◆ **Philip's street atlases cover every county in England, Wales, Northern Ireland and much of Scotland**

- ◆ Every named street is shown, including alleys, lanes and walkways
- ◆ Thousands of additional features marked: stations, public buildings, car parks, places of interest
- ◆ Route-planning maps to get you close to your destination
- ◆ Postcodes on the maps and in the index
- ◆ Widely used by the emergency services, transport companies and local authorities

Street atlases currently available

England

Bedfordshire and Luton	Surrey
Berkshire	East Sussex
Birmingham and West Midlands	West Sussex
Bristol and Bath	Tyne and Wear
Buckinghamshire and Milton Keynes	Warwickshire and Coventry
Cambridgeshire and Peterborough	Wiltshire and Swindon
Cheshire	Worcestershire
Cornwall	East Yorkshire Northern Lincolnshire
Cumbria	North Yorkshire
Derbyshire	South Yorkshire
Devon	West Yorkshire
Dorset	
County Durham and Teesside	**Wales**
Essex	Anglesey, Conwy and Gwynedd
North Essex	Cardiff, Swansea and The Valleys
South Essex	Carmarthenshire, Pembrokeshire and Swansea
Gloucestershire and Bristol	
Hampshire	Ceredigion and South Gwynedd
North Hampshire	Denbighshire, Flintshire, Wrexham
South Hampshire	
Herefordshire Monmouthshire	Herefordshire Monmouthshire
Hertfordshire	Powys
Isle of Wight	
Kent	**Scotland**
East Kent	Aberdeenshire
West Kent	Ayrshire
Lancashire	Dumfries and Galloway
Leicestershire and Rutland	Edinburgh and East Central Scotland
Lincolnshire	Fife and Tayside
Liverpool and Merseyside	Glasgow and West Central Scotland
London	Inverness and Moray
Greater Manchester	Lanarkshire
Norfolk	Scottish Borders
Northamptonshire	
Northumberland	**Northern Ireland**
Nottinghamshire	County Antrim and County Londonderry
Oxfordshire	County Armagh and County Down
Shropshire	
Somerset	Belfast
Staffordshire	County Tyrone and County Fermanagh
Suffolk	

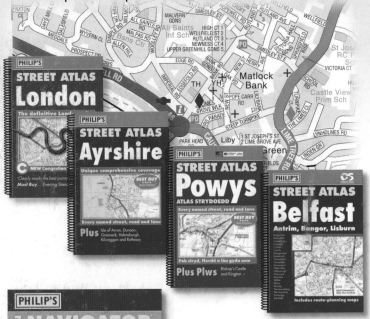

For national mapping, choose
Philip's Navigator Britain
the most detailed road atlas available of England, Wales and Scotland. Hailed by Auto Express as 'the ultimate road atlas', the atlas shows every road and lane in Britain.

How to order
Philip's maps and atlases are available from bookshops, motorway services and petrol stations. You can order direct from the publisher by phoning **0207 531 8473** or online at **www.philips-maps.co.uk**
For bulk orders only, e-mail philips@philips-maps.co.uk